G000127965

ESSENTIAL CASES ON HUN
FOR THE POLIC

THE RAOUL WALLENBERG INSTITUTE
PROFESSIONAL GUIDES TO HUMAN RIGHTS
VOLUME 4

ESSENTIAL CASES ON HUMAN RIGHTS FOR THE POLICE

Reviews and Summaries of International Cases

By

Ralph Crawshaw
Leif Holmström

In cooperation with

Human Rights Centre
University of Essex
United Kingdom

MARTINUS NIJHOFF PUBLISHERS
LEIDEN / BOSTON

A C.I.P. record for this book is available from the Library of Congress.

Printed on acid-free paper.

ISBN-13: 978-90-04-13978-7
ISBN-10: 90-04-13978-8

© 2006 Koninklijke Brill NV, Leiden, The Netherlands.

Koninklijke Brill NV incorporates the imprints Brill, Hotei Publishers,
IDC Publishers, Martinus Nijhoff Publishers and VSP.

http://www.brill.nl

All rights reserved. No part of this publication may be reproduced, stored in a
retrieval system, or transmitted in any form or by any means, electronic, mechanical,
photocopying, microfilming, recording or otherwise, without written permission
from the Publisher.

Authorization to photocopy items for internal or personal use is granted by Brill
provided that the appropriate fees are paid directly to The Copyright Clearance
Center, 222 Rosewood Drive, Suite 910, Danvers MA 01923, USA.
Fees are subject to change.

Printed and bound in The Netherlands.

In memory of Brenda Crawshaw

*who died from injuries sustained in a car crash
just before this book was completed. Brenda was a very special lady,
and she gave Ralph wholehearted encouragement and support
in his human rights work.*

TABLE OF CONTENTS

PREFACE   XV

PART I
General Introduction   1

1.   Introduction to Essential Cases on Human Rights
     for the Police   3

     A. OUTLINE OF THE SCOPE AND CONTENTS   3

     B. PRINCIPLE OF NON-DISCRIMINATION   6

     C. RIGHT TO EFFECTIVE REMEDY AND THE REQUIREMENT
         TO INVESTIGATE ALLEGATIONS OF HUMAN RIGHTS
         VIOLATIONS   8

     D. INTERNATIONAL INSTITUTIONS AND PROCEDURES   10
         (*a*) Human Rights Committee   10
         (*b*) Committee on the Elimination of Racial Discrimination   11
         (*c*) Committee on the Elimination of Discrimination against Women   13
         (*d*) Committee against Torture   14
         (*e*) Working Group on Arbitrary Detention   15
         (*f*) International Tribunal for the former Yugoslavia   17
         (*g*) International Criminal Tribunal for Rwanda   19
         (*h*) Committee on Freedom of Association   22
         (*i*) African Commission on Human and Peoples' Rights   24
         (*j*) Inter-American Court of Human Rights   26
         (*k*) European Court of Human Rights   28

     E. HUMAN RIGHTS AND POLICING   30

PART II
Police Powers and Respect for Human Rights   33

1.   Introduction to Police Powers and
     Respect for Human Rights   35

2.   Right to Life   39

     A. INTRODUCTION   39

B. REVIEW OF CASES   41
   (*a*) Human Rights Committee   41
   (*b*) Committee on Freedom of Association   48
   (*c*) African Commission on Human and Peoples' Rights   52
   (*d*) Inter-American Court of Human Rights   53
   (*e*) European Court of Human Rights   57

C. CASE SUMMARIES   67
   (*a*) *Maria Fanny Suárez de Guerrero* v. *Colombia*   67
     (Human Rights Committee)
   (*b*) Case No. 1761 (*Colombia*)   72
     (Committee on Freedom of Association)
   (*c*) *Velásquez Rodrigues* case (*Honduras*)   74
     (Inter-American Court of Human Rights)
   (*d*) *McCann and Others* v. *the United Kingdom*   86
     (European Court of Human Rights)
   (*e*) *Mahmut Kaya* v. *Turkey*   104
     (European Court of Human Rights)
   (*f*) *Nachova and Others* v. *Bulgaria*   112
     (European Court of Human Rights)

3.   Prohibition of Torture   123

   A. INTRODUCTION   123

   B. REVIEW OF CASES   127
     (*a*) Human Rights Committee   127
     (*b*) Committee against Torture   132
     (*c*) Committee on Freedom of Association   139
     (*d*) African Commission on Human and Peoples' Rights   142
     (*e*) Inter-American Court of Human Rights   144
     (*f*) European Court of Human Rights   149

   C. CASE SUMMARIES   155
     (*a*) *Hugo Rodríguez* v. *Uruguay*   155
      (Human Rights Committee)
     (*b*) *Albert Womah Mukong* v. *Cameroon*   158
      (Human Rights Committee)
     (*c*) *Celis Laureano* v. *Peru*   161
      (Human Rights Committee)
     (*d*) *Radivoje Ristic* v. *Yugoslavia*   163
      (Committee against Torture)
     (*e*) Case No. 2005 (*Central African Republic*)   168
      (Committee on Freedom of Association)
     (*f*) *Villagrán Morales* et al. case (*Guatemala*),
      the *"street children"* case   172
      (Inter-American Court of Human Rights)

(*g*) *Cantoral Benavides* case (*Peru*)   178
(Inter-American Court of Human Rights)
(*h*) *Aksoy* v. *Turkey*   184
(European Court of Human Rights)
(*i*) *Selmouni* v. *France*   186
(European Court of Human Rights)

4.   Right to Liberty and Security of Person   199

A. INTRODUCTION   199

B. REVIEW OF CASES   200
(*a*) Human Rights Committee   200
(*b*) Working Group on Arbitrary Detention   216
(*c*) Committee on Freedom of Association   222
(*d*) African Commission on Human and Peoples' Rights   225
(*e*) Inter-American Court of Human Rights   227
(*f*) European Court of Human Rights   232

C. CASE SUMMARIES   244
(*a*) *W. Delgado Páez* v. *Colombia*   244
(Human Rights Committee)
(*b*) *Chongwe* v. *Zambia*   247
(Human Rights Committee)
(*c*) *V. P. Domukovsky* et al. v. *Georgia*   248
(Human Rights Committee)
(*d*) *Spakmo* v. *Norway*   250
(Human Rights Committee)
(*e*) *Paul Kelly* v. *Jamaica*   252
(Human Rights Committee)
(*f*) *Michael and Brian Hill* v. *Spain*   255
(Human Rights Committee)
(*g*) Decision No. 38/1994 (*Turkey*)   258
(Working Group on Arbitrary Detention)
(*h*) Case No. 2116 (*Indonesia*)   262
(Committee on Freedom of Association)
(*i*) *Castillo Páez* case (*Peru*)   266
(Inter-American Court of Human Rights)
(*j*) *Brogan and Others* case (*the United Kingdom*)   270
(European Court of Human Rights)
(*k*) *K.-F.* v. *Germany*   282
(European Court of Human Rights)

5. Prohibition of Arbitrary Interference
    with Privacy   287

    A. INTRODUCTION   287

    B. REVIEW OF CASES   288
        (*a*) Human Rights Committee   288
        (*b*) European Court of Human Rights   292

    C. CASE SUMMARIES   305
        (*a*) *Rojas Garcia* v. *Colombia*   305
              (Human Rights Committee)
        (*b*) *Miguel Angel Estrella* v. *Uruguay*   308
              (Human Rights Committee)
        (*c*) *A.* v. *France*   310
              (European Court of Human Rights)
        (*d*) *Halford* v. *the United Kingdom*   313
              (European Court of Human Rights)
        (*e*) *P. G. and J. H.* v. *the United Kingdom*   322
              (European Court of Human Rights)

PART III
Police Functions and Protection of Human Rights   333

1. Introduction to Police Functions and
    Protection of Human Rights   335

2. Right to a Fair Trial   341

    A. INTRODUCTION   341

    B. REVIEW OF CASES   343
        (*a*) Human Rights Committee   343
        (*b*) Working Group on Arbitrary Detention   354
        (*c*) African Commission on Human and Peoples' Rights 359
        (*d*) Inter-American Court of Human Rights   360
        (*e*) European Court of Human Rights   365

    C. CASE SUMMARIES   374
        (*a*) *Gridin.* v. *Russian Federation*   374
              (Human Rights Committee)
        (*b*) *Bernard Lubuto* v. *Zambia*   378
              (Human Rights Committee)
        (*c*) *G. Peart and A. Peart* v. *Jamaica*   382
              (Human Rights Committee)

(*d*) Opinion No. 27/2001 (*Morocco*) 385
(Working Group on Arbitrary Detention)
(*e*) *Allenet de Ribemont* v. *France* 390
(European Court of Human Rights)
(*f*) *S.* v. *Switzerland* 395
(European Court of Human Rights)
(*g*) *Doorson* v. *the Netherlands* 400
(European Court of Human Rights)

3. Right to Freedom of Thought, Conscience
    and Religion 407

    A. INTRODUCTION 407

    B. REVIEW OF CASES 410
    (*a*) Human Rights Committee 410
    (*b*) European Court of Human Rights 414

    C. CASE SUMMARIES 417
    (*a*) *M. A. B., W. A. T. and J.-A. Y. T.* v. *Canada* 417
    (Human Rights Committee)
    (*b*) *Kalaç* v. *Turkey* 419
    (European Court of Human Rights)
    (*c*) *Metropolitan Church of Bessarabia and Others* v. *Moldova* 422
    (European Court of Human Rights)

4. Right to Freedom of Opinion
    and Expression 433

    A. INTRODUCTION 433

    B. REVIEW OF CASES 436
    (*a*) Human Rights Committee 436
    (*b*) Working Group on Arbitrary Detention 444
    (*c*) Inter-American Court of Human Rights 449
    (*d*) European Court of Human Rights 450

    C. CASE SUMMARIES 459
    (*a*) *Jong-Kyu Sohn* v. *the Republic of Korea* 459
    (Human Rights Committee)
    (*b*) *Ivcher Bronstein* case (*Peru*) 463
    (Inter-American Court of Human Rights)
    (*c*) *Thorgeir Thorgeirson* v. *Iceland* 470
    (European Court of Human Rights)
    (*d*) *Özgür Gündem* v. *Turkey* 476
    (European Court of Human Rights)

5. Right to Freedom of Peaceful Assembly
    and Association   487

    A. INTRODUCTION   487

    B. REVIEW OF CASES   489
       (*a*) Human Rights Committee   489
       (*b*) Committee on Freedom of Association   491
       (*c*) European Court of Human Rights   496

    C. CASE SUMMARIES   500
       (*a*) *Auli Kivenmaa* v. *Finland*   500
           (Human Rights Committee)
       (*b*) Case No. 2184 (*Zimbabwe*)   508
           (Committee on Freedom of Association)
       (*c*) Case No. 2189 (*China*)   511
           (Committee on Freedom of Association)
       (*d*) *Plattform "Ärzte für das Leben"* v. *Austria*   519
           (European Court of Human Rights)

PART IV
Police Behaviour in Times of Armed Conflict,
Disturbance and Tension   525

1. Introduction to Police Behaviour in Times of
    Armed Conflict, Disturbance and Tension   527

2. Respect for and Protection of Human Rights   537

    A. INTRODUCTION   537

    B. REVIEW OF CASES   541
       (*a*) Human Rights Committee   541
       (*b*) Committee against Torture   545
       (*c*) Working Group on Arbitrary Detention   547
       (*d*) African Commission on Human and Peoples' Rights   550
       (*e*) Inter-American Court of Human Rights   555
       (*f*) European Court of Human Rights   558

    C. CASE SUMMARIES   562
       (*a*) *Hajrizi Dzemajl* et al. v. *Serbia and Montenegro*   562
           (Committee against Torture)
       (*b*) Decision No. 16/1994 (*Israel*)   573
           (Working Group on Arbitrary Detention)
       (*c*) Opinion No. 25/2001 (*Pakistan*)   576
           (Working Group on Arbitrary Detention)

(*d*) *Free Legal Assistance Group* et al. v. *Zaire* 579
    (African Commission on Human and Peoples' Rights)
(*e*) *Bámaca Velásquez* case (*Guatemala*) 582
    (Inter-American Court of Human Rights)
(*f*) *Ergi* v. *Turkey* 594
    (European Court of Human Rights)

3.   International Crimes 597

A. INTRODUCTION 597

B. REVIEW OF CASES 600
    (*a*) International Tribunal for the former Yugoslavia 600
    (*b*) International Criminal Tribunal for Rwanda 610

C. CASE SUMMARIES 616
    (*a*) *Prosecutor* v. *Anto Furundzija* 616
       (International Tribunal for the former Yugoslavia)

TABLE OF CASES 637

    (*a*) Human Rights Committee 637
    (*b*) Committee on the Elimination of Racial Discrimination 638
    (*c*) Committee against Torture 638
    (*d*) Working Group on Arbitrary Detention 638
    (*e*) International Tribunal for the former Yugoslavia 639
    (*f*) International Criminal Tribunal for Rwanda 639
    (*g*) Committee on Freedom of Association 639
    (*h*) African Commission on Human and Peoples' Rights 640
    (*i*) Inter-American Court of Human Rights 640
    (*j*) European Court of Human Rights 641

TABLE OF INSTRUMENTS 643

    (*a*) Universal Declaration of Human Rights
       and universal human rights treaties 643
    (*b*) Regional human rights treaties 655
    (*c*) Non-treaty human rights instruments 664
    (*d*) Other international instruments 669

PREFACE

The present system for the protection of human rights has been in existence since the middle of the last century. International human rights standards have been agreed and promulgated; means to secure compliance by States with their obligations to secure human rights have been established; and international tribunals hold individuals to account for their criminal abuse of power. All of this means that the physical and mental integrity of countless numbers of people have been protected, and that many victims of human rights violations have been granted remedy and redress. This system is one of the highest achievements of humankind. Nevertheless, in the graphic language of the preamble to the Universal Declaration of Human Rights, disregard and contempt for human rights continue to result in barbarous acts that outrage the conscience of mankind.

The optimism and the caution and regret expressed above echo through the pages of this book, for they show how the system can restore some measure of human dignity to those from whom it has been stripped, but they also show the brutality and lawlessness of some of those vested with power.

In the preface to a companion volume to this book, *Essential Texts on Human Rights for the Police: A Compilation of International Instruments*, by the same authors, it was pointed out that as police are uniquely placed to safeguard human rights, they need to be aware of the standards embodied in international human rights and humanitarian law instruments. Those treaties and non-treaty instruments seen as essential to the police are compiled in that book. Having completed it, the authors felt that a book of essential cases was also required, hence the present volume.

The purpose of this book is to review and summarize international cases identified as being essential to police. The cases embody the jurisprudence of courts and bodies established under international law to secure compliance with international human rights and humanitarian standards, and they are essential to police, because they have a direct bearing on the exercise of police powers and the performance of police functions. Furthermore, the cases are essential to anyone seeking to understand the theory and practice of policing.

Jurisprudence from 10 international institutions is cited in this book, as well as a few other related cases. Authoritative reports of the cases are to be found in official records and reports of judgments, decisions, views and opinions. Accounts of the jurisprudence are also given in publications devoted to the various institutions and in human rights publications of a general or specific nature. However, this book is unique in that the authors here present summaries and/or reviews of about 200 cases that have arisen out of police activity.

The cases cited in the book can be seen as a catalogue of errors, negligence and, in some cases, serious criminality by police officials. However, whilst it is important to study what might be termed the pathology of policing in order to understand and to correct policing, it is also important to acknowledge the contribution that police make to the conditions necessary for the enjoyment of all human rights by maintaining peace and order. Furthermore, it is important to secure the human rights of police officials.

There are four parts to this book. Part I provides a general introduction. Parts II and III concern, respectively, police powers and respect for human rights and police functions and protection of human rights. Part IV, finally, concerns police behaviour in times of armed conflict, disturbance and tension. Introductions to the parts and their respective chapters outline scope and contents.

Essential Cases on Human Rights for the Police can be used in human rights education programmes for police and other officials with investigative or prosecutorial functions. It can be used by teachers and resource persons as a source of reference for such programmes or to supplement teaching manuals. The book can also serve as a source of reference to anyone interested in the actual application of international human rights standards to policing.

Research into the jurisprudence of the Inter-American Court of Human Rights was undertaken by Graham Dossett, who identified cases from that Court relevant to the purposes of this book. The co-authors acknowledge Graham's valuable contribution.

The preparation and dissemination of the present publication have been made possible by a grant made by the Foreign and Commonwealth Office of the United Kingdom and by the support of the Swedish International Development Cooperation Agency (Sida). We wish to acknowledge the contribution this type of funding makes towards the promotion of human rights and effective, lawful and humane policing.

    Ralph Crawshaw   *Leif Holmström*

PART I

General Introduction

1. Introduction to Essential Cases on Human Rights for the Police

A. OUTLINE OF THE SCOPE AND CONTENTS

Courts and bodies established under international law to secure compliance with international human rights and humanitarian standards are producing a continuously developing jurisprudence. The purpose of this book is to review and summarize cases embodying that jurisprudence insofar as they are essential to police practice and to the development of policy, strategy and tactics. This means that the primary focus of the book is on institutions empowered to receive complaints about human rights violations; to communicate with States about those complaints; to take their own decisions on the merits of complaints by referring to treaty and other State obligations; and whose findings on such cases are made public. In other words, they are conducting a judicial process or a process equivalent to a judicial process. The only institutions whose cases are summarized and/or reviewed in this book and which do not meet these criteria are international tribunals before which individuals are held to account for crimes.

The cases selected for summary and/or review are considered essential for police officials, because they have a direct bearing on the exercise of police powers and the performance of police functions. They are essential, because the various institutions make pronouncements expressing great legal and humanitarian principles that police are obliged to follow; they set out good practice for policing in democracies governed by the rule of law; and they reinforce provisions that prohibit bad practice, that is to say unlawful and inhumane behaviour. Some cases under international law might be of considerable interest to lawyers or others working in the field of human rights protection, because they establish important legal principles or elucidate the meaning of a particular treaty provision. However, if they are not directly relevant to police practice or to the development of policy, strategy and tactics or are otherwise important, these cases have been omitted.

In making their selection according to these criteria, the authors have endeavoured to achieve a fair balance between the jurisprudence of the various institutions and between the different rights dealt with in the book. For example, the United Nations Human Rights Committee and the European Court of Human Rights have pronounced upon large numbers of cases arising out of violations of the right to life, the

3

I:1

prohibition of torture and the right to liberty and security of person. Given the importance of these rights for police, the circumstances of each of the cases and the findings of the institutions in the cases, it might be argued that greater prominence should be given to these rights and to these institutions. However, to do so would have meant ignoring or dealing only perfunctorily with other institutions and rights that also have great significance to policing.

There has been no selection of cases on the basis of States that have been subject to scrutiny by international human rights institutions. The inclusion of a case in this book is not, *per se*, a criticism or condemnation of the State involved, or of its police agencies. The fact that a State has been subject to these procedures means that it has made itself available to such procedures. It has made the actions of its officials open to examination, consideration and judgment. This is an important step in securing respect for, and protection of, human rights generally within a State and for the development of effective, lawful and humane policing. States which have not made themselves accountable in this way can only be featured to a very limited extent in this type of publication, whatever their records on human rights. They should be encouraged to participate fully in the international system for the protection of human rights, for the benefit of people living within their jurisdiction and for the enhancement of the rule of law within and between States.

The authors have opted for a rights-based approach for the presentation of cases selected for this publication. The cases are summarized and/or reviewed in relation to a specific human right or, occasionally, to more than one right. As a consequence, issues arising out of violations of the principle of non-discrimination and other general principles of international law are not dealt with separately, but in the context of the cases when they arise. Furthermore, the cases are compiled so as to present the jurisprudence of each human rights institution in respect of the particular rights.

In this part of the book, the general introduction, the present section is followed by a brief presentation of the principle of non-discrimination and an account of the right to effective remedy and the requirement to investigate allegations of human rights violations. Next there is a section presenting the international institutions and procedures selected for the purposes of this work. Cases are cited from the following 10 institutions: the Human Rights Committee, the Committee on the Elimination of Racial Discrimination, the Committee against Torture, the Working Group on Arbitrary Detention, the International Tribunal for the former Yugoslavia, the International Criminal Tribunal for Rwanda, the Committee on Freedom of Association, the African Commission on Human and People's Rights, the Inter-American Court of Human Rights and the European Court of Human Rights. Additionally, the Committee on the Elimination of Discrimination against Women is included. Most of these institutions are established under human rights treaties. Some of them, however, are set up under the authority of the constitution of an international organization, such as the Charter of the United Nations. Finally, a section on human rights and policing completes the general introduction.

Parts II and III of the book concern, respectively, police powers and respect for human rights, and police functions and protection of human rights. Both parts have the same structure. After a brief introduction to the part, there are chapters dealing with specific human rights. Part II has separate chapters for the right to life; the prohibition of torture; the right to liberty and security of person; and the prohibition of arbitrary interference with privacy. Correspondingly, part III has chapters for the right to a fair trial; the right to freedom of thought, conscience and religion; the right to freedom of opinion and expression; and the right to freedom of peaceful assembly and association. Each chapter is divided into three sections.

Section A provides a broad introduction to the particular right and its significance to policing. Reference is made to provisions of the Universal Declaration of Human Rights protecting that right and to relevant human rights treaties and non-treaty instruments of universal or regional application. Some mechanisms established under the Charter of the United Nations are also mentioned.

Section B contains a review of cases. Under the name of the respective institutions, an account is first given of the relevant treaty and non-treaty provisions in respect of the specific right. A selection of cases essential for police is then reviewed, in format ranging from brief accounts to facts and findings in greater detail. This section also include comments pertinent to the cases presented.

Section C has summaries of cases considered to be of particular relevance to this book. These summaries are, generally, fairly extended in order to illustrate the processes, methods and reasoning by which the various institutions come to their decisions; to set out fully and clearly any observations which are essential to good police practice; and to provide a detailed account of any police action or police operation that may be included in the original account of facts and findings.

Part IV of the book, finally, concerns police behaviour in times of armed conflict, disturbance and tension. An introduction to the part provides an outline of international humanitarian law, contrasting it with international human rights law. After the introduction, there are two chapters having roughly the same structure as the presentation of cases in previous parts of the book.

The chapter dealing with respect for and protection of human rights includes cases from human rights institutions arising out of police actions in times of armed conflict, disturbance and tension. The introduction to this chapter points to the vulnera-

I:1

bility of all human rights in times of armed conflict, disturbance and tension. It also gives an account of provisions of human rights treaties on derogation by States parties from their human rights obligations in time of war or other public emergency threatening the life of the nation.

The other chapter deals with international crimes. In contrast to the rest of the book, focus here is on individual criminal responsibility rather than on State responsibility for violations of human rights. Some illustrative cases from the jurisprudence of international tribunals set up to prosecute persons responsible for serious violations of international humanitarian law have been selected for summary and/or review in that chapter of the book.

To facilitate its use, the book is provided with a table of cases as well as a table of treaties and non-treaty instruments referred to in the text. The former table indicates where in the text a particular case is summarized and/or reviewed. The latter table indicates where an instrument is cited and includes some basic information about each instrument, such as adoption particulars and, where applicable, date of its entry into force.

B. PRINCIPLE OF NON-DISCRIMINATION

The principle of non-discrimination is fundamental to the protection of human rights. Article 2 of the Universal Declaration of Human Rights stipulates that everyone is entitled to all the rights and freedoms set forth in that instrument without distinction of any kind, such as race, colour, sex, language, religion, political or other opinion, national or social origin, property, birth or other status. Similar provisions are embodied in human rights treaties in respect of the rights they protect, for example article 2, paragraph 1, of the International Covenant on Civil and Political Rights, article 2 of the African Charter on Human and Peoples' Rights, article 1, paragraph 1, of the American Convention on Human Rights and article 14 of the Convention for the Protection of Human Rights and Fundamental Freedoms (the European Convention on Human Rights).

Furthermore, in article 7 of the Universal Declaration, there is a provision stipulating that everyone is equal before the law and entitled without any discrimination to equal protection of the law. Corresponding provisions are included in article 26 of the Covenant, article 3 of the African Charter and article 24 of the American Convention. In the European Convention, however, there is no such provision, but the fundamental principle of equality before the law and equal protection of the law is now expressed in the preambular text to Protocol No. 12 to the Convention, a separate treaty with a general prohibition of discrimination. Under article 1 of the Protocol, the enjoyment of any right set forth by law shall be secured without discrimination on any ground such as sex, race, colour, language, religion, political or other opinion, national or social origin, association with a national minority, property, birth or other status. No one shall be discriminated against by any public authority on any such ground.

The United Nations Human Rights Committee, established under article 28 of the International Covenant on Civil and Political Rights, has dealt with the principle of non-discrimination in its general comment No. 18 (37).[1] The Committee pointed out that non-discrimination, together with equality before the law and equal protection of the law without any discrimination, constituted a basic and general principle relating to the protection of human rights. Indeed, it insisted, the principle was so basic that article 3 of the Covenant obligated each State party to ensure the equal right of men and women to the enjoyment of the rights set forth in the Covenant. Furthermore, while article 4, paragraph 1, allowed States parties to take measures derogating from certain obligations under the Covenant in time of public emergency, the same article required, *inter alia*, that those measures should not involve discrimination solely on the ground of race, colour, sex, language, religion or social origin. Under article 20, paragraph 2, States parties were obliged to prohibit, by law, any advocacy of national, racial or religious hatred which constituted incitement to discrimination.[2]

The principle of non-discrimination is reinforced and extended by various other human rights instruments, in particular, among the universal treaties, the International Covenant on Economic, Social and Cultural Rights, the International Convention on the Elimination of All Forms of Racial Discrimination, the Convention on the Elimination of All Forms of Discrimination against Women and the Convention on the Rights of the Child. In the field of international labour standards, there are two fundamental human rights treaties: the Convention concerning Equal Remuneration for Men and Women Workers for Work of Equal Value (No. 100) and the Convention concerning Discrimination in Respect of Employment and Occupation (No. 111). The Convention concerning Indigenous and Tribal Peoples in Independent Countries (No. 169) and the Framework Convention for the Protection of National Minorities, a regional treaty, deal with minority rights, and the Convention against Discrimination in Education is another example of a treaty prohibiting discrimination in a specific context. The Declaration on the Elimination of All Forms of Intolerance and of Discrimination Based on Religion or Belief is a non-treaty instrument protecting the right to freedom of religion or belief.

---

[1] See United Nations, *Official Records of the General Assembly, Forty-fifth Session, Supplement No. 40* (A/45/40), vol. I, annex VI, sect. A.

[2] *Ibidem*, paras. 1 and 2.

I:1

Article 2 of the Convention on the Rights of the Child may illustrate the development of non-discrimination provisions. Under this article, States parties are required to respect and ensure all rights set forth in the Convention to each child within their jurisdiction without discrimination of any kind, irrespective of the child's or his or her parent's or legal guardian's race, colour, sex, language, religion, political or other opinion, national, ethnic or social origin, property, disability, birth or other status. States parties are further required to take all appropriate measures to ensure that the child is protected against all forms of discrimination or punishment on the basis of the status, activities, expressed opinions or beliefs of the child's parents, legal guardians or family members.

C. RIGHT TO EFFECTIVE REMEDY AND THE REQUIREMENT TO INVESTIGATE ALLEGATIONS OF HUMAN RIGHTS VIOLATIONS

International human rights law not only obliges States to respect and ensure the rights enshrined in international instruments, it also requires them to provide effective remedies when those rights are violated. The right to effective remedy is set out in article 8 of the Universal Declaration of Human Rights. This provision guarantees all persons the right to an effective remedy by the competent national tribunals for violations of fundamental rights granted by the constitution or by law. Expressed in this way, the article reinforces the important principle that implementation of human rights primarily takes place at national level.

The right to effective remedy is further developed in universal and regional human rights treaties. Article 2, paragraph 3, of the International Covenant on Civil and Political Rights, article 25, paragraph 1, of the American Convention on Human Rights and article 13 of the Convention for the Protection of Human Rights and Fundamental Freedoms embody provisions expressly protecting the right to an effective remedy, notwithstanding that the violation has been committed by persons acting in an official capacity or in the course of their official duties. Furthermore, in addition to the general principle of remedy, each treaty contains rights to remedy in specific situations, for example the right to *habeas corpus*.

Human rights treaties establishing individual complaints procedures express another important principle, namely that national remedies must be exhausted before the treaty enforcement machinery can be invoked. Article 2 of the Optional Protocol to the International Covenant on Civil and Political Rights, article 46, paragraph 1 (*a*), of the American Convention on Human Rights and article 35, paragraph 1, of the Convention for the Protection of Human Rights and Fundamental Freedoms are examples of such provisions.

The right to effective remedy is essential to the effective implementation of human rights at national level, as is the requirement to investigate allegations of human rights violations. Indeed, the right to remedy implies a requirement to investigate such allegations in order to establish that a violation has occurred; to provide the most appropriate remedy; to bring perpetrators to justice; and to strengthen or introduce measures to prevent recurrences of violations.

The requirement on States to investigate allegations of human rights violations is explicit in provisions of some human rights treaties and in non-treaty instruments, for example in article 12 of the Convention against Torture and Other Cruel, Inhuman or Degrading Treatment or Punishment and article 13, paragraph 1, of the Declaration on the Protection of All Persons from Enforced Disappearance. It is also expressed in the jurisprudence and other pronouncements of treaty monitoring bodies established under various human rights treaties. Furthermore, some treaties include provisions which require each State party to ensure that certain acts and activities are fully covered under its criminal or penal law. For example, article 4 of the Convention against Torture requires States parties to make torture, attempts to commit torture and complicity or participation in torture offences under criminal law punishable by appropriate penalties that take into account their grave nature. In some cases when States have been found to be in violation of their treaty obligations, international institutions have required that the perpetrators of those violations should be prosecuted and punished.

Police officials, and especially police leaders, should be aware of these requirements, because they are often uniquely placed to know when systematic and occasional violations of human rights have occurred. They may also receive or become aware of complaints that rights have been violated. Given the nature of those violations and the tasks of police to prevent and investigate crime, there is a clear duty on police leaders to ensure that complaints or suspicions of human rights violations are promptly and effectively investigated. Some human rights violations, such as unlawful killings, torture and cruel and inhuman treatment, are crimes under domestic law. Other violations may not carry criminal liability, but may be actionable at civil law, for example arbitrary arrests and detention and invasions of privacy. Many, including these examples, would be infringements of police discipline codes. When investigations reveal evidence of human rights violations, the appropriate criminal and/or disciplinary proceedings should be initiated.

I:1

D. INTERNATIONAL INSTITUTIONS AND PROCEDURES

(*a*) Human Rights Committee

Article 28 of the International Covenant on Civil and Political Rights provides that there shall be established a Human Rights Committee to carry out the functions set forth in the Covenant. It shall consist of 18 State party nationals of high moral character and recognized competence in the field of human rights. Consideration shall be given to the usefulness of the participation of some persons having legal experience, to equitable geographical distribution of membership and to the representation of the different forms of civilization and of the principle legal systems. Elected at a meeting of States parties, members of the Committee serve in their personal capacity for a term of four years.

In the preamble to the Covenant, the States parties recognize that in accordance with the Universal Declaration of Human Rights, the ideal of free human beings enjoying civil and political freedom and freedom from fear and want can only be achieved if conditions are created whereby everyone may enjoy his civil and political rights, as well as his economic, social and cultural rights. Under article 2 of the Covenant, each State party undertakes to respect and to ensure to all individuals within its territory and subject to its jurisdiction the rights recognized in the Covenant without distinction of any kind, such as race, colour, sex, language, religion, political or other opinion, national or social origin, property, birth or other status. Each State party also undertakes to adopt such laws or other measures as may be necessary to give effect to those rights and to secure an effective remedy in cases of a violation of the rights and freedoms protected by the Covenant.

The Covenant encompasses many provisions of great significance to police, such as provisions on the right to life, the prohibition of torture, the right to liberty and security of person, the prohibition of arbitrary interference with privacy, the right to a fair trial, the right to freedom of thought, conscience and religion, the right to freedom of opinion and expression as well as the right to freedom of peaceful assembly and association. The Covenant entered into force on 23 March 1976. At present, 154 States have ratified or acceded to the Covenant.

The Committee has a number of tasks to ensure compliance by States parties with their obligations under the Covenant, including the competence to receive and consider communications. Articles 41 to 43 provide procedures to followed when a State party claims that another State party is not fulfilling its obligations under the Covenant and the latter State has declared that it recognizes the competence of the Committee to receive and consider such communications. The Committee may also deal with individual complaints against States parties under a separate treaty, the

Optional Protocol to the International Covenant on Civil and Political Rights, which came into effect at the same time as the Covenant itself. Under article 1, a State party to the Optional Protocol recognizes the competence of the Committee to receive and consider communications from individuals subject to its jurisdiction who claim to be victims of a violation by that State party of any of the rights set forth in the Covenant. At present, 105 States have ratified or acceded to the Optional Protocol.

Furthermore, under the Second Optional Protocol to the International Covenant on Civil and Political Rights, aiming at the abolition of the death penalty, the State parties to this treaty have extended the scope of application of the Committee's competence to receive and consider communications. When the Committee has such competence under article 41 of the Covenant or article 1 of the first Optional Protocol, the competence shall include the provisions of the Second Optional Protocol unless the State party has made a statement to the contrary at the moment of ratification or accession under articles 4 or 5, respectively. The Second Optional Protocol entered into force on 11 July 1991. At present, 54 States have ratified or acceded to this Optional Protocol.

The Committee has developed a rich jurisprudence. More than 1,000 communications have been filed under the first Optional Protocol. The communications are examined in closed meetings. The decisions on admissibility and the views adopted by the Committee after consideration of the merits are published in the Committee's annual reports to the General Assembly of the United Nations.

From the jurisprudence of the Committee, 59 cases are summarized and/or reviewed in this publication. This Committee is more universally cited than any other of the institutions included, apart from the European Court of Human Rights. This reflects the paramount position of the Committee in its field of competence, which is so pertinent to police.

(*b*) Committee on the Elimination of Racial Discrimination

Article 8 of the International Convention on the Elimination of All Forms of Racial Discrimination provides that there shall be established a Committee on the Elimination of Racial Discrimination. The Committee shall consist of 18 experts of high moral standing and acknowledged impartiality. Consideration shall be given to equitable geographical distribution and to the representation of the different forms of civilization as well as of the principle legal systems. Elected at a meeting of States parties, members of the Committee serve in their personal capacity for a term of four years.

I:1

Under article 1 of the Convention, the term "racial discrimination" shall mean any distinction, exclusion, restriction or preference based on race, colour, descent, or national or ethnic origin which has the purpose or effect of nullifying or impairing the recognition, enjoyment or exercise, on an equal footing, of human rights and fundamental freedoms in the political, economic, social, cultural or any other field of public life. Under article 2, States parties to the Convention condemn racial discrimination and undertake to pursue by all appropriate means and without delay a policy of eliminating racial discrimination in all its forms and promoting understanding among all races. To this end they undertake, *inter alia*, to engage in no act or practice of racial discrimination against persons, groups of persons or institutions and to ensure that all public authorities and public institutions, national and local, shall act in conformity with this obligation. Furthermore, article 6 of the Convention provides that States parties shall assure to everyone within their jurisdiction effective protection and remedies, through the competent national tribunals and other State institutions, against any acts of racial discrimination which, contrary to the Convention, violate his human rights and fundamental freedoms. The Convention entered into force on 4 January 1969. At present, 170 States have ratified or acceded to this Convention.

Articles 11 to 13 of the Convention provide procedures to be followed when a State party considers that another State party is not giving effect to the provisions of the Convention. Under article 14, a State party may declare that it recognizes the competence of the Committee to receive and consider communications from individuals or groups of individuals within its jurisdiction claiming to be victims of a violation by that State of any of the rights set forth in the Convention. So far, 46 States have made such a declaration.

The Committee has considered a relatively small number of cases under article 14 of the Convention, some 30 communications since the competence of the Committee to exercise this function became effective on 3 December 1982. The communications are considered in closed meetings. The decisions on admissibility and the opinions adopted by the Committee after consideration of the merits are published in the Committee's annual reports to the General Assembly of the United Nations.

No cases from the jurisprudence of the Committee have been selected for a summary and/or review. Two cases, however, are cited as examples in the introduction to police functions and protection of human rights.[3]

---

[3] See part III, chap. 1 (*infra*, pp. 337-339).

(c) Committee on the Elimination of Discrimination against Women

Article 17 of the Convention on the Elimination of All Forms of Discrimination a-gainst Women provides that there shall be established a Committee on the Elimination of Discrimination against Women for the purpose of considering the progress made in the implementation of the Convention. The Committee shall consists of 23 experts of high moral standing and competence in the field covered by the Convention. Consideration shall be given to equitable geographical distribution and to the representation of the different forms of civilization as well as the principle legal systems. Elected at a meeting of States parties, members of the Committee serve in their personal capacity for a term of four years.

Under article 1 of the Convention, the term "discrimination against women" shall mean any distinction, exclusion or restriction made on the basis of sex which has the effect or purpose of impairing or nullifying recognition, enjoyment or exercise by women, irrespective of their marital status, on a basis of equality of men and women, of human rights and fundamental freedoms in the political, economic, social, cultural, civil or any other field. Under article 2, States parties to the Convention condemn discrimination against women in all its forms, agree to pursue by all appropriate means and without a delay a policy of eliminating discrimination against women. To this end they undertake, *inter alia*, to adopt appropriate legislative and other measures, including sanctions, prohibiting all discrimination against women and to establish legal protection of the rights of women on an equal basis with men and to ensure through the competent national tribunals and other public institutions the effective protection of women against any act of discrimination. The Convention entered into force on 3 September 1981. At present, 180 States have ratified or acceded to this Convention.

There are no provisions in the Convention setting forth procedures for dealing with communications against States parties from other States or from individuals. In respect of the latter, however, such a system is introduced in a separate treaty, the Optional Protocol to the Convention on the Elimination of All Forms of Discrimination against Women, which entered into force on 22 December 2000. Under article 1 of the Optional Protocol, a State party recognizes the competence of the Committee on the Elimination of Discrimination against Women to receive and consider communications submitted in accordance with article 2. Communications may be submitted by or on behalf of individuals or groups of individuals, under the jurisdiction of a State party, claiming to be victims of a violation of any of the rights set forth in the Convention by that State. At present, 74 States have ratified or acceded to the Optional Protocol.

I:1

With a few filed cases, the Committee has just started to develop its jurisprudence under the Optional Protocol. The communications are considered in closed meetings. The decisions on admissibility and the views adopted by the Committee after consideration of the merits are published in the Committee's annual reports to the General Assembly of the United Nations.

There are no cases from the jurisprudence of the Committee included in the present publication.

(*d*) Committee against Torture

Article 17 of the Convention against Torture and Other Cruel, Inhuman or Degrading Treatment or Punishment provides that there shall be established a Committee against Torture to carry out the functions set forth in the Convention. The Committee shall consist of 10 experts of high moral standing and recognized competence in the field of human rights. Consideration shall be given to equitable geographical distribution and to the usefulness of the participation of some persons with legal experience. Elected at a meeting of States parties, members of the Committee serve in their personal capacity for a term of four years.

In the preamble to the Convention, the States parties made reference to the prohibition of torture and cruel, inhuman or degrading treatment or punishment set forth, *inter alia*, in article 5 of the Universal Declaration of Human Rights and article 7 of the International Covenant on Civil and Political Rights. To make more effective the struggle against torture and other cruel, inhuman or degrading treatment or punishment throughout the world, the State parties agreed to the provisions embodied in the Convention.

Provisions of particular significance to police are the definition of the term "torture" in article 1 and the extension of the application of the Convention to other acts of cruel, inhuman or degrading treatment or punishment, not amounting to torture, in article 16; the obligation that States parties shall take effective legislative, administrative, judicial and orther measures to prevent acts of torture and the principle that no exceptional circumstances whatsoever, whether a state of war or a threat of war, internal political instability or any other public emergency, may be invoked as a justification of torture, nor an order from a superior officer or a public authority, in article 2; the right to prompt and impartial investigation into acts of torture believed or alleged to have been committed, in articles 12 and 13; the right of victims of torture to obtain redress and the enforceable right to fair and adequate compensation, in article 14; and the principle that any statement which is established to have been made as a result of torture shall not be invoked as evidence in any proceedings, except against a person accused of torture as evidence that the statement was made, in article

15. The Convention entered into force on 26 June 1987. At present, 141 States have ratified or acceded to the Convention.

The Committee is entrusted with a number of tasks, including the competence to receive and consider communications. Under article 21 of the Convention, a State party may at any time declare that it recognizes the competence of the Committee to receive and consider communications to the effect that a State party claims that another State party is not fulfilling its obligations under the Convention. Correspondingly, under article 22, a State party may at any time declare that it recognizes the competence of the Committee to receive and consider communications from or on behalf of individuals subject to its jurisdiction who claim to be victims of a violation by a State party of the provisions of the Convention. Respectively, 56 and 57 States parties have made declarations under articles 21 and 22.

About 250 communications have been filed under article 22 of the Convention. The communications are considered by the Committee in closed meetings. The decisions on admissibility and the views, since 2002 called decisions, adopted by the Committee after consideration of the merits are published in the Committee's annual reports to the General Assembly of the United Nations.

In this publication, seven cases from the jurisprudence of the Committee are summarized and/or reviewed.

(*e*) Working Group on Arbitrary Detention

In 1991, the United Nations Commission on Human Rights established the Working Group on Arbitrary Detention to investigate cases of detention imposed arbitrarily or otherwise inconsistently with the relevant international standards.[4] It forms part of a system of working groups and special rapporteurs with thematic or country mandates, often referred to as the special procedures of the Commission, extraconventional procedures established under the Charter of the United Nations. The jurisprudence of the Working Group is included in this publication, because its mandate is of significant relevance to police and its working methods are equivalent to a judicial process.

The Working Group is composed of five independent experts and was set up originally for a term of three years, later extended every three years. Under its mandate,

---

[4] See Commission on Human Rights resolution 1991/42 of 5 March 1991 (United Nations, *Official Records of the Economic and Social Council, 1991, Supplement No. 2* (E/1991/22), chap. II, sect. A).

I:1

as amended in 1997,[5] the Working Group is entrusted with the task of investigating cases of deprivation of liberty imposed arbitrarily, provided that no final decision has been taken in such cases by domestic courts in conformity with domestic law, with the relevant international standards set forth in the Universal Declaration of Human Rights and with the relevant international legal instruments accepted by the States concerned.

Under its current working methods,[6] the Working Group may receive communications from the individuals concerned, their families or their representatives as well as from Governments and intergovernmental and non-governmental organizations. The Working Group may also take up cases on its own initiative. It has taken the view that the investigation of a case should be of an adversarial nature so as to assist it in obtaining the cooperation of the State concerned.

When the Working Group examines allegations of violations of human rights and finds that the allegations could be more appropriately dealt with under another thematic special procedure, it may refer them to the working group or special rapporteur concerned. In cases of concurrent competence, the Working Group may consider taking joint action. When there is a country-specific mechanism in place, the Working Group decides on the action to be taken in consultation with the rapporteur or person responsible. Communications concerned with matters already referred to a treaty body dealing with individual cases are transmitted to that body if the person and facts involved are the same.

In the discharge of its mandate, the Working Group refers to the Universal Declaration of Human Rights and the relevant international instruments accepted by the State concerned, in particular the International Covenant on Civil and Political Rights. When appropriate, the Working Group also makes reference to relevant non-treaty instruments, such as the Body of Principles for the Protection of All Persons under Any Form of Detention or Imprisonment, the Standard Minimum Rules for the Treatment of Prisoners, United Nations Rules for the Protection of Juveniles Deprived of their Liberty and the United Nations Standard Minimum Rules for the Administration of Juvenile Justice (The Beijing Rules). Situations of armed conflict covered by the Geneva Conventions of 12 August 1949 and the Protocols Additional to the Geneva Conventions do not fall within the competence of the Working Group.

---

[5] See Commission on Human Rights resolution 1997/50 of 15 April 1997 (United Nations, *Official Records of the Economic and Social Council, 1997, Supplement No. 3* (E/1997/23), chap. II, sect. A).
[6] See United Nations document E/CN.4/1998/44, annex I.

In examining situations of deprivation of liberty, the Working Group regards such deprivation as arbitrary in the following cases: when it is clearly impossible to invoke any legal basis justifying the situation (category I); when the deprivation of liberty results from prosecution or from a conviction in connection with the exercise of the rights and freedoms proclaimed in articles 7, 13, 14, 18, 19, 20 and 21 of the Universal Declaration and, where applicable, articles 12, 18, 19, 21, 22, 25, 26 and 27 of the Covenant (category II); and when the total or partial non-observance of the international norms relating to the right to a fair trial, established in the Universal Declaration and in the relevant international instruments accepted by the States concerned, is of such gravity as to give the deprivation of liberty an arbitrary character (category III).

In dealing with communications, the Working Group concludes its consideration of the merits of the case by rendering an opinion, until 1997 called decisions. Exceptionally, it may reconsider its previous views. In cases of arbitrary deprivation of liberty, the Working Group requests the State to take necessary measures to remedy the situation. The decisions and opinions of the Working Group are published in its annual reports to the Commission on Human Rights.

The Working Group has received hundreds of communications concerning a large number of individual cases of alleged arbitrary deprivation of liberty. It has developed a rich jurisprudence in its field of competence. Six decisions and 12 opinions of the Working Group are summarized and/or reviewed in this publication.

(*f*) International Tribunal for the former Yugoslavia

In 1993, the Security Council of the United Nations established the International Tribunal for the Prosecution of Persons Responsible for Serious Violations of International Humanitarian Law Committed in the Territory of the Former Yugoslavia since 1991. The Council acted under its powers with respect to threats to the peace, breaches of the peace and acts of aggression set forth in Chapter VII of the Charter of the United Nations.[7] The resolution was passed in response to the serious violations of international humanitarian law committed in the territory of the former Yugoslavia and to the threat to international peace and security posed by those serious violations. The International Tribunal functions in accordance with the provisions of its Statute, adopted in that resolution. It is based in The Hague, the Netherlands. The International Tribunal is expected to have completed all of its work in the year 2010.

Under articles 1 to 7 of the Statute, the International Tribunal has the power to prosecute persons held individually responsible for grave breaches of the Geneva Con-

---

[7] See Security Council resolution 827 (1993) of 25 May 1993.

I:1

ventions of 12 August 1949, violations of the laws or customs of war, genocide and crimes against humanity, committed in the territory of the former Yugoslavia since 1 January 1991. Article 9 provides that the International Tribunal and national courts have concurrent jurisdiction over such violations of international humanitarian law. However, the International Tribunal has primacy over national courts. At any stage of the procedure, it may request national courts to defer to its competence.

Articles 11 to 17 of the Statute lay down the organization of the International Tribunal. At present, there are three trial chambers and an appeals chamber, the prosecutor and a registry.

The chambers consist of independent judges, 16 permanent judges and a maximum at any one time of nine *ad litem* judges. The permanent judges are elected by the General Assembly of the United Nations for a term of four years. They can be re-elected. The *ad litem* judges are drawn from a pool of 27 judges. They are also elected by the General Assembly for a term of four years, but they are not eligible for re-election. The *ad litem* judges serve in the trial chambers for specific trials for a period of up to three years. The judges shall be persons of high moral character, impartiality and integrity possessing the qualifications required in their respective countries for appointment to the highest judicial offices.

Each trial chamber consists of three permanent judges and a maximum at any one time of six *ad litem* judges. Trial chambers may be divided into sections of three judges, composed of both permanent and *ad litem* judges. Sections have the same powers and responsibilities as a trial chamber under the Statute. The appeals chamber consists of seven permanent judges: five judges of the International Tribunal and two from the International Criminal Tribunal for Rwanda. These seven judges also constitute the appeals chamber of the latter tribunal. Each appeal is heard and decided by five judges.

The prosecutor is responsible for the investigation and prosecution in cases under the jurisdiction of the International Tribunal and acts independently as a separate organ. The prosecutor is appointed by the Security Council to serve for a four-year term and may be reappointed. He or she shall be of high moral character and possess the highest level of competence and experience in the conduct of investigations and prosecutions of criminal cases.

The registry is responsible for the administration and servicing of the International Tribunal. The registrar is appointed by the Secretary-General of the United Nations for a term of four years and is eligible for reappointment.

Articles 18 to 24 of the Statute deal with procedures at the trial chamber level. Investigations are initiated by the prosecutor at his or her own discretion or on the basis of information obtained from any source, particularly from Governments, United Nations organs and intergovernmental and non-governmental organizations. Indictments must be confirmed by a judge prior to becoming effective. The trial commences only once the accused is physically present before the International Tribunal. At the initial appearance before the trial chamber, the accused is instructed to enter a plea.

The trial chambers shall ensure that a trial is fair and expeditious and that proceedings are conducted in accordance with the rules of procedure and evidence adopted by the judges of the International Tribunal. As an important guarantee of a fair trial, the accused is entitled to legal assistance, if necessary at the expense of the International Tribunal. Other important elements include the presumption of innocence, the right to be tried without undue delay, the right to examine adverse witnesses and the right of the accused not be compelled to testify against himself or herself or to confess guilt. As a general rule, the hearings are public. Separate provisions provide for the protection of victims and witnesses.

The trial chambers pronounce judgments and impose sentences and penalties on persons convicted of serious violations of international humanitarian law. The penalty imposed by the trial chamber shall be limited to imprisonment.

Under article 25 of the Statute, the appeals chamber shall hear appeals from persons convicted by a trial chamber or from the prosecutor on the grounds that there has been an error on a question of law invalidating the decision or an error of fact which has occasioned a miscarriage of justice. Decisions may be affirmed, reversed or revised by the appeals chamber. Article 26 provides for review proceedings.

Decisions and judgments are published. An annual report of the International Tribunal is submitted to the Security Council and the General Assembly of the United Nations.

In dealing with police behaviour in times of armed conflict, disturbance and tension, the jurispridence of the International Tribunal for the former Yugoslavia is of great significance to police. In this publication, three cases are cited.

(g) International Criminal Tribunal for Rwanda

In 1994, the Security Council of the United Nations established the International Criminal Tribunal for Rwanda for the sole purpose of prosecuting persons responsible for genocide and other serious violations of international humanitarian law com-

I:1

mitted in the territory of Rwanda and Rwandan citizens responsible for genocide and other such violations committed in the territory of neighbouring States, between 1 January and 31 December 1994. The Council acted under its powers with respect to threats to the peace, breaches of the peace and acts of aggression set forth in Chapter VII of the Charter of the United Nations.[8] Expressing its grave concern at the reports indicating that genocide and other systematic, widespread and flagrant violations of international humanitarian law had been committed in Rwanda, the Council was determined to put an end to such crimes and to take effective measures to bring to justice the persons responsible for them. The International Tribunal is is governed by its Statute, annexed to the resolution and to a large extent modelled on the Statute of the International Tribunal for the former Yugoslavia. It is located in Arusha, Tanzania. The International Tribunal is expected to have completed all of its work in the year 2010.

Under articles 1 to 6 of the Statute, the International Tribunal has the power to prosecute persons held individually responsible for genocide, crimes against humanity and violations of article 3 common to the Geneva Conventions of 12 August 1949 and the Protocol Additional to the Geneva Conventions of 12 August 1949, and relating to the Protection of Victims of Non-International Armed Conflicts (Protocol II), committed in Rwanda or neighbouring States in 1994. Article 8 provides that the International Tribunal and national courts have concurrent jurisdiction over such violations of international humanitarian law, but it has primacy over the national courts of all States. At any stage of the procedure, the International Tribunal may formally request national courts to defer to its competence.

Article 10 of the Statute stipulates that the International Tribunal shall consist of the chambers, the prosecutor and a registry. At present, there are three trial chambers and an appeals chamber. Articles 11 to 16 comprise further provisions on the organization of the International Tribunal.

The chambers consist of independent judges, 16 permanent judges and a maximum at any one time of nine *ad litem* judges. The permanent judges are elected by the General Assembly of the United Nations for a term of four years. They can be reelected. The *ad litem* judges are drawn from a pool of 18 judges. They are also elected by the General Assembly for a term of four years, but they are not eligible for reelection. The *ad litem* judges serve in the trial chambers for specific trials for a period of up to three years. The judges shall be persons of high moral character, impartiality and integrity possessing the qualifications required in their respective countries for appointment to the highest judicial offices.

---

[8] See Security Council resolution 955 (1994) of 8 November 1994.

Each trial chamber consists of three permanent judges and a maximum at any one time of six *ad litem* judges. Trial chambers may be divided into sections of three judges, composed of both permanent and *ad litem* judges. Sections have the same powers and responsibilities as a trial chamber under the Statute. The appeals chamber consists of seven permanent judges: two judges of the International Tribunal and five judges from the International Tribunal for the former Yugoslavia. The seven judges also constitute the appeals chamber of the latter tribunal. Each appeal is heard and decided by five judges.

The Prosecutor is responsible for the investigation and prosecution in cases under the jurisdiction of the International Tribunal and acts independently as a separate organ. Originally, the prosecutor of the International Tribunal for the former Yugoslavia also served as the prosecutor of the International Criminal Tribunal for Rwanda Since 2003, however, the Security Council shall appoint a separate prosecutor to serve for a four-year term and who may be reappointed. He or she shall be of high moral character and possess the highest level of competence and experience in the conduct of investigations and prosecutions of criminal cases.

The registry is responsible for the administration and servicing of the International Tribunal. The registrar is appointed by the Secretary-General of the United Nations for a term of four years and is eligible for reappointment.

Articles 17 to 23 of the Statute deal with procedures at the trial chamber level. Investigations are initiated by the prosecutor at his or her own discretion or on the basis of information obtained from any source, particularly from Governments, United Nations organs and intergovernmental and non-governmental organizations. Indictments must be confirmed by a judge prior to becoming effective. The trial commences only once the accused is physically present before the International Tribunal. At the initial appearance before the trial chamber, the accused is instructed to enter a plea.

The trial chambers shall ensure that a trial is fair and expeditious and that proceedings are conducted in accordance with the rules of procedure and evidence adopted by the judges of the International Tribunal. As an important guarantee of a fair trial, the accused is entitled to legal assistance, if necessary at the expense of the International Tribunal. Other important elements include the presumption of innocence, the right to be tried without undue delay, the right to examine adverse witnesses and the right of the accused not be compelled to testify against himself or herself or to confess guilt. As a general rule, the hearings are public. Separate provisions provide for the protection of victims and witnesses.

I:1

The trial chambers pronounce judgments and impose sentences and penalties on persons convicted of serious violations of international humanitarian law. The penalty imposed by the trial chamber shall be limited to imprisonment.

Under article 24 of the Statute, the appeals chamber shall hear appeals from persons convicted by a trial chamber or from the prosecutor on the grounds that there has been an error on a question of law invalidating the decision or an error of fact which has occasioned a miscarriage of justice. Decisions may be affirmed, reversed or revised by the appeals chamber. Article 25 provides for review proceedings.

Decisions and judgments are published. An annual report of the International Tribunal is submitted to the Security Council and the General Assembly of the United Nations.

Like the jurispridence of the International Tribunal for the former Yugoslavia, the case law of the International Criminal Tribunal for Rwanda is pertinent to the purposes of this publication. Two cases have been selected for review.

(*h*) Committee on Freedom of Association

In 1951, the Governing Body of the International Labour Office established the Committee on Freedom of Association. The Governing Body is one of the organs of the International Labour Organization (ILO). Originally formed in 1919 and since 1946 a specialized agency of the United Nations, the ILO aims to promote social justice and internationally recognized human and labour rights. As an intergovernmental organization it has a unique structure based on a tripartite decision-making system with representation of workers and employers as well as governments.

The International Labour Conference has adopted 185 conventions related to different matters falling within its field of competence. Eight of these conventions are regarded as fundamental human rights conventions, two of each in the following four categories: freedom of association and the effective recognition of the right to collective bargaining; the elimination of all forms of forced or compulsory labour; the effective abolition of child labour; and the elimination of discrimination in respect of employment and occupation. International labour standards established in these instruments are binding on the 178 member States of the International Labour Organization, even if they have not ratified the conventions, because they have endorsed the principles set forth in the ILO Constitution, as declared in 1998 by the International Labour Conference in the ILO Declaration on Fundamental Principles and Rights at Work. The two conventions in the first category are the Convention concerning Freedom of Association and Protection of the Right to Organise (No. 87) and the Convention concerning the Application of the Principles of the Right to Organise and to Bargain Collectively (No. 98), at present ratified by 144 and 154 States, respectively.

The Committee on Freedom of Association was set up as a supervisory procedure to ensure compliance with the constitutional right to freedom of association by States not parties to Conventions No. 87 and No. 98. The Committee has the purpose of examining complaints about violations of freedom of association against any member State of the International Labour Organization, irrespective of the status of the State in relation to these conventions. The Committee is a Governing Body committee composed of ten members: an independent chairperson and three representatives each of governments, employers and workers. It forms part of a system of different mechanisms for monitoring State compliance with international labour standards.

The Committee examines, in private meetings, complaints submitted to the Governing Body by employers' and/or workers' organizations. It establishes the facts of the case in dialogue with the Government concerned. A case may include several complaints and involve a large number of people, and new allegations may be added to the original complaints. A case may be considered together with other cases against the same State. Based on the complaint or complaints, the Government's reply and the Committee's conclusions, recommendations are made to the Governing Body for approval. The Committee may conclude its consideration of a case by making definitive recommendations, but often the Committee makes interim recommendations or requests to be informed by the Government of developments and reconsiders the case at subsequent sessions. In substance, unless the case does not call for further examination, the recommendations to the Governing Body include requests to the Government in respect of the case, reflecting the Committee's conclusions. For each case considered by the Committee during a session there is a report published in the Committee's report on the session to the Governing Body.

The Committee has developed a rich jurisprudence in its field of competence. It has examined more than 2,000 cases. Many of the complaints relate to police intervention and police behaviour in labour and industrial relations disputes, alleging violations of the right to life, acts of torture or other grave violations of the human rights of workers and employers. Other complaints concern infringement by police of the rights of trade unions and employer's organizations and their members. In response to such allegations of non-compliance with the principles of freedom of association, the Committee has made a number pronouncements of great significance to police. In this publication, 24 cases from the Committee's jurisprudence are cited.

I:1

(*i*) African Commission on Human and Peoples' Rights

Article 30 of the African Charter on Human and Peoples' Rights provides that an African Commission on Human and Peoples' Rights shall be established within the Organization of African Unity (OAU). The Commission shall promote human and people's rights and ensure their protection in Africa. In 1998, the OAU Assembly of Heads of State and Government adopted the Protocol to the African Charter on Human and Peoples' Rights on the Establishment of an African Court on Human and Peoples' Rights, a separate treaty in force since 25 January 2004. The Court is expected to come into operation in 2006 and shall complement the protective mandate of the Commission. In respect of the human rights of women, the provisions of the Charter are reinforced by the Protocol to the African Charter on Human and Peoples' Rights on the Rights of Women in Africa, a treaty in force since 25 November 2005. At present, there are 22 and 17 States parties to the Protocols, respectively. In 2002, the Organization of African Unity was replaced by the African Union, following the entry into force of the Constitutive Act of the African Union. The Charter entered into force on 21 October 1986. At present, all 53 member States of the African Union are parties to the Charter. The Commission is based in Banjul, The Gambia.

Articles 31 to 44 of the Charter contain further provisions on the establishment and organization of the Commission. It shall be composed of 11 members elected by the Assembly of Heads of State and Government for a term of six years and eligible for re-election. They shall be chosen from amongst African personalities of the highest reputation, known for their high morality, integrity, impartiality and competence in matters of human and peoples' rights, particularly, consideration being given to persons having legal experience. Members of the Commission serve in their personal capacity.

Under article 45 of the Charter, the Commission has the mandate to promote human and peoples' rights; to ensure the protection of human and peoples' rights; to interpret the provisions of the Charter; and to perform any other tasks entrusted to it by the Assembly of Heads of State and Government.

The Charter is a regional human rights treaty open to African States. Under article 1 of the Charter, the States parties shall recognize the rights, duties and freedoms enshrined in it and undertake to adopt legislative or other measures to give effect to them. Civil, cultural, economic, political and social rights as well as collective rights are set forth in the Charter. Provisions of particular relevance to police are, for example, those on the right to life, the prohibition of torture and the right to liberty and security of person. In discharging its mandate, the Commission shall draw inspiration from international law on human and peoples' rights, from the provisions of the Charter as well as other international instruments, and it shall take into consideration, as subsidiary measures to determine the principles of law, *inter alia*, customs generally accepted as law, general principles of law recognized by African States as well as legal precedents and doctrine, as stipulated in articles 60 and 61.

Articles 47 to 54 of the Charter lay down the procedure for dealing with inter-State complaints. If a State party has good reasons to believe that another State party has violated the provisions of the Charter, the matter may be referred to the Commission. The States concerned may be asked by the Commission to provide all relevant information, and they may submit written or oral representations before it. The Commission shall seek all necessary information and try to reach an amicable solution before it prepares a report on facts and findings. When transmitting the report to the Assembly of Heads of States and Government, the Commission may make recommendations deemed useful.

Articles 55 to 59 concern the procedure for dealing with other communications received by the Commission. If the majority of the members so decide, such communications shall be considered, provided certain conditions of admissibility are met and the States concerned are informed. If the Commission finds that communications apparently relate to special cases revealing the existence of a series of serious or massive violations of human and peoples' rights, the Commission shall draw the attention of the Assembly of Heads of States and Governments to these cases. The Assembly may then request the Commission to make an in-depth study of the cases and make a factual report, accompanied by its finding and recommendations. For cases of emergency, there is a special procedure.

All measures taken in relation to communications are confidential until the Assembly of Heads of State and Government otherwise decides. Reports on communications are published upon the decision of the Assembly. The Commission's annual report on its activities is published after it has been considered by the Assembly. In fact, the decisions of the Commission in respect of communications are included in the annual report, which the Assembly routinely takes note of and authorizes for publication.

Hundreds of communications have been filed with the Commission under the Charter. For the purposes of this publication, however, rather few cases are pertinent for summary and/or review, as the decisions of the Commission often do not contain a great deal of detail on the circumstances that led to the complaints. Clearly, the findings of the Commission are relevant and important in the African context. They are interesting to a wider audience for comparative purposes and because the African system for the protection of human rights has some unique features which are illustrated by these cases. From the jurisprudence of the Commission, seven cases are cited in this book.

I:1

(j) Inter-American Court of Human Rights

Under article 33 of the American Convention on Human Rights, the Pact of San José, Costa Rica, there shall be two organs competent in respect of matters relating to the fulfillment of State party commitments: the Inter-American Commission on Human Rights and the Inter-American Court of Human Rights. The Court was established by the Convention, but the Commission had already been set up under the Charter of the Organization of American States.

Articles 52 to 60 of the Convention contain provisions on the organization of the Court. It shall consist of seven judges. They shall be jurists of the highest moral authority and of recognized competence in the field of human rights, and they shall possess the qualifications required for the exercise of the highest judicial functions. The judges are elected in an individual capacity by the States parties to the Convention, in the General Assembly of the Organization of American States, for a term of six years, and they may be re-elected once. Under certain conditions, an *ad hoc* judge may be appointed by a State party to a case to serve on the Court in that case. The Court is located in San José, Costa Rica.

Under articles 34 to 37 of the Convention, the Inter-American Commission on Human Rights shall be composed of seven members. They shall be persons of high moral character and recognized competence in the field of human rights. They shall be elected in a personal capacity by the General Assembly of the Organization of American States for a term of four years and may be re-elected once. The Commission shall represent all member States.

The Convention is a regional human rights treaty open to the 35 member States of the Organization of American States. It entered into force on 18 July 1978. At present, there are 24 States parties to the Convention. Under article 1 of the Convention, States parties undertake to respect the rights and freedoms recognized in it and to ensure the free and full exercise of those rights and freedoms without discrimination. They also undertake, under article 2, to adopt such legislative and other measures as may be necessary to give effect to such rights and freedoms.

Civil and political rights are dealt with in articles 3 to 25 of the Convention. Many of the provisions are significant to police, such as those on the right to life, the right to humane treatment, the right to personal liberty, the right to a fair trial and the right to privacy. Article 25 stipulates that everyone has the right to simple and prompt recourse, or any other effective recourse, to a competent court or tribunal for protection against acts that violate his fundamental rights recognized by national law or the Convention, even though such violation may have been committed by persons in the course of their official duties. The States parties undertake to grant effective remedy.

Economic, social and cultural rights are mentioned in article 26. The States parties undertake to adopt measures for the progressive achievement of such rights. This provision is now supplemented by the Additional Protocol to the American Convention on Human Rights in the Area of Economic, Social and Cultural Rights, the Protocol of San Salvador. It entered into force on 16 November 1999 and has, at present, 13 States parties.

Under articles 61 and 62 of the Convention, only States parties and the Commission may submit cases to the Court, which has jurisdiction in all cases concerning the interpretation and application of the provisions of the Convention, provided that the States parties to the case recognize such jurisdiction. The Court may also have jurisdiction in cases under article 19 of the Additional Protocol.

Under article 44 of the Convention, any person or non-governmental organization legally recognized in one or more member States may lodge petitions with the Commission alleging violations of the Convention by a State party. Correspondingly, under article 45, the Commission may receive and examine communications from one State party against another when the States concerned have declared that they recognize such competence of the Commission.

Articles 48 to 51 of the Convention set out the procedure for the consideration of petitions or communications received by the Commission. In cases where the petition or communication is not found inadmissible, the record is not closed and there is no friendly settlement reached, the Commission draws up a report setting forth the facts and stating its conclusions. In transmitting the report to the States concerned, the Commission may make proposals and recommendations. If the matter has not been settled or submitted to the Court within a three-month period from the transmittal of the report, the Commission may take further action to conclude its consideration of the petition or communication.

Under article 63 of the Convention, if the Court finds that there has been a violation of a right or freedom protected by the Convention, it shall rule that the injured party shall be ensured the enjoyment of the right or freedom that was violated. It shall also rule, if appropriate, that the consequences of the measure or situation that constituted the breach shall be remedied and that fair compensation shall be paid to the injured party. For cases of extreme gravity and urgency, a fast procedure is provided.

Articles 66 to 69 of the Convention contain provisions on procedure. Reasons shall be given for the judgment of the Court, and it shall be final and not subject to appeal. However, at the request of any of the parties to the case, the Court shall interpret its judgment if there is a disagreement as to the meaning or scope of it. The

I:1

States parties undertake to comply with the judgment of the Court in any case to which they are parties. Decisions and judgments of the Court are published.

The Commission has registered a large number of complaints under the Convention. However, relatively few cases have been heard by the Court. There are judgments in about 50 reported cases. Many of them are of great interest to police. From the jurisprudence of the Court, judgments on the merits in 12 cases have been selected for summary and/or review.

(k) European Court of Human Rights

Article 19 of the Convention for the Protection of Human Rights and Fundamental Freedoms, or the European Convention on Human Rights as it is generally known, prescribes the setting up of the European Court of Human Rights to ensure the observance of the engagements undertaken by the States parties to the Convention. It shall function on a permanent basis. Under articles 20 to 23, the Court shall consists of a number of judges equal to that of States parties to the Convention, at present 45 States. The judges sit on the Court in their individual capacity. They shall be of high moral character and must either possess the qualifications required for appointment to high judicial office or be jurisconsults of recognized competence. The judges are elected by the Parliamentary Assembly of the Council of Europe for a term of six years, and they may be re-elected. The term of office shall expire when the judge reaches the age of 70. Under article 27, in considering cases before it, the Court shall sit in committees of three judges, in chambers of seven judges and in a grand chamber of 17 judges. The Court is based in Strasbourg, France.

The Convention is a regional human rights treaty open to members of the Council of Europe. In fact, it is ratified by all member States but one, a new member that has signed the Convention. It entered into force on 3 September 1953. The original Convention has been supplemented by a number of Protocols. Protocol No. 11 to the Convention for the Protection of Human Rights and Fundamental Freedoms, restructuring the control machinery established thereby, entered into force on 1 November 1998. Apart from introducing new mechanisms for the consideration of State compliance with the obligations under the Convention, this Protocol included many other changes in the structure and text of the Convention. In this publication, the Convention is cited as amended by the Protocol unless otherwise indicated.

Under the previous system, there were two organs set up to ensure the observance by States parties of the provisions of the Convention: the European Commission of Human Rights and the European Court of Human Rights. Both organs consisted of a number of members, serving in their individual capacity, equal to that of the States parties. None of the organs functioned on a full-time basis. The Commission was authorized to receive inter-State complaints as well as petitions from any person, non-governmental organization or group of individuals claiming to be the victim of a violation of the rights set forth in the Convention by a State party which had recognized such competence of the Commission. In admissible cases not already completed, the Commission transmitted to the Committee of Ministers of the Council of Europe a report on the facts and its view on whether they disclosed a breach of the obligations under the Convention. The States parties and the Commission had an exclusive right to bring a case before the Court under certain conditions. If the case was not referred to the Court within a three-month period from the transmission of the report, the Committee of Ministers had to decide on the question of a violation of the Convention.

Under article 1 of the Convention, the States parties shall ensure to everyone within their jurisdiction the rights and freedoms defined in it. Articles 2 to 18 deal with the rights protected by the Convention, all civil and political rights. Provisions of particular interest to police are, *inter alia*, those dealing with the right to life, the prohibition of torture, the right to liberty and security, the right to a fair trial and the right to respect for private and family life. In cases of a violation, everyone shall have the right to an effective remedy before a national authority notwithstanding that the violation has been committed by persons acting in an official capacity.

Article 32 of the Convention provides that the Court's jurisdiction shall extend to all matters concerning the interpretation and application of the Convention and its protocols. Any State party may refer to the Court, under article 33, any alleged breach of the provisions of the Convention and the protocols by another State party. Under article 34, the Court may also receive applications from any person, non-governmental organization or group of individuals claiming to be the victim of a violation by a State party of the rights set forth in the Convention or the protocols. Article 35 sets out the admissibility criteria. If the Court declares the application admissible, it shall, under article 38, pursue the examination of the case and place itself at the disposal of the parties concerned for confidential friendly settlement proceedings. Hearings shall be public unless otherwise decided, as stated in article 40.

Articles 42 to 46 include provisions on judgments and decisions. Reasons shall be given for judgments and decisions on admissibility. The judgment of a chamber of the Court is final when the parties declare that they will not refer the case to the grand chamber, when there is no request to refer the case to the grand chamber within three months after the judgment or when such a request is rejected. A panel of five judges of the grand chamber may accept the request if the case raises a serious question affecting the interpretation or application of the Convention and its protocols or a serious issue of general importance. A chamber may also, under article 30, before rendering its judgment, relinquish its jurisdiction to the grand chamber in certain cases. Judgments of the grand chamber are final. The final judgment of the Court shall be published.

Article 41 of the Convention provides that the Court, if it finds that there has been a violation of the Convention or the protocols and the internal law of the State party concerned allows only partial reparation to be made, shall, if necessary, afford just satisfaction to the injured party. Under article 46, final judgments of the Court are legally binding on States parties to the Convention in any case to which they are parties. Furthermore, final judgments shall be transmitted to the Committee of Ministers, which shall supervise their execution.

Many thousands of applications have been lodged under the European Convention on Human Rights, and the Court has delivered judgments and decisions in a large number of cases. Although it is a regional system for the protection of human rights, cases under this Convention are the most frequently cited in this publication. They include many pronouncements of the Court on standards and principles of universal application of great significance to police, and sometimes other international institutions make reference to the Court's jurisprudence in their own work. From the jurisprudence of the Court, 60 cases, including one inter-State case, are summarized and/or reviewed. Additionally, three cases declared inadmissible by the Commission and two cases, including one inter-State case, decided upon by the Committee of Ministers, under the then article 32 of the Convention, are cited because of their relevance for the development of the Court's case law.

E. HUMAN RIGHTS AND POLICING

The cases summarized and/or reviewed in this book can be seen as a catalogue of errors, negligence and, in some cases, serious criminality by police officials. In some respects, this is inevitable in a publication of this nature, devoted as it is to cases in which people have, generally successfully, claimed to have been the victims of human rights violations. Furthermore, one of the reasons that the international system for the protection of human rights came into being was to protect people from abuse of power by the State. As state officials empowered to use force and to deprive people of their liberty, it is axiomatic that the exercise of powers by the police will be scrutinized by the institutions of that system.

Police are typically expected and required to provide instant but temporary solutions to emergencies that occur in the societies they regulate and protect. These emergencies arise out of the complexities and exigencies of individual human behaviour and human societies. The laws that police seek to apply in response to such situations cannot reflect and respond to human behaviour in all its diversity. Furthermore, a variety of other factors come into play in the processes of policing, for example, the exploitation by politicians of public concerns about policing, criminality and social disorder for political advantage; the underlying causes of criminality and social disorder in a society that are beyond the influence or control of police; and the adequacy of resources allocated to police and of education and training of police.

None of this justifies human rights violations, especially egregious violations of the right to life and the prohibition of torture, but it does begin to explain why and how even well meaning police officials can violate human rights. Policing generally, and the enforcement of law in particular, can be a messy, untidy business, especially when attempted in chaotic and dangerous conditions.

However, it is much too simplistic to portray the relationship between human rights and policing as one where police are seen simply as actual or potential violators of human rights. It is more accurately depicted by the notions of respect, protection, investigation and entitlement. Of course, police must respect human rights when they exercise their powers. Otherwise, a contradiction arises in which police, law enforcers, break the law protecting human rights in order to enforce the law. When this happens, police are not reducing criminality. They are adding to it.

Concerning the protection of human rights, police do this in the performance of their various functions. In fact, the protection of human rights is a police function. Police protect human rights in a general sense, because in their efforts to contain crime and disorder, they contribute to conditions that are necessary for the enjoyment of all human rights. Police also protect specific human rights in very specific ways. For example, in preventing and investigating crimes of homicide, police protect the right to life. After all, human rights treaties require States parties to protect the right to life by law, and such protection cannot be provided without adequate policing.

The investigative function of police includes a duty to investigate human rights violations, because, in the first instance, some violations, such as violations of the right to life and of the prohibition of torture, are very serious crimes. Furthermore, human rights instruments and the jurisprudence of human rights institutions require that alleged or suspected violations of human rights should be investigated. Whilst it has not been specified that police should carry out these investigations, indeed in some cases it would not be appropriate for them to do so, in many cases it is inevitable that police will investigate. Prompt, impartial and effective investigation of human rights abuse reinforces other measures to ensure respect for and protection of human rights, including human rights of police.

Finally, police are entitled, as are all members of the human family, to human rights and especially to the full range of economic, social and cultural rights as well as civil and political rights. Above and beyond this, politicians and police leaders need to

I:1

be aware that the nature of police work is such that police officials have particular human rights entitlements. Police work has its own dangers, difficulties and discomforts. Not all of these can be removed, but, for example, inadequacies in training, equipment, briefing or deployment that lead to the death of a police official are, at first view, a violation of that official's right to life. It is not appropriate in this publication to examine the full range of human rights from the point of view of police entitlements, but on the question of police pay and conditions of service, politicians and members of societies generally need to ask themselves whether these are sufficient to maintain the human dignity of police officials and to provide a bulwark against corruption.

PART II

Police Powers and Respect for Human Rights

1. Introduction to Police Powers and Respect for Human Rights

Powers to use force, to deprive people of their liberty as well as to search and carry out surveillance activities are essential to the processes of policing. These powers are some of the necessary and legitimate means a society has at its disposal to contain criminality and social disorder. Furthermore, lawful and humane exercise of powers by police reinforces the rule of law and enhances security. However, unlawful and inhumane exercise of powers undermines the rule of law and creates a climate of insecurity and fear. Such actions are generally serious forms of criminality in themselves and particularly reprehensible forms of social disorder.

The extent to which police officials in any police agency exercise their powers lawfully and humanely is a measure of their professionalism. It is also a measure of the capacity of that agency to be an effective servant of the people in a democratic society governed by the rule of law.

There are reviews and summaries of cases involving the exercise of police powers from a wide variety of international human rights institutions in the ensuing chapters of this part of the book. Apart from the Working Group on Arbitrary Detention and the Committee on Freedom of Association, they are all courts and bodies established under universal or regional human rights treaties.

The jurisprudence of these various institutions is extremely rich and interesting in respect of human rights violations arising out of the exercise of police powers. This reflects characteristics that are common to policing everywhere. It also reflects differences in policing as it is practised in the various States with their diverse political and legal systems and their distinctive social groupings and cultures. Whilst such diversity and distinctiveness are recognized and even applauded, and it is acknowledged that the implementation of human rights must take into account local circumstances and cultures, the human rights standards protected by international human rights institutions are, nevertheless, universal. Political, social and economic elites in States do invoke differences between States, and especially cultural differences, to justify serious human rights violations committed by them or on their behalf in defence of their own selfish and sectional interests. Police are used, or misused, to these ends.

II:1

Many of the States featuring in the cases selected for this book are, to varying degrees, democracies governed by the rule of law, or States aspiring to that condition. Some States that were in the grip of authoritarian regimes when these cases were brought are undergoing processes of transition to more democratic forms of governance. Whatever the type of political regime, human rights violations are an affront to human dignity, and in democratic States, or States making the transition to democracy, human rights violations undermine democracy and the rule of law. A professional, public police serves democracy and the rule of law, and in that way is the servant of the people. The cases summarized and/or reviewed in the following chapters reinforce the need for professional policing, which is effective, lawful and humane, and they reinforce the great legal and humanitarian principles by which police should operate.

The following chapters in this part of the book deal with, respectively, the right to life; the prohibition of torture; the right to liberty and security of person; and the prohibition of arbitrary interference with privacy.

In many of the cases there are allegations that a number of human rights have been violated. Such cases are normally cited only in the chapter where it is most appropriate to include them for the purposes of this publication. Occasionally, however, the circumstances of a case are such that it merits inclusion in more than one chapter. In this connection, it seems appropriate to make some general observations about the phenomenon of enforced or involuntary disappearances, as they involve multiple human rights violations of the most serious kind, typically violations of the right to life, the prohibition of torture, the right to humane conditions of detention as well as the right to liberty and security of person.

In the leading case of the Inter-American Court of Human Rights on enforced or involuntary disappearance of persons, the *Velásquez Rodríguez* case (*Honduras*),[1] summarized in connection with the right to life[2] and also cited in connection with the prohibition of torture[3] and the right to liberty and security of person,[4] the Court observed that the phenomenon of disappearance was a complex form of human rights violation that had to be understood and confronted in an integral fashion. Although this practice existed virtually world-wide, it had occurred with exceptional intensity in Latin America in the last few years.

---

[1] See Inter-American Court of Human Rights, Series C: *Decisions and Judgments*, No. 4 (1988), petition No. 7920, judgment of 29 July 1988.
[2] See part II, chap. 2, sect. C (*c*) (*infra*, pp. 74-85).
[3] See part II, chap. 3, sect. B (*e*) (*infra*, p. 146).
[4] See part II, chap. 4, sect. B (*e*) (*infra*, p. 228).

The Court made reference to the Working Group on Enforced or Involuntary Disappearances, established in 1980 by the United Nations Commission on Human Rights to examine questions relevant to enforced or involuntary disappearances of persons.[5] The establishment of the Working Group was seen by the Court as a clear demonstration of general censure and repudiation of the practice of disappearances. The main purpose of the Working Group, which like the Working Group on Arbitrary Detention forms part of the special procedures of the Commission, is to assist families in determining the fate and whereabouts of their missing relatives who, having disappeared, are situated outside the protective precinct of the law. The Court also mentioned references to disappearances, repeatedly made within the inter-American system, to the effect that the practice should be investigated and stopped.

Furthermore, the Court made the point that whilst international practice and doctrine had often categorized disappearances as a crime against humanity, there was no treaty using that terminology in force and applicable to the States parties to the American Convention on Human Rights. Since that judgment, however, there have been some developments in this respect.

In the inter-American system for the promotion and protection of human rights, the Inter-American Convention on Forced Disappearance of Persons is in force since 1996. In the preamble to the Convention, the States parties reaffirm that the systematic practice of the forced disappearance of persons constitutes a crime against humanity. A less emphatic pronouncement was made in 1992 by the General Assembly of the United Nations in a non-treaty instrument. In the preamble to the Declaration on the Protection of All Persons from Enforced Disappearance, the systematic practice of acts of enforced disappearance was considered to be of the nature of a crime against humanity. Finally, in article 7 of the Rome Statute of the International Criminal Court, a treaty in force since 2002, enforced disappearance of persons is categorized as a crime against humanity when the act is committed as part of a widespread or systematic attack directed against any civilian population, with knowledge of the attack.

Article II of the Inter-American Convention contains a definition of forced disappearance similar to the description of enforced disappearance in article 1 of the Declaration. Further developed in article 7 of the Rome Statute, the term "enforced disappearance of persons" is defined as the arrest, detention or abduction of persons by, or with the authorization, support or acquiescence of, a State or a political organization, followed by a refusal to acknowledge that the deprivation of freedom or to give

---

[5] See Commission on Human Rights resolution 20 (XXXVI) of 29 February 1980 (United Nations, *Official Records of the Economic and Social Council, 1980, Supplement No. 3* (E/1980/ 13 and Corr.1), chap. XXVI, sect. A).

II:1

information on the fate or whereabouts of those persons, with the intention of removing them from the protection of the law for a prolonged period of time.

The cases on enforced or involuntary disappearances cited in the following chapters should be seen in the context of this array of measures taken to prevent a particularly wicked form of human rights abuse and to bring to justice perpetrators of these crimes.

2. Right to Life

A. INTRODUCTION

The primary purpose of the right to life is to protect people from being unlawfully killed by the State. It is enshrined in article 3 of the Universal Declaration of Human Rights, and it is protected by various universal and regional human rights treaties as well as by non-treaty instruments. The right to life is elaborated, developed and delineated in the jurisprudence of international human rights institutions. It is considered to express a general principle of international law binding on all States. Major human rights treaties protect the right to life as a non-derogable right. Article 4 of the International Covenant on Civil and Political Rights, for example, states that no derogation may be made from the provisions on the the right to life in article 6 of the Covenant, not even in time of public emergency threatening the life of the nation. Under international humanitarian law, murder and other forms of unlawful killing are prohibited in times of international and non-international armed conflict, as stated in the Geneva Conventions of 12 August 1949 and the Protocols Additional to the Geneva Conventions. Unlawful killings may also constitute international crimes under the Rome Statute of the International Criminal Court.

The Convention on the Rights of the Child may illustrate different aspects of the right to life in the context of a treaty of general application, as it contains a number of measures designed, directly or indirectly, to protect the right to life of children. Under article 6, for example, the States parties recognize that every child has the inherent right to life, and they shall ensure to the maximum extent possible the survival and development of the child. Article 24 sets out a number of measures to ensure the health of children. In particular, the States parties are required to take approriate measures to diminish infant and child mortality. Article 38 contains a number of provisions to protect children in times of armed conflict. For example, the States parties undertake to respect and ensure respect for rules of international humanitarian law applicable to them in armed conflicts, which are relevant to the child, and they shall take all feasible measures to ensure that persons who have not attained the age of 15 years do not take a direct part in hostilities. The application of the latter rule is extended to 18 years by article 1 of the Optional Protocol to the Convention on the Rights of the Child on the involvement of children in armed conflict. Under article 1 of the Convention, a child means every human being below the age of 18 years unless, under the law applicable, majority is attained earlier.

II:2

A number of non-treaty instruments are of great significance to police, because they set out standards on the use of force. Compliance with these reinforces protection of the right to life and enhances the professionalism and effectiveness of police. The Code of Conduct for Law Enforcement Officials requires, in article 3, police to use force only when strictly necessary and to the extent required for the purpose. In the explanatory commentary to this article, it is stated that firearms should not be used except when a suspected offender offers armed resistance or otherwise jeopardizes the lives of others and less extreme measures would be ineffective. The 26 principles constituting the Basic Principles on the Use of Force and Firearms by Law Enforcement Officials set out professional standards on this aspect of policing. Principle 9 stipulates, *inter alia*, that law enforcement officials shall not use firearms against persons except in self-defence or defence of others against imminent threat of death or serious injury. Under the European Code of Police Ethics, a regional instrument more recently adopted, police may use force only when strictly necessary and only to the extent required to obtain a legitimate objective, as stated in article 37 of the Code.

Finally, of great relevance to the right to life is the question of extrajudicial, arbitrary and summary executions. A universal non-treaty instrument, the Principles on the Effective Prevention and Investigation of Extra-legal, Arbitrary and Summary Executions has been designed to prevent unlawful killings by State officials and to ensure that any such killings are thoroughly investigated. Governments shall prohibit by law all extralegal, arbitrary and summary executions and ensure that any such executions are recognized as criminal offences punishable by appropriate penalties. Executions of this nature shall not be carried out whatever the cirumstances. Governments shall ensure strict control, including a clear chain of command over all officials responsible for apprehension, arrest, detention, custody and imprisonment, as well as those officials authorized by law to use force and firearms.

The Special Rapporteur on extrajudicial, summary or arbitary executions implements a thematic special procedure of the United Nations Commission on Human Rights, originally established in 1982.[1] Under the mandate, as amended in 1992,[2] the Special Rapporteur is entrusted with the task of examining situations of extrajudicial, summary or arbitrary executions. The Special Rapportuer is required to submit

---

[1] See Commission on Human Rights resolution 1982/29 of 11 March 1992 (United Nations, *Official Records of the Economic and Social Council, 1982, Supplement No. 2* (E/1982/12 and Corr.1), chap. XXVI, sect. A) and Economic and Social Council resolution 1982/35 of 7 May 1982.

[2] See Commission on Human Rights resolution 1992/72 of 5 March 1992 (United Nations, *Official Records of the Economic and Social Council, 1992, Supplement No. 2* (E/1992/22), chap. II, sect. A).

his or her findings on an annual basis, together with conclusions and recommendations, to the Commission and to respond effectively to information received, in particular when an extrajudicial, summary or arbitrary execution is imminent or seriously threatened or when such an execution has occured.

Situations in which the Special Rapporteur has acted have included the following: genocide; violations of the right to life during armed conflict, especially of the civilian population and other non-combatants, contrary to international humanitarian law; deaths due to attacks or killings by security forces of the State or by paramilitary groups, death squads or other private forces cooperating with or tolerated by one or several States; deaths due to the use of force by law enforcement officials or persons acting in direct or indirect compliance with the State when the use of force is inconsistent with the criteria of absolute necessity and proportionality; deaths in custody due to torture, neglect or use of force or life-threatening conditions of detention; death threats and fear of imminent extrajudicial executions by State officials, paramilitary groups, private individuals or groups cooperating with or tolerated by the Government; and breach of the obligation to investigate alleged violations of the right to life and to bring those responsible to justice.[3]

Powers granted to police under national laws to use force, including lethal force, are essential to the purposes of policing. The cases summarized and/or reviewed in this chapter of the book indicate how these laws, and the application of lethal force by police, are scrutinized and judged by international institutions. They also show how State authorities, including the police, are expected to take positive steps to protect the right to life.

B. REVIEW OF CASES

(*a*) Human Rights Committee

Article 6 of the International Covenant on Civil and Political Rights protects the right to life. Under paragraph 1, every human being has the inherent right to life, and this right shall be protected by law. No one shall be arbitrarily deprived of life.

In the remainder of the article, paragraphs 2 to 6, there are provisions on the death penalty and on the crime of genocide. The Covenant does not prohibit the capital punishment, and thus it does not provide an absolute protection for the right to life. However, it does require that it is imposed only for the most serious crimes and that it is carried out pursuant to a final judgment rendered by a competent court. Furthermore, it stipulates that there shall be a right to seek pardon or commutation of the

---

[3] See e.g. United Nations document E/CN.4/2002/74, para. 8.

II:2

sentence and that it shall not be carried out on persons below 18 years of age or on pregnant women.

The provisions of article 6 are protected from derogation under article 4 of the Covenant. Not even in time of public emergency threatening the life of the nation may a State party take measures derogating from its obligations under article 6.

The provisions on the death penalty are complemented by the Second Optional Protocol to the International Covenant on Civil and Political Rights, aiming at the abolition of the death penalty, open to States parties to the Covenant and in force since 1991. Under this treaty, no one shall be executed within the territory of a State party to the Protocol, and all necessary measures shall be taken to abolish the death penalty within its jurisdiction. However, reservations are allowed for the application of the death penalty in time of war.

Article 6, paragraph 1, of the Covenant, in addition to proclaiming the inherent right to life, places obligations on States to enact laws guaranteeing that right and to ensure that such laws are not applied so as arbitrarily to deprive an individual of his life. The term "arbitrary" has a wider meaning than "unlawful" in that a killing may breach article 6 even though it is within the domestic law of a State. In its general comment No. 6 (16) concerning article 6 of the Covenant,[4] the Human Rights Committee has described the protection against arbitrary deprivation of life as one of paramount importance.[5]

In the same general comment, the Committee has characterized the right to life as the supreme right from which no derogation is permitted.[6] Whilst this chapter is concerned primarily with the right to life as it is affected by acts or omissions of the police, the Committee has favoured a broad interpretation of the right and given the reduction of infant mortality and the elimination of malnutrition as examples of positive measures States can take to protect the right to life.[7]

The Committee has considered that States parties should take measures not only to prevent and punish deprivation of life by criminal acts, but also to prevent arbitrary killing by their own security forces. It has added that the deprivation of life by the authorities of the State is a matter of the utmost gravity and that, therefore, the law must strictly control and limit the circumstances in which a person may be deprived

---

[4] See United Nations, *Official Records of the General Assembly, Thirty-seventh Session, Supplement No. 40* (A/37/40), annex V.
[5] *Ibidem*, para. 3.
[6] *Ibidem*, para. 1.
[7] *Ibidem*, para. 5.

of his life by such authorities.[8] Whilst there may be good reasons for distinguishing between deprivation of life by criminal acts and arbitrary killings by security forces, it is, perhaps, unfortunate that general comment No. 6 (16) is worded in this way, because arbitrary killings by security forces are also criminal acts. Nevertheless, the message is clear. Deprivation of life by the State is an extremely grave matter to be strictly limited and controlled by law.

Much of the jurisprudence of the Committee on article 6 has concerned cases brought by prisoners on death row in countries in the Caribbean region and cases against States in Latin America arising out of killings and disappearances perpetrated by members of security forces in the 1970's and 1980's. In many of the former cases, submissions are made, sometimes successfully, claiming that to carry out a sentence of death following a trial conducted in breach of the right to a fair trial set forth in article 14 of the Covenant would breach both articles.

The case *María Fanny Suárez de Guerrero* v. *Colombia*,[9] summarized in section C[10] and also cited in connection with the respect for and protection of human rights in times of armed conflict, disturbance and tension,[11] is included primarily because of the views the Committee expressed on the use of force by police. The communication was submitted on behalf the victim's husband and concerned the premeditated and calculated slaughter by police of seven unarmed people, among them Mrs. Suárez de Guerrero, in connection with a raid carried out on 13 April 1978 at a house where a kidnapped person was believed to be held prisoner. Whilst the actions that led to this case are shocking, they are not unique, and they are not confined to States where democracy and the rule of law are weak. This is an example of what can, and does, happen when police and other security forces are given extraordinary powers under emergency legislation.

Police leaders and those responsible for securing the accountability of police and security forces need to be aware of the various factors that can lead to egregious violations of fundamental human rights. Such factors include the granting of emergency powers; the pressures on police to provide effective responses to the activities of armed opposition groups or terrorists; the undoubted dangers that police face when confronting such groups; and a propensity in some cases to overreact to their provocations. The need for leadership, supervision and oversight is very strong when such circumstances exist.

---

[8] *Ibidem*, para. 3.
[9] *Ibidem*, annex XI, communication No. 45/1979, views adopted on 31 March 1982.
[10] See part II, chap. 2, sect. C (*a*) (*infra*, pp. 67-72).
[11] See part IV, chap. 2, sect. B (*a*) (*infra*, pp. 541-542).

II:2

In the *María Fanny Suárez de Guerrero* case, the Committee observed that there was no evidence that the action of the police was necessary in their own defence, or that of others, or that it was necessary to effect the arrest or prevent the escape of the persons concerned. It was the Committee's view that the action of the police resulting in the death of Mrs. Suárez de Guerrero was disproportionate to the requirements of law enforcement in the circumstances. These are all-important principles on the use of force, and especially on the use of lethal force, that police should follow.

Another significant observation made by the Committee in this case was that the victims were no more than suspects of a crime. Their killing by the police deprived them of all the protections of due process of law laid down by the Covenant. As one of the purposes of policing is to protect the rule of law, it is manifestly important that police actions should reinforce and not subvert the due process of law.

The Committee concluded that Mrs. Suárez de Guerrero was arbitrarily deprived of her life in violation of article 6, paragraph 1, of the Covenant. If the police action was justifiable under Colombian law, the right to life was not adequately protected by law as required by the same provision of the Covenant.

The Committee has expressed some important principles on the question of enforced or involuntary disappearances. For example, in the case *Herrera Rubio* v. *Colombia*,[12] also cited in connection with the respect for and protection of human rights in times of armed conflict, disturbance and tension,[13] the author, Joaquín Herrera Rubio, a Colombian citizen, claimed that his parents, José Herrera and Emma Rubio de Herrera, were abducted on 27 March 1981 from their home by force and subsequently killed, thus revealing a violation of article 6 of the Covenant. The Committee referred to its general comment No. 6 (16), providing, *inter alia*, that States parties should take specific and effective measures to prevent the disappearance of individuals. Furthermore, they should establish effective facilities and procedures to investigate thoroughly cases of missing and disappeared persons in circumstances which might involve a violation of the right to life.[14]

The author further claimed to be a victim of torture and ill-treatment in violation of articles 7 and 10 of the Covenant. Following his arrest on 17 March 1981 by members of the Colombian armed forces on suspicion of being a "guerrillero", he was

---

[12] See United Nations, *Official Records of the General Assembly, Forty-third Session, Supplement No. 40* (A/43/40), annex VII, sect. B, communication No. 161/1983, views adopted on 2 November 1987.

[13] See part IV, chap. 2, sect. B (*a*) (*infra*, p. 542).

[14] See United Nations, *Official Records of the General Assembly, Thirty-seventh Session, Supplement No. 40* (A/37/40), annex V, para. 4.

tortured by the military authorities. They also threatened to kill his parents unless he signed a confession. He gave a very detailed description of the ill-treatment to which he had been subjected, and he provided the names of those allegedly responsible.

The State party made submissions on investigations carried out into the deaths, duly noted by the Committee. However, the Committee observed, the investigations appeared to have been inadequate in the light of the State party's obligations under article 2 of the Covenant. According to this article, each State party undertakes, *inter alia*, to respect and ensure to all individuals within its territory and subject to its jurisdiction the rights recognized in the Covenant; to adopt laws or other measures to give effect to such rights; and to provide an effective remedy to any person whose rights or freedoms have been violated.

An important element of the obligations under article 2 is that the protection of Covenant rights must be effective, and this requires a variety of measures. Effective protection of the right to life includes effective protection against abduction, torture and killing by forces of the State, and effective remedy requires an effective investigation. The Committee found a violation of article 6 of the Covenant, because the State party had failed to take appropriate measures to prevent the disappearance and subsequent killings of the parents of Mr. Herrera Rubia. It also found that he had been subjected to torture and ill-treatment during his detention, in violation of articles 7 and 10, paragraph 1, of the Covenant.

The Committee made similar reference to its general comment No. 6 (16) and to article 2 of the Covenant in the case *Nydia Bautista de Arellana* v. *Colombia*,[15] another case involving a situation of disappearance. The author of the communication was instructed by the relatives and family of Nydia Erika Bautista de Arellana, a Colombian citizen who disappeared on 30 August 1987 and whose body was subsequently recovered. It was claimed that she was the victim of violations by Colombia of, *inter alia*, article 6 of the Covenant.

In this case, the Committee noted that two Colombian institutions, the national delegate for human rights and an administrative tribunal, had clearly established the responsibility of State agents for the disappearance and subsequent death of the victim. It concluded that the State party was directly responsible for her disappearance and subsequent assassination, thus revealing a violation of article 6, paragraph 1, of the Covenant. The Committee then not only stressed the duty of the State party to investigate thoroughly alleged violations of human rights, and in particular forced disappearances of persons and violations of the right to life, but it insisted that the State

---

[15] *Ibidem, Fifty-first Session, Supplement No. 40* (A/51/40), vol. II, annex VIII, sect. S, communication No. 563/1993, views adopted on 27 October 1995.

should prosecute criminally, try and punish those held responsible for such violations. The Committee also found other violations of the Covenant in this case.

The next two cases in this review concern the duty of the State to protect the right to life of detainees.

In the case *Guillermo Ignacio Dermit Barbato and Hugo Haroldo Dermit Barbato* v. *Uruguay*,[16] also cited in connection with the respect for and protection of human rights in times of armed conflict, disturbance and tension,[17] the author, Hugo Gilmet Dermit, a Uruguayan citizen, submitted the communication on behalf of his cousins who were the alleged victims. As to Hugo Haroldo Dermit Barbato, a Uruguayan student of medicine, the author stated that he had completed an eight-year sentence of imprisonment in July 1980. Nevertheless, he was kept in detention pursuant to so-called "prompt security measures" and was informed that he would be released only if he left the country. After he had obtained an entry visa from the Swedish Government, the Uruguayan authorities informed him that he would be released. Some days after he should have been released, however, his mother was called to a military hospital to identify his body. She was told that he had committed suicide. The author alleged violations of article 6 and a number of other articles of the Covenant.

The State party did not submit any report on the circumstances in which the victim died or any information as to what inquiries had been made or the outcome of such enquiries. Consequently, the Committee gave appropriate weight to the information submitted by the author indicating that a few days before Hugo Haroldo Dermit Barbato died, he had been seen by other prisoners and was reported to have been in good spirits. While the Committee could not arrive at a definite conclusion as to whether the victim had committed sucide, was driven to suicide or was killed by others while in custody, the inescapable conclusion was that the Uruguayan authorities, either by act or ommission, were responsible for not taking adequate measures to protect his life, as required by article 6, paragraph 1, of the Covenant.

The Committee concluded, in respect of Hugo Haroldo Dermit Barbato, that the State party was under an obligation to take effective steps to establish the facts of his death; to bring to justice any persons found to be responsible for it; and to pay appropriate compensation to his family.

---

[16] *Ibidem, Thirty-eighth Session, Supplement No. 40* (A/38/40), annex IX, communication No. 84/1981, views adopted on 21 October 1982.

[17] See part IV, chap. 2, sect. B (*a*) (*infra*, p. 542).

In the case *Rickly Burrell* v. *Jamaica*,[18] also cited in connection with the respect for and protection of human rights in times of armed conflict, disturbance and tension,[19] the victim, a Jamaican citizen, was awaiting execution at a prison when, on 31 October 1993, he was shot and killed by a warder during a prison disturbance in which some warders had been taken hostage by prisoners. It was alleged by his counsel that Mr. Burrell's death constituted a violation of article 6, paragraph 1, of the Covenant.

In this case, it is interesting to note counsel's submissions to the Committee. He argued that the shooting was not necessary in the particular circumstances and not proportional to the requirements of law enforcement. The State party had failed to take adequate measures to protect the life of Mr. Burrell while he was in custody. In this context, counsel made reference to the lack of training received by warders in restraint techniques and the use of different levels of force, as well as to the ready access warders had to weapons. He also referred to international requirements with regard to the use of force in three non-treaty instruments, namely the Code of Conduct for Law Enforcement Officials, the Basic Principles on the Use of Force and Firearms by Law Enforcement Officials and the Principles on the Effective Prevention and Investigation of Extra-legal, Arbitrary and Summary Executions.

The Committee noted that counsel had alleged, on the basis of letters received from other inmates in the prison, that Mr. Burrell was shot after the warders who had been taken hostage were already released, and thus the need for force no longer existed. The Committee also noted that the State party itself had acknowledged that Mr. Burrell's death was the unfortunate result of confusion on the part of the warders. They panicked when seeing some of their colleagues being threatened by the inmates. The report submitted by the State party acknowledged that the shooting continued after the warders were rescued.

In the circumstances, the Committee concluded that the State party had failed in taking effective measures to protect Mr. Burrell's life, in violation of article 6, paragraph 1, of the Covenant. The Committee also found other violations of the Covenant in this case. As to the obligation to provide an effective remedy in article 2, paragraph 3 (*a*), of the Covenant, the Committee was of the opinion that in the circumstances of the case, that obligation entailed to pay compensation to the family of Mr. Burrell and to ensure that similar violations did not occur in the future.

---

[18] See United Nations, *Official Records of the General Assembly, Fifty-first Session, Supplement No. 40* (A/51/40), vol. II, annex VIII, sect. R, communication No. 546/1993, views adopted on 18 July 1996.

[19] See part IV, chap. 2, sect. B (*a*) (*infra*, p. 542).

II:2

The final case reviewed here, *John Khemraadi Baboeram* et al. v. *Suriname*,[20] concerned eight prominent people including lawyers, professors, businessmen and a journalist, who were arrested in their homes in Paramaribo, the capital of Suriname, on 8 December 1982 by military police and subjected to violence. Following an announcement by State authorities that a coup attempt had been foiled and that a number of detainees had been killed while trying to escape, their bodies were delivered to a mortuary. The bodies were seen by family members and other people who testified that they showed numerous wounds. Neither autopsies, nor official investigations into the killings, had taken place. The communications were submitted by close relatives of John Khemraadi Baboeram and seven other victims claimed to have been killed by military police, and they alleged violations by Suriname of article 6 and a number of other articles of the Covenant.

The Committee observed that the right enshrined in article 6, paragraph 1, of the Covenant was the supreme right of the human being and that the deprivation of life by the authorities of a State party was a matter of utmost gravity. This followed from the article as a whole. In particular, it was the reason for the provision in paragraph 2 of the article that the death penalty might be imposed only for the most serious crimes. The requirements that the right should be protected by law and that no one should be arbitrarily deprived of his life meant that the law had strictly to control and limit the circumstances in which a person might be deprived of his life by State authorities. It was evident from the fact that 15 prominent persons, including the victims in the present case, lost their lives as a result of the deliberate actions of the military police, that the deprivation of life was intended. The Committee concluded that the victims were arbitrarily deprived of their lives contrary to article 6, paragraph 1, of the Covenant.

As the State party had failed to submit any evidence proving that these persons were shot whilst trying to escape, the Committee urged the State to take effective steps to investigate the killings; to bring to justice any persons found to be responsible for the death of the victims; to pay compensation to the surviving families; and to ensure that the right to life was duly protected in Suriname.

(*b*) Committee on Freedom of Association

The protection of the right to life and the physical security of leaders and members of trade unions and employers' organizations are clearly prerequisites for the enjoy-

---

[20] See United Nations, *Official Records of the General Assembly, Fortieth Session, Supplement No. 40* (A/40/40), annex X, communications No. 146/1983, No. 148/1983, No. 149/1983, No. 150/1983, No. 151/1983, No. 152/1983, No. 153/1983 and No. 154/1983, views adopted on 4 April 1985.

ment of the right to freedom of association. In its jurisprudence, the Committee on Freedom of Association has adopted a number of decisions and principles on these matters to which it, when appropriate, makes reference in its reports on cases to the Governing Body of the International Labour Office.

The circumstances of the human rights violations alleged in complaints to the Committee are not explored by it in such forensic detail as those examined by other institutions featured in this publication. This practice is consistent with the Committee's main responsibility, which is to consider, with a view to making a recommendation to the Governing Body, whether cases are worthy of examination by that Body. The Committee carries out preliminary examinations of complaints submitted to it; takes account of government observations, if any; determines the compliance of any given legislation or practice with the principles laid down in the Convention concerning Freedom of Association and Protection of the Right to Organise (No. 87) and the Convention concerning the Application of the Principles of the Right to Organise and to Bargain Collectively (No. 98); and based on its conclusions, makes recommendations to the Governing Body.

In accordance with the purpose of this procedure, to promote respect for the rights of trade unions and employers' organizations in law and in fact, the Committee may recommend the Governing Body to draw the attention of the Government concerned to problems found and to invite the Government to take measures to resolve them. The Government may be requested to enquire into the allegations, determine the responsibility and punish the perpetrators. As with many serious human rights violations, especially those involving unlawful killings by State officials, the question of impunity of perpetrators is of particular concern. In its reports, the Committee is adding its voice to that of the other institutions calling for proper accountability of the authors of such egregious human rights violations.

In a report on case No. 1233 (*El Salvador*),[21] the Committee examined a complaint concerning the arrest of a trade union leader by three armed people who, it was presumed, were members of the state security police force. His corpse was discovered some two weeks after his arrest and, in their communications, the complainants alleged that he had been tortured to death. According to the Government, the perpetrators were members of a right-wing death squad. In its conclusions, the Committee deeply deplored the murder, especially in view of the circumstances in which, according to the complainants, it had occurred. The Committee drew to the attention of the Government the fact that freedom of association could only be exercised in con-

---

[21] See International Labour Office, *Official Bulletin*, vol. LXVII, Series B, No. 1 (1984), p. 204, interim report.

II:2

ditions in which fundamental human rights, and in particular those relating to human life and personal safety, were fully respected and guaranteed.

In a report on case No. 1700 (*Nicaragua*),[22] the Committee considered allegations including the assassination of a leader of an organization of employers, the bombing of the headquarters of that organization and the use of death threats against its members. Allegedly, preliminary enquiries indicated that those responsible were members of the Nicaraguan army. In its conclusions, the Committee regretted the return to a climate of violence in Nicaragua and deeply deplored the murder of this leader. It took note of the information supplied by the Government that judicial proceedings were being taken against those responsible for the murder. As to the bomb attack, the Committee pointed out that a climate of violence, such as one in which the premises and property of workers' and employers' organizations were attacked, was a serious obstacle to the exercise of their rights and that such acts required severe measures to be taken by the authorities. The Committee also drew the attention of the Government to the fact that the rights of workers' and employers' organizations could only be exercised in a climate free from violence, pressure or threats of any kind against the leaders and members of such organizations. It was for the Government to ensure that this principle was respected.

In a report on case No. 1192 (*Philippines*),[23] and another case against the same State, the arrest, torture and unexplained disappearance of trade union leaders and members were among the allegations. In its conclusions, the Committee recalled, as it had done in several cases concerning the disappearance of trade union officials, that it deplored a climate of insecurity in which there were unexplained disappearances. The Committee pointed out that such a climate inevitably represented a serious impediment to the exercise of trade union rights. The Government was requested to continue its investigations into these unexplained disappearances and to keep the Committee informed about the outcome.

In a report on case No. 1598 (*Peru*),[24] and two other cases against the same State, also cited in connection with the right to freedom of peaceful assembly and association,[25] the Committee expressed its most profound dismay that in view of the extremely serious nature of the allegations dating back as far as 1988 and relating to such deplorable actions as killings, disappearances, arrests, physical ill-treatment and torture of trade union leaders and members, the Government had not submitted

---

[22] *Ibidem*, vol. LXXVI, Series B, No. 3 (1993), p. 117, request report.

[23] *Ibidem*, vol. LXVII, Series B, No. 3 (1984), p. 85, request report.

[24] *Ibidem*, vol. LXXVIII, Series B, No. 1 (1995), p. 38, request report.

[25] See part III, chap. 5, sect. B (*b*) (*infra*, pp. 493-494).

any detailed and precise information on the majority of these or had done so in an incomplete and imprecise manner.

The Committee reiterated that a climate of violence giving rise to the killing or the disappearance of trade union leaders constituted a severe obstacle to the exercise of trade union rights. Such actions called for severe measures on the part of the authorities, like the institution of independent judicial inquiries in order to shed full light, at the earliest date, on the facts and circumstances in which killings such as these occured and in this way, to the extent possible, determine where responsibilities lay, punish those guilty and prevent the repetition of similar events. The Committee also recalled that the absence of judgments against the guilty parties created, in practice, a situation of impunity which reinforced the climate of violence and insecurity, extremely damaging to the exercise of trade union rights.

In a report on case No. 1434 (*Colombia*),[26] and four other cases against the same State, the Committee expressed its deep concern over the allegations involving the violent death and disappearance of over 200 trade union leaders and members since 1986, the assaults, arrests and threats to the lives of hundreds of trade unionists and the attack on the headquarters of a trade union. It was shocked by the very high number of murders and disappearances. There was no doubt that the Committee found itself confronted with one of the most serious cases it had received concerning the respect for the right to life.

As to the threats to the lives of hundreds of trade unionists, identified by name, the Government stated that these threats were part of the wave of violence sweeping over the country and that it would investigate the seriousness of reported threats. The Committee emphasized that the fear induced by such threats had inevitable repercussions on the exercise of trade union activities and that the exercise of these activities was possible only in a context of respect for basic human rights and in an atmosphere free of violence, pressure and threats of any kind.

In a report on case No. 1888 (*Ethiopia*),[27] the Committee examined a complaint concerning the killing of a trade union leader, the arrest and detention of other leaders of the trade union and the interference in the internal administration of the union. This report is also cited in connection with the right to liberty and security of person[28] and with the right to freedom of peaceful assembly and association.[29] In its conclusions,

---

[26] See International Labour Office, *Official Bulletin*, vol. LXXI, Series B, No. 3 (1988), p. 201, interim report.

[27] *Ibidem*, vol. LXXXVI, Series B, No. 1 (2003), p. 226, request report.

[28] See part II, chap. 4, sect. B (*c*) (*infra*, p. 224).

[29] See part III, chap. 5, sect. B (*b*) (*infra*, p. 494).

II:2

the Committee recalled that a climate of violence such as that surrounding the murder or disappearance of trade union leaders constituted a serious obstacle to the exercise of trade union rights. The absence of judgments against the guilty parties created, in practice, a situation of impunity, reinforcing the climate of violence and insecurity and being extremely damaging to the exercise of trade union rights

In a report on case No. 1761 (*Colombia*),[30] summarized in section C,[31] the Committee considered allegations including murders and other acts of violence against trade union officials and members. The report illustrates well the nature of the examinations carried out by the Committee under its mandate. Deeply deploring and repudiating the assassination of three trade union officials, the Committee noted that the Government only gave vague information on the existence of inquiries into two of the murders. It wished to insisit on the need for judicial inquiries to be carried out in all the cases to clarify the facts, determine responsibilities and punish the guilty parties. The Committee requested the Government to take the necessary steps to this end and to keep it informed of the outcome of such investigations

(*c*) African Commission on Human and Peoples' Rights

Article 4 of the African Charter on Human and Peoples' Rights states that human beings are inviolable. Every human being is entitled to respect for his life and the integrity of his person, and no one may be arbitrarily deprived of this right.

There is no provision on the death penalty in the Charter, nor is there any provision allowing States parties to derogate from their treaty obligations.

The African Commission on Human and Peoples' Rights has considered a number of cases on the right to life that are important and interesting from a policing perspective. Some of these are summarized and/or reviewed in connection with the respect for and protection of human rights in times of armed conflict, disturbance and tension,[32] because they arose in such a context. An early decision by the Commission in a case on violations of a number of human rights protected by the Charter, including the right to life, is cited in this review.

---

[30] See International Labour Office, *Official Bulletin*, vol. LXXVII, Series B, No. 2 (1994), p. 194, interim report.
[31] See part II, chap. 2, sect. C (*b*) (*infra*, pp. 72-74).
[32] See part IV, chap. 2, sects. B (*d*) and C (*d*) (*infra*, pp. 550-555 and 579-582, respectively).

In the case *Krischna Achutan and Amnesty International* v. *Malawi*,[33] also cited in connection with the prohibition of torture[34] and with the right to a fair trial,[35] three communications were considered jointly by the Commission. The first communication was filed with the Commission by Krischna Achutan on behalf of Aleke Banda, his father-in-law, and the two others by Amnesty International on behalf of Orton and Vera Chirwa. Allegations included violations of various human rights in respect of Mr. Banda, Mr. Chirwa and his wife. All three had been imprisoned for many years. Additionally, Amnesty International reported, *inter alia*, that trade union leaders were imprisoned and that peacefully striking workers were shot and killed by the police. Police also raided student dormitories and arrested students who were beaten and tortured.

On the right to life, the Commission laconically pronounced that shootings by police officers were a violation of the right of every human being to respect for his life. No other reason was given for holding that there had been a violation by Malawi of article 4 of the Charter. The Commission also held that other provisions of the Charter had been violated.

In view of important political changes in Malawi since the communications were submitted, the Commission made some observations in respect of State responsibility for treaty obligations. Under principles of international law, change of government did not affect such responsibility, including the responsibility for mismanagement by a previous government. Although the present Government did not commit the human rights abuses complained of in the communications, it was responsible for the reparation of them.

(d) Inter-American Court of Human Rights

Article 4 of the American Convention on Human Rights protects the right to life. The scope of this article is similar to that of article 6 of the International Covenant on Civil and Political Rights. Under paragraph 1, every person has the right to have his life respected. This right shall be protected by law and, in general, from the moment of conception. No one shall be arbitrarily deprived of his life.

Paragraphs 2 to 6 of the article contain, like the Covenant, provisions on the death penalty, with the additional requirement that it shall not be inflicted for political offences.

---

[33] See *Review of the African Commission on Human and Peoples' Rights*, vol. 5 (1995), p. 186, communications No. 64/92, No. 68/92 and No. 78/92.
[34] See part II, chap. 3, sect. B (*d*) (*infra*, pp. 142-143).
[35] See part III, chap. 2, sect. B (*c*) (*infra*, p. 360).

II:2

The provisions of article 4 are protected from derogation under article 27 of the Convention. Not even in time of war, public danger or other emergency threatening the independence or security of the State party may article 4 be suspended.

In respect of the application of death penalty, there is a facultative Protocol to the A-merican Convention on Human Rights to Abolish the Death Penalty, open to States parties to the Convention and in force since 1991. In this treaty, it is proclaimed that States parties to the Protocol shall not apply the death penalty in their territory to any person subject to their jurisdiction. Exemptions are provided for in wartime.

The *Velásquez Rodríguez* case *(Honduras)*[36] concerns the disappearance in 1981 of Angel Manfredo Velásquez Rodríguez, a Honduran student, in violation of the right to life in article 4 of the Convention, but it also deals with breaches of the right to humane treatment in article 5 and the right to personal liberty in article 7, all read in conjunction with article 1, paragraph 1, on the obligation to respect rights. In fact, this case could be considered as a paradigm case on a situation of forced disappear-ance, one of the reasons for its inclusion in this context. It is summarized at some length in section C,[37] because the judgment sets out very detailed and explicit ac-counts of how a systematic and selective practice of disappearances was put into ef-fect in the State and how this particular victim was disappeared. The case is also cit-in connection with the prohibition of torture[38] and the right to liberty and security of person.[39]

In this case, the Inter-American Court of Human Rights made some trenchant obser-vations on the phenomenon of disappearances, especially in Latin America. Without question, the State had the right and duty to guarantee its security, the Court noted, but regardless of the seriousness of certain actions and the culpability of the perpe-trators of certain crimes, the power of the State was not unlimited, nor could the State resort to any means to attain its ends. In its observations on disappearances, the Court also described the responses of international institutions to such atrocities.

The Court mentioned that forced disappearances were not new in the history of hu-man rights violations. However, their systematic and repeated nature and their use not only for causing certain individuals to disappear, either briefly or permanently, but also as a means of creating a general state of anguish, insecurity and fear, was a recent phenomenon. Although this practice existed virtually world-wide, it had oc-

---

[36] See Inter-American Court of Human Rights, Series C: *Decisions and Judgments*, No. 4 (1988), petition No. 7920, judgment of 29 July 1988.
[37] See part II, chap. 2, sect. C *(c)* *(infra*, pp. 74-85).
[38] See part II, chap. 3, sect. B *(e)* *(infra*, p. 146).
[39] See part II, chap. 4, sect. B *(e)* *(infra*, p. 228).

curred with exceptional intensity in Latin American countries in the few years preceding this case.

Another reason for the relatively extensive summary of the case in this publication is the inclusion of some of the Court's comments on the burden of proof and the general criteria considered in its evaluation and finding of the facts in the proceeding. Furthermore, in its analysis of the obligation of States parties in article 1, paragraph 1, to respect the rights set forth in the Convention, the Court expressed the conditions under which a particular act or omission violating one of those rights could be imputed to a State. These are observations made by the Court also in other judgments, but they have been retained only in this summary. They are interesting and useful, not only because of the insights they give into the reasoning of the Court, but because of what they tell us about the international regime for the protection of human rights generally.

In this judgment, finally, it is important to note the Court's assertion that the duty of the State to investigate human rights violations is a part of the fulfillment of its duty to ensure public order. Some human rights violations are serious forms of criminality and of social disorder. Clearly, the State has the duty to prevent such criminality and disorder, to investigate it when it occurs and to prosecute and punish the offenders. Indeed, the duty to punish those who violate human rights is a constant theme in the jurisprudence of the Court.

The *Velásquez Rodríguez* case is frequently referred to in other cases before the Court arising out of situations of forced disappearance. One such case, the *Bámaca Velásquez* case (*Guatemala*),[40] summarized in connection with the respect for and protection of human rights in times of armed conflict, disturbance and tension[41] and also cited in connection with the prohibition of torture,[42] concerned the capture, torture and killing in 1992, by agents of the State's armed forces, of Efraín Bámaca Velásquez, the leader of a guerilla group engaged in an internal armed conflict against the State.

Before concluding that the State had violated, *inter alia*, article 4 of the Convention, the Court reiterated that involuntary or forced disappearance constituted a multiple and continuing violation of a number of rights protected by the Convention. Not only did it produce an arbitrary deprivation of liberty, but it also endangered personal integrity, safety and the very life of the detainee. Frequently, it involved secret exe-

---

[40] See Inter-American Court of Human Rights, Series C: *Decisions and Judgments*, No. 70 (2001), petition No. 11129, judgment of 25 November 2000.
[41] See part IV, chap. 2, sect. C (*e*) (*infra*, pp. 582-593).
[42] See part II, chap. 3, sect. B (*e*) (*infra*, pp. 148 and 149).

cution of those detained, without trial, following the concealment of the corpse in order to eliminate any material evidence of the crime and to ensure the impunity of those responsible. The Court also made reference to the definition of forced disappearance in the Inter-American Convention on Forced Disappearance of Persons, in force since 1996, although this treaty was not directly applicable in the case.

The *Neira Allegría* et al. case (*Peru*)[43] concerned the responses of the Peruvian authorities, represented by the republican guard, the navy and the police, to a serious riot in a prison located on an island that caused the death of many of the inmates. The alleged victims in the case, Victor Neira Allegría, Edgar Zenteno Escobar and William Zenteno Escobar, were being detained in the prison and had been missing since the riot broke out on 18 June 1986. Based on the proceeding, the Court concluded that they lost their lives due to the effects of the crushing of the uprising by Government forces and as a consequence of the disproportionate use of force. This included the demolition by explosives of a building occupied by prisoners. Whilst endorsing the right and duty of the State to suppress the riot, the Court ultimately, in the circumstances, found that the victims were arbitrarily deprived of their lives in violation of article 4, paragraph 1, of the Convention.

Although those detained in the prison were highly dangerous and in fact armed, it was the opinion of the Court that these circumstances were not reasons sufficient to justify the amount of force used. It then reiterated the point made in the *Velásquez Rodríguez* case that whilst the State had the right and duty to gurantee its security, the power of the State was not unlimited. It could not resort to any means to attain its ends. The State was subject to law and morality, and disrespect for human dignity could not serve as the basis for any of its actions.

As the right to *habeas corpus* in effect had been suspended to the detriment of the alleged victims in the case, the Court also found that Peru had violated article 7, paragraph 6, of the Convention, in relation to the prohibition of suspension of guarantees in article 27, paragraph 2.

The *Villagrán Morales* et al. case (*Guatemala*), the *"street children"* case,[44] is summarized in connection with the probition of torture[45] and also cited in connection with the right liberty and security of person.[46] This case concerns the killing of Anstraum Villagrán Morales and the abduction, torture and killing of four other youths,

---

[43] See Inter-American Court of Human Rights, Series C: *Decisions and Judgments*, No. 20 (1995), petition No. 10078, judgment of 19 January 1995.

[44] *Ibidem*, No. 63 (2000), petition No. 11383, judgment of 19 November 1999.

[45] See part II, chap. 3, sect. C (*f*) (*infra*, pp. 172-178).

[46] See part II, chap. 4, sect. B (*e*) (*infra*, pp. 231-232).

"street children", in 1990 by members of the State's national police force. It is referred to here because of what the Court said about the right to life, particularly in relation to children.

The Court observed that the right to life was a fundamental human right and that the exercise of this right was essential for the exercise of all other human rights. The right to life included not only the right of every human being not to be arbitrarily deprived of his life, but also the right not to be prevented from having access to the conditions guaranteeing a dignified existence. States had the obligation to guarantee the creation of conditions required for violations of this basic right not to occur and, in particular, the duty to prevent its agents from violating it.

In respect of the latter point, the Court referred to general comment No. 6 (16) by the Human Rights Committee, on article 6 of the International Covenant on Civil and Political Rights.[47] In this general comment, the Committee observed that States parties to the Covenant should take measures not only to prevent and punish deprivation of life by criminal acts, but also to prevent arbitrary killing by their own security forces. It went on to say that the deprivation of life by authorities of the State was a matter of utmost gravity and that the State had strictly to control and limit the circumstances in which a person might be deprived of his life by such authorities.[48]

Finding a violation of the right to life of the five victims in the *"street children"* case, the Court stated that it wished to indicate the particular gravity of the case. The victims were youths, three of them children. The conduct of the State not only violated the express provision of article 4 of the Convention, but also numerous international instruments that devolved to the State the obligation to adopt special measures of protection and assistance for the children within its jurisdiction. The Court also found a number of other violations in this case.

(*e*) European Court of Human Rights

Article 2 of the Convention for the Protection of Human Rights and Fundamental Freedoms protects the right to life. Under paragraph 1, everyone's right to life shall be protected by law. No one shall be deprived of his life intentionally save in the execution of a sentence of a court following his conviction of a crime for which this penalty is provided by law.

---

[47] See United Nations, *Official Records of the General Assembly, Thirty-seventh Session, Supplement No. 40* (A/37/40), annex V.
[48] *Ibidem*, para. 3.

II:2

As to the death penalty, it should be noted, however, that there are two facultative Protocols to the Convention concerning the abolition of the death penalty, open to States parties to the Convention. Protocol No. 6, in force since 1985, proclaims that the death penalty shall be abolished and that no one shall be condemned to such penalty or executed, but the death penalty may be applied in time of war. Protocol No. 13, in force since 2003, extends the abolition of the death penalty to all circumstances.

There is no specific reference to arbitrary deprivation of life in this Convention, in contrast to the corresponding provisions in the International Covenant on Civil and Political Rights, the African Charter on Human and Peoples' Rights and the American Convention on Human Rights. However, in article 2, paragraph 2, of the Convention, specific circumstances are set out under which the taking of life will not contravene the Convention when it results from the use of force which is no more than absolutely necessary. Those circumstances are: in defence of any person from unlawful violence; in order to effect a lawful arrest or to prevent the escape of a person lawfully detained; or in action lawfully taken for the purpose of quelling a riot or insurrection.

The provisions of article 2 are protected from derogation under article 15 of the Convention. Not even in time of war or other public emergency threatening the life of the nation may a State party take measures derogating from its obligations under article 2, except in respect of deaths resulting from lawful acts of war.

In a decison on the application *Stewart v. the United Kingdom,*[49] the European Commission of Human Rights, before declaring the application inadmissible, made some important statements on the interpretation of article 2 of the Convention, later referred to by the European Court of Human Rights in its case law. Having reviewed the wording of article 2, and the jurisprudence of both the Commission and the Court, it was the Commission's opinion that the text of this article, read as a whole, indicated that paragraph 2 did not primarily define situations where it was permitted intentionally to kill an individual, but it defined the situations where it was permissible to use force which might result, as the unintended outcome of the use of force, in the deprivation of life.

The use of force, however, had to be no more than absolutely necessary for the achievement of one of the purposes set out in article 2, paragraph 2 (*a*), (*b*) or (*c*), of the Convention. In this respect, the Commission observed that the use of the term "absolutely necessary" in that paragraph indicated that a stricter and more compel-

---

[49] See European Commission of Human Rights, *Decisions and Reports*, No. 39 (1984), p. 162, application No. 10044/82, decision of 10 July 1984.

ling test of necessity had to be employed from that normally applicable when determining whether State action was necessary in a democratic society under paragraph 2 of articles 8 to 11. In particular, the force used had to be strictly proportionate to the achievement of the aims set out in article 2, paragraph 2 (*a*), (*b*) and (*c*). In assessing whether the use of force was strictly proportionate, regard had to be had to the nature of the aim pursued, the dangers to life and limb inherent in the situation and the degree of the risk that the force employed might result in loss of life.

These observations on the wording of article 2 of the Convention were cited in the case *McCann and Others* v. *the United Kingdom*,[50] summarized in section C[51] and also cited in connection with the respect for and protection of human rights in times of armed conflict, disturbance and tension.[52] This judgment of the Court, sitting as a grand chamber, has been selected for an extended summary for a variety of reasons. It concerns a fairly complex anti-terrorist operation that took place in 1988 in Gibraltar. It required careful analysis of intelligence, detailed planning and cooperation between various authorities in different jurisdictions. In this operation, three terrorist supects, Daniel McCann, Mairead Farrell and Sean Savage, were killed, and the applicants, representing the estates of the victims, claimed that the killing of the suspects disclosed a violation of article 2 of the Convention. The Court, in finding a violation of the right to life, attributed that violation to defects in the control and organization of the operation and not to the actions of four soldiers who actually killed the terrorist suspects.

The Court considered that the use of force by agents of the State in pursuit of one of the aims delineated in article 2, paragraph 2, of the Convention might be justified where it was based on an honest belief, perceived, for good reasons, to be valid at the time, but which subsequently turned out to be mistaken. However, having carefully scrutinized the way in which the authorities interpreted the intelligence available to them, the briefing given to the four soldiers and the way in which events unfolded during the operation, it appeared to the Court that there had been a lack of appropriate care in the control and organization of the arrest operation. The Court was not persuaded that the killing of the three suspects constituted the use of force no more than absolutely necessary in defence of persons from unlawful violence within the meaning of article 2, paragraph 2 (*a*).

The Court held, by ten votes to nine, that there had been a violation of article 2 of the Convention. In their joint dissenting opinion, the nine judges forming the minor-

---

[50] See *Publications of the European Court of Human Rights*, Series A: *Judgments and Decisions*, vol. 324 (1996), application No. 18984/91, judgment of 27 September 1995.
[51] See part II, chap. 2, sect. C (*d*) (*infra*, pp. 86-104).
[52] See part IV, chap. 2, sect. B (*f*) (*infra*, p. 559).

II:2

ity were unable to subscribe to the opinion of the majority that there had been such a violation. While agreeing that the actions of the four soldiers did not, in themselves, give rise to a violation of that article, they disagreed with the evaluation made by the majority of the way in which the control and organization of the operation were carried out by the authorities. They considered it unjustified to conclude that there was a lack of appropriate care in the control and organization of the arrest operation.

The *McCann and Others* case can be contrasted with the case *Andronicou and Constantinou* v. *Cyprus*.[53] It concerned the alleged unlawful killing in 1993 of a young man, Lefteris Andronicou, and young woman, Elsie Constantinou, in the course of a rescue operation by officers of a special police unit, trained to shoot to kill if fired at. The man, who was armed with a firearm, was holding the woman hostage in a flat, and the police feared that he would kill her if they did not intervene. The applicants, four Cypriot nationals, were close relatives of the victims.

The Commission acknowledged that in view of the atmosphere of crisis that developed throughout the day, it might be possible to make allowances for some of the mistakes, omissions and errors of judgment which had occurred in the authorities' handling of the situation. Nevertheless, it concluded, the decision to deploy the special unit officers to deal with a domestic quarrel was a fundamental flaw in the planning and control of the operation. Furthermore, before the Court, the Commission was also critical of the chaotic way in which the negotiations phase had been conducted. It was argued that the authorities' failure to use a trained negotiator and to control third-party contacts with the hostage taker, as well as the crowds milling around the location of the incident, suggested a lack of professionalism.

In its judgment, the Court stated that its sole concern had to be to evaluate whether, in the circumstances, the planning and control of the rescue operation, including the decision to deploy the special unit officers, showed that the authorities had taken appropriate care to ensure that any risk to the lives of the couple had been minimized and that they were not negligent in their choice of action. It considered that there might have been shortcomings regarding, for example, the lack of crowd control or the absence of a dedicated telephone line between the police negotiator and the hostage taker. However, the negotiations were, nevertheless, in general conducted in a manner which could be said to be reasonable in the circumstances.

The rescue operation was launched just before midnight, and the Court accepted that the authorities were persuaded that the hostage taker intended to kill the young woman and then to commit suicide at midnight. In the Court's view, the authorities'

---

[53] See European Court of Human Rights, *Reports of Judgments and Decisions*, 1997-VI, p. 2059, application No. 25052/94, judgment of 9 October 1997.

decision to use the special unit officers, in the circumstances as they were known at the time, was justified. Whilst these officers were trained to kill if fired at, they were issued with clear instructions as to when to use their weapons. They were told to use only proportionate force and to fire only if the hostage's life or their own lives were in danger. Having regard to these and other considerations, the Court was of the view that it had not been shown that the rescue operation was not planned and organized in a way that minimized to the greatest extent possible any risk to the lives of the couple.

In its assessment of the application of force by the police officials, the Court noted that their use of lethal force in the circumstances was the direct result of the hostage taker's violent reaction to the storming of the flat. He had sought to take the life of the first officer who entered the room. The Court ultimately considered that the use of lethal force in the circumstances, however regrettable, did not exceed what was absolutely necessary for the purposes of defending the lives of the officers and that of the hostage and did not amount to a breach by the respondent State of the obligations under article 2, paragraph 2 (*a*), of the Convention. It found, by five votes to four, that there had been no violation of that article.

In spite of the Court's finding, one is left wondering whether the two people would have lost their lives if the management of the scene of the incident and the conduct of negotiations had been of a higher professional standard.

In the case *McKerr* v. *the United Kingdom*,[54] the applicant, Jonathan McKerr, alleged that his father, Gervaise McKerr, had been shot and killed on 11 November 1982 by police officers. The Court held that there had been a violation of the right to life because of a failure of the State to conduct a proper investigation into the circumstances of the death of Gervaise McKerr. The judgment in this case was delivered on the same date as the judgments in three similar cases against the United Kingdom.

The Court did not pronounce on the responsibility of the State for the death, noting, *inter alia*, that a number of key factual issues arose in the case, at the time under examination in domestic procedures. The Court did not consider that it should duplicate proceedings in the civil courts. They were better placed and equipped as fact-finding tribunals. However, the Court noted that under article 2 of the Convention, investigations capable of leading to the identification and punishment of those responsible had to be be undertaken into allegations of unlawful killings.

---

[54] *Ibidem*, 2001-III, p. 475, application No. 28883/95, judgment of 4 May 2001.

II:2

In examining this procedural aspect of article 2, the Court found that the investigative procedures had not struck the right balance between legitimate interests, such as national security or the protection of material relevant to other investigations, and providing for the necessary safeguards in an accessible and effective manner. It listed various shortcomings of the investigations in the case. Those included a lack of independence of the police officers investigating the incidents from those officers implicated in the incidents. The Court observed that proper procedures for ensuring accountability of State agents were indispensible in maintaining public confidence and meeting the legitimate concerns that might arise from the use of lethal force.

The case *Osman* v. *the United Kingdom*,[55] also cited in connection with the right to a fair trial,[56] concerned the killing of Ali Osman and the wounding of his son, on 7 March 1988, by a schoolteacher who had formed an attachment to the boy. The applicants were Mr. Osman's widow, Mulkiye Osman, and the son, Ahmet Osman, both British nationals. In this case, the Court, sitting as a grand chamber, considered the positive duty on the State to protect the right to life.

The Court noted that the first sentence of article 2, paragraph 1, of the Convention enjoined the State not only to refrain from the intentional and unlawful taking of life, but also to take appropriate steps to safeguard the lives of those within its jurisdiction. It pointed out that the State's obligation in this respect extended beyond its primary duty to secure the right to life by putting in place effective criminal law provisions to deter the commission of offences against the person, backed up by law enforcement machinery for the prevention, suppression and sanctioning of breaches of such provisions. Accordingly, article 2 might also imply, in certain well-defined circumstances, a positive obligation on the authorities to take preventive operational measures to protect an individual whose life was at risk from the criminal acts of another individual.

However, bearing in mind the difficulties involved in policing modern societies, the unpredictability of human conduct and the operational choices that had to be made in terms of priorities and resources, the Court pointed out that such an obligation had to be interpreted in a way not imposing an impossible or disproportionate burden on the authorities. Accordingly, not every claimed risk to life could entail for the authorities a requirement under the Convention to take operational measures to prevent that risk from materializing. Another relevant consideration for the Court was the need to ensure that the police exercised their powers in a manner which fully respected the due process and other guarantees which legitimately placed restraints on the scope of their action to investigate crime and bring offenders to justice, including

---

[55] *Ibidem*, 1998-VIII, p. 3124, application No. 23452/94, judgment of 28 October 1998.
[56] See part III, chap. 2, sect. B (*e*) (*infra*, pp. 366-367).

the guarantees in articles 5 and 8 of the Convention, on the right to liberty and security and the right to respect for private and family life, respectively.

The Court stated that where there was an allegation that the authorities had violated their positive obligation to protect the right to life in the context of their duty to prevent and suppress offences against the person, a number of points had to be established. The Court had to be satisfied that the authorities knew or ought to have known at the time of the existence of a real and immediate risk to the life of an identified individual or individuals from the criminal acts of a third party and that they failed to take measures within the scope of their powers which, judged reasonably, might have been expected to avoid that risk.

In the view of the Court, the applicants had failed to point to any decisive stage when it could be said that the police knew or ought to have known that the lives of the Osman family were at real and immediate risk from the teacher. It concluded, by seventeen votes to three, that there had been no violation of article 2 of the Convention in this case.

In respect of the right to a fair trial, however, the Court unanimously found a violation of article 6, paragraph 1, of the Convention.

In the case *Paul and Audrey Edwards* v. *the United Kingdom*,[57] the applicants, two United Kingdom nationals, alleged in particular that the authorities had failed to protect the life of their son, Christopher Edwards, who had been killed in 1994 while he was detained in prison by a dangerous, mentally ill prisoner. Both men had been arrested at different times and at different places by police, remanded in custody by magistrates and then confined in the same prison cell. In its deliberations, the Court recalled the *Osman* case and the principles it took into account in deciding whether or not a State had met its positive obligation to protect the right to life. Furthermore, it pointed out that in the context of prisoners, it had on previous occasions emphasized that persons in custody were in a vulnerable position and that the authorities were under a duty to protect them.

In applying these principles to the present case, the Court examined whether the authorities knew or ought to have known of the existence of a real and immediate risk to the life of Mr. Edwards from the acts of his cellmate and whether they failed to take measures within the scope of their powers which, judged reasonably, might have been expected to avoid that risk.

---

[57] See European Court of Human Rights, *Reports of Judgments and Decisions*, 2002-II, p. 137, application No. 46477/99, judgment of 14 March 2002.

II:2

Regarding the state of knowledge of the authorities, the Court noted that it was considered in the report of an inquiry into the case, set up by the prison service, local government authority and local health authority, the three State agencies with statutory responsibilities towards Mr. Edwards, that any prisoner sharing a cell with the perpetrator on the night in question would have been at risk to his life. Therefore, it seemed to the Court that the essential question was whether the prison authorities knew or ought to have known of his extreme dangerousness at the time the decision was taken to place him in the same cell as Mr. Edwards. In this respect, the Court was satisfied that information was available which identified the perpetrator as suffering from a mental illness with a record of violence, serious enough to merit proposals for compulsory detention. This, in combination with his bizarre and violent behaviour on and following arrest, demonstrated that he was a real and serious risk to others and, in the circumstances of this case, to Mr. Edwards when placed in his cell.

Regarding the measures they might reasonably have been expected to take to avoid that risk, the Court observed that the information concerning the perpetrator's medical history and perceived dangerousness ought to have been brought to the attention of the prison authorities and, in particular, those responsible for deciding whether to place him in the health care centre or in ordinary location with other prisoners. It was not. There was a series of shortcomings in the transmission of information, from the failure of the psychiatric registrar to consult the perpetrator's notes in order to obtain the full picture; the failure of the police to fill in an official form designed to identify and bring to notice detainees considered to be an exceptional risk on ground of mental illness; and the failure of the police, prosecution or magistrates' court to take into account the perpetrators's suspected dangerousness and instability.

It was also apparent that there were numerous failings in the way in which Mr. Edwards was treated from his arrest to allocation to a shared cell. In particular, despite his disturbed mental state, no doctor was called to examine him in the police station, no official form was filled in by the police and there was a failure to pass onto the prison screening officer information provided informally by the applicants, the probation service at the court and an individual police officer. However, though it would obviously have been desirable for Mr. Edwards to be detained either in a hospital or the health care centre of the prison, his life was placed at risk by the introduction into his cell of a dangerously unstable prisoner. The shortcomings in that regard were most relevant to the issues in this case. On the same basis, the Court considered that on the information available to the authorities, the perpetrator should not have been placed in Mr. Edwards' cell in the first place.

The Court concluded that the failure of the agencies involved in this case - medical profession, police, prosecution and court - to pass on information about the perpetrator to the prison authorities and the inadequate nature of the screening process on his arrival in prison disclosed a breach of the State's obligation to protect the life of Christopher Edwards. Therefore, there had been a breach of article 2 of the Convention in this regard.

The Court also found that there had been a failure to comply with the requirements of article 2 to hold an effective investigation into the death of Mr. Edwards because of the lack of power of the inquiry to compel witnesses and the private character of the proceedings from which the applicants were excluded, save when they were giving evidence. Accordingly, in those respects, there had been a violation of the procedural obligation in article 2. The Court also found a violation of the right to an effective remedy set forth in article 13 of the Convention.

In the case *Mahmut Kaya* v. *Turkey*,[58] summarized in section C,[59] the applicant, a Turkish national, alleged that his brother, Hasan Kaya, in 1993 was kidnapped, tortured and killed by, or with the connivance of, State agents and that there was no effective investigation or remedy for his complaints. The Court applied the principles set out in the *Osman* case to killing by individuals or groups who, it seemed, were acting with the knowledge or acquiescence of elements in the security forces. This phenomenon, here referred to as "unknown perpetrator killing", has been alleged in other conflicts, particularly where the State is responding to terrorism or other acts of insurgency. The Court's observations on the State's duty to protect the right to life in such cases are especially important, for they include the trenchant comment that the authorities were aware or ought to have been aware of the criminal collusion between killers and security forces. The Court's analysis of the inept and dilatory investigation by the authorities into the murder from which this case emanated is particularly telling.

As to article 2 of the Convention, the Court found, by six votes to one, that the respondent State failed to protect the life of Hasan Kaya and, unanimously, that the authorities failed to conduct an effective investigation into the circumstances of his death. The Court also found, by six votes to one, violations of the prohibition of torture and the right to an effective remedy set forth in articles 3 and 13, respectively.

Finally, the case *Nachova and Others* v. *Bulgaria*,[60] summarized in section C,[61] concerned the killing by a military police officer, in an arrest operation on 19 July 1996,

---

[58] *Ibidem*, 2000-III, p. 149, application No. 22535/93, judgment of 28 March 2000.
[59] See part II, chap. 2, sect. C (*e*) (*infra*, pp. 104-112).
[60] See European Court of Human Rights, applications No. 43577/98 and No. 43579/98, judgment 6 July 2005.
[61] See part II, chap. 2, sect. C (*f*) (*infra*, pp. 112-122).

II:2

of two men of Roma origin, Kuncho Angelov and Kiril Petkov, conscripts in the Bulgarian army. The applicants, Anelia Kunchova Nachova and three other Bulgarian nationals, close relatives of the alleged victims, invoked articles 2, 13 and 14 of the Convention. Following a judgment by the the Court sitting as a chamber, the final judgment was delivered by the Court sitting as a grand chamber.

The Court found that the State was responsible for the deprivation of life of the victims, in violation of article 2 of the Convention. In this case, firearms were used to arrest people who were suspected of non-violent offences, were not armed and did not pose any threat to the arresting officers or others. The Court expressed grave concern that the relevant regulations on the use of firearms by the military police effectively permitted lethal force to be used when arresting a member of the armed forces for even the most minor offence. Furthermore, the violation was aggravated by the fact that excessive firepower was used, and the State was responsible for the failure to plan and control the arrest operation in a manner compatible with article 2. Under the same article, the Court also found a violation of the State's obligation to investigate deprivations of life effectively.

The applicants alleged that the events leading to the deaths of Mr. Angelov and Mr. Petkov constituted an act of racial violence. The Court held, by eleven votes to six, that there had been no violation in that respect of article 14 of the Convention, in conjunction with article 2. It could not exclude the possibility that the police officer was simply adhering strictly to the regulations and would have acted as he did in any similar context, regardless of ethnicity. However, the Court held unanimously that there had been a violation in respect of these provisions in that the authorities failed to investigate possible racist motives behind the events.

The Court endorsed the analysis, in the chamber's judgment, of the procedural obligation of States parties to investigate possible racist motives for acts of violence. When investigating violent incidents and, in particular, deaths at the hands of State agents, State authorities had the additional duty to take all reasonable steps to unmask any racist motive and to establish whether or not ethnic hatred or prejudice might have played a role in the events. Failing to do so and treating racially induced violence and brutality on an equal footing with cases that had no racist overtones would be to turn a blind eye to the specific nature of acts that were particularly destructive of fundamental rights.

The Court also reiterated an observation of great significance to police officials and police agencies. In order to maintain public confidence in their law enforcement machinery, States parties had to ensure that in the investigation of incidents involving the use of force, a distinction was made both in their legal systems and in practice between cases of excessive use of force and of racist killing.

C. CASE SUMMARIES

(a) *María Fanny Suárez de Guerrero* v. *Colombia*
(Human Rights Committee)[62]

The author of the communication was Pedro Pablo Camargo, a law professor who submitted the communication to the Human Rights Committee on 5 February 1979, writing on behalf of the husband of María Fanny Suárez de Guerrero. The author alleged violations by Colombia of article 6 on the right to life and other provisions of the International Covenant on Civil and Political Rights.

The facts

The author submitted, *inter alia*, the following. On 13 April 1978, the judge of a military criminal court of investigation, himself a member of the police, ordered a raid to be carried out at a house in a district of Bogotá, the capital of Colombia. The order for the raid was issued to a major, a chief of police of the Bogotá police department. The raid was ordered in the belief that a former ambassador of Colombia to France, who had been kidnapped some days earlier by a guerrilla organization, was being held prisoner in that house.

In the police raid, two captains, two lieutenants, a corporal, five constables and a driver took part. In spite of the fact that the former ambassador was not found, the police squad decided to hide in the house to await the arrival of the suspected kidnappers. Seven people, including María Fanny Suárez de Guerrero, arrived at the house at intervals and, as they arrived, they were each shot. The author described the circumstances of the killings and alleged that they were arbitrarily killed by the police, that the police action was unjustified and that it had been inadequately investigated by the Colombian authorities. He claimed that the case was initially shelved under Legislative Decree No. 0070 of 20 January 1978, because the Colombian authorities considered that the police had acted within the powers granted by that Decree.

Legislative Decree No. 0070 amended the Colombian penal code by declaring that an act would be justified if it was committed by members of the police force in the course of operations planned with the object of, *inter alia*, preventing and curbing the offences of extortion and kidnapping.

---

[62] See United Nations, *Official Records of the General Assembly, Thirty-seventh Session, Supplement No. 40* (A/37/40), annex XI, communication No. 45/1979, views adopted on 31 March 1982.

II:2

The author stated that this Decree had established a new ground of defence against a criminal charge, so as to justify crimes committed by members of the police force when they were taking part in operations to repress certain types of offences. In other words, an act that would otherwise be criminal would be justified and would not give rise to criminal responsibility when it was committed by members of the police force. He stated that domestic remedies to declare the Decree unconstitutional had been exhausted.

On 9 August 1979, the Committee transmitted the communication to the State party requesting information and observations relevant to the question of admissibility.

In denying that the Decree constituted a breach of the Covenant, the State party cited a ruling by the Supreme Court of Justice to the effect, *inter alia*, that the Decree was a temporary addition to the penal code and obviously related to the fact that the national territory was in a state of siege. The Decree had been adopted for the purpose of creating a new defence to a criminal charge, and the Supreme Court ruled that it was legitimate that members of armed forces should be protected by a justification of the punishable acts that they were constrained to commit.

Concerning the specific incident involving the death of Mrs. Suárez de Guerrero, the State party agreed that she was one of seven people killed in a police operation, and it stated that an administrative inquiry into the case had been instituted by the office of the state counsel for the national police. Furthermore, as a result of a criminal investigation, nine police officials were subject to criminal proceedings, but the trial had still to be completed. Consequently, the State party submitted, domestic remedies had not yet been exhausted.

In his response, the author pointed out that it was left to the police authorities themselves to determine whether or not acts were justified and that up to that time all extrajudicial deaths caused by the police had been justified by the police force itself, without any intervention of the ordinary courts.

Regarding the police operation that took place on 13 April 1978 in Bogotá, the author maintained that it was the police themselves who had entrusted the criminal investigation to a judge of a military criminal court and that the judge, after more than two years, had not summoned those involved to appear in court. The author argued that the criminal proceedings were not genuine, as the police had carried out the investigation with respect to themselves, and that the military criminal procedure did not permit civilian victims to be represented. Ordinary criminal procedure provided both for a criminal action and for a civil action for damages. The author maintained that the Government had not permitted the institution of civil proceedings on behalf of the victims in the military criminal case and that the application of domestic proceedings was unreasonably prolonged.

On 25 July 1980, the Committee requested the State party to provide information as to how the state of siege affected the present case; whether the institution of civil proceedings for damages had been permitted and, if not, the reasons for any refusal to permit such proceedings; and the reasons for the delay, of more than two years, in the adjudication of the military court in the matter.

The State party responded that the state of siege might affect the case if those responsible for the deaths in the police operation invoked Legislative Decree No. 0070 in justification and if the appropriate military tribunal agreed that the ground invoked was applicable. It agreed that no civil action could be instituted in conjunction with the military proceedings. However, persons who had suffered loss or injury might apply to an administrative tribunal to obtain appropriate damages, and thus, with another remedy available, the institution of a civil action in conjunction with military criminal proceedings was unimportant. The State party submitted that the delay in the adjudication of the military court was due to the heavy work load of all the judges and prosecutors and not to negligence. The administrative inquiry had, however, been completed and the dismissal of all of the members of the police squad involved in the operation had been requested and carried out.

The author provided additional information. He pointed out that the investigation into the killings on 13 April 1978 was conducted by the very police official who had led the raid. He further stated that the Inspector General of Police, acting as a judge of the first instance, had ordered all criminal proceedings against those charged with the killings to be discontinued on the basis of the military criminal justice code. This was allowed for on a number of grounds, and the author alleged that the Inspector General of Police had invoked the ground of justification of the criminal act provided for in Legislative Decree No. 0070. A higher military court had later annulled this decision, but, the author informed the Committee, a military court had acquitted the 11 police officials involved, an acquittal based on the Decree. The author further stated that as a result of the acquittal, no administrative suit for compensation could be filed and that the police officials who had been dismissed at the request of the administrative enquiry would be reinstated.

As to the admissibility of the communication, the Committee found, on the basis of the information submitted by the State party and the author, that it was unable to conclude that there were still effective remedies available which could be invoked on behalf of the alleged victim. Accordingly, the Committee concluded that the communication was not inadmissible, but it stated that this decision could be reviewed in the light of any further explanations the State party might submit. Howev-

II:2

er, no such submission was received from the State party by the date set by the Committee for that purpose.

The Committee's views on the merits

The Committee based its views on, *inter alia*, the following facts that were not in dispute or had not been refuted by the State party.

Legislative Decree No. 0070 had established a new ground of defence that might be pleaded by members of the police force to exonerate them for an otherwise punishable act committed in the course of operations planned with the object of preventing and curbing the offences of extortion and kidnapping.

On 13 April 1978, the judge of a military criminal court of investigation, himself a member of the police, ordered a raid to be carried out at a house in a district of Bogotá, in the belief that a former ambassador of Colombia to France was being held prisoner in the house, having been kidnapped some days earlier by a guerrilla organization. In spite of the fact that he had not been found, the police patrol hid in the house to await the arrival of the suspected kidnappers. Seven people who subsequently entered the house, including Mrs. Suárez de Guerrero, were then shot and killed by the police.

Although the police had originally claimed that the victims had died whilst resisting arrest, and brandishing and firing various weapons, the report of the Institute of Forensic Medicine, ballistic reports and the results of a paraffin test showed that none of the victims had fired a shot and that they had all been killed at point blank range. Some of them had been shot in the back or in the head. It was also established that the victims were not all killed at the same time, but at intervals as they arrived at the house, and that most of them had been shot while trying to save themselves from the unexpected attack. In the case of Mrs. Suárez de Guerrero, the forensic report showed that she had been shot several times after she had already died from a heart attack.

A request of the administrative inquiry for the dismissal of the members of the police squad involved in the operation was ordered, but the Inspector General of Police, acting as a judge of the first instance, issued an order for criminal proceedings against the police officials to be discontinued. A higher military court annulled this decision, but a military tribunal again acquitted the 11 members of the police department on the basis of Legislative Decree No. 0070. In view of this acquittal, no civil or administrative suit could be filed to obtain compensation.

In formulating its views, the Committee also took into account the following considerations.

The Committee noted that the Decree referred to a situation of disturbed public order in Colombia. It also noted that the Government of Colombia, in compliance with the requirements of article 4, paragraph 3, of the Covenant, on 18 July 1980 had declared to the Secretary-General of the United Nations that in view of the state of siege in the national territory, temporary measures had been adopted to the effect of limiting the application of articles 19, paragraph 2, and 21 of the Covenant. The Committee observed that the present case was not concerned with those provisions and that there were several rights recognized by the Covenant which could not be derogated from by the State party. These included articles 6 and 7, both invoked in this case.

The Committee pronounced that the right to life enshrined in article 6, paragraph 1, of the Covenant was the supreme right of the human being. It followed that the deprivation of life by the authorities of the State was a matter of the utmost gravity. This followed from the article as a whole and, in particular, was the reason why paragraph 2 of the article laid down that the death penalty might be imposed only for the most serious crimes. The requirements that the right should be protected by law and that no one should be arbitrarily deprived of his life meant that the law had strictly to control and limit the circumstances in which a person might be deprived of his life by the authorities of a State.

In the present case, it was evident from the fact that seven persons lost their lives as a result of the deliberate action of the police that the deprivation of life was intentional. Moreover, the police action was apparently taken without warning to the victims and without giving them any opportunity to surrender to the police patrol or to offer any explanation of their presence or intentions. There was no evidence that the action of the police was necessary in their own defence, or that of others, or that it was necessary to effect the arrest or prevent the escape of the persons concerned. Furthermore, the victims were no more than suspects of the kidnapping that had occurred some days earlier, and their killing by the police deprived them of all the protections of due process of law laid down by the Covenant. In the case of Mrs. Suárez de Guerrero, the forensic report showed that she had been shot several times after she had already died from a heart attack. There can be no reasonable doubt that her death was caused by the police patrol.

For these reasons, the Committee was of the view that the action of the police resulting in the death of Mrs. Suárez de Guerrero was disproportionate to the requirements of law enforcement in the circumstances of the case and that she was arbitrarily deprived of her life contrary to article 6, paragraph 1, of the Covenant. Inasmuch as the

II:2

police action was made justifiable as a matter of Colombian law by Legislative Decree No. 0070, the right to life was not adequately protected by the law of Colombia
as required by article 6, paragraph 1.

It was not necessary to consider further alleged violations, arising from the same
facts, of other articles of the Covenant. Any such violations were subsumed by the e-
ven more serious violations of article 6.

The Committee was accordingly of the view that the State party should take the necessary measures to compensate the husband of María Fanny Suárez de Guerrero for
the death of his wife and to ensure that the right to life was duly protected by a-
mending the law.

(*b*) Case No. 1761 (*Colombia*)
(Committee on Freedom of Association)[63]

The complaints against the Goverment of Colombia were submitted, respectively, on
1 and 10 November 1993 and 17 February 1994 by the Latin American Central of
Workers (CLAT) and on 24 February 1994 by the World Confederation of Trade
Unions (WFTU). The Government sent some observations in a communication dated 28 April 1994.

Colombia had ratified the Convention concerning Freedom of Association and Protection of the Right to Organise (No. 87) and the Convention concerning the Application of the Principles of the Right to Organise and to Bargain Collectively (No.
98).

The facts

The CLAT alleged that Rodrigo Rojas Acosta was assassinated on 25 October 1993
at 9.30 p.m. outside his house. Two hired assassins killed him at point-blank range.
He was 28 years old and an active member of the Revolutionary Independent Workers' Movement (MOIR). He joined the Ecopetrol enterprise as a labourer in 1987
and was subsequently elected member of the executive committee of the petroleum
refining branch of the Workers' Trade Union (USO). The CLAT added that Israel
Perea was assassinated on 11 October 1993. He was president of a branch of the Association of Port and Field Labourers. He was 70 years old and an active member of
the Colombian Liberal Party.

---

[63] See International Labour Office, *Official Bulletin*, vol. LXXVII, Series B, No. 2 (1994), p.
194, interim report.

The WFTU alleged that Reinaldo Maiguel Camelo, a trade union official, was assassinated on 14 February 1994 at his home; that 12 trade union officials and trade unionists had been arrested under various specified circumstances; that a number of workers had been expelled from the premises of a trade union's headquarters; and that members of the State security had carried out inspection visits to trade union meetings and headquarters.

The Government stated that the trade union officials Israel Perea and Reinaldo Maiguel Camelo were assassinated and that information had been requested on the present state of the investigations. It also gave an account of the reasons for the arrests of the various trade union officials.

The Committee's conclusions and recommendations

The Committee on Freedom of Association noted with concern the serious nature of the allegations concerning the assassination of three trade union officials, the arrest of 12 trade union officials and trade unionists, the expulsion of workers from the headquarters of a trade union, and the carrying out of inspection visits by members of the State security to trade union meetings and headquarters.

In general, the Committee pointed out to the Government that trade union rights could only be exercised in a climate that was free from violence, pressure or threats of any kind against trade unionists or members of such organizations and that it was the responsibility of governments to ensure that this principle was respected. Furthermore, freedom of association could be exercised only in conditions in which fundamental human rights, and in particular those relating to human life and personal safety, were fully respected and guaranteed.

More specifically, regarding the allegations of attacks on the right to life, the Committee deeply deplored the assassinations of the trade union officials Rodrigo Rojas Acosta, Israel Perea and Reinaldo Maiguel Camelo. It noted that the Government had given only vague information on the existence of inquiries into the last two mentioned murders. The Committee wished to insist on the need for judicial inquiries to be carried out in all the cases to clarify the facts, determine responsibilities and punish the guilty parties. It requested the Government to take the necessary steps to this end and to keep it informed of the outcome of such investigations. The Committee recalled that the absence of judgments against the guilty parties created, in practice, a situation of impunity which reinforced the climate of violence and insecurity, extremely damaging to the exercise of trade union rights.

The Committee also made observations on the arrests of the 12 trade union officials, emphasizing that the detention of trade unionists and trade union leaders for reasons

II:2

connected with their activities to defend the interests of workers was contrary to the principles of freedom of association.

Finally, the Committee requested the Government to send its observations on the other allegations to which it had not replied: the expulsion of workers from the premises of a trade union's headquarters and the carrying out of inspection visits by members of the State security to trade union meetings and headquarters.

In the light of these conclusions, the Committee invited the Governing Body of the International Labour Office to approve a number of recommendations.

Recalling that trade union rights could be exercised only where fundamental human rights, and in particular the right to life and the security of the person were fully respected and guaranteed, the Government was requested to take steps to ensure that judicial inquiries were carried out to clarify the facts, determine responsibilities and punish the authors of the assassination of the trade union officials Rodrigo Rojas Acosta, Israel Perea and Reinaldo Maiguel Camelo, which the Committee deeply deplored and repudiated. The Government was also requested to keep the Committee informed in this regard. It was recalled that the absence of judgments against the guilty parties created, in practice, a situation of impunity, which reinforced the climate of violence and insecurity, extremely damaging to the exercise of trade union rights.

The Committee also set out its recommendations on the arrest of the 12 trade union officials and requested the Government to send its observations on the allegations to which it had not replied.

(c) *Velásquez Rodríguez* case (*Honduras*)
(Inter-American Court of Human Rights)[64]

On 24 April 1986, the Inter-American Commission on Human Rights submitted to the Inter-American Court of Human Rights an application against the Republic of Honduras. It originated in a petition received by the Commission on 7 October 1981. It was based on the alleged violation of the American Convention on Human Rights suffered by Angel Manfredo Velásquez Rodríguez who had disappeared, violently detained without a warrant for his arrest by members of the armed forces of the State, a detention denied by the police and security forces. The Commission requested the Court to determine whether Honduras had violated the provisions on the right to life in article 4, the right to humane treatment in article 5 and the right to personal

---

[64] See Inter-American Court of Human Rights, Series C: *Decisions and Judgments*, No. 4 (1988), petition No. 7920, judgment of 29 July 1988.

liberty in article 7 of the Convention. The Court was also asked to rule that the consequences of the situation that constituted the breach of such a right or freedom should be remedied and that fair compensation should be paid to the injured party or parties.

Proceedings and conclusions of the Court

During the proceedings, the Court considered documentary evidence and the evidence of witnesses, including parliamentarians, lawyers, persons who had been disappeared and relatives of disappeared persons, as well as members of the armed forces. The Commission presented witnesses before the Court to testify on specific facts related to the case and as to whether there were in Honduras, at the time when Manfredo Velásquez disappeared, numerous cases of persons who were kidnapped and then disappeared in actions imputable to the armed forces and enjoying the acquiescense of the Government; and whether there existed at the relevant time in Honduras effective domestic remedies to protect those persons who were kidnapped and then disappeared in such actions.

An eyewitness, the victim's sister, gave a detailed account of how, on 12 September 1981, Manfredo Velásquez, a Honduran student, was kidnapped and taken away. According to the testimony of a former member of the armed forces, based on what he had been told by an officer who took part in the action, Mr. Velásquez was kidnapped in an operation of the armed forces. During the struggle, Mr. Velásquez was wounded in the leg when a gun went off. He was taken to a military establishment where he was tortured and then turned over to those in charge of carrying out executions. They took him out of the area, allegedly at the orders of the chief of the armed forces, and killed him with a knife and machete, dismembered his body and buried the remains in different places.

Before weighing the evidence, the Court addressed some questions regarding the burden of proof and the general criteria to be considered in its evaluation and finding of the facts in the proceedings. It noted that because the Commission was accusing the Government of the disappearance of Manfredo Velásquez, in principle, it should bear the burden of proving the facts underlying its petition.

The Court observed that the Commission's argument relied upon the proposition that the policy of disappearances, supported or tolerated by the Government, was designed to conceal and destroy evidence of disappearances. When the existence of such a policy or practice had been shown, the disappearance of a particular individual might be proved through circumstantial or indirect evidence or by logical inference. Otherwise, it would be impossible to prove that an individual had been disappeared.

II:2

If it could be shown that there was an official practice of disappearances in Honduras, carried out by the Government or at least tolerated by it, and if the disappearance of Mr. Velásquez could be linked to that practice, the Commission's allegations would have been proven to the Court's satisfaction, so long as the evidence presented on both points met the standard of proof required in cases such as this.

The Court had to determine what the standards of proof should be in the present case. Neither the Convention, the Statute of the Court nor its Rules of Procedure spoke to this matter. International jurisprudence had recognized the power of the courts to weigh the evidence freely, although it had always avoided a rigid rule regarding the amount of proof necessary to support the judgment. Standards of proof were less formal in international legal proceedings than in the domestic ones.

Whilst direct evidence was not the only type of evidence that might be legitimately considered in reaching a decision, circumstantial or presumptive evidence was especially important in allegations of disappearances, because this type of repression was characterized by an attempt to suppress all information about the kidnapping or the whereabouts and fate of the victim.

The Court, as an international tribunal, had its own specialized procedures and all the elements of domestic legal procedures were therefore not automatically applicable. Furthermore, the international protection of human rights should not be confused with criminal justice. States did not appear before the Court as defendants in a criminal action. The objective of international human rights law was not to punish those individuals guilty of violations, but rather to protect victims and to provide for the reparation of damages resulting from the acts of the States responsible.

In contrast to domestic criminal law, in proceedings to determine human rights violations, the State could not rely on the defense that the complainant had failed to present evidence when it could not be obtained without the State's cooperation. The State controlled the means to verify acts occurring within its territory, and although the Commission had investigatory powers, it could not exercise them within the jurisdiction of the State unless having the cooperation of that State.

Since the Government had only offered some documentary evidence in support of its preliminary objections, but none on the merits, the Court had to reach its decision without the valuable assistance of a more active participation by Honduras, which might otherwise have resulted in a more adequate presentation of its case.

Furthermore, the manner in which the Government conducted its defense would have sufficed to prove many of the Commission's allegations by virtue of the principle that the silence of the accused, or elusive or ambiguous answers on its part, might be interpreted as an acknowledgment of the truth of the allegations, so long as the contrary was not indicated by the record or not compelled as a matter of law.

In its own proceedings, the Commission had invoked article 42 of its Regulations. The facts reported in the petition, the pertinent parts of which had been transmitted to the Government of the State, should be presumed to be true if, during the maximum period set by the Commission, the Government had not provided the pertinent information, as long as other evidence did not lead to a different conclusion.

In the instant case, the Court accepted the validity of the documents presented by the Commission and by Honduras, particularly because the parties did not oppose or object to those documents, nor did they question their authenticity or veracity.

During the hearings, the Government had attempted to show that some witnesses were not impartial because of ideological reasons, origin or nationality, family relations or a desire to discredit Honduras. It was even insinuated that testifying against the State in these proceedings was disloyal to the nation. Furthermore, the Government had cited criminal records or pending charges to show that some witnesses were not competent to testify. Whilst it was true that certain factors might influence the truthfulness of a witness, the Government had not presented any concrete evidence to show that the witnesses had not told the truth. It had limited itself to making general observations regarding their alleged incompetence or lack of impartiality, and this was insufficient to rebut testimony which was fundamentally consistent with that of other witnesses.

Moreover, some of the Government's arguments were unfounded within the context of human rights law. The insinuation that persons who, for any reason, resorted to the inter-American system for the protection of human rights were disloyal to their country was unacceptable and could not constitute a basis for any penalty or negative consequence. Making reference to the American Declaration of the Rights and Duties of Man and the American Convention on Human Rights, the Court cited that human rights were higher values not derived from the fact that an individual was a national of a certain State, but were based upon attributes of his human personality. Neither was it sustainable that having a criminal record or charges pending was sufficient to find that a witness was not competent to testify in the Court.

Many of the press clippings offered by the Commission could not be considered as documentary evidence. However, many of them contained public and well-known facts which, as such, did not require proof. Others were of evidentiary value insofar as they textually reproduced public statements, especially those of high-ranking members of the armed forces, of the Government or even of the Supreme Court of Honduras. Finally, others were important as a whole insofar as they corroborated

II:2

testimony regarding the responsibility of the Honduran military and police for disappearances.

As to the alleged violations of the Convention, the Court found, *inter alia*, the following facts to have been proven.

During the period 1981 to 1984, 100 to 150 persons disappeared in Honduras, and many were never heard from again. Those disappearances followed a similar pattern, beginning with the kidnapping of the victims by force, often in broad daylight and in public places, by armed men in civilian clothes and disguises, acting with apparent impunity and using vehicles without any official identification, with tinted windows and with false license plates or no plates at all. It was public and notorious knowledge in Honduras that the kidnappings were carried out by military personnel or the police, or persons acting under their orders.

The disappearances were carried out in a systematic manner. The Court considered the following circumstances particularly relevant. The victims were usually persons considered dangerous to state security by Honduran officials. In addition, the victims had usually been under surveillance for long periods of time. The arms employed were reserved for the official use of the military and police. The vehicles used had tinted glass which required special official authorization. In some cases, government agents carried out the detentions openly and without any pretense or disguise. In others, government agents had cleared the areas where the kidnappings were to take place, and on at least one occasion, when government agents stopped the kidnappers, they were allowed to continue freely on their way after showing their identification.

The kidnappers blindfolded the victims, took them to secret, unofficial detention centres and moved them from one centre to another. They interrogated the victims and subjected them to cruel and humiliating treatment and torture. Some were ultimately murdered and their bodies were buried in clandestine cemeteries. When queried by relatives, lawyers and persons or entities interested in the protection of human rights or by judges charged with executing writs of *habeas corpus*, the authorities systematically denied any knowledge of the detentions or the whereabouts or fate of the victims. That attitude was seen even in the cases of persons who later reappeared in the hands of the same authorities that had systematically denied holding them or knowing their fate.

Military and police officials as well as those from the executive and judicial branches either denied the disappearances or were incapable of preventing or investigating them, punishing those responsible, or helping those interested to discover the whereabouts and fate of the victims or the location of their remains. The investigative committees created by the Government and the armed forces did not produce any results. The judicial proceedings brought were processed slowly with a clear lack of interest, and some were ultimately dismissed.

On 12 September 1981, between 4.30 and 5.00 p.m., several heavily-armed men in civilian clothes driving a white Ford without license plates kidnapped Manfredo Velásquez. He remained disappeared, creating a reasonable presumption that he was dead. Persons connected with the armed forces or under its direction carried out that kidnapping.

The kidnapping and disappearance of Mr. Velásquez fell within the systematic practice of disappearances referred to by the facts deemed to have been proven. To wit, Manfredo Velásquez was a student involved in activities the authorities considered dangerous to national security. The kidnapping of him was carried out in broad daylight by men in civilian clothes who used a vehicle without license plates. In the present case, there were the same type of denials by his captors and the armed forces, the same omissions of the latter and of the Government in investigating and revealing his whereabouts and the same ineffectiveness of the courts where three writs of *habeas corpus* and two criminal complaints were brought. There was no evidence in the record that Mr. Velásquez had disappeared in order to join subversive groups, other than a mayor's letter containing rumors to that effect. The letter itself showed that the Government had associated him with activities it considered a threat to national security. However, the Government did not corroborate the view expressed in the letter with any other evidence. Nor was there any evidence that he was kidnapped by common criminals or other persons unrelated to the practice of disappearances existing at that time.

In short, the Court found that the following facts had been proven in the proceedings: a practice of disappearances carried out or tolerated by Honduran officials existed between 1981 and 1984; Manfredo Velásquez had disappeared at the hands of or with the acquiescence of those officials within the framework of that practice; and the Government of Honduras had failed to guarantee the human rights affected by that practice.

As to the phenomenon of disappearances, the Court made a number of observations. Disappearances were not new in the history of human rights violations. However, their systematic and repeated nature and their use not only for causing certain individuals to disappear, either briefly or permanently, but also as a means of creating a general state of anguish, insecurity and fear, was a recent phenomenon. Although this practice existed virtually world-wide, it had occurred with exceptional intensity in Latin America in the few years preceding this case.

II:2

The phenomenon of disappearances was a complex form of human rights violation that had to be understood and confronted in an integral fashion. In this context, the Court referred to the establishment of the Working Group on Enforced or Involuntary Disappearances, set up in 1980 by the United Nations Commission on Human Rights. The Court observed that this was a clear demonstration of general censure and repudiation of the practice of disappearances. This phenomenon had already received world attention within the United Nations. The practice of disappearances should be stopped, the victims reappear and those responsible be punished.

As to the inter-American system, the General Assembly of the Organization of American States and the Inter-American Commission on Human Rights had repeatedly referred to the practice of disappearances and urged that disappearances should be investigated and the practice be stopped.

International practice and doctrine had often categorized disappearances as a crime against humanity, although there was no treaty in force, in which this terminology was used, applicable to the States parties to the American Convention on Human Rights.

Without question, the Court observed, the State had the right and duty to guarantee its security. It was also indisputable that all societies suffered some deficiencies in their legal orders. However, regardless of the seriousness of certain actions and the culpability of the perpetrators of certain crimes, the State's power was not unlimited, nor could the State resort to any means to attain its ends. The State was subject to law and morality, and disrespect for human dignity could not serve as the basis for any State action.

The forced disappearance of human beings was a multiple and continuous violation of many rights under the Convention that the States parties were obliged to respect and guarantee. The kidnapping of a person was an arbitrary deprivation of liberty, an infringement of a detainee's right to be taken without delay before a judge and to invoke the appropriate procedures to review the legality of the arrest, all in violation of article 7 recognizing the right to personal liberty.

Moreover, prolonged isolation and deprivation of communication were in themselves cruel and inhuman treatment, harmful to the psychological and moral integrity of the person and a violation of the right of any detainee to respect for his inherent dignity as a human being. Such treatment, therefore, violated article 5 of the Convention recognizing the right to the integrity of the person. Investigations into the practice of disappearances, and the testimony of victims who had regained their liberty, showed that those disappeared often were subjected to merciless treatment, including all types of indignities, torture and other cruel, inhuman and degrading treatment, in violation of the right to physical integrity recognized in article 5.

The practice of disappearances often involved secret execution without trial, followed by concealment of the body to eliminate any material evidence of the crime and to ensure the impunity of those responsible. This was a flagrant violation of the right to life, recognized in article 4 of the Convention.

The Court concluded that the practice of disappearances, in addition to directly violating many provisions of the Convention, constituted a radical breach of the treaty in that it showed a crass abandonment of the values emanating from the concept of human dignity and of the most basic principles of the inter-American system and the Convention. The existence of this practice, moreover, evinced a disregard of the duty to organize the State in such a manner as to guarantee the rights recognized in the Convention.

The Court went on to examine the conditions under which a particular act violating one of the rights recognized by the Convention could be imputed to a State party, thereby establishing its international responsibility. The Commission had asked the Court to find that Honduras had violated the rights guaranteed to Manfredo Velásquez by articles 4, 5 and 7 of the Convention. The Government had denied the charges.

The obligation assumed by the States parties in relation to each of the rights protected by the Convention was specified in article 1, paragraph 1. Each claim alleging that one of those rights had been infringed necessarily implied also a violation of that provision. Article 1, paragraph 1, was essential in determining whether a violation of the human rights recognized by the Convention could be imputed to a State party. In effect, that article charged the States parties with the fundamental duty to respect and guarantee the rights recognized in the Convention. Any impairment of those rights that could be attributed under the rules of international law to the action or omission of any public authority constituted an act imputable to the State, and thus it assumed responsibility in the terms provided by the Convention.

The first obligation assumed by States under article 1, paragraph 1, was to respect the rights and freedoms recognized by the Convention. The exercise of public authority had certain limits derived from the fact that human rights were inherent attributes of human dignity and, therefore, superior to the power of the State. The second obligation was to ensure the free and full exercise of the rights recognized by the Convention to every person subject to its jurisdiction. This obligation implied the duty to organize the governmental apparatus and, in general, all the structures through which public power was exercised, so that they were capable of juridically

II:2

ensuring the free and full enjoyment of human rights. As a consequence of this obligation, the States had to prevent, investigate and punish any violation of the rights recognized by the Convention. Moreover, if possible, they had to attempt to restore the right violated and provide compensation as warranted for damages resulting from the violation.

The obligation to ensure the free and full exercise of human rights was not fulfilled by the existence of a legal system designed to make it possible to comply with this obligation. The Government was also required to conduct itself so as to effectively ensure the free and full exercise of human rights. The obligation of States parties was, thus, much more direct than that concerning domestic legal effects contained in article 2 of the Convention.

According to article 1, paragraph 1, any exercise of public power violating the rights recognized by the Convention was illegal. Whenever a State organ, official or public entity violated one of those rights, this constituted a failure of the duty to respect the rights and freedoms set forth in the Convention. This conclusion was independent of whether the organ, official or public entity had contravened provisions of internal law or overstepped the limits of authority. Under international law, the State was responsible for the acts of its agents undertaken in their official capacity and for their omissions, even when those agents acted outside the sphere of their authority or violated internal law. This principle suited perfectly the nature of the Convention. It was violated whenever public power was used to infringe the rights recognized therein. If acts of public power exceeding the State's authority or being illegal under its own laws were not considered to compromise that State's obligations under the treaty, the system of protection provided for in the Convention would be illusory.

Thus, in principle, any violation of rights recognized by the Convention carried out by an act of public authority or by persons using their position of authority was imputable to the State. However, this did not define all the circumstances in which a State was obliged to prevent, investigate and punish human rights violations, nor all the cases in which the State might be found responsible for an infringement of those rights. An illegal act violating human rights and being initially not directly imputable to a State, for example, because it was the act of a private person or because the person responsible had not been identified, could lead to international responsibility of the State, not because of the act itself, but because of the lack of due diligence to prevent the violation or to respond to it as required by the Convention.

Violations of the Convention could not be founded upon rules that took psychological factors into account in establishing individual culpability. For the purposes of analysis, the intent or motivation of the agent who had violated the rights recognized by the Convention was irrelevant. The violation could be established even if the identity of the individual perpetrator was unknown. What was decisive was whether a violation of the rights recognized by the Convention had occurred with the support or the acquiescence of the Government or whether the State had allowed the act to take place without taking measures to prevent it or to punish those responsible. Thus, the Court's task was to determine whether the violation was the result of a State's failure to fulfill its duty to respect and guarantee those rights, as required by article 1, paragraph 1, of the Convention.

The State had a legal duty to take reasonable steps to prevent human rights violations and to use the means at its disposal to carry out a serious investigation of violations committed within its jurisdiction, to identify those responsible, to impose the appropriate punishment and to ensure the victim adequate compensation.

This duty to prevent included all those means of a legal, political, administrative and cultural nature that promoted the protection of human rights and ensured that any violations were considered and treated as illegal acts, which, as such, could lead to the punishment of those responsible and the obligation to indemnify the victims for damages. While the State was obliged to prevent human rights abuses, the existence of a particular violation did not, in itself, prove the failure to take preventive measures. On the other hand, subjecting a person to official, repressive bodies practising torture and assassination with impunity was itself a breach of the duty to prevent violations of the rights to life and physical integrity of the person, even if that particular person was not tortured or assassinated or if those facts could not be proven in a concrete case.

The State was obliged to investigate every situation involving a violation of the rights protected by the Convention. If the State apparatus acted in such a way that the violation went unpunished and the victim's full enjoyment of such rights was not restored as soon as possible, the State had failed to comply with its duty to ensure the free and full exercise of those rights to the persons within its jurisdiction. The same was true when the State allowed private persons or groups to act freely and with impunity to the detriment of the rights recognized by the Convention.

In certain circumstances, it might be difficult to investigate acts violating an individual's rights. The duty to investigate, like the duty to prevent, was not breached merely because the investigation did not produce a satisfactory result. Nevertheless, it had to be undertaken in a serious manner and not as a mere formality preordained to be ineffective. An investigation had to have an objective and be assumed by the State as its own legal duty, not as a step taken by private interests that depended upon the initiative of the victim or his family or upon their offer of proof, without an effective search for the truth by the Government. This was true regardless of what agent was eventually found responsible for the violation. Where the acts of private

II:2

parties that had violated the Convention were not seriously investigated, those parties were aided in a sense by the Government, thereby making the State responsible on the international plane.

As to the responsibility of the State party in the present case, the evidence showed a complete inability of the procedures of Honduras, theoretically adequate, to carry out an investigation into the disappearance of Manfredo Velásquez and of the fulfillment of its duties to pay compensation and punish those responsible, as set out in article 1, paragraph 1, of the Convention.

As the Court had verified in the present judgment, the failure of the judicial system to act upon the writs brought before various tribunals had been proven. Not one writ of *habeas corpus* was processed. No judge had access to the places where Mr. Velásquez might have been detained. The criminal complaint was dismissed.

The organs of the executive branch did not carry out any serious investigation to establish the fate of Mr. Velásquez. There was no investigation of public allegations of a practice of disappearances, nor a determination of whether Mr. Velásquez had been a victim of that practice. The Commission's requests for information were ignored to the point that it had to presume, under article 42 of its Regulations, that the allegations were true. An investigation had been carried out by the armed forces, the same body accused of direct responsibility for the disappearances. This raised grave questions regarding the seriousness of the investigation. The Government had often resorted to asking relatives of the victims to present conclusive proof of their allegations even though those allegations, because they involved crimes against the person, should have been investigated on the Government's own initiative in fulfillment of the State's duty to ensure public order. This was especially true when the allegations referred to a practice carried out within the armed forces, not subject to private investigations because of its nature. No proceeding was initiated to establish responsibility for the disappearance of Mr. Velásquez and apply punishment under internal law. All of the above led to the conclusion that the Honduran authorities did not take effective action to ensure respect for human rights within the jurisdiction of the State as required by article 1, paragraph 1, of the Convention.

The duty to investigate facts of this type continued as long as there was uncertainty about the fate of the person who had disappeared. Even in the hypothetical case that those individually responsible for crimes of this type could not be legally punished under certain circumstances, the State was obliged to use the means at its disposal to inform the relatives of the fate of the victims and, if they had been killed, the location of their remains.

The Court was convinced, and had so found, that the disappearance of Manfredo Velásquez was carried out by agents who acted under cover of public authority. However, even had that fact not been proven, the failure of the State apparatus to act, clearly proven, was a failure on the part of Honduras to fulfill the duties it had assumed under article 1, paragraph 1, of the Convention. It obliged the State to ensure Mr. Velásquez the free and full exercise of his human rights.

The Court noted that the legal order of Honduras did not authorize such acts and that internal law defined them as crimes. The Court also recognized that not all levels of government were necessarily aware of those acts, nor was there any evidence that such acts were the result of official orders. Nevertheless, those circumstances were irrelevant for the purposes of establishing whether Honduras was responsible under international law for the violations of human rights perpetrated within the practice of disappearances.

According to the principle of the continuity of the state in international law, responsibility existed both independently of changes of government over a period of time and continuously from the time of the act that created responsibility to the time when the act was declared illegal. The foregoing was also valid in the area of human rights although, from an ethical or political point of view, the attitude of the new government might be much more respectful of those rights than that of the government in power when the violations occurred.

The Court, therefore, concluded that the facts found in these proceedings showed that Honduras was responsible for the involuntary disappearance of Mr. Velásquez. Thus, the State had violated articles 4, 5 and 7 of the Convention.

The Court declared that Honduras had violated, in the case of Angel Manfredo Velásquez Rodríguez, its obligations to respect and to ensure the right to personal liberty set forth in article 7, its obligations to respect and to ensure the right to humane treatment set forth in article 5 and its obligation to ensure the right to life set forth in article 4 of the Convention, all read in conjunction with article 1, paragraph 1, on the obligation to respect rights. Honduras was required to pay fair compensation to the victim's next of kin.

II:2

(*d*) *McCann and Others* **v.** *the United Kingdom*
(European Court of Human Rights)[65]

The case was referred to the European Court of Human Rights on 20 May 1994 by the European Commission of Human Rights. It originated in an application against the United Kingdom of Great Britain and Northern Ireland lodged with the Commission on 14 August 1991 by representatives of the estates of Daniel McCann, Mairead Farrell and Sean Savage. The object of the Commission's request was to obtain a decision as to whether the facts of the case disclosed a breach by the respondent State of its obligations to protect the right to life under article 2 of the Convention for the Protection of Human Rights and Fundamental Freedoms. The Court delivered its judgment sitting as a grand chamber.

The facts

Before 4 March 1988, the United Kingdom, Spanish and Gibraltar authorities were aware that a terrorist attack on Gibraltar was being planned by the Provisional IRA (Irish Republican Army). It appeared that the target was to be an area where the Royal Anglian Regiment assembled to carry out the changing of the guard at 11 a.m. every Tuesday

An advisory group was formed to advise and assist the Gibraltar Commissioner of Police. It consisted of soldier F. (senior military adviser and officer in the Special Air Service, SAS), soldier E. (SAS attack commander), soldier G. (bomb-disposal adviser), an acting deputy commissioner of police, a detective chief inspector and security service officers. The Commissioner issued instructions for an operational order to be prepared to deal with the situation.

According to the military rules of engagement issued to soldier F. by the Ministry of Defence, the purpose of the military forces being in Gibraltar was to assist the Gibraltar police to arrest the IRA active service unit should the police request such military intervention. The rules also instructed soldier F. to operate as directed by the Commissioner.

The rules specified the circumstances in which the use of force by the soldiers would be permissible as follows:

---

[65] See *Publications of the European Court of Human Rights*, Series A: *Judgments and Decisions*, vol. 324 (1996), application No. 18984/91, judgment of 27 September 1995.

Use of force

4. You and your men will not use force unless requested to do so by the senior police officer(s) designated by the Gibraltar Police Commissioner; or unless it is necessary to do so in order to protect life. You and your men are not then to use more force than is necessary in order to protect life ...

Opening fire

5. You and your men may only open fire against a person if you or they have reasonable grounds for believing that he/she is currently committing, or is about to commit, an action which is likely to endanger your or their lives, or the life of any other person, and if there is no other way to prevent this.

Firing without warning

6. You and your men may fire without warning if the giving of a warning or any delay in firing could lead to death or injury to you or them or any other person, or if the giving of a warning is clearly impracticable.

Warning before firing

7. If the circumstances in paragraph 6 do *not* apply, a warning is necessary before firing. The warning is to be as clear as possible and is to include a direction to surrender and a clear warning that fire will be opened if the direction is not obeyed.

The operational order of the Commissioner stated that it was suspected that a terrorist attack was planned in Gibraltar and that the target would be the band and guard of the first battalion of the Royal Anglian Regiment during a ceremony on 8 March 1988. It was expected that a car bomb would be used. The intention of the operation was stated to be: (*a*) to protect life; (*b*) to foil the attempt; (*c*) to arrest the offenders; and (*d*) the securing and safe custody of the prisoners. The order further stated that the suspects were to be arrested by using minimum force, that they were to be disarmed and that evidence was to be gathered for a court trial. Annexed to the order were lists of attribution of police personnel, firearms rules of engagement and a guide to firearms use by police.

A plan for evacuation of the expected area of attack was drawn up. It was to be put into effect on Monday or Tuesday, 7 or 8 March 1988.

II:2

In the Gibraltar joint operations room, there were three groups: the army or military group, the police group and the surveillance or security service group. Each had its own separate means of communication with its personnel on the ground. The two principal means of communication were the two radio-communication networks, known as the surveillance net and the tactical or military net. The police net was not considered secure, and a telephone appeared to have been used for communications with the central police station.

On 4 March 1988, there was a reported sighting of the IRA active service unit in Málaga, Spain, and surveillance was mounted. At midnight between 5 and 6 March 1988, the Commissioner held a briefing attended by officers from the security services, military personnel and members of the Gibraltar police. The Commissioner explained the rules of engagement and firearms procedures and expressed the importance of gathering evidence for a subsequent trial.

The briefing by the security services representative included the following assessments. The IRA intended to attack the changing of the guard ceremony in an assembly area on the morning of Tuesday, 8 March 1988. An active service unit consisting of Daniel McCann, Mairead Farrell and Sean Savage would carry out the attack. Mr. McCann and Ms. Farrell had been previously sentenced to terms of imprisonment for offences concerned with explosives. Mr. Savage was described as an expert bomb-maker. Photographs were shown of the three suspects. The three individuals were believed to be dangerous terrorists who would almost certainly be armed and would use their weapons if confronted by security forces. The attack would be by way of a car bomb that would be brought across the border in a vehicle. It was thought that the use of a blocking car, i.e. a car not containing a bomb but parked in the assembly area in order to reserve a space for the car containing the bomb, was unlikely.

At the briefing, it was said that the use of a remote-control device was considered to be the most likely means of detonating the bomb. According to a soldier's statement, they were briefed that the bomb would be initiated by a "button job", i.e. a remote-control device. He stated that the soldiers had expressed the view that there was more chance they would have to shoot to kill in view of the very short time factor a "button job" would impose.

Various soldiers stated that they had been briefed that the suspects might, if confronted, seek to detonate the bomb; that any one of the three suspects could be carrying a device to detonate it by remote control; that they were ruthless, dangerous and dedicated; that the device would be small enough to conceal on the person; that it could be detonated by the pressing of just one button; and that the equipment the

IRA had was capable of detonating a radio-controlled bomb over a distance of a mile and a half.

As to the events on 6 March 1988, the operations room opened at 8 a.m., and members of the surveillance teams were on duty in the streets of Gibraltar, as were soldiers A., B., C. and D. and members of the police force involved in the operation. The soldiers, working in pairs, were in civilian clothing and were each equipped with a 9mm Browning pistol and a radio. Police officers P., Q. and R., on duty to support the soldiers in any arrest, were also in plain clothes and armed.

There was surveillance at the Spanish immigration post from 8 a.m., and, on the Gibraltar side of the border, there was another surveillance team and an arrest group. While soldiers E. and F. referred to the preferred military option as being to intercept and arrest the suspects in the frontier area, this did not appear to have been pursued with any conviction because of the brief time available for identification to be made. Soldier F. stated that the military option had been refined down to the preferred option to arrest all of the suspects in the assembly area once they had parked a car, to disarm them and then to defuse the bomb.

Police and security service officials saw that a white Renault car had been parked in the assembly area under observation. A man, later identified as Sean Savage, was seen to fiddle with something between the seats of the car, lock the car door and walk away. He was followed for approximately an hour by security service officials who recalled that he was using anti-surveillance techniques.

A security service official stated that Daniel McCann and Mairead Farrell passed the frontier on foot at about 2.30 p.m., and that they were followed. At about 2.50 p.m., it was reported that Mr. McCann and Ms. Farrell had met Mr. Savage and that they were looking at the white Renault car in the assembly area. The possibility of arresting them then was considered but rejected, because they moved away from the car, and it was felt that they might have been on reconnaissance and might return to the car.

After the three suspects had left the assembly area, soldier G. examined the suspect car from the exterior briefly without touching it. He noted that the aerial, which was rusty, did not seem to accord with the age of the car. He reported that he regarded the car as a suspect car bomb. He later explained that this was a way of describing a car parked in suspicious circumstances, where there was every reason to believe that it was a car bomb and where it could not be said that it was not. Soldier G. was described as the bomb-disposal adviser, because he had experience in dealing with car bombs, but he stated that he was neither a radio-communications expert nor an explosives expert. Soldiers A., C. and D. stated that it had been confirmed to them that there was a bomb in the assembly area which could be detonated by a remote-controlled device.

Having received the report from soldier G., and in view of the subsequent movements of the three suspects, the Commissioner decided that they should be arrested on suspicion of conspiracy to murder. At 3.40 p.m., he signed a form requesting the military to apprehend the suspects. In the form, it was acknowledged that the military option might include the use of lethal force for the preservation of life. At that time, soldiers C. and D. were monitoring the movement of the three suspects, and soldiers A. and B. were making their way towards them. The soldiers were informed that control had passed to them to make an arrest. As the soldiers approached the suspects, Mr. Savage split away from Mr. McCann and Ms. Farrell. According to evidence given, the soldiers had practised arrest procedures with the police before the operation, and a suitable place had been identified in Gibraltar for the detention of the terrorists.

Soldiers A. and B. stated that they followed Mr. McCann and Ms. Farrell. When soldier A. was approximately ten metres behind Mr. McCann, the suspect looked back over his left shoulder, looking directly at soldier A. and seeming to realize who he was and that he was a threat. Soldier A. stated that he drew his pistol intending to shout a warning at the same time, though he was uncertain if the words actually came out. Mr. McCann's hand moved suddenly across the front of his body. The soldier thought that the suspect was going for the button to detonate the bomb and opened fire, shooting one round into Mr. McCann's back from a distance of three metres. The soldier then saw Ms. Farrell make a half turn to the right towards Mr. McCann, grabbing for the handbag under her left arm. The soldier thought that she was also going for a button and shot one round into her back. He then turned back to the other suspect and shot him once more in the body and twice in the head. He fired a total of five shots.

Soldier B. stated that they were three to four metres away from the suspects when he saw Mr. McCann look over his shoulder and heard what he presumed was a shout from soldier A., thought to be the start of the arrest process. At almost the same instant, there was firing to his right, and Ms. Farrell made a sharp movement to her right, drawing the bag she had under her left arm across her body. The soldier feared that she was going for the button, and he opened fire on her. He deemed that Mr. McCann was in a threatening position and switched fire to him. The soldier then turned back to Ms. Farrell and continued firing until he was certain that she was no longer a threat, namely, her hands away from her body. He fired a total of seven shots.

Both soldiers denied that Mr. McCann or Ms. Farell had made any attempt to surrender with their hands up in the air or that they had fired at the suspects lying on the ground. Soldier A. stated expressly that his intention had been to kill Mr. McCann to stop him becoming a threat and detonating the bomb.

After the shooting, a number of police officials arrived on the scene. Two police officials placed their jackets over the bodies, and another carried out a search of the bodies.

The shootings were witnessed by a considerable number of people. Evidence given by three witnesses suggested that the suspects had been shot while lying on the ground, although none of the other witnesses saw the soldiers so firing at the suspects. While the soldiers were not sure that any words of warning were uttered by soldier A., four witnesses had a clear recollection of hearing the words "police, stop", or words to that effect. One police offical who was approaching the scene stated that he saw Mr. McCann make a move as if going for a gun and that Ms. Farell made a move towards her handbag, making him think that she was going for a detonator. Another two police officials also saw Ms. Farell make a move towards her handbag.

As to Mr. Savage, soldiers C. and D. stated that they had followed him. When soldier D. approached him to make the arrest, he heard gunfire, and at the same time soldier C. shouted "stop". The suspect spun round, and his arm went down towards his right hand hip area. Soldier D. believed that Mr. Savage was going for a detonator and opened fire from about two to three metres. He fired nine rounds at rapid rate, initially aiming into the centre of the suspect's body, with the last two at his head. Mr. Savage corkscrewed as he fell. The soldier acknowledged that it was possible that the suspect's head was inches away from the ground as he finished firing. He kept firing until Mr. Savage was motionless on the ground and his hands were away from his body.

Soldier C. recalled that he had followed Mr. Savage, slightly behind soldier D., and heared shots from the direction in which Mr. McCann and Ms. Farell had headed. When Mr. Savage spun round, soldier C. shouted "stop" and drew his pistol. The suspect moved his right arm down to the area of his jacket pocket, and the soldier opened fire, as he feared the suspect was about to detonate the bomb. He fired six times as Mr. Savage spiraled down, aiming at the mass of his body. One shot went into his neck and another into his head as he fell. Soldier C. continued firing until he was sure that the suspect was no longer in a position to initiate a device.

Under cross-examination, both soldiers stated that once it became necessary to open fire, they would continue shooting until the person was no longer a threat. Soldier C.

II:2

agreed that the best way to ensure this result was to kill. Soldier D. stated that he was firing at the suspect to kill him and that this was the way that all soldiers were trained. Both soldiers, however, denied that they had shot Mr. Savage while he was on the ground.

Soldier E., the attack commander, stated that the intention at the moment of opening fire was to kill, since this was the only way to remove the threat.

Witnesses H., I. and J., involved in the surveillance of the three suspects, were following Mr. Savage at the time of the shooting. Witnesses H. and J. heard the sound of a police siren before the shooting. They all heard the shots directed at Mr. Mc-Cann and Ms. Farrell, but witnesses H. and J. did not witness the shooting of Mr. Savage. Witness I. saw one or two shots being fired at Mr. Savage on the ground. A number of other witnesses gave various accounts of what they had seen, confirming in some ways the accounts of the officials involved in the operation, but conflicting with them in other ways.

At about 4.05 p.m., control of the operation was returned to the police. A bomb-disposal team then opened the white Renault car, but they found no explosive device or bomb. The bodies of the three suspects were searched and no weapons or detonating devices were discovered.

At the scene of the shootings of Mr. McCann and Ms. Farrell, the shell cases and cartridges were picked up without marking their location or otherwise recording their position. The positions of the bodies were not marked. At the scene of the shooting of Mr. Savage, only some of the cartridge positions were marked. A police official had made a chalk outline of the position of Mr. Savage's body. Within that outline, there were five strike marks, three in the area of the head. No police photographs were taken of the bodies' positions.

Inside Ms. Farrell's handbag was found a key ring with two keys and a tag bearing a registration number of a car. Enquiries to trace this vehicle led to the discovery on 8 March 1988 of a second car, in a car park in Marbella, Spain. That car contained an explosive device in the boot. The device consisted of Semtex explosive to which were attached four detonators and around which were packed 200 rounds of ammunition. There were two timers but the device was not primed or connected. It was believed that the device was set to explode at the time of the military parade on 8 March 1988.

Post-mortem examinations of the bodies of the three deceased suspects were conducted by a pathologist from the United Kingdom. His report was provided to a pathologist instructed by the applicants. Comment was later made by both pathologists with regard to defects in the post-mortem procedures. In particular, the bodies had been stripped before the examining pathologist saw them, depriving him of possible aid in establishing entry and exit wounds, and there had been no X-ray facilities.

An inquest into the killings was held by the Gibraltar Coroner, with a jury, from 6 to 30 September 1988. Evidence was heard from seventy-nine witnesses, including soldiers, police officials, surveillance personnel, pathologists, forensic scientists and experts on explosive devices.

The legal representative of the applicants questioned the witnesses and made submissions to the effect, *inter alia*, that either the decision to shoot to kill the suspects had been made by the Government of the United Kingdom prior to the incident, and the soldiers were ordered to carry out the shootings, or the operation was planned and implemented in such a way that the killing of the suspects by the soldiers was the inevitable result. In any event, in light of the circumstances, the use of lethal force by the soldiers was not necessary or, if it was necessary, the force used was excessive and therefore not justified.

Soldier F., the senior military commander, and Soldier E., the tactical commander, denied that there had been a plan, express or tacit, to execute the suspects. When it was put to soldiers A., B., C. and D., they also denied that they had been sent out either expressly or on the basis of a nod or a wink to kill the suspects.

At the conclusion of the inquest, the Coroner addressed the jury in respect of the applicable law and summed up the respective propositions of the applicants' representatives and the representatives of the soldiers and the Crown. He concluded from the evidence given by the soldiers that when they opened fire, they shot intending to kill, and he directed the jury as to the range of possible verdicts. Finally, he advised them that there were only three verdicts reasonably open to a jury: (*a*) killed unlawfully, i.e. unlawful homicide; (*b*) killed lawfully, i.e. justifiable, reasonable homicide; or (*c*) open verdict. The jury returned verdicts of lawful killing by a majority of nine to two.

The applicants were dissatisfied with these verdicts and commenced actions in the High Court of Justice in Northern Ireland against the Ministry of Defence for loss and damage as a result of the deaths. However, the Secretary of State for Foreign and Commonwealth Affairs issued certificates under law that excluded proceedings in Northern Ireland against the Crown in respect of liability arising otherwise than in respect of Her Majesty's Government in the United Kingdom. The applicants challenged the legality of the certificates, but later they withdrew their challenge on the basis that the application had no reasonable prospects of success.

II:2

Other evidence was produced before the Commission and the Court.

The Government provided the Commission with a copy of a statement made by a Spanish police officer in Málaga. According to this statement, at the beginning of March 1988, the United Kingdom police had provided the Spanish police with photographs of the possible members of the IRA active service unit, named as Daniel McCann, Mairead Farrell and Sean Savage. The three individuals were observed arriving at Málaga Airport on 4 March 1988, but trace of them was lost as they left. There was then a search to locate the three suspects during 5 to 6 March 1988.

A statement, made by a journalist, was supplied on behalf of the applicants. It concerned surveillance by the Spanish authorities of the white Renault car used by the active service unit, and it alleged that the authorities in Gibraltar were aware of the car's arrival at the border. The applicants submitted a further opinion of their witness on the detonation of explosive devices. He reiterated his view that it would have been impossible for the three suspects to have detonated a bomb in the target area from the location where they were shot, using an ICOM or any other conceivable concealable transmitter/aerial combination.

In its report, the Commission made the following findings on questions of fact.

The suspects were effectively allowed to enter Gibraltar to be picked up by the surveillance operatives in place in strategic locations for that purpose. There was no evidence to support the applicants' contention of a premeditated design to kill Mr. McCann, Ms. Farrell and Mr. Savage. There was no convincing support for any allegation that the soldiers shot Mr. McCann and Ms. Farrell when they were attempting to surrender or when they were lying on the ground. However, the soldiers carried out the shooting from close proximity. The forensic evidence indicated a distance of as little as three feet in the case of Ms. Farrell.

Ms. Farrell and Mr. McCann were shot by soldiers A. and B. at close range after the two suspects had made what appeared to the soldiers to be threatening movements. They were shot as they fell to the ground but not when they were lying on the ground. It was probably either the sound of a police siren or the sound of the shooting of Mr. McCann and Ms. Farrell, or indeed both, that caused Mr. Savage to turn round to face the soldiers who were behind him. It was not likely that soldiers C. and D. witnessed the shooting of Mr. McCann and Ms. Farrell before proceeding in pursuit of Mr. Savage. There was insufficient material to rebut the version given by soldiers C. and D. of the shooting. Mr. Savage was shot at close range until he hit the ground and probably in the instant as or after he hit the ground. This conclusion was supported by the pathologists' evidence at the subsequent inquest.

Soldiers A. to D. opened fire with the purpose of preventing the threat of detonation of a car bomb in the centre of Gibraltar by suspects who were known to them to be terrorists with a history of previous involvement with explosives. A timer must in all probability have been mentioned at the Commissioner's operational briefing. For whatever reason, however, it was not a factor which was taken into account in the soldiers' view of the operation.

As to relevant domestic law and practice, relevant provisions of article 2 of the Gibraltar Constitution provided, *inter alia*, that there would be no contravention of that article if a person died as a result of the use of force, lawful and reasonably justifiable in the circumstances, and applied for a number of specified purposes. These included the defence of the person from violence, in order to effect a lawful arrest and in order to prevent the commission by that person of a criminal offence. The relevant domestic case law on what constituted reasonableness in the use of force was set out and discussed in this part of the judgment.

The final item included in this context was an account of the document, providing rules on the use of force and firearms, that was annexed to the operational order of the Commissioner of Police.

Two international non-treaty instruments were also referred to in this part of the judgment: the Basic Principles on the Use of Force and Firearms by Law Enforcement Officials, providing, in principle 9, intentional lethal use of firearms to be made only when strictly unavoidable in order to protect life; and the Principles on the Effective Prevention and Investigation of Extra-legal, Arbitrary and Summary Executions, requiring, in principle 9, thorough, prompt and impartial investigations of all suspected cases of extralegal, arbitrary and summary executions.

In its final submissions to the Court, the Government held that the deprivations of life to which the applications related were justified under article 2, paragraph 2 (*a*), of the Convention as resulting from the use of force which was no more than absolutely necessary in defence of the people of Gibraltar from unlawful violence.

The applicants submitted that the Government had not shown beyond reasonable doubt that the planning and execution of the operation was in accordance with article 2, paragraph 2, of the Convention. Accordingly, the killings were not absolutely necessary within the meaning of this provision.

The law

As to the alleged violation of article 2 of the Convention and the interpretation of that provision, the Court referred to a number of other cases brought under that arti-

II:2

cle. The Court noted that the provisions of the Convention had to be interpreted and applied so as to make its safeguards practical and effective. Article 2 ranked as one of the most fundamental provisions in the Convention, an article being non-derogable in peacetime and enshrining one of the basic values of the democratic societies making up the Council of Europe.

The Court considered that the exceptions delineated in paragraph 2 of the article indicated that this provision extended to, but was not concerned exclusively with, intentional killing. Referring to the Commission's decision on the application *Stewart v. the United Kingdom*, the Court noted that the text of article 2, read as a whole, demonstrated that paragraph 2 did not primarily define instances where it was permitted intentionally to kill an individual, but described the situations where it was permitted to use force that might result, as an unintended outcome, in the deprivation of life. However, the use of force had to be no more than absolutely necessary for the achievement of one of the purposes set out in paragraph 2 (*a*), (*b*) or (*c*).

In this respect, the use of the term "absolutely necessary", in article 2, paragraph 2, indicated that a stricter and more compelling test of necessity had to be employed from that normally applicable when determining whether State action was necessary in a democratic society under paragraph 2 of articles 8 to 11 of the Convention. In particular, the force used had to be strictly proportionate to the achievement of the aims set out in article 2, paragraph 2 (*a*), (*b*) and (*c*).

In keeping with the importance of this provision in a democratic society, the Court observed that in making its assessment, it had to subject deprivations of life to the most careful scrutiny, particularly where deliberate lethal force was used. It had to take into consideration not only the actions of the agents of the State who actually administered the force, but also all the surrounding circumstances, including such matters as the planning and control of the actions under examination.

Concerning the obligation in article 2, paragraph 1, of the Convention to protect life, the applicants submitted that this provision imposed a positive duty on States to protect life. In particular, the national law had strictly to control and limit the circumstances in which a person might be deprived of his life by agents of the State. Furthermore, the State had to give appropriate training, instructions and briefing to its agents, who might use force, and exercise strict control over any operations that might involve the use of lethal force. They argued that the relevant domestic law did not encompass the standard of absolute necessity, set forth in article 2, and that this constituted a violation of the article. There was also a violation of this provision in that the law did not require that the agents of the State should be trained in accordance with the strict standards of article 2, paragraph 1.

Referring to a number of cases, the Court recalled that the Convention did not oblige States parties to incorporate its provisions into national law. It held that the difference between article 2 of the Gibraltar Constitution and article 2 of the Convention was not sufficiently great that a violation of article 2, paragraph 1, could be found on this ground alone.

Regarding the applicants' arguments concerning the training, instruction and operational control of the agents of the State, the Court considered that these were matters that raised issues under article 2, paragraph 2, concerning the proportionality of the State's response. It sufficed to note in this respect that the rules of engagement issued to the soldiers and the police provided a series of rules governing the use of force, carefully reflecting the national standard as well as the substance of the Convention standard.

The adequacy of inquest proceedings as an investigative mechanism was also an item discussed. The Court noted that a general legal prohibition of arbitrary killing by the agents of the State would be ineffective, in practice, if there existed no procedure for reviewing the lawfulness of the use of lethal force by State authorities. The obligation to protect the right to life under article 2 of the Convention, read in conjunction with the State's general duty under article 1 to secure to everyone within its jurisdiction the rights and freedoms defined in the Convention, required by implication that there should be some form of effective official investigation when individuals had been killed as a result of the use of force by agents of the State.

The Court felt, however, that it was not necessary in the present case to decide what form such an investigation should take and under what conditions it should be conducted, since public inquest proceedings did in fact take place. Moreover, the proceedings lasted 19 days and involved a detailed review of the events surrounding the killings. As to the alleged shortcomings in these inquest proceedings, the Court did not consider that they substantially hampered the carrying out of a thorough, impartial and careful examination of the circumstances surrounding the killings. It followed that there had been no breach of article 2, paragraph 1, of the Convention on this ground.

As to the application of article 2 to the facts of the case, the Government submitted that the verdicts of the inquest jury were of central importance to any subsequent examination of the deaths of the deceased and that the Court should give substantial weight to those verdicts. The applicants, on the other hand, maintained that inquests were ill-equipped to be full and detailed inquiries into controversial killings.

The Court recalled that under the scheme of the Convention, the then articles 28, paragraph 1, and 31, the establishment and verification of the facts was primarily a

II:2

matter for the Commission,. The Court was not, however, bound by the Commission's findings of fact and remained free to make its own appreciation in the light of all the material before it. A number of cases supporting this view were cited by the Court. Having regard to the submissions of those appearing before the Court and to the inquest proceedings, the Court took the Commission's establishment of the facts and findings, summarized in the judgment, to be accurate and reliable.

Regarding the appreciation of these facts from the standpoint of article 2, the Court observed that the inquest jury had the benefit of assessing the value of the witnesses' testimony at first hand. Nevertheless, the jury's finding was limited to a decision of lawful killing and did not provide reasons for the conclusion it reached. In addition, the focus of concern of the inquest proceedings and the standard applied by the jury was whether the killings by the soldiers were reasonably justified in the circumstances as opposed to whether they were absolutely necessary under article 2, paragraph 2, of the Convention.

Against this background, the Court stated that it must make its own assessment as to whether the facts as established by the Commission disclosed a violation of article 2 of the Convention. In accordance with its usual practice, it would assess the issues in the light of all the material placed before it by the applicants and by the Government or, if necessary, material obtained of its own motion. A number of cases were cited in the judgment in support of this conclusion.

The applicants claimed that there was strong circumstantial evidence to support their allegation that there had been a premeditated plan to kill the deceased. The Government submitted that it was implicit in the jury's verdicts of lawful killing that they found that there was no plot to kill the three terrorists. The aim of the operation was to effect their lawful arrest. The Commission had concluded that there was no evidence to support the applicants' claim of a premeditated plot to kill the suspects.

The Court observed that it would need to have convincing evidence before it could conclude that there was a premeditated plan, in the sense developed by the applicants. It did not find it established that there had been an execution plot at the highest level of command in the Ministry of Defence or in the Government, that soldiers A., B., C. and D. had been so encouraged or instructed by the superior officers who had briefed them prior to the operation or, indeed, that they had decided on their own initiative to kill the suspects irrespective of the existence of any justification for the use of lethal force and in disobedience to the arrest instructions they had received. Nor was there evidence that there was an implicit encouragement by the authorities or hints and innuendoes to execute the three suspects. The Court therefore rejected as unsubstantiated the applicants' allegations that the killing of the three suspects was premeditated or the product of a tacit agreement amongst those involved in the operation.

As to conduct and planning of the operation, the applicants submitted that it would be wrong for the Court to limit its assessment to the question of the possible justification of the soldiers who actually killed the suspects. It had to examine the liability of the Government for all aspects of the operation. Indeed, the soldiers might well have been acquitted at a criminal trial if they could have shown that they honestly believed the ungrounded and false information given to them. The applicants referred in particular to the fact that the soldiers had been told as a matter of certainty that the suspects had planted a car bomb; that they could detonate it by flicking a switch; and that they would not hesitate to do so if challenged. In sum, the applicants submitted that the killings came about as a result of incompetence and negligence in the planning and conduct of the anti-terrorist operation to arrest the suspects, as well as a failure to maintain a proper balance between the need to meet the threat posed and the right to life of the suspects.

The Government submitted that the actions of the soldiers were absolutely necessary in defence of persons from unlawful violence within the meaning of article 2, paragraph 2 (*a*), of the Convention. If it was accepted that the soldiers honestly and reasonably believed that the terrorists, upon whom they opened fire, might have been about to detonate a bomb by pressing a button, then they had no alternative but to open fire.

The Government further submitted that in examining the planning of the anti-terrorist operation, it should be borne in mind that intelligence assessments were necessarily based on incomplete information; that in the IRA, they were exceptionally ruthless and skilled in counter-surveillance techniques; that the IRA was constantly and rapidly developing new technology; that the authorities had to take into account the possibility that the terrorists might be equipped with more sophisticated radio-controlled devices than the IRA had previously been known to use; and that, finally, the consequences of underestimating the threat posed by the active service unit could have been catastrophic.

The Government then made a number of observations to support their submission that the intelligence assessments made in the course of the operation were reasonable in the light of the limited information available to the authorities and the potentially devastating consequences of underestimating the terrorists' abilities and resources.

The Commission considered that given the soldiers' perception of the risk to the lives of the people of Gibraltar, the shooting of the three suspects could be regarded

II:2

as absolutely necessary for the legitimate aim of the defence of others from unlawful violence. It also concluded that the planning and execution of the operation by the authorities did not disclose any deliberate design or lack of proper care that might have rendered the use of lethal force disproportionate to the aim of saving lives.

In carrying out its examination under article 2 of the Convention, the Court observed that it had to bear in mind that the information the authorities had received, that there would be a terrorist attack in Gibraltar, presented them with a fundamental dilemma. On the one hand, they were required to have regard to their duty to protect the lives of the people in Gibraltar, including their own military personnel, and, on the other, to have minimum resort to the use of lethal force against those suspected of posing this threat in the light of the obligations flowing from both domestic and international law. Other factors also to be taken into account were the fact that the authorities were confronted by an active service unit of the IRA composed of persons who had been convicted of bombing offences and a known explosives expert and that the IRA had demonstrated a disregard for human life. Furthermore, the authorities had prior warning of the impending terrorist action and thus had ample opportunity to plan their reaction and to take measures to foil the attack and arrest the suspects. Inevitably, however, the security authorities could not have been in possession of the full facts and were obliged to formulate their policies on the basis of incomplete hypotheses.

Against this background, in determining whether the force used was compatible with article 2 of the Convention, the Court had to scrutinize carefully not only whether the force used by the soldiers was strictly proportionate to the aim of protecting persons against unlawful violence, but also whether the anti-terrorist operation was planned and controlled by the authorities so as to minimize, to the greatest extent possible, recourse to lethal force. The Court considered each of these points in turn.

Regarding the actions of the soldiers, the Court recalled that the four soldiers who carried out the shootings were informed by their superiors that there was a car bomb in place. It could be detonated by any of the three suspects by means of a concealed radio-control device, which could be activated by pressing a button. The suspects would be likely to detonate the bomb if challenged, thereby causing heavy loss of life and serious injuries, and they were also likely to be armed and to resist arrest. The Court then recalled the Commission's findings concerning the shootings of the three suspects and the fact that it was subsequently discovered that the suspects were unarmed, that they did not have a detonator device on their persons and that there was no bomb in the car.

The Court accepted that the soldiers honestly believed, in the light of the information that they had been given, that it was necessary to shoot the suspects in order to prevent them from detonating a bomb and causing serious loss of life. The actions which they took, in obedience to superior orders, were thus perceived by them as absolutely necessary in order to safeguard innocent lives.

The Court considered that the use of force by agents of the State, in pursuit of one of the aims delineated in article 2, paragraph 2, of the Convention, might be justified under this provision where it was based on an honest belief, perceived, for good reasons, to be valid at the time, but which subsequently turned out to be mistaken. To hold otherwise would be to impose an unrealistic burden on the State and its law enforcement personnel in the execution of their duty, perhaps to the detriment of their lives and those of others. Having regard to the dilemma confronting the authorities in the circumstances of the case, it followed that the actions of the soldiers did not, in themselves, give rise to a violation of article 2.

The question arose, however, whether the anti-terrorist operation as a whole was controlled and organized in a manner that respected the requirements of article 2 and whether the information and instructions given to the soldiers, in effect rendering inevitable the use of lethal force, took adequately into consideration the right to life of the three suspects.

The Court first observed that it had been the intention of the authorities to arrest the suspects at an appropriate stage. Indeed, evidence was given at the inquest that arrest procedures had been practised by the soldiers before 6 March 1988 and that efforts had been made to find a suitable place in Gibraltar to detain the suspects after their arrest.

It might be questioned why the three suspects were not arrested at the border immediately on their arrival in Gibraltar and why the decision was taken not to prevent them from entering Gibraltar if believed to be on a bombing mission. On this issue, the Government submitted that at that moment there might not have been sufficient evidence to warrant the detention and trial of the suspects. Moreover, to release them, having alerted them to the authorities' state of awareness but leaving them or others free to try again, would obviously increase the risks. Nor could the authorities be sure that those three were the only terrorists they had to deal with or of the manner in which it was proposed to carry out the bombing.

The Court confined itself in this respect to observing that the danger to the population of Gibraltar in not preventing the suspects' entry had to be considered to outweigh the possible consequences of having insufficient evidence to warrant their detention and trial. In its view, either the authorities knew that there was no bomb in the car, which the Court had already discounted, or there was a serious miscalculation by those responsible for controlling the operation. As a result, the scene was set

II:2

in which the fatal shooting, given the intelligence assessments made, was a foreseeable possibility if not a likelihood. The decision not to stop the three terrorists from entering Gibraltar was thus a relevant factor to take into account in this context.

The Court noted that at the briefing on 5 March, attended by soldiers A., B., C., and D., it was considered likely that the attack would be by way of a large car bomb. A number of key assessments were made. In particular, it was thought that the bomb would be detonated by a radio-control device; that the detonation could be effected by the pressing of a button; that it was likely that the suspects would detonate the bomb if challenged; and that they would be armed and would be likely to use their arms if confronted. In the event, all of these crucial assumptions, apart from the terrorists' intentions to carry out an attack, turned out to be erroneous. Nevertheless, as had been demonstrated by the Government, on the basis of the experience in dealing with the IRA, they were all possible hypotheses in a situation where the true facts were unknown and where the authorities operated on the basis of limited intelligence information.

In fact, the Court observed, it appeared that insufficient allowances had been made for other assumptions. For example, since the bombing was not expected until 8 March when the changing of the guard ceremony was to take place, there was equally the possibility that the three terrorists were on a reconnaissance mission. While this was a factor briefly considered, it did not appear to have been regarded as a serious possibility. In addition, at the briefings or after the suspects had been spotted, it might have been thought unlikely that they would have been prepared to explode the bomb as Mr. McCann and Ms. Farrell strolled towards the border area, since this would have increased the risk of detection and capture. It might also have been thought improbable that at that point, they would have set up the transmitter in anticipation to enable them to detonate the supposed bomb immediately if confronted. Moreover, even if allowances were made for the technological skills of the IRA, the description of the detonation device as a "button job" without the qualifications subsequently described by the experts at the inquest, of which the competent authorities must have been aware, oversimplified the true nature of these devices.

The Court felt it further disquieting in this context that the assessment made by soldier G. after a cursory external examination of the car, that there was a suspect car bomb, was conveyed to the soldiers as a definite identification that there was such a bomb. It was recalled that while soldier G. had experience in car bombs, it transpired that he was not an expert in radio-communications or explosives and that his assessment, that there was a suspect car bomb, was more in the nature of a report that a bomb could not be ruled out.

In the absence of sufficient allowances being made for alternative possibilities and the definite reporting of the existence of a car bomb that according to the assessments made, could be detonated at the press of a button, a series of working hypotheses were conveyed to soldiers A., B., C. and D. as certainties, thereby making the use of lethal force almost unavoidable. However, the Court observed, the failure to make provision for a margin of error also had to be considered in combination with the training of the soldiers to continue shooting once they opened fire until the suspect was dead. As noted by the Coroner in his summing-up to the jury at the inquest, all four soldiers shot to kill the suspects. Soldier E. testified that it had been discussed with the soldiers that there was an increased chance that they would have to shoot to kill, since there would be less time where there was a "button" device.

Against this background, the authorities were bound by their obligation to respect the right to life of the suspects to exercise the greatest of care in evaluating the information at their disposal before transmitting it to soldiers whose use of firearms automatically involved shooting to kill. Their reflex action in this vital respect lacked the degree of caution in the use of firearms to be expected from law enforcement personnel in a democratic society, even when dealing with dangerous terrorist suspects. It stood in marked contrast to the standard of care reflected in the instructions in the use of firearms by the police, which had been drawn to their attention and which emphasized the legal responsibilities of the individual officer in the light of conditions prevailing at the moment of engagement. This failure by the authorities also suggested a lack of appropriate care in the control and organization of the arrest operation.

In sum, having regard to the decision not to prevent the suspects from travelling into Gibraltar, to the failure of the authorities to make sufficient allowances for the possibility that their intelligence assessments might, in some respects at least, be erroneous and to the automatic recourse to lethal force when the soldiers opened fire, the Court was not persuaded that the killing of the three suspects constituted the use of force not more than absolutely necessary in defence of persons from unlawful violence within the meaning of article 2, paragraph 2 (*a*), of the Convention. Accordingly, the Court held, by ten votes to nine, that there had been a violation of article 2.

The minority, in a joint dissenting opinion, was unable to subscribe to the opinion of the majority that there had been such a violation. They agreed with the conclusion that the actions of the four soldiers who carried out the shootings did not, in themselves, give rise to a violation of article 2 of the Convention. However, they disagreed with the evaluation made by the majority of the way in which the control and organization of the operation were carried out by the authorities. They considered the conclusion, that there was a lack of appropriate care in the control and organization of the arrest operation, to be unjustified.

II:2

As to the then article 50 of the Convention, allowing the Court to afford just satisfaction to an injured party, under specified circumstances, when there had been a violation of the Convention, the Court dismissed the applicants' claim for damages. It referred to the fact that the three suspects who were killed had been intending to plant a bomb in Gibraltar. The Court did, however, make an order for the United Kingdom to pay to the applicants costs and expenses, incurred during the Strasbourg proceedings only, less the amount received by way of legal aid from the Council of Europe.

(e) *Mahmut Kaya* v. *Turkey* (European Court of Human Rights)[66]

The case was referred to the European Court of Human Rights on 8 March 1999 by the European Commission of Human Rights. It originated in an application against the Republic of Turkey lodged with the Commission on 20 August 1993 by Mahmut Kaya, a Turkish national. The application concerned the applicant's allegations that his brother, Hasan Kaya, was kidnapped, tortured and killed by, or with the connivance of, State agents and that there was no effective investigation or remedy for his complaints. The applicant invoked the right to life in article 2, the prohibition of torture in article 3, the right to an effective remedy in article 13 and the prohibition of discrimination in article 14 of the Convention for the Protection of Human Rights and Fundamental Freedoms.

The facts

Hasan Kaya practised medicine in southeast Turkey. From November 1990 to May 1992 he had worked in Sirnak. He had treated demonstrators injured in clashes with the security forces during the Kurdish New Year celebrations. Following this, he was transferred to another town in the same region. He had told the wife of a friend, Metin Can, that prior to the transfer, he had been threatened and put under considerable pressure.

Following the transfer, Hasan Kaya worked in a health centre. He often met with Metin Can, who was a lawyer and the president of a human rights organization. Mr. Can had been representing persons suspected of being members of the Workers' Party of Kurdistan (PKK). He had told his wife that he had received threats and that an official had warned him that steps had been planned against him.

---

[66] See European Court of Human Rights, *Reports of Judgments and Decisions*, 2000-III, p. 149, application No. 22535/93, judgment of 28 March 2000.

II:2

In December 1992, a man was taken into detention by police officers and interrogated to find out what he knew about the PKK. He was asked whether two medical doctors, one of whom was Hasan Kaya, had been treating wounded members of that organization. A threat was made that Mr. Kaya would be punished. He was also asked about lawyers, particularly Metin Can. On his release, he told Mr. Can what had occurred.

During Christmas 1992, Hasan Kaya told the applicant that he felt that his life was in danger. He believed that the police were making reports on him and keeping him under surveillance. Around the same time, Metin Can told the applicant that his flat had been searched while he was out and that he thought he was under surveillance.

On or about 20 February 1993, Mr. Can received a telephone call. The callers said that they had been to his flat earlier and wanted to come and see him immediately. He told them to come to his office the next day.

On 21 February 1993, after receiving a phone call at his office, Mr. Can met two men in a coffee house. They said that there was a wounded member of the PKK hidden outside town. Mr. Can took the men back to his flat and called Hasan Kaya on the telephone. Mr. Kaya arrived at the flat. It was arranged that the two men would take the wounded man to a village nearby and that they would call when they were ready. The two men left. At about 7 p.m., there was a phone call. Metin Can left with Hasan Kaya, who was carrying his medical bag. Mr. Can told his wife that they would not be long. They drove off in the car of Mr. Kaya's brother.

They did not return that night. Around mid-day on 22 February 1993, Mr. Can's wife received a phone call. The speaker sounded like one of the men who had come to the flat. He said that Metin Can and his friend had been killed. Mrs. Can and a friend went to the security directorate to report that the two men were missing. On the same day, the car belonging to Hasan Kaya's brother was traced.

On 27 February 1993, the bodies of Hasan Kaya and Metin Can were found. The reports of two autopsies carried out on each of the bodies, on 27 and 28 February 1993, indicated that they had died of gunshot wounds to the head, but the reports provided contradictory information on the injuries they had sustained.

In the judgment, it is described how various people provided information to the authorities and how the authorities responded. For example, Ahmet Kaya, the father of Hasan Kaya, provided an account to public prosecutors of his son's arrest. He stated that the two men had been taken in a vehicle 138 km through eight official checkpoints, and the circumstances indicated that the State authorities were involved. He also reported details of an incident in which a wanted terrorist had announced in a

II:2

beer house that he had killed the two men. He had then called for help over a radio, and two gendarmes had arrived and taken him away.

When requested by prosecutors to respond to or to investigate the information, police and gendarmerie either disclaimed knowledge of the incidents, denied that they had occurred or carried out ineffective investigations.

A number of domestic investigation documents were placed before the Commission, including, provided by the applicant, a copy of the so-called "Susurluk report", produced at the request of the Prime Minister within his office. After receiving the report in January 1998, he made it available to the public, although 11 pages and certain annexes were withheld.

Susurluk was the scene of a road accident in November 1996 involving a car in which a member of parliament, a former deputy director of the Istanbul security services, a notorious far-right extremist, a drug trafficker wanted by Interpol and his girlfriend had been travelling. The latter three were killed. The fact that they had all been travelling in the same car had so shocked public opinion that it had been necessary to start more than 16 judicial investigations at different levels and a parliamentary inquiry.

In the introduction, it was stated that the report was not based on a judicial investigation and did not constitute a formal investigative report. It was intended for information purposes and purported to do no more than describe certain events that had occurred mainly in southeast Turkey, tending to confirm the existence of unlawful dealings between political figures, government institutions and clandestine groups.

The report analyzed a series of events, such as murders carried out under orders, the killings of well-known figures or supporters of the Kurds and deliberate acts by a group of informants supposedly serving the State. It concluded that there was a connection between the fight to eradicate terrorism in the region and the underground relations that had been formed as a result, particularly in the drug-trafficking sphere. One of a number of murders referred to in the report was that of Metin Can.

The report ended with numerous recommendations, such as improving coordination and communication between the different branches of the security, police and intelligence departments; identifying and dismissing security force personnel implicated in illegal activities; limiting the use of confessors; reducing the number of village guards; terminating the use of a special operations bureau outside the southeast region and incorporating it into the police outside that area; opening investigations into various incidents; and taking steps to suppress gang and drug-smuggling activities.

II:2

The law

The Court observed that the Commission's overall conclusion was that there was insufficient evidence to support a finding beyond reasonable doubt that State officials carried out the killing of Hasan Kaya. It accepted the facts as established by the Commission.

As to alleged violations of article 2 of the Convention, the applicant claimed that the State was responsible for the death of his brother, Hasan Kaya, through the lack of protection and failure to provide an effective investigation into his death. He invoked the provisions of article 2. The Government disputed those allegations. The Commission concluded that the State had failed to comply with the positive obligation to protect Mr. Kaya's life.

In respect of the alleged failure to protect the right to life, the Court first recalled that under article 2, paragraph 1, of the Convention, everyone's right to life had to be protected by law. This provision enjoined the State not only to refrain from the intentional and unlawful taking of life, but also to take appropriate steps to safeguard the lives of those within its jurisdiction. This involved a primary duty on the State to secure the right to life by putting in place effective criminal law provisions to deter the commission of offences against the person, backed up by law enforcement machinery for the prevention, suppression and punishment of breaches of such provisions. It also extended in appropriate circumstances to a positive obligation on the authorities to take preventive operational measures to protect an individual, or individuals, whose life was at risk from the criminal acts of another individual.

Bearing in mind the difficulties in policing modern societies, the unpredictability of human conduct and the operational choices to be made in terms of priorities and resources, the Court stated that the positive obligation had to be interpreted in a way not imposing an impossible or disproportionate burden on the authorities. Accordingly, not every claimed risk to life could entail for the authorities a requirement under the Convention to take operational measures to prevent that risk from materializing. For a positive obligation to arise, it had to be established that the authorities knew or ought to have known at the time of the existence of a real and immediate risk to the life of an identified individual or individuals from the criminal acts of a third party and that they failed, within the scope of their powers, to take measures which, judged reasonably, might have been expected to avoid that risk.

The Court recalled that it had not been established beyond reasonable doubt that any State agent was involved in the killing of Hasan Kaya. There were, however, strong inferences that could be drawn on the facts of the case that the perpetrators of the murder were known to the authorities. The Court referred to the fact that Metin Can

II:2

and Hasan Kaya were transported by their kidnappers over more than 130 km through a series of official checkpoints. It noted also the evidence in the investigation file that a suspected terrorist, who claimed involvement in the killing, was seen by two witnesses to receive assistance from gendarmes. The Court was struck by the consistency of the oral testimony of a number of witnesses about the disappearance of Metin Can and Hasan Kaya. Furthermore, the Susurluk report took the position that the murder of Mr. Can, and therefore by implication that of Mr. Kaya, was one of the extrajudicial executions carried out with the knowledge of the authorities.

The question to be determined by the Court was whether in the circumstances the authorities failed in a positive obligation to protect Hasan Kaya from a risk to his life.

The Court noted that Mr. Kaya believed that his life was at risk and that he was under surveillance by the police. He was under suspicion by the police of treating wounded members of the PKK. His friend, Mr. Can, a lawyer who had acted for PKK suspects as well as being the president of a human rights organization regarded as suspect by the authorities, had also received threats and feared that he was under surveillance.

The Government claimed that Hasan Kaya was not more at risk than any other person in the southeast region. The Court noted the tragic number of victims to the conflict in that region. It recalled, however, that in 1993 there were rumours current alleging that contra-guerrilla elements were involved in targeting persons suspected of supporting the PKK. It was undisputed that in a significant number, there were killings, the phenomenon of "unknown perpetrator killing", which included prominent Kurdish figures. The Court was satisfied that Hasan Kaya, as a medical doctor suspected of aiding and abetting the PKK, was at that time at particular risk of falling victim to an unlawful attack. Moreover, this risk could in the circumstances be regarded as real and immediate. The Court was equally satisfied that the authorities had to be regarded as being aware of this risk.

Furthermore, the authorities were aware, or ought to have been aware, of the possibility that this risk derived from the activities of persons or groups acting with the knowledge or acquiescence of elements in the security forces. The Susurluk report, for example, informed the Prime Minister that the authorities were aware of killings being carried out to eliminate alleged supporters of the PKK, including the murder of Metin Can. The Government insisted that this report did not have any judicial or evidential value. However, even the Government described the report as providing information on the basis of which the Prime Minister was to take further appropriate measures. It might therefore be regarded as a significant document.

The Court did not rely on this report as establishing that any State official was implicated in any particular killing. The report did, however, provide further strong substantiation for allegations, current at the time and since, that contra-guerrilla groups involving confessors or terrorist groups were targeting individuals perceived to be acting against State interests, with the acquiescence, and possible assistance, of members of the security forces.

The Court further considered whether the authorities did all that could reasonably be expected of them to avoid the risk to Hasan Kaya.

It recalled that there was a large number of security forces in the southeast region pursuing the aim of establishing public order. They faced the difficult task of countering the violent armed attacks of the PKK and other groups. There was a framework of law in place with the aim of protecting life. The Turkish criminal code prohibited murder, and there were police and gendarmerie forces with the functions of preventing and investigating crime, under the supervision of the judicial branch of public prosecutors. There were also courts applying the provisions of the criminal law in trying, convicting and sentencing offenders.

The Court observed, however, that the implementation of the criminal law in respect of unlawful acts, allegedly carried out with the involvement of the security forces, disclosed particular characteristics in the southeast region in this period.

Firstly, where offences were committed by State officials in certain circumstances, the competence to investigate was removed from the public prosecutor in favour of administrative councils, which took the decision whether to prosecute. These councils were made up of civil servants, under the orders of the governor, who was himself responsible for the security forces whose conduct was in issue. The investigations they instigated were often carried out by gendarmes linked hierarchically to the units concerned in the incident. The Court accordingly, in two previous cases, had found that the administrative councils did not provide an independent or effective procedure for investigating deaths involving members of the security forces.

Secondly, the cases concerning the region at this time examined by the Convention organs had produced a series of findings of failure by the authorities to investigate allegations of wrongdoing by the security forces, both in the context of the procedural obligations under article 2 and the requirement of effective remedies imposed by article 13 of the Convention. A common feature of these cases was a finding that the public prosecutor failed to pursue complaints by individuals claiming that the security forces had been involved in an unlawful act, for example in not interviewing or taking statements from implicated members of the security forces, in accepting at

II:2

face value the reports of incidents submitted by members of the security forces and in attributing incidents to the PKK on the basis of minimal or no evidence.

Thirdly, the attribution of responsibility for incidents to the PKK had particular significance regarding the investigation and judicial procedures that ensued since jurisdiction for terrorist crimes had been given to the national security courts. In a series of cases, the Court had found that those courts did not fulfil the requirement of independence imposed by article 6 of the Convention, due to the presence of a military judge whose participation gave rise to legitimate fears that the court might be unduly influenced by considerations having nothing to do with the nature of the case.

The Court found that these defects undermined the effectiveness of the protection afforded by the criminal law in the southeast region during the period relevant to this case. It considered that this permitted or fostered a lack of accountability of members of the security forces for their actions. That was not compatible with the rule of law in a democratic society respecting the fundamental rights and freedoms guaranteed under the Convention. Consequently, these defects removed the protection that Hasan Kaya should have received by law.

The Government had disputed that they could in any event have effectively provided protection against attacks. The Court was not convinced by this argument. A wide range of preventive measures would have been available to the authorities regarding the activities of their own security forces and those groups allegedly acting under their auspices or with their knowledge. The Government had not provided any information concerning steps taken by them prior to the Susurluk report to investigate the existence of contra-guerrilla groups and the extent to which State officials were implicated in unlawful killings carried out during this period, with a view to taking appropriate measures of prevention.

The Court concluded, by six votes to one, that in the circumstances of the case, the authorities failed to take reasonable measures available to them to prevent a real and immediate risk to the life of Hasan Kaya. Accordingly, there had been a violation of article 2 of the Convention.

In respect of the alleged inadequacy of the investigation, the Court reiterated that the obligation to protect life under article 2, read in conjunction with the State's general duty under article 1 to secure to everyone within its jurisdiction the rights and freedoms defined in the Convention, required by implication that there should be some form of effective official investigation when individuals had been killed as a result of the use of force.

In the present case, the investigation into the disappearance was conducted by a public prosecutor. It then changed hands four times, being transferred finally to a national security court.

The investigation at the scene of discovery of the bodies involved two autopsies. The first was cursory and included the remarkable statement that there were no marks of ill-treatment on the bodies. The second autopsy was more detailed and did record marks on both bodies. It omitted, however, to provide explanations or conclusions regarding certain of the injuries.

There was no forensic examination of the scene or report regarding whether the victims were killed at the scene or how they were deposited at the scene. Nor was there any investigation concerning how the two victims had been transported, a journey that would have involved stopping at a series of official checkpoints along the more than 130 km route. The Court observed that there was no evidence in the investigation file to document any attempts to check custody records or to take statements from potential eyewitnesses at the place where the car was found.

It was noticeable that the only leads in the investigation concerned alleged contra-guerrilla and security force involvement and were provided by information from Ahmet Kaya and Anik Can, relatives of the victims, who passed on what they had heard from others and from the press. Information was also provided by a lawyer and the president of a branch of a human rights organization when they read an article in the press concerning the alleged perpetrators of the killings. The editor of a newspaper submitted a petition, drawing attention to interviews published in the newspaper alleging contra-guerrilla and State security-officer involvement. The public prosecutors concerned did take steps in response, but these steps were often limited and superficial. For example, instructions were given to locate a suspected contra-guerrilla. However, the reports by the police were contradictory. The first stated that he had left his address while the second claimed that the address did not exist. No steps were taken to clarify this.

The information concerning the alleged sighting of a wanted terrorist, who had claimed participation in the killings, was also not pursued, in particular, the apparent report of a police officer confirming the eyewitness statements that the terrorist had been staying at the district gendarmerie headquarters. No further enquiry was made of the gendarmes, notwithstanding the fact that one of the eyewitnesses had given the first names of two gendarmes whom he had claimed to recognize.

The investigation was also dilatory. There were significant delays in seeking statements from witnesses, and there was no apparent activity between 5 May 1993 and September 1993 and no significant step taken from April 1994 until 13 March 1995.

II:2

The Court did not underestimate the difficulties facing public prosecutors in the southeast region at that time. Nonetheless, where there were serious allegations of misconduct and infliction of unlawful harm implicating State security officers, it was incumbent on the authorities to respond actively and with reasonable expedition.

The Court was not satisfied that the investigation carried out into the killing of Hasan Kaya and Metin Can was adequate or effective. It failed to establish significant elements of the incident or clarify what happened to the two men, and it had not been conducted with the diligence and determination necessary for there to be any realistic prospect of identifying and apprehending the perpetrators. It had remained from the early stages within the jurisdiction of the national security court prosecutors, who investigated primarily terrorist or separatist offences.

The Court concluded unanimously that in this respect, there had been a violation of article 2 of the Convention. It further concluded, by six votes to one, that there had been breaches of the prohibition of torture in article 3 and the right to an effective remedy in article 13. However, the Court did not find it necessary to examine whether there had been also a violation of the prohibition of discrimination set forth in article 14.

As to article 41 of the Convention, allowing the Court to afford just satisfaction to an injured party, under specified circumstances, when there had been a violation of the Convention, the Court accepted that the applicant had himself suffered non-pecuniary damage, which could not be compensated solely by the findings of violations, and awarded him the sum of 2,500 pounds sterling. For costs and expenses, the Court also awarded the applicant the sum of 22,000 pounds, together with any value-added tax that might be chargeable, less the amount received by way of legal aid from the Council of Europe.

(f) *Nachova and Others* v. *Bulgaria* (European Court of Human Rights)[67]

The case was transmitted to the European Court of Human Rights on 1 November 1998. It originated in two applications against the Republic of Bulgaria lodged with the European Commission of Human Rights on 15 May 1998 by Anelia Kunchova Nachova, Aksiniya Hristova, Todorka Petrova Rangelova and Rangel Petkov Rangelov, Bulgarian nationals of Roma origin. The applicants alleged that Kuncho Angelov and Kiril Petkov, their respective close relatives shot by military police trying

---

[67] See European Court of Human Rights, applications No. 43577/98 and No. 43579/98, judgment 6 July 2005.

to arrest them, were deprived of their lives in violation of article 2 of the Convention for the Protection of Human Rights and Fundamental Freedoms. They further alleged that the investigation into the events was ineffective, thus in breach of articles 2 and 13 of the Convention, and that the respondent State had failed in its obligation to protect life by law. They also alleged that the events complained of were the result of discriminatory attitudes towards persons of Roma origin and entailed a violation of article 14 of the Convention, read in conjunction with article 2.

On 26 February 2004, the Court, sitting as a chamber, delivered its judgment in the case, but the Government then requested the case to be referred to the grand chamber. The Court delivered its final judgment sitting as a grand chamber.

The facts

Kuncho Angelov and Kiril Petkov were conscripts in a division of the army dealing with the construction of apartment blocks and other civilian projects. Early in 1996, they were arrested for repeated absences without leave and sentenced to short terms of imprisonment. Both had previous convictions for theft. On 15 July 1996, they escaped from a construction site outside the prison where they had been brought for work and went to the home of Mr. Angelov's grandmother. Neither man was armed. Their absence was reported, and a warrant for their arrest was received on 16 July 1996 by a unit of military police.

On 19 July 1996, an anonymous telephone message was received at the police unit indicating where Mr. Angelov and Mr. Petkov were hiding. Four military police officers, under the command of a major, were dispatched to arrest the men. At least two of the officers knew one or both of them. The major apparently knew the location, since his mother was from that village. In a briefing from the commanding officer, a colonel, before they left, the officers were informed that Mr. Angelov and Mr. Petkov were "criminally active", a euphemism used to denote persons with previous convictions or persons suspected of offences, and that they had escaped from detention. The officers were instructed that all means and methods dictated by the circumstances were to be used to arrest them.

For the purposes of the operation, two officers wore uniforms while the others were in civilian clothes. The major wore a bulletproof vest. He was armed with a personal handgun and a 7.62mm Kalashnikov automatic rifle. The other men carried handguns. Three Kalashnikov automatic rifles remained in the boot of the vehicle throughout the operation.

When the officers arrived in the village, they drove to the Roma district where one of them recognized the house of Mr. Angelov's grandmother, since he had previous-

II:2

ly arrested Mr. Angelov there. Mr. Angelov and Mr. Petkov ran from the house, trying to escape. After warning them several times that he would shoot if they did not surrender, the major gunned them down. They were taken to a hospital where they were pronounced dead.

An eyewitness claimed that because his grandson was in the area where the shooting occurred, he had asked the major for permission to remove the young boy from danger. The major had pointed his gun at him saying "you damn Gypsies". Another witness testified that he saw Mr. Angelov and Mr. Petkov fall to the ground and the man who had shot them emerge from behind the house holding an automatic rifle. The witness also said that other men in uniform then started remonstrating with the officer who had shot Mr. Angelov and Mr. Petkov, telling him that he should not have fired and that he should not have come with them.

A criminal investigation into the deaths was opened the same day. The autopsy report found that both men had died from chest wounds, caused by an automatic rifle fired from a distance. The investigator concluded that the major had acted in accordance with military police regulations and had not committed an offence. He recommended that the investigation should be closed. The military prosecutor followed this recommendation and concluded that the major had warned the two men several times and fired shots in the air. He had shot them only because they had not surrendered, as there had been a danger they might escape, and he had tried to avoid inflicting fatal injuries. No one else had been hurt. The applicants appealed unsuccessfully.

The law

In the request for referral of the case to the grand chamber, the Government asked for re-examination of the issues raised by the case under article 14 of the Convention. The findings under articles 2 and 13 of the Convention were accepted. The applicants also asked the Court to deal with the issues under article 14 alone, as the conclusions under articles 2 and 13 were not contested. The Court ruled, however, that it had also to deal with the issues raised under articles 2 and 13 of the Convention.

The applicants complained that Mr. Angelov and Mr. Petkov had been killed in violation of article 2 of the Convention. It was alleged that they had died as a result of the failure of domestic law and practice to regulate the use of firearms by State agents in a manner compatible with the Convention. In effect, State agents had been authorized to use lethal force in circumstances where this was not absolutely necessary. This fact alone violated article 2. The applicants also complained that the authorities had failed to conduct an effective investigation into the deaths.

The chamber held that article 2 of the Convention prohibited the use of firearms to arrest persons who, like Mr. Angelov and Mr. Petkov, were suspected of having committed non-violent offences, were not armed and did not pose any threat to the arresting officers or others. The respondent State was accordingly responsible for the deprivation of life in the case, as lethal force had been used in violation of article 2. The violation of this article was further aggravated by the fact that excessive fire-power had been used and by the failure of the authorities to plan and control the arrest operation in a manner compliant with article 2.

The chamber also found that the State had violated its obligation under article 2, paragraph 1, of the Convention to investigate effectively the deaths of Mr. Angelov and Mr. Petkov. In particular, the investigation had been characterized by serious unexplained omissions and inconsistencies, and its approach had been flawed in that it had applied a standard not comparable to that required by article 2, paragraph 2.

The Government and the applicants accepted the findings of the chamber in respect of article 2 of the Convention.

The Court observed that Mr. Angelov and Mr. Petkov were shot and killed by a military police officer trying to arrest them after their escape from detention. The case fell to be examined under article 2, paragraph 2 (*b*), of the Convention.

The Court noted as a matter of grave concern that the relevant regulations on the use of firearms by the military police effectively permitted lethal force to be used when arresting a member of the armed forces for even the most minor offence. Not only were the regulations not published, they contained no clear safeguards to prevent the arbitrary deprivation of life. Under the regulations, it was lawful to shoot any fugitive who did not surrender immediately in response to an oral warning and the firing of a warning shot in the air. The laxity of these regulations and the manner in which they tolerated the use of lethal force were clearly exposed by the events that led to the fatal shooting in the case and by the response of the investigating authorities to those events. Such a legal framework was fundamentally deficient and fell well short of the level of protection by law of the right to life required by the Convention.

The Court thus found that there was a general failure by the respondent State to comply with its obligation under article 2 of the Convention to secure the right to life by putting in place an appropriate legal and administrative framework on the use of force and firearms by military police.

As to the manner in which the arrest operation had been planned, the Court endorsed the chamber's finding that the authorities failed to comply with their obligation to minimize the risk of loss of life, since the arresting officers were instructed to use all

II:2

available means to arrest Mr. Angelov and Mr. Petkov, in disregard of the fact that the fugitives were unarmed and posed no danger to life or limb. The chamber had rightly stated that a crucial element in the planning of an arrest operation had to be the analysis of all the available information about the surrounding circumstances, including, as an absolute minimum, the nature of the offence committed by the person to be arrested and the degree of danger, if any, posed by that person. The question whether and in what circumstances recourse to firearms should be envisaged if the person to be arrested tried to escape had to be decided on the basis of clear legal rules, adequate training and in the light of that information.

The Court highlighted the absence of a clear legal and regulatory framework defining the circumstances in which military police officers might have recourse to potentially deadly force. It agreed with the chamber that the relevant regulations did not make use of firearms dependent on an assessment of the surrounding circumstances and, most importantly, did not require an evaluation of the nature of the offence committed by the fugitive and of the threat he or she posed.

In the event, the Court noted, the regulations in place permitted a team of heavily armed officers to be dispatched to arrest the two men in the absence of any prior discussion of the threat, if any, they posed or of clearing warnings on the need to minimize any risk to life. In short, the manner in which the operation was planned and controlled betrayed a deplorable disregard for the pre-eminence of the right to life.

It was undisputed that Mr. Angelov and Mr. Petkov had served in a special army institution in which conscripts discharged their duties as construction workers on non-military sites. They had been sentenced to short terms of imprisonment for non-violent offences. They had escaped without using violence, simply by leaving their place of work, which was outside the detention facility. While they had previous convictions for theft and had repeatedly been absent without leave, they had no record of violence. Neither man was armed nor represented a danger to the arresting officers or third parties, a fact of which the arresting officers must have been aware on the basis of the information available to them. In any event, upon encountering the men in the village, the officers, or at least the major, observed that they were unarmed and not showing any signs of threatening behaviour.

Having regard to these facts, the Court considered that in the circumstances, any resort to potentially lethal force was prohibited by article 2 of the Convention, regardless of any risk that Mr. Angelov and Mr. Petkov might escape. Recourse to potentially deadly force could not be considered as absolutely necessary where it was known that the person to be arrested did not pose any threat to life or limb and was not suspected of having committed a violent offence. Additionally, the conduct of the major called for serious criticism in that he used grossly excessive force. In particular, it appeared that there were other means available to effect the arrest; that the major chose to use his automatic rifle and switched it to automatic mode although he also carried a handgun; and that Mr. Petkov was wounded in the chest, a fact for which no plausible explanation was provided.

The Court found that the respondent State failed to comply with its obligations under article 2 of the Convention in that the relevant legal framework on the use of force was fundamentally flawed and Mr. Angelov and Mr. Petkov were killed in circumstances in which any use of firearms to effect their arrest was incompatible with this provision. Furthermore, grossly excessive force was used. Therefore, there had been a violation of article 2 regarding the deaths of Mr. Angelov and Mr. Petkov.

As to the investigation into the killings, the Court saw no reason to depart from the chamber's findings. It observed that the investigation into the deaths of Mr. Angelov and Mr. Petkov assessed the lawfulness of the officers' conduct in the light of the relevant regulations. The fact that the investigation validated the use of force in the circumstances only served to confirm the fundamentally defective nature of those regulations and their disregard of the right to life. By basing themselves on the strict letter of the regulations, the investigating authorities did not examine relevant matters such as the fact that the victims were known to be unarmed and represented no danger to anyone, still less whether it was appropriate to dispatch a team of heavily armed officers in pursuit of two men whose only offence was to go absent without leave. In short, there was no strict scrutiny of all the material circumstances.

Quite apart from the excessively narrow legal framework in which the investigation was conducted, the Court further observed that a number of indispensable and obvious investigative steps were not taken. In particular, the sketch map relied upon by the authorities did not indicate the characteristics of the terrain. Relevant measurements were missed. No reconstruction of the events was staged. Without the information that could thereby have been obtained, it was not possible to check the arresting officers' accounts of the events.

Moreover, the investigator and the prosecutors ignored highly relevant facts, such as that Mr Petkov had been shot in the chest, that the spent cartridges were found in a yard only a few metres from the spot where Mr Angelov and Mr Petkov fell and that the major used grossly excessive force by firing in automatic mode. The authorities ignored those significant facts and, without seeking any proper explanation, merely accepted the major's statements and terminated the investigation. The investigator and the prosecutors thus effectively shielded the major from prosecution.

The Court endorsed the chamber's view that such conduct on the part of the authorities was a matter of grave concern, as it cast serious doubts on the objectivity and

II:2

impartiality of the investigators and prosecutors involved. It reiterated that a prompt and effective response by the authorities in investigating the use of lethal force was essential in maintaining public confidence in their adherence to the rule of law and in preventing any appearance of collusion in or tolerance of unlawful acts. In the present case, the respondent State had violated its obligation under article 2, paragraph 1, of the Convention to investigate the deprivation of life effectively.

With regard to the grounds on which the Court found a violation of the procedural aspect of article 2, no separate issue arose under article 13 of the Convention.

In cases of deprivation of life, the chamber noted, articles 2 and 14 of the Convention combined imposed a duty on State authorities to conduct an effective investigation irrespective of the victim's racial or ethnic origin. It also considered that the authorities had the additional duty to take all reasonable steps to unmask any racist motive in an incident involving the use of force by law enforcement agents. In the present case, despite evidence which should have alerted the authorities to the need to investigate possible racist motives, no such investigation had been undertaken. The authorities had on that account failed in their duty under article 14 of the Convention, taken together with article 2.

Particular evidentiary difficulties involved in proving discrimination called for a specific approach to the issue of proof in cases where the authorities had not pursued lines of inquiry that had been clearly warranted in their investigation into acts of violence by State agents, and had disregarded evidence of possible discrimination. The Court might, when examining complaints under article 14 of the Convention, draw negative inferences or shift the burden of proof to the respondent Government.

On the facts of the case, the chamber considered that the conduct of the investigating authorities warranted a shift of the burden of proof. It thus fell to the Government to satisfy the Court, on the basis of additional evidence or a convincing explanation of the facts, that the events complained of had not been shaped by discrimination on the part of State agents. As the Government had not offered a convincing explanation, and noting previous cases in which the Court had found that law enforcement officers in Bulgaria had subjected Roma to violence resulting in death, the chamber concluded that there had also been a violation of the substantive aspect of article 14 of the Convention, taken together with article 2.

Having recalled these findings of the chamber, the Court then considered whether or not the respondent State was liable for deprivation of life on the basis of the victims' race or ethnic origin. It observed that discrimination was treating differently persons in relevantly similar situations, without an objective and reasonable justification. Racial violence was a particular affront to human dignity and, in view of its perilous consequences, required from the authorities special vigilance and a vigorous reaction. For this reason, the authorities had to use all available means to combat racism and racist violence, thereby reinforcing democracy's vision of a society in which diversity was not perceived as a threat but as a source of its enrichment.

Faced with the applicants' complaint of a violation of article 14, the Court's task was to establish whether or not racism was a causal factor in the shooting that led to the deaths of Mr. Angelov and Mr. Petkov so as to give rise to a breach of this article, in conjunction with article 2 of the Convention.

The applicants referred to several separate facts and they maintained that sufficient inferences of a racist act could be drawn from them.

The major had discharged bursts of automatic fire in a populated area, in disregard of the public's safety. Considering that there was no rational explanation for such behaviour, the applicants were of the view that racist hatred on the part of the major was the only plausible explanation and that he would not have acted in that manner in a non-Roma neighbourhood.

The Court noted, however, that the use of firearms in the circumstances at issue was regrettably not prohibited under the relevant domestic regulations, a flagrant deficiency already condemned. The military police officers carried their automatic rifles in accordance with the rules, and they were instructed to use all necessary means to effect the arrest. The possibility that the major was simply adhering strictly to the regulations and would have acted as he did in any similar context, regardless of the ethnicity of the fugitives, could not therefore be excluded. While the relevant regulations were fundamentally flawed and fell well short of the requirements of the Convention to protect the right to life, there was nothing to suggest that the major would not have used his weapon in a non-Roma neighbourhood. It was true that the major's conduct during the arrest operation called for serious criticism, as he had used grossly excessive force. Nonetheless, it could not be excluded either that his reaction was shaped by the inadequacy of the legal framework governing the use of firearms and by the fact that he was trained to operate within that framework.

The applicants also stated that the officers' attitude had been strongly influenced by their knowledge of the victims' Roma origin. However, it was not possible to speculate on whether or not their Roma origin had any bearing on the officers' perception of them. Furthermore, there was evidence that some of the officers knew one or both of the victims personally.

The applicants referred to the statement given by a neighbour of one of the victims who reported that the major had shouted at him, "you damn Gypsies", immediately

II:2

after the shooting. While such evidence of a racial slur being uttered in connection with a violent act should have led the authorities in this case to verify the statement, that statement was of itself an insufficient basis for concluding that the respondent State was liable for a racist killing.

Lastly, the applicants relied on information about numerous incidents involving the use of force against Roma by Bulgarian law enforcement officers that had not resulted in the conviction of those responsible. It was true that a number of organizations had expressed concern about the occurrence of such incidents. However, the Court could not lose sight of the fact that its sole concern was to ascertain whether in the case at hand, the killing of Mr. Angelov and Mr. Petkov was motivated by racism.

The chamber decided to shift the burden of proof to the Government on account of the authorities' failure to carry out an effective investigation into the alleged racist motive for the killing. The inability of the Government to satisfy the chamber that the events complained of were not shaped by racism resulted in finding a substantive violation of article 14 of the Convention, taken together with article 2.

The Court reiterated that in certain circumstances, the burden of proof might be regarded as resting on the authorities to provide a satisfactory and convincing explanation of the causes of the death of a person within their control in custody. It could not exclude the possibility that in certain cases of alleged discrimination, it might require the Government to disprove an arguable allegation of discrimination and, if it failed to do so, find a violation of article 14 of the Convention on that basis. However, where alleged, as here, that a violent act was motivated by racial prejudice, such an approach would amount to requiring the Government to prove the absence of a particular subjective attitude on the part of the person concerned. While in the legal systems of many countries, proof of the discriminatory effect of a policy or decision would dispense with the need to prove intent in respect of alleged discrimination in employment or the provision of services, such an approach was difficult to transpose to a case where allegedly an act of violence was racially motivated.

The Court did not consider that the alleged failure of the authorities to carry out an effective investigation into the alleged racist motive for the killing should shift the burden of proof to the Government with regard to the alleged violation of article 14 of the Convention, in conjunction with the substantive aspect of article 2. Having assessed all relevant elements, the Court did not consider that it had been established that racist attitudes played a role in the deaths of Mr. Angelov and Mr. Petkov. It thus found no violation of the Convention in that respect.

The Court then considered whether the respondent State had complied with its obligation to investigate possible racist motives. It endorsed the chamber's analysis of the procedural obligation of States parties to investigate possible racist motives for acts of violence. When investigating violent incidents and, in particular, deaths at the hands of State agents, State authorities had the additional duty to take all reasonable steps to unmask any racist motive and to establish whether or not ethnic hatred or prejudice might have played a role in the events. Failing to do so and treating racially induced violence and brutality on an equal footing with cases that had no racist overtones would be to turn a blind eye to the specific nature of acts that were particularly destructive of fundamental rights. A failure to make a distinction in the way in which essentially different situations were handled might constitute unjustified treatment irreconcilable with article 14 of the Convention. In order to maintain public confidence in their law enforcement machinery, States parties had to ensure that in the investigation of incidents involving the use of force, a distinction was made both in their legal systems and in practice between cases of excessive use of force and of racist killing.

The Court also said that proving racial motivation would often be extremely difficult in practice. The respondent State's obligation to investigate possible racist overtones to a violent act was an obligation to use best endeavours and not absolute. The authorities had to do what was reasonable in the circumstances to collect and secure the evidence, explore all practical means of discovering the truth and deliver fully reasoned, impartial and objective decisions, without omitting suspicious facts that might be indicative of a racially induced violence. The Court added that the duty to investigate the existence of a possible link between racist attitudes and an act of violence was an aspect of the procedural obligations arising under article 2 of the Convention, but it might also be seen as implicit in the responsibilities under article 14, taken in conjunction with article 2, to secure the enjoyment of the right to life without discrimination. Owing to the interplay of the two provisions, issues such as those in the present case might fall to be examined under one of the two provisions only, with no separate issue arising under the other, or might require examination under both articles.

The authorities had before them the statement of a neighbour of the victims, who stated that the major had shouted "you damn Gypsies" while pointing a gun at him immediately after the shooting. That statement, seen against the background of the many published accounts of the existence in Bulgaria of prejudice and hostility against Roma, called for verification.

The Court considered that any evidence of racist verbal abuse being uttered by law enforcement agents in an operation involving the use of force against persons from an ethnic or other minority was highly relevant to the question whether or not unlawful, hatred-induced violence had taken place. Where such evidence came to light in the investigation, it had to be verified and, if confirmed, a thorough examination

II:2

of all the facts should be undertaken in order to uncover any possible racist motives. Furthermore, the fact that the major used grossly excessive force against two unarmed and non-violent men also called for a careful investigation.

In sum, the investigator and the prosecutors involved in this case had before them plausible information sufficient to alert them to the need to carry out an initial verification and, depending on the outcome, an investigation into possible racist overtones in the events that led to the death of the two men. However, the authorities did nothing to verify the statement of the witness. They omitted to question other witnesses about it. The major was not asked to explain why he had considered it necessary to use such a degree of force. No attempt was made to verify his record and to ascertain, for example, whether he had previously been involved in similar incidents or whether he had ever been accused in the past of displaying anti-Roma sentiment. Those failings were compounded by the behaviour of the investigator and the prosecutors who, as the Court had already found, disregarded relevant facts and terminated the investigation, thereby shielding the major from prosecution. The Court thus found that the authorities failed in their duty under article 14 of the Convention, taken together with article 2, to take all possible steps to investigate whether or not discrimination might have played a role in the events.

The Court held unanimously that there had been a violation of article 2 in respect of the deaths of Mr. Angelov and Mr. Petrov and the failure of the authorities to conduct an effective investigation into the deaths, as well as a violation of article 14, in conjunction with article 2, as to the failure to investigate possible racist motives behind the events leading to those deaths. Regarding the allegation that the events leading to the deaths of Mr. Angelov and Mr. Petrov constituted an act of racial violence, the Court held, however, by eleven votes to six, that there had been no violation.

As to article 41 of the Convention, allowing the Court to afford just satisfaction to an injured party, under specified circumstances, when there had been a violation of the Convention, the Court held that the respondent State should pay, in respect of pecuniary and non-pecuniary damage, jointly to Ms. Nachova and Ms. Hristova 25,000 euros and jointly to Ms. Rangelova and Mr. Rangelov 22,000 euros, and in respect of costs and expenses, jointly to all the applicants 11,000 euros.

3. Prohibition of Torture

A. INTRODUCTION

Whilst police are empowered to use force, up to and including lethal force, there are no circumstances whatsoever under which torture may be practised lawfully. Torture is a crime under international law and the domestic laws of States. It is the obscene exemplar of the violation of the physical and mental integrity of an individual. An individual will say whatever his or her torturer requires in order to bring an end to the torture. Such is the "truth" elicited through torture.

Article 5 of the Universal Declaration of Human Rights provides that no one shall be subjected to torture or to cruel, inhuman or degrading treatment or punishment. Torture is prohibited in similar terms in the International Covenant on Civil and Political Rights and in the regional human rights treaties of general application. Like the right to life, the prohibition of torture is considered to express a general principle of international law binding on all States, and it is enshrined in major human rights treaties as a non-derogable provision. Article 4 of the Covenant, for example, states that no derogation may be made from the prohibition of torture in article 7, not even in time of public emergency threatening the life of the nation. Under international humanitarian law, torture is prohibited in times of international and non-international armed conflict, as stated in the Geneva Concentions of 12 August 1949 and the Protocols Additional to the Geneva Conventions. Acts of torture may also constitute international crimes under the Rome Statute of the International Criminal Court.

The general provisions on the prohibition of torture are supplemented by treaties and non-treaty instruments specifically designed to reinforce the struggle against torture and other cruel, inhuman or degrading treatment or punishment, notably the Convention against Torture and Other Cruel, Inhuman or Degrading Treatment or Punishment, in force since 1987. This universal human rights treaty sets out a definition of the term "torture".

Article 1, paragraph 1, of the Convention reads:

> For the purposes of this Convention, the term "torture" means any act by which severe pain or suffering, whether physical or mental, is intentionally

inflicted on a person for such purposes as obtaining from him or a third person information or a confession, punishing him for an act he or a third person has committed or is suspected of having committed, or intimidating or coercing him or a third person, or for any reason based on discrimination of any kind, when such pain or suffering is inflicted by or at the instigation of or with the consent or acquiescence of a public official or other person acting in an official capacity. It does not include pain or suffering arising only from, inherent in or incidental to lawful sanctions.

Article 16, paragraph 1, of the Convention extends the obligations of States parties to prevent other acts of cruel, inhuman or degrading treatment or punishment, not amounting to torture, when such acts are committed by or at the instigation of or with the consent or acquiescence of a public official or other person acting in an official capacity.

The imperative character of the prohibition of torture is unambiguously expressed in article 2, paragraphs 2 and 3, of the Convention. No exceptional circumstances whatsoever may be invoked as a justification of torture, not even a state of war or a threat of war, internal political instability or any other public emergency, nor may an order from a superior officer or a public authority.

The system of protection under the Convention embodies a number of mechanisms, including the procedure for consideration of individual complaints. A separate treaty, the Optional Protocol to the Convention against Torture and Other Cruel, Inhuman or Degrading Treatment or Punishment, not yet in force, was adopted in 2002 to strengthen the protection by introducing non-judicial means of a preventive nature, based on regular visits to places of detention.

The Convention was preceded by the Declaration on the Protection of All Persons from Being Subjected to Torture and Other Cruel, Inhuman or Degrading Treatment or Punishment, a non-treaty instrument adopted in 1975 by the General Assembly of the United Nations. Treaties of regional application are the Inter-American Convention to Prevent and Punish Torture, in force since 1987, and the European Convention for the Prevention of Torture and Inhuman or Degrading Treatment or Punishment, in force since 1989. The latter instrument has established a system for examining the treatment of persons deprived of their liberty, by means of visits.

Some non-treaty instruments are of particular relevence to police, because they include signficant provisions on the treatment of detainees and of people suspected of crime. The Code of Conduct for Law Enforcement Officials enshrines, in article 5, the prohibition of torture and the provision that no law enforcement official may invoke superior orders or exceptional circumstances as a justification of torture. In the

Basic Principles on the Use of Force and Firearms by Law Enforcement Officials, principle 15 prohibits law enforcement officials from using force on detainees except when striclty necessary for maintaining security order within the institution or when personal safety is threatened. The Body of Principles for the Protection of All Persons under Any Form of Detention or Imprisonment reiterates the prohibition of torture in principle 6. Principle 21, paragraph 2, stipulates that no detained person while being interrogated shall be subject to violence, threats or methods of interrogation which impair his capacity of decision or his judgment. In the European Code of Police Ethics, the most recent instrument, the prohibition of torture is expressed in article 36. The explanatory memorandum, published together with the Code, includes the following paragraph on the prohibition of torture:

> In addition to the fact that torture, inhuman or degrading treatment or punishment is a serious offence against human dignity and a violation of human rights, such measures, when used for the purpose of obtaining a confession or similar information, may, and are even likely to, lead to incorrect information from the person who is subject to torture or similar methods. Thus, there is no rational justification for using such methods in a state governed by the rule of law.

Finally, the Principles on the effective investigation and documentation of torture and other cruel, inhuman or degrading treatment or punishment (the Istanbul Principles) should be noted as a useful tool in the efforts to combat torture. They outline minimum standards for States in order to ensure the effective documentation of torture. This set of principles is annexed to the Istanbul Protocol, the manual on the same subject submitted in 1999 to the United Nations High Commissioner for Human Rights by a large number of organizations.

The Special Rapporteur on the question of torture implements a thematic special procedure of the United Nations Commission on Human Rights. Under the mandate, originally established in 1985,[1] the Special Rapporteur shall examine questions relevant to torture and respond effectively to credible and reliable information that comes before him. The methods of work of the Special Rapporteur describe the activities carried out under the mandate.[2] He seeks and receives credible and reliable information from Governments, the specialized agencies and from intergovernmental and non-governmental organizations. He makes urgent appeals to Governments to clarify the situation of individuals whose circumstances give grounds to fear that

---

[1] See Commission on Human Rights resolution 1985/33 of 13 March 1985 (United Nations, *Official Records of the Economic and Social Council, 1985, Supplement No. 2* (E/1985/22), chap. II, sect. A).
[2] See United Nations document E/CN.4/1997/7, annex.

II:3

treatment falling within the mandate might occur or be occurring. He transmits to Governments information indicating that acts within the mandate may have occurred or that legal or administrative measures are needed to prevent such acts to occur, and he carries out visits *in situ* with the consent of the Government concerned.

The urgent appeal procedure is not *per se* accusatory, but essentially preventive in nature and purpose. The Government concerned is merely requested to look into the matter and to take steps aimed at protecting the right to physical and mental integrity of the person concerned, in accordance with the international human rights standards.

The Special Rapporteur transmits to Governments summaries of all credible and reliable information adressed to him alleging individual cases as well as practices of torture. He requests the Governments to look into those allegations and to provide him with relevant information. Additionally, he may urge Governments to take steps to investigate the allegations, to prosecute and impose appropriate sanctions, to take effective steps to prevent the recurrence of such acts and to compensate the victims or their relatives.

The Special Rapporteur reports annually to the Commission on his activities and makes observations on specific situations, as well as conclusions and recommendations. He also presents interim reports to the General Assembly of the United Nations on overall trends and developments with regard to his mandate.

The absolute nature of the prohibition of torture is illustrated by the cases summarized and/or reviewed in this chapter of the book. The international institutions have insisted that torture and and other cruel, inhuman or degrading treatment or punishment remain forbidden regardless of the situation faced by the State, and regardless of what the victim has done or is alleged to have done.

Finally, it is also important at this point to be aware of cases cited in the context of police behaviour in times of armed conflict, disturbance and tension. In the case *Prosecutor* v. *Furundzija*,[3] summarized in connection with international crimes,[4] the International Tribunal for the former Yugoslavia, in applying the law to the circumstances of the case, delivered a comprehensive account of the prohibition of torture under international law. In particular, it considered torture under international humanitarian law and human rights law and identified some specific elements pertaining to torture as considered from the viewpoint of international criminal law relating

---

[3] See case No. IT-95-17/1-T, judgment of 10 December 1998 (trial chamber); see also case No. IT-95-17/1-A, judgment of 21 July 2000 (appeals chamber).
[4] See part IV, chap. 3, sect. C (*a*) (*infra*, pp. 616-636).

to armed conflicts. The International Tribunal also discussed rape as torture and as a distinct crime under international criminal law.

B. REVIEW OF CASES

(*a*) Human Rights Committee

Article 7 of the International Covenant on Civil and Political Rights embodies the prohibition of torture. Under this provision, no one shall be subjected to torture or to cruel, inhuman or degrading treatment or punishment. In particular, no one shall be subjected without his free consent to medical or scientific experimentation.

This article is protected from derogation under article 4 of the Covenant. Not even in time of public emergency threatening the life of the nation may a State party take measures derogating from its obligations under article 7.

As with the prohibition of torture in the Universal Declaration of Human Rights and similar provisions in the regional treaties, article 7 of the Covenant includes a variety of forms of ill-treatment, and these are not defined in the instruments. Indeed, the Human Rights Committee, in its general comment No. 20 (44) on article 7 of the Covenant,[5] stated that the Covenant did not contain any definition of the concepts covered by that article, nor did the Committee consider it necessary to draw up a list of prohibited acts or to establish sharp distinctions between the different kinds of punishment or treatment. The distinctions depended on the nature, purpose and severity of the treatment applied.[6] In much of its jurisprudence arising out of article 7, the Committee has followed this principle and simply found violations of this article, although in some cases it has concluded specifically that torture or inhuman treatment had been inflicted.

In the case *Hugo Rodríguez* v. *Uruguay,*[7] summarized in section C,[8] the Committee was concerned that in adopting a law granting amnesties for human rights violations committed under the rule of a former military dictatorship, the State party had contributed to an atmosphere of impunity which might undermine the democratic order and give rise to further grave human rights violations.

---

[5] See United Nations, *Official Records of the General Assembly, Forty-seventh Session, Supplement No. 40* (A/47/40), annex VI, sect. A.

[6] *Ibidem*, para. 4.

[7] *Ibidem, Forty-ninth Session, Supplement No. 40* (A/49/40), vol. II, annex IX, sect. B, communication No. 322/1988, views adopted on 19 July 1994.

[8] See part II, chap. 3, sect. C (*a*) (*infra*, pp. 155-158).

II:3

The author, a Uruguayan citizen, claimed that in June 1983, he was arrested by police and taken to the secret police headquarters where he was subjected to torture detailed in the communication. He was brought before a military judge and indicted on unspecified charges. He remained detained until 27 December 1984. No judicial investigation of his case could be initiated until the reintroduction of constitutional guarantees in March 1985, but it was in fact barred by amnesty provisions. He contended that he had been denied appropriate redress and invoked violations by Uruguay of a number of articles of the Covenant, in particular article 7.

Bearing in mind that the author's allegations were substantiated and not disputed by the State party, the Committee found that Uruguay had violated article 7. As to an effective remedy under article 2, paragraph 3, of the Covenant, the Committee observed that the adoption of amnesty provisions and their subsequent enforcement had rendered the realization of the author's right extremely difficult. In fact, he had not had an effective remedy. It further reaffirmed its position that amnesties for gross violations of human rights were incompatible with the obligations of States parties under the Covenant. The Committee called for an official investigation into the allegations of Mr. Rodrígues in order to identify the persons responsible for torture and ill-treatment and to enable him to seek civil redress. The State party should also grant him appropriate compensation and ensure that similar violations did not occur in the future.

Whilst the Committee was expressing its concern in relation to law-based amnesties, it is important to recognize that an atmosphere of impunity can arise out of any generalized failure to secure accountability of those who violate human rights, whether or not that failure arises out of such an amnesty. Furthermore, it can be argued that abuse of human rights undermines the democratic and legal order of any country, whether it is a country making the transition to democracy or a country with long established democratic traditions.

In the case *Albert Womah Mukong* v. *Cameroon*,[9] likewise summarized in section C[10] and also cited in connection with the right to liberty and security of person[11] and with the right to freedom of opinion and expression,[12] the author, a citizen of Cameroon and journalist, writer and opponent of the political system in the country, was arrested on 16 June 1988 and detained until 5 May 1989. He was again arrested on

---

[9] See United Nations, *Official Records of the General Assembly, Forty-ninth Session, Supplement No. 40* (A/49/40), vol. II, annex IX, sect. AA, communication No. 458/1991, views adopted on 21 July 1994.

[10] See part II, chap. 3, sect. C (*b*) (*infra*, pp. 158-161).

[11] See part II, chap. 4, sect. B (*a*) (*infra*, p. 207).

[12] See part III, chap. 4, sect. B (*a*) (*infra*, pp. 439-440).

26 February 1990 and released on 23 March 1990. He claimed, *inter alia*, that the conditions of detention, the deprivation of food and clothing, the death threats and incommunicado detention to which he had been subjected amounted to a violation by Cameroon of article 7 of the Covenent. He also invoked a number of other provisions of the Covenant.

As to the conditions of detention, the State party argued that they had to be linked to the state of economic and social development of Cameroon. The Committee stated that certain minimum standards regarding conditions of detention had to be observed regardless of a State party's level of development. Referring to specific provisions of the Standard Minimum Rules for the Treatment of Prisoners, the Committee considered that these were minimum requirements always to be observed, even if economic or budgetary considerations made compliance with the obligations difficult. Furthermore, Mr. Mukong had been singled out for exceptionally harsh and degrading treatment. The Committee concluded that he had been subjected to cruel, inhuman and degrading treatment, in violation of article 7 of the Covenant. It also found violations by Cameroon of the right to liberty and security of person in article 9 and the right to freedom of opinion and expression in article 19. The State party was urged, under article 2, paragraph 3 (*a*), of the Covenant, to grant the author appropriate compensation, to investigate his allegations of ill-treatment in detention and to ensure that similar violations did not occur in the future.

In the case *Celis Laureano* v. *Peru*,[13] the third Committee case summarized in section C,[14] the author, Basilio Laureano Atachahua, a Peruvian citizen, claimed that his granddaughter, Ana Rosario Celis Laureano, had been subjected to unlawful detention and subsequent disappearence that was attributed to the armed forces of Peru. On 13 August 1993, she was abducted by masked men believed to belong to the military and/or special police forces. She was suspected of guerrilla activities. The author alleged violations by Peru of, *inter alia*, article 6 on the right to life and article 7 of the Covenant.

The Committee concluded that the abduction and disappearance of Ms. Laureano and the prevention of contact with her family and with the outside world constituted cruel and inhuman treatment, in violation of article 7, *juncto* article 2, paragraph 1, of the Covenant. It also found violations by Peru of other provisions of the Covenant, notably on the right to life. The Committee urged the State party, under article 2, paragraph 3 (*a*), of the Covenant, to open a proper investigation into the disap-

---

[13] See United Nations, *Official Records of the General Assembly, Fifty-first Session, Supplement No. 40* (A/51/40), vol. II, annex VIII, sect. P, communication No. 540/1993, views adopted on 25 March 1996.

[14] See part II, chap. 3, sect. C (*c*) (*infra*, pp. 161-163).

II:3

pearance of Ms. Laureano and her fate, to provide for appropriate compensation to the victim and her family and to bring to justice those responsible for her disappearance, notwithstanding any domestic amnesty legislation to the contrary.

Another case involving abduction and disapperance is the case *Elena Quinteros and M. C. Almeida de Quinteros* v. *Uruguay*.[15] The author, María del Carmen Almeida de Quinteros, a Uruguayan national, submitted, *inter alia*, that her daughter, Elena Quinteros Almeida, was arrested on 24 June 1976 and that she could not obtain any official information about her daughter's whereabouts. The author claimed that Elena Quinteros was the victim of torture and other violations by Uruguay of Covenant provisions. She also claimed that she was herself a victim of article 7 of the Covenant, because her daughter had disappeared.

The Committee found that the information before it revealed breaches of article 7 and other articles of the Covenant in respect of Elena Quinteros. As to the author's claim on her own behalf, the Committee understood the anguish and stress caused to the mother by the disappearance of her daughter and by the continuing uncertainty concerning her fate and whereabouts. The author had the right to know what had happened to her daughter. Consequently, the author was also a victim of the violations by Uruguay of the Covenant suffered by her daughter, in particular of article 7.

The Committee concluded, *inter alia*, that the Government should take immediate and effective steps to establish what had happened to the victim, to bring to justice any persons found to be responsible for her disappearance and to ensure that similar violations did not occur in the future. This case is an example of a violation of article 7 of the Covenant somewhat different to the more typical violation where the physical or mental integrity of a detainee is abused.

Another such case, *Rojas García* v. *Colombia*,[16] is summarized in connection with the prohibition of arbitrary interference with privacy.[17] The author, Rafael Armando Rojas García, a Colombian citizen, submitted on his own behalf and on behalf of his family that on 5 January 1993, at 2 a.m., a group of armed men from the public prosecutor's office, wearing civilian clothes, forcibly entered the author's house through the roof. The group carried out a room-by-room search of the premises, terrifying and verbally abusing the members of the author's family, including small children.

---

[15] See United Nations, *Official Records of the General Assembly, Thirty-eighth Session, Supplement No. 40* (A/38/40), annex XXII, communication No. 107/1981, views adopted on 21 July 1983.

[16] *Ibidem, Fifty-sixth Session, Supplement No. 40* (A/56/40), vol. II, annex X, sect. D, communication No. 687/1996, views adopted on 3 April 2001.

[17] See part II, chap. 5, sect. C (*a*) (*infra*, pp. 305-307).

One of the officials fired a gunshot. The State party argued that this rather dramatic search in the course of a murder investigation was lawful under its criminal procedure code. The author claimed that the events constituted violations by Colombia of, *inter alia*, article 7 of the Convention as well as article 17 on arbitrary or unlawful interference or attacks.

After noting the treatment received by the Rojas García family at the hands of the police, not refuted by the State party, the Committee decided that there had been a violation of article 7 of the Covenant in this case. It also found that Colombia had violated article 17, paragraph 1. In an individual opinion, two members of the Committee disagreed in respect of article 7, because, under the circumstances, they could not conclude that the search party had an intent to terrify the author's family. Under article 2, paragraph 3 (*a*), of the Covenant, the Committee pronounced that the State party was under an obligation to provide the author and his family with an effective remedy, including reparation, and to take steps to prevent similar violations occurring in the future.

Finally on the jurisprudence of the Committee, one early case, *Sergio Rubén López Burgos* v. *Uruguay*,[18] also cited in connection with the right to liberty and security of person,[19] is of particular relevance to this publication. The author, Delia Saldías de López, claimed that her husband, Mr. López Burgos, a Uruguayan trade union leader, was kidnapped on 13 July 1976 in Argentina by members of the Uruguayan security and intelligence forces. Subsequently, he was illegally and clandestinely transported to Uruguay where he was detained. The author further claimed that Mr. López Burgos, during his detention of approximately four months in Argentina and Uruguay, was continuously subjected to physical and mental torture and other cruel, inhuman or degrading treatment, detailed in the communication. It was alleged that the Uruguayan authorities in this case had violated, *inter alia*, article 7 of the Convention as well as article 9 on the right to liberty and security of person.

In relation to this type of abduction, the Committee observed that although the arrest and initial detention and mistreatment allegedly took place on foreign territory, it was not barred from considering these allegations inasmuch as the acts were perpetrated by Uruguayan agents acting on foreign soil. It noted that the reference made in article 1 of the Optional Protocol to the Covenant to individuals subject to the State party's jurisdiction did not refer to the place where the violation occurred. This rather referred to the relationship between the individual and the State party in re-

---

[18] See United Nations, *Official Records of the General Assembly, Thirty-sixth Session, Supplement No. 40* (A/36/40), annex XIX, communication No. 52/1979, views adopted on 29 July 1981.
[19] See part II, chap. 4, sect. B (*a*) (*infra*, p. 207).

II:3

spect of a violation of any of the rights set forth in the Covenant, wherever they occurred. Article 2, paragraph 1, of the Covenant placed an obligation on a State party to respect and ensure the rights to all individuals within its territory and subject to its jurisdiction. However, this did not imply that the State party concerned could not be held accountable for violations of rights under the Covenant committed by its agents on the territory of another State. The Committee concluded that the communication disclosed violations by Uruguay of, *inter alia*, articles 7 and 9, paragraph 1, of the Covenant.

This statement by the Committee on territorial application is a significant point which could become even more significant in the future. It seems inevitable that police officials will be operating, legitimately and with increasing frequency, in foreign jurisdictions under arrangements designed to secure effective operational collaboration between police agencies to combat terrorism and other forms of international and transnational crimes.

(*b*) Committee against Torture

The Convention against Torture and Other Cruel, Inhuman or Degrading Treatment or Punishment embodies, for the purposes of the Convention, a definition of the term "torture" in article 1, paragraph 1, quoted in the introduction to this chapter of the book.[20] Under article 16, paragraph 1, the application of the Convention is extended, in specified circumstances, to include other acts of cruel, inhuman or degrading treatment or punishment which do not amount to torture. In particular, this is the case with the obligations contained in articles 10 to 13 of the Convention.

Under article 2 of the Convention, each State party is required to take effective legislative, administrative, judicial and other measures to prevent acts of torture in any territory under its jurisdiction. The Convention also includes provisions in articles 5 to 9 for bringing persons accused of torture to justice, regardless of their nationality or of where the crime is alleged to have been committed, i.e. provisions on universal jurisdiction.

Article 12 of the Convention requires each State party to ensure that its competent authorities proceed to a prompt and impartial investigation, wherever there are reasonable grounds to believe that an act of torture has been committed in any territory under its jurisdiction. Under article 13, the State party shall ensure that any individual alleging that he has been subjected to torture in any territory under the State's jurisdiction has the right to complain to, and to have his case promptly and impartially examined by, its competent authorities.

---

[20] See part II, chap. 3, sect. A (*supra*, pp. 123-124).

As torture is a very serious crime, it is clearly a policing function to carry out these types of investigation. Furthermore, it is essential for police leaders to recognize the importance of having in place proper supervisory systems to prevent torture from being committed by officials for whom they are responsible. Full records of the conditions and circumstances of detainees, including the identity of the officials who detained them and those responsible for their welfare, are essential elements of such systems. The effectiveness and promptness of investigations carried out in accordance with articles 12 and 13 of the Convention would, of course, be enhanced by supervisory systems and records designed to protect detainees. Cases on the application of articles 12 and 13 brought before the Committee against Torture illustrate the points.

For example, in the case *Qani Halimi-Nedzibi* v. *Austria*,[21] the author of the communication, a Yugoslav citizen, was convicted of offences connected with drug trafficking and imprisoned in Austria in 1991. He alleged that he had been tortured by police and coerced into making incriminating statements. His complaint was that the failure of the Austrian authorities promptly to investigate his allegations of torture and the refusal of the courts to exclude as evidence against him statements allegedly made by him as a result of torture constituted a violation of articles 12 and 15 of the Convention, respectively. Article 15 requires each State party to ensure that any statement established to have been made as a result of torture shall not be invoked as evidence in any proceedings, except against a person accused of torture as evidence that the statement was made.

The Committee found no violation of article 15 of the Convention. However, concerning the State party's duty to proceed to a prompt and impartial investigation of allegations of torture, the Committee noted that the allegations were made before an investigating judge on 5 December 1988. Although the investigating judge questioned the police officers about the allegations on 16 February 1989, no investigation took place until 5 March 1990. The Committee considered that a delay of 15 months before an investigation of allegations of torture was initiated was unreasonably long and that there had been a breach of article 12 of the Convention.

In the case *Encarnación Blanco Abad* v. *Spain*,[22] the author of the communication claimed to be the victim of violations by Spain of articles 12, 13 and 15 of the Convention, having been detained on 29 January 1992 by officers of the Guardia Civil

---

[21] See United Nations, *Official Records of the General Assembly, Forty-ninth Session, Supplement No. 44* (A/49/44), annex V, sect. A, communication No. 8/1991, views adopted on 18 November 1993.

[22] *Ibidem, Fifty-third Session, Supplement No. 44* (A/53/44 and Corr.1), annex X, sect. A.3, communication No. 59/1996, views adopted on 14 May 1998.

II:3

on suspicion of involvement in activities on behalf of ETA, the Basque separatist movement. She alleged to have been mistreated between 29 January and 2 February 1992 while she was kept incommunicado under anti-terrorist legislation. Investigative proceedings into her complaints of mistreatment and torture were commenced but, ultimately, shelved definitively.

The Committee observed that under article 12 of the Convention, the authorities had the obligation to proceed to an investigation ex officio wherever there were reasonable grounds to believe that acts of torture or ill-treatment had been committed and whatever the origin of the suspicion. The investigation should be prompt and impartial. Promptness was essential to ensure that the victim could not continue to be subjected to such acts and also because in general, unless the methods employed had permanent or serious effects, the physical traces of torture, and especially of cruel, inhuman or degrading treatment, soon disappeared.

The Committee found that the lack of investigation of the allegations made by Mrs. Blanco Abad, first to a forensic physician and then to a judge of the national high court, on 2 February 1992, and the amount of time that passed between the reporting of the facts and the initiation of proceedings by a court, on 21 February 1992, were incompatible with the obligation to proceed to a prompt investigation, as provided for in article 12 of the Convention, and revealed a violation of this article.

The Committee further observed that article 13 of the Convention did not require either the formal lodging of a complaint of torture under a procedure laid down in national law or an express statement of intent to institute and sustain a criminal action arising from the offence. It was enough for the victim simply to bring the facts to the attention of an authority of the State for the latter to be obliged to consider it as a tacit but unequivocal expression of the victim's wish that the facts should be promptly and impartially investigated, as prescribed by this provision of the Convention.

The Committee noted that while a court had examined the complaint, it had not done so with the requisite promptness. The Committee considered that the chronology of the investigative measures into the complaint had not satisfied the requirement for promptness in examining complaints, as prescribed by article 13 of the Convention.

The Committee also observed that during the preliminary proceedings, up to the time when they were discontinued, the court had taken no steps to identify and question any of the Guardia Civil officers who might have taken part in the acts complained of by the author. The Committee found this omission inexcusable, since a criminal investigation had to seek both to determine the nature and circumstances of

the alleged acts and to establish the identity of any person who might have been involved therein, as required by the State party's own domestic legislation.

The Committee considered this ommission, and a variety of other ommissions, to be
incompatible with the obligation to proceed to an impartial investigation as provided
for in article 13 of the Convention. It took the view that the facts before it revealed a
violation of this article.

Both of the above cases are cited in the case *Radivoje Ristic* v. *Yugoslavia*,[23] summarized in section C.[24] The author of this communication, a citizen of Yugoslavia,
claimed that an act of torture resulting in the death of his son, Milan Ristic, had been
committed by police officials and that the authorities had failed to carry out a
prompt and impartial investigation. The author invoked several provisions of the
Convention, in particular articles 12, 13 and 14.

On 13 February 1995, three police officials allegedly arrested Milan Ristic while
looking for a murder suspect. One of the officials struck his son with a blunt object,
presumably a pistol or rifle butt, behind the left ear, killing him instantly. The officials moved the body and, with a blunt instrument, broke both thighbones. They then
called an ambulance and a police investigation team, including a forensic technician.
The police officials told the investigators that Milan Ristic had committed suicide by
jumping from the roof of a nearby building and that they had an eyewitness to that
effect. A medical doctor who attended with the ambulance pronounced Milan Ristic
dead and then left the scene. Thereafter, the police officials struck the deceased on
the chin, causing injury to his face.

Noting the deficiencies of the investigation conducted by the State party's authorities following the incident, the Committee considered that the investigation was neither effective nor thorough. A proper investigation would indeed have entailed an
exhumation and a new autopsy, allowing the cause of death to be medically established with a satisfactory degree of certainty. Moreover, the incident took place six
years ago, and no proper investigation had been conducted by the State party. In the
cirumstances, the Committee found violations of articles 12 and 13 of the Convention.

This case is included for a summary, because it underlines the importance of prompt
and impartial investigations into claims that torture has been committed and because
it provides a good illustration of how the Committee functions in response to indi-

---

[23] *Ibidem, Fifty-sixth Session, Supplement No. 44* (A/56/44), annex VII, sect. A.2, communication No. 113/1998, views adopted on 11 May 2001.
[24] See part II, chap. 3, sect. C (*d*) (*infra*, pp. 163-168).

II:3

vidual communications. In particular, it shows how the Committee identified and responded to various shortcomings in the investigation into the allegation of torture and to inconsistencies in the State party's response to the Committee.

Most of the cases considered by the Committee relate to article 3 of the Convention. Paragraph 1 prohibits any State party from expelling, returning or extraditing a person to another State where there are substantial grounds for believing that he or she would be in danger of being subjected to torture. For the purpose of determining whether there are such grounds, paragraph 2 of the article requires the competent authorities to take into account all relevant considerations including, where applicable, the existence in the State concerned of a consistent pattern of gross, flagrant or mass violations of human rights.

In the case *Ismail Alan* v. *Switzerland*,[25] the author was a Turkish citizen of Kurdish background, residing in Switzerland. He submitted that in Turkey, he had been, *inter alia*, arrested, tortured, imprisoned and internally exiled, because he had been a sympathizer of an outlawed Kurdish organization. In 1990, he requested asylum in Switzerland. It was rejected in 1993, and his appeal was dismissed in 1994. He claimed to be a victim of a violation by Switzerland of article 3 of the Convention.

In considering the author's claim, the Committee had to decide whether there were substantial grounds for believing that he would be in danger of being subject to torture upon return to Turkey. In making this decision the Committee pointed out that it had to take into account all relevant considerations pursuant to article 3, paragraph 2, including the existence of a consistent pattern of gross, flagrant or mass violations of human rights. The aim of that determination was, however, to establish whether the individual concerned would be personally at risk of being subjected to torture in the country to which he or she would return. It followed that the existence of a consistent pattern of gross, flagrant or mass violations of human rights in a country did not, as such, constitute a sufficient ground for determining that a person would be in danger of being subjected to torture upon his or her return to that country. Specific grounds had to exist indicating that the individual concerned would be personally at risk. Similarly, the absence of a consistent pattern of gross violations of human rights did not mean that a person could not be considered to be in danger of being subjected to torture in the specific circumstances

In the instant case, the Committee considered that Mr. Alan's ethnic background, his alleged political affiliation, his history of detention and his internal exile should be

---

[25] See United Nations, *Official Records of the General Assembly, Fifty-first Session, Supplement No. 44* (A/51/44), annex V, sect. [B], communication No. 21/1995, views adopted on 8 May 1996.

taken into account. In the circumstances, the Committee found that he had sufficiently substantiated that he personally was at risk of being subjected to torture if returned to Turkey.

Finally, the Committee regretfully noted that the practice of torture remained systematic in Turkey, as attested to in the Committee's findings in its inquiry under article 20 of the Convention.[26] The Committee observed that the main aim and purpose of the Convention was to prevent torture, not to redress torture once it had occurred. It concluded that the expulsion or return of Mr. Alan to Turkey in the prevailing circumstances would constitute a violation of article 3 of the Convention. Consequently, the State party had an obligation to refrain from forcibly returning him to Turkey.

The Committee made the same points arising out of article 3, paragraph 2, of the Convention in the case *Gorki Ernesto Tapia Paez* v. *Sweden*.[27] The author of this communication, a Peruvian citizen residing in Sweden, applied in 1990 for political asylum, but it was finally rejected by the Swedish Government in 1995. He claimed that his forced return to Peru would constitute a violation by Sweden of article 3 of the Convention.

The Committee noted that Mr. Tapia Paez was a member of the Shining Path, an organization of the Communist Party of Peru. He had participated in a demonstration in Peru where he had handed out leaflets and distributed handmade bombs. Subsequently, the police searched his house, and he went into hiding and left the country to seek asylum in Sweden. Furthermore, Mr. Tapia Paez came from a politically active family. One of his cousins had disappeared, another had been killed for political reasons and his mother and sisters had been granted de facto refugee status by Sweden.

The Committee considered that the test of article 3 of the Convention was absolute. Whenever substantial grounds existed for believing that an individual would be in danger of being subjected to torture upon expulsion to another State, the State party was under an obligation not to return the person concerned to that State. The nature of the activities in which the person concerned was engaged could not be a material consideration when making a determination under article 3 of the Convention. In the light of the circumstances in this case, the Committee took the view that the State party had an obligation to refrain from forcibly returning Mr. Tapia Paez to Peru.

---

[26] *Ibidem, Forty-eighth Session, Supplement No. 44A* (A/48/44/Add.1).

[27] *Ibidem, Fifty-second Session, Supplement No. 44* (A/52/44), annex V, sect. B.4, communication No. 39/1996, views adopted on 28 April 1997.

II:3

The author's membership of a group in conflict with a State also arose in the case *Josu Arkauz Arana* v. *France*.[28] The author, a Spanish national of Basque origin, had taken up residence in France. In 1991, Mr. Arkauz was arrested on a charge of belonging to ETA, the Basque separatist movement, and sentenced to eight years' imprisonment for criminal conspiracy. Before his release, he was further sentenced to a three-year ban from French territory, but he argued that his deportation to Spain would constitute a violation by France of article 3 of the Convention. Following a ministerial order, Mr. Arkauz was forcibly deported and handed over to Spanish security forces on 13 January 1997. He reported to the Committee that he had been ill-treated and threatened by the French police, and he described incidents that had occurred in Spain after his deportation.

The Committee noted the specific circumstances under which the deportation of Mr. Arkauz had taken place. It mentioned, *inter alia*, that there had been suspicions, expressed in particular by some non-governmental organizations, that other persons in the same circumstances as Mr. Arkauz had been subjected to torture on being returned to Spain and during their incommunicado detention. The deportation had been effected under an administrative procedure, later found illegal by a French administrative court, entailing a direct handover from police to police without the intervention of a judicial authority and without any possibility for Mr. Arkauz to contact his family or his lawyer. This meant that the detainee's rights had not been respected and that Mr. Arkauz had been placed in a situation where he was particularly vulnerable to possible abuse. The Committee recognized the need for close cooperation between States in the fight against crime and for effective measures to be agreed upon for that purpose. However, it believed that such measures had to respect fully the rights and fundamental freedoms of the individuals concerned.

The Committee took the view that the expulsion of Mr. Arkauz to Spain, in the circumstances in which it took place, constituted a violation by France of article 3 of the Convention.

Whilst these examples are interesting, especially as they show the reasoning behind some of the Committee's decisions, it should be pointed out that in considering most of the communications alleging violations of article 3 of the Convention, the Committee finds that there is no risk to the applicant and, therefore, no violation of the article.

---

[28] *Ibidem, Fifty-fifth Session, Supplement No. 44* (A/55/44), annex VIII, sect. A.2, communication No. 63/1997, views adopted on 9 November 1999.

Finally, another important and interesting case considered by the Committee, *Hajrizi Dzemajl* et al. v. *Serbia and Montenegro*,[29] is summarized in connection with the respect for and protection of human rights in times of armed conflict, disturbance and tension.[30] The complainants in this case were 65 nationals of Serbia and Montenegro, all of Roma origin.

On 15 April 1995, several hundred non-Roma people attacked a Roma settlement. This resulted in the levelling of the entire settlement and the burning or complete destruction of all proporties belonging to its Roma residents. A number of police officers were present at the scene of these events when they occured, but they did not intervene. Investigations into the incident were discontinued, and no perpetrators were tried by any court. The State failed to enable the victims to obtain redress and to provide them with compensation. The complainants alleged violations by Serbia and Montenegro of a number of articles of the Convention

The Committee considered that the burning and destruction of houses, in the circumstances, constituted acts of cruel, inhuman or degrading treatment or punishment, committed with the acquiescence of police officers, in violation of article 16, paragraph 1, of the Convention. In an individual opinion, two members of the Committee expressed the view that the acts amounted to torture within the meaning of article 1, paragraph 1. The Committee also found violations of articles 12 and 13 of the Convention.

(*c*) Committee on Freedom of Association

The prohibition of torture is frequently reflected in the jurisprudence of the Committee on Freedom of Association. In cases involving allegations that leaders or members of trade unions or employers' organizations have been subjected to torture or other ill-treatment, the Committee makes reference, in particular, to those of its decisions and principles that focus on accountability of perpetrators. In its reports on such cases, the Committee recommends the Governing Body of the International Labour Office to call on the Governments concerned to initiate independent inquiries so that those responsible may be identified and punished and crimes of torture and other forms of ill-treatment prevented in the future.

Procedural aspects of the Committee's examination of complaints alleging violations of freedom of association have been dealt with above in connection with the

---

[29] *Ibidem, Fifty-eighth Session, Supplement No. 44* (A/58/44), annex VI, sect. A, complaint No. 161/2000, decision adopted on 21 November 2002.
[30] See part IV, chap. 2, sect. C (*a*) (*infra*, pp. 562-572).

II:3

right to life.[31] What is said there is equally relevant in respect of the prohibition of torture.

The reports on cases where violations of the prohibition of torture are alleged reveal a distressing catalogue of criminality and abuse directed at severely violating the victim's physical and mental integrity.

In a report on case No. 1341 (*Paraguay*),[32] the Committee examined a number of complaints relating to the detention of trade union activists and leaders, to violent repression of peaceful trade union demonstrations and to acts of interference and pressure exerted against trade unions and their leaders. In particular, the climate of violence and repression affected the trade union movement in the hospital, banking, transport, press, teaching and agricultural sectors. For example, it was alleged that a trade union leader had been arbitrarily imprisoned in a police station, subjected to physical and psychological torture and deprived of visiting rights. Responding to alleged acts of violence and death threats by members of the police force against trade union members, the Committee considered that in the event of assaults on the physical or moral integrity of individuals, the Government concerned should immediately institute an independent judicial inquiry with a view to clarifying the facts, determining responsibility, punishing those responsible and preventing the repetition of such acts.

In a report on case No. 1508 (*Sudan*),[33] the Committee considered serious allegations about measures taken by the Sudanese authorities after a military coup. The complainants alleged various infringements of freedom of association, including the dissolution of all trade union organizations by military decree; the imprisonment of a great number of trade union leaders and activists, apparently without charges and without trial; and the imposition by military tribunals of heavy sentences, including the death sentence, on named trade union leaders. Other allegations related to the death in prison, as a result of torture, of a prominent trade union leader, a medical doctor; the arrest and detention of several union leaders in extremely poor conditions; and the kidnapping and disappearance of another union leader. As to the alleged death under torture of the medical doctor, the Committee noted that the Government had not yet provided a copy of the autopsy report. In view of the extremely serious nature of the allegation, the Committee regretted that the Government had not provided any further information on the proceedings as requested. Furthermore, the Committee stressed the importance, in situations of this kind, of proceedings be-

---

[31] See part II, chap. 2, sect. B (*b*) (*supra*, p. 49).

[32] See International Labour Office, *Official Bulletin*, vol. LXXII, Series B, No. 3 (1989), p. 103, interim report.

[33] *Ibidem*, vol. LXXV, Series B, No. 3 (1992), p. 123, definitive report.

ing brought to a speedy conclusion, since justice delayed was justice denied. In a previous report on this case,[34] the Committee recalled that in past cases of alleged torture or ill-treatment of detainees, it had stressed that governments should carry out inquiries into complaints of this kind so that appropriate measures, including compensation for damages suffered and sanctioning of those responsible, were taken to ensure that no detainee was subjected to such treatment.

In a report on case No. 1527 *(Peru)*,[35] the Committee responded to complaints arising out of allegations of exploitation of workers in the mining industry, including references to murder of named trade unionists and detention and ill-treatment of others. It was alleged that those detained had been humiliated and tortured, some showing signs of burns and injuries caused by electric shocks. Concerning allegations of this type, the Committee recalled that governments should give precise instructions and apply effective sanctions where cases of ill-treatment were found, so as to ensure that no detainee was subjected to such treatment. It also emphasized the importance to be attached to the principle laid down in the International Covenant on Civil and Political Rights according to which all persons deprived of their liberty must be treated with humanity and with respect for the inherent dignity of the human person.

A report on case No. 2005 *(Central African Republic)*[36] is summarized in section C.[37] It concerns allegations of violations of trade union rights, as well as of the arbitrary arrest and detention, torture and physical ill-treatment of a trade union official.

The Committee made a number of observations on the facts of this case that should guide police responses to industrial disputes generally, perhaps the most important being that trade union activities should not in themselves be used by the public authorities as a pretext for arbitrary arrest or detention of trade unionists. In addition to the fact that such deprivations of liberty are, in any event, serious human rights violations, they may lead to the infliction of torture, as other cases featured in this publication show.

In the light of its conclusions, the Committee invited the Governing Body to approve a number of recommendations. These included deploring the Government's failure to provide any details concerning the procedures, and reasons involved in the trade union official's arrest and detention, and reaffirming that the Government should give precise instructions to the effect that no detainee should be subjected to ill-treatment and apply effective sanctions where cases of ill-treatment were found. The

---

[34] *Ibidem*, vol. LXXIV, Series B, No. 1 (1991), p. 106, interim report.
[35] *Ibidem*, No. 2 (1991), p. 97, interim report.
[36] *Ibidem*, vol. LXXXII, Series B, No. 3 (1999), p. 35, interim report.
[37] See part II, chap. 3, sect. C *(e)* *(infra*, pp. 168-172).

II:3

Government was urged to set up an independent judicial inquiry and to forward its observations concerning these allegations.

(*d*) African Commission on Human and Peoples' Rights

Article 5 of the African Charter on Human and Peoples' Rights requires that every individual shall have the right to the respect of the dignity inherent in a human being and to the recognition of his legal status. It prohibits all forms of exploitation and degradation of man, in particular slavery, slave trade, torture, cruel, inhuman or degrading punishment and treatment.

There is no provision in the Charter allowing States parties to derogate from their treaty obligations.

In its jurisprudence, the African Commission on Human and Peoples' Rights has considered a number of communications in which States parties are alleged to have violated article 5 of the Charter in respect of the prohibition of torture and other cruel, inhuman or degrading treatment or punishment.

In the case *Krischna Achutan and Amnesty International* v. *Malawi*,[38] also cited in connection with the right to life[39] and with the right to a fair trial,[40] three communications were considered jointly by the Commission. The first communication was filed with the Commission by Krischna Achutan on behalf of Aleke Banda, his father-in-law, and the two others by Amnesty International on behalf of Orton and Vera Chirwa. The Commission examined allegations of, *inter alia*, torture and ill-treatment.

In 1981, Orton Chirwa, a prominent political figure in the country before independence, and his wife had been abducted from Zambia, where they lived in exile, and taken into custody by Malawi security officials. They were subsequently sentenced to death for treason, later commuted to life imprisonment. It was alleged that Mr. and Mrs. Chirwa were held in almost complete solitary confinement, given extremely poor food, inadequate medical care, shackled for long periods of time within their cells and prevented from seeing each other for years. Amnesty International also described extremely poor prison conditions, including overcrowding and torture consisting of beatings and electric shocks, and it reported that police had raided student dormitories and arrested students who had been beaten and tortured.

---

[38] See *Review of the African Commission on Human and Peoples' Rights*, vol. 5 (1995), p. 186, communications No. 64/92, No. 68/92 and No. 78/92.
[39] See part II, chap. 2, sect. B (*c*) (*supra*, p. 53).
[40] See part III, chap. 2, sect. B (*c*) (*infra*, p. 360).

The Commission held that conditions of overcrowding and acts of beating and torture that took place in prisons in Malawi contravened the prohibition in article 5 of the Charter of torture, cruel, inhuman or degrading punishment and treatment. Aspects of the treatment of Orton and Vera Chirwa, such as excessive solitary confinement, shackling within a cell, extremely poor quality of food and denial of access to medical care, were also in contravention of this article. The Commission concluded that there had been a violation of article 5 as well as of other articles of the Charter.

In the case *John D. Ouko* v. *Kenya*,[41] the complainant, a students' union leader, alleged that he was forced to flee the country in 1997 for his political opinions. Prior to leaving Kenya, he was arrested and detained without trial for 10 months in the basement cells of the secret service department in Nairobi. The detention facility was a two by three metre cell with a 250-watt electric bulb, which was left on throughout the entire period of his detention. Mr. Ouko further alleged that he was denied bathroom facilities and was subjected to both physical and mental torture.

The Commission found that such conditions contravened the right to respect for dignity and freedom from inhuman and degrading treatment under article 5 of the Charter. It also observed that those conditions and the treatment were contrary to the minimum standards contained in the Body of Principles for the Protection of All Persons under Any Form of Detention or Imprisonment. In particular, the Commission referred to principle 1, requiring that detainees shall be treated in a humane manner and with respect for the inherent dignity of the human person, and principle 6 prohibiting torture and cruel, inhuman or degrading treatment or punishment.

As to a violation of the complainant's right to freedom from torture, the Commission found, however, that Mr. Ouku had not substantiated his claim. Clearly, the conditions and treatment alleged in this case did not amount to torture. The Commission concluded that the Republic of Kenya had violated article 5 and other articles of the Charter.

In the case *Malawi African Association* et al. v. *Mauritania*,[42] also cited in connection with the respect for and protection of human rights in times of armed conflict, disturbance and tension,[43] the Commission considered 38 communications lodged against Mauritania. In conclusion, the Commission declared that during the years

---

[41] See Organization of African Unity document AHG/229 (XXXVII), annex V, p. 73, communication No. 232/99.

[42] See Organization of African Unity document AHG/222 (XXXVI), annex V, p. 138, communications No. 54/91, No. 61/91, No. 96/93, No. 98/93, Nos. 164/97-196/97 and No. 210/98.

[43] See part IV, chap. 2, sect. B (*d*) (*infra*, pp. 553-555).

II:3

1989 to 1992, there were grave or massive violations of human rights in that State, in particular of, *inter alia*, article 5 of the Charter.

In respect of article 5 of the Charter, the Commission noted that all of the communications detailed instances of torture and cruel, inhuman and degrading treatment. Allegations included that the detainees were beaten and denied sleep; that they were kept in chains, locked up in overpopulated cells; that they were burnt and buried in sand and left to die a slow death; that electrical shocks were administered to their genital organs and that they had weights tied on to them; that their heads were plunged into water to the point of provoking suffocation; and that the women were raped. The Government did not produce any argument to counter this. Taken together or in isolation, the acts referred to in the communications were proof of widespread utilization of torture and of cruel, inhuman and degrading forms of treatment. They constituted a violation of article 5 of the Charter.

(*e*) Inter-American Court of Human Rights

Article 5 of the American Convention on Human Rights protects the right to humane treatment. Under paragraph 1, every person has the right to have his physical, mental and moral integrity respected. Paragraph 2 states that no one shall be subjected to torture or to cruel, inhuman or degrading punishment or treatment. Furthermore, all persons deprived of their liberty shall be treated with respect for the inherent dignity of the human person. The remaning four paragraphs deal with other aspects of the right to humane treatment.

The provisions of article 5 are protected from derogation under article 27 of the Convention. Not even in time of war, public danger or other emergency threatening the independence or security of the State party may article 5 be suspended.

The prohibition of torture and cruel, inhuman or degrading punishment or treatment in article 5 of the Convention is further developed in a separate instrument, the Inter-American Convention to Prevent and Punish Torture. In article 2 of this Convention, torture is defined as any act intentionally performed whereby physical or mental pain or suffering is inflicted on a person for purposes of criminal investigation, as a means of intimidation, as personal punishment, as a preventive measure, as a penalty or to any other purpose. Torture shall also be understood to be the use of methods upon a person intended to obliterate the personality of the victim or to diminish his physical or mental capacities, even if they do not cause him physical pain or mental anguish. However, the concept of torture shall not include physical or mental pain or suffering that is inherent in or solely the consequence of lawful measures, provided that they do not include the performance of the acts or use of the methods referred to in the provision.

States parties to the Convention undertake to prevent and punish torture (article 1). The Convention includes, *inter alia*, provisions requiring that any public servant or employee acting in that capacity, or anyone else at the instigation of such a person, who orders, instigates or induces the use of torture, directly commits it or fails to prevent it shall be held guilty of the crime of torture (article 3); that superior orders shall not provide exemption from criminal liability (aricle 4); that the existence of public emergencies or disasters shall not be invoked or admitted as justification for the crime of torture (article 5); that effective measures are taken to prevent and punish torture and other cruel, inhuman or degrading treatment or punishment and to make such acts punishable by severe penalties that take into account their serious nature (article 6); that in the training of police officers, special emphasis shall be put on the prohibition of the use of torture in interrogation, detention or arrest (article 7); and that any person making an accusation of having been subjected to torture shall have the right to an impartial examination of the case, and the authorities shall proceed properly and immediately to conduct an investigation into the case and to initiate the corresponding criminal process when there is an accusation or well-grounded reason to believe that an act of torture has been committed (article 8).

No enforcement body is established under this Convention, but under article 8, paragraph 3, a case may be submitted to the international fora competent to consider it, after the exhaustion of domestic remedies. Consequently, the Inter-American Court of Human Rights may apply the Convention in cases brought before it against a State party.

As with cases on the right to life considered by the Court, many of the cases concerning violations of the prohibition of torture arise out of situations of disappearance. One such case, the *Villagrán Morales* et al. case (*Guatemala*), the *"street children"* case,[44] summarized in section C,[45] is also cited in connection with the right to life[46] and with the right to liberty and security of person.[47] This case concerns the killing of Anstraum Villagrán Morales and the abduction, torture and killing of four other youths, "street children", in 1990 by members of the State's national police force. In cases of this kind, the Court has expressed concern about the vulnerability of detainees kept in isolation from contact with the outside world. Prolonged isolation and incommunicado detention have, in themselves, been considered to be forms of cruel and inhuman treatment.

---

[44] See Inter-American Court of Human Rights, Series C: *Decisions and Judgments*, No. 63 (2000), petition No. 11383, judgment of 19 November 1999.
[45] See part II, chap. 3, sect. C (*f*) (*infra*, pp. 172-178).
[46] See part II, chap. 2, sect. B (*d*) (*supra*, pp. 56-57).
[47] See part II, chap. 4, sect. B (*e*) (*infra*, pp. 231-232).

II:3

In the *"street children"* case, the Court recalled that four of the victims had been retained clandestinely for up to 21 hours. While they were detained they were isolated from the external world and certainly aware that their lives were in danger. The Court felt it was reasonable to infer that merely owing to these circumstances, they had experienced extreme psychological and moral suffering during those hours. It concluded that the physical and mental integrity of the youths was violated and that they were victims of ill-treatment and torture, in violation of article 5, paragraphs 1 and 2, of the Convention, in relation to the obligation to respect rights in article 1, paragraph 1. The Court also found that a number of other provisions of the Convention had been violated in the case, notably article 4 on the right to life.

Another case, the *Cantoral Benavides* case (*Peru*),[48] summarized in section C,[49] also involved a situation of disappearance, but one not resulting in the death of the victim. In 1993, Luis Alberto Cantoral Benavides was detained by members of the national police of Peru without an arrest warrant issued by a competent authority. For the first eight or nine days of his detention, he was held incommunicado and subjected to acts of violence to get him to confess. He was charged with treason and terrorism and finally sentenced to 20 years in prison. He was incarcerated until his release in 1997.

In respect of article 5 of the Convention, the Court stated that under international human rights law, it had been established that people were to be held incommunicado during detention only in exceptional situations. It might constitute an act contrary to human dignity to be held incommunicado. The Court referred to a number of its earlier judgments, including those in the *Velásquez Rodríguez* case (*Honduras*),[50] summarized in connection with the right to life[51] and also cited in connection with the right to liberty and security of person,[52] and the *Suárez Rosero* case (*Ecuador*),[53] in which it noted the serious impact that being held incommunicado had on a detainee. In this case, reviewed in connection with the right to liberty and security of person,[54] the Court said that isolation from the outside world caused moral and psychological trauma and made the detainee particularly vulnerable to aggression and arbitrariness.

---

[48] See Inter-American Court of Human Rights, Series C: *Decisions and Judgments*, No. 69 (2001), petition No. 11377, judgment of 18 August 2000.

[49] See part II, chap. 3, sect. C (*g*) (*infra*, pp. 178-183).

[50] See Inter-American Court of Human Rights, Series C: *Decisions and Judgments*, No. 4 (1988), petition No. 7920, judgment of 29 July 1988.

[51] See part II, chap. 2, sect. C (*c*) (*supra*, pp. 74-85).

[52] See part II, chap. 4, sect. B (*e*) (*infra*, p. 228).

[53] See Inter-American Court of Human Rights, Series C: *Decisions and Judgments*, No. 35 (1999), petition No. 11273, judgment of 12 November 1997.

[54] See part II, chap. 4, sect. B (*e*) (*infra*, pp. 229-231).

The Court found that there were sufficient reasons to assert that in addition to being held communicado and having been subjected to very hostile and restictive prison conditions, Mr. Cantoral Benavides was on several occasions beaten and physically mistreated in other ways. This casused him severe bodily injury and emotional suffering. In the circumstances of the case and the context in which the facts took place, the Court considered, beyond a reasonable doubt, that at least some of the acts of aggression examined in the case could be classified as physical and psychological torture. It concluded that the State had violated article 5, paragraphs 1 and 2, of the Convention. The Court also found a number of other violations in the case.

In decisions reflecting the views adopted by the Human Rights Committee in the case *Elena Quinteros and M. C. Almeida de Quinteros* v. *Uruguay*,[55] reviewed above,[56] the Court additionally have found violations of article 5 of the Convention in relation to the next of kin of the victims, for example in the *"street children"* and *Cantoral Benavides* cases.

In the *"street children"* case, the Court found that a variety of factors had amounted to cruel and inhuman treatment of the families of the "street children". These included failure of the authorities to establish the identity of the victims, to notify the next of kin of their deaths, to deliver their bodies to the families and to provide the families with information on the development of the investigations. Added to these and other failures was the feeling of insecurity and impotence caused to the next of kin by the failure of the authorities to investigate the crimes and punish those responsible. In the *Cantoral Benavides* case, the Court recognized that the detention and imprisonment of the victim caused his mother and brother severe suffering and anguish.

In considering human rights violations in the context of terrorism, the Court has recalled that a true international system prohibiting all forms of torture has been put in place. It has referred to its own jurisprudence and to the case law of the European Court of Human Rights, citing, for example, the case *Selmouni* v. *France*,[57] summarized in section C.[58] In the *Cantoral Benavides* case, it noted that the European Court had insisted that even in the most difficult circumstances, such as the fight against terrorism and organized crime, acts of torture and inhuman or degrading treatment

---

[55] See United Nations, *Official Records of the General Assembly, Thirty-eighth Session, Supplement No. 40* (A/38/40), annex XXII, communication No. 107/1981, views adopted on 21 July 1983.

[56] See part II, chap. 3, sect. B (*a*) (*supra*, p. 130).

[57] See European Court of Human Rights, *Reports of Judgments and Decisions*, 1999-V, p. 149, application No. 25803/94, judgment of 28 July 1999.

[58] See part II, chap. 3, sect. C (*i*) (*infra*, pp. 186-197).

II:3

or punishment were strictly prohibited, regardless of what the victim had done. The Inter-American Court itself has pronounced that the fact that a State is confronted with terrorism should not lead to restrictions on the protection of the physical integrity of the person. The need to conduct investigations and the undeniable difficulties inherent to combatting terrorism were not grounds for placing such restrictions.

In this respect, it is interesting to refer to the *Bámaca Velásquez* case *(Guatemala)*,[59] summarized in connection with the respect for and protection of human rights in times of armed conflict, disturbance and tension[60] and also cited in connection with the right to life.[61] In this case, Efraín Bámaca Velásques, the leader of a guerrilla group engaged in an internal armed conflict against the State, was captured, tortured and killed in 1992 by agents of the State's armed forces. Even in these circumstances, when the State was faced with a situation of internal upheaval, the Court insisted that there should be no restrictions on the protection of the physical integrity of the individual. In this case, the Court also reviewed its own jurisprudence, and that of the Human Rights Committee and the European Court of Human Rights, on the question of the right to humane treatment of the next of kin of victims.

The Court considered that the acts denounced in the case were deliberately prepared and inflicted in order to obtain information from the victim. He was subjected to grave acts of physical and mental violence for this purpose, and he was thus intentionally placed in a situation of anguish and intense physical suffering that could only be qualified as both physical and mental torture. The Court concluded that the State had violated, *inter alia*, article 5, paragraphs 1 and 2, of the Convention to the detriment of Mr. Bámaca Velásques, his wife and next of kin.

In finding violations of article 5 of the Convention, the Court, in accordance with its usual practice, decides that the State concerned should conduct an investigation to determine the persons responsible for the violations and punish them.

Finally, in a number of cases before the Court where torture has been alleged against States parties to the Inter-American Convention to Prevent and Punish Torture, the provisions of this treaty have also been invoked to establish that the State concerned has violated its obligations.

In the *"street children"* case, for example, the Court found that the State had violated articles 1, 6 and 8 of that Convention. It was clear from the evidence that the

---

[59] See Inter-American Court of Human Rights, Series C: *Decisions and Judgments*, No. 70 (2001), petition No. 11129, judgment of 25 November 2000.
[60] See part IV, chap. 2, sect. C (*e*) (*infra*, pp. 582-593).
[61] See part II, chap. 2, sect. B (*d*) (*supra*, pp. 55-56).

State authorities had not adopted any formal decision to initiate a criminal investigation into the alleged perpetration of the crime of torture, neither had they investigated it in practice, although a great deal of evidence had been collected on the cruel treatment and torture of the victims when the homicides were investigated. In the *Cantoral Benavides* and *Bámaca Velásquez* cases, the Court also found violations of the Inter-American Convention to Prevent and Punish Torture

(f) European Court of Human Rights

Article 3 of the Convention for the Protection of Human Rights and Fundamental Freedoms expresses the prohibition of torture. Under this provision, no one shall be subjected to torture or to inhuman or degrading treatment or punishment.

This article is protected from derogation under article 15 of the Convention. Not even in time of war or other public emergency threatening the life of the nation may a State party take measures derogating from its obligations under article 3.

The *Greek* case (*Greece*),[62] is a complex inter-State case that originated in three identical applications lodged against the Government of Greece by the Governments of Denmark, Norway and Sweden as well as in a similar application by the Government of the Netherlands. On 21 April 1967, a new Government came to power in Greece, and several articles of the Constitution were suspended by a royal decree in view of internal dangers threatening public order and the security of the State. Under article 15 of the Convention, the Secretary General of the Council of Europe was notified of the measure. The applicant Governments alleged that the respondent Government had violated a number of articles of the Convention by legislative and administrative measures. Additionally, the Scandinavian Governments later submitted, *inter alia*, that article 3 of the Convention had also been violated, as political prisoners in a number cases had been tortured or subjected to inhuman or degrading treatment by police officers acting under the authority of the respondent Government.

In respect of article 3, the European Commission of Human rights made an interesting pronouncement on the meaning of this provision of the Convention. Clearly, there might be treatment to which all descriptions in the article applied, for all torture must be inhuman and degrading treatment, and inhuman treatment also degrading. The notion of inhuman treatment covered at least such treatment as deliberately caused severe suffering, mental or physical, in the particular situation being unjusti-

---

[62] See *Yearbook of the European Convention on Human Rights, 1969* [vol. 12 *bis*]: *The Greek Case*, applications No. 3321/67, No. 3322/67, No. 3323/67 and No. 3344/67, European Commission of Human Rights, report adopted on 5 November 1969, and Committee of Ministers of the Council of Europe, resolution DH (70) 1 adopted on 15 April 1970.

II:3

fiable. The word "torture" was often used to describe inhuman treatment for a purpose, such as the obtaining of information or confessions or the infliction of punishment. It was generally an aggravated form of inhuman treatment. Furthermore, treatment or punishment of an individual might be said to be degrading if it grossly humiliated him before others or drove him to act against his will or conscience.

Having made these distinctions, the Commission found it established beyond doubt that torture or ill-treatment contrary to article 3 had been inflicted in a number of situations examined in the case. Subsequently, acting under the then article 32 of the Convention, the Committee of Ministers of the Council of Europe decided, *inter alia*, that there had been a violation of article 3.

In another inter-State case, *Ireland* v. *the United Kingdom*,[63] the Irish Government alleged violations by the United Kingdom of article 3 and a number of other articles of the Convention. The case had its roots in the conflict in Northern Ireland. From August 1971 until December 1975, the authorities in Northern Ireland exercised a series of extrajudicial powers of arrest, detention and internment. This case concerned the scope and the operation in practice of those measures as well as the alleged ill-treatment of persons thereby deprived of their liberty.

In respect of five interrogation techniques, referred to variously as interrogation in depth, disorientation or sensory deprivation techniques, the Commission concluded that the combined use of those techniques constituted a practice of inhuman treatment and of torture in breach of article 3 of the Convention. The techniques were described as, respectively, wall standing, forcing a detainee to remain for long periods in a stress position; hooding, putting a dark coloured hood over the detainees' heads; subjection to continuous, loud noise; deprivation of sleep; and deprivation of food and drink. The two determining factors in this decision were the use of techniques sufficient to break the will and their purpose, to obtain information.

In its report on this case, the Commission referred to the term "unjustifiable" that it had used in the *Greek* case. Noting that this term, in the particular situation, had given rise to some misunderstanding, it found it necessary to state clearly that it did not have in mind the possiblity that there could be justification for any treatment in breach of article 3 of the Convention. It went on to state that under the Convention, war or other state of emergency did not authorize a State party to derogate from its obligations under article 3. The prohibition of torture and ill-treatment was absolute. There could never be under the Convention or under international law a justification for acts in breach of that provision.

---

[63] See *Publications of the European Court of Human Rights*, Series A: *Judgments and Decisions*, vol. 25 (1978), application No. 5310/71, judgment of 18 January 1978.

In determining whether the five techniques should be qualified as torture, the European Court of Human Rights, sitting in plenary, held that it had to have regard to the distinction embodied in article 3 between this notion and that of inhuman or degrading treatment. This distinction derived principally from a difference in the intensity of the suffering inflicted. It was the intention that the Convention, by the term "torture", should attach a special stigma to deliberate inhuman treatment causing very serious and cruel suffering. The Court held, by sixteen votes to one, that the use of the five techniques constituted a practice of inhuman and degrading treatment in breach of article 3 of the Convention and, by thirteen votes to four, that the use of those techniques did not constitute a practice of torture within the meaning of the same article.

Furthermore, the Court found that in the autumn of 1971, quite a large number of those held in custody at a military camp had been subjected to violence by members of the police and that it definitely constituted a practice. The violence led to intense suffering and to physical injury that occasionally was substantial, but it did not amount to torture. The Court held unanimously that this practice of inhuman treatment was in breach of article 3, but, by fourteen votes to three, not one of torture.

This case can be contrasted with a later case, *Tomasi* v. *France.*[64] The applicant, Félix Tomasi, a French national, was suspected of having taken part in an attack on 11 February 1982 against a rest centre of the Foreign Legion, located in Corsica. Two unarmed soldiers were shot, one being killed and the other suffering serious injuries. The attack had been carried out by a commando of several people wearing balaclava helmets to conceal their features. The following day, the Corsican National Liberation Front, a movement seeking independence for Corsica, claimed responsibility for this attack and 24 other bomb attacks perpetrated the same night. Mr. Tomasi was arrested in 1983 and charged with several serious criminal offences including murder and possessing firearms. The investigation and trial, resulting in the applicant's acquittal, lasted five years and seven months. Throughout that time the applicant was kept in detention.

The applicant alleged, *inter alia*, that he was beaten and badly treated in police custody after arrest, an ill-treatment incompatible with article 3 of the Convention. He was examined by four different physicians in the days immediately after the period spent in police custody, and they found evidence of slight physical injuries consistent with the allegations made.

In relation to the applicant's complaint of ill-treatment, the Court found that the evidence of medical examination of the applicant and complaints by him indicated that

---

[64] *Ibidem*, vol. 241-A (1993), application No. 12850/87, judgment of 27 August 1992.

II:3

his injuries related to the period when he was held in police custody. Furthermore, the Court noted that no claims had been made to the contrary. This was held to be sufficient to establish a causal connection between the injuries and the period in police custody.

As to the gravity of the treatment, the Court found it sufficient to observe that the medical certificates and reports, drawn up in total independence by medical practitioners, attested to the large number of blows inflicted on Mr. Tomasi and their intensity. These were two elements sufficiently serious to render such treatment inhuman and degrading. The requirements of the investigation and the undeniable difficulties inherent in the fight against crime, particularly with regard to terrorism, could not result in limits being placed on the protection to be afforded in respect of the physical integrity of individuals. Accordingly, the Court concluded that there had been a violation of article 3 of the Convention. It also found other violations of the Convention.

In a concurring opinion, one of the judges observed that it would be unfortunate if some elements of the judgment were to leave the impression that blows inflicted on a suspect in police custody were prohibited only insofar as they exceeded a certain minimum level of severity, for example on account of the large number of such blows and their intensity. Recalling, *inter alia*, the *Greek* case and the *Ireland* v. *the United Kingdom* case, he pointed out that any use of physical force in respect of a person deprived of his liberty not made strictly necessary as a result of his own conduct violated human dignity and had therefore to be regarded as a breach of the right guaranteed under article 3 of the Convention. At the most, the severity of the treatment was relevant in determining, where appropriate, whether or not there had been torture.

In the case *Aksoy* v. *Turkey*,[65] summarized in section C[66] and also cited in connection with the right to liberty and security of person,[67] the applicant, Zeki Aksoy, a Turkish citizen, complained, *inter alia*, that he had been subjected to treatment contrary to article 3 of the Convention during his detention in police custody in 1992. The Court found that the victim had been subjected to ill-treatment of such a serious and cruel nature that it could only be described as torture. It held, by eight votes to one, that there had been a violation of article 3. In this case, the Court said that article 3 enshrined one of the fundamental values of democratic society and that even in the most difficult of circumstances, such as the fight against terrorism and organized

---

[65] See European Court of Human Rights, *Reports of Judgments and Decisions*, 1996-VI, p. 2260, application No. 21987/93, judgment of 18 December 1996.
[66] See part II, chap. 3, sect. C (*h*) (*infra*, pp. 184-186).
[67] See part II, chap. 4, sect. B (*f*) (*infra*, pp. 240-241).

crime, the Convention prohibited in absolute terms torture or inhuman or degrading treatment or punishment. The Court observed that where an individual was taken into police custody in good health but found to be injured at the time of release, it was incumbent on the State to provide a plausible explanation as to the causing of the injury. Failing to do so raised a clear issue under article 3 of the Convention. In this case, the Court also found that other provisions had been violated.

In a more recent case, *Selmouni* v. *France*,[68] also summarized in section C,[69] the applicant, Ahmed Selmouni, a Netherlands and Moroccan national, alleged, *inter alia*, that the manner in which he had been treated while in police custody in 1991 had given rise to a violation of article 3 of the Convention. The case provides a revealing account of how domestic courts and the European Court of Human Rights responded to allegations of torture against police officials. For example, a court of appeal observed that the offences of which the defendants were found guilty were exceptionally serious. They had to be regarded as instances of particularly degrading treatment. Having been committed by senior officials responsible for enforcing the laws of the Republic, they had to be punished firmly. Such a conduct could not be justified, irrespective of the personality of the offenders in their charge and the degree of their corruption and dangerousness.

Under the circumstances of this case, the Court was satisfied that the physical and mental violence, considered as a whole, committed against Mr. Selmouni during police custody caused severe pain and suffering and was particularly serious and cruel. Such conduct had to be regarded as acts of torture for the purposes of article 3 of the Convention. In coming to its conclusions, the Court set out a detailed account of what constituted torture. It also made a significant pronouncement on the ways in which human rights standards might be developing, especially in relation to the protection of the physical and mental integrity of individuals. Certain acts classified in the past as inhuman and degrading treatment as opposed to torture could be classified differently in the future. The Court took the view that the increasingly high standard being required in the area of the protection of human rights and fundamental liberties correspondingly and inevitably required greater firmness in assessing breaches of the fundamental values of democratic societies. The Court also found a violation of article 6 of the Convention on account of the length of the proceedings.

It is a shocking case, not only because of the nature of the treatment to which the Court found the victim had been subjected, but also because the situation arose in a

---

[68] See European Court of Human Rights, *Reports of Judgments and Decisions*, 1999-V, p. 149, application No. 25803/94, judgment of 28 July 1999.
[69] See part II, chap. 3, sect. C (*i*) (*infra*, pp. 186-197).

II:3

long established democracy where the rule of law prevails and where the various police agencies generally work to high professional standards.

Perhaps the most important conclusion to draw from this case is that police leaders, and others with responsibilities for ensuring effective, lawful and humane policing, need to develop and sustain within police agencies an ethos completely intolerant of bad behaviour by police and continuously supportive of good behaviour. This is a warning against complacency, because no State, whatever its traditions of governance, and no police agency, whatever its traditions of professionalism, is immune from abuse of power and the perpetration of serious human rights violations by its officials.

It is interesting to compare this case with another case, *Ribitsch* v. *Austria*,[70] where a police official accused of torture was acquitted, on appeal, by a domestic court. The applicant, Ronald Ribitsch, an Austrian national, was arrested in 1988 for drug trafficking, and he later claimed that he was beaten and ill-treated whilst being interrogated by police.

In its deliberations on the case, the Court observed that it was not disputed that Mr. Ribitsch's injuries were sustained during his detention in police custody, which was in any case unlawful, while he was entirely under the control of police officers. The Court pointed out that the police official's acquittal in the criminal proceedings by a domestic court bound by the principle of presumption of innocence did not absolve Austria from its responsibility under the Convention. Accordingly, the Government was under an obligation to provide a plausible explanation of how the applicant's injuries were caused. However, the Government did no more than refer to the outcome of the domestic criminal proceedings. The high standard of proof necessary to secure a criminal conviction was not found to have been satisfied. In that context, it was also clear that significant weight had been given to the explanation that the injuries were caused by a fall against a car door. Like the Commission, the Court found this explanation unconvincing. It considered that even if Mr. Ribitsch had fallen while being moved under escort, this could only have provided a very incomplete, and therefore insufficient, explanation of the injuries concerned.

The Court emphasized that in respect of a person deprived of his liberty, any recourse to physical force not having been made strictly necessary by his own conduct diminished human dignity and was in principle an infringement of the right set forth in article 3 of the Convention. The injuries suffered by Mr. Ribitsch showed that he

---

[70] See *Publications of the European Court of Human Rights*, Series A: *Judgments and Decisions*, vol. 336 (1996), application No. 18896/91, judgment of 4 December 1995.

had undergone ill-treatment amounting to both inhuman and degrading treatment. The Court held, by six votes to three, that there had been a breach of article 3.

C. CASE SUMMARIES

(a) *Hugo Rodríguez* v. *Uruguay* (Human Rights Committee)[71]

The author of the communication was Hugo Rodríguez, a Uruguayan citizen. He submitted the communication to the Human Rights Committee on 23 July 1988. Although the author invoked violations by Uruguay of a number of articles of the International Covenant on Civil and Political Rights, he requested the Committee to focus on his allegations concerning article 7 of the Covenant and on the State party's alleged failure properly to investigate his case, to punish the guilty and to award him appropriate compensation.

The facts

The author submitted, *inter alia*, the following. In June 1983, he was arrested by the Uruguayan police. He was taken by plainclothes policemen to the headquarters of the secret police. There he was kept handcuffed for several hours, tied to a chair with his head hooded. He alleged that he was forced to stand naked, still handcuffed, and buckets of cold water were poured over him. The next day, he was forced to lie naked on a metal bedframe, his arms and legs were tied to the frame and electric charges were applied to his eyelids, nose and genitals. He stated that a series of other brutalities were inflicted on him. This treatment continued for a week after which he was relocated to another cell. There he remained incommunicado for another week. He was then brought before a military judge and indicted on unspecified charges. He remained detained at a prison until 27 December 1984.

During his detention and even thereafter, until the transition from military to civilian rule in the country, no judicial investigation of his case could be initiated. After the re-introduction of constitutional guarantees in March 1985, a formal complaint was filed with the competent authorities. No judicial investigation was, however, initiated because of a dispute over jurisdiction of the courts. Ultimately, this was because Parliament enacted a law, effectively providing for the immediate end of judicial investigations into such matters and making impossible the pursuit of this category of crimes committed during the years of military rule.

---

[71] See United Nations, *Official Records of the General Assembly, Forty-ninth Session, Supplement No. 40* (A/49/40), vol. II, annex IX, sect. B, communication No. 322/1988, views adopted on 19 July 1994.

II:3

The author contended that he had been denied appropriate redress in the form of investigation of the abuses allegedly committed by the military authorities, punishment of those held responsible and compensation as victim. He further contended that the State party could not, by simple legislative act, violate its international commitments and thus deny justice to all the victims of human rights abuses committed under the previous military regime.

The State party, arguing that the communication should be declared inadmissible on the ground of non-exhaustion of domestic remedies, claimed, *inter alia*, that the amnesty law did not necessarily result in the suspension of investigations into allegations of torture. Whilst this law did not permit criminal prosecution of offenders, it did not leave the victims of the alleged offences without a remedy, because victims of torture could file claims for compensation through other judicial or administrative channels. The State party explained that the object of the law was to consolidate the institution of democracy and to ensure the social peace necessary for the establishment of a solid foundation of respect for human rights. In a later submission, the State party also contended that to investigate past events was tantamount to reviving the confrontation between persons and groups and that this would not contribute to reconciliation, pacification and the strengthening of democratic institutions.

As to the admissibility of the communication, the Committee found that the author had plausibly submitted that the strict application of the amnesty law frustrated any attempt to obtain compensation, as the enforcement of the law barred an official investigation of his allegations. Furthermore, in the light of the gravity of the allegations, it was the State party's responsibility to carry out investigations even if, as a result of that law, no penal sanctions could be imposed on persons responsible for torture and ill-treatment of prisoners. The absence of such investigation constituted a considerable impediment to the pursuit of civil remedies. The Committee decided that the communication was admissible insofar as it appeared to raise issues under article 7 of the Covenant.

The Committee's views on the merits

The Committee noted that the State party had not disputed the author's allegations that he was subjected to torture by the authorities of the then military regime in Uruguay. Bearing in mind that the author's allegations were substantiated, the Committee found that the facts as submitted sustained a finding that the military regime in Uruguay had violated article 7 of the Covenant. In this context, the Committee noted that although the Optional Protocol to the Covenant laid down a procedure for the examination of individual communications, the State party had not addressed the issues raised by the author as a victim of torture nor submitted any information concerning an investigation into the author's allegations of torture. Instead, the State party had limited itself to justifying, in general terms, the decision to adopt an amnesty law.

As to the appropriate remedy that the author might claim pursuant to article 2, paragraph 3, of the Covenant, the Committee found that the adoption of amnesty legislation and subsequent practice in Uruguay had rendered extremely difficult the realization of the author's right to an adequate remedy.

The Committee could not agree with the State party that it had no obligation to investigate violations of Covenant rights by a prior regime, especially when those included crimes as serious as torture. Article 2, paragraph 3 (*a*), of the Covenant clearly stipulated an undertaking by each State party to ensure that any person whose rights or freedoms, as recognized in it, were violated should have an effective remedy, notwithstanding that the violation had been committed by persons acting in an official capacity. In this context, the Committee referred to its general comment No. 20 (44) on article 7 of the Covenant.[72] The right to lodge complaints against maltreatment prohibited by this article had to be recognized in the domestic law, and complaints had to be investigated promptly and impartially by competent authorities so as to make the remedy effective. In this general comment, the Committee also noted that some States had granted amnesty in respect of acts of torture. Amnesties were generally incompatible with the duty of States to investigate such acts; to guarantee freedom from such acts within their jurisdiction; and to ensure that they did not occur in the future. States might not deprive individuals of the right to an effective remedy, including compensation and such full rehabilitation as might be possible.[73]

The State party had suggested that Mr. Rodríguez might still conduct private investigations into his torture. The Committee found that the responsibility for investigations fell under the State party's obligation to grant an effective remedy. Having examined the specific circumstances of this case, the Committee found that the author had not had an effective remedy.

The Committee reaffirmed its position that amnesties for gross violations of human rights, and legislation such as the amnesty law in the present case, were incompatible with the obligations of a State party under the Covenant. The Committee noted with deep concern that the adoption of this law effectively excluded in a number of cases the possibility of investigation into past human rights abuses, thereby preventing the State party from discharging its responsibility to provide effective remedies to the victims of those abuses. Moreover, the Committee was concerned that in a-

---

[72] *Ibidem, Forty-seventh Session, Supplement No. 40* (A/47/40), annex VI, sect. A.
[73] *Ibidem*, paras. 14 and 15.

II:3

dopting this law, the State party had contributed to an atmosphere of impunity which might undermine the democratic order and give rise to further grave human rights violations.

The Committee was of the view that the facts before it disclosed a violation of article 7, in connection with article 2, paragraph 3, of the Covenant.

Furthermore, under article 2, paragraph 3 (*a*), of the Covenant, Mr. Rodríguez was entitled to an effective remedy. The Committee urged the State party to take effective measures to carry out an official investigation into his allegations of torture, in order to identify the persons responsible for torture and ill-treatment and to enable him to seek civil redress; to grant him appropriate compensation; and to ensure that similar violations did not occur in the future.

(*b*) *Albert Womah Mukong* v. *Cameroon* (Human Rights Committee)[74]

The author of the communication was Albert Womah Mukong, a citizen of Cameroon. He submitted the communication to the Human Rights Committee on 26 February 1991. He claimed to be a victim of violations by Cameroon of article 7 and a number of other provisions of the International Covenant on Civil and Political Rights, including article 19 on the right to freedom of opinion and expression.

The facts

The author submitted, *inter alia*, the following. He was a journalist, writer and opponent of the one-party system in Cameroon. He had frequently and publicly advocated the introduction of multi-party democracy and worked towards the establishment of a new political party in his country. Some of the books he had written were either banned or prohibited from circulation. In the summer of 1990, he left Cameroon, and in October 1990 he applied for asylum in the United Kingdom of Great Britain and Northern Ireland.

On 16 June 1988, he was arrested, after an interview given to a correspondent of the British Broadcasting Corporation (BBC), in which he had criticized both the President of Cameroon and the Government. He claimed that in detention, he was interrogated about this interview and subjected to cruel and inhuman treatment. He indicated that from 18 June to 12 July 1988, he was continuously held in a cell measuring approximately 25 square metres, together with 25 to 30 other detainees. The cell did

---

[74] *Ibidem, Forty-ninth Session, Supplement No. 40* (A/49/40), vol. II, sect. AA, communication No. 458/1991, views adopted on 21 July 1994.

not have sanitary facilities and, as the authorities initially refused to feed him, he was without food for several days until his friends and family located him.

From 13 July to 10 August 1988, he was detained in a cell at police headquarters. He claimed that he was not allowed to keep his clothes and that he was forced to sleep on a concrete floor. Within two weeks of detention under these conditions, he fell ill with a chest infection. Thereafter, he was allowed to wear his clothes and to use old cartons as a sleeping mat.

On 5 May 1989, he was released, but on 26 February 1990, he was again arrested, following a meeting on 23 January during which several people, himself included, had publicly discussed ways and means of introducing multi-party democracy in Cameroon.

Between 26 February and 23 March 1990, he was detained at a brigade camp. There he allegedly was not allowed to see either his lawyer, his wife or his friends. He claimed that he was subjected to intimidation and mental torture. He was threatened that he would be taken to the torture chamber or shot, should any unrest among the population develop. He took these threats seriously, as two of his opposition colleagues, detained with him, had in fact been tortured. On one day, he allegedly was locked in his cell for 24 hours, suffering from the heat (temperatures above 40 degrees C). On another day, he allegedly was beaten by a prison warder when he refused to eat.

The author alleged a violation of article 7 of the Covenant on account of the treatment he was subjected to between 18 June and 10 August 1988 and during his detention at the brigade camp. He made further allegations and submissions regarding other violations of the Covenant.

The State party contended that Mr. Mukong had not availed himself of judicial remedies in respect of claims of ill-treatment and of inhuman and degrading treatment in detention. As to the alleged violation of article 7, the State party noted, *inter alia*, that article 1 of the Convention against Torture and Other Cruel, Inhuman or Degrading Treatment or Punishment stipulated that the term "torture" did not include pain or suffering arising only from, inherent in or incidental to lawful sanctions. It added that the situation and comfort in the country's prisons had to be linked to the state of economic and social development of Cameroon.

The State party categorically denied that Mr. Mukong was, at any time during his detention in June 1988 or in February/March 1990, subjected to torture or cruel, inhuman or degrading treatment. It submitted that the burden of proof for the allegations laid with the author.

II:3

The Committee declared the communication admissible. However, it reserved the right to review the decision in respect of the author's claim under article 7. Subsequently, responding to a request by the State party for such a review and taking note of further clarifications about the availability of judicial remedies for the author's claims, the Committee saw no reason to revise its decision on admissibility.

The Committee's examination of the merits

In respect of alleged violations of article 7 of the Covenant, the Committee made the following observations. The author had contended that the conditions of his detention in 1988 and 1990 amounted to a violation of this article, in particular because of insalubrious conditions of detention facilities, overcrowding of a cell, deprivation of food and of clothing, death threats and incommunicado detention. The State party had replied that the burden of proof for these allegations laid with the author and that as far as conditions of detention were concerned, they were a factor of the underdevelopment of Cameroon.

The Committee did not accept the State party's views. As it had held on previous occasions, the burden of proof could not rest alone with the author of a communication, especially considering that the author and the State party did not always have equal access to the evidence and that frequently the State party alone had access to the relevant information. Mr. Mukong had provided detailed information about the treatment to which he was subjected. In the circumstances, it was incumbent upon the State party to refute the allegations in detail, rather than shifting the burden of proof to the author.

As to the conditions of detention in general, the Committee observed that certain minimum standards regarding the conditions of detention had to be observed regardless of a State party's level of development. These included, in accordance with rules 10, 12, 17, 19 and 20 of the Standard Minimum Rules for the Treatment of Prisoners, minimum floor space and cubic content of air for each prisoner, adequate sanitary facilities, clothing in no manner degrading or humiliating, provision of a separate bed and provision of food of nutritional value adequate for health and strength. It should be noted that these were minimum requirements always to be observed, even if economic or budgetary considerations might make compliance with these obligations difficult. It transpired from the file that these requirements were not met during the detention of Mr. Mukong in the summer of 1988 and in February/March 1990.

The Committee further noted that quite apart from the general conditions of detention, Mr. Mukong had been singled out for exceptionally harsh and degrading treatment. Thus he was kept detained incommunicado, threatened with torture and death, intimidated, deprived of food and kept locked in his cell for several days on end without the possibility of recreation. In this context, the Committee recalled its general comment No. 20 (44) on article 7 of the Convention, recommending that States parties should make provision against incommunicado detention and noting that total isolation of a detained or imprisoned person might amount to acts prohibited by this article.[75] In view of the above, the Committee found that Mr. Mukong had been subjected to cruel, inhuman and degrading treatment, in violation of article 7.

The Committee was of the opinion that the facts before it revealed violations by Cameroon of article 7. The Committee also responded to other allegations by the author of violations of the Covenant not included in this summary of the case.

Under article 2, paragraph 3 (*a*), of the Covenant, the State party was under an obligation to provide Mr. Mukong with an effective remedy. The Committee urged the State party to grant him appropriate compensation for the treatment to which he had been subjected; to investigate his allegations of ill-treatment in detention; to respect his rights under article 19 of the Covenant; and to ensure that similar violations did not occur in the future.

(c) Celis Laureano v. Peru
(Human Rights Committee)[76]

The author of the communication was Basilio Laureano Atachahua, a Peruvian citizen. He submitted the communication to the Human Rights Committee on 22 October 1992 on behalf of his granddaughter, Ana Rosario Celis Laureano, also a Peruvian citizen. The author claimed that his granddaughter was a victim of violations by Peru of article 7 and a number of other provisions of the International Covenant on Civil and Political Rights, including article 24, paragraph 1, as the State party had failed to provide her with such measures of protection as were required by her status as a minor.

The facts

The author presented, *inter alia*, the following facts. In March 1992, his granddaughter, then 16 years old, was abducted by unknown armed men, presumably guerrillas of the Shining Path movement. She returned after six days. In May 1992, she was once again forced to to accompany the guerrillas but managed to escape.

---

[75] *Ibidem, Forty-seventh Session, Supplement No. 40* (A/47/40), annex VI, sect. A, paras. 6 and 11.

[76] *Ibidem, Fifty-first Session, Supplement No. 40* (A/51/40), vol. II, annex VIII, sect. P, communication No. 540/1993, views adopted on 25 March 1996.

II:3

On 23 June 1992, Ms. Laureano was detained by the military on suspicion of collaboration with the guerrilla movement. On 5 August 1992, a judge of a civil court ordered her release on the ground that she was a minor. However, on 13 August 1992, Ms. Laureano was abducted from the house where she and the author were staying. It was strongly suspected that her abductors were state officials and, in spite of considerable efforts to trace her, she was never seen again.

The Committee's examination of the merits

The Committee regretted the absence of cooperation on the part of the State party in respect of the merits of the communication. It was implicit in article 4, paragraph 2, of the Optional Protocol to the Covenant that a State party should investigate thoroughly, in good faith and within the imparted deadlines, all the allegations of violations of the Covenant against it and that it should make available to the Committee all the information at its disposal. In the instant case, the State party had not furnished any information other than that Ms. Laureano's disappearance was being investigated. In the circumstances, due weight had to be given to the author's allegations, to the effect that they had been substantiated.

With regard to the claim under article 7 of the Covenant, the Committee recalled that Ms. Laureano disappeared and had no contact with her family or, on the basis of the information available to it, with the outside world. In the circumstances, the Committee concluded that the abduction and disappearance of the victim and prevention of contact with her family and with the outside world constituted cruel and inhuman treatment, in violation of article 7, *juncto* article 2, paragraph 1, of the Covenant.

Concerning the author's claim that article 24, paragraph 1, of the Covenant had been violated, as the State party had failed to protect his granddaughter's status as a minor, the Committee made the following observations. It noted that during the investigations initiated after Ms. Laureano's initial detention by the military, a civil court judge had ordered her provisional release, because she was a minor. However, subsequent to her later disappearance, the State party did not adopt any particular measures to investigate her disappearance or to determine her whereabouts to ensure her security and welfare, given that Ms. Laureano was under age at the time of her disappearance. In the cirumstances, the Committee concluded that Ms. Laureano did not benefit from such special measures of protection as she was entitled to because of her status as a minor. Accordingly, there had been a violation of article 24, paragraph 1, of the Covenant.

The Committee was of the view that the facts before it revealed, *inter alia*, violations of article 7, *juncto* article 2, paragraph 1, and of article 24, paragraph 1, of the Covenant.

Under article 2, paragraph 3, of the Covenant, the State party was under an obligation to provide the victim and the author with an effective remedy. The Committee urged the State party to open a proper investigation into the disappearance of Ms. Laureano and her fate; to provide for appropriate compensation to the victim and her family; and to bring to justice those responsible for her disappearance, notwithstanding any domestic amnesty legislation to the contrary.

Finally, the Committee recalled that by becoming a State party to the Optional Protocol, the State had recognized the competence of the Committee to determine whether or not there had been a violation of the Covenant. Pursuant to article 2 of the Covenant, the State had undertaken to ensure to all individuals within its territory and subject to its jurisdiction the rights recognized in the Covenant and to provide an effective and enforceable remedy in case a violation had been established. Bearing this in mind, the Committee wished to receive from the State party, within 90 days, information about the measures taken to give effect to the Committee's views.

(d) Radivoje Ristic v. Yugoslavia (Committee against Torture)[77]

The author of the communication was Radivoje Ristic, a citizen of Yugoslavia. He submitted the communication to the Committee against Torture on 22 July 1998. The author claimed that an act of torture resulting in the death of his son, Milan Ristic, had been committed by police officials and that the authorities had failed to carry out a prompt and impartial investigation. He invoked several provisions of the Convention against Torture and Other Cruel, Inhuman or Degrading Treatment or Punishment, in particular articles 12, 13 and 14.

The facts

The author submitted, *inter alia*, the following. On 13 February 1995, three police officials allegedly arrested Milan Ristic while looking for a murder suspect. One of the officials struck his son with a blunt object, presumably a pistol or rifle butt, behind the left ear, killing him instantly. The officials moved the body and, with a blunt instrument, broke both thighbones. They then called an ambulance and a police investigation team, including a forensic technician.

---

[77] *Ibidem, Fifty-sixth Session, Supplement No. 44* (A/56/44), annex VII, sect. A.2, communication No. 113/1998, views adopted on 11 May 2001.

II:3

The police officials told the investigators that Milan Ristic had committed suicide by jumping from the roof of a nearby building and that they had an eyewitness to that effect. A medical doctor who attended with the ambulance pronounced Milan Ristic dead and then left the scene in the ambulance. The body was collected later by a mortuary van. The author claimed that after the departure of the ambulance, the police officials struck the deceased on the chin, causing injury to his face.

The author provided a copy of the autopsy report and a copy of a report by the doctor who had attended the incident with the ambulance. He contended that these reports did not tally with each other. Whereas the ambulance doctor stated that he had noticed no injuries to the face, the autopsy report had listed a laceration and bruise on the chin. The author challenged these reports, noting that it was hardly possible that a person could have fallen from the roof of the building (a height of 14.65 metres) without suffering any injury to the face, heels, pelvis, spine or internal organs and without internal haemorrhaging.

At the request of the parents, two forensic experts examined the autopsy report and found it superficial and contradictory. They reported that the autopsy had not been performed in accordance with the principles of forensic and medical science and practice and that the conclusion was not in agreement with the findings. They proposed the exhumation of the remains and another autopsy by a forensic expert. In a written statement dated 18 July 1995, addressed to the public attorney's office, the pathologist who had carried out the autopsy agreed that the remains should be exhumed for forensic examination. He pointed out that as he was not a specialist in forensic medicine, he might have made a mistake or missed some details.

The parents filed criminal charges against a number of police officials before a public prosecutor. On 19 February 1996, the prosecutor dismissed the charges. Under Yugoslav law, following dismissal of a criminal complaint, the victim or the person acting on his behalf might either request the institution of investigative proceedings or file an indictment and proceed directly to trial. In this case, the parents presented their own indictment on 25 February 1996.

An investigating judge questioned the police officials involved as well as witnesses and found no grounds for believing that a criminal offence had been committed. A district court endorsed the decision of the investigating judge. The court did not find it necessary to hear the testimony of the two forensic experts and did not consider the possibility of ordering an exhumation and a new autopsy. Furthermore, the investigating judge delivered an unsigned statement to the parents, allegedly made by the pathologist in court when they were not present, which contradicted the one he had made in writing on 18 July 1995.

The parents appealed the decision to the Serbian Supreme Court. On 29 October 1996, it dismissed the appeal as unfounded. According to the ruling, the testimony of the eyewitness showed that Milan Ristic was alive at the time when two police officials arrived at the scene of the incident and that they and the witness saw Milan Ristic jump from the roof. There was nothing they could do to stop him.

The parents again tried to bring the case before the judiciary, but without success.

The author considered that first the police and, subsequently, the judicial authorities had failed to ensure a prompt and impartial investigation into the incident. All domestic remedies had been exhausted without a court ever having ordered or formally instituted proper investigative proceedings.

The author claimed that the State party had violated several articles of the Convention, in particular articles 12, 13 and 14. He stated that although he and his wife had the possibility of seeking compensation, the prospect of their being awarded damages was de facto non-existent in the absence of a criminal court judgment.

The State party informed the Committee that all domestic remedies had been exhausted, but the communication did not fulfil other necessary conditions provided for by the Convention. In particular, no act of torture had been committed, since the deceased did not have any contact with State authorities, the police. Accordingly, the communication was not admissible.

The Committee declared the communication admissible.

Subsequently, on the merits, the State party reiterated that the alleged victim had not been subjected to torture, because he had at no time been in contact with the police officials. Therefore, there had been no violation of the Convention. The State party also emphasized that its courts operated independently. They had concluded rightfully and in accordance with the law that no investigation should be initiated against the alleged authors of the acts of torture.

The State party then gave its version of the facts which, it claimed, showed that the death of Milan Ristic had been the result of suicide and that no acts of torture had been committed. Concerning the judicial proceedings that followed the death of the victim, the State party noted that the main reason that an investigation had not been ordered was the lack of strong evidence to prove a causal link between the behaviour of the police officials and the death of the victim. The State party contended that the proper procedures had been scrupulously followed at all stages.

II:3

Finally, the State party emphasized that certain omissions that might have occurred during the events immediately following the death of Milan Ristic, and referred to by the author of the communication, were not important, because they did not prove that Mr. Ristic had died as a result of torture.

In comments submitted by the author on the merits, he pointed out that the State party had limited itself to arguing that the police officials were not involved in the death of his son. It had not addressed the main issue of the communication, the failure to carry out a prompt, impartial and comprehensive investigation. He focused on a number of factual elements supporting his claim, including delays in collecting evidence and in initiating an investigation and a failure to order the exhumation of the body and a new autopsy.

Concerning the obligation to investigate incidents of torture and cruel, inhuman or degrading treatment or punishment, the author referred to the Committee's jurisprudence. The Committee had observed that under article 12 of the Convention, the authorities had the obligation to proceed to an investigation ex officio wherever there were reasonable grounds to believe that acts of torture or ill-treatment had been committed and whatever the origin of the suspicion. The obligation of a prompt and impartial investigation existed even when torture had merely been alleged by the victim, without the existence of a formal complaint. The author further referred to a statement by the Committee that a delay of 15 months before the initiation of an investigation was unreasonable and contrary to article 12 of the Convention

As to the principle of impartiality of the judicial authorities, the author stated that a body could not be impartial if it was not sufficiently independent. He referred to the case law of the European Court of Human Rights to define both the impartiality and the independence of a judicial body in accordance with articles 6, paragraph 1, and 13 of the Convention for the Protection of Human Rights and Fundamental Freedoms. He underlined that the authority capable of providing a remedy should be sufficiently independent from the alleged author of the violation.

Concerning the existence of reasonable grounds to believe that an act of torture or other ill-treatment had been committed, the author again relied on the jurisprudence of the European Court of Human Rights. He pointed to the existence of facts or information which would satisfy an objective observer that the person concerned might have committed the offence.

The author stressed that at the time of his submission, five years had already elapsed since his son's death. He contended that notwithstanding strong indication that grave police brutality had caused the death of Milan Ristic, the Yugoslav authorities had failed to conduct a prompt, impartial and comprehensive investigation able to lead to the identification and punishment of those responsible, and they had thus failed to provide the author with any redress.

Referring to a number of sources, the author argued that police brutality in Yugoslavia was systematic and that public prosecutors were not independent and rarely instituted criminal proceedings against police officers accused of violence and/or misconduct towards citizens. In such cases, the action was very often limited to a request for information directed to the police authorities alone, and the use of dilatory tactics was common.

Finally, the author specifically referred to the most recent examination of the periodic report submitted by Yugoslavia to the Committee. In its concluding observations, the Committee had stated that it was extremely concerned over the numerous accounts of the use of torture by the State police forces that it had received from non-governmental organizations. It was gravely concerned over the lack of sufficient investigation, prosecution and punishment by the competent authorities of suspected torturers or those breaching article 16 of the Convention and with the insufficient reaction to the complaints of such abused persons, resulting in the de facto impunity of the perpetrators of acts of torture.

Issues and proceedings before the Committee

The Committee regretted that the State party had limited itself to providing the Committee with a different account of the event to that provided by the author of the complaint. It noted that more precise information concerning the conduct of the investigation was necessary, including an explanation of why a new autopsy had not been carried out.

With regard to the alleged violations of articles 12 and 13 of the Convention, the Committee noted the following elements on which both parties had been able to submit observations.

There were apparent differences and inconsistencies as to the cause of death of the alleged victim between the statement made by the ambulance doctor, the autopsy report and the report by the two forensic experts submitted at the request of the parents of the alleged victim. Although the investigating judge, appointed when the parents of the alleged victim proceeded in the capacity of private prosecutor, had stated that the autopsy had not been performed in accordance with the principles of forensic medicine, there had been no order of exhumation of the body for a new forensic examination. There was a difference between the statement made by one police official, according to which the police department had been called for a person who had committed suicide, and the statements made by other police officials and

II:3

the witness, according to which the police department had been called for a person who might jump from the roof of a building. The police had not immediately informed the investigating judge on duty of the incident, in order for him to oversee the on-site investigation, in compliance with the State party's criminal procedure code.

Moreover, the Committee was especially concerned by the fact that the doctor who carried out the autopsy admitted, in a statement dated 18 July 1995, that he was not a specialist in forensic medicine.

Noting the above elements, the Committee considered that the investigation conducted by the State party's authorities had been neither effective nor thorough. A proper investigation would indeed have entailed an exhumation and a new autopsy. That would in turn have allowed the cause of death to be medically established with a satisfactory degree of certainty. The Committee noted that six years had elapsed since the incident took place and that the State party had had ample time to conduct a proper investigation.

In the circumstances, the Committee found that the State party had violated its obligations under articles 12 and 13 of the Convention to investigate promptly and effectively allegations of torture or severe police brutality.

With regard to allegations of a violation of article 14, the Committee found that in the absence of a proper criminal investigation, it was not possible to determine whether the rights to compensation of the alleged victim or his family had been violated. Such an assessment could only be made after the conclusion of proper investigations. The Committee therefore urged the State party to carry out such investigations without delay.

Finally, the Committee urged the State party to provide the author of the communication with an appropriate remedy and to inform it, within 90 days, of the steps the State party had taken in response to the observations made by the Committee.

(*e*) Case No. 2005 (*Central African Republic*)
(Committee on Freedom of Association)[78]

The complaints against the Government of the Central African Republic were submitted on 12 February 1999 by the Organization of African Trade Union Unity (OATUU) and on 10 May 1999 by the National Central African Confederation of

---

[78] See International Labour Office, *Offical Bulletin*, vol. LXXXII, Series B, No. 3 (1999), p. 35, interim report.

Workers (CNTC). The Government sent its observations in communications dated 19 March and 3 June 1999, respectively. The Trade Union of Central African Workers (USTC) supported the complaint by the OATUU in a communication of 24 June 1999.

The Central African Republic had ratified the Convention concerning Freedom of Association and Protection of the Right to Organise (No. 87) and the Convention concerning the Application of the Principles of the Right to Organise and to Bargain Collectively (No. 98).

The facts

The complainants' allegations included the following. The OATUU reported the arrest of Sony Cole, the USTC's secretary-general, on 9 January 1999 by members of the presidential guard. The OATUU further alleged that after being tortured by the latter, Mr. Cole was detained by the local Bangui police and was not allowed any visits other than from the Central African League for Human Rights. According to the OATUU, Mr. Cole's only crime was to demand payment of the wages of public sector workers that were several months overdue.

The CNTC reported the problem of the unpaid wages affecting state employees. According to this organization, the public sector service wage backlog was 25 months, while the pension backlog was 18 months. The CNTC further reported that teachers had held several strikes since 1997 in response to the non-payment of salaries. The Government's response was to use supply teachers to replace permanent teachers. The CNTC also alleged that five teachers holding trade union office were the victims of anti-trade union discrimination. In addition, the organization accused the Government of refusing to negotiate in good faith concerning the wage backlogs and the deadlock in the education system. Finally, it alleged that its premises were broken into on 6 January 1999.

The Government replied that the USTC, and especially its secretary-general, Mr. Cole, had been pursuing a strategy intended to disturb law and order. In particular, the Government considered the leadership of this trade union to be violating article 6 of the trade union statutes, laying down the fundamental principle of independence and a non-political stance for the trade union movement. It explained that the secretary-general of the USTC was co-signatory to a political convention with a number of opposition political parties and that the USTC put forward trade union candidates at the general elections, using trade union apparatus and funds to finance the campaign. The Government declared that it intended to take appropriate measures, if such abuses occurred again, in order to uphold law and order. Finally, as regarded the arrest of Mr. Cole, the Government declared that the reason lay outside his trade

II:3

union activities and was connected with the move into politics. In a later communication, the Government specified that the case of Mr. Cole was being pursued at the judicial level and that it would be inappropriate to comment before a verdict was reached.

The Committee's conclusions and recommendations

The Committee on Freedom of Association observed that the allegations in this case referred to the arrest and detention of a trade union official, violations of the right to strike and the right to collective bargaining and breaking into trade union premises.

Regarding the arrest and detention of Mr. Cole, the Committee noted that the Government provided no detailed information on these allegations, stating merely that Mr. Cole was arrested for political reasons and for disturbing law and order and not for reasons connected to his trade union activities. The Government specified that the matter was being pursued at the judicial level. In this connection, the Committee reaffirmed that while persons engaged in trade union activities or holding trade union office could not claim immunity in respect of the ordinary criminal law, trade union activities should not in themselves be used by the public authorities as a pretext for the arbitrary arrest or detention of trade unionists.

Noting that the Government referred to a strategy intended to disturb law and order and to the political activities of the USTC to justify the action against Mr. Cole, the Committee emphasized that arrests on the grounds of disturbing law and order could, given the general nature of the charge, make it possible to punish activities of the trade union type. The Committee reaffirmed that in the interests of the normal development of the trade union movement, it would be desirable to have regard to the principles on the independence of the trade union movement adopted by the International Labour Conference. The Committee also reaffirmed that governments should not attempt to transform the trade union movement into an instrument for the pursuance of political aims, nor should they attempt to interfere with the normal functions of a trade union because of its freely established relationship with a political party.

In relation to Mr. Cole's situation, the Committee reminded the Government that accused trade unionists, like anyone else, should benefit from normal judicial proceedings and have the right to due process, in particular the right to be informed of the charges against them; the right to have adequate time and facilities for the preparation of their defence and to communicate freely with counsel of their own choosing; and the right to a prompt trial by an impartial and independent judicial authority.

Additionally, concerning the physical ill-treatment and torture allegedly inflicted on Mr. Cole, the Committee deplored that the Government had not provided a response to these allegations. It reaffirmed that the Government should give precise instructions to the effect that no detainee should be subjected to ill-treatment and apply effective sanctions where cases of ill-treatment were found. Likewise, the Committee emphasized the importance that should be attached to the principle laid down in the International Covenant on Civil and Political Rights according to which all persons deprived of their liberty must be treated with humanity and with respect for the inherent dignity of the human person. To this end, the Committee urged the Government to send its observations with regard to the allegations that Mr. Cole had been tortured and to set up an independent judicial inquiry. Finally, deploring the Government's failure to provide any details concerning the procedures and reasons involved in Mr. Cole's arrest and detention, the Committee urged the Government to send its observations on these aspects of the case and to keep it informed of the development of the judicial case.

The Committee then set out its observations on the allegations of violations of the right to strike and the right to collective bargaining; forced entry into trade union premises; conscription of workers and anti-trade union discrimination against workers having exercised their right to strike in response to the non-payment of their wages; and the Government's refusal to negotiate in good faith on the matter of the wage backlog.

Regarding the allegations of breaking into the home of a trade union leader and the union's premises, the Committee emphasized that the rights of workers' and employers' organizations could only be exercised in a climate that was free from violence, pressure or threats of any kind against the leaders and members of such organizations. It was for governments to ensure that this principle was respected. In addition, the Committee reaffirmed that the entry by the public authorities into trade union premises without a judicial warrant constituted a serious and unjustifiable interference in trade union activities.

The Committee asked the Government to communicate without delay its observations on the CNTC's allegations so that it could examine these allegations in full knowledge of all the facts.

In the light of these conclusions, the Committee invited the Governing Body of the International Labour Office to approve a number of recommendations.

Deploring the Government's failure to provide any details concerning the procedures and reasons involved in Mr. Cole's arrest and detention, the Goverment was

II:3

urged to send its observations on these aspects of the case and to keep the Committee informed of the development of the judicial case.

Concerning the physical ill-treatment and torture allegedly inflicted on Mr. Cole, it was reaffirmed that the Government should give precise instructions to the effect that no detainee should be subjected to ill-treatment and it should apply effective sanctions where cases of ill-treatment were found. The Government was urged to set up an independent judicial inquiry and to send its observations concerning these allegations.

The Committee also set out its recommendations on the allegations of violations of the right to strike and the right to collective bargaining, of forced entry into trade union premises and of the Government's refusal to negotiate in good faith on the matter of the wage backlog.

(f) *Villagrán Morales* et al. case (*Guatemala*), the *"street children"* case (Inter-American Court of Human Rights)[79]

On 30 Ianuary 1997, the nter-American Commission on Human Rights submitted to the nter-American Court of Human Rights an application against the Republic of Guatemala. t originated in a petition received by the Commission on 15 September 1994, and it was based on the murder of Anstraum Aman Villagrán Morales and the abduction, torture and murder of four other youths, Henry Giovanni Contreras, Federico Clemente Figueroa Túnchez, Iulio Roberto Caal Sandoval and Iovito Iosué Iuárez Cifuentes. The alleged violations of the American Convention on Human Rights also included the failure of State mechanisms to deal appropriately with the violations and provide the families of the victims with access to justice.

The case was referred for the Court to determine whether Guatemala had violated, *inter alia*, the provisions on the right to humane treatment in article 5, the right to life in article 4 and the obligation in article 1 to respect the rights set forth in the Convention. As two of the victims were minors when abducted, tortured and murdered and one of them was a minor when killed, the Commission also alleged that the State had violated the provision on the rights of the child in article 19 of the Convention. Furthermore, in its application, the Commission cited violations of articles 1, 6 and 8 of the nter-American Convention to Prevent and Punish Torture.

---

[79] See Inter-American Court of Human Rights, Series C: *Decisions and Judgments*, No. 63 (2000), petition No. 11383, judgment of 19 November 1999.

II:3

Proceedings and conclusions of the Court

In coming to its conclusions, the Court received documentary evidence and heard the testimony of witnesses, including mothers of the victims, a street child, officials of the State's national police force and expert witnesses, on forensic science and on legal matters.

In relation to the alleged violation of article 5 of the Convention, the Court stated, *inter alia*, the following.

In its application, the Commission alleged that the State had violated article 5, because four of the victims had been abducted by State agents responsible for the physical integrity of the victims while they were in their custody. The Commission observed that so-called "street children" were subject to different forms of abuse and persecution by agents from certain State security forces and that it had previously referred to this situation in several of its reports. When answering the application during the proceeding, the State did not offer any defense regarding the violation of the right to humane treatment and, in particular, did not contest that the victims had been tortured.

In its final arguments, the Commission declared that the four young victims of torture had been retained incommunicado, a situation which, in itself, had clearly resulted in great anxiety and suffering. It made special reference to the tender age of the victims of torture in the case, two of them minors, 15 and 17 years old respectively, and to the fact that they had lived on the streets.

Furthermore, the Commission added that the circumstances surrounding the deaths of these youths had caused a great deal of suffering to the families of the victims. The way in which the bodies had been abandoned and the lack of information about the situation had caused the families anxiety and fear. In the Commission's opinion, the evidence made it clear that the authorities had not attempted to communicate with the families or to provide them with further information once the proceedings were underway.

The Court considered that the violation of article 5 of the Convention should be examined from two angles. It should decide whether or not article 5, paragraphs 1 and 2, had been violated to the detriment of four of the victims and it should decide whether or not the families of the victims had, themselves, been subjected to cruel, inhuman and degrading treatment.

The Court noted that there was considerable evidence that the physical integrity of these four youths had been violated and that before they died, they had been victims

II:3

of serious ill-treatment and physical and psychological torture by the State agents and, more specifically, members of the national police force.

The dead bodies of the youths had been found with signs of serious physical violence that the State had been unable to explain. The file contained photographs of the faces and necks of the bodies of the youths. In these photographs, different injuries were clearly visible, including those made by the bullets that were the cause of death and other signs of physical violence. The four autopsies identified the location of the bullet wounds and, in two cases, referred to other injuries that could be clearly seen in the photographs or were located in other parts of the bodies. These were attributed to animal bites. The size and depth of the wounds, the type of animal that could have produced them and whether the wounds had occurred before or after death had not been specified. The autopsies of the other two youths provided no explanation of the injuries to their bodies.

The Court referred to an Amnesty International report, included with the file and not contested by the State. In this report, it was mentioned, *inter alia*, that the bodies presented signs of torture: the ears and tongues had been cut off and the eyes had been burned or extracted. Furthermore, it appeared that some kind of burning liquid had been thrown on the chest and chin of one of the victims. According to the office of the Prosecutor-General, the mutilations, to which the four had been subjected, corresponded to the treatment that the police usually used on those who informed against this security force. It was concluded in the report that the mutilation of the ears, eyes and tongue signified that the person had heard or seen or spoken of something inadvisable.

One of the expert witnesses appearing before the Court had observed that there were no photographs of the whole body of any of the four victims. Regarding the injuries to the eyes, the expert witness stated that based on what could be seen in the photographs, in all cases, they were produced by the shots received in the head. Concerning the tongue of one of the victims, the only one that was visible in the photographs, he stated that although a little out of focus, he could not affirm that it had been mutilated. With regard to two of the bodies, this expert witness stressed that they bore wounds that were not found in the autopsy, although they were clearly visible in the photographs. Moreover, he stated that there were no signs that the youths had tried to defend themselves.

A witness who had given evidence in the domestic proceedings referred to facts that, taken in conjunction with statements of other witnesses and points from related documents, allowed the Court to infer the existence of a general pattern of violence against the "street children". This witness had described an abduction prior to the one that was the subject of this case. She and two of the victims in the present case had been taken to a cemetery, and she provided information on the painful mistreatment to which they had been submitted.

The Court recalled that the youths had been retained clandestinely by their captors for between 10 and 21 hours. This lapse of time had occurred between two extremely violent circumstances, forced seizure and then death from bullet wounds, which the Court had already declared proved. It was reasonable to conclude that the treatment they received during those hours was extremely aggressive, even if there was no other evidence in this regard.

While they were detained, the four youths were isolated from the external world and certainly aware that their lives were in danger. It was reasonable to infer that merely owing to these circumstances, they had experienced extreme psychological and moral suffering during those hours.

In this respect, the Court recalled that it had stated in a previous case that the mere fact of being placed in the trunk of a car constituted an infringement of article 5 of the Convention. Even if no other physical or ill treatment occurred, that action alone had clearly to be considered to contravene the respect due to the inherent dignity of the human person. In another case on the deprivation of liberty, the Court had stated that one of the reasons for incommunicado detention to be considered an exceptional instrument was the grave effects it had on the detained person. Indeed, isolation from the outside world produced moral and psychological suffering in any person, placed him in a particularly vulnerable position and increased the risk of aggression and arbitrary acts in prisons.

Similarly, the Court recalled, the European Court of Human Rights had stated that the mere threat of a behaviour prohibited by article 3 of the Convention for the Protection of Human Rights and Fundamental Freedoms, corresponding to article 5 of the American Convention on Human Rights, when it was sufficiently real and imminent, might in itself be in conflict with the norm. In other words, creating a threatening situation or threatening an individual with torture might, at least in some circumstances, constitute inhuman treatment.

The Court further recalled that it had previously stated that a person who had been unlawfully detained was extremely vulnerable and that there was a risk that his other rights, such as the right to humane treatment and to be treated with dignity, would be violated.

Finally, it was clear to the Court from the evidence that the events in this case had occurred in a context of great violence against children and youths who lived on the streets, violence that very often included different types of torture and ill-treatment.

II:3

It having been proved that the physical and mental integrity of the four youths had been violated and that they were victims of ill-treatment and torture, the Court proceeded to determine the responsibility for these violations.

The Court believed that the ill-treatment and torture was practised by the same persons who abducted and killed the youths. Since the Court had established that those responsible for these acts were members of the national police force, it was pertinent to conclude that the perpetrators of the ill-treatment and torture, carried out in the time between the seizure and the murders, were State agents, whether they were those investigated and charged in the domestic proceedings or others. In this respect, the Court referred to the presumption established by the European Court to the effect that the State was responsible for injuries inflicted on a person who had been in the custody of State agents if the authorities were incapable of demonstrating that those agents had not inflicted the injuries.

The Court then recalled the Commission's argument that the circumstances of the death of the five victims in the case, together with the lack of action by the State, had caused the victims' next of kin anxiety and also considerable fear.

In this respect, the Court made a number of deductions from the records of the proceedings and the statements of witnesses. Furthermore, it was evident that the national authorities had not taken any steps to establish the identity of the victims, who remained registered as XX until their next of kin had identified them, even though three of the youths had criminal records. The authorities had not made adequate efforts to locate the victims' next of kin, to notify them of their deaths, to deliver the bodies to them and to provide them with information on the development of the investigations. All these omissions had delayed and, in some cases, denied the next of kin the opportunity to bury the youths in accordance with their traditions, values and beliefs. Therefore, the suffering of all of the victims' families had been increased. Added to this was the feeling of insecurity and impotence caused to the next of kin by the failure of the authorities to fully investigate the crimes and punish those responsible.

The Court made particular reference to how the corpses of four of the youths had been treated. The bodies were discovered in a wood. The youths had not only been victims of extreme violence that had resulted in their deaths, but their bodies had also been abandoned in an uninhabited spot, exposed to the weather and to animals. It was clear that this treatment of the remains of the victims, sacred to their families, constituted cruel and inhuman treatment of the families.

The Court also recalled its statement in another case against the same State. The burning of the victim's mortal remains to destroy all traces that could reveal his whereabouts was an assault on the cultural values prevailing in Guatemalan society, handed down from generation to generation, with regard to respecting the dead. This action increased the suffering of the victim's relatives.

Finally, the Court referred to a judgment of the European Court in which it was ruled that the mother of a young woman, who had been abducted by State authorities and who had disappeared, was herself a victim of a violation of article 3 of the European Convention.

Owing to the foregoing, the Court concluded that the State had violated article 5, paragraphs 1 and 2, of the Convention, in relation to the obligation to respect rights in article 1, paragraph 1, to the detriment of four of the victims in the case, and violated article 5, paragraph 2, in relation to article 1, paragraph 1, to the detriment of the mothers of all five victims in the case. The Court also found violations of article 4 on the right to life and other articles of the Convention.

In relation to the alleged violations of articles 1, 6 and 8 of the Inter-American Convention to Prevent and Punish Torture, the Court stated, *inter alia*, the following.

The Court recalled that the Commission alleged that the State had also violated these provisions, because an investigation into the crime of torture had never been initiated, nor had the perpetrators been prosecuted or punished. This was in spite of the fact that the State was fully aware of the events and of the identity of two police officials against whom there was evidence that they had committed torture and other crimes. The Commission had also cited various provisions that established the obligation to investigate, prosecute and punish those responsible for the crime of torture, including articles 7 and 12 of the Convention against Torture and Other Cruel, Inhuman or Degrading Treatment or Punishment.

Under the Inter-American Convention to Prevent and Punish Torture, State parties were required, *inter alia*, to undertake to prevent and punish torture in accordance with the terms of the Convention (article 1); to ensure that all acts of torture and attempts to commit torture were offences under their criminal law and to make such acts punishable by severe penalties, taking into account their serious nature (article 6); and to guarantee that any person making an accusation of having been subjected to torture within their jurisdiction should have the right to an impartial examination of his case (article 8). Furthermore, if there was an accusation or well-grounded reason to believe that an act of torture had been committed within their jurisdiction, the States parties were to guarantee that their respective authorities would proceed properly and immediately to conduct an investigation into the case and to initiate, whenever appropriate, the corresponding criminal process.

II:3

Noting that Guatemala had accepted the jurisdiction of the Court and ratified the Inter-American Convention to Prevent and Punish Torture, the Court proceeded to interpret and apply the Convention in this particular case.

The Court observed that it was clear from the documents, testimonies and expert witness reports in the file, that the Guatemalan administrative and judicial authorities had not adopted any formal decision to initiate a criminal investigation into the alleged perpetration of the crime of torture, neither had they investigated it in practice, although a great deal of evidence had been collected on the cruel treatment and torture of the victims when the homicides were investigated.

Article 8 of the Convention expressly embodied the State's obligation to proceed *de oficio* and immediately in cases such as this one. The Court had previously declared that in proceedings on human rights violations, the State's defence could not rest on the impossibility of the plaintiff to obtain evidence that in many cases could not be obtained without the State's cooperation. However, the State had not acted in accordance with these provisions.

The Court concluded, therefore, that the State had violated articles 1, 6 and 8 of the Convention to the detriment of four of the youths.

Finally, the Court declared that the State had violated article 1, paragraph 1, of the American Convention on Human Rights regarding the obligation to investigate human rights violations. The State should conduct a real and effective investigation to determine the persons responsible for the human rights violations referred to in its judgment and eventually punish them.

(g) *Cantoral Benavides* case (*Peru*)
(Inter-American Court of Human Rights)[80]

On 8 August 1996, the Inter-American Commission on Human Rights submitted to the Inter-American Court of Human Rights an application against the Republic of Peru. It originated in a petition received by the Commission on 20 April 1994. It was based on the alleged violations of the American Convention of Human Rights suffered by Luis Alberto Cantoral Benavides due to the unlawful deprivation of his liberty, following his arbitrary detention and incarceration, cruel, inhuman and degrading treatment, violation of the judicial gurantees, as well as double jeopardy based on the same facts. The Court was requested to decide whether the State had violated, *inter alia*, the provisions on the right to humane treatment in article 5 of the Conven-

---

[80] *Ibidem*, No. 69 (2001), petition No. 11377, judgment of 18 August 2000.

tion. Furthermore, in its application, the Commission invoked violations of articles 2, 6 and 8 of the Inter-American Convention to Prevent and Punish Torture.

Proceedings and conclusions of the Court

During the proceedings, the Court considered documentary evidence and the evidence of witnesses, including the victim, his mother, a co-defendant of the victim, a judge, lawyers, journalists, representatives of human rights organizations and a retired commandant of the Peruvian police.

As to the alleged violation of article 5 of the Convention, the Court considered, *inter alia*, the following facts to have been proven.

On 6 February 1993, Mr. Cantoral Benavides was detained, without an arrest warrant issued by a competent authority, by agents of the national anti-terrorism bureau of the State's national police. At the time of the detention, a state of emergency was in effect in parts of the State's territory. A number of guarantees protected by the Peruvian Constitution had been suspended. Mr. Cantoral Benavides was held incommunicado at the bureau for eight or nine days, beginning on 6 February 1993, and it was not until 15 days after his detention that he was allowed to see a lawyer. While being held incommunicado, he was subjected, by the police and naval personnel, to acts of violence in order to get him to confess. He was, for example, blindfolded, cuffed with his hands behind his back, forced to remain standing, struck in several parts of his body and taken to the beach at night where he was subjected to physical and psychological torture. He was also held with animals at the veterinary section of a military base.

Two days after his detention at the police station, he was visited by a physician, but he was not examined thoroughly. He was displayed before the media, wearing the striped garb of a prisoner, as the perpetrator of the crime of treason even though he had not yet been legally tried or convicted. He was subjected to physical violence, including beatings with a club, during his transfer and upon his arrival at a prison. The first year of his incarceration, he spent in solitary confinement, in a small cell with no ventilation or natural light, being permitted to see his relatives only once a month, but denied physical contact with them. At the time of the arrest, physical and psychological aggression against people being investigated for the crimes of treason against the fatherland and terrorism was a common practice. The State had knowledge of the acts of physical and psychological aggression committed against Mr. Cantoral Benavides, yet no attempt was made to investigate them.

The Court noted that Mr. Cantoral Benavides had been held incommunicado for the first eight days of his detention. Under international human rights law, it had been

II:3

established that people were to be held incommunicado during detention only in exceptional situations and that such detention might constitute an act contrary to human dignity.

In a number of judgments, the Court had established that prolonged isolation and being held incommunicado constituted, in themselves, forms of cruel and inhuman treatment, harmful to the mental and moral integrity of the person and to the right of all detainees of respect for the inherent dignity of the human being. One reason for viewing the holding of a person incommunicado as an exceptional instrument was the serious impact it had on the detainee. Isolation from the outside world caused any person to suffer moral and psychological trauma, making him or her particularly vulnerable and increasing the risk of aggression and arbitrariness in jails.

Regarding prison conditions, the Court noted that the Human Rights Committee had held that the detention of a prisoner with other persons, in conditions that posed a threat to his or her health, constituted a violation of article 7 of the International Covenant on Civil and Political Rights.

Furthermore, the Court had stated that all persons detained had the right to live in prison conditions that were in keeping with personal dignity. The State had to guarantee their right to life and personal integrity. Consequently, the State, responsible for detention facilities, was the guarantor of these rights of detainees.

In the provisional measures related to the case of a woman tried in Peru at the same time as Mr. Cantoral Benavides for the crimes of treason and terrorism, the Court had concluded that the prison conditions for persons accused of such crimes did not comply with the provisions of the Convention. The State was ordered to modify the conditions in which she was being held, especially regarding her isolation in cell(s), for the purpose of bringing such conditions into line with the provisions of article 5 of the Convention. The Court also ordered the State to provide the prisoner with medical attention, both physical and psychological, as soon as possible.

The Court had established, in the same case, that holding a person incommunicado, public exhibition in defamatory clothing before the media, isolation in a small cell, without ventilation or natural light, and restriction of visiting rights constituted forms of cruel, inhuman and degrading treatment under article 5, paragraph 2, of the Convention.

The Court then considered the facts of the case in the context of practices prevailing at the time in Peru *vis-à-vis* persons accused of the crimes of treason and terrorism. It noted that in another judgment, it had affirmed that cruel, inhuman and degrading treatment during criminal investigations into the crimes of treason against the fatherland and terrorism then was common practice in Peru.

In this respect, the Court also recalled that the European Court of Human Rights had noted that article 3 of the Convention for the Protection of Human Rights and Fundamental Freedoms strictly prohibited torture and inhuman or degrading punishment or treatment regardless of what the victim had done. Article 3 did not provide for any exceptions, in contrast with most of the principles of that Convention, and did not permit derogation even in the case of a public danger threatening the life of the nation. The European Court had specified, on repeated occasions, that the prohibition applied even in the most difficult of circumstances for the State, such as those involving aggression by terrorist groups or large-scale organized crime.

Along the same lines, the Inter-American Court had warned that the fact that a State was confronted with terrorism should not lead to restrictions on the protection of the physical integrity of the person. Specifically, the Court had stated that any use of force not strictly necessary, given the behaviour of the person detained, constituted an affront to human dignity in violation of article 5 of the Convention. The need to conduct investigations and the undeniable difficulties inherent to combatting terrorism were not grounds for placing restrictions on the protection of the physical integrity of the person.

The European Court had underscored the fact that one of the elements considered in defining the term "torture" in article 1 of the Convention against Torture and Other Cruel, Inhuman or Degrading Treatment or Punishment was the intentional infliction of physical or mental pain or suffering for certain purposes, such as obtaining information from a person or intimidating or punishing him or her. The Inter-American Court recalled the definition of the term "torture" in article 2 of the Inter-American Convention to Prevent and Punish Torture.

Furthermore, the European Court had pointed out that certain acts in the past classified as inhuman or degrading treatment, but not as torture, in the future might be classified differently, i.e. as torture. The growing demand for the protection of fundamental rights and freedoms had to be accompanied by a more vigorous response in dealing with infractions of the basic values of democratic societies.

The Inter-American Court further observed that according to international standards, torture could be inflicted not only through physical violence, but also through acts that produced severe physical, psychological or moral suffering in the victim. In both the Convention against Torture and Other Cruel, Inhuman or Degrading Treatment or Punishment and the American Convention on Human Rights, reference was made to this possibility. Also, by institutionalizing the right to personal integrity, the

II:3

latter of these two international instruments made explicit reference to respect for the psychological and moral integrity of the person.

In the international jurisprudence, the notion of psychological torture had been developing. The European Court had established that the mere possibility of the commission of one of the acts prohibited in article 3 of the European Convention was sufficient to consider that the article had been violated, although the risk had to be real and imminent. In line with this, to threaten someone with torture might constitute, in certain circumstances, at least inhuman treatment. For the purposes of determining whether article 3 of the Convention had been violated, not only physical suffering, but also moral anguish had to be considered. Furthermore, having examined communications received from individuals, the Human Rights Committee had classified the threat of serious physical injury as a form of psychological torture.

The Inter-American Court concluded from the references it had recalled that a true international system prohibiting all forms of torture had been put in place.

Considering the circumstances of this case, and the context in which the events took place, the Court considered, beyond a reasonable doubt, that at least some of the acts of aggression examined in the case could be classified as physical and psychological torture. The Court also considered that the acts were planned and inflicted deliberately upon Mr. Cantoral Benavides for at least two purposes. Prior to his conviction, the purpose was to wear down his psychological resistance and force him to incriminate himself or to confess to certain illegal activities. After he was convicted, the purpose was to subject him to other types of punishment in addition to imprisonment.

Concerning the alleged violation of article 5, paragraphs 1 and 2, of the Convention *vis-à-vis* the relatives of the victim, the Court recognized that the situation his mother and brother went through as a result of his detention and imprisonment caused them severe suffering and anguish. It would assess this when setting necessary reparations for proven violations of the Convention.

The Court concluded that the State had violated, to the detriment of Mr. Cantoral Benavides, article 5, paragraphs 1 and 2, of the Convention. The Court also found violations of other articles of the Convention.

In relation to the alleged violations of articles 2, 6 and 8 of the Inter-American Convention to Prevent and Punish Torture, the Court stated, *inter alia*, the following.

Under that Convention, State parties were required, *inter alia*, to undertake to prevent and punish torture in accordance with the terms of the Convention (article 1); to ensure that all acts of torture and attempts to commit torture were offences under their criminal law and to make such acts punishable by severe penalties, taking into account their serious nature (article 6); and to guarantee that any person making an accusation of having been subjected to torture within their jurisdiction should have the right to an impartial examination of his case (article 8). Furthermore, if there was an accusation or well-grounded reason to believe that an act of torture had been committed within their jurisdiction, the States parties were to guarantee that their respective authorities would proceed properly and immediately to conduct an investigation into the case and to initiate, whenever appropriate, the corresponding criminal process.

The Court declared that in this case, it was appropriate for the Court to exercise its jurisdiction to apply this Convention, as it had done already on previous occasions.

The Commission alleged that Mr. Cantoral Benavides had been subjected to physical and psychological torture. The Court noted that on different occasions, the Peruvian authorities had been asked to investigate allegations of mistreatment or torture which had been proven in this case. However, the evidence revealed that the administrative and judicial authorities in Peru did not make a formal decision to initiate a criminal investigation of the alleged crime of torture. They did not conduct such an investigation despite the existence of evidence of cruel, inhuman and degrading treatment and of torture committed to the detriment of the victim.

After having studied the State's violation of article 5 of the American Convention on Human Rights, the Court concluded that Peru, through its State agents, had subjected Mr. Cantoral Benavides to torture and other cruel, inhuman and degrading treatment. Therefore, it was clear that the State had not effectively prevented such acts and, by not investigating them, had failed to punish those responsible.

Consequently, the Court concluded that the State had violated, to the detriment of Mr. Cantoral Benavides, articles 2, 6 and 8 of the Inter-American Convention to Prevent and Punish Torture.

Finally, the Court decided that the State should order an investigation to determine the persons responsible for the violations of human rights referred to in its judgment and punish them.

II:3

(h) *Aksoy* v. *Turkey*
(European Court of Human Rights)[81]

The case was referred to the European Court of Human Rights on 4 December 1995 by the Government of Turkey and on 12 December 1995 by the European Commission of Human Rights. It originated in an application against Turkey lodged with the Commission on 20 May 1993 by Zeki Aksoy, a Turkish citizen. The object of the Commission's request and of the Goverments's application was to obtain a decision as to whether the facts disclosed a breach by the respondent State of its obligations under, *inter alia*, article 3 of the Convention for the Protection of Human Rights and Fundamental Freedoms.

The facts

Mr. Aksoy was arrested by Turkish security forces towards the end of November 1992 and released on 10 December 1992. He was shot and killed on 16 April 1994, and thereafter his father indicated that he wished to pursue the case.

The Commission heard evidence from witnesses in Turkey, and it heard oral submissions on the admissibility and merits at hearings in Strasbourg. After evaluating the evidence, the Commission came to a number of conclusions with regard to the facts in the case.

It was not possible to make a definite finding as to the date on which Mr. Aksoy was arrested, although this clearly took place no later than 26 November 1992. He was released on 10 December 1992, and therefore he was detained for at least 14 days.

On 15 December 1992, he was admitted to hospital and diagnosed with bilateral radial paralysis. He left hospital on 31 December 1992 on his own initiative, without having been properly discharged. There was no evidence that he had suffered any disability prior to his arrest, nor any evidence of any untoward incident during the five days between his release from police custody and his admission to hospital.

The Commission noted that the medical evidence indicated that Mr. Aksoy's injuries could have various causes, but one of these could be the trauma suffered by a person who had been strung up by his arms. Moreover, radial paralysis affecting both arms was apparently not a common condition, although it was consistent with the form of ill-treatment known as "Palestinian hanging".

---

[81] See European Court of Human Rights, *Reports of Judgments and Decisions*, 1996-VI, p. 2260, application No. 21987/93, judgment of 18 December 1996.

As to evidence heard from one of the policemen who interrogated Mr. Aksoy and from the public prosecutor who saw him prior to his release, both claimed that it was inconceivable he could have been ill-treated in any way. The Commission found this evidence unconvincing, since it gave the impression that the two public officers were not prepared even to consider the possibility of ill-treatment occurring at the hands of the police. The Government offered no alternative explanation for Mr. Aksoy's injuries.

There was insufficient evidence to enable any conclusions to be drawn with regard to the applicant's other allegations of ill-treatment by electric shocks and beatings. However, it did seem clear that he was detained in a small cell with two other people, all of whom having to share a single bed and blanket, and that he was kept blindfolded during interrogation.

The law

In the circumstances, the Court considered that it should accept the facts as established by the Commission.

Concerning the alleged violation of article 3 of the Convention, the applicant claimed to have been subjected to treatment contrary to this provision. The Government considered the allegations of ill-treatment to be unfounded. The Commission, however, found that the applicant had been tortured.

Making reference to its case law, the Court considered that where an individual was taken into police custody in good health but found to be injured at the time of release, it was incumbent on the State to provide a plausible explanation as to the causing of the injury. Failing to do so, a clear issue arose under article 3 of the Convention.

Article 3, as the Court had observed on many occasions, enshrined one of the fundamental values of democratic society. Even in the most difficult of circumstances, such as the fight against terrorism and organized crime, the Convention prohibited in absolute terms torture or inhuman or degrading treatment or punishment. Unlike most of the substantive clauses of the Convention and of the first Protocol and Protocol No. 4 to the Convention, article 3 made no provision for exceptions, and no derogation from it was permissible under article 15, paragraph 2, even in the event of a public emergency threatening the life of the nation.

In order to determine whether any particular form of ill-treatment should be qualified as torture, the Court observed that it had to have regard to the distinction drawn in article 3 between this notion and that of inhuman or degrading treatment. As it

II:3

had remarked before, this distinction would appear to have been embodied in the Convention to allow the special stigma of torture to attach only to deliberate inhuman treatment causing very serious and cruel suffering.

The Court recalled that the Commission found, *inter alia,* that Mr. Aksoy had been subjected to "Palestinian hanging", in other words, that he had been stripped naked, with his arms tied together behind his back, and suspended by his arms.

In the view of the Court, this treatment could only have been deliberately inflicted. Indeed, a certain amount of preparation and exertion would have been required to carry it out. It would appear to have been administered with the aim of obtaining admissions or information from Mr. Aksoy. In addition to the severe pain it must have caused at the time, the medical evidence showed that it led to a paralysis of both arms lasting for some time. The Court considered that this treatment was of such a serious and cruel nature that it could only be described as torture.

In view of the gravity of this conclusion, the Court considered that it was not necessary for it to examine the applicant's complaints of other forms of ill-treatment. In conclusion, the Court held, by eight votes to one, that there had been a violation of article 3 of the Convention.

The Court also responded to other allegations submitted by the applicant. Those parts of the judgment are not included in this summary of the case.

As to the then article 50 of the Convention, allowing the Court to afford just satisfaction to an injured party, under specified circumstances, when there had been a violation of the Convention, the Court took the following decision. In view of the extremely serious violations of the Convention suffered by Mr. Aksoy and the anxiety and distress that these undoubtedly caused to his father, who had continued with the application after his son's death, the Court, by eight votes to one, decided to award the full compensation sought, pecuniary and non-pecuniary damage amounting to 4,283,450,000 Turkish lira, altogether. The applicant's claim for costs and expenses was also awarded.

(*i*) *Selmouni* v. *France*
(European Court of Human Rights)[82]

The case was referred to the European Court of Human Rights on 16 March 1998 by the European Commission of Human Rights and on 14 April 1998 by the Netherlands Government. It originated in an application against the French Republic

---

[82] *Ibidem*, 1999-V, p. 149, application No. 25803/94, judgment of 28 July 1999.

lodged with the Commission on 28 December 1992 by Ahmed Selmouni, a Netherlands and Moroccan national. The object of the Commission's request and of the Government's application was to obtain a decision as to whether the facts of the case disclosed a breach by the respondent State of its obligations under article 3 of the Convention for the Protection of Human Rights and Fundamental Freedoms, as well as of article 6, paragraph 1, on the right to a fair trial in respect of the length of the proceedings.

The facts

On 21 November 1991, the police arrested two men and a woman in connection with drug trafficking. One of the men told the police that he had bought heroin from a man in Amsterdam. He gave the police a telephone number in Amsterdam that enabled them to identify the applicant.

On 25 November 1991, Mr. Selmouni was arrested in Paris, but he denied any involvement in drug trafficking. He was held in police custody from 8.30 p.m. on the day of his arrest to 7 p.m. on 28 November 1991, and he was questioned by the police officials against whom he later made complaints.

Mr. Selmouni was questioned on five separate occasions on 26 November, between 12.40 a.m. and 11.30 p.m., and further questioned on 27 and 28 November. During that period he was medically examined at the casualty department of a hospital and on the police premises where he was being detained. He complained of being assaulted. On each occasion, bruising and tenderness were found on various parts of his body.

Following an examination on 29 November 1991, a doctor drew up a certificate to the effect that Mr. Selmouni claimed to have been assaulted. The certificate stated:

> Headaches, bruises under left and right eyes, on left and right arms, back, thorax, left and right thighs and left knee. All areas painful.

On the same day, the applicant was brought before an investigating judge, who charged him with offences against the dangerous drugs legislation and remanded him in custody. On 7 December, an expert in forensic medicine, apppointed by the investigating judge, because Mr. Selmouni had complained of assault, examined him in prison. Mr. Selmouni described to the doctor a series of assaults committed on him, consisting of punches, kicks and blows from a wooden instrument, by police officials during a series of interrogations at a police station.

II:3

The doctor noted in his report bruises, swellings, abrasions, lesions and superficial wounds to various parts of the body. The report, attached to the investigation file o-pened in respect of Mr. Selmouni, concluded that he had stated to have been ill-treated while in police custody and presented lesions of traumatic origin on his skin sustained at a time corresponding to the period of police custody. On 17 February 1992, the public prosecutor's office instructed the national police inspectorate to question the police officers concerned.

On 1 December 1992, when interviewed in prison by an officer of the inspectorate, Mr. Selmouni described in his statement how he was arrested at gun point by two police officials at about 8.30 p.m. on 25 November 1991. He said he was then taken to his hotel room and that whilst the police officials were searching his room, one of the officers punched him on the left temple. He was subsequently taken to a drugs squad station where he was subjected to a body search. His interrogation by five po-lice officials then began.

Mr. Selmouni went on to describe a series of brutalities and assaults he alleged were committed by police officials during the interrogation sessions that took place on the nights of 25 and 26 November 1991. On the first night, these included being made to kneel on the floor and having his hair pulled; being struck in the ribs with a stick re-sembling a baseball bat and continuously tapped on the head with the bat; being punched; and having his feet crushed by police officials standing on them. The state-ment continued with an account of what happened on the following night. It de-scribed how the officer he presumed to be in charge, a detective chief inspector, grabbed him by the hair and made him run along a corridor while the others posi-tioned themselves on either side, tripping him up. He then related how the police of-ficials took him into an office where a woman was sitting and made him kneel down; how they pulled his hair, saying to the woman, "look, you're going to hear somebody sing"; how he was taken back into the corridor where one of the police officers took out his penis and came up to him saying, "here, suck this"; and how that officer then urinated over him.

Other brutalities and indignities alleged to have taken place during the second ses-sion of interrogation included the placing of two ignited blowlamps close to his shoeless feet; being threatened with injection by a syringe; and, after being told by one of the police officials, "you Arabs enjoy being screwed", being made to undress and having a small black truncheon inserted into his anus by a police official. At the latter point, the officer of the inspectorate noted that Mr. Selmouni started crying when relating the scene.

Mr. Selmouni's statement referred to medical examinations between the interroga-tion sessions, at a hospital where he was taken by two uniformed police officials after complaining to them of injuries sustained during the night of 25 November and later by a doctor on the premises of the drugs squad. He stated that he could identify the police officials having mistreated him and describe the part played by each one. The record of the interview was sent to the public prosecutor on 2 December 1992.

On 7 December 1992, a criminal court sentenced the applicant to 15 years' imprisonment and permanent exclusion from French territory. On 16 September 1993, a court of appeal reduced the prison sentence to 13 years.

On 1 February 1993, the applicant lodged a criminal complaint together with an application to join the criminal proceedings as a civil party. He adduced assault occasioning actual bodily harm resulting in total unfitness for work for more than eight days; assault and wounding with a weapon, namely a baseball bat; indecent assault; assault occasioning permanent disability; and rape aided and abetted by two or more accomplices, all of which offences committed between 25 and 29 November 1991 by police officers in the performance of their duties. On 27 April 1993, the investigating judge to whom the case had been allocated instructed the director of the national police inspectorate to investigate the case.

On 9 June 1993, the forensic medicine expert re-examined Mr. Selmouni at the request of the investigating judge. On that occasion, Mr. Selmouni said that he did not mention the sexual assault previously, because he felt ashamed of it. An examination of the anal sphincter did not reveal any lesion such as to corroborate or invalidate Mr. Selmouni's statements, mainly owing to the amount of time elapsed since the alleged acts.

The medical doctor reported that the lesions recorded in the first medical certificate did necessitate sick leave on grounds of total unfitness for work of five days. As Mr. Selmouni had claimed that his sight in his left eye was impaired, the doctor stated that an examination by an eye specialist was necessary if to establish a causal link with the alleged acts.

At an identity parade organized on 10 February 1994 to identify the police officials against whom the allegations were made, Mr. Selmouni picked out four officials from the ten who took part.

The case was subsequently transferred to a judge of a *tribunal de grande instance* in the interests of the proper administration of justice. On 21 June 1994, the public prosecutor reopened the investigation into offences of assault by public servants occasioning total unfitness for work for more than eight days and sexual assault by

II:3

several assailants or accomplices against any persons identified as a result of the investigation.

On 19 September 1995, Mr. Selmouni underwent an operation on his left eye, and a few days later the investigating judge appointed an eye specialist to examine him. The specialist's report, filed on 18 January 1996, included the observation that Mr. Selmouni's eyesight had deteriorated since the operation, but it could not be said with certainty that it really deteriorated between 25 November 1991 and the end of September 1995.

On 21 October 1996, the investigating judge officially informed the police officials implicated by the applicant that they were being placed under investigation for assault by public servants occasioning total unfitness for work for more than eight days and for sexual assault.

On 24 April 1998, in view of the denials by the police officials maintaining that a struggle ensued when Mr. Selmouni was arrested, the investigating judge instructed the forensic medicine expert to examine all Mr. Selmouni's medical files and certificates. The expert was requested to give his opinion as to whether the injuries found could have been caused in a struggle when Mr. Selmouni was arrested, or they supported the applicant's allegations.

The expert's report, filed on 3 July 1998, concluded that an examination of the medical file showed that a number of the injuries could have been caused during a struggle when the applicant was arrested. However, some would certainly have been sustained after that arrest and support the applicant's statements. As regarded the acts of sodomy, the negative result of the test carried out in June 1993 neither disproved nor proved that they had occurred. The investigation file was sent to the public prosecutor's office on 15 September 1998.

On 21 October 1998, the investigating judge committed the four police officials concerned for trial at a criminal court on charges of assault occasioning total unfitness for work for less than eight days and indecent assault committed collectively and with violence and coercion.

On 25 March 1999, the police officers were convicted of the offences charged. The court considered itself bound to apply the criminal law in a way that would serve as an example to others and sentenced three of the police officials to three years' imprisonment. The court deemed it necessary to punish the fourth police official, the detective chief inspector, more severely, because he had been in charge of the group and responsible for the conduct of the investigation. He was sentenced to four years' imprisonment. The police officials appealed.

In a judgment of 8 April 1999, a court of appeal dismissed an application for release made by the detective chief inspector. The offences in question had resulted in serious and continuing prejudice to public order because of their exceptionally serious nature, having regard to the status, the accused possessed, of senior police official responsible for enforcing the laws of the Republic.

Subsequently, in a judgment of 1 July 1999, after which the detective chief inspector was released, the court of appeal acquitted the policemen for lack of evidence on the charge of indecent assault. However, it held them to be guilty of assault and wounding with or under the threat of the use of a weapon, occasioning total unfitness for work for less than eight days by police officers in the course of their duty and without legitimate reason. It sentenced the detective chief inspector to 18 months' imprisonment, of which 15 months were suspended. Two of the other police officials were sentenced to 15 months' imprisonment suspended and the fourth to 12 months' imprisonment suspended. Concerning the sentence, the court of appeal stated, *inter alia*, that the defendants were guilty of offences being exceptionally serious, to be regarded as instances of particularly degrading treatment. Having been committed by senior officials responsible for enforcing the laws of the Republic, they had to be punished firmly. Such conduct could not be justified, irrespective of the personality of the offenders in their charge and the degree of their corruption and dangerousness.

The law

In its application to the Commission, Mr. Selmouni alleged a violation of articles 3 and 6, paragraph 1, of the Convention. The Commission expressed the unanimous opinion that there had been a violation of these provisions.

With respect to the complaint based on article 3 of the Convention, the Government asked the Court to state that the applicant had failed to exhaust domestic remedies and, in the alternative, that the offences with which the police officers in question were charged could not be classified as torture. The Government acknowledged that the total length of the proceedings was excessive from the standpoint of article 6, paragraph 1.

Concerning the alleged violation of article 3 of the Convention, the applicant complained that the manner in which he had been treated while in police custody had given rise to a violation of this article.

The Government's main submission was that the complaint based on article 3 could not be examined by the Court, because the applicant had not exhausted domestic remedies. In support of this submission, it cited previous cases before the Commis-

II:3

sion and the Court. It concluded that the excessive length of time taken to examine the applicant's complaint could not *ipso facto* lead to a finding that the remedy was ineffective; that due consideration should be given in the present case to the fact that the police officers in question were having to answer for their acts before the national criminal courts; and that the application brought before the Court was therefore premature.

The applicant replied that he had satisfied the obligation to exhaust domestic remedies, and he indicated how this had been done.

It was the opinion of the Court that the issue was not so much whether there had been an inquiry, but as to whether the inquiry had been conducted diligently, whether the authorities had been determined to identify and prosecute those responsible and, accordingly, whether the inquiry had been effective. It considered that Mr. Selmouni's allegations were particularly serious in respect of both the alleged facts and the status of the persons implicated. The Court concluded that the authorities had not taken the positive measures required in the circumstances of the case to ensure that the remedy referred to by the Government was effective and that the Government's objection on grounds of failure to exhaust domestic remedies could not be upheld.

As to the merits of the complaint, the applicant described the various forms of ill-treatment to which he had been subjected. He submitted that the medical evidence established a causal link with the events that occurred while he was in police custody and gave credibility to his allegations.

The Commission considered that the medical certificates and reports, drawn up in total independence by medical practitioners, attested to the large number of blows inflicted on the applicant and their intensity.

In its observations in the alternative, the Government pointed out that there was not yet a final ruling in respect of the offences alleged. The police officers in question should have the benefit of the presumption of innocence, in accordance with article 6, paragraph 2, of the Convention.

Making reference to its case law, the Court considered that where an individual taken into police custody in good health was found to be injured at the time of release, it was incumbent on the State to provide a plausible explanation of how those injuries were caused. If failing to do so, a clear issue arose under article 3 of the Convention. It also pointed out that in his criminal complaint and application to join the proceedings as a civil party, Mr. Selmouni directed his allegations against the police officers in question and that the issue of their guilt was a matter for the jurisdiction of the French courts, in particular the criminal courts, alone. Whatever the outcome of the domestic proceedings, the police officers' conviction or acquittal did not absolve the respondent State from its responsibility under the Convention. It was accordingly under an obligation to provide a plausible explanation of how Mr. Selmouni's injuries were caused.

The Court considered that it should accept, in the main, the facts as established by the Commission. However, the Court's analysis differed from the Commission's opinion, because it considered, unlike the Commission, that it was required to rule on those of the allegations in Mr. Selmouni's statements that were not supported by the medical reports. In that connection, it noted that the Government submitted arguments in the alternative on the seriousness of the facts and the ways in which they might be classified under article 3 of the Convention. In those observations, the Government debated the seriousness of the alleged injuries, but it did not at any time contest the other facts alleged by Mr. Selmouni. Accordingly, the Court was of the opinion that with regard to the complaint submitted to it, those facts could be assumed to have been established.

The Court considered, however, that it had not been proved that Mr. Selmouni was raped, as the allegation was made too late for it to be proved or disproved by medical evidence. Likewise, a causal link could not be established on the basis of the medical report between the applicant's alleged loss of visual acuity and the events that occurred during police custody.

As to the gravity of the treatment, the applicant submitted, *inter alia*, that the threshold of severity required for the application of article 3 of the Convention was attained in the present case. He considered that the motive for the police officials' actions was to obtain a confession. He contended that the police officials deliberately ill-treated him, given their constant questioning by day and, above all, by night.

The applicant submitted that he had been subjected to both physical and mental ill-treatment. In his view, it was well known that such police practices existed. They required preparation, training and deliberate intent and were designed to obtain a confession or information. He argued that in the light of the facts of the case, the severity and cruelty of the suffering inflicted on him justified classifying the acts as torture within the meaning of article 3 of the Convention.

The Commission considered that the blows inflicted on the applicant had caused him actual injuries and acute physical and mental suffering. In its opinion, that treatment must have been inflicted on him deliberately and, moreover, with the aim of obtaining a confession or information. In the Commission's view, such treatment was of such a serious and cruel nature that it could only be described as torture, without it

II:3

being necessary to give an opinion regarding the other offences, in particular of rape, alleged by the applicant.

The Government contended, in the light of both the Court's case law and the circumstances of the case, that the ill-treatment allegedly inflicted by the police officers did not amount to torture within the meaning of article 3 of the Convention.

The Court reiterated, making reference to its case law, that article 3 enshrined one of the most fundamental values of democratic societies. Even in the most difficult circumstances, such as the fight against terrorism and organized crime, the Convention prohibited in absolute terms torture and inhuman or degrading treatment or punishment. Article 3 made no provision for exceptions, and no derogation from it was permissible under article 15, paragraph 2, even in the event of a public emergency threatening the life of the nation.

In order to determine whether a particular form of ill-treatment should be qualified as torture, the Court had to have regard to the distinction, embodied in article 3, between this notion and that of inhuman or degrading treatment. As the Court had previously found, it appeared to have been the intention that the Convention should, by means of this distinction, attach a special stigma to deliberate inhuman treatment causing very serious and cruel suffering. In this context, the Court referred to articles 1 and 16 of the Convention against Torture and Other Cruel, Inhuman or Degrading Treatment or Punishment, also expressing such a distinction

The Court found that all the injuries recorded in the various medical certificates and the applicant's statements regarding the ill-treatment while in police custody established the existence of physical and, undoubtedly, mental pain or suffering, notwithstanding the regrettable failure, after the events complained of, to order a psychological report on Mr. Selmouni. The course of the events also showed that the pain or suffering was inflicted on the applicant intentionally for the purpose of, *inter alia*, making him confess to the offence that he was suspected of having committed. Lastly, the medical certificates showed clearly that the numerous acts of violence were directly inflicted by police officers in the performance of their duties.

The acts complained of were such as to arouse in the applicant feelings of fear, anguish and inferiority capable of humiliating and debasing him and possibly breaking his physical and moral resistance. Therefore, making reference to its case law, the Court found elements sufficiently serious to render such treatment inhuman and degrading. In any event, the Court reiterated that in respect of a person deprived of his liberty, recourse to physical force not being made strictly necessary by his own conduct diminished human dignity. It was in principle an infringement of the right set forth in article 3 of the Convention.

194

In other words, it remained to be established in the instant case whether the pain or suffering inflicted on Mr. Selmouni could be defined as severe within the meaning of article 1 of the Convention against Torture. The Court considered that this severity was, like the minimum severity required for the application of article 3, in the nature of things, relative. It depended on all the circumstances of the case, such as the duration of the treatment, its physical or mental effects and, in some cases, the sex, age and state of health of the victim.

The Court had previously examined cases and concluded that there had been treatment which could only be described as torture. However, having regard to the fact that the Convention was a living instrument to be interpreted in the light of present-day conditions, the Court considered that certain acts classified in the past as inhuman and degrading treatment as opposed to torture could be classified differently in the future. It took the view that the increasingly high standard being required in the area of the protection of human rights and fundamental liberties correspondingly and inevitably required greater firmness in assessing breaches of the fundamental values of democratic societies.

The Court was satisfied that a large number of blows were inflicted on Mr. Selmouni. Whatever a person's state of health, it could be presumed that such intensity of blows would cause substantial pain. Moreover, a blow did not automatically leave a visible mark on the body. However, it could be seen from the report of the forensic medicine expert of 7 December 1991 that the marks of the violence Mr. Selmouni had endured covered almost all of his body.

The Court also noted that the applicant was dragged along by his hair; that he was made to run along a corridor with police officers positioned on either side to trip him up; that he was made to kneel down in front of a young woman to whom someone said, "look, you're going to hear somebody sing"; that one police officer then showed him his penis, saying, "here, suck this", before urinating over him; and that he was threatened with a blowlamp and then a syringe. Besides the violent nature of the above acts, the Court was bound to observe that they would be heinous and humiliating for anyone, irrespective of their condition.

The Court noted, lastly, that the above events were not confined to any one period of police custody during which, without this in any way justifying them, heightened tension and emotions might have led to such excesses. It had been clearly established that Mr. Selmouni endured repeated and sustained assaults over a number of days of questioning.

Under these circumstances, the Court was satisfied that the physical and mental violence, considered as a whole, committed against the applicant's person caused se-

II:3

vere pain and suffering and was particularly serious and cruel. Such conduct must be regarded as acts of torture for the purposes of article 3 of the Convention. It concluded, therefore, that there had been a violation of this provision.

Concerning the alleged violation of article 6, paragraph 1, of the Convention, the applicant held that the proceedings in respect of his complaint against the police officers were not conducted within a reasonable time as required by this article.

The Court considered that the period to be taken into consideration in examining the length of the proceedings with regard to the requirement "reasonable time" laid down in article 6, paragraph 1, of the Convention began when the applicant expressly lodged a complaint while being interviewed by an officer of the national police inspectorate, i.e. on 1 December 1992. The Court noted that this simple form of criminal complaint was a remedy afforded by French law. The public prosecutor was informed of the applicant's complaint as early as 2 December 1992, when the record of the interview by the officer was transferred to him. Having regard to the nature and extreme seriousness of the alleged acts, the Court did not consider that it should take 1 February 1993 as the starting-point, the date on which the applicant lodged a criminal complaint and an application to join the proceedings as a civil party, or, *a fortiori*, the date on which that complaint and application were registered.

The Court considered that the reasonableness of the length of proceedings was to be assessed in the light of the particular circumstances of the case, regard being had to the criteria laid down in the Court's case law, in particular the complexity of the case and the conduct of the applicant and of the relevant authorities. Having heard the arguments of the applicant, the Government and the Commission on this point, the Court agreed with the applicant that neither the complexity of the case nor the applicant's conduct justified the length of the proceedings.

As it had already noted in respect of the preceding complaint, the Court reiterated that where an individual had an arguable claim that there had been a violation of article 3 of the Convention, the notion of an effective remedy entailed, on the part of the State, a thorough and effective investigation capable of leading to the identification and punishment of those responsible.

The Court considered that the overall length of the proceedings was excessive. It concluded that the reasonable time prescribed by article 6, paragraph 1, of the Convention had been exceeded. Accordingly, there had been a violation of this provision on account of the length of the proceedings.

As to article 41 of the Convention, allowing the Court to afford just satisfaction to the injured party, under specified circumstances, when there had been a violation of the Convention, the Court considered that the applicant had suffered personal injury and non-pecuniary damage for which the findings of violations in the judgment did not afford sufficient satisfaction. It awarded him 500,000 French francs. It also considered reasonable the applicant's claim for costs and expenses incurred before the Commission and the Court, namely 113,364 francs. It awarded him that amount in full, less the amounts received in legal aid from the Council of Europe that had not already been taken into account in the claim.

4. Right to Liberty and Security of Person

A. INTRODUCTION

The powers to arrest people and to detain them subsequent to arrest are fundamental to the purposes of policing. These are necessary powers for the purposes of preventing and investigating crime and for maintaining and restoring public order. In many jurisdictions, police are also empowered to deprive certain people of their liberty for their own protection. These include juveniles, people of unsound mind as well as alcoholics and drug addicts.

Article 9 of the Universal Declaration of Human Rights provides that no one shall be subjected to arbitrary arrest, detention or exile. The terms "arrest" and "detention" are not defined in the Universal Declaration or in the human rights treaties referred to in this publication, but they are defined in a non-treaty instrument, the Body of Principles for the Protection of All Persons under Any Form of Detention or Imprisonment. For the purposes of this instrument, "arrest" means the act of apprehending a person for the alleged commission of an offence or by the action of an authority. A "detained person" means any person deprived of personal liberty except as a result of conviction for an offence, and "detention" means the condition of detained persons defined in this way. The terms "imprisoned person" and "imprisonment" refer to any person deprived of personal liberty as a result of conviction for an offence and to the condition of such an imprisoned person, respectively.

At the same time as recognizing the necessity and significance of power to deprive people of their liberty for the purposes of policing, it is also important to acknowledge that the right to liberty of person is a fundamental human right. It is enshrined in article 3 of the Universal Declaration, stating that everyone has the right to life, liberty and security of person. Other articles of the Universal Declaration that deal with liberty of person are article 10 on right to a fair trial, article 11 expressing the presumption of innocence and other principles of criminal proceedings and article 13 protecting the right to freedom of movement.

Furthermore, universal and regional human rights treaties protect personal liberty by stipulating that everyone has the right to liberty and security of person and by prohibiting arbitrary arrest or detention and unlawful deprivations of liberty. Such provisions are, for example, article 9 of the International Covenant on Civil and Politi-

II:4

cal Rights, article 37 of the Convention on the Rights of the Child, article 6 of the African Charter on Human and Peoples' Rights, article 7 of the American Convention on Human Rights and article 5 of the Convention for the Protection of Human Rights and Fundamental Freedoms. They also bestow a number of other rights on people who have been deprived of their liberty, designed to ensure the lawfulness and necessity of their arrest or detention. Additionally, there are non-treaty instruments with provisions on different aspects of the right to liberty and security of person, instruments like the United Nations Rules for the Protection of Juveniles Deprived of their Liberty and the Declaration on the Protection of All Persons from Enforced Disappearance.

The right to liberty and security of person does not express general principles of international law of the same absolute nature as the right to life and the prohibition of torture. Some instruments protecting the right to liberty and security of person allow States to derogate from their obligations in respect of this right. Under article 4 of the Covenant, for example, States parties may take such measures in time of public emergency threatening the life of the nation. However, in any event, the right to liberty and security of person does express principles of great significance to any police agency seeking high professional standards.

The meanings of the term "security of person" in this context, the term "arbitrary" and indeed other terms used in these treaties and non-treaty instruments are elucidated in the cases summarized and/or reviewed in this chapter of the book.

B. REVIEW OF CASES

(*a*) Human Rights Committee

The right to liberty and security of person is protected by article 9 of the International Covenant on Civil and Political Rights. Under paragraph 1, everyone has the right to liberty and security of person. No one shall be subjected to arbitrary arrest or detention, and no one shall be deprived of his liberty except on such grounds and in accordance with such procedures as are established by law.

The remaining four paragraphs of this article require, *inter alia*, those arrested to be informed, at the time of arrest, of the reasons for their arrest and, promptly, of any charges against them (paragraph 2); those arrested or detained on a criminal charge to be brought promptly before a judge or other judicial officer and entitled to trial within a reasonable time or to release (paragraph 3); those arrested or detained to have an entitlement to test the lawfulness of their detention before a court (paragraph 4); and compensation for victims of unlawful arrest or detention (paragraph 5).

II:4

In time of public emergency threatening the life of the nation, States parties may take measures derogating from their obligations under article 9, but only on the conditions set forth in article 4 of the Covenant.

The right to liberty of person needs to be contrasted with the right to liberty of movement protected by article 12 of the Covenant. This article protects the right of everyone lawfully within the territory of a State to liberty of movement and freedom to choose his residence, and it protects the freedom of everyone to leave any country, including his own. Paragraph 3 of the article stipulates that these rights may not be subject to restrictions other than those prescribed by law and necessary to protect national security, public order, public health or morals or the rights and freedoms of others, and they have to be consistent with the other rights recognized in the Covenant. Article 12, paragraph 4, prohibits arbitrary deprivation of the right of a person to enter his own country. In its general comment No. 27 (67) on article 12, the Human Rights Committee pointed out that freedom of movement was an indispensible condition for the free development of a person.[1] Whilst distinguishing between the provisions of articles 9 and 12 of the Covenant, the Committee observed that in some circumstances they might come into play together.[2]

However, it is clear from the case *Ismet Celepli* v. *Sweden*[3] that article 9, paragraph 1, of the Covenant concerns severe restrictions on liberty, such as arrest or detention, rather than mere restrictions on liberty of movement

The author, a Turkish citizen of Kurdish origin, arrived in Sweden in 1975 and obtained permission to stay there, but he was not granted refugee status. On 10 December 1984, an expulsion order against him was issued under aliens legislation, but it was not enforced, as it was believed that he could become exposed to political persecution upon his return to Turkey. Instead, the Swedish authorities prescribed limitations and conditions concerning his place of residence, namely that he was confined to his home municipality (a town of 10,000 inhabitants 25 kilometres south of Stockholm) and had to report to the police three times a week. He could not leave or change his town of residence, nor change employment, without prior permission from the police. The restrictions on Mr. Celepli's freedom of movement were reviewed several times and finally abolished in 1990. The author did not invoke any specific provisions, but it appeared that he claimed to be a victim of a violation by Sweden of, *inter alia*, articles 9 and 12 of the Covenant.

---

[1] See United Nations, *Official Records of the General Assembly, Fifty-fifth Session, Supplement No. 40* (A/55/40), vol. I, annex VI, sect. A, para. 1.

[2] *Ibidem*, para. 7.

[3] *Ibidem, Forty-ninth Session, Supplement No. 40* (A/49/40), vol. II, annex IX, sect. Z, communication No. 456/1991, views adopted on 18 July 1994.

II:4

The Committee declared that his claim under article 9 was inadmissible, as it was incompatible with the provisions of that article. As to article 12, the communication was declared admissible. However, bearing in mind that the State party had invoked reasons of national security to justify the restrictions on Mr. Celepli's freedom of movement, the Committee found that the restrictions to which he was subjected were compatible with those allowed pursuant to article 12, paragraph 3, of the Covenant. As already indicated, this provision allows States parties to place legal restrictions on the right to liberty of movement provided that they are necessary to protect, *inter alia*, national security and are consistent with the other rights recognized in the Covenant.

The case *W. Delgado Páez* v. *Colombia*,[4] summarized in section C,[5] concerned, *inter alia*, the right to security of person. The author, William Eduardo Delgado Páez, a Colombian national, was appointed in 1983 to be teacher of religion and ethics at a secondary school. He alleged to have been a victim of discrimination by the authorities because of his social views. After having received death threats and been attacked personally, he left Colombia and obtained political asylum in France in 1986. He claimed to be a victim of a number of violations of the Covenant.

It is a landmark case in which the Committee reasoned that the concept of right to security did not apply only to situations of formal deprivation of liberty, even though it was expressed in an article addressing such situations. The Committee argued that States could not be allowed to ignore known threats to the life of persons within their jurisdiction, just because he or she was not arrested or detained. States parties to the Covenant had a duty to take reasonable and appropriate measures to protect people whose lives had been threatened. The Committee found that Colombia in this case had not taken, or had been unable to take, appropriate measures to ensure Mr. Delgado's right to security of his person under article 9, paragraph 1, of the Covenant.

In the case *Barbarín Mojica* v. *the Dominican Republic*,[6] the author, a citizen of the Dominican Republic and well-known labour leader, alleged that his son, Rafael Mojica, disappeared on 6 May 1990 following death threats from military officers. According to witnesses, he boarded a taxi in which other, unidentified, men were trav-

---

[4] *Ibidem, Forty-fifth Session, Supplement No. 40* (A/45/40), vol. II, annex IX, sect. D, communication No. 195/1985, views adopted on 12 July 1990.

[5] See part II, chap. 4, sect. C (*a*) (*infra*, pp. 244-246).

[6] See United Nations, *Official Records of the General Assembly, Forty-ninth Session, Supplement No. 40* (A/49/40), vol. II, annex IX, sect. W, communication No. 449/1991, views adopted on 15 July 1994.

elling. It was presumed that he had been killed. The author's claims under articles 6, 7 and 9, paragraph 1, of the Covenant were declared admissible.

In finding a violation by the Dominican Republic of article 9, paragraph 1, of the Covenant, the Committee pointed out that it had held in its prior jurisprudence that the right to liberty and security of person might be invoked not only in the context of arrest and detention. An interpretation which would allow States parties to tolerate, condone or ignore threats made by persons in authority to the personal liberty and security of non-detained individuals within the State party's jurisdiction would render ineffective the guarantees of the Covenant. The Committee concluded that the State party had failed to ensure Rafael Mojica's right under this provision.

In respect of article 6, paragraph 1, of the Covenant, protecting the right to life, the Committee recalled its general comment No. 6 (16) concerning article 6, in which it had stated, *inter alia*, that States parties should take specific and effective measures to prevent the disappearance of individuals and establish effective facilities and procedures to investigate thoroughly cases of missing and disappeared persons in circumstances that might involve a violation of that right.[7] It observed that the State party in this case had not denied that the disappearance of Rafael Mojica was caused by individuals belonging to the Government's security forces. In the circumstances, the Committee found that the right to life enshrined in article 6 had not been effectively protected by the Dominican Republic, especially considering that this was a case where the victim's life had previously been threatened by military officers.

As to article 7 of the Covenant, prohibiting torture and cruel, inhuman or degrading treatment or punishment, the Committee noted that the circumstances in the case gave rise to a strong inference that Rafael Mojica had been subjected to such treatment. Aware of the nature of enforced or involuntary disappearances in many countries, the Committee felt confident in concluding that the disappearance of persons was inseparably linked to treatment that amounted to a violation of that provision.

Pursuant to article 2, paragraph 3, of the Covenant, the Committee urged the State party to investigate thoroughly the disappearance of Rafael Mojica, to bring to justice those responsible for his disappearance and to pay appropriate compensation to his family.

In considering the merits of a more recent case involving the enforced disappearance of a person, *Sarma* v. *Sri Lanka*,[8] the Committee cited the definition of that phenom-

---

[7] *Ibidem, Thirty-seventh Session, Supplement No. 40* (A/37/40), annex V, para. 4.
[8] *Ibidem, Fifty-eighth Session, Supplement No. 40* (A/58/40), vol. II, annex V, sect. V, communication No. 950/2000, views adopted on 16 July 2003.

II:4

enon set out in article 7, paragraph 2 (*i*), of the Rome Statute of the International Criminal Court. The definition is referred to in the introduction to this part of the book where situations of disappearance are discussed in more detail.[9] The author, S. Jegatheeswara Sarma, a Sri Lankan citizen, claimed that his son, J. Thevaraja Sarma, was a victim of a violation by Sri Lanka of articles 6, 7, 9 and 10 of the Covenant and that he and his family also were victims of a violation of article 7.

The author alleged that his son, himself and three others were detained on 23 June 1990 by military personnel. The author's son was apparently suspected of being a member of the Liberation Tigers of Tamil Eelam (LTTE). Whilst in military detention, he was allegedly tortured, hooded and forced to identify other suspects. In fact, the author and other detainees were forced to parade before the author's hooded son before being released. In May 1991, the author's wife was told that her son was dead. The author, however, claimed that he saw his son on 9 October 1991 in a military van. As the author tried to talk to him, the son signalled with his head to prevent his father from approaching.

The Committee noted that the State party had not denied that J. Thevaraja Sarma was abducted on 23 June 1990 by an officer of the Sri Lankan army and had remained unaccounted for since then. It concluded that in the circumstances, the State party was responsible for the disappearance of the author's son.

Noting the definition of enforced disappearance of persons, contained in article 7, paragraph 2 (*i*), of the Rome Statute, the Committee observed that any act of such disappearance constituted a violation of many of the rights enshrined in the Covenant. These included the right to liberty and security of person in article 9; the right not to be subjected to torture or to cruel, inhuman or degrading treatment or punishment in article 7; and the right of all persons deprived of their liberty to be treated with humanity and with respect for the inherent dignity of the human person in article 10. It also violated or constituted a grave threat to the right to life set forth in article 6.

The facts of the present case, the Committee stated, clearly illustrated the applicability of the provisions on liberty and security of person in article 9 of the Covenant. The State party had itself acknowledged that the arrest of J. Thevaraja Sarma was illegal. Not only was there no legal basis for his arrest, there evidently was none for the continuing detention. Such a gross violation of article 9 could never be justified. In the Committee's opinion, the facts before it clearly revealed a violation of that ar-

---

[9] See part II, chap. 1 (*supra*, pp. 36-38).

ticle in its entirety. The Committee also found a violation by Sri Lanka of article 7 of the Covenant, both with regard to J. Thevaraja Sarma and to his parents.

As to the possible violation of article 6 of the Covenant, the Committee noted that the author had not asked the Committee to conclude that his son was dead. Moreover, while invoking article 6, the author also asked for the release of his son, indicating that he had not abandoned hope for his son's reappearance. The Committee considered that in such circumstances, it was not for it to appear to presume the death of the author's son. Therefore, it would be appropriate in this case not to make any finding in respect of article 6.

The State party was under an obligation under article 2, paragraph 3 (*a*), of the Covenant to provide S. Jegatheeswara Sarma and his family with an effective remedy, including a thorough and effective investigation into the disappearance and fate of the J. Thevaraja Sarma, his immediate release if still alive, adequate information resulting from its investigation and adequate compensation for the violations suffered by him, his father and the family. The State party had also the obligation to ensure the prompt trial of all persons responsible for the abduction of the J. Thevaraja Sarma and to bring to justice any other person who had been implicated in the disappearance, as well as to prevent similar violations in the future.

In the case *Chongwe* v. *Zambia*,[10] the author, Rodger Chongwe, a Zambian advocat and chaiman of a 13-party opposition alliance, received a life threatening wound when he was shot by police on 23 August 1997 whilst attending a political rally. He survived what he regarded as an assassination attempt. Although his life was not taken, the Committee found violations by Zambia of articles 6, paragraph 1, and 9, paragraph 1, of the Covenant. The case is summarized in section C.[11] The Committee's observations on the obligation that article 6, paragraph 1, of the Covenant places on States parties to protect the right to life replicate its observations in cases where the victims have been actually killed.

This case can be contrasted with an earlier case, *Leehong* v. *Jamaica*,[12] where the author, Anthony Leehong, a Jamaican citizen awaiting execution, claimed, *inter alia*, that on 20 December 1988, he was shot by the police from behind, without any

---

[10] See United Nations, *Official Records of the General Assembly, Fifty-sixth Session, Supplement No. 40* (A/56/40), vol. II, annex X, sect. K, communication No. 821/1998, views adopted on 25 October 2000.

[11] See part II, chap. 4, sect. C (*b*) (*infra*, pp. 247-248).

[12] See United Nations, *Official Records of the General Assembly, Fifty-fourth Session, Supplement No. 40* (A/54/40), vol. II, annex XI, sect. G, communication No. 613/1995, views adopted on 13 July 1999.

II:4

warning, before being arrested. The author alleged violations by Jamaica of article 9 and a number of other articles of the Covenant. With respect to Mr. Leehong's right to security of his person, the Committee found that there had been a violation of article 9, paragraph 1, as the claim concerning the shooting remained uncontested by the State party. It also found other violations of the Covenant. The obligation to protect the right to life in accordance with article 6, paragraph 1, was not an issue in this case.

In addition to protecting liberty and security of person, article 9, paragraph 1, of the Covenant prohibits arbitrary arrest and detention, and it requires deprivations of liberty to be lawful.

The case *Hugo van Alphen* v. *the Netherlands*[13] is one of a number of cases in which the notion of arbitrariness has been considered. The author, a Netherlands solicitor, was arrested on 5 December 1983 on suspicion of having committed a number of crimes, including having been an accessory or accomplice to the offence of forgery. At various stages during the investigation, he was remanded in custody. He claimed, *inter alia*, that his detention was arbitrary, in violation of article 9 of the Covenant.

The principle issue before the Committee was whether the detention of Mr. van Alphen from 5 December 1983 to 9 February 1984 was arbitrary. It was uncontested that the judicial authorities of the Netherlands, in their repeated considerations as to prolongation of his detention, observed the rules governing pre-trial detention laid down in the State's criminal procedure code. However, it remained to be determined whether other factors might render arbitrary an otherwise lawful detention. In considering this point, the Committee noted that the drafting history of article 9, paragraph 1, of the Covenant confirmed that arbitrariness was not to be equated with against the law, but it had to be interpreted more broadly to include elements of inappropriateness, injustice and lack of predictability. This meant that remand in custody pursuant to lawful arrest had to be not only lawful but reasonable and necessary in all the circumstances, for example to prevent flight, interference with evidence or recurrence of crime. As the State party had not shown that these factors were present in the case of Mr. van Alphen, the Committee found that his continued detention was arbitrary and in violation of article 9, paragraph 1. In an individual opinion, one member of the Committee disagreed.

---

[13] *Ibidem, Forty-fifth Session, Supplement No. 40* (A/45/40), vol. II, annex IX, sect. M, communication No. 305/1988, views adopted on 23 July 1990.

In a later case, *Albert Womah Mukong* v. *Cameroon*,[14] the Committee followed the same line of reasoning. This case is summarized in connection with the prohibition of torture because of the treatment to which the author was subjected during his detention,[15] and it is also cited in connection with the right to freedom of opinion and expression.[16] The author, a journalist, writer and opponent of the political system in Cameroon, was arrested on 16 June 1988 after an interview given to a correspondent of the BBC, in which he had criticized the President of Cameroon and the Government. On 5 May 1989, he was released, but he was again arrested on 26 February 1990 following a public meeting on introducing multi-party democracy in Cameroon. In the summer of 1990, he left his country.

The Committee concluded that the detention of Mr. Mukong was neither reasonable nor necessary in the cirumstances of the case, thus revealing a violation by Cameroon of article 9, paragraph 1, of the Covenant. It also found violations of the prohibition of torture in article 7 and the right to freedom of opinion and expression in article 19.

In the case *Sergio Rubén López Burgos* v. *Uruguay*,[17] also cited in connnection with the prohibition of torture,[18] the author, Delia Saldías de López, claimed that her husband, Mr. López Burgos, a Uruguayan trade union leader, was kidnapped on 13 July 1976 in Argentina by members of the Uruguayan security and intelligence forces. Subsequently, he was illegally and clandestinely transported to Uruguay where he was detained. The author alleged that the Uruguayan authorities in this case had violated, *inter alia*, articles 7 and 9 of the Covenant.

In respect of the act of abduction into Uruguayan territory, the Committee found that it constituted an arbitrary arrest and detention perpetrated by State agents acting on foreign soil. The communication disclosed a violation by Uruguay of article 9, paragraph 1, of the Covenant. The Committee also found a number of other violations of the Covenant in this case.

---

[14] *Ibidem, Forty-ninth Session, Supplement No. 40* (A/49/40), vol. II, annex IX, sect. AA, communication No. 458/1991, views adopted on 21 July 1994.

[15] See part II, chap. 3, sect. C (*b*) (*supra*, pp. 158-161).

[16] See part III, chap. 4, sect. B (*a*) (*infra*, pp. 439-440).

[17] See United Nations, *Official Records of the General Assembly, Thirty-sixth Session, Supplement No. 40* (A/36/40), annex XIX, communication No. 52/1979, views adopted on 29 July 1981.

[18] See part II, chap. 3, sect. B (*a*) (*supra*, pp. 131-132).

II:4

In a similar case, *V. P. Domukovsky* et al. v. *Georgia*,[19] summarized in section C,[20] one of the authors, Victor P. Domukovsky, a Russian national, claimed that in 1993, the Government of Azerbaijan had refused Georgia's request to extradite him and one of the other authors. Thereupon, he was kidnapped from Azerbaijan and illegally arrested. In respect of this operation carried out by Georgian special services, the Committee considered that in the absence of a more specific explanation than that given by the State party of the legal basis for the arrest of Mr. Domukovsky in Azerbaijan, due weight should be given to his detailed allegations. It found that the arrest was unlawful, in violation of article 9, paragraph 1, of the Covenant. The Committee concluded that Georgia had violated a number of provisions of the Covenant in respect of all four authors in this case.

Whilst, clearly, arrests must be lawful according to national law, the continuing detention of a person must also be lawful. The case *Spakmo* v. *Norway*,[21] summarized in section C,[22] illustrates this point. The author, Aage Spakmo, a Norwegian citizen, was commissioned by a landlord to carry out repairs on a building. An injunction order was issued under tenancy legislation, but the work continued. On 27 July 1984, Mr. Spakmo was ordered by police to stop his work, as it disturbed the peace in the neighbourhood. He refused to do so and was arrested, but he was released after an hour. The next day, he was arrested again for the same reason and detained for eight hours.

The Committee concluded that the arrest of Mr. Spakmo was not unlawful. However, for an arrest to be in compliance with article, 9, paragraph 1, of the Covenant, it had also to be reasonable and necessary in all the circumstances. It found that the eight-hour detension of Mr. Spakmo was unreasonable and constituted a violation by Norway of that provision. In an individual opinion, six members of the Committee disagreed with this conclusion. It is interesting to note their observations on the relationship of the Committee to national courts and the logic behind their opinion that the facts of the case did not constitute a violation of article 9, paragraph 1.

---

[19] See United Nations, *Official Records of the General Assembly, Fifty-third Session, Supplement No. 40* (A/53/40), vol. II, annex XI, sect. M, communications No. 623/1995, No. 624/1995, No. 626/1995 and No. 627/1995, views adopted on 6 April 1998.

[20] See part II, chap. 4, sect. C (*c*) (*infra*, pp. 248-250).

[21] See United Nations, *Official Records of the General Assembly, Fifty-fifth Session, Supplement No. 40* (A/55/40), vol. II, annex IX, sect. B, communication No. 631/1996, views adopted on 5 November 1999.

[22] See part II, chap. 4, sect. C (*d*) (*infra*, pp. 250-252).

Article 9, paragraph 2, of the Covenant requires that anyone who is arrested shall be informed, at the time of arrest, of the reasons for his arrest. Furthermore, he shall be promptly informed of any charges against him.

In the case *Adolfo Drescher Caldas* v. *Uruguay*,[23] the author, Ivonne Ibarburu de Drescher, claimed that her husband, Mr. Drescher Caldas, a Uruguayan national and trade union official, was arrested on 3 October 1978 by officials who did not identify themselves or produce any judicial warrant. He was informed that he was being arrested under so-called "prompt security measures", but he was not given more specific reasons for his arrest. The author invoked a number of provisions of the Covenant, including article 9, paragraph 2.

It was the opinion of the Committee that article 9, paragraph 2, of the Covenant required that anyone arrested should be informed sufficiently of the reasons for his arrest to enable him to take immediate steps to secure his release if he believed that the reasons given were invalid or unfounded. It was not sufficient simply to inform Mr. Drescher Caldas that he was being arrested under certain security measures, without any indication of the substance of the complaint against him. Consequently, there was a violation by Uruguay of article 9, paragraph 2. The Committee also found other violations of the Covenant in this case.

In the case *Peter Grant* v. *Jamaica*,[24] the Committee observed that the State party was not absolved from its obligation under article 9, paragraph 2, of the Covenant to inform a person of the reasons for his arrest and of the charges against him, because the arresting officer was of the opinion that the arrested person was aware of them. The author, a Jamaican citizen, was arrested on 13 July 1987, some weeks after a murder with which he was subsequently charged. He was convicted and sentenced to death, later commuted to life imprisonment. The State party did not contest that he was not informed of the reasons for his arrest until seven days later. In the circumstances, the Committee concluded that there had been a violation by Jamaica of article 9, paragraph 2, as well as violations of other provisions of the same article.

This case can be contrasted with the case *Gerald J. Griffin* v. *Spain*.[25] The author, a Canadian citizen, was arrested on 17 April 1991 in Spain in connection with illegal

---

[23] See United Nations, *Official Records of the General Assembly, Thirty-eighth Session, Supplement No. 40* (A/38/40), annex XVIII, communication No. 43/1979, views adopted on 21 July 1983.

[24] *Ibidem, Fifty-first Session, Supplement No. 40* (A/51/40), vol. II, annex VIII, sect. Z, communication No. 597/1994, views adopted on 22 March 1996.

[25] *Ibidem, Fiftieth Session, Supplement No. 40* (A/50/40), vol. II, annex X, sect. G, communication No. 493/1992, views adopted on 4 April 1995.

II:4

drugs found in his camper vehicle. He claimed, *inter alia*, that there was no inter-preter present at the time of his arrest and that he was not informed of the reasons for his arrest and of the charges against him. The Committee noted that Mr. Griffin was arrested and taken into custody after the police, in his presence, had searched the camper vehicle and discovered illegal drugs. Furthermore, the police refrained from taking his statement in the absence of an interpreter, and the following morning the drugs were weighed in the presence of Mr. Griffin. He was then brought before an examining magistrate and, through an interpreter, informed of the charges against him.

The Committee observed that although no interpreter was present during the arrest, it was wholly unreasonable to argue that the author was unaware of the reasons for his arrest. In any event, he was promptly informed, in his own language, of the charges against him. Therefore, the Committee found no violation by Spain of arti-cle 9, paragraph 2, of the Covenant. However, it concluded that Mr. Griffin's rights under article 10, paragraph 1, had been violated because of the conditions during his detention.

In the case *Michael and Brian Hill* v. *Spain*,[26] summarized in section C[27] and also cited in connection with the right to a fair trial,[28] the authors, both British citizens, were on holiday in Spain when, on 16 July 1985, they were arrested by police on suspicion of having firebombed a bar, an accusation they had denied since the time of their arrest. They alleged that they were not properly informed of the reasons for their detention until an interpreter was made available, seven and eight hours, re-spectively, after their arrest. They also complained that they did not understand the charges because of the lack of a competent interpreter. The State party asserted that the delay was of three hours and that the official interpreter was appointed under rules ensuring competence. The Committee accepted the State party's arguments and found no violation of article 9, paragraph 2, of the Covenant. It found, however, that Spain had violated other provisions of the Covenant in respect of Michael and Brian Hill, including article 9, paragraph 3, dealt with below.

Another case, *Paul Kelly* v. *Jamaica*,[29] likewise summarized in section C[30] and cited in connection with the right to a fair trial,[31] is also relevant to issues arising out of

---

[26] *Ibidem, Fifty-second Session, Supplement No. 40* (A/52/40), vol. II, annex VI, sect. B, com-munication No. 526/1993, views adopted on 2 April 1997.

[27] See part II, chap. 4, sect. C (*f*) (*infra*, pp. 255-258).

[28] See part III, chap. 2, sect. B (*a*) (*infra*, p. 349).

[29] See United Nations, *Official Records of the General Assembly, Forty-sixth Session, Supple-ment No. 40* (A/46/40), annex XI, sect. D, communication No. 253/1987, views adopted on 8 April 1991.

more than one paragraph of article 9 of the Covenant. The author, a Jamaican citizen awaiting execution, was arrested on 20 August 1981 and detained without formal charges being brought against him until 15 September 1981 when he was charged with murder. He was subsequently convicted and sentenced to death. The author invoked a number of provisions of the Covenant.

The Committee found a violation by Jamaica of article 9, paragraph 2, because Paul Kelly was not apprised in any detail of the reasons for his arrest for several weeks following his detention. He was not informed about the facts of the crime or about the identity of the victim. In coming to its conlusion, the Committee compared the requirements of article 9, paragraph 2, with those of article 14, paragraph 3 (*a*), of the Covenant, which required any individual under criminal charges to be informed promptly and in detail of the nature and cause of the charges against him. However, the latter provision only applied once the individual had been formally charged with a criminal offence. It did not apply to those remanded in custody pending the result of police investigations. That situation was covered by article 9, paragraph 2.

The Committee also found violations by Jamaica of article 9, paragraphs 3 and 4, of the Covenant. Paul Kelly was not brought before a judge or judicial official for some five weeks. That was in contravention of paragraph 3, requiring that anyone arrested on a criminal charge should be brought promptly before a judge or other officer authorized by law to exercise judicial power. Furthermore, as throughout this period he was denied access to legal representation and contact with his family, his right under paragraph 4 was also violated, since he was not in due time afforded the opportunity to obtain, on his own initiative, a decision by the court on the lawfulness of his detention as required by that provision. Clearly, these contacts were considered necessary for the right of *habeas corpus* to be exercised. The Committee also found that other provisions of the Covenant had been violated in this case, including the right to a fair trial.

Apart from requiring anyone arrested or detained on a criminal charge to be brought promptly before a judge or other judicial official, article 9, paragraph 3, of the Covenant gives such a person an entitlement to trial within a reasonable time or to release. It also gives a right to release pending trial, stating that it shall not be the general rule that persons awaiting trial shall be detained in custody. Release may, however, be made subject to guarantees to appear for trial.

The Committee has considered the meaning of the term "promptly" for the purposes of judicial review of detention in a number of cases, without laying down an exact

---

[30] See part II, chap. 4, sect. C (*e*) (*infra*, pp. 252-255).
[31] See part III, chap. 2, sect. B (*a*) (*infra*, p. 348).

II:4

period of time for this standard. In its general comment No. 8 (16) concerning article 9 of the Covenant, the Committee pronounced on this issue that delays must not exceed a few days.[32]

In the case *Nicole Fillastre* v. *Bolivia*,[33] the Committee observed that what constituted a reasonable time for the purposes of pre-trial detention was a matter of assessment for each particular case. The lack of adequate budgetary appropriations for the administration of criminal justice, alluded to by the State party in this case, did not justify unreasonable delays in the adjudication of criminal cases. Nor did the fact that investigations into criminal cases were carried out by way of written proceedings justify such delays.

The author, a French citizen residing in France, claimed that her husband, André Fillastre, also a French national and a private detective, and a colleague of his, Pierre Bizouarn, on a mission in Bolivia were arrested by police on 3 September 1987 after allegations that they, together with the mother in a child custody dispute, had abducted the child in his father's home. They were held in custody for 10 days before being brought before any judicial instance and without being informed of the charges against them. A decision at first instance had not been reached some four years after the victims' arrest, and they were still detained. Considerations of evidence-gathering did not justify such prolonged detention. The Committee concluded that there had been a violation by Bolivia of article 9, paragraphs 2 and 3, of the Covenant and that in the circumstances, the victims should be granted remedy in the form of immediate release. There was also a violation in this case of the right to a fair trial.

In the case *Ronald H. van der Houwen* v. *the Netherlands*,[34] the author, a citizen of the Netherlands, was arrested on 12 February 1993 after police officers had entered his appartment where he was selling cocaine to visitors. The next day, he was charged and placed in detention. On 16 February 1993, he was brought before the examining magistrate. The author claimed that 73 hours of detention without being brought before a judge was in violation of the State party's obligation under article 9, paragraph 3, of the Covenant. The Committee, however, considered that the facts did not raise any issue under that provision and that the communication therefore was inadmissible.

---

[32] See United Nations, *Official Records of the General Assembly, Thirty-seventh Session, Supplement No. 40* (A/37/40), annex V, para. 2.

[33] *Ibidem, Forty-seventh Session, Sup-plement No. 40* (A/47/40), annex IX, sect. N, communication No. 336/1988, views adopted on 5 November 1991.

[34] *Ibidem, Fiftieth Session, Supplement No. 40* (A/50/40), vol. II, annex XI, sect. L, communication No. 583/1994, decision adopted on 14 July 1995.

On the other hand, in a more recent case, *Borisenko* v. *Hungary*,[35] the Committee found that the detention for three days before being brought before a judicial officer constituted a violation of article 9, paragraph 3, of the Covenant. The author, Rostislav Borisenko, a Ukrainian citizen temporarily in Hungary, was arrested on 29 April 1996 by police in plain clothes who suspected him of pickpocketing. He was charged with theft and, on 2 May 1996, brought before a court. In the absence of an explanation from the State party on the necessity to detain Mr. Borisenko for this period, the Committee found that Hungary had violated article 9, paragraph 3. It also found a breach of the right to a fair trial.

This case may indicate that the Committee now is setting the standard required for compliance with this provision at less than three days. However, two members of the Committee held dissenting opinions in this respect. One of them stated in his individual opinion that he was unable to agree that article 9, paragraph 3, envisaged a rigid, inexorable rule that a person detained must be produced before a judicial officer within 48 hours of his arrest. He added that the determination of compliance or non-compliance with the requirement of this paragraph had ultimately to depend on the facts of each case.

In another case, *Neville Lewis* v. *Jamaica*,[36] there was a 23-month delay between arrest and trial. The author, a Jamaican citizen awaiting execution, was arrested by police on 11 November 1992 and subsequently charged with murder. On 14 October 1994, he was convicted and sentenced to death. He claimed that Jamaica had violated a number of articles of the Covenant.

As to the delay between arrest and trial, the Committee took the view that in the absence of any satisfactory explanation by the State party, a delay of 23 months during which Mr. Lewis was in detention was unreasonable. Therefore, it constituted a violation by Jamaica of article 9, paragraph 3, of the Covenant. In individual opinions, three members of the Committee disagreed. The Committee also found a violation of the Covenant in respect of the treatment of Mr. Lewis during his detention.

The question of detention or release pending trial also arose in the *Michael and Brian Hill* case. The authors, both British citizens residing in the United Kingdom, were charged on 19 July 1985 with arson and causing damage to private property. They were detained in custody awaiting trial. They complained that they were not granted

---

[35] *Ibidem, Fifty-eighth Session, Supplement No. 40* (A/58/40), vol. II, annex V, sect. J, communication No. 852/1999, views adopted on 14 October 2002.
[36] *Ibidem, Fifty-second Session, Supplement No. 40* (A/52/40), vol. II, annex VI, sect. X, communication No. 708/1996, views adopted on 17 July 1997.

II:4

bail. As they could not return to the United Kingdom, their construction firm there was declared bankrupt.

The Committee reaffirmed its prior jurisprudence under article 9, paragraph 3, of the Covenant that pre-trial detention should be the exception. Bail should be granted, except in situations where the likelihood existed that the accused would abscond or destroy evidence, influence witnesses or flee from the jurisdiction of the State party. The mere fact that the accused was a foreigner did not of itself imply that he might be held in detention pending trial. Furthermore, the mere conjecture of a State party that a foreigner might leave its jurisdiction if released on bail did not justify an exception to the rule laid down in this provision of the Covenant. In these circumstances, the Committee found that this right had been violated by Spain in respect of Michael and Brian Hill.

In another case, *Famara Koné* v. *Senegal*,[37] the author's detention was also found to be incompatible with article 9, paragraph 3, of the Covenant. Mr. Koné, a Senegalese citizen, was arrested on 15 January 1982 in Gambia by Senegalese soldiers, allegedly for protesting against the intervention of Senegalese troops in that country. He was transferred to Senegal and detained for more than four years. No date for his trial was set throughout this period.

The Committee held that such a delay, during which Mr. Koné was kept in custody, could not be deemed compatible with article 9, paragraph 3. Special circumstances, such as impediments to the investigation attributable to the accused or to his representative, could be such a justification, but no such circumstances existed in this case. The Committee concluded that there was a violation by Senegal of this provision of the Covenant.

Finally, in respect of article 9 of the Covenant, paragraph 4 embodies the right to *habeas corpus*, giving anyone deprived of his liberty an entitlement to legal proceedings in order that a court may decide without delay on the lawfulness of his detention and to release if the detention is not lawful.

The case *Eric Hammel* v. *Madagascar*[38] is interesting for a number of reasons. The author, a French national, was a practising lawyer in Madagascar until his expulsion in 1982. On 8 February 1982, he was arrested and kept in incommunicado detention until 11 February 1982 when he was notified of an expulsion order against him is-

---

[37] *Ibidem, Fiftieth Session, Supplement No. 40* (A/50/40), vol. II, annex X, sect. A, communication No. 386/1989, views adopted on 21 October 1994.
[38] *Ibidem, Forty-second Session, Supplement No. 40* (A/42/40), annex VIII, sect. A, communication No. 155/1983, views adopted on 3 April 1987.

sued by the Minister of the Interior. He was deported on the same evening to France. He was not indicted nor brought before a magistrate on any charge, neither was he afforded an opportunity to challenge the expulsion order prior to its execution. Following a subsequent application by Mr. Hammel to have the expulsion order revoked, the Supreme Court of Madagascar rejected his application. It found the expulsion order valid on the grounds that he allegedly made, as quoted by the Committee, "use both of his status as a corresponding member of Amnesty International and of the Human Rights Committee [*sic*] at Geneva, and as a barrister" to discredit Madagascar.

In this context, the Committee made reference to article 13 of the Covenant. An alien lawfully in the territory of a State party might be expelled only in pursuance of a decision reached in accordance with law and should, except where compelling reasons of national security otherwise required, be allowed to have his case reviewed by the competent authority. The Committee noted that Mr. Hammel was not given an effective remedy to challenge his expulsion and that the State party had not shown that there were compelling reasons of national security to deprive him of that remedy.

The Committee further noted with concern that the decision to expel Mr. Hammel would appear to have been linked to the fact that he had represented persons in cases before it. If that was the case, the Committee observed, it would be both untenable and incompatible with the spirit of the Covenant, and with the Optional Protocol to the Covenant, if States parties to these instruments were to take exception to anyone acting as legal counsel for persons placing their communications before the Committee for its consideration.

With respect to article 9, paragraph 4, of the Covenant, the Committee found that the facts disclosed a violation by Madagascar, because Mr. Hammel had been unable to challenge his arrest before a court. The Committee also found a violation of article 13 of the Covenant.

In the case *Albert Berry* v. *Jamaica*,[39] also cited in connection with the right to a fair trial,[40] the author, a Jamaican citizen, was awaiting execution after having been arrested on 27 March 1984 on a murder charge and subsequently convicted and sentenced to death. On 15 June 1984, the preliminary hearing was held. He claimed to be the victim of violations by Jamaica of a number of provisions of the Covenant, including article 9, paragraphs 3 and 4.

---

[39] *Ibidem, Forty-ninth Session, Supplement No. 40* (A/49/40), vol. II, annex IX, sect. D, communication No. 330/1988, views adopted on 7 April 1994.
[40] See part III, chap. 2, sect. B (*a*) (*infra*, p. 353).

II:4

The State party did not contest that Mr. Berry was detained for two and a half months before he was brought before a judge or judicial officer authorized to decide on the lawfulness of his detention. It simply contended that he could have applied to the courts for a writ of *habeas corpus.* The Committee noted, however, that throughout this period he had no access to legal representation. It considered that a delay of over two months violated the requirement in article 9, paragraph 3, of the Covenant that anyone arrested on a criminal charge should be brought promptly before a judge or other officer authorized by law to exercise judicial power. In the circumstances, the Committee concluded that Mr. Berry's right under article 9, paragraph 4, was also violated, since he was not in due time afforded the opportunity to obtain, on his own initiative, a decision by a court on the lawfulness of his detention. Furthermore, the facts of the case disclosed other violations by Jamaica of provisions of the Covenant.

(*b*) Working Group on Arbitrary Detention

It is recalled that the Working Group on Arbitrary Detention regards deprivation of liberty as arbitrary in the following cases:

(*a*) When it manifestly cannot be justified on any legal basis, such as continued detention after the sentence has been served or despite an applicable amnesty act (category I);

(*b*) When the deprivation of liberty is the result of a judgment or sentence for the exercise of the rights or freedoms proclaimed by articles 7, 13, 14, 18, 19, 20 and 21 of the Universal Declaration of Human Rights and also, in respect of States parties, in articles 12, 18, 19, 21, 22, 25, 26 and 27 of the International Covenant on Civil and Political Rights (category II); and

(*c*) When the complete or partial non-observance of the international standards relating to a fair trial set forth in the Universal Declaration and in the relevant international instruments accepted by the States concerned is of such gravity as to confer on the deprivation of liberty, of whatever kind, an arbitrary character (category III).

In order to evaluate the arbitrary character of cases of deprivation of liberty falling within category III, the Working Group considers, in addition to the general principles set out in the Universal Declaration, several criteria drawn from the Body of Principles for the Protection of All Persons under Any Form of Detention or Imprisonment and, for States parties, in particular the criteria laid down in articles 9 and 14 of the Covenant.

II:4

When the Working Group concludes that a person has been arbitrarily deprived of his or her liberty, the Government concerned is typically requested to take the necessary steps to remedy the situation and to bring it into conformity with the standards and principles set forth in the Universal Declaration and, where applicable, the Covenant. States non-parties to the Covenant are encouraged to become a party to it. Cases involving allegations of torture are often brought to the attention of the Special Rapporteur on the question of torture.

From the rich jurisprudence of the Working Group, seven cases have been selected for inclusion in this chapter of the book.

An early case, decision No. 38/1994 *(Turkey)*,[41] summarized in section C,[42] is important and subsequently referred to by the Working Group. In this case, the alleged victim, Soner Onder, a Turkish student aged 17, was arrested by police, following a demonstration on 25 December 1991, and charged with a number of crimes, including possessing an explosive substance and multiple killing. Reportedly, he signed a confession whilst in police custody. When brought before a prosecutor, he retracted, claiming that he had signed the confession, while being kept blindfolded and without any knowledge of its contents, because he had been tortured.

The Working Group considered that the case raised a question of principle, whether the fact that the detention was ordered on the basis of evidence resulting from a confession extracted under torture conferred on it an arbitrary character. In coming to its decision, the Working Group examined further information within the United Nations system on the issue contained in relevant general comments of the Human Rights Committee, reports of the Special Rapporteur on the question of torture and reports of the Committee against Torture, in particular concerning Turkey.

The Working Group also took into account international provisions referring to the inadmissibility of evidence obtained under torture or requiring that no one should be compelled to testify against himself or to confess guilt; appearances of the representative of Turkey before the Committee against Torture; and provisions of Turkish law prohibiting torture and punishing those found guilty of the crime of torture.

Ultimately, the Working Group declared that the detention of Soner Onder was arbitrary. It was in contravention of article 5 of the Universal Declaration, article 7 of the Covenant and article 15 of the Convention against Torture and Other Cruel, Inhuman or Degrading Treatment or Punishment, the latter ratified by Turkey. It fell

---

[41] See United Nations document E/CN.4/1996/40/Add.1, p. 11, decision adopted on 1 December 1994.

[42] See part II, chap. 4, sect. C *(g)* *(infra*, pp. 258-262).

II:4

within category III of the principles applicable in the consideration of cases submitted to the Working Group. Turkey was not a party to the Covenant.

In another case allegedly involving torture, opinion No. 18/2001 (*Mexico*),[43] it was reported that Rodolfo Montiel Flores and Teodoro Cabrera García were arrested on 2 May 1999 by members of the armed forces and accused of a variety of crimes, including planting marijuana and carrying arms without a licence. The alleged victims were founder members of an organization set up in response to widespread and illegal logging in the region. It was claimed, *inter alia*, that they were subjected to torture in order to make them sign incriminating confessions. They were sentenced to long terms of imprisonment.

In considering this case, the Working Group recalled its above decision No. 38/1994 (*Turkey*). In addition to the international instruments and procedures referred to in that case, it cited guideline 16 of the Guidelines on the Role of Prosecutors. This provision reads:

> When prosecutors come into possession of evidence against suspects that they know or believe on reasonable grounds was obtained through recourse to unlawful methods, which constitute a grave violation of the suspect's human rights, especially involving torture or cruel, inhuman or degrading treatment or punishment, or other abuses of human rights, they shall refuse to use such evidence against anyone other than those who used such methods, or inform the Court accordingly, and shall take all necessary steps to ensure that those responsible for using such methods are brought to justice.

The Working Group found that the detention of Mr. Montiel and Mr. Cabrera was ordered in flagrant violation of article 5 of the Universal Declaration, as well as articles 7 and 14 (*g*) of the Covenant and article 15 of the Convention against Torture, treaties to which Mexico was a party. These violations were of such gravity as to confer on the detention an arbitrary character, falling within category III. The Government of Mexico was requested not only to take the necessary steps to remedy the situation, but also to take measures for the punishment of the authors of the violations.

Different human rights provisions were invoked in another case with allegations of torture against the same State, opinion No. 37/2000 (*Mexico*).[44] It was claimed that Jacobo Silva Nogales, a rural schoolteacher and social activist, was arrested on 18

---

[43] See United Nations document E/CN.4/2002/77/Add.1, p. 85, opinion adopted on 14 September 2001.

[44] *Ibidem*, p. 28, opinion adopted on 27 November 2000.

October 1999 by police. Gloria Arena Agis, Fernando Gatica Chino and Felicitas Padilla Navas were arrested four days later. All of them were arrested in a violent manner, without any arrest warrant from a competent body. Allegedly, they were tortured while being in detention. They were charged with terrorism and other criminal activities.

The Working Group recalled that it could not render an opinion on the innocence of a person deprived of his liberty, but on the arbitrary nature of an arrest in which the principles of due process were not complied with by the authorities. In the present case, the Working Group considered that the right of the detainees to the presumption of innocence was not respected inasmuch as they were forced to incriminate themselves under torture. Furthermore, during the first four weeks of their detention, the right to be assisted by counsel was not respected, and their subsequent trial was not conducted with the safeguards of impartiality. The violation in this case of these principles of due process was so serious that the Working Group determined that the deprivation of liberty was arbitrary. It constituted a breach of articles 9 and 10 of the Universal Declaration and articles 9 and 14 of the Covenant, to which Mexico was a party, and fell within category III.

In a case concerning 12 detainees arrested in the years 1989 to 1994, decision No. 45/1995 (*Egypt*),[45] it was reported that they had been regularly transferred from one prison to another and that some of them had been tortured or brutally beaten. The Working Group noted that all the detainees concerned were being kept in detention without being charged or tried. For seven of them there were orders for their release, but the Egyptian authorities instead each time issued new detention orders.

In the Working Group's view, there were grave violations in this case of the right to a fair trial, and in particular of the provisions of articles 9, 10, and 11 of the Universal Declaration and articles 9, paragraphs 2 and 3, and 14, paragraphs 1, 2 and 3, of the Covenant, to which Egypt was a party. Their gravity was such that it conferred on the detentions an arbitrary character, falling within category III. Moreover, since the release of some of the detainees had been regularly ordered and the authorities had systematically refused to execute these orders, their detention was also declared arbitrary as falling within category I.

In a similar case, opinion No. 16/1997 (*Bolivia*),[46] it was claimed that Juan Carlos Pinto Quintanilla, arrested by police on 13 April 1992, was tortured and had no ac-

---

[45] See United Nations document E/CN.4/1997/4/Add.1, p. 24, decision adopted on 29 November 1995.
[46] See United Nations document E/CN.4/1998/44, annex III, p. 23, opinion adopted on 28 November 1997.

II:4

cess to counsel during the eight days he was on police premises. Furthermore, although he had been deprived of liberty for five and a half years, his case had not gone beyond the investigation stage, basically due to the fact that the relevant documents were transferred successively to various courts owing to problems of competence. Allegedly, he faced charges of rebellion and sedition, but in fact he was accused of militancy in a guerilla group. The complaint also referred to 34 named persons allegedly being in similar situations as Mr. Pinto.

The Working Group stated that the facts of the case constituted such serious violations of the rules of the due process of law that the imprisonment might be considered arbitrary. It concluded that the deprivation of liberty of Mr. Pinto was arbitrary, as being in contravention of articles 9, 10 and 11 of the Universal Declaration and articles 9, 10 and 14 of the Covenant, to which Bolivia was a party, and falling within category III. The other 34 cases were brought to the attention of the Government.

In a number of cases, the Working Group has considered situations where people have been detained for having engaged in peaceful activities undertaken in the exercise of their fundamental rights. One such case, decision No. 46/1995 (*China*),[47] concerned the detention of a large number of people for their exercise of the freedom of thought, conscience and religion, the freedom of opinion and expression or the freedom of peaceful assembly and association. The case included situations such as Buddhist nuns expressing their attachment to their religion by demonstrating or attempting to demonstrate in public; individuals having contacts with foreign journalists or having sent information abroad regarding human rights issues; activists drafting and distributing prodemocracy leaflets; a person attempting to organize a meeting of veteran prodemocracy campaigners; and people being active in unrecognized non-violent associations of a political or trade union character.

In coming to its decision on these matters, the Working Group noted that the Government did not contest the nature of the facts of which the persons concerned were accused. It further noted that neither in the description of the facts as presented by the source nor in the Government's reply was it alleged or asserted that the deeds imputed had been carried out by violent means or by inciting violence. Therefore, these activities were exercised peacefully. The detentions were based on the exercise by people of their fundamental rights and freedoms guaranteed by articles 18, 19 and 20 of the Universal Declaration and articles 18, 19, 21 and 22 of the Covenant. Accordingly, where applicable, the detentions were declared arbitrary in terms of category II. China was not a party to the Covenant.

---

[47] See United Nations document E/CN.4/1997/4/Add.1, p. 28, decision adopted on 30 November 1995.

The final case included in this review, opinion No. 11/2001 (*Viet Nam*),[48] concerned the peaceful exercise of human rights guaranteed by international instruments and the house arrest of Thich Quang Do, a monk of the banned Unified Buddhist Church of Viet Nam. According to the source, on 31 May 2001, he was condemned to two years' administrative detention under the provisions of a government decree and forbidden to leave his pagoda. This decree reportedly empowered the police to order the detention of citizens suspected of threatening national security without formal charges or trial.

On 1 June 2001, the police blocked the entry to the monastery, and members of the Church trying to visit the monk were turned away. Police officers cut the monastery's telephone lines and seized the monk's mobile phone. 10 security police officers were placed inside the monastery, and others were stationed outside. They intensified controls around the monastery residence and were closely searching visitors and blocking communications. Two officers kept permanent guard outside the monk's room, blocking all access so that he could not leave the monastery.

From this, it appeared to the Working Group, the communication related to a case of house arrest. In this regard, it had to consider, in the light of its deliberation No. 1/1993 on house arrest,[49] whether such a measure in the case of Thich Quang Do constituted deprivation of liberty and, if so, whether it was of an arbitrary character.

With regard to the first point, the Working Group recalled that in accordance with its deliberation, house arrest constituted a measure of deprivation of liberty when it was carried out in closed premises which the person was not allowed to leave. In this case, the Working Group noted that according to the information transmitted to it by the source and not contested by the Government in its reply, the monk had been under house arrest in his monastery. The Working Group considered that in the circumstances, the house arrest of Thich Quang Do was indeed a measure of deprivation of liberty within the meaning of deliberation No. 1/1993.

According to the source, the measure depriving Thich Quang Do of his liberty was put into effect just when he was preparing to lead a demonstration in support of the Patriarch of the Unified Buddhist Church of Viet Nam. The Government maintained that the house arrest was the result of a court order. The Working Group noted that the Government admitted that in 1998, the monk benefited from an amnesty when he still had two years' imprisonment to serve. As a result, his house arrest should have been put into effect on the day of his release, in 1998. That was not the case,

---

[48] See United Nations document E/CN.4/2002/77/Add.1, p. 60, opinion adopted on 12 September 2001.
[49] See United Nations document E/CN.4/1993/24, para. 20.

II:4

and this supported the source's theory that it was the monk's intention to take part in a peaceful demonstration that gave rise to his house arrest.

The detainee merely had peacefully exercised the rights guaranteed by articles 18 and 19 of the Universal Declaration and articles 18 and 19 of the Covenant, to which Viet Nam was a party. In view of this, the Working Group rendered the opinion that the house arrest of Thich Quang Do was an arbitrary deprivation of his liberty, falling within category II.

(*c*) Committee on Freedom of Association

The jurisprudence of the Committee on Freedom of Association serves as a reminder that police powers, and especially the powers to arrest and detain, shall only be exercised for legitimate policing purposes. During the course of a dispute between employers and employees, a professional, public police service should not be used, or rather misused, to defend the sectional interests of either party to such a dispute. Police intervention is appropriate only when it is genuinely necessary to prevent or investigate crime or to maintain or restore public order.

Labour standards of the International Labour Organization provide a basis for the adoption of national standards and procedures to resolve labour and industrial relations disputes, and these do not fall within the framework of criminal law. The primary purpose of any police action in a dispute between employers and employees is to maintain order so that the dispute can be resolved within the appropriate framework. On most occasions, of course, such disputes are settled without the need for police intervention. In its reports to the Governing Body of the International Labour Office, the Committee has applied, in a number of case reports, important principles relevant to police intervention in labour and industrial relations disputes and activities of trade unions and employers and their organizations.

In a report on cases No. 1007 (*Nicaragua*) and No. 1208 (*Nicaragua*) as well as three other cases brought against the same State,[50] the Committee responded to different complaints concerning matters such as arrest and imprisonment of employer leaders and arrest, persecution and harassment of trade union leaders. In its general recommendations concerning these cases, the Committee stated that freedom of association could only be exercised in conditions in which fundamental human rights, and in particular the right to freedom from arbitrary arrest, were fully respected and guaranteed. More specifically, in case No. 1007, the Committee recalled that the preventive detention of leaders of workers' and employers' organizations for activi-

---

[50] See International Labour Office, *Official Bulletin*, vol. LXVII, Series B, No. 1 (1984), p. 59, interim report.

ties connected with the exercise of their rights was contrary to the principles of freedom of association. In case No. 1208, the Committee drew attention to the fact that preventive detention of union leaders entailed a serious risk of interference in the activities of trade union organizations.

In a report on case No. 1258 (*El Salvador*) and another nine cases against that State,[51] the Committee examined complaints concerning attempts on the lives and physical integrity, disappearances and arrests of peoples connected with the trade union movement. In case No. 1258, the Committee drew the attention of the Government to the fact that the detention of leaders or members for reasons connected with their activities in defence of the interests of workers constituted a serious interference with civil liberties in general and with trade union rights in particular. In its general recommendations, the Committee called on the Government to adopt appropriate measures to guarantee that trade union rights might be exercised in a normal fashion. This would only be possible in conditions in which fundamental human rights were respected and in a climate free of violence, pressures and threats of any kind.

In the report on case No. 1285 (*Chile*),[52] also cited in connection with the right to freedom of peaceful assembly and association,[53] the Committee examined allegations that a number of trade union organizers and leaders had been detained for such reasons as holding a peaceful, public demonstration during the course of a legal strike; carrying placards at a peaceful demonstration; distributing leaflets on a public highway; and heading a peaceful protest march. In its recommendations, the Committee reminded the Government of the importance it attached to, *inter alia*, the principle that measures depriving trade unionists of their freedom on grounds related to their trade union activity, even where they were merely summoned or questioned for a short period, constituted an obstacle to the exercise of trade union rights.

The imposition of a curfew on the area around a trade union building, barring trade union leaders from union activities, repeated summonsing of trade union leaders for interrogation as well as threats and other harassment were among the matters alleged in the report on case No. 1414 (*Israel*).[54] Responding to these allegations, as in previous cases involving repeated summonsing by the authorities, the Committee drew the Government's attention to the principle that the apprehension and systematic or

---

[51] *Ibidem*, vol. LXIX, Series B, No. 1 (1986), p. 94, interim report.
[52] *Ibidem*, vol. LXVIII, Series B, No. 3 (1985), p. 115, definitive report.
[53] See part III, chap. 5, sect. B (*b*) (*infra*, p. 493).
[54] See International Labour Office, *Official Bulletin*, vol. LXXI, Series B, No. 2 (1988), p. 26, definitive report.

II:4

arbitrary interrogation by the police of trade union leaders and unionists involved a danger of abuse and could constitute a serious attack on trade union rights.

In the report on case No. 1308 (*Grenada*),[55] the Committee responded to an allegation that the president of a trade union had been arrested for the purpose of deporting him in order to deprive the trade union movement of one of its leaders. Noting that the detainee had been released following appeal court proceedings, the Committee recalled, as it had pronounced in analogous cases in the past, that the arrest of a trade union leader against whom no charge was brought involved restrictions on the freedom of association. Governments should adopt measures for issuing appropriate instructions to prevent the danger involved for trade union activities by such arrests. Furthermore, it was also clear that such arrests created an atmosphere of intimidation and fear prejudicial to the normal development of trade union activities.

In a report on case No.1888 (*Ethiopia*),[56] the Committee examined a complaint concerning the killing of a trade union leader, the arrest and detention of other leaders of the trade union and the interference in the internal administration of the union. This report is also cited to in connection with the right to life[57] and with the right to freedom of peaceful assembly and association.[58] In its conclusions, the Committee recalled that freedom of association implied not only the right of workers' and employers' organizations to form freely organizations of their own choosing, but also the right of organizations to pursue lawful activities for the defence of their occupational interests. Furthermore, the arrest, even if only briefly, of trade union leaders and trade unionists for exercising legitimate trade union activities constituted a violation of the principles of freedom of association.

The report on case No. 2074 (*Cameroon*)[59] concerned alleged discrimination against a trade union and arbitrary detention of trade union officers. In its conclusions regarding the latter allegation, the Committee reminded the parties to the dispute that persons engaged in trade union activities or holding trade union office could not claim immunity in respect of the ordinary criminal law. However, trade union activities should not in themselves be used by the authorities as a pretext for the arbitrary arrest or detention of trade unionists.

---

[55] *Ibidem*, vol. LXIX, Series B, No. 1 (1986), p. 15, definitive report.
[56] *Ibidem*, vol. LXXXVI, Series B, No. 1 (2003), p. 226, request report.
[57] See part II, chap. 2, sect. B (*b*) (*supra*, pp. 51-52).
[58] See part III, chap. 5, sect. B (*b*) (*infra*, p. 494).
[59] See International Labour Office, *Official Bulletin*, vol. LXXXIII, Series B, No. 3 (2000), p. 30, definitive report.

Another recent case report, case No. 2116 (*Indonesia*),[60] is summarized in section C.[61] It concerns a dispute between the management and employees of a hotel. Apart from the observations of the Committee on the arrest and detention of some of the trade unionists, it is also interesting to note its analysis of the dispute and its views on the obligations of the Government concerned under the Convention concerning Freedom of Association and Protection of the Right to Organise (No. 87) and the Convention concerning the Application of the Principles of the Right to Organise and to Bargain Collectively (No. 98), the two fundamental human rights conventions on the freedom of association.

(*d*) African Commission on Human and Peoples' Rights

Article 6 of the African Charter on Human and Peoples' Rights states that every individual shall have the right to liberty and security of his person. It prohibits depriving a person of his freedom except for reasons and conditions previously laid down by law. In particular, it prohibits arbitrary arrest or detention.

There is no provision in the Charter allowing States parties to derogate from their treaty obligations.

With regard to the jurisprudence of the African Commission on Human and Peoples' Rights, one decision on two communications concerning alleged violations of article 6 of the Charter is included in this review. Although these allegations derived from governmental decrees rather than police action, the decision is reviewed here because of the observations made by the Commission on the right to *habeas corpus*, on the need to interpret the Charter in a culturally sensitive way and on how extreme measures to curtail rights simply created greater unrest.

In the case *Constitutional Rights Project and Civil Liberties Organisation* v. *Nigeria*,[62] the Commission examined allegations that decrees by the Government of Nigeria violated article 6 of the Charter. The State Security (Detention of Persons) Amended Decree No. 14, 1994 prohibited any court in Nigeria from issuing a writ of *habeas corpus* or any prerogative order for the production of any person detained under State Security (Detention of Persons) Decree No. 2, 1984. The latter Decree provided for persons endangering state security to be detained for a reviewable period of three months.

---

[60] *Ibidem*, vol. LXXXIV, Series B, No. 3 (2001), p. 104, interim report.

[61] See part II, chap. 4, sect. C (*h*) (*infra*, pp. 262-266).

[62] See Organization of African Unity document AHG/222 (XXXVI), annex V, p. 63, communications No. 143/95 and No. 150/96.

II:4

The Commission observed that the problem of arbitrary detention had existed for hundreds of years and that the writ of *habeas corpus* was developed as the response of common law to arbitrary detention. It permitted detained persons and their representatives to challenge such detention and demand the authority either to release or justify all imprisonment.

The Commission further observed that deprivation of the right to *habeas corpus* alone did not automatically violate article 6 of the Charter. Indeed, if article 6 were never violated, there would be no need for *habeas corpus* provisions. However, where violations of the article were widespread, *habeas corpus* rights were essential in ensuring that individuals' rights were respected. The question thus became whether the right to *habeas corpus*, as it had developed in common law systems, was a necessary corollary to the protection of article 6 and whether its suspension thus violated that article. On this point, the Commission stated that the Charter should be interpreted in a culturally sensitive way, taking into full account the differing legal traditions of Africa and finding its expression through the laws of each country. The Commission pointed out that the Government of Nigeria had conceded that the right to *habeas corpus* was important in Nigeria and emphasized that it would be reinstated as society became democratized.

The Commission considered that the importance of *habeas corpus* was demonstrated in the communication filed by the Civil Liberties Organisation. The Government had argued that no one had actually been denied the right under the 1994 Decree, whereas the communication provided a list of such people who had been detained without charges in very poor conditions, some incommunicado. They were unable to challenge their detention owing to the suspension of *habeas corpus*.

The Commission held that the detention of individuals without charge or trial was a clear violation of articles 6 and 7, paragraph 1 (*a*) and (*d*), of the Charter, the latter two provisions protecting the right to appeal to competent national organs against acts violating fundamental rights and the right to be heard within a reasonable time, respectively.

These and other circumstances dramatically illustrated how a deprivation of rights under articles 6 and 7 were compounded by the deprivation of the right to apply for a writ of *habeas corpus*. Furthermore, given the history of *habeas corpus* in the common law to which Nigeria was an heir and its acute relevance in modern Nigeria, the Commission stated that suspending it had to be seen as further violations of articles 6 and 7, paragraph 1 (*a*) and (*d*), of the Charter.

The Government had argued that *habeas corpus* actions were still available to most detainees in Nigeria and that the right to bring *habeas corpus* actions was denied only to those detained for state security reasons under the 1984 Decree. However, the Commission observed, whilst this did not create a situation as serious as when all detainees were denied the right to challenge their detention, the limited application of a provision did not guarantee its compatibility with the Charter. To deny a fundamental right to a few was just as much a violation as denying it to many.

The Commission noted that the Government had attempted to justify the 1994 Decree with the necessity for state security. However, whilst the Commission was sympathetic to all genuine attempts to maintain public peace, it had to note that too often extreme measures to curtail rights simply created greater unrest. It considered that it was dangerous for the protection of rights for the executive branch of government to operate without such checks as usually performed by the judiciary.

The Commission found that there were violations of, *inter alia*, articles 6 and 7, paragraph 1 (*a*) and (*d*), of the Charter. It recommended the Government of Nigeria to bring its laws in line with the Charter.

(*e*) Inter-American Court of Human Rights

Article 7 of the American Convention on Human Rights protects the right to personal liberty. Paragraph 1 of this article states that every person has the right to personal liberty and security. Paragraph 2 prohibits deprivation of physical liberty except for the reasons and under the conditions established beforehand by the constitution of the State party concerned or by a law established pursuant thereto. Paragraph 3 prohibits arbitrary arrest or imprisonment.

The next three paragraphs of this article set out rights of people deprived of their liberty. Paragraph 4 requires that detainees shall be informed of the reasons for their detention and promptly notified of the charge or charges against them; paragraph 5 stipulates that a detainee shall be brought promptly before a judge or other judicial officer, and it sets out the entitlement to a trial within a reasonable time or release pending trial; and paragraph 6 requires that anyone deprived of his liberty shall be entitled to recourse to a competent court in order that the court may decide without delay on the lawfulness of the arrest or detention and order his release if the arrest or detention is unlawful.

Finally, paragraph 7 states that no one shall be detained for debt.

In time of war, public danger or other emergency threatening the independence or security of a State party, it may take measures derogating from its obligations under article 7, but only on the conditions set forth in article 27 of the Convention.

II:4

Three cases of the jurisprudence of the Inter-American Court of Human Rights are reviewed in this chapter. Two of the cases arise out of situations of disappearance. In this context, it is interesting to recall what the Court has said about this phenomenon in the *Velásquez Rodríguez* case (*Honduras*),[63] the leading case on disappearances summarized in connection with the right to life[64] and also cited in connection with the prohibition of torture.[65] The forced disappearance of human beings was a multiple and continuous violation of many rights under the Convention that the States parties were obligated to respect and guarantee. The kidnapping of a person was an arbitrary deprivation of liberty, an infringement of a detainee's right to be taken without delay before a judge and to invoke the appropriate procedures to review the legality of the arrest, all in violation of article 7 of the Convention recognizing the right to personal liberty.

The *Castillo Páez* case (*Peru*),[66] summarized in section C,[67] concerned the alleged abduction and subsequent disappearance in 1990 of Ernesto Rafael Castillo Páez by the Peruvian police. It is a typical case on disappearance, involving violations of article 7 on the right to personal liberty as well as articles 4 on the right to life, 5 on the right to humane treatment, 8 on the right to a fair trial and 25 on the right to judicial protection, all in relation to the obligation under article 1 to respect the rights recognized in the Convention. The focus of the summary is on violations of articles 7 and 25.

In this disturbing and distressing case, the Court considered it to have been demonstrated that the police authorities had denied the arrest and hidden the victim so that he could not be located by a magistrate. Furthermore, in relation to article 25 of the Convention, the Court considered that the remedy of *habeas corpus*, filed against the detention of Mr. Castillo Páez by his next of kin, had been obstructed by State agents through the adulteration of the logs of entry of detainees, making it impossible to locate the victim. Consequently, this remedy was ineffective for securing the release of the victim and, perhaps, for saving his life. The Court found that Peru had violated, *inter alia*, articles 7 and 25 of the Convention, in relation to article 1, paragraph 1.

---

[63] See Inter-American Court of Human Rights, Series C: *Decisions and Judgments*, No. 4 (1988), petition No. 7920, judgment of 29 July 1988.

[64] See part II, chap. 2, sect. C (*c*) (*supra*, pp. 74-85).

[65] See part II, chap. 3, sect. B (*e*) (*supra*, p. 146).

[66] See Inter-American Court of Human Rights, Series C: *Decisions and Judgments*, No. 34 (1998), petition No. 10733, judgment of 3 November 1997.

[67] See part II, chap. 4, sect. C (*i*) (*infra*, pp. 266-269).

The *Suárez Rosero* case (*Ecuador*),[68] also cited to in connection with the prohibition of torture,[69] concerns, *inter alia,* a number of provisions in article 7 of the Convention and the provision on the right to judicial protection in article 25. Rafael Iván Suárez Rosero was arrested on 23 June 1992 by officers of the Ecuadoran national police in connection with a police operation to disband an international drug-trafficking organization. He was arrested without a warrant from a competent authority, and he was not captured *in flagrante delicto.* He was held incommunicado. On 22 July 1992, a commissioner-general of police ordered that he should be detained until a court issued an order to the contrary. The next day, Mr. Suárez Rosero was transferred to another place of detention where he remained incommunicado for five more days.

During the entire period of his incommunicado detention, from 23 June to 28 July 1992, Mr. Suárez Rosero was not allowed to receive visits from his family or communicate with a lawyer. His contact with relatives was limited to the exchange of clothes and scribbled notes censored by the security staff. From 28 July 1992, Mr. Suárez Rosero was allowed to receive his family, lawyer and members of human rights organizations on visiting days. The interviews with his lawyer were conducted in the presence of police officers. On 12 August 1992, a criminal court issued an order of preventive detention against Mr. Suárez Rosero. On 29 March 1993, he filed a writ of *habeas corpus* with the Supreme Court of Justice of Ecuador but, on 10 June 1994, this was denied. Mr. Suárez Rosero was eventually released on 29 April 1996. On 9 September 1996, he was found guilty of illegal trafficking in narcotic drugs, fined and sentenced to a term of imprisonment. At no time had Mr. Suárez Rosero been summoned to appear before a competent judicial authority to be informed of the charges brought against him.

The Court, referring to article 7, paragraphs 2 and 3, of the Convention and to Ecuador's Political Constitution and criminal procedure code, noted that Mr. Suárez Rosero had not been apprehended *in flagrante delicto.* His arrest should therefore have been effected with a warrant issued by a competent judicial authority. However, the first judicial proceeding relating to his detention took place on 12 August 1992, over a month after his arrest, in violation of procedures previously established by the domestic law of the State. For these reasons, the Court found that Mr. Suárez Rosero's arrest and subsequent detention from 23 June 1992 were in violation of article 7, paragraphs 2 and 3, of the Convention.

---

[68] See Inter-American Court of Human Rights, Series C: *Decisions and Judgments,* No. 35 (1999), petition No. 11273, judgment of 12 November 1999.
[69] See part II, chap. 3, sect. B (*e*) (*supra,* p. 146).

II:4

The Court further noted that according to the Political Constitution of Ecuador, the incommunicado detention of a person might not exceed 24 hours. Nevertheless, Mr. Suárez Rosero was held incommunicado from 23 June to 28 July 1992, for a total of 35 days in excess of the maximum period established by the Constitution. The Court observed that incommunicado detention was an exceptional measure, the purpose of which was to prevent any interference with the investigation of the facts. Such isolation had to be limited to the period of time expressly established by law. Even in that case, the State was obliged to ensure that the detainee enjoyed the minimum and non-derogable guarantees established in the Convention and, specifically, the right to question the lawfulness of the detention and the guarantee of access to effective defence during his incarceration.

The Court found that incommunicado detention of Mr. Suárez Rosero's from 23 June to 28 July 1992 violated article 7, paragraph 2, of the Convention. The Court further deemed that as he had not been brought before a competent judicial authority as required by article 7, paragraph 5, that provision had also been violated.

Turning to article 7, paragraph 6, of the Convention, the Court observed that the right it enshrined was not exercised with the mere formal existence of the remedies it governed as those remedies had to be effective. In an advisory opinion, the Court had held that in order for *habeas corpus* to achieve its purpose, to obtain a judicial determination of the lawfulness of a detention, it was necessary for the detained person to be brought before a competent judge or tribunal with jurisdiction over him. Here *habeas corpus* performed a vital role in ensuring that a person's life and physical integrity were respected, in preventing his disappearance or the keeping of his whereabouts secret and in protecting him against torture or other cruel, inhuman or degrading punishment or treatment.

The Court considered it proven that the writ of *habeas corpus* filed by Mr. Suárez Rosero was disposed of by the Supreme Court of Justice of Ecuador more than 14 months after it was filed. The application was ruled inadmissible on the ground that he had omitted certain information, whereas, under the domestic law of the State, such information was not a prerequisite for admissibility.

As to article 25 of the Convention, providing everyone with the right to simple and prompt recourse, or any other effective recourse, to a competent court or tribunal, the Court in the *Castillo Páez* case had ruled that this provision constituted one of the basic pillars not only of the Convention, but of the very rule of law in a democratic society in the sense of the Convention. Article 25 was closely linked to the general obligation to respect the rights, contained in article 1, paragraph 1, of the Convention, in assigning protective functions to the domestic law of States parties. The purpose of *habeas corpus* was not only to ensure respect for the right to personal liberty and physical integrity, but also to prevent the person's disappearance or the keeping of his whereabouts secret and, ultimately, to ensure his right to life.

On the basis of this, and especially since Mr. Suárez Rosero had not had access to simple, prompt and effective recourse, the Court found that the State had violated articles 7, paragraph 6, and 25 of the Convention.

In the *Villagrán Morales* et al. case (*Guatemala*),[70] the *"street children"* case, summarized in connection with the prohibition of torture[71] and also cited in connection with the right to life,[72] the five victims were killed, four of them after abduction and torture. In coming to its conclusions, the Court observed that there was abundant concurring evidence that the abduction of four of the youths was perpetrated by State agents and, more specifically, by members of the State's national police force.

With regard to the arrests, the Court reiterated what it had said in a previous case. Article 7 of the Convention contained in its paragraphs 2 and 3, as specific guarantees, the prohibition of detention and unlawful or arbitrary arrest, respectively. According to the first of these regulatory provisions, no one should be deprived of his physical liberty, except for the reasons, cases or circumstances specifically established by law (material aspect) and under strict conditions established beforehand by law (formal aspect). In the second provision, there was a condition according to which no one should be subject to arrest or imprisonment for causes or methods that although qualified as legal, might be considered incompatible with respect for the fundamental rights of the individual, because they were among other matters unreasonable, unforeseeable or out of proportion.

In this case, it was clear that in contravention of the provisions of article 7, paragraph 2, of the Convention, the four youths had been arrested although the causes or conditions established by the Guatemalan Constitution were not present. Under article 6 of the Constitution, a person might only be deprived of his liberty under an order issued according to the law by a competent judicial authority or because he was caught *in fraganti* while committing a crime or offence. Neither ground was present in this case. Moreover, the Court noted that those arrested were not brought before the competent judicial authority within six hours, as also ordered in that article, and what was more, the same article expressly established that those arrested might not be subject to any other authority. In comparing the facts of this case with the basic procedural regulation, it was clear that it was not complied with. Consequently, the

---

[70] See Inter-American Court of Human Rights, Series C: *Decisions and Judgments*, No. 63 (2000), petition 11383, judgment of 19 November 1999.
[71] See part II, chap. 3, sect. C (*f*) (*supra*, pp. 172-178).
[72] See part II, chap. 2, sect. B (*d*) (*supra*, pp. 56-57).

II:4

Court concluded that neither the material nor the formal aspect of the legal rules for detention were observed in the detention of the four youths.

The Court further noted that the European Court of Human Rights had remarked that the emphasis on the promptness of judicial control of arrests was of special importance for the prevention of arbitrary arrests. Prompt judicial intervention allowed the detection and prevention of threats against life or serious ill-treatment that violated fundamental guarantees contained in the Convention for the Protection of Human Rights and Fundamental Freedoms and in the American Convention on Human Rights. The protection of both the physical liberty of the individual and his personal safety were in play, in a context where the absence of guarantees might result in the subversion of the rule of law and deprive those arrested of the minimum legal protection. In this respect, the European Court particularly stressed that the failure to acknowledge the arrest of an individual was a complete negation of these guarantees and a very serious violation of the article in question.

Consequently, in this case, the Court concluded that the State had violated article 7 of the Convention, in relation to article 1, paragraph 1, to the detriment of the four youths arrested. The Court also found violations of other articles of the Convention as well as of articles of the Inter-American Convention to Prevent and Punish Torture. Furthermore, the Court declared that the State had violated article 1, paragraph 1, regarding the obligation to investigate and that the State should conduct a real and effective investigation to determine the persons responsible for the human rights violations referred to in its judgment and eventually punish them.

(*f*) European Court of Human Rights

Article 5 of the Convention for the Protection of Human Rights and Fundamental Freedoms protects the right to liberty and security of person. Paragraph 1 of the article affirms this right and requires that no one shall be deprived of his liberty save in cases mentioned in the provision and in accordance with a procedure prescribed by law. The six categories of permissible deprivations of liberty include, as stated in paragraph 1 (*c*), the lawful arrest or detention of a person for the purpose of bringing him before the competent legal authority on reasonable suspicion of having committed an offence or when it is reasonably necessary to prevent his committing an offence or fleeing after having done so.

Paragraph 2 stipulates that everyone who is arrested shall be informed promptly, in a language he understands, of the reasons for his arrest and of any charge against him. Under paragraph 3, everyone arrested or detained in accordance with the provisions of paragraph 1 (*c*) shall be brought promptly before a judge or other officer authorized by law to exercise judicial power. Furthermore, he shall be entitled to trial within a reasonable time or to release pending trial, and release may be conditioned by guarantees to appear for trial.

Paragraph 4 gives everyone deprived of his liberty by arrest or detention the entitlement to take proceedings by which the lawfulness of his detention shall be decided speedily by a court. His release shall be ordered if the detention is not lawful. Finally, under paragraph 5, victims of arrest or detention in breach of article 5 shall have an enforceable right to compensation.

In time of war or other public emergency threatening the life of the nation, any State party may take measures derogating from its obligations under article 5, but only on the conditions set forth in article 15 of the Convention.

In the *Guzzardi* case (*Italy*),[73] the European Court of Human Rights was required to consider what consituted a deprivation of liberty. The applicant, Michele Guzzardi, a national of Italy, complained that in 1975, a court placed him under special supervision for three years under legislation directed against the mafia. Mr. Guzzardi was ordered to reside on a small Italian island and, whilst not detained in a cell, he could only move around an extremely small part of the island. The Court pointed out that the difference between deprivation of liberty and restriction upon liberty was one of degree or intensity, and not one of nature or substance. On balance, it considered that the case was to be regarded as one involving deprivation of liberty. The Court, sitting in plenary, held, by eleven votes to seven, that there was a deprivation of liberty within the meaning of article 5 of the Convention. It further held, *inter alia*, by ten votes to eight, that Mr. Guzzardi was the victim of a breach of article 5, paragraph 1.

The situations of permissible deprivations of liberty are exhaustively listed in article 5, paragraph 1, of the Convention. In other situations, deprivations are prohibited as has been indicated, for example, in the *Ciulla* case (*Italy*).[74] The applicant, Salvatore Ciulla, an Italian citizen, alleged violations of article 5, paragrahps 1 and 5, of the Convention. Under the same legislation as in the previous case, a court ordered the arrest of Mr. Ciulla as a preventive measure. On 8 May 1984, he was taken into custody at a prison. On 24 May 1984, the court made a compulsory residence order in a specific location. The European Court found that the arrest of Mr. Ciulla was designed to obviate the risk that he might evade any possible preventive measure, and there were no concrete and specific offences mentioned. Whilst not underestimating the importance of Italy's struggle against organized crime, the Court observed that

---

[73] See *Publications of the European Court of Human Rights*, Series A: *Judgments and Decisions*, vol. 39 (1981), application No. 7367/76, judgment of 6 november 1980.
[74] *Ibidem*, vol. 148 (1989), application No. 11152/84, judgment of 22 February 1989.

II:4

the exhaustive list of permissible exceptions in article 5, paragraph 1, had to be interpreted strictly. The Court, sitting in plenary, held, *inter alia*, by fifteen votes to two, that there had been a violation of that provision.

In a number of cases, the Court has insisted that whether a detention is lawful within the meaning of article 5, paragraph 1, including whether it is effected in accordance with a procedure prescribed by law, refers essentially to national law. However, it also requires that any measure depriving an individual of liberty must be compatible with the purposes of article 5, namely to protect the individual from arbitrariness.

In the case *Lukanov* v. *Bulgaria,*[75] the Court was not persuaded that the conduct for which Mr. Lukanov was prosecuted constituted a criminal offence under Bulgarian law. It did not find that his deprivation of liberty was a lawful detention effected on reasonable suspicion of having committed an offence. The applicant, Andrei Karlov Lukanov, a Bulgarian citizen and former member of the Government, was charged in 1992 with having, in concert with other Government members, misappropriated funds allocated for certain developing countries, in breach of his official duties. The prosecutor ordered his detention on remand. The Court observed that the provisions of the criminal code did not imply that anyone could incur criminal liability by taking part in collective decisions of this nature, and there was no evidence that such decisions were unlawful, taken in excess of powers or contary to the law on the national budget. There had been a violation of article 5, paragraph 1, of the Convention.

Some of the categories of permissible deprivations of liberty under article 5, paragraph 1, reflect more closely police powers to arrest and detain than others. For example, the lawful arrest or detention of a person for non-compliance with the lawful order of a court or in order to secure the fulfilment of any obligation prescribed by law, as allowed for by paragraph 1 (*b*), is an action that police could be expected to undertake. However, such an obligation must be specific, not general.

In an early case of the Court, the *Lawless* case (*Ireland*),[76] the applicant, G. R. Lawless, a national of Ireland, was detained without trial under emergency legislation between 13 July and 11 December 1957 in a military camp. The Court said, *inter alia*, that the detention of Mr. Lawless on suspicion of being engaged in activities prejudicial to the preservation of public peace and order or to the security of the State could not be deemed to be a measure taken in order to secure the fulfilment of

---

[75] See European Court of Human Rights, *Reports of Judgments and Decisions*, 1997-II, p. 529, application No. 21915/93, judgment of 20 March 1997.
[76] See *Publications of the European Court of Human Rights*, Series A: *Judgments and Decisions*, [vol. 3] (1961), application No. 332/57, judgment of 1 July 1961.

an obligation prescribed by law. This was the case, because paragraph 1 (*b*) did not contemplate arrest or detention for the prevention of offences against public peace and public order or against the security of the State, but for securing the execution of specific obligations imposed by law. For this and other reasons, the Court concluded that article 5 of the Convention did not provide any legal foundation for the detention of Mr. Lawless, but it was founded on the right to derogation duly exercised by the Irish Government under article 15 of the Convention.

The *Lawless* case can be contrasted with another case, *McVeigh, O'Neill and Evans* v. *the United Kingdom*.[77] The applicants, Bernard Leo McVeigh, a United Kingdom citizen, Oliver Anthony O'Neill, an Irish citizen, and Arthur Walter Evans, a United Kingdom citizen, were post-office employees. They were arrested on 22 February 1977 upon their arrival in the United Kingdom from Ireland, under emergency legislation designed to counter acts of terrorism. They were detained for 45 hours at a police station where they were searched, fingerprinted, photographed and questioned as permitted under that legislation. The European Commission of Human Rights decided that the measures were, in principle, permissible under article 5, paragraph 1 (*b*), of the Convention. They could be justified in this particular situation, because the obligation imposed on the applicants to submit to examination was a specific and concrete obligation. Subsequently, acting under the then article 32 of the Convention, the Committee of Ministers of the Council of Europe decided that there had been no violation of article 5 in the case.[78]

Article 5, paragraph 1 (*c*), of the Convention allows the lawful arrest or detention of a person effected for the purpose of bringing him before the competent legal authority on reasonable suspicion of having committed an offence or when it is reasonably considered necessary to prevent his committing an offence or fleeing after having done so. The meaning of this subparagraph is also addressed in the *Lawless* case. It was evident, the Court said, that the expression "effected for the purpose of bringing him before the competent legal authority" qualified every category of cases of arrest or detention referred to in the subparagraph. In other words, deprivation of liberty was permitted for the purpose of bringing a person before the competent judicial authority irrespective of whether that person had been arrested or detained on reasonable suspicion of having committed an offence, or because it was reasonably considered necessary to prevent his committing an offence or fleeing after having done so.

In the *Guzzardi* case, the Court observed that if the grounds for the detention of Mr. Guzzardi were because it was reasonably considered necessary to prevent his com-

---

[77] See European Commission of Human Rights, *Decisions and Reports*, No. 25 (1982), p. 15, applications No. 8022/77, No. 8025/77 and No. 8027/77, report adopted on 18 March 1981.
[78] *Ibidem*, p. 57, resolution DH (82) 1 adopted on 24 March 1982.

II:4

mitting an offence, a question would arise as to the measure's lawfulness. The phrase "lawful" was not adapted to a policy of general prevention directed against an individual or a category of individuals who, like mafiosi, presented a danger on account of their continuing propensity to crime. It did no more than afford the States a means of preventing a concrete and specific offence. The Court held, by twelve votes to six, that the deprivation of liberty in this case was not justified under article 5, paragraph 1 (*c*), of the Convention.

In the *Ciulla* case, the Court also pointed out that article 5, paragraph 1 (*c*), permitted deprivation of liberty only in connection with criminal proceedings. This was apparent from its wording, which had to be read in conjunction both with paragraphs 1 (*a*) and 3 that formed a whole with it. The preventive procedure provided for in the domestic law applied in this case was designed for purposes different from those of criminal proceedings. The deprivation of Mr. Ciulla's liberty preceding the court's cumpulsory residence order could not be equated with pre-trial detention as governed by article 5, paragraph 1 (*c*), of the Convention.

The question of what constitutes reasonable suspicion has been considered by the Court in the *Fox, Campbell and Hartley* case (*the United Kingdom*).[79] The applicants, Bernhard Fox, Marie Campbell and Samuel Hartley, all Irish citizens, were arrested in 1986 under emergency legislation in Northern Ireland, suspected of being terrorists. They were questioned about suspected involvement in activities of the Provisional IRA (Irish Republican Army). No charges were brought against them, and they were released, Mr. Fox and Ms. Campbell after 44 hours and Mr. Hartley after 30 hours. In respect of article 5, paragraph 1 (*c*), of the Convention, the applicants argued that they had not been arrested and detained on reasonable suspicion of having committed an offence.

The Court stated that having a reasonable suspicion presupposed the existence of facts or information which would satisfy an objective observer that the person concerned might have committed the offence. What might be regarded as reasonable would, however, depend upon all the circumstances. In this respect, terrorist crime fell into a special category. Because of the attendant risk of loss of life and human suffering, the police were obliged to act with utmost urgency in following up all information, including that from secret sources. Furthermore, the police might frequently have to arrest a suspected terrorist on the basis of reliable information that could not be revealed to the suspect or produced in court to support a charge, because doing so could put in jeopardy the source of information. The reasonableness

---

[79] See *Publications of the European Court of Human Rights*, Series A: *Judgments and Decisions*, vol. 182 (1990), applications No. 12244/86, No. 12245/86 and No. 12383/86, judgment of 30 August 1990.

of the suspicion justifying such arrests could not always be judged according to the same standards as were applied in dealing with conventional crime. The Court cautioned, however, that the exigencies of dealing with terrorist crime could not justify stretching the notion of reasonableness to the point, where the essence of the safeguard secured by article 5, paragraph 1 (*c*), of the Convention was impaired.

The fact that the suspected terrorists in this case were questioned about specific terrorist attacks confirmed that the arresting officers had a genuine suspicion of involvement in those acts, but it could not satisfy an objective observer that the suspects might have committed these acts. The minimum standard set by article 5, paragraph 1 (*c*), of the Convention for judging the reasonableness of a suspicion for the arrest of an individual was not met in this case. The Court held, by four votes to three, that there had been a breach of this provision.

The concept of reasonableness in relation to ordinary, non-terrorist, criminality is addressed in the case *K.-F.* v. *Germany*,[80] summarized in section C,[81] which also provides a good account of what is required for a detention to be lawful under article 5. The applicant, Mr. K.-F., a German national, and his wife were arrested on 4 July 1991 at 9.45 a.m. by police after a landlady had complained that they were about to leave without paying the rent for a flat. They were taken to a police station for their identities to be checked. They were suspected of rent fraud, and there was a risk that they would abscond. On the next day, at 10.30 a.m., they were released, since the public prosecutor had informed the police that he did not intend to issue an arrest warrant. The applicant claimed, *inter alia*, that his arrest and subsequent detention were unlawful under article 5, paragraph 1, of the Convention.

The Court accepted that in the cirumstances, Mr. K.-F. was detained on reasonable suspicion of having committed an offence within the meaning of article 5, paragraph 1 (*c*), and it pursued the purpose indicated in that provision. However, in respect of whether or not his arrest and detention were lawful, the Court came to the conclusion that there had been a breach of paragraph 1 (*c*), because Mr. K.-F. had been detained for more than 12 hours. Under domestic law, 12 hours' detention was the maximum period of time for the purpose of checking identity, and it was absolute.

Article 5, paragraph 1 (*e*), of the Convention allows the lawful detention of persons for the prevention of infectious diseases, of persons of unsound mind, alcoholics or

---

[80] See European Court of Human Rights, *Reports of Judgments and Decisions*, 1997-VII, p. 2657, application No. 25629/94, judgment of 27 November 1997.
[81] See part II, chap. 4, sect. C (*k*) (*infra*, pp. 282-286).

II:4

drug addicts or vagrants. In the *Winterwerp* case (*the Netherlands*),[82] the notion of unsound mind was considered. The applicant, Frits Winterwerp, a Netherlands national, was in 1968 committed to a psychiatric hospital under an emergency procedure. On his wife's application, a district court ordered his confinement to the same hospital. On further application by his wife and subsequently at the request of the public prosecutor, the order was renewed by a regional court from year to year on the basis of medical reports. The applicant complained that he was a victim of breaches of article 5, paragraphs 1 and 4, of the Convention.

As to the term "persons of unsound mind", the Court pointed out that no definitive interpretation could be given to this expression in article 5, paragraph 1 (*e*), of the Convention. It was a term whose meaning was continually evolving as research in psychiatry progressed, increasing flexibility in treatment was devloping and society's attitude to mental illness changed. In any event, the Court stated, paragraph 1 (*e*) could not be taken as permitting the detention of a person simply because his views or behaviour deviated from the norms prevailing in a particular society.

As to the lawfulness of a detention under article 5, paragraph 1 (*e*), the Court insisted that a person should not be deprived of his liberty unless he had been reliably shown to be of unsound mind. This required objective medical expertise. Furthermore, the mental disorder had to be of a kind or degree that warranted compulsory confinement, and the validity of continued confinement depended upon the persistence of such a disorder.

In the circumstances of the case, the Court concluded that the confinment of Mr. Winterwerp constituted the lawful detention of a person of unsound mind and that he was detained in accordance with a procedure prescribed by law. There was no violation of article 5, paragraph 1, of the Convention.

Article 5, paragraph 2, of the Convention stipulates that everyone who is arrested shall be informed promptly, in a language which he understands, of the reasons for his arrest and of any charge against him. This paragraph was interpreted in the *Fox, Campbell and Hartley* case. The applicants claimed that they were not given at the time of their arrest adequate and understandable information of the substantive grounds for their arrest. They were left to deduce from the subsequent interrogation the reasons for their arrest.

The Court pronounced that this provision contained the elementary safeguard that any person arrested should know why he was being deprived of his liberty. The pro-

---

[82] See *Publications of the European Court of Human Rights*, Series A: *Judgments and Decisions*, vol. 33 (1980), application No. 6301/73, judgment of 24 October 1979.

vision was an integral part of the scheme of protection afforded by article 5. By virtue of paragraph 2, any person arrested had to be told, in simple, non-technical language that he could understand, the essential legal and factual grounds for his arrest, so as to be able, if fit, to apply to a court to challenge its lawfulness in accordance with paragraph 4 of the same article. Whilst this information had to be conveyed promptly, it needed not to be related in its entirety by the arresting officer at the very moment of the arrest. Whether the content and promptness of the information conveyed were sufficient was to be assessed in each case according to its special features. In this case, the Court found no violation of article 5, paragraph 2, of the Convention.

Article 5, paragraph 3, of the Convention states that everyone arrested or detained in accordance with the provisions of paragraph 1 (*c*) of this article shall be brought promptly before a judge or other officer authorized by law to exercise judicial power. He shall be entitled to trial within a reasonable time or to release pending trial. Release may be conditioned by guarantees to appear for trial.

The notion of being brought promptly before a juge was considered by the Court in the *Brogan and Others* case (*the United Kingdom*),[83] where the four applicants, Terence Brogan and three other British citizens living in Northern Ireland, were arrested in 1984 under emergency legislation designed to counter acts of terrorism. They were detained by police for periods ranging from four days and six hours to six days and sixteen and a half hours. None of them were brought before a judge or judicial officer during the time they spent in police custody. This case is summarized in section C,[84] where it can be seen that the applications also raised issues under article 5, paragraphs 1 (*c*), 4 and 5, of the Convention. The Court delivered its judgment sitting in plenary.

The Court, noting the growth of terrorism in modern society, recognized the need, inherent in the Convention system, for a proper balance between the defence of the institutions of democracy in the common interest and the protection of individual rights. It acknowledged that the investigation of terrorist offences presented the authorities with special problems. In this case, the Court took note of safeguards of ministerial control, monitoring by Parliament of the need for emergency legislation and reviews of the operation of legislation. Furthermore, it accepted that the context of terrorism in Northern Ireland had the effect of prolonging the permissible period of detention prior to appearance before a judge or judicial authority. Nevertheless, the Court decided that even the shortest of the four periods of detention fell outside

---

[83] *Ibidem*, vol. 145-B (1989), application No. 11209/84, No. 11234/84, No. 11266/84 and No. 11386/85, judgment of 29 November 1988.

[84] See part II, chap. 4, sect. C (*j*) (*infra*, pp. 270-281).

II:4

the strict time constraints permitted by the notion of promptness. It concluded that none of the applicants were brought promptly before a judicial authority, nor were they released promptly following arrest. The Court held, by twelve votes to seven, that there had been a violation of article 5, paragraph 3, of the Convention in respect of all four applicants.

Similar issues arose in the case *Aksoy* v. *Turkey*,[85] summarized in connection with the prohibition of torture.[86] The applicant, Zeki Aksoy, was arrested by Turkish security forces towards the end of November 1992, held without judicial intervention and released on 10 December 1992. The inability of the authorities to state exactly when Mr. Aksoy was deprived of his liberty is a point to be noted. He was shot and killed on 16 April 1994, and thereafter his father indicated that he wished to pursue the case. The Court, recalling its judgment in the *Brogan and Others* case, observed that clearly, the period of 14 or more days during which Mr. Aksoy was detained without being brought before a judge or other judicial officer did not satisfy the requirement of promptness in article 5, paragraph 3, of the Convention.

The Government had argued that there was no violation of this provision, as Turkey, under article 15 of the Convention, had derogated from its obligations under article 5. The Court, however, responded that States parties did not enjoy an unlimited discretion in determining whether a public emergency existed and, if so, how far it was necessary to go in attempting to overcome the emergency. It was for the Court to rule whether a State had gone beyond the extent strictly required by the exigencies of the crisis. The domestic margin of appreciation was thus accompanied by a European supervision. In exercising this supervision, the Court had to give appropriate weight to such relevant factors as the nature of the rights affected by the derogation and the circumstances leading to the emergency situation and its duration.

The Court considered that the extent and impact of terrorist activity in the southeast of Turkey had undoubtedly created, in the region concerned, a public emergency threatening the life of the nation.

As to the right to liberty of person, the Court stressed the importance of article 5 in the Convention system. It reiterated that this provision enshrined a fundamental human right, namely the protection of the individual against arbitrary interference by the State with his or her right to liberty. Judicial control of interference by the executive with the individual's right to liberty was an essential feature of the guarantee embodied in article 5, paragraph 3, intended to minimize the risk of arbitrariness and

---

[85] See European Court of Human Rights, *Reports of Judgments and Decisions*, 1996-VI, p. 2260, application No. 21987/93, judgment of 18 December 1996.

[86] See part II, chap. 3, sect. C (*h*) (*supra*, pp. 184-186).

to ensure the rule of law. Furthermore, prompt judicial intervention might lead to the detection and prevention of serious ill-treatment.

The Court also reiterated its view that the investigation of terrorist offences undoubtedly presented the authorities with special problems. However, it could not accept that it was necessary to hold a suspect for 14 days without judicial intervention. This period was exceptionally long and left the applicant vulnerable not only to arbitrary interference with his right to liberty, but also to torture. Moreover, the Government did not adduce any detailed reasons before the Court as to why the fight against terrorism in southeastern Turkey rendered judicial intervention impracticable.

The Court considered that in this case, there were insufficient safeguards available to Mr. Aksoy, being detained over a long period of time. In particular, the denial of access to a lawyer, doctor, relative or friend and the absence of any realistic possibility of being brought before a court to test the legality of the detention meant that he was left completely at the mercy of those holding him. As can be seen from the summary of this case in connnection with the prohibition of torture, this "mercy" also led to finding a violation of article 3 of the Convention.

The Court took account of the unquestionably serious problem of terrorism in southeastern Turkey and the difficulties faced by the State in taking effective measures against it. However, it was not persuaded that the exigencies of the situation necessitated the holding of Mr. Aksoy on suspicion of involvement in terrorist offences for 14 days or more in incommunicado detention without access to a judge or other judicial officer. Accordingly, the Court held, by eight votes to one, that there had been a violation of article 5, paragraph 3, of the Convention.

The question of who can be qualified as an officer authorized by law to exercise judicial power has been considered in a number of cases, for example in the *Schiesser* case *(Switzerland)*.[87] The applicant, Friedrich Schiesser, a Swiss citizen, was brought by police before a district attorney who heard him without his lawyer being present and ordered him to be placed in detention on remand. He was suspected of having committed several offences, and it was feared that he might suppress evidence. The applicant contended that the district attorney could not be regarded as an officer authorized by law to exercise judicial power in the meaning of article 5, paragraph 3, of the Convention.

The Court observed that whilst such an officer was not identical with a judge, he nevertheless had to have some of the latter's attributes. He had to satisfy certain con-

---

[87] See *Publications of the European Court of Human Rights*, Series A: *Judgments and Decisions*, vol. 34 (1980), application No. 7710/76, judgment of 4 December 1979.

II:4

ditions constituting a guarantee for the person arrested. These included independence of the executive and of the parties; an obligation that the officer himself heard the individual brought before him; and an obligation to review the cirmcumstances militating for or against detention to decide, by reference to legal criteria, whether there were reasons to justify detention and to order release if there were no such reasons.

The Court was of the opinion that in the present case, the district attorney offered the guarantees of independence as well as the procedural and substantive guarantees required under article 5, paragraph 3, of the Convention. The Court held, by five votes to three, that there had been no breach of that provision.

On the question of the right to trial within a reasonable time or release, it is important to note the *Neumeister* case (*Austria*).[88] The applicant, Fritz Neumeister, an Austrian national, was detained on remand from 24 February to 12 May 1961. On 12 July 1962, he was again arrested and placed in detention on remand because of a danger of flight. Several requests for his release were rejected. On 16 September 1964, finally, he was released on bail.

In this case, the Court pointed out that article 5, paragraph 3, of the Convention could not be understood as giving the judicial authorities a choice between bringing the accused to trial or granting him provisional release even subject to guarantees. The reasonableness of the time spent by an accused in detention up to the beginning of the trial had to be assessed in relation to the very fact of his detention. Until conviction, an accused had to be presumed innocent. The purpose of this particular provision was essentially to require his provisional release once his continuing detention ceased to be reasonable.

The Court was of the opinion that the danger that Mr. Neumeister would avoid appearing at the trial by absconding was, in October 1962 when he proposed a bank guarantee for the first time, no longer so great that it was necessary to dismiss as quite ineffective the taking of guarantees which, under article 5, paragraph 3, might condition a grant of provisional release in order to reduce the risks that it entailed. The Court found that Mr. Neumeister's detention constituted a violation of that provision.

In the case *W. v. Switzerland*,[89] the Court recalled that the reasonableness of the continued detention of an accused person had to be assessed in each case according to its specific features. The applicant, Mr. W., a Swiss national, was a businessman

---

[88] *Ibidem*, [vol. 8] (1968), application No. 1936/63, judgment of 27 June 1968.
[89] *Ibidem*, vol. 254-A (1993), application No. 14379/88, judgment of 26 January 1993.

who with 11 accomplices was prosecuted for a series of economic offences, including a large number of frauds. On 27 March 1985, he was arrested and placed in pre-trial detention on the grounds that there was a risk of absconding, collusion and repetition of offences. From 24 May 1985 to 18 May 1988, he submitted eight applications for release. All of them were rejected. On 30 March 1989, he was sentenced to 11 years' imprisonment. The applicant claimed that the length of his pre-trial detention had been in breach of article 5, paragraph 3, of the Convention.

The Court stated that continued detention could be justified in a given case only when specific indications of a genuine requirement of public interest outweighed the rule of respect for individual liberty, notwithstanding the presumption of innocence. It went on to observe that the persistence of reasonable suspicion that the person arrested had committed an offence was a condition *sine qua non* for the lawfulness of the continued detention, but after a certain lapse of time it no longer sufficed. The Court then had to establish whether the other grounds given by the judicial authorities continued to justify the deprivation of liberty.

The Court accepted the reasons for the continued detention of Mr. W. and the conduct of the proceedings. It held, by five votes to four, that there had been no violation of article 5, paragraph 3, of the Convention.

Article 5, paragraph 4, entitles everyone deprived of his liberty by arrest or detention to take proceedings by which the lawfulness of his detention shall be decided speedily by a court. If the detention is not lawful, his release shall be ordered.

In the *Winterwerp* case that concerned the detention of a person of unsound mind, the Court observed that the reasons justifying the detention within the meaning of paragraph 1 might cease to exist and that the application of paragraph 4 had to be subject to review. The Court pointed out that the very nature of the deprivation of liberty under consideration would appear to require a review of lawfulness to be available at reasonable intervals.

Furthermore, the Court reiterated that in order to satisfy article 5, paragraph 4, interventions had to follow a procedure of judicial character and give to the individual concerned guarantees appropriate to the deprivation of liberty in question. In this case, Mr. Winterwerp was never associated personally or through a representative in the proceedings leading to the detention orders; he was never notified of the proceedings or of their outcome; and he was not heard by the courts or given the opportunity to argue his case. In this respect, the guarantees demanded by this provison of the Convention were lacking both in law and in practice. The Court found that the procedure did not meet the requirements of article 5, paragraph 4.

II:4

In the *Brogan and Others* case, the applicants claimed that an effective review of the lawfulness of their detention was precluded, as article 5 of the Convention had not been incorporated into domestic law. However, the remedy of *habeas corpus* was available to them, though they had not availed themselves of it. Making reference to its case law, the Court said that lawfulness under article 5, paragraph 4, of the Convention had the same meaning as in paragraph 1. Whether an arrest or a detention could be regarded as lawful had to be determined in the light not only of domestic law, but also of the text of the Convention, the general principles embodied therein and the aim of the restrictions permitted by paragraph 1 of the article. Paragraph 4 gave an entitlement to a review bearing upon the procedural and substantive conditions essential for the lawfulness of the deprivation of liberty, in the sense of the Convention. In this case, the applicants should have had available to them a remedy allowing the competent court to examine not only compliance with the procedural requirements set out in domestic law, but also the reasonableness of the suspicion grounding the arrest and the legitimacy of the purpose pursued by the arrest and the ensuing detention.

The Court reiterated that these conditions were met in the practice of Northern Ireland courts in relation to the remedy of *habeas corpus*. Accordingly, it held that there had been no violation of article 5, paragraph 4, of the Convention.

C. CASE SUMMARIES

(a) *W. Delgado Páez* v. *Colombia* (Human Rights Committee)[90]

The author of the communication was William Eduardo Delgado Páez, a Colombian national. He submitted the communication to the Human Rights Committee on 4 October 1985, claiming violations by Colombia of a number articles of the International Covenant on Civil and Political Rights, including in respect of the right to security of person.

The facts

The author submitted, *inter alia*, the following. In 1983, he was appointed to be teacher of religion and ethics at a secondary school in Leticia, Colombia, but as an advocate of "liberation theology", his social views differed from those of the then apostolic prefect of Leticia. Following a series of incidents, the author became con-

---

[90] See United Nations, *Official Records of the General Assembly, Forty-fifth Session, Supplement No. 40* (A/45/40), vol. II, annex IX, sect. D, communication No. 195/1985, views adopted on 12 July 1990.

vinced that he was a victim of discrimination by the ecclesiastical and educational authorities of Leticia. To remedy the situation, he took steps that included making complaints against the apostolic prefect and the educational authorities. Subsequently, while away from Leticia, he received anonymous phone calls threatening him with death if he returned and did not withdraw his complaints. He also received other threats which he reported to the military authorities, the teachers' union, the Ministry of Education and the President of Colombia. A work colleague was then shot and killed, and the author was himself attacked. Fearing for his own life, he left the country and obtained political asylum in France in 1986.

The issues and proceedings before the Committee

In considering this communication, the Committee noted that although the author had not specifically invoked article 9 of the Covenant, a further submission in 1987 raised important questions under that article. Even though the State party had been requested to address these issues, it had not done so.

The Committee observed that the first sentence of article 9, paragraph 1, of the Covenant did not stand as a separate paragraph. Its location as a part of paragraph 1 could lead to the view that the right to security arose only in the context of arrest and detention. The *travaux préparatoires* indicated that the discussions of the first sentence did indeed focus on matters dealt with in the other provisions of article 9. The Universal Declaration of Human Rights, in article 3, referred to the right to life, liberty and security of person. These elements had been dealt with in separate clauses in the Covenant. Although the only reference in the Covenant to the right to security of person was to be found in article 9, there was no evidence that it was intended to narrow the concept of the right to security only to situations of formal deprivation of liberty. At the same time, States parties had undertaken to guarantee the rights enshrined in the Covenant. It could not be the case that as a matter of law, States could ignore known threats to the life of persons under their jurisdiction, just because he or she was not arrested or otherwise detained. States parties were under an obligation to take reasonable and appropriate measures to protect them. An interpretation of article 9 allowing a State party to ignore threats to the personal security of non-detained persons within its jurisdiction would render totally ineffective the guarantees of the Covenant.

In applying this finding to the facts of the case under consideration, the Committee observed that there appeared to have been an objective need for Mr. Delgado to be provided by the State with protective measures to guarantee his security, given the threats made against him, the attack on his person and the murder of a close colleague. It was arguable that in seeking to secure this protection, Mr. Delgado had failed to address the competent authorities, making his complaints to the military au-

II:4

thorities, the teachers' union, the Ministry of Education and the President of Colombia, rather than to the general prosecutor or the judiciary. It was unclear to the Committee whether these matters were reported to the police. Furthermore, it did not know with certainty whether any measures had been taken by the Government. However, the Committee noted that the author claimed that there was no response to his request to have these threats investigated and to receive protection. The State party had not informed the Committee otherwise. Indeed, the State party had failed to comply with the request by the Committee to provide it with information on any of the issues relevant to article 9 of the Covenant. Whilst the Committee was reluctant to make a finding of a violation in the absence of compelling evidence as to the facts, it was for the State party to inform the Committee if alleged facts were incorrect, or if they would not, in any event, indicate a violation of the Covenant.

The Committee had in its past jurisprudence made clear that circumstances might cause it to assume facts in the author's favour if the State party failed to reply or to address them. The pertinent factors in this case were that Mr. Delgado had been engaged in a protracted confrontation with the authorities over his teaching and his employment. Criminal charges, later proved unfounded, had been brought against him, and he had been suspended from his employment. Furthermore, he was known to have instituted a variety of complaints against the ecclesiastical and scholastical authorities. Coupled with these factors were threats to his life. If the State party neither denied the threats nor cooperated with the Committee to explain whether the relevant authorities were aware of them and, if so, what was done about them, the Committee had necessarily to treat as correct allegations that the threats were known and that nothing was done. Accordingly, while fully understanding the situation in Colombia, the Committee found that the State party had not taken, or had been unable to take, appropriate measures to ensure Mr. Delgado's right to security of his person under article 9, paragraph 1, of the Covenant.

The Committee also found a violation of article 25 (*c*), because the constant harassment and the threats against Mr. Delgado, in respect of which the State party failed to provide protection, made his continuation in public service teaching impossible.

The Committee concluded, therefore, that the facts of the communication disclosed violations of articles 9, paragraph 1, and 25 (*c*) of the Covenant. The State party was under an obligation to take effective measures to remedy the violations, including the granting of appropriate compensation, and to ensure that similar violations did not occur in the future.

(*b*) *Chongwe* v. *Zambia*
(Human Rights Committee)[91]

The author of the communication was Rodger Chongwe, a citizen of Zambia. He submitted the communication to the Human Rights Committee on 7 November 1997, claiming to be the victim of an assassination attempt that constituted a violation by Zambia of article 6 of the the International Covenant on Civil and Political Rights. He also raised, *inter alia*, the issue of security of person to be considered in relation to article 9.

The facts

The author submitted, *inter alia*, the following. He was a Zambian advocate and chairman of a 13-party opposition alliance. He stated that during the afternoon of 23 August 1997, he and Dr. Kenneth Kaunda, for 27 years the President of Zambia, were shot and wounded by the police. He stated that the incident occurred in a town called Kabwe when the author and Dr. Kaunda were to attend a major political rally to launch a civil disobedience campaign. He annexed reports by Human Rights Watch and Inter-African Network for Human Rights and Development as part of his communication.

The author further stated that the police fired on the vehicle on which he was travelling, slightly wounding former President Kaunda and inflicting a life threatening wound on himself. The police force subsequently promised to undertake its own investigation. The Zambian Human Rights Commission was also said to be investigating the incident, but no results of any investigations had been produced. He further referred to a Human Rights Watch report that, including 10 pages on the so-called "Kabwe shooting", confirmed the shooting incident by quoting witness statements and medical reports.

The Committee's consideration of the merits

The Committee observed that article 6, paragraph 1, of the Covenant entailed the obligation of a State party to protect the right to life of all persons within its territory and subject to its jurisdiction. In the present case, the author had claimed, and the State party failed to contest before the Committee, that the State party authorized the use of lethal force without lawful reasons that could have led to the killing of him. In the circumstances, the Committee found that the State party had not acted in accord-

---

[91] *Ibidem, Fifty-sixth Session, Supplement No. 40* (A/56/40), vol. II, annex X, sect. K, communication No. 821/1998, views adopted on 25 October 2000.

II:4

ance with its obligation to protect Mr. Chongwe's right to life under article 6, paragraph 1.

The Committee recalled its jurisprudence that article 9, paragraph 1, of the Covenant protected the right to security of person also outside the context of formal deprivation of liberty. The interpretation of article 9 did not allow a State party to ignore threats to the personal security of non-detained persons subject to its jurisdiction. In the present case, it appeared that persons acting in an official capacity within the Zambian police forces shot at Mr. Chongwe, wounded him and barely missed killing him. The State party had refused to carry out independent investigations, and the investigations initiated by the Zambian police had still not been concluded and made public, more than three years after the incident. No criminal proceedings had been initiated, and Mr. Chongwe's claim for compensation appeared to have been rejected. In the circumstances, the Committee concluded that Mr. Chongwe's right to security of his person under article 9, paragraph 1, had been violated.

The Committee was of the view that the facts before it disclosed a violation of articles 6, paragraph 1, and 9, paragraph 1, of the Covenant.

Under article 2, paragraph 3 (*a*), of the Covenant, the State party was under the obligation to provide Mr. Chongwe with an effective remedy and to take adequate measures to protect his personal security and life from threats of any kind. The Committee urged the State party to carry out independent investigations of the shooting incident and to expedite criminal proceedings against the persons responsible for the shooting. If the outcome of the criminal proceedings revealed that persons acting in an official capacity were responsible for the shooting and hurting of Mr. Chongwe, the remedy should include damages to him. The State party was under an obligation to ensure that similar violations did not occur in the future.

(c) *V. P. Domukovsky* et al. v. *Georgia* (Human Rights Committee)[92]

The authors of the communications were, respectively, Victor P. Domukovsky, a Russian national, and Zaza Tsiklauri, Petre Gelbakhiani and Irakli Dokvadze, all Georgian nationals. They submitted their communications to the Human Rights Committee on 22 and 23 December 1994 and 9 July 1995. On 5 July 1996, the Committee decided to join the consideration of the communications. The authors claimed

---

[92] *Ibidem, Fifty-third Session, Supplement No. 40* (A/53/40), vol. II, annex XI, sect. M, communications No. 623/1995, No. 624/1995, No. 626/1995 and No. 627/1995, views adopted on 6 April 1998.

II:4

to be victims of violations by Georgia of article 9 and a number of other articles of the International Covenant on Civil and Political Rights.

The facts

Mr. Dumokovsky submitted, *inter alia*, the following. On 5 October 1993, he and 18 others were brought to trial before the Supreme Court of Georgia on charges of participating in terrorist acts with the aim of weakening the Government's power and of killing the Head of State. On 6 March 1995, he was found guilty and sentenced to 14 years' imprisonment.

He stated that on 3 February 1993, when he was residing in Azerbaijan where he had sought refuge, the Government of Azerbaijan refused Georgia's request to extradite him and Mr. Gelbakhiani, one of the other authors. Thereupon, he was kidnapped from Azerbaijan and illegally arrested. In this context, he stated that the President of Georgia had publicly praised the special services that performed the kidnapping as having carried out a splendid operation. He further stated that he was beaten upon arrest and kept in detention from 6 April 1993 to 27 May 1993, after which he was transferred to solitary confinement until August 1993. Furthermore, he claimed that his arrest was illegal, because he was a deputy member of the Supreme Soviet of Georgia and as such protected by immunity.

On 13 August and 11 December 1994, he was severely beaten in his cell, as a result of which he sustained a concussion. He claimed, without giving any details, that he was forced to testify against himself.

Issues and proceedings before the Committee

With regard to the claim made by Mr. Domukovsky and Mr. Gelbakhiani that they had been illegally arrested when residing in Azerbaijan, the Committee noted that the State party had submitted that they were arrested following an agreement with the Azerbaijan authorities on cooperation in criminal matters. The State party had provided no specific information about the agreement, nor had it explained how the agreement was applied to the instant case. Counsel for Mr. Domukovsky, however, had produced a letter from the Azerbaijan Ministry of Internal Affairs to the effect that it was not aware of any request for their arrest. In the absence of a more specific explanation from the State party of the legal basis of their arrest in Azerbaijan, the Committee considered that due weight should be given to the authors' detailed allegations. It found that their arrest was unlawful and in violation of article 9, paragraph 1, of the Covenant.

II:4

In the circumstances, the Committee did not need to address the question whether Mr. Domukovsky's arrest was also illegal because of his claimed parliamentary immunity or that it violated article 25 of the Covenant.

The Committee was of the view that the facts before it disclosed a violation of article 9, paragraph 1, of the Covenant in respect of Mr. Domukovsky and Mr. Gelbakhiani. It also found that a number of other provisions of the Covenant had been violated in respect of the four authors. Furthermore, they were entitled, under article 2, paragraph 3 (*a*), to an effective remedy, including their release, and the State party was under an obligation to ensure that similar violations did not occur in the future.

Finally, the Committe recalled that by becoming a State party to the Optional Protocol to the Covenant, the State had recognized the competence of the Committee to determine whether or not there had been a violation of the Covenant. Pursuant to article 2 of the Covenant, the State had undertaken to ensure to all individuals within its territory and subject to its jurisdiction the rights recognized in the Covenant and to provide an effective and enforceable remedy in case a violation had been established. Bearing this in mind, the Committee wished to receive from the State party, within 90 days, information about the measures taken to give effect to the Committee's views.

(*d*) *Spakmo* v. *Norway*
(Human Rights Committee)[93]

The author of the communication was Aage Spakmo, a Norwegian citizen. He submitted the communication to the Human Rights Committee on 28 November 1994. He claimed to be the victim of violations of article 9 of the International Covenant on Civil and Political Rights.

The facts

The author submitted, *inter alia*, the following. He was commissioned by a landlord to carry out repairs to a building, including the demolition and replacement of three balconies. However, two tenants applied for an injunction delaying the work until such time as the owner guaranteed that the balconies would be restored to their original appearance. The injunction was granted. He then contacted the judge to ascertain how to proceed. He was told that the owner could either request an oral negotiation in court, or the municipal building authorities could issue a ruling authorizing the demolition of the balconies. The author further stated that a municipal inspector,

---

[93] *Ibidem, Fifty-fifth Session, Supplement No. 40* (A/55/40), vol. II, annex IX, sect. B, communication No. 631/1996, views adopted on 5 November 1999.

after having examined the building, gave an oral order to continue with the demolition.

He recommenced the work. After having received a complaint from one of the tenants in the building, the police came to the site at 10.30 p.m. and formed the opinion that the work was disturbing the peace in the neighbourhood. When they ordered him to stop his work, he refused to do so, claiming that he was working legally. Having been repeatedly ordered to stop his activities and refusing to do so, he was arrested and then released after one hour.

The next day, a Saturday, he continued with his demolition work. Again, the police ordered him to stop, and he refused. On this occasion, he was arrested at about 2.30 p.m. and released eight hours later.

Issues and proceedings before the Committee

The question before the Committee was whether the arrest of Mr. Spakmo was in violation of article 9 of the Covenant. The author had argued that there was no legal basis for his arrest and that the police were exceeding their competence in detaining him. The Committee had noted the State party's explanations in this respect and examined the Courts' decisions. It concluded that Mr. Spakmo was arrested in accordance with Norwegian law and that his arrest was thus not unlawful.

The Committee then recalled that for an arrest to be in compliance with article 9, paragraph 1, of the Covenant, it had not only to be lawful, but also reasonable and necessary in all the circumstances. In this case, it was not disputed that the police had ordered Mr. Spakmo several times to stop the demolition and that he refused to comply. In the circumstances, the Committee considered that his arrest on the first occasion was reasonable and necessary in order to stop the demolition that the police considered unlawful and a disturbance of the peace in the neighbourhood. Mr. Spakmo's arrest on the next day was again a result of him refusing to follow the orders of the police. While accepting that his arrest by the police on that occasion might also have been reasonable and necessary, the Committee considered that the State party had failed to show why it was necessary to detain Mr. Spakmo for eight hours to make him stop his activities. In the circumstances, the Committee found that his detention for eight hours was unreasonable and constituted a violation of article 9, paragraph 1, of the Covenant.

The Committee recalled that the State party was under the obligation to provide Mr. Spakmo with an effective remedy, including compensation, and to take measures to prevent similar violations in the future. It also requested the State party to publish the Committee's views.

II:4

Six members of the Committee were unable to agree with the conclusion that Mr. Spakmo's detention for eight hours was unreasonable and constituted a violation of article 9, paragraph 1, of the Covenant.

In their individual opinion, the dissenting members emphasized that the role of the Committee was to apply provisions of the Covenant to particular cases and that it was not a fourth instance of any judicial proceedings. According to the established jurisprudence of the Committee, it was not for the Committee but for national courts to evaluate facts and evidence. In fact, they observed, the Committee had seldom rejected the national courts' findings or interpretation or application of domestic law if it was, as such, in conformity with the Covenant, unless the interpretation or application was manifestly unreasonable or disproportionate or constituted denial of justice.

The Norwegian courts' decisions in the present case did not disclose any such defect. On the contrary, the courts had taken all the relevant factors into account in reaching their decisions. After his arrest on the first occasion, Mr. Spakmo was released one hour later around midnight. After his arrest on the next occasion, he was released eight hours later, again around midnight. It might be, the members observed, that the police on the latter occasion had little choice but to hold Mr. Spakmo until after nightfall, given the length of daylight hours in Norway in July and his previous conduct. They could thus have prevented another disturbance to the peace of the neighbourhood.

(e) *Paul Kelly* v. *Jamaica* (Human Rights Committee)[94]

The author of the communication was Paul Kelly, a Jamaican citizen awaiting execution at a prison in Jamaica. He submitted the communication to the Human Rights Committee on 15 September 1987. He claimed to be the victim of violations by Jamaica of, *inter alia*, articles 9, 10 and 14 of the International Covenant on Civil and Political Rights.

The facts

The author submitted, *inter alia*, the following. He was arrested on 20 August 1981 and detained until 15 September 1981 without formal charges being brought against him. Following a statement to the police given on 15 September 1981, he was charged with murder. He was tried between 9 and 15 February 1983, found guilty and sentenced to death. His appeal against conviction was dismissed.

---

[94] *Ibidem, Forty-sixth Session, Supplement No. 40* (A/46/40), annex XI, sect. D, communication No. 253/1987, views adopted on 8 April 1991.

Between his arrest and the filing of formal charges against him, 26 days passed. During this time, he was not allowed to contact his family nor to consult with a lawyer, in spite of his requests to meet with one. After he was charged, another week elapsed before he was brought before a judge. During this period, his detention was the sole responsibility of the police, and he was unable to challenge it. This situation, he contended, revealed violations of article 9, paragraphs 3 and 4, of the Covenant in that he was not brought promptly before a judge or other officer authorized by law to exercise judicial power, and because he was denied the means of challenging the lawfulness of his detention during the first five weeks following his arrest.

Furthermore, the State party had violated article 14, paragraph 3 (*a*), of the Covenant, because he was not informed promptly and in detail of the nature of the charges against him. Upon his arrest, he was held for several days at central lock-up, pending "collection" by the police, and merely told that he was wanted in connection with a murder investigation. It was only on 15 September 1981 that he was informed that he was charged with murder.

The author also contended that he had been the victim of a violation of article 14, paragraph 3 (*c*), of the Covenant in that he was not tried without undue delay. Thus, almost 18 months elapsed between his arrest and the start of the trial. During the whole period, he was in police custody.

Finally, the author alleged that he was the victim of a violation of article 10 of the Covenant, since the treatment he was subjected to on death row was incompatible with the respect for the inherent dignity of the human person. In this context, he enclosed a copy of a report about the conditions of detention on death row at the prison, prepared by a non-governmental organization, which described the deplorable living conditions prevailing on death row. More particularly, the author claimed that these conditions put his health at considerable risk, adding that he received insufficient food, of very low nutritional value, that he had no access to recreational or sporting facilities and that he was locked in his cell virtually 24 hours a day. It was further submitted that the prison authorities did not provide for even basic hygienic facilities, adequate diet, medical or dental care or any type of educational services. Taken together, these conditions were said to constitute a breach of article 10 of the Covenant.

Issues and proceedings before the Committee

In respect of the allegations pertaining to article 9, paragraphs 3 and 4, of the Covenant, the State party had not contested that Paul Kelly was detained for some five weeks before he was brought before a judge or judicial officer entitled to decide on the lawfulness of his detention. The delay of over one month violated the require-

II:4

ment, in article 9, paragraph 3, that anyone arrested on a criminal charge should be brought promptly before a judge or other officer authorized by law to exercise judicial power. The Committee considered it to be an aggravating circumstance that throughout this period, Paul Kelly was denied access to legal representation and any contact with his family. As a result, his right under article 9, paragraph 4, was also violated, since he was not in due time afforded the opportunity to obtain, on his own initiative, a decision by the court on the lawfulness of his detention.

As to the author's claim under article 10 of the Covenant, the Committee reaffirmed that the obligation to treat individuals with respect for the inherent dignity of the human person encompassed the provision of, *inter alia*, adequate medical care during detention. The provision of basic sanitary facilities to detained persons equally fell within the ambit of article 10. The Committee further considered that the provision of inadequate food to detained individuals and the total absence of recreational facilities did not, save under exceptional circumstances, meet the requirements of article 10. In the case of Paul Kelly, the State party had not refuted the allegation that he had contracted health problems as a result of a lack of basic medical care and that he was only allowed out of his cell for 30 minutes each day. As a result, his right under article 10, paragraph 1, had been violated.

On article 14, paragraph 3 (*a*), of the Covenant, requiring any individual under criminal charges to be informed promptly and in detail of the nature and the charges against him, the Committee pronounced that the requirement of prompt information only applied once the individual had been formally charged with a criminal offence. It did not apply to those remanded in custody pending the result of police investigations. The latter situation was covered by article 9, paragraph 2, of the Covenant. In the present case, the State party had not denied that Paul Kelly was not apprised in any detail of the reasons for his arrest for several weeks following his apprehension and that he was not informed about the facts of the crime in connection with which he was detained or about the identity of the victim. The Committee concluded that the requirements of article 9, paragraph 2, were not met.

With respect to the claim of undue delay in the proceedings against the author, two issues arose. The author contended that his right, under article 14, paragraph 3 (*c*), of the Covenant, to be tried without undue delay was violated, because almost 18 months elapsed between his arrest and the opening of the trial. While the Committee reaffirmed that all stages of the judicial proceedings should take place without undue delay, it could not conclude that a lapse of a year and a half between the arrest and the start of the trial constituted undue delay, as there was no suggestion that pre-trial investigations could have been concluded earlier or that Paul Kelly complained in this respect to the authorities.

II:4

The Committee was of the view that the facts before the Committee disclosed violations of, *inter alia*, articles 9, paragraphs 2 to 4, and 10 of the Covenant.

Furthermore, in capital punishment cases, States parties had an imperative duty to observe rigorously all the guarantees for a fair trial set out in article 14 of the Covenant. Because of violations of article 14 of the Covenant, not included in this summary, the Committee was of the view that Paul Kelly was entitled to a remedy entailing his release. In coming to this view, it reiterated its opinion that the imposition of a sentence of death upon the conclusion of a trial in which the provisions of the Covenant had not been respected constituted, if no further appeal against the sentence was available, a violation of article 6.

(f) *Michael and Brian Hill* v. *Spain* (Human Rights Committee)[95]

The authors of the communication were Michael and Brian Hill, British citizens residing in the United Kingdom of Great Britain and Northern Ireland. They submitted the communication to the Human Rights Committee on 1 October 1992, claiming to be victims of violations by Spain of, *inter alia*, articles 9 and 10 of the International Covenant on Civil and Political Rights.

The facts

The authors submitted, *inter alia*, the following. They owned a construction firm in the United Kingdom which declared bankruptcy whilst they were held in detention in Spain. In 1985, they went on holiday to Spain. On 16 July 1985, the Gandía police arrested them on suspicion of having firebombed a bar in Gandía, an accusation they had denied since the time of their arrest. They claimed that they were in the bar until 2.30 a.m., but they did not return at 4 a.m. to set fire to the premises as was alleged.

At the police station, they requested the police to allow them to contact the British Consulate so as to obtain the aid of a consular representative who could assist as an independent interpreter. The request was denied and an interpreter, who they alleged was unqualified, was called to assist in the interrogation which took place without the presence of defence counsel. They stated that they could not express themselves properly, as they did not speak Spanish, and the interpreter's English was very poor. As a result, serious misunderstandings allegedly arose. They denied having been informed of their rights at the time of their arrest or during the interrogation. They al-

---

[95] *Ibidem, Fifty-second Session, Supplement No. 40* (A/52/40), vol. II, annex VI, sect. B, communication No. 526/1993, views adopted on 2 April 1997.

II:4

leged that they were not properly informed of the reasons for their detention until seven and eight hours, respectively, after the arrest.

On 19 July 1985, they were formally charged with arson and causing damage to private property. The indictment stated that on 16 July 1985 at 3 a.m., they had left the bar, driven away in their camper vehicle, returned at 4 a.m. and thrown a bottle containing petrol and petrol-soaked paper through a window of the bar.

On 20 July 1985, they appeared before the examining magistrate in order to submit a statement denying their involvement in the crime. After having been held in police custody for 10 days, for five of which they were allegedly left without food and with only warm water to drink, they were transferred to a prison in Valencia.

On 17 November 1986, they were tried in a provincial high court, convicted as charged, sentenced to six years and one day of imprisonment and ordered to payment of 1,935,000 pesetas in damages to the owner of the bar. They subsequently initiated a process of appeal. Having petitioned for release under a provision of the criminal procedure code which provided that a prisoner might be released pending the outcome of his or her appeal, they were released on 6 July 1988 and returned to the United Kingdom.

As to the question of interpretation between English and Spanish, the State party explained that the interpreter was not a person selected ad hoc by the local police. She was a person designated by the Instituto Nacional de Empleo (INEM) upon agreement with the Ministry of Interior. Interpreters had to have satisfied professional criteria before being employed by INEM. The records indicated that the interpreter was a properly designated interpreter and that she was qualified to interpret for the Michael and Brian Hill at the time of their arrest.

As to their desire to communicate with the British Consulate, the State party contended that the documents revealed that the Consulate was duly informed of their detention.

The State party rejected the allegation that Michael and Brian Hill had been kept for 10 days without food and enclosed a statement from the chief of the Gandía police and receipts they allegedly had signed.

The authors maintained that the intepreter who attended at the time of their initial arrest and detention made crucial mistakes of interpretation that ultimately led to their conviction.

They reaffirmed that they did not receive any food or drink for a period of five days and very little thereafter, because the funds allocated specifically for this purpose were misappropriated. They pointed out what they regarded to be defects in the documentation produced by the State party on this matter.

Examination of the merits

With regard to the authors' allegations of violations of article 9 of the Covenant, the Committee considered that the arrest of Michael and Brian Hill was not illegal or arbitrary. Article 9, paragraph 2, required that anyone who was arrested should be informed, at the time of arrest, of the reasons for his arrest and should be promptly informed of any charges against him. The authors specifically alleged that seven and eight hours, respectively, elapsed before they were informed of the reason for their arrest, and they complained that they did not understand the charges because of the lack of a competent interpreter. The documents submitted by the State party showed that police formalities were suspended from 6 a.m. until 9 a.m., when the interpreter arrived, so that the accused could be duly informed in the presence of legal counsel. Furthermore, from the documents sent by the State, it appeared that the interpreter was not an ad hoc interpreter. She was an official interpreter appointed according to rules that should ensure her competence. In these circumstances, the Committee found that the facts before it did not reveal a violation of article 9, paragraph 2.

As to article 9, paragraph 3, of the Covenant, stipulating that it should not be the general rule that persons awaiting trial should be detained in custody, the authors complained that they were not granted bail and that because they could not return to the United Kingdom, their construction firm was declared bankrupt. The Committee reaffirmed its prior jurisprudence that pre-trial detention should be the exception and that bail should be granted, except in situations where the likelihood existed that the accused would abscond or destroy evidence, influence witnesses or flee from the jurisdiction of the State party. The mere fact that the accused was a foreigner did not of itself imply that he might be held in detention pending trial.

The State party had indeed argued that there was a well-founded concern that Michael and Brian Hill would leave Spanish territory if released on bail. However, it had provided no information about what this concern was based upon and why it could not be addressed by setting an appropriate sum of bail and other conditions of release. The mere conjecture of a State party that a foreigner might leave its jurisdiction if released on bail did not justify an exception to the rule laid down in article 9, paragraph 3. In these circumstances, the Committee found that this right had been violated in respect of Michael and Brian Hill.

II:4

With respect to the authors' allegations regarding their treatment during detention, particularly during the first 10 days in police custody, the Committee noted that the information and documents submitted by the State party did not refute the authors' claim that they were not given any food during the first five days of police detention. The Committee concluded that such treatment amounted to a violation of article 10 of the Covenant. One member of the Committee disagreed.

The Committee found that the facts before it revealed a violation of, *inter alia*, articles 9, paragraph 3, and 10 of the Covenant in respect of both Michael and Brian Hill. Pursuant to article 2, paragraph 3 (*a*), they were entitled to an effective remedy, entailing compensation.

(g) Decision No. 38/1994 (*Turkey*)
(Working Group on Arbitrary Detention)[96]

The communication, addressed to the Government of Turkey on 20 September 1993, concerned Soner Onder, a Turkish student aged 17. Allegedly, he was being subjected to arbitrary detention that had involved torture. Turkey had ratified the Convention against Torture and Other Cruel, Inhuman or Degrading Treatment or Punishment. Turkey was not a party to the International Covenant on Civil and Political Rights.

The Working Group on Arbitrary Detention welcomed the cooperation of the Government. Having transmitted the Government's reply to the source and received its comments, the Working Group believed that it was in a position to take a decision on the facts and circumstances of the case.

The facts

According to the source, Soner Onder, who studied at a technical university in Istanbul, was detained by police following a demonstration on 25 December 1991. He was reportedly taken to Istanbul police headquarters and interrogated at the anti-terror branch until 8 January 1992, when he was formally arrested by a state security court and sent to a prison.

The demonstration was held, according to the source, by the youth organization of the illegal Kurdish Workers' Party (PKK). Following the demonstration, an arson attack, in which 12 people died, was carried out on a department store. Soner Onder was detained by police in the vicinity of the incident, along with several hundred

---

[96] See United Nations document E/CN.4/1996/40/Add.1, p. 11, decision adopted on 1 December 1994.

other youths whose identity papers showed a birthplace in the southeastern (mainly Kurdish) provinces. His trial began in February 1992 before a state security court. Reportedly, there were 22 defendants in the trial. Except for seven of them, all had been conditionally released.

Soner Onder was charged with membership of an armed organization, possession of an explosive substance, multiple killing, criminal damage and criminal damage for seditious purposes. He reportedly signed a confession while in police custody, but he retracted when brought before the prosecutor on 8 January 1992. He claimed that he had signed the confession, while being kept blindfolded and without any knowledge of its contents, because he had been tortured. The source alleged that there was evidence to support the claim of torture, including an examination by the Forensic Medicine Institute, 24 days after he was taken into police custody, which revealed that he still had considerable swelling on one testicle.

The source further noted that there were several contradictions between the confession and the version given by Soner Onder. According to the confession, on 25 December 1991, he met a person named in his statement, before the attack on the store, and received from him several Molotov cocktails in a bag. He then participated in the demonstration and threw a Molotov cocktail at a shop. The official police report of his detention stated that he was captured at the scene of the crime, together with five other defendants, holding a Molotov cocktail. But according to the version of Soner Onder, on the morning of 25 December 1991, being a Syriac Christian, he attended a Christmas service. He then caught a minibus to return to his sister's home. The minibus was stopped by police, and the identity cards of all the passengers were checked. He was then detained and taken for questioning as his card revealed that he had been born in the southeastern province of Mardin, a centre of PKK armed activity. The Working Group was subsequently informed that on 18 October 1994, Soner Onder was sentenced to life imprisonment.

In its reply, the Government pointed out that the demonstration turned violent when Molotov cocktails were thrown, setting fire to several shops and banks. In the fire, 12 people died. According to the Government, Soner Onder was searched and found to be in possession of a Molotov cocktail. When he was questioned, he admitted to have taken part in the demonstration and thrown the Molotov cocktail at the shop where the 12 people died. The Government confirmed that when the accused appeared in court on 9 January 1992, he pleaded not guilty. He denied the charges, protesting that the statement in which he confessed to the charges had been taken under duress, while he was blindfolded. The witnesses for the defence, as well as the people who had signed the report concerning the arrest of Soner Onder, were heard by the court and their statements were given due consideration.

II:4

Further information and comments were provided by the source on the Government's observations. According to one observer who had attended a hearing in the state security court on 10 May 1994, the public prosecutor told him in a conversation that he was going to request the death sentence, as the accused had been identified by an eyewitness. However, the prosecutor admitted to the observer that the report of arrest, according to which Soner Onder was picked up at the scene of the attack holding a Molotov cocktail, had been signed by mistake by a police officer who was tired, because he had been on duty too long. He further admitted that in point of fact, the student had been picked up in a minibus some distance from the scene of the attack, which was what the accused and other witnesses had been claiming from the outset.

In conclusion, the source considered that the accused's version, namely that he had to retract his confession in court because it had been obtained under torture, was backed up by the following circumstantial evidence. Soner Onder was held incommunicado while being questioned in breach of justice ministry circulars then in force; the medical certificate confirming ill-treatment was drawn up by an authorized medical service; and no inquiry was ordered when the accused claimed that he had confessed under torture.

When the witness was called on to identify him at the first hearing, Soner Onder was not put in the middle of a group of people unconnected with the trial, as was customary to ensure the credibility of the test, but he was placed in the middle of the other persons accused, in the dock. However, a number of them, also identified by the witness, were able to prove that they had not taken part in the attack and were released. Other witnesses stated that they had seen Soner Onder elsewhere at the time of the attack, yet the prosecutor did not ask any questions to evaluate that testimony.

Issues and proceedings before the Working Group

The Working Group considered that the question of principle raised by the case was whether or not the fact that the detention was ordered on the basis of evidence resulting from confessions extracted under torture conferred on it an arbitrary character.

Before reaching its decision, the Working Group examined further information within the United Nations system on the issue contained in relevant general comments of the Human Rights Committee, reports of the Special Rapporteur on the question of torture and reports of the Committee against Torture, in particular concerning Turkey.

The Working Group considered that the question of principle raised had to be examined not only in relation to international provisions prohibiting torture under any circumstances, but also in relation to provisions either explicitly referring to the inadmissibility of evidence obtained under torture or, with a view to preventing torture, requiring that no one should be compelled to testify against himself or to confess guilt. The Working Group here made reference to article 14, paragraph 3 (*g*), of the Covenant, principle 21 of the Body of Principles for the Protection of All Persons under Any Form of Detention or Imprisonment and, above all, article 15 of the Convention against Torture.

The Working Group noted that the latter article, prohibiting the use of statements made under torture as evidence, could be invoked in this case under international and internal provisions, as Turkey had ratified the Convention against Torture, and this rule was also set out in several texts of internal law to which the Working Group referred.

Furthermore, the Working Group had taken into consideration provisions in the national legislation punishing the crime of torture by imprisonment, disqualifying the perpetrator temporarily from holding public office and providing for imprisonment with hard labour and permanent disqualification from holding office when torture was used to extract a confession. The Working Group also referred to decisions of the Supreme Court of Appeal on cases brought under these provisions. This case law was reinforced by legislation prohibiting torture and similar practices during questioning and providing that the judge could not take into consideration statements obtained under duress.

Finally, the Working Group concluded that it was difficult to challenge the certificate testifying to the blows received by Soner Onder, since it was drawn up by a physician from the Forensic Institute, bearing in mind that physicians from that Institute, as reported by the State, were fully independent and accorded an exclusive position in the criminal procedure. Furthermore, the prosecution did not initiate any investigation of the alleged torture, as prosecutors were reported to have a responsibility to do, nor did it prove that the confession reflected the free will of the accused person, supported by other evidence.

In view of the application in this case of article 15 of the Convention against Torture and provisions of internal law, the Working Group considered that the fact that the detention was ordered on the basis of evidence obtained from a confession extracted under torture conferred on it an arbitrary character.

The detention of Soner Onder was declared to be arbitrary, being in contravention of article 5 of the Universal Declaration of Human Rights, article 7 of the Covenant

II:4

and article 15 of the Convention against Torture, to which Turkey was a party. It fell within category III of the principles applicable in the consideration of cases submitted to the Working Group.

Consequently, the Working Group requested the Government of Turkey to take the necessary steps to remedy the situation in order to bring it into conformity with the provisions and principles incorporated in the Universal Declaration and in the Covenant, as well as in article 15 of the Convention against Torture, in particular by taking measures towards the release of Soner Onder from prison.

(*h*) Case No. 2116 (*Indonesia*)
(Committee on Freedom of Association)[97]

The complaint against the Government of Indonesia were submitted on 23 February 2001 by the International Union of Food, Agricultural, Hotel, Restaurant, Catering, Tobacco and Allied Workers' Associations (IUF). The IUF submitted new allegations in communications dated 24 July as well as 15 and 16 October 2001. The Government sent its observations in communications dated 15 June and 31 August 2001, respectively.

Indonesia had ratified the Convention concerning Freedom of Association and Protection of the Right to Organise (No. 87) and the Convention concerning the Application of the Principles of the Right to Organise and to Bargain Collectively (No. 98).

The facts

The IUF stated that it was presenting the complaint on behalf of its Indonesian affiliate, the Shangri-la Hotel Independent Workers' Union (SPMS), against the Government of Indonesia for violations of Conventions No. 87 and No. 98. The complainant's allegations included the following.

The SPMS in Jakarta had initiated negotiations with the management of the Shangri-la Hotel regarding the establishment of a pension scheme, the granting of an annual indemnity and the equitable distribution of a percentage of gratuities, but these negotiations had been unproductive.

The management refused to have the president of the union attend the negotiations. On 22 December 2000, he was dismissed from his employment and prohibited from

---

[97] See International Labour Office, *Official Bulletin*, vol. LXXXIV, Series B, No. 3 (2001), p. 104, interim report.

entering the hotel. The employees met together in the hotel lobby and signed a petition protesting against this action. On the same day, the management transferred the guests to other hotels, declared the hotel closed and locked out all the employees.

On 26 December 2000 at 1.15 a.m., approximately 350 police officials attacked the striking workers and, at the request of the hotel management, evacuated the hotel by force. Around 20 unionists, including the IUF representative in Indonesia, were detained at the police station for a day.

At the beginning of January 2001, the management sent approximately 400 trade unionists a letter stating that they would lose their jobs for participating in the strike unless they were prepared to resign from the union. Since then, the management had refused to take part in any negotiations.

On 20 February 2001, the treasurer of the union, an employee of the hotel, was admitted to hospital after having been attacked by the head of the hotel's bodyguards. The police released one of the assailants without laying any charges.

The IUF asserted that despite the union's repeated requests, neither the Ministry of Labour nor the labour tribunal intervened to protect the workers' rights to freedom of association and to bargain collectively. In the IUF's view, the Indonesian Government had failed to meet its obligation to ensure respect for the laws concerning freedom of association and protection of trade unionists, particularly with regard to the use of a lockout as a means of resolving a collective dispute and the collective dismissal of over 400 employees because of their trade union membership. It also denounced the use of governmental police forces to assist the employer and to break up the collective protest action of the employees.

In subsequent communications, the IUF further stated, *inter alia*, that the SPMS comprised nearly 500 employees of the hotel who were dismissed after holding the strike pursuant to which the management closed the hotel for almost three months. The strike was not illegal. The objective of the workers' spontaneous action on 22 December 2000 was to protest against the dismissal of the union's president. Since the protest did not involve all members of the SPMS on duty at the time, it was not intended to bring all of the hotel's activities to a halt. In fact, the strike, called because of the management's refusal to negotiate, was planned for 31 December 2000. The management had anticipated the union members' protest. From the early morning of 22 December 2000, it had prepared to increase the number of security personnel and requested the presence of police and military. The majority of SPMS members kept working as usual until they were sent home or dismissed by the company on 23 December 2000.

II:4

The IUF contested that the workers' protest amounted to an occupation of the hotel lobby; that it had caused the cessation of hotel activities; and that the workers had caused physical damage to hotel facilities or broken hotel glass doors. It argued that the company had put into effect a lockout on 23 December 2000. The police had broken the glass doors when hundreds of police personnel in the early morning of 26 December 2000 rushed into the hotel, attacked the workers and conveyed them to the police station.

After having described the background to the conflict, the Government maintained, *inter alia*, the following.

On 22 December 2000, the management decided to suspend the president of the union as an employee of the hotel because of serious violations of provisions of the prevailing collective labour agreement. Under that agreement, any employee seriously violating it might be immediately dismissed from employment. On the same date, about 500 employees affiliated to the SPMS went on strike and demonstrated at the hotel. They occupied areas of the hotel and closed all the hotel entrances, and they searched all people entering and leaving the hotel. As such actions frightened guests, the management closed the hotel

The Government explained that the police had expelled the workers from the hotel, because employees affiliated to SPMS had occupied the hotel area. The police then carried out an investigation, suspecting criminal activity in the hotel. Furthermore, around 20 members of the SPMS and the representative of IUF in Indonesia were arrested and detained for a day merely to obtain information about the suspected criminal activity in the hotel.

Concerning the correspondence sent by the management to a number of SPMS members allegedly asking them to resign from their union, the Government stated that in January 2001, the management sent a letter to the employees involved in the illegal strike and the demonstration and occupation of the hotel area, stating that they had committed a serious violation of the provisions of the collective labour agreement. Their cases would be processed through the district office of the department of manpower. The Government indicated that the conflict at the hotel resulted in the application for termination of employment of 580 workers submitted by the management to two labour dispute settlement committees, both of which giving permission to terminate the employment of those who had not already resigned on their own initiative.

In conclusion, the Government stressed that it was striving to improve the industrial relations climate, but there were many constraints on the process of improvement, as Indonesia was undergoing a period of transition.

264

II:4

The Committee's conclusions and recommendations

Responding to the complainant's allegations and the Government's reply, the Committee on Freedom of Association drew, *inter alia*, the following conclusions.

As to the alleged large-scale dismissal of SPMS members, it appeared to the Committee that in effect 580 members were dismissed for their involvement in the strike action in late December 2000, but there was nothing to indicate that the strike action was illegal. The hotel industry was not an essential service, in the strict sense of the term, in which strikes could be prohibited. Moreover, the reasons put forward by the labour dispute settlement committees, namely that the occupation of the hotel lobby by striking unionists disturbed hotel activities and resulted in losses for the employer, did not, in the Committee's view, constitute grounds sufficient to justify the termination of employment of the unionists concerned. In this respect, the Committee drew the Government's attention to the principle that the dismissal of a worker because of a strike, a legitimate trade union activity, constituted serious discrimination in employment and was contrary to Convention No. 98. When trade unionists or trade union leaders were dismissed for having exercised the right to strike, the Committee could only conclude that they had been punished for their trade union activities and had been discriminated against.

Furthermore, the Committee reiterated, it would not appear that sufficient protection against acts of anti-union discrimination, as set out in Convention No. 98, was granted by legislation in cases where employers could, in practice, on condition that they paid the compensation prescribed by law for cases of unjustified dismissal, dismiss any worker if the true reason was the worker's trade union membership or activities.

Concerning the the police intervention on 26 December 2000, allegedly resulting in the arrest and detention of approximately 20 unionists, including the IUF representative in Indonesia, the Committee noted the Government's statement that these people were arrested and detained for a day merely to obtain information about suspected criminal events in the hotel. The Committee failed to see what criminal activities could have been committed by unionists occupying the lobby of a hotel that had been completely evacuated of its guests and employees by the management a few days earlier. In this regard, the Committee reminded the Government that the arrest and detention, even if only briefly, of trade union leaders and trade unionists for exercising legitimate trade union activities constituted a violation of the principles of freedom of association. Moreover, the Committee reiterated, measures depriving trade unionists of their freedom on grounds related to their trade union activity, even where they were merely summoned or questioned for a short period, constituted an obstacle to the exercise of trade union rights.

II:4

Regarding the alleged assault on the treasurer of the union by one of the hotel's bodyguards and the release by the police of one of the assailants without any charges being laid, the Government contended that the security guards of the hotel were not responsible for that assault and that the treasurer was involved in a fight with an unknown party not related to the events that had occurred in the hotel. The Committee noted, nevertheless, that the Government had not denied that he had been assaulted. In this respect, the Committee recalled that the rights of workers' and employers' organizations could only be exercised in a climate that was free from violence, pressure or threats of any kind against the leaders and members of these organizations, and it was for governments to ensure that this principle was respected. Moreover, in the event of assaults on the physical or moral integrity of individuals, the Committee had considered that an independent judicial inquiry should be instituted immediately with a view to fully clarifying the facts, determining responsibility, punishing those responsible and preventing the repetition of such acts.

In the light of these conclusions, the Committee invited the Governing Body of the International Labour Office to approve a number of recommendations.

The Government was requested to indicate exactly how many members of the SPMS, dismissed pursuant to their involvement in strike action, were demanding reinstatement in their jobs and to take steps to ensure the reinstatement of these persons if they so wished.

The Government was reminded of what the Committtee said in the its conclusions about arrest and detention in relation to the police intervention. The Government was urged to institute without delay an independent judicial inquiry into the physical assault on the treasurer of the SPMS with a view to fully clarifying the facts, determining responsibility, punishing those responsible and preventing the repetition of such acts. The Government was requested to keep the Committee informed of the results of such an inquiry.

There were also other recommendations not included in the present summary.

(*i*) *Castillo Páez* v. *Peru*
(Inter-American Court of Human Rights)[98]

On 13 January 1995, the Inter-American Commission on Human Rights submitted to the Inter-American Court of Human Rights an application against the Republic of Peru. It originated in a petition received by the Commission on 16 November 1990.

---

[98] See Inter-American Court of Human Rights, Series C: *Decisions and Judgments*, No. 34 (1998), petition No. 10733, judgment of 3 November 1997.

It was based on the alleged abduction and subsequent disappearance of Ernest Rafael Castillo Páez by the Peruvian police in violation of the American Convention on Human Rights. The Commission referred the case for a ruling by the Court as to whether Peru had violated, *inter alia*, the provisions on the right to personal liberty in article 7 and the right to judicial protection in article 25 of the Convention, both in relation to article 1 on the obligation to respect the rights.

Proceedings and conclusions of the Court

The Court considered the relevant facts that it deemed to have been proven or not to have been disputed, from the study of the actions of the State and the Commission and from the documentary, personal and expert evidence submitted in the case.

On the basis of the documentary and personal evidence, the Court deemed it to be proven that during the period in question, there existed in Peru a practice on the part of the forces of law and order which consisted in the forced disappearance of persons thought to be members of subversive groups. Likewise, students were the victims of such disappearances. In the early nineties, the security forces also placed the detainees in the trunks of police cars, as had occurred in this case

The Court studied the documentary and personal evidence submitted by the parties in order to decide whether the alleged facts demonstrated that members of the police had detained Mr. Castillo Páez and whether that detention was the cause of his disappearance. In that regard, the Court considered it proven that he left his home on 21 October 1990 and that on the same day the subversive group "Shining Path" detonated explosives in Lima, the capital of Peru. Shortly after the explosions, the Peruvian security forces organized an operation to detain those responsible. During that action, a white patrol vehicle approached Mr. Castillo Páez. He was wearing dark pants, a white shirt and a beige jacket. He was identified by several witnesses. Two policemen wearing green uniforms and red berets got out of the patrol vehicle. One of them arrested Mr. Castillo Páez, who did not resist, and minutes later he was placed in the trunk of the patrol vehicle. Shortly afterwards, another police vehicle arrived at the scene of the arrest, and the policemen exchanged words. The second vehicle left, followed by the vehicle carrying Mr. Castillo Páez, to an unknown destination. These events lasted approximately ten minutes.

The Court found that the victim's parents had initiated an unsuccessful search to find their son at different police precincts and instituted the appropriate judicial measures for locating him. On 25 October 1990, the victim's father filed a petition of *habeas corpus* with an examining court. On 31 October 1990, it declared the action well-founded on the basis of the evidence and of a series of irregularities discovered in the proceeding that obstructed the investigation. Subsequently, a trial was

II:4

held in a criminal court for the crime of abuse of authority against several members of the police force allegedly involved in the disappearance of Mr. Castillo Páez. That court found that the victim had been stopped by a vehicle of the Peruvian national police on the morning of 21 October 1990 and that his whereabouts were since unknown. However, in the judgment it was declared that there was no evidence to prove the defendants' responsibility. The case was, therefore, closed without anyone being punished and without an order being made for payment of compensation to the next of kin of Mr. Castillo Páez.

Since the victim's disappearance, he was not released by the police, nor was any information about him provided, although a process had been instituted to ascertain his whereabouts and secure his release.

The Court found that Peru had violated, to the detriment of Mr. Castillo Páez, several paragraphs of article 7 of the Convention. It was proven that the victim was detained by members of the national police in contravention of the Political Constitution of Peru, inasmuch as that fundamental law provided that no one might be arrested except by written order issued by a judicial authority, which did not occur in this case. It had not been proven, nor had the State so claimed, that detention of Mr. Castillo Páez took place when he was surprised *in flagrante delicto* or that there was a state of emergency in force at the time, circumstances which would have justified the victim's detention by police officers without any judicial intervention. The foregoing had its basis in article 7, paragraphs 2 and 3, of the Convention and in the Constitution of Peru.

It did not appear from the acts of the proceedings that the detainee had been brought before a competent court within 24 hours or otherwise, if distance was a factor, nor within 15 days on suspicion of terrorism, pursuant to article 7, paragraph 5, of the Convention and to the Constitution of Peru. On the contrary, with the statements by a judge during the public hearing, it was demonstrated that the police authorities had denied the arrest and hidden the detainee so that he could not be located by the magistrate. The judge's testimony was confirmed by the victim's father who also had conducted a fruitless search for his son in the police establishments. The State had simply denied the arrest and, in support of the denial, presented evidence in the form of reports from policemen on duty at a precinct station and from other units involved in the operation of 21 October 1990. However, the Court considered the evidence to be insufficient to refute the statements of the witnesses.

As to the alleged violation of article 25 of the Convention, the Court stated, *inter alia*, the following.

The Court considered that the remedy of *habeas corpus* filed against the detention of Mr. Castillo Páez by his next of kin was obstructed by State agents through the adulteration of the logs of entry of detainees, thus making it impossible to locate the victim. Furthermore, although the appeal of *habeas corpus* was favourably disposed of in two instances, the Supreme Court of Justice had nullified the ruling in a judgement of 7 February 1991.

Consequently, it had been proven that the remedy of *habeas corpus* had been ineffective for securing the release of the victim and, perhaps, for saving his life. The fact that the ineffectiveness of *habeas corpus* was due to forced disappearance did not exclude the violation of article 25 of the Convention. This provision on the right to effective recourse to a competent national court or tribunal was one of the fundamental pillars not only of the Convention, but of the very rule of law in a democratic society in the terms of the Convention.

The Court further stated that article 25 was closely linked to the general obligation to respect the rights, contained in article 1, paragraph 1, of the Convention, in that it assigned duties of protection to the States parties through their domestic legislation. The purpose of *habeas corpus* was not only to guarantee personal liberty and humane treatment, but also to prevent disappearance or failure to determine the place of detention and, ultimately, to ensure the right to life.

It was found proven that Mr. Castillo Páez was detained by members of the Peruvian police force and that consequently, he was in the custody of the police. They hid him so that he would not be located. The Court concluded that the ineffectiveness of the remedy of *habeas corpus* was imputable to the State and constituted a violation of article 25 of the Convention, in connection with article 1, paragraph 1.

The Court decided that the State had violated, *inter alia*, the right to personal liberty, recognized in article 7 of the Convention, in relation to article 1, paragraph 1, to the detriment of Mr. Castillo Páez. Furthermore, the State had violated the right to effective recourse to a competent national court or tribunal, recognized in article 25 of the Convention, in relation to article 1, paragraph 1, to the detriment of the victim and his next of kin.

The Court also decided that the State was obliged to repair the consequences of the violations it had found and to compensate the victim's next of kin and reimburse them for any expenses they might have incurred in their representations to the Peruvian authorities in connection with the case.

II:4

(j) *Brogan and Others* case (*the United Kingdom*)
(European Court of Human Rights)[99]

The case was brought before the European Court of Human Rights on 15 July 1987 by the European Commission of Human Rights and on 3 August 1987 by the Government of the United Kingdom of Great Britain and Northern Ireland. It originated in four applications against the United Kingdom lodged with the Commission by Terence Brogan, Dermot Coyle, William McFadden and Michael Tracey, all British citizens, on 18 October 1984, 22 October 1984, 22 November 1984 and 8 February 1985, respectively.

The object of the Commission's request and of the Government's application was to obtain a decision as to whether or not the facts of the case disclosed a breach by the respondent State of its obligations under article 5 of the Convention for the Protection of Human Rights and Fundamental Freedoms and, as far as the request was concerned, article 13 of the Convention. The Court delivered its judgment sitting in plenary

The facts

Mr. Brogan was arrested on 17 September 1984. Mr. Coyle, Mr. McFadden and Mr. Tracey were arrested on 1 October 1984. They were arrested under section 12 of the Prevention of Terrorism (Temporary Provisions) Act, 1984. Within hours of their arrest, they were questioned, respectively, about the attack on a police mobile patrol resulting in the death of a police sergeant and serious injuries to another police officer; the the planting of a land mine intended to kill members of the security forces and a blast incendiary bomb attack; the murder of a soldier in a bomb attack and of another soldier during a petrol bomb and gunfire attack; and about the armed robbery of two post offices and the conspiracy to murder members of the security forces. Three of them were interrogated about the suspected membership of the Provisional IRA (Irish Republican Army) and one of them about the suspected membership of the Irish National Liberation Army (INLA), both proscribed terrorist organizations for the purposes of the 1984 Act. During detention, each one of them was visited by his solicitor.

They were informed by the arresting officer that they were being arrested under section 12 of the 1984 Act and that there were reasonable grounds for suspecting them to have been involved in the commission, preparation or instigation of acts of terror-

---

[99] See *Publications of the European Court of Human Rights*, Series A: *Judgments and Decisions*, vol.145-B (1989), applications No. 11209/84, No. 11234/84, No. 11266/84 and No. 11386/85, judgment of 29 November 1988.

ism connected with the affairs of Northern Ireland. They were cautioned that they did not need to say anything, but anything they did say might be used in evidence. In principle, they remained silent during the interviews.

On the day following his arrest, each one of them was informed by police officers that the Secretary of State for Northern Ireland had agreed to extend his detention by a further five days under section 12 (4) of the 1984 Act. They were released after periods of detention ranging from four days and six hours to six days and sixteen and a half hours. None of them was brought before a judge or other officer authorized by law to exercise judicial power, nor charged after his release.

The emergency situation in Northern Ireland in the early 1970s and the attendant level of terrorist activity formed the background to the introduction of the Prevention of Terrorism (Temporary Provisions) Act, 1974. Between 1972 and 1983, over two thousand deaths were attributable to terrorism in Northern Ireland as compared with about one hundred in Great Britain. In the mid 1980s, the number of deaths was significantly lower than in the early 1970s, but organized terrorism continued to thrive.

The 1974 Act proscribed the IRA and made it an offence to display support in public for that organization in Great Britain. The IRA was already a proscribed organization in Northern Ireland. The Act also conferred special powers of arrest and detention on the police so that they could deal more effectively with the threat of terrorism. The 1974 Act was subject to renewal every six months by Parliament so that, *inter alia*, the need for the continued use of the special powers could be monitored. The Act was thus renewed until March 1976 when it was re-enacted with certain amendments.

Under section 17 of the 1976 Act, the special powers were subject to parliamentary renewal every twelve months. The 1976 Act was in turn renewed annually until 1984 when it was re-enacted with certain amendments. The 1984 Act, in force since March 1984, proscribed the INLA as well as the IRA. It was renewed every year, but it would expire in March 1989 when the Government intended to introduce permanent legislation.

The 1976 Act was reviewed in reports published in July 1978 and January 1983. Annual reports on the 1984 Act were presented to Parliament in 1984, 1985, 1986 and 1987 when a wider-scale review of the operation of the 1984 Act was also completed. These reviews were commissioned by the Government and presented to Parliament to assist consideration of the continued need for the legislation. The authors of these reviews concluded in particular that in view of the problems inherent in the prevention and investigation of terrorism, the continued use of the special powers of

II:4

arrest and detention was indispensable. The suggestion that decisions extending detention should be taken by the courts was rejected, notably because the information grounding those decisions was highly sensitive and could not be disclosed to the persons in detention or their legal advisers. For various reasons, the decisions fell properly within the sphere of the executive.

The relevant provisions of section 12 of the 1984 Act, substantially the same as those of the 1974 and 1976 Acts, empowered a constable to arrest without warrant any person whom he had reasonable grounds for suspecting to be a person concerned in the commission, preparation or instigation of acts of terrorism connected with the affairs of Northern Ireland. A person arrested under this section could not be detained for more than 48 hours after his arrest, but the Secretary of State could, in any particular case, extend the period of 48 hours by a period or periods specified by him. Any such further period or periods could not exceed five days in all. The provision requiring that an accused person should be brought before court after his arrest did not apply to a person detained in these circumstances.

According to the definition given in section 14 (1) of the 1984 Act, terrorism meant the use of violence for political ends, and it included any use of violence for the purpose of putting the public or any section of the public in fear.

In order to make a lawful arrest under section 12 (1) (*b*) of the 1984 Act, the arresting officer had to have a reasonable suspicion that the person being arrested was or had been concerned in the commission, preparation or instigation of acts of terrorism. In addition, an arrest without warrant was subject to the applicable common law rules, namely, that a person being arrested had in ordinary circumstances to be informed of the true ground of his arrest at the time he was taken into custody or, if special circumstances existed excusing this, as soon thereafter as it was reasonably practicable to inform him. This did not require technical or precise language to be used, provided the person being arrested knew in substance why.

Under ordinary law, there was no power to arrest and detain a person merely to make enquiries about him. In domestic jurisprudence, it was held that the questioning of a suspect on the ground of a reasonable suspicion that he had committed an arrestable offence was a legitimate cause for arrest and detention without warrant where the purpose of such questioning was to dispel or confirm such a reasonable suspicion, provided he was brought before a court as soon as practicable. In a domestic case, it was held that under the 1984 Act no specific crime needed be suspected to ground a proper arrest under section 12 (1) (*b*) and that no charge might follow an arrest under section 12 (1). Thus, an arrest was not necessarily the first step in a criminal proceeding against a suspected person on a charge which was intended to be judicially investigated.

In Northern Ireland, applications for extended detention beyond the initial 48-hour period were processed at senior police level in Belfast and then forwarded to the Secretary of State for Northern Ireland for approval by him. There were no criteria in the 1984 Act (or its predecessors) governing decisions to extend the initial period of detention, though strict criteria developed in practice were listed in the reports and reviews appended to the Government's memorial. According to statistics, just over two percent of police requests for extended detention in Northern Ireland were refused by the Secretary of State.

The principal remedies available to persons detained under the 1984 Act were an application for a writ of *habeas corpus* and a civil action claiming damages for false imprisonment.

Under section 12 (4) and (5) of the 1984 Act, a person might be arrested and detained for a total period of seven days. Paragraph 5 (2) of Schedule 3 to the 1984 Act provided that a person detained pursuant to an arrest under section 12 of the Act should be deemed to be in legal custody when he was so detained. However, the remedy of *habeas corpus* was not precluded by paragraph 5 (2). If the initial arrest was unlawful, so also was the detention grounded upon that arrest. *Habeas corpus* was a procedure whereby a detained person might make an urgent application for release from custody on the basis that his detention was unlawful.

A person claiming that he had been unlawfully arrested and detained might in addition bring an action seeking damages for false imprisonment. Where the lawfulness of the arrest, according to domestic jurisprudence, depended upon reasonable cause for suspicion, it was for the defendant authority to prove the existence of such reasonable cause. Furthermore, in false imprisonment proceedings, the reasonableness of an arrest might be examined on the basis of the well-established principles of judicial review of the exercise of executive discretion.

The law

The Court, having taken notice of the growth of terrorism in modern society, recognized the need, inherent in the Convention system, for a proper balance between the defence of the institutions of democracy in the common interest and the protection of individual rights.

The Government had informed the Secretary General of the Council of Europe on 22 August 1984 of the withdrawal of a notice of derogation under article 15 of the Convention relying on an emergency situation in Northern Ireland. Accordingly, the Government indicated that the provisions of the Convention were being fully executed. In any event, the derogation did not apply to the area of law in issue in the

II:4

present case. Consequently, there was no call in the present proceedings to consider whether any derogation from the United Kingdom's obligations under the Convention might be permissible under article 15 by reason of a terrorist campaign in Northern Ireland.

Examination of the case had to proceed on the basis that the articles of the Convention, in respect of which complaints had been made, were fully applicable. This did not, however, preclude proper account being taken of the background circumstances of the case. In the context of article 5 of the Convention, it was for the Court to determine the significance to be attached to those circumstances and to ascertain whether, in the instant case, the balance struck complied with the applicable provisions of that article in the light of their particular wording and its overall object and purpose.

The applicants alleged breach of article 5, paragraph 1, of the Convention. There was no dispute that the applicants' arrest and detention were lawful under Northern Ireland law and, in particular, in accordance with a procedure prescribed by law. The applicants argued that the deprivation of liberty they suffered by virtue of section 12 of the 1984 Act failed to comply with article 5, paragraph 1 (*c*), on the ground that they were not arrested on suspicion of an offence, nor was the purpose of their arrest to bring them before the competent legal authority.

Under the first head of argument, the applicants maintained that their arrest and detention were grounded on suspicion, not of having committed a specific offence, but rather of involvement in unspecified acts of terrorism. This did not constitute any breach of the criminal law in Northern Ireland and could not be regarded as an offence under article 5, paragraph 1 (*c*), of the Convention.

The Government did not dispute that the 1984 Act did not require an arrest to be based on suspicion of a specific offence, but it argued that the definition of terrorism in the Act was compatible with the concept of an offence and satisfied the requirements of paragraph 1 (*c*) in this respect, as the Court's case law confirmed. In this connection, the Government pointed out that the applicants were not in fact suspected of involvement in terrorism in general, but of membership of a proscribed organization and involvement in specific acts of terrorism, each of which constituted an offence under the law of Northern Ireland and each of which was expressly put to the applicants during the course of their interviews following their arrests.

Section 14 of the 1984 Act defined terrorism as the use of violence for political ends, which included the use of violence for the purpose of putting the public or any section of the public in fear. The same definition of acts of terrorism, as contained in the Detention of Terrorists (Northern Ireland) Order, 1972 and the Northern Ireland

(Emergency Provisions) Act, 1973, had already been found by the Court in another judgment to be well in keeping with the idea of an offence.

In addition, all of the applicants were questioned within a few hours of their arrest about their suspected involvement in specific offences and their suspected membership of proscribed organizations. Accordingly, the Court found that the arrest and subsequent detention of the applicants were based on a reasonable suspicion of commission of an offence within the meaning of article 5, paragraph 1 (*c*), of the Convention.

This provision also required that the purpose of the arrest or detention should be to bring the person concerned before the competent legal authority. The Government and the Commission argued that such an intention was present and that if sufficient and usable evidence had been obtained during the police investigation that followed the applicants' arrest, they would undoubtedly have been charged and brought to trial.

The applicants contested these arguments and referred to the fact that they were neither charged nor brought before a court during their detention. No charge had necessarily to follow an arrest under section 12 of the 1984 Act, and the requirement under the ordinary law to bring the person before a court had been made inapplicable to detention under this Act. In the applicants' contention, this was therefore a power of administrative detention exercised for the purpose of gathering information, as the use in practice of the special powers corroborated.

The Court noted that it was not required to examine the impugned legislation *in abstracto*, but had to confine itself to the circumstances of the case before it.

The fact that the applicants were neither charged nor brought before a court did not necessarily mean that the purpose of their detention was not in accordance with article 5, paragraph 1 (*c*), of the Convention. As the Government and the Commission had stated, the existence of such a purpose had to be considered independently of its achievement, and article 5, paragraph 1 (*c*), did not presuppose that the police should have obtained sufficient evidence to bring charges, either at the point of arrest or while the applicants were in custody.

Such evidence might have been unobtainable or, in view of the nature of the suspected offences, impossible to produce in court without endangering the lives of others. There was no reason to believe that the police investigation in this case was not in good faith or that the detention of the applicants was not intended to further that investigation by way of confirming or dispelling the concrete suspicions that, as the Court had found, grounded their arrest. Had it been possible, the police would, it

II:4

could be assumed, have laid charges, and the applicants would have been brought before the competent legal authority.

Their arrest and detention had, therefore, to be taken to have been effected for the purpose specified in paragraph 1 (*c*). In conclusion, there had been no violation of article 5, paragraph 1, of the Convention.

Under the 1984 Act, a person arrested under section 12 on reasonable suspicion of involvement in acts of terrorism might be detained by police for an initial period of 48 hours and, on the authorization of the Secretary of State for Northern Ireland, for a further period or periods of up to five days.

The applicants claimed, as a consequence of their arrest and detention under this legislation, to have been the victims of a violation of article 5, paragraph 3, of the Convention. They noted that a person arrested under the ordinary law of Northern Ireland had to be brought before a magistrates' court within 48 hours. Under the ordinary law in England and Wales, the maximum period of detention permitted without charge was four days, judicial approval being required at the 36-hour stage. In their submission, there was no plausible reason why a seven-day detention period was necessary, marking as it did such a radical departure from ordinary law and even from the three-day period permitted under the special powers of detention embodied in the Northern Ireland (Emergency Provisions) Act, 1978. Nor was there any justification for not entrusting such decisions to the judiciary of Northern Ireland.

The Government argued that in view of the nature and extent of the terrorist threat and the resulting problems in obtaining evidence sufficient to bring charges, the maximum statutory period of detention of seven days was an indispensable part of the effort to combat that threat, as successive parliamentary debates and reviews of the legislation had confirmed. In particular, they drew attention to the difficulty faced by the security forces in obtaining evidence that was both admissible and usable in consequence of training in anti-interrogation techniques adopted by those involved in terrorism. Time was also needed to undertake necessary scientific examinations, to correlate information from other detainees and to liaise with other security forces. The Government claimed that the need for a power of extension of the period of detention was borne out by statistics. For instance, in 1987, extensions were granted in Northern Ireland in respect of 365 persons. Some 83 were detained in excess of five days, and of this number, 39 were charged with serious terrorist offences during the extended period.

Regarding the suggestion that extensions of detention beyond the initial 48-hour period should be controlled or even authorized by a judge, the Government pointed out the difficulty, in view of the acute sensitivity of some of the information on which the suspicion was based, of producing it in court. Not only would the court have to sit *in camera*, but neither the detained person nor his legal advisers could be present or told any of the details. This would require a fundamental and undesirable change in the law and procedure of the United Kingdom under which an individual deprived of his liberty was entitled to be represented by his legal advisers at any proceedings before a court relating to his detention. If entrusted with the power to grant extensions of detention, the judges would be seen to be exercising an executive rather than a judicial function. It would add nothing to the safeguards against abuse that the existing arrangements were designed to achieve, and it could lead to unanswerable criticism of the judiciary. In all the circumstances, the Secretary of State was better placed to take such decisions and to ensure a consistent approach. Moreover, the merits of each request to extend detention were personally scrutinized by the Secretary of State.

The Commission, in its report, cited its established case law to the effect that a period of four days in cases concerning ordinary criminal offences and of five days in exceptional cases could be considered compatible with the requirement of promptness in article 5, paragraph 3, of the Convention. In the Commission's opinion, a somewhat longer period of detention than in normal cases was justified, given the context in which the applicants were arrested and the special problems associated with the investigation of terrorist offences. The Commission concluded that the periods of detention in this case of four days and six hours and four days and eleven hours did satisfy the requirement of promptness, whereas the periods of five days and eleven hours and six days and sixteen and a half hours did not.

The Court observed that the fact that a detained person was not charged or brought before a court, did not in itself amount to a violation of the first part of article 5, paragraph 3, of the Convention. No violation of this provision could arise if the arrested person was released promptly before any judicial control of his detention would have been feasible. If the arrested person was not released promptly, he was entitled to a prompt appearance before a judge or judicial officer.

The assessment of promptness had to be made in the light of the object and purpose of article 5. The Court had regard to the importance of this article in the Convention system. It enshrined a fundamental human right, namely the protection of the individual against arbitrary interferences by the State with his right to liberty. Judicial control of interferences by the executive with the individual's right to liberty was an essential feature of the guarantee embodied in article 5, paragraph 3, intended to minimize the risk of arbitrariness. Judicial control was implied by the rule of law, one of the fundamental principles of a democratic society, expressly referred to in the preamble to the Convention, and from which the whole Convention drew its inspiration.

II:4

The obligation expressed in English by the word "promptly" and in French by the word "aussitôt" was clearly distinguishable from the less strict requirement in the second part of article 5, paragraph 3, "reasonable time"/"délai raisonnable", and even from that in paragraph 4, "speedily"/"à bref délai". The term "promptly" also occured in the English text of article 5, paragraph 2, where the French text used the words "dans le plus court délai". As indicated by the Court in another judgment, the term "promptly" in paragraph 3 might be understood as having a broader significance than "aussitôt", literally meaning immediately. Thus confronted with versions of a law-making treaty being equally authentic but not exactly the same, the Court had to interpret them in a way that reconciled them as far as possible and was most appropriate in order to realize the aim and achieve the object of the treaty.

The use in the French text of the word "aussitôt", with its constraining connotation of immediacy, confirmed that the degree of flexibility attaching to the notion of promptness was limited, even if the attendant circumstances could never be ignored for the purposes of the assessment under article 5, paragraph 3, of the Convention. Whereas promptness was to be assessed in each case according to its special features, the significance to be attached to those features could never be taken to the point of impairing the very essence of the right guaranteed by that provision, to the point of effectively negativing the State's obligation to ensure a prompt release or a prompt appearance before a judicial authority.

This case was exclusively concerned with the arrest and detention, by virtue of powers granted under special legislation, of persons suspected of involvement in terrorism in Northern Ireland. The requirements under the ordinary law in Northern Ireland as to bringing an accused before a court were expressly made inapplicable to such arrest and detention by section 12 (6) of the 1984 Act. There was no call to determine in the judgment whether in an ordinary criminal case any given period, such as four days, in police or administrative custody would as a general rule be capable of being compatible with the first part of article 5, paragraph 3, of the Convention. None of the applicants was in fact brought before a judge or judicial officer during his time in custody. The issue to be decided was therefore whether, having regard to the special features relied on by the Government, each applicant's release could be considered as prompt for the purposes of article 5, paragraph 3.

The investigation of terrorist offences undoubtedly presented the authorities with special problems, partial reference to which had already been made. The Court took full judicial notice of the factors adverted to by the Government in this connection. It was also true that in Northern Ireland the referral of police requests for extended detention to the Secretary of State and the individual scrutiny of each police request by a Minister did provide a form of executive control. In addition, the need for the continuation of the special powers had been constantly monitored by Parliament and their operation regularly reviewed by independent personalities. The Court accepted that subject to the existence of adequate safeguards, the context of terrorism in Northern Ireland had the effect of prolonging the period during which the authorities might, without violating article 5, paragraph 3, of the Convention, keep a person suspected of serious terrorist offences in custody before bringing him before a judge or other judicial officer.

The difficulties, alluded to by the Government, of judicial control over decisions to arrest and detain suspected terrorists might affect the manner of implementation of article 5, paragraph 3, for example in calling for appropriate procedural precautions in view of the nature of the suspected offences. However, they could not justify, under this provision, dispensing altogether with prompt judicial control.

As the Court had indicated, the scope for flexibility in interpreting and applying the notion of promptness was very limited. In the Court's view, even the shortest of the four periods of detention, namely the four days and six hours spent in police custody by one of the applicants, fell outside the strict constraints as to time permitted by the first part of article 5, paragraph 3. To attach such importance to the special features of this case as to justify so lengthy a period of detention without appearance before a judge or other judicial officer would be an unacceptably wide interpretation of the plain meaning of the word "promptly". An interpretation to this effect would import into that paragraph a serious weakening of a procedural guarantee to the detriment of the individual and would entail consequences impairing the very essence of the right protected by the provision. The Court thus had to conclude that none of the applicants was either brought promptly before a judicial authority or released promptly following his arrest. The undoubted fact that the arrest and detention of the applicants were inspired by the legitimate aim of protecting the community as a whole from terrorism was not on its own sufficient to ensure compliance with the specific requirements of the provision. Thus, there had been a breach of article 5, paragraph 3, of the Convention in respect of all four applicants.

As to article 5, paragraph 4, of the Convention, the applicants argued that an effective review of the lawfulness of their detention, as required by that provision, was precluded, because article 5 had not been incorporated into United Kingdom law.

The remedy of *habeas corpus* was available to the applicants in the present case, though they chose not to avail themselves of it. Such proceedings would have led to a review of the lawfulness of their arrest and detention under the terms of the 1984 Act and the applicable principles developed by case law. The Commission found that the requirements of article 5, paragraph 4, were satisfied, since the review available in Northern Ireland would have encompassed the procedural and substantive

II:4

basis, under the Convention, for their detention. The Government adopted the same reasoning.

According to the Court's established case law, the notion of lawfulness under article 5, paragraph 4, had the same meaning as in paragraph 1. Whether or not an arrest or detention could be regarded as lawful had to be determined in the light not only of domestic law, but also of the text of the Convention, the general principles embodied therein and the aim of the restrictions permitted by article 5, paragraph 1. By virtue of article 5, paragraph 4, arrested or detained persons were entitled to a review bearing upon the procedural and substantive conditions essential for the lawfulness, in the sense of the Convention, of their deprivation of liberty. This meant that the applicants in this case should have had available to them a remedy allowing the competent court to examine not only compliance with the procedural requirements set out in section 12 of the 1984 Act, but also the reasonableness of the suspicion grounding the arrest and the legitimacy of the purpose pursued by the arrest and the ensuing detention.

As was shown by the Court's case law, these conditions were met in the practice of the Northern Ireland courts in relation to the remedy of *habeas corpus*. Accordingly, there had been no violation of article 5, paragraph 4, of the Convention.

The applicants further alleged breach of article 5, paragraph 5. A claim for compensation for unlawful deprivation of liberty could be made in the United Kingdom in respect of a breach of domestic law. As article 5 of the Convention was not considered part of the domestic law of the United Kingdom, no claim for compensation lay for a breach of any provision of article 5 not at the same time constituting a breach of United Kingdom law.

The Government argued, *inter alia*, that the aim of article 5, paragraph 5, was to ensure that the victim of an unlawful arrest or detention should have an enforceable right to compensation. In this regard, it was also contended that the term "lawful" for the purposes of the various paragraphs of article 5 was to be construed as essentially referring back to domestic law and in addition as excluding any element of arbitrariness. Even in the event of a violation being found of any of the first four paragraphs of article 5, there had been no violation of paragraph 5, it was concluded, because the applicants' deprivation of liberty was lawful under Northern Ireland law and was not arbitrary.

The Court, like the Commission, considered that such a restrictive interpretation was incompatible with the terms of paragraph 5 referring, as it did, to arrest or detention in contravention of the provisions of article 5 of the Convention.

In this case, the applicants were arrested and detained lawfully under domestic law but in breach of article 5, of paragraph 3. This violation could not give rise, either before or after the findings made by the Court in the present judgment, to an enforceable claim for compensation by the victims before the domestic courts, and this was not disputed by the Government. Accordingly, there had also been a breach of article 5, paragraph 5, of the Convention in this case in respect of all four applicants. This finding was without prejudice to the Court's competence under the then article 50 of the Convention in the matter of awarding compensation by way of just satisfaction.

Furthermore, the applicants claimed before the Commission that they had no effective remedy in Northern Ireland in respect of their complaints under article 5 and that consequently, there was also a breach of article 13 of the Convention.

In the light of the finding that there had been no violation of article 5, paragraph 4, of the Convention in this case, the Court did not deem it necessary to inquire whether the less strict requirements of article 13 were complied with, especially as the applicants did not pursue this complaint before the Court.

The Court held, by sixteen votes to three, that there had been no violation of article 5, paragraph 1, of the Convention; by twelve votes to seven, that there had been a violation of article 5, paragraph 3, in respect of all four applicants; unanimously, that there had been no violation of article 5, paragraph 4; by thirteen votes to six, that there had been a violation of article 5, paragraph 5, in respect of all four applicants; and unanimously, that it was not necessary to consider the case under article 13 of the Convention.

As to the then article 50, allowing the Court to afford just satisfaction to an injured party, under specified circumstances, when there had been a violation of the Convention, the Government requested the Court to reserve the matter. In the circumstances of the case, the Court considered that the question of the application of article 50 was not ready for decision in relation to the claim for compensation for prejudice suffered. It considered it necessary to reserve the matter, taking due account of the possibility of an agreement between the respondent State and the applicants.

II:4

(k) *K.-F.* v. *Germany*
(European Court of Human Rights)[100]

The case was referred to the European Court of Human Rights on 28 October 1996 by the European Commission of Human Rights. It originated in an application a-gainst Germany lodged with the Commission on 14 December 1993 by Mr. K.-F., a German national. The applicant asked the Court not to reveal his identity. The ob-ject of the request was to obtain a decision as to whether the facts of the case dis-closed a breach by the respondent State of its obligations under article 5, paragraph 1, of the Convention for the Protection of Human Rights and Fundamental Free-doms.

The facts

In May 1991, Mr. K.-F. and his wife rented a holiday flat. On 4 July 1991, the land-lady of the flat complained to the police that they were about to leave without pay-ing the rent for the flat. The police attended and, at 9.45 p.m., arrested Mr. K.-F. and his wife. They were taken to a police station for their identities to be checked.

In a report made at 11.30 p.m., the police stated that they strongly suspected Mr. and Mrs. K.-F. of rent fraud and that there was a risk that they would abscond. They were questioned until 12.45 a.m. and then between 8.30 a.m. and 9.40 a.m. on 5 July 1991. At 9.25 a.m., the public prosecutor informed the police that he did not intend to issue a warrant for arrest. At 10.30 a.m., Mr. and Mrs. K.-F. were released. On 13 September 1991, the public prosecutor decided to discontinue criminal proceedings against them.

On 6 April 1992, Mr. K.-F. applied to a court of appeal for an order that police of-ficials involved in the case should be prosecuted for attempted coercion and false imprisonment. On 21 May 1992, the appeal court dismissed his application on the ground that there was insufficient cause to prosecute the police officers. A further application was dismissed on 30 November 1993 for the same reason. On that occa-sion, the court noted that under the criminal procedure code, a person arrested for the purposes of checking his identity could not be deprived of his liberty for more than 12 hours, in all. However, the applicant had been detained on 4 July at 9.45 p.m. and released next day at 10.30 a.m., a period exceeding 12 hours.

---

[100] See European Court of Human Rights, *Reports of Judgments and Decisions*, 1997-VII, p. 2657, application No. 25629/94, judgment of 27 November 1997.

The law

The applicant claimed that his detention overnight from 4 to 5 July 1991 had infringed article 5, paragraph 1, of the Convention,

In his submission, the applicant argued that both his arrest and his detention were unlawful, as he had not committed any offence, disputes over the amount of rent belonging, in his view, to the realm of civil law. Furthermore, he had not made any attempt to flee, nor had he sought at any stage to conceal his identity. Indeed, he had supplied the police with all necessary information. In any event, the time he had spent in detention exceeded the statutory maximum by 45 minutes.

The Government drew a distinction between, on the one hand, the applicant's arrest and detention from 9.45 p.m. to 9.40 a.m. on the following day and, on the other hand, the period between 9.45 a.m. and 10.30 a.m. that same day when his personal details were being recorded. It drew attention to the provisions of domestic law that set out the various grounds for arrest and detention of the applicant.

The Commission expressed the view that the applicant was arrested and detained on reasonable suspicion of having committed an offence, within the meaning of article 5, paragraph 1 (*c*), of the Convention and for the purpose set out in that article. Moreover, it found nothing to persuade it that the relatively minor delay of 45 minutes in releasing the applicant had resulted in the arbitrary deprivation of his liberty contrary to the object and purpose of article 5, paragraph 1.

Firstly, the Court considered whether the arrest and detention of Mr. K.-F. were based on reasonable suspicion that he had committed an offence. In this connection, the Court reiterated that the reasonableness of the suspicion on which an arrest had to be based formed an essential part of the safeguard against arbitrary arrest and detention laid down in article 5, paragraph 1 (*c*). Having a reasonable suspicion presupposed the existence of facts or information satisfying an objective observer that the person concerned might have committed the offence. However, the facts raising a suspicion needed not be of the same level as those necessary to justify a conviction or even to bring of charge. That came at a later stage of the process of criminal investigation.

In the present case, the Court noted that the landlady informed the police that Mr. and Mrs. K.-F. rented her flat without intending to perform their obligations as tenants and that they were about to make off without paying what they owed. Initial inquiries revealed that the address of Mr. and Mrs. K.-F. was merely a post office box and that Mr. K.-F. had previously been under investigation for fraud. The police arrested the couple and took them to the police station so that their identities could be

II:4

checked. In their report drawn up at 11.30 p.m. on the day of the arrest, the police stated that they strongly suspected the couple of rent fraud and that there was a risk that they would abscond.

Having regard to those circumstances, the Court stated that it could, in principle, follow the reasoning of the domestic court of appeal when it, in its judgments of 21 May 1992 and 30 November 1993, held that the police officers' suspicions of rent fraud and the danger that Mr. K.-F. would abscond were justified. Consequently, he was detained on reasonable suspicion of having committed an offence within the meaning of article 5, paragraph 1 (*c*), of the Convention.

However, it was also a requirement under that provision that the arrest and detention should be effected for the purpose of bringing the person concerned before the competent legal authority. In this connection, the Court reiterated that the fact that Mr. K.-F. was neither charged nor brought before a court did not necessarily mean that the purpose of his detention was not in accordance with article 5, paragraph 1 (*c*). The existence of such a purpose had to be considered independently of its achievement. This provision did not presuppose that the police should have obtained sufficient evidence to bring charges, either at the point of arrest or while Mr. K.-F. was in custody.

In the case under review, the Court held that there was nothing to suggest that the police inquiries were not conducted in good faith or that the arrest and detention of Mr. K.-F. were effected for a purpose other than to complete the inquiries by checking his identity and investigating the allegations made against him. To that end, Mr. K.-F. and the landlady were questioned further during the morning of 5 July 1991. Accordingly, it might legitimately be supposed that had it been possible to confirm the suspicions of rent fraud, Mr. K.-F. would have been brought before the relevant judicial authority.

Therefore, the Court found that the deprivation of liberty in issue pursued the purpose indicated in article 5, paragraph 1 (*c*), of the Convention.

Lastly, the Court had to determine whether the arrest and detention of Mr. K.-F. were lawful, including whether they were effected in accordance with a procedure prescribed by law. The Court reiterated that the Convention here referred essentially to national law and laid down an obligation to comply with its substantive and procedural provisions. It also required that any measure depriving the individual of his liberty had to be compatible with the purpose of article 5, namely to protect the individual from arbitrariness. In order to resolve that issue, the Court reviewed the various grounds for arrest and detention put forward by the Government. The Court observed that the court of appeal, a national court in a position better to verify compliance with domestic law than the institutions under the Convention, had found that the arrest and detention of Mr. K.-F. were lawful. The Court saw no reason to come to a different conclusion.

The appeal court had left open the question whether it was necessary to hold the applicant until the following morning. It had been established, however, that the police continued to make inquiries throughout the night and up until the release of Mr. K.-F., partly in order to check whether an arrest warrant had been issued against him. Having regard to those circumstances, the Court concluded that the detention of Mr. K.-F. from 9.45 p.m. to 9.45 a.m. on the following day was justifiable.

On the other hand, the Court noted that the length of time Mr. K.-F. spent in detention had, by 45 minutes, exceeded the legal maximum laid down by the criminal procedure code. The appeal court had come to the same conclusion in its judgment of 30 November 1993.

The Court reiterated in this connection that the list of exceptions to the right to liberty secured in article 5, paragraph 1, of the Convention was exhaustive. Only a narrow interpretation of those exceptions was consistent with the aim of that provision, namely to ensure that no one was arbitrarily deprived of his or her liberty.

It was true that the Court had accepted that in certain circumstances, there might be some limited delay before a detained person was released. However, this had been in cases where the period of detention was not laid down in advance by statute and ended as a result of a court order. Practical considerations relating to the running of the courts and the completion of special formalities meant that the execution of such a court order might take time. However, in the instant case, the maximum period of 12 hours' detention for the purposes of checking identity was laid down by law and was absolute. Since the maximum period of detention was known in advance, the authorities responsible for the detention were under a duty to take all necessary precautions to ensure that the permitted duration was not exceeded. That applied also to the recording of Mr. K.-F.'s personal details. Being included among the measures for checking identity, it should have been carried out during the period of detention allotted for that purpose.

Having regard to those factors, the Court held that because the maximum period laid down by law for detaining the applicant was exceeded, there had been a breach of article 5, paragraph 1 (*c*), of the Convention.

Under the then article 50, allowing the Court to afford just satisfaction to an injured party, under specified circumstances, when there had been a violation of the Con-

II:4

vention, the Court considered that in this case the finding of a violation of article 5, paragraph 1 (*c*), constituted sufficient compensation.

5. Prohibition of Arbitrary Interference with Privacy

A. INTRODUCTION

Powers of lawful search, seizure and surveillance are, like the other powers referred to in this part of the book, essential to policing and routinely exercised by police. Indeed, covert policing operations, without which acts of terrorism and organized crime and could not be countered, are crucially dependent on these powers. At the same time, the right of a person to have his or her private life respected is a precious freedom. Governments and individuals should interfere with it only for very good reason and solely on legal grounds.

In recent years, the technological means to intrude on privacy have expanded considerably, especially through the rapid development of electronic surveillance measures and the establishment of computerized filing systems and data banks. These developments bring undoubted benefits in terms of public safety and public protection, while at the same time increasing possiblities for abuse of power.

Article 12 of the Universal Declaration of Human Rights states that no one shall be subjected to arbitrary interference with his privacy, family, home or correspondence, nor to attacks upon his honour and reputation. It further states that everyone shall have the right to protection of the law against such interference or attacks. Similar provisions are contained in universal and regional treaties, for example, article 17 of the International Covenant on Civil and Political Rights and article 8 of the Convention for the Protection of Human Rights and Fundamental Freedoms.

Non-treaty instruments set out more specific guidance for police on the question of privacy. Under article 4 of the Code of Conduct for Law Enforcement Officials, matters of a confidential nature in the possession of law enforcement officials shall be kept confidential unless the performance of duty or the needs of justice strictly require otherwise. In the explanatory commentary to this article, it is acknowledged that by the nature of their duties, law enforcement officials obtain information that may relate to private lives or be potentially harmful to the interests and reputation of others. Information of this kind should be safeguarded and only disclosed in the performance of duty or to serve the needs of justice. In the commentary, it is pointed out that any disclosure of such information for other purposes is wholly improper.

II:5

Under article 41 of the European Code of Police Ethics, police shall interfere with an individual's right to privacy only when strictly necessary and only to obtain a legitimate objective. The commentary to that article, in the explanatory memorandum published together with the Code, includes the observation that interference in peoples' privacy must always be considered as an exceptional measure, and even when justified, it should involve no more interference than absolutely necessary.

Article 42 of the Code requires that the collection, storage and use of personal data by the police shall be carried out in accordance with international data protection principles and, in particular, be limited to the extent necessary for the performance of lawful, legitimate and specific purposes. This requirement is clarified in the explanatory memorandum. Here it is pointed out that the use of new information technologies largely facilitates police action against different forms of criminality. The registration and the analysis of personal data, in particular, allows the police to cross-check information. Without resort to these tools, the existence of networks would thus remain obscure. However, it is added, the uncontrolled use of personal data may constitute violations of the right to privacy of the individuals concerned. In order to avoid abuse at the stages of collection, storage and use of personal data, such police activities must be guided by principles for the protection of data.

The cases summarized and/or reviewed in this chapter of the book reflect the jurisprudence of the Human Rights Committee and that of the European Court of Human Rights. These two institutions have a rich case law on the prohibition of arbitrary interference with privacy relevant to the purposes of this publication.

B. REVIEW OF CASES

(*a*) Human Rights Committee

Article 17 of the International Covenant on Civil and Political Rights protects the right to privacy. Under paragraph 1, no one shall be subjected to arbitrary or unlawful interference with his privacy, family, home or correspondence, nor to unlawful attacks on his honour and reputation.

Paragraph 2 establishes a corresponding right to protection of the law against such interference or attacks.

In time of public emergency threatening the life of the nation, States parties may take measures derogating from their obligations under article 17 on the conditions set forth in article 4 of the Covenant.

In its general comment No. 16 (32) on article 17 of the Covenant,[1] the Human Rights Committee elucidated the meaning of a number of terms used in this article. The term "unlawful" meant that no interference could take place except in cases envisaged by the law. Interference authorized by States could only take place on the basis of law, which itself had to comply with the provisions, aims and objectives of the Covenant. The expression "arbitrary interference" was also relevant to the protection of the right provided for in article 17. In the Committee's view, this expression could also extend to interference provided for under the law. The introduction of the concept of arbitrariness was intended to guarantee that even interference provided for by the law should be in accordance with the provisions, aims and objectives of the Covenant and should be, in any event, reasonable in the particular circumstances.[2]

Regarding the term "family", the Committee stated that the objectives of the Covenant required that for the purposes of article 17, the term should be given a broad interpretation to include all those comprising the family as understood in the society of the State party concerned. The term "home" in English, "manzel" in Arabic, "zhù-zhái" in Chinese, "domicile" in French, "zhilishche" in Russian and "domicilio" in Spanish, as used in article 17 in the six equally authentic languages, respectively, was to be understood to indicate the place where a person resided or carried out his usual occupation.[3]

In the case *Rojas García* v. *Colombia*,[4] summarized in section C[5] and also cited in connection with the prohibition of torture,[6] the State party argued that the rather dramatic search, carried out by a group of armed men in plain clothes from the public prosecutor's office in the course of a murder investigation, was lawful under its criminal procedure code. The author, Rafael Armando Rojas García, a Colombian citizen, submitted that on 5 January 1993, at 2 a.m., the group forcibly entered his house through the roof and carried out a room-by-room search of the premises, terrifying and verbally abusing the members of his family. He claimed that he and his family were the victims of violations by Colombia of, *inter alia*, articles 7 and 17 of the Covenant.

---

[1] See United Nations, *Official Records of the General Assembly, Forty-third Session, Supplement No. 40* (A/43/40), annex VI.

[2] *Ibidem*, paras. 3 and 4, respectively.

[3] *Ibidem*, para. 5.

[4] *Ibidem, Fifty-sixth Session, Supplement No. 40* (A/56/40), vol. II, annex X, sect. D, communication No. 687/1996, views adopted on 3 April 2001.

[5] See part II, chap. 5, sect. C (*a*) (*infra*, pp. 305-307).

[6] See part II, chap. 3, sect. B (*a*) (*supra*, pp. 130-131).

II:5

The Committee considered that any interference in the home had to be not only lawful, but also not arbitrary. Recalling the notion of arbitrariness as defined in its general comment No. 16 (32) and considering that the State party's arguments failed to justify the conduct described, the Committee found a violation by Colombia of article 17, paragraph 1, of the Covenant. It also found that the State party had violated article 7 in respect of the Rojas García family, but in an individual opinion, two members of the Committee disagreed about this conclusion.

In another case, *Miguel Angel Estrella* v. *Uruguay*,[7] also summarized in section C,[8] the Committee linked censorship of, and restrictions on, correspondence of detainees with the right of a detainee to humane treatment as required by article 10, paragraph 1, of the Covenant. The author, an Argentine national, claimed that on 15 December 1977, he was kidnapped at his home by heavily armed people in civilian clothes. He was detained on suspicion of subversive activities and subjected to torture and other ill-treatment. Finally, he was convicted and sentenced to a term of imprisonment by a military court. On 15 February 1980, he was released and expelled from Uruguay. He alleged that Uruguay had violated a number of provisions of the Covenant, including articles 17 and 10 in respect of severe censorship of his correspondence.

The Committee accepted that it was normal for prison authorities to control and censor prisoners' correspondence, but such measures should be subject to satisfactory legal safeguards against arbitrary application. The degree of restriction had to be consistent with the standard of humane treatment of detained persons required by article 10, paragraph 1, of the Covenant. In this case, the Committee found that the correspondence of Miguel Angel Estrella was censored and restricted to an extent not justified by Uruguay as compatible with article 17, read in conjunction with article 10, paragraph 1. It also found other violations of the Covenant.

Another early case involving the issue of correspondence of a detainee is the case *Larry James Pinkney* v. *Canada*.[9] The author, a citizen of the United States of America, was serving a prison sentence in Canada. He described himself as a black political activist. On 10 May 1976, he was arrested and remanded in custody pending trial on certain criminal charges. He alleged that Canada had violated a number

---

[7] See United Nations, *Official Records of the General Assembly, Thirty-eighth Session, Supplement No. 40* (A/38/40), annex XII, communication No. 74/1980, views adopted on 29 March 1983.

[8] See part II, chap. 5, sect. C (*b*) (*infra*, pp. 308-310).

[9] See United Nations, *Official Records of the General Assembly, Thirty-seventh Session, Supplement No. 40* (A/37/40), annex VII, communication No. 27/1977, views adopted on 29 October 1981.

of provisions of the Covenant, including article 17, paragraph 1, as he was prevented from communicating with outside officials during his pre-trial detention.

When Mr. Pinkney was detained, there existed a domestic legal provision governing the regulation of detainees' correspondence that was expressed in very general terms. The Committee observed that in prohibiting arbitrary or unlawful interference with correspondence, article 17 of the Covenant also required that everyone should have the right to the protection of the law against such interference. Even though there was no evidence to establish that Mr. Pinkney was himself the victim of a violation of the Covenant in this respect, the provision did not, in the opinion of the Committee, in itself provide satisfactory legal safeguards against arbitrary application.

In the case *Nicholas Toonen v. Australia*,[10] a violation of article 17, paragraph 1, of the Covenant was found also because of legal provisions, but not their actual application. The author, an Australian citizen and activist for the rights of homosexuals, resided in Tasmania, one of the constitutive states of Australia. In 1991, he challenged Tasmanian criminal code provisions criminalizing various forms of sexual contact between men.

The Committee observed that it was undisputed that adult consensual sexual activity in private was covered by the concept of privacy under article 17 of the Covenant. Furthermore, Mr. Toonen was actually and currently affected by the continued existence of the Tasmanian laws. The Committee considered that the challenged provisions interfered with the author's privacy, even if they had not been enforced for a decade, and their continued existence continuously and directly interfered with his privacy.

As to whether the prohibition against private homosexual behaviour in Tasmanian law might be deemed arbitrary, the Committee recalled its general comment No. 16 (32). The introduction of the concept of arbitrariness was intended to guarantee that even interference provided for by the law should be in accordance with the provisions, aims and objectives of the Covenant and should be, in any event, reasonable in the circumstances.[11] The Committee interpreted the requirement of reasonableness to imply that any interference with privacy had to be proportional to the end sought and necessary in the circumstances of any given case.

---

[10] *Ibidem, Forty-ninth Session, Supplement No. 40* (A/49/40), vol. II, annex IX, sect. EE, communication No. 488/1992, views adopted on 31 March 1994.

[11] *Ibidem, Forty-third Session, Supplement No. 40* (A/43/40), annex VI, para. 4.

II:5

The State party acknowledged that the impugned provisions constituted an arbitrary interference with Mr. Toonen's privacy, but the Tasmanian authorities submitted that those provisions were justified on public health and moral grounds.

For the purposes of article 17 of the Covenant, the Committee could not accept that moral issues were exclusively a matter of domestic concern, as this would open the door to withdrawing from the Committee's scrutiny a potentially large number of statutes interfering with privacy. In the circumstances of the case, the Committee ultimately concluded that the challenged provisions did not meet the test of reasonableness, *inter alia*, as they were not currently enforced, thus implying that they were not deemed essential to the protection of morals in Tasmania. They arbitrarily interfered with Mr. Toonen's right under article 17, paragraph 1, of the Covenant. The Committee found a violation by Australia of this provision *juncto* article 2, paragraph 1, of the Covenant. It further stated that an effective remedy under article 2, paragraph 3 (*a*), would be to repeal the provisions. One member of the Committee submitted an individual opinion in the case.

(*b*) European Court of Human Rights

Article 8 of the Convention for the Protection of Human Rights and Fundamental Freedoms protects the right to respect for private and family life. Under paragraph 1, everyone has the right to respect for his private and family life, his home and his correspondence.

Paragraph 2 states that there shall be no interference by a public authority with the exercise of this right except such as is in accordance with the law and is necessary in a democratic society in the interests of national security, public safety or the economic well-being of the country, for the prevention of disorder or crime, for the protection of health or morals or for the protection of the rights and freedoms of others.

In time of war or other public emergency threatening the life of the nation, States parties may take measures derogating from their obligations under article 8 on the conditions set forth in article 15 of the Convention.

The terms "private life" and "home" were analyzed in the case *Niemietz* v. *Germany*.[12] The applicant, Gottfried Niemietz, a German citizen and practising lawyer, alleged that a search of his law office had given rise to a breach of article 8 of the Convention. On 13 November 1986, his office had been searched by representatives of the public prosecutor's office and the police in the context of criminal proceed-

---

[12] See *Publications of the European Court of Human Rights*, Series A: *Judgments and Decisions*, vol. 251-B (1993), application No. 13710/88, judgment of 16 December 1992.

ings. He claimed, *inter alia*, that the search had violated his right to respect for his home and correspondence guaranteed by article 8.

As to the term "private life", the European Court of Human Rights did not consider it possible or necessary to attempt an exhaustive definition. However, it would be too restrictive to limit the notion to an inner circle in which the individual might live his life as chosen and to exclude therefrom entirely the outside world not encompassed within that circle. Respect for private life had also to comprise the right to establish and develop relationships with other human beings. Furthermore, there appeared to the Court to be no reason of principle why this understanding of the notion of private life should exclude activities of a professional or business nature, since it was in the course of their working lives that the majority of people had a significant opportunity of developing relationships with the outside world.

Furthermore, the Court stated that it might not always be possible to draw precise distinctions concerning the notion of home. Activities related to a profession or business might well be conducted from a person's private residence, and activities not so related might well be carried on in an office or commercial premises.

Making reference to its case law, the Court said that interpreting the words "private life" and "home" as including certain professional or business activities or premises would be consonant with the essential object and purpose of article 8, namely to protect the individual against arbitary interference by the public authorities. In the circumstances of the case, the Court concluded that the search of the office of Mr. Niemietz constituted an interference with his rights under article 8 and a breach of that article.

The jurisprudence deriving from article 8 of the Convention is rich and well-developed. Cases relevant to policing can be conveniently categorized under four broad headings: surveillance and data collection; home searches; correspondence; and criminalization of homosexuality.

With regard to surveillance and data collection, there are numerous cases, often focussing on the adequacy of domestic law to protect people from intrusive action by the State party. In the *Klass and Others* case (*Germany*),[13] Gerhard Klass and four other German citizens, all of them lawyers, claimed in an application lodged with the European Commission of Human Rights in 1971 that, *inter alia*, article 8 of the Convention was violated by the State party, because national law permitted surveillance measures without obliging the authorities in every case to notify the persons

---

[13] *Ibidem*, vol. 28 (1979), application No. 5029/71, judgment of 6 September 1978.

II:5

concerned after the event and because it excluded any remedy before the courts a-gainst the ordering and execution of such measures.

In finding interference of the right to privacy in this case to be in accordance with article 8, paragraph 2, of the Convention, the Court, sitting in plenary, took judicial notice of two important facts. The first consisted of the technical advances made in the means of espionage and, correspondingly, of surveillance; the second was the development of terrorism in Europe in recent years. The Court observed that democratic societies found themselves threatened by highly sophisticated forms of espionage and by terrorism. As a result, the State had to be able to undertake the secret surveillance of subversive elements operating within its jurisdiction in order to counter effectively such threats. The Court therefore accepted that the existence of some legislation granting powers of secret surveillance over the mail, post and telecommunications was, under exceptional conditions, necessary in a democratic society in the interests of national security and/or for the prevention of disorder or crime.

In the *Malone* case (*the United Kingdom*),[14] the applicant, James Malone, a United Kingdom citizen, complained, *inter alia*, that his telephone calls had been intercepted by police and that a register of numbers called from his telephone had been maintained. On 22 March 1977, Mr. Malone was charged with a number of offences relating to dishonest handling of stolen goods. In a subsequent trial, it emerged that a telephone conversation with Mr. Malone as a party had been intercepted at the request of the police under a warrant issued by the Home Secretary.

The Court, sitting in plenary, found in this case that neither the interception of telephone calls, nor the practice of metering such calls, was in accordance with the law under article 8, paragraph 2, of the Convention. Citing earlier cases, the Court reiterated its opinion that the phrase "in accordance with the law" did not merely refer back to domestic law. It also related to the quality of the law, requiring it to be compatible with the rule of law. The Court observed that the phrase implied that there had to be a measure of legal protection in domestic law against arbitrary interference by public authorities with the rights safeguarded by article 8, paragraph 1. This followed from the object and purpose of that article.

In relation to the interception of telephone calls, the Court focused on the notions of foreseeability and precision. It pointed out that the requirement of foreseeability could not mean that an individual should be enabled to foresee when the authorities were likely to intercept his communications so that he could adapt his conduct accordingly. Nevertheless, the Court observed, the law had to be sufficiently clear in its terms to give citizens an adequate indication as to the circumstances in which,

---

[14] *Ibidem*, vol. 82 (1984), application No. 8691/79, judgment of 2 August 1984.

and the conditions on which, public authorities were empowered to resort to this secret and potentially dangerous interference with the right to respect for private life and correspondence.

On the question of precision, the Court noted that since the implementation in practice of measures of secret surveillance of communications was not open to scrutiny by the individuals concerned or the public at large, it would be contrary to the rule of law for the legal discretion granted to the executive to be expressed in terms of an unfettered power. Consequently, the law had to indicate the scope of any such discretion conferred on the competent authorities and the manner of its exercise with sufficient clarity, having regard to the legitimate aim of the measure in question, to give the individual adequate protection against arbitrary interference.

Ultimately, in relation to the interception of telephone calls, the Court found that the domestic law in question did not indicate with reasonable clarity the scope and manner of exercise of the relevant discretion conferred on the public authorities. To that extent, the minimum degree of legal protection to which citizens were entitled under the rule of law in a democratic society was lacking.

In relation to the register of numbers called from Mr. Malone's telephone, the Court concluded that apart from the simple absence of prohibition, there would appear to be no legal rules concerning the scope and manner of exercise of the discretion enjoyed by the public authorities. Consequently, although lawful in terms of domestic law, the interference resulting from the existence of this practice was not in accordance with the law within the meaning of article 8, paragraph 2, of the Convention.

The case *A*. v. *France*,[15] summarized in section C,[16] concerns measures of surveillance. The applicant, Mrs. A., a French national, claimed to be the victim of a violation of article 8 of the Convention. In 1980, a senior police official was informed by Mr. G. that Mrs. A. had hired him to kill a named person. Mr. G. volunteered to make a telephone call to Mrs. A.'s home to discuss possible methods for carrying out the crime and to record the telephone conversation. The police official accepted the offer. Once the recording was made, he informed his superiors of the threat, but he did not reveal the identity of his informant nor the existence of the cassette. The recording was later handed over to an investigating judge. Mrs. A. took the view that the recording of her telephone conversation with Mr. G. was incompatible with her right to respect for her private life and correspondence, guaranteed by article 8.

---

[15] *Ibidem*, vol. 277-B (1994), application No. 14838/89, judgment of 23 November 1993.
[16] See part II, chap. 5, sect. C (*c*) (*infra*, pp. 310-313).

II:5

The Court observed that the undertaking complained of by the applicant depended on Mr. G. and the police official working together. They could hardly be dissociated from each other. The police official made a crucial contribution to executing the scheme by making available for a short time his office, his telephone and his tape recorder. Admittedly, he did not inform his superiors of his actions, and he had not sought the prior authorization of an investigating judge, but he was acting in the performance of his duties as a high-ranking police officer. It followed that the public authorities were involved to such an extent that the State's responsibility under the Convention was engaged.

In any event, the recording represented an interference in respect of which Mrs. A. was entitled to the protection of the French legal system. Referring to its case law, the Court reiterated that this interference undoubtedly concerned Mrs. A.'s right to respect for her correspondence, a point not disputed by the Government. In these circumstances, it was not necessary to consider whether it also affected her private life.

Like the Commission, the Court noted that the contested recording had no basis in domestic law. It therefore found a breach of article 8 of the Convention. This finding made it unnecessary for the Court to rule on compliance with the other requirements of paragraph 2 of that article.

In another case on surveillance, *Halford* v. *the United Kingdom*,[17] also summarized in section C,[18] the applicant, Alison Halford, a British citizen and a senior police official, claimed that calls made from her home and her office telephones were intercepted for the purposes of obtaining information to use against her in proceedings she was bringing at an industrial tribunal. She had instituted those proceedings in 1990 alleging that she had been discriminated against on grounds of sex. She alleged that the interception of her telephone calls amounted to a violation of article 8 of the Convention.

Citing previous cases and considering the circumstances of the case, the Court concluded that the conversations held by Ms. Halford on her office telephones fell within the scope of the notions of private life and correspondence. Evidence justified the conclusion that there was a reasonable likelihood that her calls had been intercepted for the purposes she had claimed. As domestic law did not provide adequate protection against interferences by the police in respect of telephone calls made on internal communication systems operated by public authorities, the Court found that the interference in this case could not be said to be in accordance with the law under arti-

---

[17] See European Court of Human Rights, *Reports of Judgments and Decisions*, 1997-III, p. 1004, application No. 20605/92, judgment of 25 June 1997.

[18] See part II, chap. 5, sect. C (*d*) (*infra*, pp. 313-322).

cle 8, paragraph 2, of the Convention. It held that there had been a violation of that article in relation to the interception of calls made on Ms. Halford's office telephones.

In respect of the alleged interception of telephone calls made from Ms. Halford's home, however, the Court, having considered all the evidence, did not find it established that there was an interference with her rights to respect for her private life and correspondence. There was no breach of article 8 in relation to the home telephone.

The applicant also claimed that she had been denied an effective domestic remedy for her complaints, in violation of article 13 of the Convention. It is interesting to note how the Court applied this provision to the circumstances of the case, finding a breach in relation to the office telephones but not the home telephone.

The case *P. G. and J. H.* v. *United Kingdom*,[19] the last case summarized in section C,[20] concerned a police operation in 1995 that led to the conviction of three men for conspiracy to carry out a robbery. Two of those convicted, the applicants Mr. P. G. and Mr. J. H., both United Kingdom nationals, complained that covert listening devices had been used to record their conversations at a flat and while detained in a police station. Furthermore, information concerning the use of a telephone had been obtained by the police by means of a process of metering the calls.

Concerning the use of the listening device at the flat, the Court ruled that as there was no domestic law regulating the use of covert listening devices at the relevant time, the interference in this case was not in accordance with the law, as required by article 8, paragraph 2, of the Convention. Therefore, there had been a violation of that provision. In deciding that the use of the listening device inside the police station also violated the same article, the Court considered the notion of private life in some detail, and various circumstances in which measures effected outside a person's home or private premises could be said to impinge upon it.

The information obtained about the use of the telephone was found to be in accordance with the law and necessary in a democratic society for the protection of public safety, the prevention of crime and the protection of the rights of others. The Court found, accordingly, that there had been no violation of article 8 in this respect.

The final two cases reviewed in relation to surveillance and data collection concern the recording of secret information about individuals by security services.

---

[19] See European Court of Human Rights, *Reports of Judgments and Decisions*, 2001-IX, p. 195, application No. 44787/98, judgment of 25 September 2001.

[20] See part II, chap. 5, sect. C (*e*) (*infra*, pp. 322-332).

II:5

In the *Leander* case (*Sweden*),[21] the applicant, Torsten Leander, a Swedish citizen, complained about the retention of secret information about him and its use in 1979 to deny him employment that required security clearance. He claimed, *inter alia*, that the personnel control procedure, as applied in the case, gave rise to a breach of article 8 of the Convention.

It was clear that the storing and release of secret information about Mr. Leander amounted to an interference with his right to respect for private life, as guaranteed by article 8, paragraph 1, of the Convention. The Court observed that the aim of the Swedish personnel control system was legitimate for the purposes of article 8, namely the protection of national security. It then had to decide whether the interference was in accordance with the law and necessary in a democratic society, and it is important to note the Court's observations on these concepts in this specific context.

In relation to the question whether the interference was in accordance with the law, the Court referred to criteria set out in the above *Malone* case, in particular to the requirements of accessibility and foreseeability. It acknowledged that the requirement of foreseeability in the special context of secret controls of staff in sectors affecting national security could not be the same as in many other fields. Thus, it could not mean that individuals should be enabled to foresee precisely what checks would be made in their regard by the special police service in its efforts to protect national security. Nevertheless, the law had to be sufficiently clear in its terms to give them an adequate indication as to the circumstances in which, and the conditions on which, the public authorities were empowered to resort to this kind of secret and potentially dangerous interference with private life.

As to whether the interference was necessary in a democratic society in the interests of security, the Court recalled that the notion of necessity implied that the interference corresponded to a pressing social need and, in particular, that it was proportionate to the legitimate aim pursued. However, the Court recognized that the national authorities enjoyed a margin of appreciation, the scope of which depended not only on the nature of the legitimate aim pursued, but also on the particular nature of the interference involved. In this case, the Court observed, the interest of the respondent State in protecting its national security had to be balanced against the seriousness of the interference with Mr. Leander's right to respect for his private life.

The Court reviewed the range of legal, political and administrative safeguards established against the arbitrary exercise of state power in Sweden, and it concluded that these met the requirements of article 8, paragraph 2, of the Convention. Having re-

---

[21] See *Publications of the European Court of Human Rights*, Series A: *Judgments and Decisions*, vol. 116 (1987), application No. 9248/81, judgment of 26 March 1987.

gard to the wide margin of appreciation available to it, the respondent State was entitled to consider that in the present case the interests of national security prevailed over the individual interests of the applicant. The interference to which Mr. Leander was subjected could not be said to have been disproportionate to the legitimate aim pursued, and there had been no breach of article 8.

In the case *Rotaru* v. *Romania*,[22] the applicant, Aurel Rotaru, a Romanian national, alleged a violation of his right to respect for his private life on account of the holding and use by the Romanian intelligence service of a file containing personal information about him, as had happened in 1990. Some of this information, recorded by security services of previous regimes, was false and defamatory. Whilst the case hinged upon many of the points made in previous cases on article 8 of the Convention, set out above, it is important to note the observations of the Court, sitting as a grand chamber, in this case on intelligence services and their supervision.

In the Court's opinion, information about Mr. Rotaru's life, in particular his studies, political activities and criminal record, some of which gathered more than 50 years earlier, when systematically collected and stored in a file held by agents of the State, fell within the scope of private life for the purposes of article 8, paragraph 1, of the Convention. This was all the more so in the applicant's case, as some of the information had been declared false and was likely to injure his reputation.

Referring to its judgment in the *Klass and Others* case, the Court recognized that intelligence services might legitimately exist in a democratic society. However, it reiterated, the powers of secret surveillance of citizens were tolerable under the Convention only insofar as strictly necessary for safeguarding the democratic institutions.

The Court also pointed out that in order to be compatible with article 8 of the Convention, systems of secret surveillance had to contain safeguards established by law applicable to the supervision of activities of the relevant services. Supervision procedures had to follow the values of a democratic society as faithfully as possible, in particular the rule of law, referred to in the preamble to the Convention. The rule of law implied, *inter alia*, that interference by the executive authorities with an individual's rights should be subject to effective supervision. This should normally be carried out by the judiciary, at least in the last resort, since judicial control afforded the best guarantees of independence, impartiality and proper procedures.

---

[22] See European Court of Human Rights, *Reports of Judgments and Decisions*, 2000-V, p. 109, application No. 28341/95, judgment of 4 May 2000.

II:5

In the *Rotaru* case, the Court noted that the Romanian system for gathering and ar-
chiving information did not provide such safeguards. It concluded that the holding
and use by the intelligence service of information on Mr. Rotaru's private life were
not in accordance with the law. The Court held, by sixteen votes to one, that there
had been a violation of article 8 of the Convention. It also held, unanimously, that
other provisions of the Convention had been violated in this case.

Concerning the regulation of home searches, it is worth noting two cases.

In the *Chappell* case (*the United Kingdom*),[23] the applicant, Anthony Richard Mal-
colm Chappell, a British citizen, had his home and office searched on 2 March 1981
by 11 or 12 police officials investigating a crime and, at the same time, by private
solicitors in connection with a civil matter concerning infringement of copyright. In
its judgment, the Court expressed some concern about the actual execution of the order and whether it could be regarded as a necessary and proportionate to the legitimate aim pursued.

In these respects, the Court felt that the manner in which the plaintiffs in the civil
case gained entry to Mr. Chappell's premises and the fact that they were searched simultaneously by 16 or 17 people were of some consequence. The Court noted that
Mr. Chappell was not afforded a proper opportunity to refuse the plaintiffs' entry to
his premises at the door, since members of their party entered together with a detective chief inspector. However, Mr. Chappell subsequently raised no objection on this
score. The Court also observed that the simultaneous searches by the police and the
plaintiffs must have been distracting for Mr. Chappell and have created difficulties
for him with regard to supervision and taking advice from, and giving instructions
to, his solicitor.

Against this, the Court weighed the following factors. Firstly, it was clear that the
two searches concerned at least partly the same materials. Secondly, the applicant
made no request for one of the searches to be deferred until the other had been completed. Thirdly, the domestic courts found that Mr. Chappell was able to look after
his interests whilst the order was being implemented. Finally, domestic courts also
found that there was nothing inherently wrong with the mode of execution of the order and that it was not necessary to set the order aside for the purpose of doing justice to Mr. Chappell.

In view of these considerations, the Court was of the opinion that the shortcomings
in the procedure followed, which were bound to cause some difficulties for the Mr.

---

[23] See *Publications of the European Court of Human Rights*, Series A: *Judgments and Decisions*, vol. 152-A (1989), application No. 10461/83, judgment of 30 March 1989.

Chappell, were not so serious that the execution of the order could be regarded as disproportionate to the legitimate aim pursued. No breach of article 8 of the Convention had been established.

In the case *Murray* v. *the United Kingdom*,[24] there were six applicants, Margaret and Thomas Murray and their four children, all Irish citizens, residing together in the same house in Belfast, Northern Ireland. On 26 July 1982, their home was searched in the course of an arrest operation carried out by army personnel investigating terrorist-linked crime. Mrs. Murray complained of the manner in which she was treated both in her home and at the army centre, objecting to the recording of personal details concerning herself and her family, as well as a photograph taken of her without her knowledge or consent. All six applicants contended that the entry into and search of their family home by the army, including the confinement of five of them for a short while in one room, violated article 8 of the Convention. Mrs. Murray also alleged other breaches of the Convention.

It was not contested that the measures adopted had interfered with the applicants' exercise of their right to respect for their private and family life and their home. The Court, sitting as a grand chamber, proceeded to consider whether they were in accordance with the law and necessary in a democratic society. In respect of the former point, the Court observed that the entry into and search of a home by army personnel and the other measures objected to by the applicants all had a basis in domestic law. Therefore, they were in accordance with the law. As to whether they were necessary in a democratic society and, in particular, whether the means employed were proportionate to the legitimate aim pursued, it was not for the Court in this connection to substitute for the assessment of the national authorities its own assessment of what might be the best policy for the investigation of terrorist crime. A certain margin of appreciation in deciding what measures to take both in general and in particular cases should be left to the national authorities

The Court acknowledged the responsibility of an elected government in a democratic society to protect its citizens and institutions against the threats posed by organized terrorism and the special problems involved in the arrest and detention of persons suspected of terrorist-linked offences. These two factors affected the fair balance to be struck between the exercise by the individual of the right guaranteed under article 8, paragraph 1, of the Convention and the necessity, under paragraph 2 of the article, for the State to take effective measures for the prevention of terrorist crimes.

---

[24] *Ibidem*, vol. 300-A (1995), application No. 14310/88, judgment of 28 October 1994.

II:5

The Court noted that domestic courts had held that Mrs. Murray was genuinely and honestly suspected of the commission of a terrorist-linked crime. For its part, the Court had found that this suspicion could be regarded as reasonable for the purposes of article 5, paragraph 1 (*c*), of the Convention. Furthermore, the Court recognized the conditions of extreme tension under which such arrests were carried out in Northern Ireland. This had been referred to by a domestic court, which had pointed out that a search could not be limited solely to looking for the person to be arrested. A search had also to embrace the objective of securing a peaceable arrest. The domestic court had stated that it was an entirely reasonable precaution that all the occupants of the house should be asked to assemble in one room, as it was in everyone's best interest for the arrest to be peaceably effected.

The Court observed that these were legitimate considerations, explaining and justifying the manner in which the entry into and search of the Murray family's home were carried out. The Court did not find that the means employed by the authorities in this regard were disproportionate to the aim pursued. Neither could it be regarded as falling outside the legitimate bounds of the process of investigation of terrorist crime for the competent authorities to record and retain basic personal details concerning the arrested person or even other persons present at the time and place of arrest. None of the personal details taken during the search of the family home, or during Mrs. Murray's stay at the army centre, would appear to have been irrelevant to the procedures of arrest and interrogation. Similar conclusions applied to the taking and retention of a photograph of Mrs. Murray at the army centre. In this connection too, the Court did not find that the means employed were disproportionate to the aim pursued.

The Court concluded that the various measures complained of were necessary in a democratic society for the prevention of crime, within the meaning of article 8, paragraph 2, of the Convention. It held, by fifteen votes to three, that there had been no violation of article 8.

Concerning correspondence, the most relevant case to the purposes of this publication is the *Schönenberger and Durmaz* case *(Switzerland)*.[25] Edmund Schönenberger, a Swiss national, was a lawyer acting for Mehmet Durmaz, a Turkish national, who had been arrested in 1984 on suspicion of drugs-related offences. Mr. Schönenberger wrote to Mr. Durmaz advising him that it would be to his advantage to exercise his right not to make any statement. This letter was witheld from Mr. Durmaz by a prosecutor. However, Mr. Durmaz was subsequently freed because of doubts about mistaken identity.

---

[25] *Ibidem*, vol. 137 (1988), application No. 11368/85, judgment of 20 June 1988.

The Court accepted the Government's argument that the interference with this correspondence was in accordance with the law, as the stopping of the letter had as its aim the prevention of disorder or crime. Recalling a previous judgment, the Court observed that the pursuit of this objective might justify wider measures of interference in the case of a convicted prisoner than in that of a person at liberty. It stated that the same reasoning might be applied to a person, such as Mr. Durmaz, being held on remand and against whom inquiries with a view to bringing criminal charges were being made, since in such a case there was often a risk of collusion.

The Court then considered whether the interference satisfied the two further requirements of article 8, paragraph 2, of the Convention, namely that it pursued one of the aims set out in that provision and was necessary in a democratic society. It pointed out that to be necessary in a democratic society, an interference must be founded on a pressing social need and, in particular, be proportionate to the legitimate aim pursued.

The Court was not convinced by the Government's argument that the advice given to Mr. Durmaz relating to the criminal proceedings was of such a nature as to jeopardize their proper conduct. It observed that Mr. Schönenberger had sought to inform Mr. Durmaz of his right to refuse to make any statement, advising him that to exercise it would be to his advantage. In that way, he was recommending him to adopt a certain tactic, lawful under under domestic law of Switzerland and other States parties. In the Court's view, advice given in these terms was not capable of creating a danger of connivance between the sender of the letter and its recipient, and it did not pose a threat to the normal conduct of the prosecution. Consequently, the contested interference was not justifiable as necessary in a democratic society. There had been a breach of article 8 of the Convention.

Concerning the criminalization of homosexuality, two cases under the Convention pre-dated the findings of the Human Rights Committee in the case *Nicholas Toonen* v. *Australia*,[26] reviewed above.[27] The Court held, in these cases, that the prohibition of homosexual acts, between consenting adults over the age of 21, constituted an interference with private life under article 8 of the Convention.

---

[26] See *Official Records of the General Assembly, Forty-ninth Session, Supplement No. 40* (A/ 49/40), vol. II, annex IX, sect. EE, communication No. 488/1992, views adopted on 31 March 1994.

[27] See part II, chap. 5, sect. B (*a*) (*supra*, pp. 291-292).

II:5

In the *Dudgeon* case *(the United Kingdom)*,[28] the applicant, Jeffrey Dudgeon, a United Kingdom national residing in Belfast, 35 years of age, was a homosexual who together with others conducted a campaign against the law in Northern Ireland on homosexuality. On 21 January 1976, police went to his address to execute a warrant under law directed at misuse of drugs, and personal papers belonging to him were seized. As homosexual acts were described in these papers, he was asked to go to a police station where he was questioned, on the basis of the papers, about his sexual life. A file was prepared for prosecution to be considered, but ultimately, proceedings were not taken.

The applicant complained, *inter alia*, that under the law in force in Northern Ireland he was liable to criminal prosecution on account of his homosexual conduct and that he had experienced fear, suffering and psychological stress directly caused by the very existence of the laws. He further complained that he was questioned by police about certain homosexual activities and that personal papers were seized during the search and not returned until more than a year later.

The Court, sitting in plenary, found that the impugned legislation constituted a continuing interference with Mr. Dudgeon's right to respect for his private life, including his sexual life, within the meaning of article 8, paragraph 1, of the Convention. As to the existence of a justification for the interference, the Court said that the restriction imposed on Mr. Dudgeon under Northern Ireland law because of its breadth and absolute character was, quite apart from the severity of possible penalties provided for, disproportionate to the aims sought to be achieved. It held, by fifteen votes to four, that there was a breach of article 8 of the Convention.

In the *Norris* case *(Ireland)*,[29] the applicant, David Norris, an Irish citizen born in 1944, was an active homosexual who, since 1971, had been a campaigner for homosexual rights in Ireland. In 1974, Mr. Norris became a founder member and chairman of the Irish Gay Rights Movement. No attempt was made to institute a prosecution against him or the organization. In fact, Mr. Norris informed the police authorities of his organization's activities, but he was met with a sympathetic response and was never subjected to police questioning. Unlike Mr. Dudgeon, Mr. Norris was not, therefore, the subject of any police investigation.

The applicant complained that under the law in force in Ireland he was liable to criminal prosecution on account of his homosexual conduct. He alleged that he had

---

[28] See *Publications of the European Court of Human Rights*, Series A: *Judgments and Decisions*, vol. 45 (1982), application No. 7525/76, judgment of 22 October 1981.
[29] *Ibidem*, vol. 142 (1989), application No. 10581/83, judgment of 26 October 1988.

thereby suffered, and continued to suffer, an unjustified interference with his right under article 8 of the Convention.

The Court, sitting in plenary, found that the case was indistinguishable from the *Dudgeon* case that concerned identical legislation then in force in Northern Ireland. Therefore, it found that the legislation interfered with Mr. Norris' right to respect for his private life under article 8, paragraph 1, of the Convention. As to justification for the interference, the Court considered that there was no pressing social need in Ireland for the legislation. On the issue of proportionality, the Court cited its judgment in the *Dudgeon* case. The justification for retaining the law unamended was outweighed by the detrimental effects the provisions could have on the life of a person of homosexual orientation. Although members of the public who regarded homosexuality as immoral might be shocked, offended or disturbed by the commission by others of private homosexual acts, this could not on its own warrant the application of penal sanctions when consenting adults alone were involved. The Court held, by eight votes to six, that there was a breach of article 8 of the Convention.

C. CASE SUMMARIES

(a) *Rojas García* v. *Colombia*
(Human Rights Committee)[30]

The author of the communication was Rafael Armando Rojas García, a Colombian citizen. He submitted the communication to the Human Rights Committee on 30 August 1995, writing on his own behalf and on behalf of various members of his family. He claimed that they were the victims of violations by Colombia of, *inter alia*, article 7, on the prohibition of torture, and article 17, paragraphs 1 and 2, of the International Covenant on Civil and Political Rights.

The facts

The author submitted, *inter alia*, the following. On 5 January 1993 at 2 a.m., a group of armed men from the office of the public prosecutor, wearing civilian clothes, forcibly entered the his house through the roof. The group carried out a room-by-room search of the premises, terrifying and verbally abusing the members of his family, including small children. In the course of the search, one of the officials fired a gunshot. Two more people then entered the house through the front door. One typed out a statement and forced the only adult male in the family to sign it. He was not al-

---

[30] See United Nations, *Official Records of the General Assembly, Fifty-sixth Session, Supplement No. 40* (A/56/40), vol. II, annex X, sect. D, communication No. 687/1996, views adopted on 3 April 2001.

II:5

lowed to read it or to keep a copy. Only at that stage was the family informed that the house was being searched as part of an investigation into the murder of the mayor of a municipality.

The author claimed that the violent assaults on the family home resulted in a severe nervous trauma, psychologically affecting his sister, an invalid. She subsequently died on 8 August 1993, and the violent search was considered to be an indirect cause of her death. Similarly, his mother, aged 75, never quite recovered from the shock of the search.

The author stated that the authorities, far from conducting a diligent investigation into the matter, did everything possible to cover up the incident. No attempt was made to establish the responsibility either of the authorities that authorized the raid or of those who carried it out, including the officer who fired a gun in a room where there were young children.

The State party argued that the entry into the house of Mr. Rojas García fulfilled all the legal requirements of the criminal procedure code and was therefore within the scope of the law. The search was ordered by an officer of the court, and it was carried out in the presence of a prosecutor.

The author reiterated that the search was illegal since the criminal procedure code did not provide for nighttime "commando-like" actions, rooftop entries and firing into the air. He stated that the prosecutor was not present, having appeared only at the very end of the events and then only to draw up a record of which no copy was supplied. The author reiterated the repercussions that the house search had on his family. He argued that forcible entry through the roof at 2 a.m. and the firing of a gunshot constituted violations of the right to life, family life and other rights and freedoms guaranteed by the Constitution of Colombia.

The Committee found the allegations under articles 7 and 17, paragraphs 1 and 2, of the Covenant to be sufficiently substantiated to be considered on their merits.

Examination of the merits

The Committee first had to determine whether the specific circumstances of the raid on the Rojas García family's house, hooded men entering through the roof at 2 a.m., constituted a violation of article 17 of the Covenant. The State party stated that the raid on the house was carried out according to the criminal procedure code. The Committee did not enter into the question of the legality of the raid. However, it considered that under article 17 of the Covenant, it was necessary for any interference in the home not only to be lawful, but also not to be arbitrary. The concept of arbitrariness in article 17 was intended to guarantee that even interference provided for by law should be in accordance with the provisions, aims and objectives of the Covenant and should be, in any event, reasonable in the particular circumstances. The Committee further considered that the State party's arguments failed to justify the conduct described. Consequently, the Committee concluded that there had been a violation of article 17, paragraph 1, insofar as there was arbitrary interference in the home of the Rojas García family.

As the Committee found a violation of article 17 of the Covenant in respect of the arbitrariness of the raid on the house of Mr. Rojas García, it did not consider it necessary to decide whether the raid constituted an attack on the family's honour and reputation.

With regard to the alleged violation of article 7 of the Covenant, the Committee noted that the treatment received by the Rojas García family at the hands of the police was not refuted by the State party. Therefore, the Committee decided that there had been a violation of article 7 of the Covenant in this case.

The Committee was of the view that the facts before it disclosed a violation of articles 7 and 17, paragraph 1, of the Covenant in respect of the Rojas García family. In an individual opinion, two members of the Committee disagreed in respect of article 7, because, under the circumstances, they could not conclude that the search party had an intent to terrify the author's family. Therefore, they found that there had been no violation of that article in the case.

In accordance with article 2, paragraph 3 (*a*), of the Covenant, the State party was under an obligation to provide the author and his family with an effective remedy, which had to include reparation. The State party was also under an obligation to take steps to prevent similar violations occurring in the future.

Finally, the Committee recalled that by becoming a State party to the Optional Protocol to the Covenant, the State had recognized the competence of the Committee to determine whether or not there had been a violation of the Covenant. Pursuant to article 2 of the Covenant, the State had undertaken to ensure to all individuals within its territory and subject to its jurisdiction the rights recognized in the Covenant and to provide an effective and enforceable remedy in case a violation had been established. Bearing this in mind, the Committee wished to receive from the State party, within 90 days, information about the measures taken to give effect to the Committee's views.

II:5

(b) Miguel Angel Estrella v. Uruguay
(Human Rights Committee)[31]

The author of the communication was Miguel Angel Estrella, an Argentine national. He submitted the communication to the Human Rights Committee on 17 July 1980, claiming violations by Uruguay of the International Covenant on Civil and Political Rights, but he did not specify which provisions of the Covenant.

The facts

The author submitted, *inter alia*, the following. He became a member of the Peronist movement in Argentina in 1966, because he wished to contribute to the wider dissemination of knowledge, in his case of music, among the deprived sectors of the population. His activities, unpaid, involved giving courses, lectures and public concerts. However, these activities were considered to be subversive by the new military Government that came to power in 1976. In 1977, the author found that his name was on a list of Argentine intellectuals who could not participate in activities under the bilateral agreements that his country had signed with other States and that he had been denounced as a subversive member of the Montoneros Organization. Following an investigation into these accusations, requested by him, he was informed that he could continue to exercise his profession freely and participate under bilateral agreements.

He subsequently went to Uruguay, where he had been invited to give concerts and run courses for Uruguayan pianists. However, his engagements with a symphony orchestra were suddenly cancelled. He was officially informed that he was under observation in Uruguay, that there were unfavourable reports about him and that his position as a Peronist made it obvious that he was opposed to the Uruguayan Government. He was also told that as there was no record of him undertaking political activities in Uruguay, his safety would be assured as long as this situation did not change. He was free to give private lessons to local pianists, but he was prohibited from undertaking any official concert or teaching activity.

The author further stated that having left the country briefly, on 10 December 1977, he returned to Uruguay to hand over the house he had rented, as he intended to go back to his own country before travelling abroad on work assignments. On 15 December, he completed the necessary arrangements to travel to Buenos Aires, but at 11 p.m. that day he was violently arrested, blindfolded, hooded and taken away in a vehicle.

---

[31] *Ibidem, Thirty-eighth Session, Supplement No. 40* (A/38/40), annex XII, communication No. 74/1980, views adopted on 29 March 1983.

Whilst in detention he was severely tortured. In particular, he was subjected to mock amputation with an electric saw and told that they were going to do the same to him as to Víctor Jara, a well-known Chilean singer and guitarist, in 1973 found dead in a stadium in Santiago, Chile, with his hands completely smashed. The author alleged that he was interrogated for the purpose of forcing him to admit that he had been involved in plans to carry out armed operations in Uruguay and Argentina.

In his submissions to the Committee, the author gave detailed descriptions of the conditions in the various places of detention where he was held and the punishments to which detainees were subjected. These included physical ill-treatment, bans on receiving correspondence and the suppression of visits. The author stated that the detainees' correspondence was subjected to severe censorship, that they could not write to their lawyers or to international organizations and that prison officials arbitrarily deleted sentences and even refused to dispatch letters.

The author claimed that he was subjected to continuous ill-treatment and arbitrary punishments, including 30 days in solitary confinement in a punishment cell and seven months without mail or recreation. His correspondence was severely censored. During the entire period of his detention, he was given only 35 letters, though he certainly received hundreds.

On 12 February 1980, he was told that he would be expelled from the country for having exposed Uruguay to a risk of war against another State. On 15 February, he was taken to an airport where he boarded an aircraft bound for France.

The State party objected to the admissibility of the communication for a number of reasons, concluding that the author did not have the right of recourse to the mechanisms provided for in the Covenant and its Optional Protocol. Accordingly, it would make no answer concerning the substance of the matter.

In declaring the communication admissible, the Committee noted that the facts and allegations, as submitted by the author, appeared to raise issues under various provisions of the Covenant, including articles 7, 9, 10 and 14.

Examination of the merits

As to the conditions of imprisonment to which Miguel Angel Estrella was subjected, the Committee was in a position to conclude, on the basis of the detailed information submitted by him, that they were inhuman.

With regard to the censorship of his correspondence, the Committee accepted that it was normal for prison authorities to exercise measures of control and censorship

II:5

over prisoners' correspondence. Nevertheless, article 17 of the Covenant provided that no one should be subjected to arbitrary or unlawful interference with his correspondence. This required that any such measures of control or censorship should be subject to satisfactory legal safeguards against arbitrary application. Furthermore, the degree of restriction had to be consistent with the standard of humane treatment of detained persons required by article 10, paragraph 1, of the Covenant. In particular prisoners should be allowed, under necessary supervision, to communicate with their family and reputable friends at regular intervals, by correspondence as well as by receiving visits. On the basis of the information before it, the Committee found that the correspondence of Miguel Angel Estrella was censored and restricted to an extent not justified by the State party as compatible with article 17, read in conjunction with article 10, paragraph 1, of the Covenant.

The Committee was of the view that the facts disclosed a number of violations of the Covenant, including article 7, because Miguel Angel Estrella was subjected to torture during the first days of his detention; article 10, paragraph 1, because he was detained under inhuman prison conditions; and article 17, read in conjunction with article 10, paragraph 1, because of the extent to which his correspondence was censored and restricted.

Accordingly, the Committee held that the State party was under an obligation to provide the victim with effective remedies, including compensation, for the violations he had suffered and to take steps to ensure that similar violations did not occur in the future.

(c) A. v. France
(European Court of Human Rights)[32]

The case was referred to the European Court of Human Rights on 26 October 1992 by the European Commission of Human Rights. It originated in an application against the French Republic lodged with the Commission on 15 February 1989 by Mrs. A., a French national. The applicant requested the Court not to disclose her identity. The object of the Commission's request was to obtain a decision as to whether the facts of the case disclosed a breach by the respondent State of its obligations under article 8 of the Convention for the Protection of Human Rights and Fundamental Freedoms.

---

[32] See *Publications of the European Court of Human Rights*, Series A: *Judgments and Decisions*, vol. 277-B (1994), application No. 14838/89, judgment of 23 November 1993.

The facts

Mrs. A. lived in Paris. On 23 July 1981, an investigating judge charged her, together with Mr. G. and four other persons, with attempted murder, infringement of the arms and ammunition legislation and infringement of the law on the protection and control of nuclear substances. On the same day, the investigating judge remanded Mrs. A. in custody. She was released, subject to court supervision, on 26 March 1982 by decision of a court of appeal. On 7 March 1991, the judge made an order finding that the six persons charged, the applicant included, had no case to answer, as there was insufficient evidence against them.

In July or August 1980, Mr. G. went to the Paris police headquarters. He there informed the head of the central office for the prevention of serious crime, a chief superintendent, that Mrs. A. had hired him to kill Mr. Pierre De Varga, a person facing charges in relation to the attempted murder of Prince Jean de Broglie and in custody in the Santé prison in Paris. Mr. G. volunteered to make a telephone call to Mrs. A.'s home to discuss possible methods for carrying out the crime and to record the telephone conversation.

The chief superintendent accepted Mr. G.'s offer. Once the recording was in his possession, he informed his superiors of the threat to Mr. De Varga. However, he did not reveal the identity of his informant or the existence of the cassette.

When questioned on 22 September 1981 in connection with the investigation into the attempted murder of Mr. De Varga, the chief superintendent told the investigating judge that Mr. G. called Mrs. A. at 10.30 p.m. from the office of the chief superintendent. He said that Mr. G. got her to talk about the case and that the conversation lasted a good quarter of an hour. The chief superintendent further said that he recorded this conversation with a tape recorder and that he kept the recording. He added that he did not report this tape recording to his superior officer. The next day the chief superintendent handed over the recording to the investigating judge.

On 9 November 1981, Mrs. A. laid a complaint, together with an application to join the proceedings as a civil party, against Mr. G. and the chief superintendent for invasion of privacy and breach of the confidentiality of telephone communications. She relied on certain articles of the criminal code and the post and telecommunications code.

Having investigated the complaint, the judge made an order finding that there was no case to answer. The conversation did not concern private life as required by the criminal code, and the protection of secrecy under the post and telecommunications code was extended to the person making the call or its recipient only if neither of

II:5

them consented to the revelation concerned. In this case, the person making the call had consented to the revelation.

Mrs. A. appealed the judge's order and subsequent court decisions rejecting her appeals, up to the Court of Cassation, but she was unsuccessful.

The law

Mrs. A. claimed to be the victim of a violation of article 8 of the Convention. She took the view that the recording of her telephone conversation with Mr. G. was incompatible with her right to respect for her private life and correspondence, guaranteed by that article.

The Government in substance contested the applicability of article 8, maintaining that there had been neither invasion of privacy nor interference by a public authority.

On the first point, the Government drew attention to the fact that the recording in question had been made on the initiative and with the consent of one of the interlocutors. It was further argued that the conversation intercepted had dealt exclusively and deliberately with matters, namely preparations of a criminal nature, falling outside the scope of private life.

As to the second, the Government affirmed that Mr. G., who bore sole responsibility for instigating and carrying out the contested scheme, was not an official of the French State and was not acting on the latter's behalf. The fact that the public authorities had provided resources, such as premises and equipment, and had not opposed the undertaking in question was not sufficient to render them responsible for the interference.

The Commission and the applicant rejected this argument. They considered that a telephone conversation did not lose its private character solely because its content concerned or might concern the public interest. In addition, the recording was made on police premises with the assistance of a chief superintendent who retained in his possession the relevant tape.

The Court observed that the undertaking complained of by the applicant depended on Mr. G. and the chief superintendent working together. They could hardly be dissociated from each other. The former played a decisive role in conceiving and putting into effect the plan to make the recording by going to see the chief superintendent and then telephoning Mrs. A. The chief superintendent, for his part, was an official of a public authority. He made a crucial contribution to executing the scheme by making available for a short time his office, his telephone and his tape recorder. Admittedly, he did not inform his superiors of his actions, and he had not sought the prior authorization of an investigating judge, but he was acting in the performance of his duties as a high-ranking police officer. It followed that the public authorities were involved to such an extent that the State's responsibility under the Convention was engaged.

In any event, the recording represented an interference in respect of which Mrs. A. was entitled to the protection of the French legal system. Referring to its case law, the Court reiterated that this interference undoubtedly concerned Mrs. A.'s right to respect for her correspondence. The Government did not dispute that. In these circumstances, it was not necessary to consider whether it also affected her private life.

The Government conceded that the interference, if there had been any, had not been in accordance with the law. It had not been consistent with the French law at the time, because it had not been effected pursuant to a judicial procedure and had not been ordered by an investigating judge. Subsequent legislation made an interception of the type in question a punishable offence.

Like the Commission, the Court noted that the contested recording had no basis in domestic law. It therefore found a breach of article 8 of the Convention. This finding made it unnecessary for the Court to rule on compliance with the other requirements of paragraph 2 of that article.

Under the then article 50 of the Convention, allowing the Court to afford just satisfaction to an injured party, under specified circumstances, when there had been a violation of the Convention, the Court was of the opinion that the applicant might have sustained non-pecuniary damage. However, it considered that the present judgment afforded her sufficient just satisfaction in that respect. Having regard to the criteria it applied in this field, the Court awarded the applicant 50,000 French francs for all her costs and expenses.

(d) Halford v. the United Kingdom
(European Court of Human Rights)[33]

The case was referred to the European Court of Human Rights on 28 May 1996 by the European Commission of Human Rights. It originated in an application against the United Kingdom of Great Britain and Northern Ireland lodged with the Commission on 22 April 1992 by Alison Halford, a British citizen. The object of the request was to obtain a decision as to whether the facts of the case disclosed a breach by the

---

[33] See European Court of Human Rights, *Reports of Judgments and Decisions*, 1997-III, p. 1004, application No. 20605/92, judgment of 25 June 1997.

II:5

respondent State of its obligations under, *inter alia*, articles 8 and 13 of the Convention for the Protection of Human Rights and Fundamental Freedoms.

The facts

Ms. Halford worked in the police service from 1962 until her retirement in 1992. In May 1983, she was appointed to the rank of assistant chief constable with the Merseyside police. As such she became the most senior-ranking female police officer in the United Kingdom.

On eight occasions during the following seven years, Ms. Halford applied unsuccessfully to be appointed to the rank of deputy chief constable, in response to vacancies arising within Merseyside and other police authorities. In order to be considered for promotion to this rank, Home Office approval was required. However, according to the applicant, this was consistently withheld on the recommendation of the Chief Constable of the Merseyside police, who objected to her commitment to equality of treatment between men and women.

Following a further refusal to promote her in February 1990, Ms. Halford commenced proceedings on 4 June 1990 in the Industrial Tribunal against, *inter alia*, the Chief Constable of Merseyside and the Home Secretary, claiming that she had been discriminated against on grounds of sex. On 14 June 1990, the chairman and vice-chairman of the Merseyside Police Authority were designated a special committee to handle the issues arising from the discrimination case.

Ms. Halford alleged that a campaign was launched against her by certain members of the Merseyside Police Authority in response to her complaint to the Industrial Tribunal. This took the form of, *inter alia*, leaks to the press, interception of her telephone calls and the decision to bring disciplinary proceedings against her.

On 14 September 1990, the special committee referred to the senior officers' disciplinary committee a report written by the Chief Constable about an alleged incident of misconduct on the part of Ms. Halford on 24 July 1990. The disciplinary committee resolved, on 20 September 1990, to hold a formal investigation and to refer the matter to the Police Complaints Authority and, on 8 February 1991, to press charges. Ms. Halford was suspended from duty on full pay from 12 December 1990.

She challenged the above decisions by way of judicial review in the High Court. The matter was adjourned in September 1991 in view of a possible settlement. However, the parties failed to reach agreement, and the matter came back before the High Court on 20 December 1991. The Court found that the chairman and vice-chairman of the Police Authority had acted beyond their legal power or authority. Without imputing ill-motive to them, it was held that there had been an element of unfairness. The relevant decisions were therefore quashed.

The hearing before the Industrial Tribunal took place in June 1992, but the proceedings were adjourned pending negotiation between the parties which led to settlement of the case. Ms. Halford was given an *ex gratia* payment of 10,000 pounds sterling by the Chief Constable (the statutory maximum that the Industrial Tribunal could have awarded), together with 5,000 pounds towards her personal expenses by the Home Secretary. It was agreed that she would retire from the police force on medical grounds, arising out of an injury to her knee in 1989. In addition, the Home Office agreed to implement various proposals put by the Equal Opportunities Commission, *inter alia*, to update and review selection procedures for senior posts within the police force.

As assistant chief constable, Ms. Halford was provided with her own office and two telephones, one of which for private use. These telephones were part of the Merseyside police internal telephone network, a telecommunications system outside the public network. No restrictions were placed on the use of these telephones and no guidance was given to her, save for an assurance she sought and received from the Chief Constable shortly after she instituted the proceedings in the Industrial Tribunal that she had authorization to attend to the case while on duty, including by telephone.

In addition, since she was frequently on call, a substantial part of her home telephone costs were paid by the Merseyside police. Her home telephone was connected to the public telecommunications network.

The applicant alleged that calls made from her home and her office telephones were intercepted for the purposes of obtaining information to use against her in the discrimination proceedings. In support of these allegations, she adduced various items of evidence before the Commission. Additionally, she informed the Court that she was told by an anonymous source on 16 April 1991 that shortly before, the source had discovered the Merseyside police checking transcripts of conversations made on her home telephone.

For the purposes of the case before the Court, the Government accepted that the applicant had adduced sufficient material to establish a reasonable likelihood that calls made from her office telephones were intercepted. They did not, however, accept that she had adduced sufficient material to establish such a reasonable likelihood in relation to her home telephone.

II:5

Ms. Halford raised her concerns about the interception of her calls before the Industrial Tribunal on 17 June 1992. On 2 July 1992, in the course of the hearing, counsel for the Home Secretary expressed the opinion that it was not possible for Ms. Halford to adduce evidence about the alleged interceptions before the Industrial Tribunal. The Interception of Communications Act, 1985 expressly excluded the calling of evidence before any court or tribunal which tended to suggest that an offence under section 1 of the Act had been committed.

On 6 December 1991, Ms. Halford applied to the Interception of Communications Tribunal for an investigation to be carried out under the 1985 Act. In a letter dated 21 February 1992, the Tribunal informed her that its investigation had satisfied it that there had been no contraventions of the sections of the Act applicable to her case. In a letter dated 27 March 1992, the Tribunal confirmed that it could not specify whether any interception had in fact taken place.

The Interception of Communications Act, 1985 came into force following a judgment of the European Court of Human Rights in a case against the United Kingdom. The objective of that Act was to provide a clear statutory framework within which the interception of communications on public systems would be authorized and controlled in a manner commanding public confidence. It was a criminal offence for anyone intentionally to intercept a communication in the course of its transmission by means of a public communications system. However, the Secretary of State might issue warrants for the interception of communications and the disclosure of intercepted material on such grounds as national security, preventing or detecting serious crime or for safeguarding the economic well-being of the United Kingdom.

The 1985 Act provided for the establishment of an Interception of Communications Tribunal. Any person who believed, *inter alia*, that communications made by or to him might have been intercepted in the course of their transmission by means of a public telecommunications system could apply to the Tribunal for an investigation. The 1985 Act also made provision for the appointment of a commissioner. His functions included reviewing the issue of warrants under the Act by the Secretary of State, reporting to the Prime Minister certain breaches of the Act and making an annual report to the Prime Minister.

The 1985 Act did not apply to telecommunications systems outside the public network, such as the internal system at Merseyside police headquarters, and there was no other legislation to regulate the interception of communications on such systems.

The law

The applicant alleged that the interception of her telephone calls amounted to violations of article 8 of the Convention.

The Commission agreed that there had been a violation as far as the interception of calls from her office telephones was concerned. The Government denied that there had been any violation.

Regarding the office telephones, the applicant argued, and the Commission agreed, that the calls made on the telephones in Ms. Halford's office at Merseyside police headquarters fell within the scope of private life and correspondence in article 8, paragraph 1, of the Convention. In its case law, the Court had adopted a broad construction of these expressions.

The Government submitted that telephone calls made by Ms. Halford from her workplace fell outside the protection of article 8, because she could have had no reasonable expectation of privacy in relation to them. At the hearing before the Court, counsel for the Government expressed the view that an employer should in principle, without the prior knowledge of the employee, be able to monitor calls made by the latter on telephones provided by the employer.

In the Court's view, it was clear from its case law that telephone calls made from business premises as well as from the home might be covered by the notions of private life and correspondence within the meaning of article 8, paragraph 1, of the Convention.

There was no evidence of any warning having been given to Ms. Halford as a user of the internal telecommunications system operated at the Merseyside police headquarters that calls made on that system would be liable to interception. The Court considered that she would have a reasonable expectation of privacy for such calls, an expectation moreover reinforced by a number of factors. As assistant chief constable she had sole use of her office with two telephones, one of which specifically designated for her private use. Furthermore, she was given the assurance, in response to a memorandum, that she could use her office telephones for the purposes of her sex-discrimination case.

For these reasons, the Court concluded that the conversations held by Ms. Halford on her office telephones fell within the scope of the notions of private life and correspondence. Therefore, article 8 was applicable to this part of the complaint.

II:5

As to the existence of an interference, the Government conceded that the applicant had adduced sufficient material to establish a reasonable likelihood that calls made from her office telephones had been intercepted. The Commission also considered that an examination of the application revealed such a reasonable likelihood.

The Court agreed. The evidence justified the conclusion that there was a reasonable likelihood that calls made by Ms. Halford from her office were intercepted by the Merseyside police with the primary aim of gathering material to assist in the defence of the sex-discrimination proceedings brought against them. This interception constituted an interference by a public authority, within the meaning of article 8, paragraph 2, of the Convention, with the exercise of Ms. Halford's right to respect for her private life and correspondence.

Article 8, paragraph 2, further provided that any interference by a public authority with an individual's right to respect for private life and correspondence had to be in accordance with the law.

According to the Court's well-established case law, this expression did not only necessitate compliance with domestic law, but also related to the quality of that law, requiring it to be compatible with the rule of law. In the context of secret measures of surveillance or interception of communications by public authorities, because of the lack of public scrutiny and the risk of misuse of power, the domestic law had to provide some protection to the individual against arbitrary interference with rights under article 8. Thus, the domestic law had to be sufficiently clear in its terms to give citizens an adequate indication as to the circumstances in, and conditions on, which public authorities were empowered to resort to any such secret measures.

In the present case, the Government accepted that if, contrary to its submission, the Court would conclude that there had been an interference with the applicant's rights under article 8 in relation to her office telephones, such interference was not in accordance with the law. Domestic law did not provide any regulation of interceptions of calls made on telecommunications systems outside the public network.

The Court noted that the 1985 Act did not apply to internal communications systems operated by public authorities, such as that at Merseyside police headquarters, and that there was no other provision in domestic law to regulate interceptions of telephone calls made on such systems. It could not therefore be said that the interference was in accordance with the law for the purposes of article 8, paragraph 2, of the Convention. The domestic law did not provide adequate protection to Ms. Halford against interferences by the police with her right to respect for her private life and correspondence. It followed that there had been a violation of article 8 in relation to the interception of calls made on Ms. Halford's office telephones.

Regarding the applicant's home telephone, it was clear from the Court's case law that telephone conversations made from the home were covered by the notions of private life and correspondence under article 8 of the Convention. Indeed, this was not disputed by the Government. Therefore, article 8 was applicable to this part of the complaint.

As to the existence of an interference, the applicant alleged that calls made from her telephone at home also were intercepted by the Merseyside police for the purposes of defending the sex-discrimination proceedings. She referred to the evidence of interception adduced before the Commission and to the further specification made to the Court. In addition, she submitted that contrary to the Commission's approach, she should not be required to establish that there was a reasonable likelihood that calls made on her home telephone were intercepted. Such a requirement would be inconsistent with the Court's pronouncement in a previous case that the menace of surveillance could in itself constitute an interference with rights under article 8 of the Convention. In the alternative, she contended that if the Court did require her to show some indication that she had been affected, the evidence brought by her was satisfactory. Given the secrecy of the alleged measures, it would undermine the effectiveness of the protection afforded by the Convention to set the threshold of proof too high.

The Government explained that they could not disclose whether or not there had been any interception of calls made from the telephone in Ms. Halford's home. The finding that the Interception of Communications Tribunal was empowered to make under the 1985 Act was deliberately required to be couched in terms not revealing whether there had been an interception on a public telecommunications system properly authorized under the Act or whether there had in fact been no interception. However, the Government could confirm that the Tribunal was satisfied that there had been no contravention of the 1985 Act applicable to Ms. Halford's case.

The Court recalled that in a previous case it was called upon to decide, *inter alia*, whether legislation empowering the authorities secretly to monitor the correspondence and telephone conversations of the applicants, who were unable to establish whether such measures had in fact been applied to them, amounted to an interference with their rights under article 8. The Court held in that case that in the mere existence of the legislation itself there was involved, for all those to whom the legislation could be applied, a menace of surveillance. This menace necessarily struck at freedom of communication between users of the postal and telecommunication services. It thereby constituted an interference by a public authority with the exercise of the applicants' right to respect for private and family life and for correspondence.

II:5

The Court further recalled its judgment in a previous case against the United Kingdom. In addition to finding that one telephone conversation to which the applicant had been a party had been intercepted at the request of the police under a warrant issued by the Home Secretary, it observed in that case that the existence in England and Wales of laws and practices permitting and establishing a system for effecting secret surveillance of communications amounted in itself to an interference.

However, the essence of Ms. Halford's complaint was not that her rights under article 8 were menaced by the very existence of admitted law and practice permitting secret surveillance, but instead that measures of surveillance were actually applied to her. Furthermore, she alleged that the Merseyside police intercepted her calls unlawfully, for a purpose unauthorized by the 1985 Act.

In these circumstances, since the applicant's complaint concerned specific measures of telephone interception which fell outside the law, the Court must be satisfied that there was a reasonable likelihood that some such measure was applied to her.

In this respect the Court noted that the Commission, the organ under the Convention primarily charged with the establishment and verification of the facts, considered the evidence presented to it not to indicate a reasonable likelihood that calls made on the applicant's home telephone were being intercepted.

The Court observed that the only item of evidence tending to suggest that calls made from Ms. Halford's home telephone were being intercepted was the information concerning the discovery of the Merseyside police checking transcripts of conversations. Before the Court, the applicant provided more specific details regarding this discovery, namely that it was made on a date after she had been suspended from duty. However, the Court noted that this information might be unreliable, since its source had not been named. Furthermore, even if it was assumed to be true, the fact that the police were discovered checking transcripts of Ms. Halford's telephone conversations on a date after she had been suspended did not necessarily lead to the conclusion that these were transcripts of conversations made from her home.

The Court did not find it established that there was an interference with the rights of Ms. Halford to respect for her private life and correspondence in relation to her home telephone. In view of this conclusion, the Court did not find a violation of article 8 of the Convention with regard to telephone calls made from her home.

Ms. Halford further alleged that she had been denied an effective domestic remedy for her complaints, in violation of article 13 of the Convention.

The applicant, with whom the Commission agreed, contended that there had been a violation of article 13 in view of the fact that there was no avenue in domestic law by which to complain about interceptions of calls made on telecommunications systems outside the public network.

The Court recalled that the effect of article 13 was to require the provision of a remedy at national level allowing the competent domestic authority both to deal with the substance of the relevant complaint under the Convention and to grant appropriate relief. States parties were afforded some discretion as to the manner in which to conform to their obligations under that article. However, such a remedy was only required in respect of grievances which could be regarded as arguable in terms of the Convention.

The Court observed that the applicant undoubtedly had an arguable claim that calls made from her office telephones were intercepted and that this amounted to a violation of article 8 of the Convention. Therefore, she was entitled to an effective domestic remedy within the meaning of article 13. However, there was no provision in domestic law to regulate interceptions of telephone calls made on internal communications systems operated by public authorities, such as the Merseyside police. The applicant was therefore unable to seek relief at national level in relation to her complaint concerning her office telephones. It followed that there had been a violation of article 13 of the Convention in relation to the applicant's office telephones.

The applicant also complained that there was no remedy available to her against an interception of telephone calls made from her home by the police acting without a warrant. She referred to the first report of the Commissioner appointed under the 1985 Act. He observed that he was not concerned with the offence of unlawful interception created by that Act. He could not in the nature of things know, nor could he well find out, whether there had been an unlawful interception. That was, he said, a job for the police.

The Court recalled its observation that in order to find an interference within the meaning of article 8 in relation to Ms. Halford's home telephone, it must be satisfied that there was a reasonable likelihood of some measure of surveillance having been applied to the applicant. It referred in addition to its assessment of the evidence adduced by the applicant in support of her claim that calls made from her home telephone were intercepted.

The Court considered that this evidence was not sufficient to found an arguable claim within the meaning of article 13. It held, by eight votes to one, that there had been no violation of article 13 of the Convention in relation to the applicant's complaint concerning her home telephone.

II:5

Under the then article 50 of the Convention, allowing the Court to afford just satisfaction to an injured party, under specified circumstances, when there had been a violation of the Convention, the Court took the following decision. The Court considered that 10,000 pounds sterling was a just and equitable amount of compensation. It decided to award 600 pounds in respect of pecuniary damage and 25,000 pounds for costs and expenses.

(e) *P. G. and J. H.* v. *the United Kingdom* (European Court of Human Rights)[34]

The case was transmitted to the European Court of Human Rights on 1 November 1998. It originated in an application against the United Kingdom of Great Britain and Northern Ireland lodged with the European Commission of Human Rights on 7 May 1997 by Mr. P. G. and Mr. J. H., nationals of the United Kingdom. The applicants requested their names not be disclosed. They complained, *inter alia*, that covert listening devices had been used to record conversations at a flat and while detained in a police station and that information had been obtained by the police concerning the use of a telephone. They invoked article 8 and other provisions of the Convention for the Protection of Human Rights and Fundamental Freedoms.

The facts

On 28 February 1995, a detective inspector received information that an armed robbery of a security firm's cash collection van was going to be committed around 2 March 1995 by Mr. P. G., one of the applicants, and by Mr. B. at one of several possible locations. The police knew where the latter lived and began visual surveillance of the premises on the same day. The detective inspector learnt that Mr. B. was suspected of being a drug dealer and that previous surveillance operations mounted against him in the past had proved unsuccessful because they had been compromised. It was therefore concluded that he was surveillance conscious. He was suspected of being responsible for the shooting of a police officer with a shot-gun in the course of a robbery. This was something all the officers, and particularly the Chief Constable, were aware of when the police operation was being planned.

No robbery took place on 2 March 1995. The next day, however, the police received further information that the robbery was to take place somewhere on 9 March 1995. Further information as to the location or target of the proposed robbery could not be obtained during 3 March 1995. In order to obtain further details about the proposed robbery, the detective inspector prepared a report for the Chief Constable in support of an application for authorization to install a covert listening device in Mr. B.'s flat.

---

[34] *Ibidem*, 2001-IX, p. 195, application No. 44787/98, judgment of 25 September 2001.

Some of the contents of this report were the subject of a successful application for non-disclosure by the Crown on the ground that serious damage would be caused to the public interest if made public.

The use of covert listening devices was governed by guidelines on the use of equipment in police surveillance operations, issued by the Home Office in 1984. On 3 March 1995, the Chief Constable decided that the use of such a device was justified under the guidelines, but he would not authorize its use until he was satisfied that its installation was feasible. Reconnaissance on that night established that it was feasible.

On 4 March 1995, the Chief Constable gave oral authorization to proceed with its use. However, he did not provide written confirmation as stated in the guidelines, because he was then absent on annual leave, so he gave the authority on the telephone from home. He stated that the use of the device was to be reviewed on a daily basis. He said that he had asked the deputy chief constable to look after the written side and to ensure, *inter alia*, that there was written confirmation of the message that the installation of the device was feasible. He did not receive this confirmation until 8 March 1995. Then the deputy chief constable gave retrospective written authorization for use of the listening device.

A covert listening device was therefore installed in a sofa in Mr. B.'s flat on 4 March 1995 before the deputy chief constable had confirmed the authorization in writing. Conversations between Mr. B. and others in his living room were monitored and recorded until 15 March 1995.

On 14 March 1995, the police made a request to British Telecommunications PLC (BT) for itemized billing in relation to Mr. B.'s telephone number at his flat for the period of 1 January 1995 to the date of the request. The data protection form was countersigned by a police superintendent in line with BT's requirements, stating that the information was necessary to assist in the identification of members of a team of suspected armed robbers. While the request was originally made in an effort to identify the unknown third person in the conspiracy, now known to have been Mr. J. H., the other applicant, the data was also used later in court to corroborate the times and dates recorded by the officers in relation to the covert listening device in the flat.

On 15 March 1995, Mr. B. and others who were with him in his home discovered the listening device and abandoned the premises. The robbery did not take place. The police had been continuing visual surveillance of the premises, taking photographs and video footage whilst the audio surveillance was in progress. The applicants were identified by various officers going in and out of the flat and observed on occasions to be carrying various holdalls. The police had also been observing a

II:5

cache in a rural location and observed Mr. P. G. collecting an item from this location on the evening of 15 March 1995. An officer had earlier inspected the hidden item, which he stated he could tell through the plastic bag was a revolver. It appeared that the vehicle Mr. P. G. used for transport that evening was a stolen vehicle.

On 16 March 1995, the Mr. P. G. and Mr. J. H. were arrested while in the stolen car. In the boot of the vehicle were found two holdalls containing, *inter alia*, two black balaclavas, five black plastic cable ties, two pairs of leather gloves and two army kitbags. Following legal advice, they declined to comment during interview and refused to provide speech samples to the police. The police obtained a search warrant for the flat and searched it. Fingerprints of Mr. P. G. and Mr. J. H. were found, as well as items such as a pair of overalls and a third balaclava. Three vehicles were recovered and examined. The items retained included balaclavas, holdalls, overalls and a broken petrol cap.

As the police wished to obtain speech samples to compare with the tapes, they applied for authorization to install covert listening devices in the cells being used by Mr. P. G. and Mr. J. H. and to attach covert listening devices to the police officers to be present when Mr. P. G. and Mr. J. H. were charged. Written authorization was given by the Chief Constable in accordance with the Home Office guidelines. Samples of the speech of Mr. P. G. and Mr. J. H. were recorded without their knowledge or permission. In the case of Mr. J. H., the conversations recorded included, on one occasion, his taking advice from his solicitor. The Government stated that when the police officer realized what the conversation concerned, it was not listened to. That recording was not adduced in evidence at trial.

The voice samples of Mr. P. G. and Mr. J. H. were sent to an expert who compared them with the voices featured on the taped recordings of conversations held in Mr. B.'s home between 4 and 15 March 1995. The expert concluded that it was likely that Mr. P. G.'s voice featured on the taped recordings and very likely that Mr. J. H.'s voice featured on them.

Mr. B., Mr. P. G. and Mr. J. H. were charged with conspiracy to rob the security firm of monies. The police submitted statements of evidence from those police officers who had conducted the audio and visual surveillance of the flat and the searches of the flat and vehicles recovered. There was also evidence from officers who had conducted surveillance of the cache, including evidence from the officer who had identified the hidden object as a revolver. Mr. P. G. was seen to collect this item on the evening of 15 March 1995.

On 9 August 1996, the applicants were convicted of conspiracy to commit armed robbery and sentenced to 15 years' imprisonment.

At the relevant time, the Home Office guidelines provided that only chief constables or assistant chief constables were entitled to give authority for the use of equipment in police surveillance operations. The guidelines were available in the library of the House of Commons and were disclosed by the Home Office on application. They provided, *inter alia,* that the authorizing officer should satisfy himself that the investigation concerned serious crime; that normal methods of investigation had been tried and failed, or would be unlikely to succeed if tried; that there was good reason to think that use of the equipment would be likely to lead to an arrest and a conviction, or where appropriate, to the prevention of acts of terrorism; and that the use of equipment was operationally feasible.

In judging how far the seriousness of the crime under investigation justified the use of a particular surveillance technique, authorizing officers were required to satisfy themselves that the degree of intrusion into the privacy of those affected was commensurate with the seriousness of the offence. The guidelines also stated that there might be circumstances in which material so obtained could appropriately be used in evidence at subsequent court proceedings.

The Telecommunications Act, 1984 prohibited the disclosure by a person engaged in a telecommunications system of any information concerning the use made of the telecommunications services provided for any other person by means of that system. However, the Data Protection Act, 1984 exempted from non-disclosure provisions any case in which the disclosure was for the prevention or detection of crime or the apprehension or prosecution of offenders and the application of those provisions would be likely to prejudice any of those matters.

The law

The applicants complained, *inter alia*, that covert listening devices were used by the police to monitor and record their conversations at a flat; that information was obtained by the police concerning the use of a telephone at the flat; and that listening devices were used while they were at the police station to obtain voice samples. In this regard, they invoked article 8 of the Convention.

Regarding the use of a covert listening device at Mr. B.'s flat to monitor and record conversations, the applicants submitted that it was an interference with their rights under article 8, paragraph 1, not justified under paragraph 2 of the article. At the time of the events in their case, there existed no statutory system to regulate the use of covert listening devices, although the Police Act, 1997 now provided such a statutory framework. The Home Office guidelines that provided the relevant instructions to the police were neither legally binding nor directly publicly accessible. The inter-

II:5

ference with their right to respect for their private life was therefore not in accordance with the law, and there had been a violation of article 8 in that respect.

The Government acknowledged that the use of this device interfered with the applicants' right to respect for private life. It submitted that it was justifiable under the article 8, paragraph 2, as being necessary in a democratic society in the interests of public safety, for the prevention of crime and/or for the protection of the rights of others. The Goverment referred to, *inter alia*, the serious nature of the crime under investigation, the fact that Mr. B. was regarded as being surveillance conscious, rendering conventional forms of surveillance insufficient, and the fact that the conversations proved that an armed robbery was being planned. However, it recalled, in a previous case against the United Kingdom, the Court found that the Home Office guidelines did not satisfy the requirement to be in accordance with the law. It recognized that the Court was liable to reach the same conclusion in the present case.

The Court noted that it was not disputed that the surveillance carried out by the police at Mr. B.'s flat amounted to an interference with the right of Mr. P. G. and Mr. J. H. to respect for their private life. Regarding conformity with the requirements of article 8, paragraph 2, that any such interference had to be in accordance with the law and necessary in a democratic society for one or more of the specified aims, it was conceded by the Government that the interference was not in accordance with the law. At the time of the events, there existed no statutory system to regulate the use of covert listening devices. Such measures were governed by the Home Office guidelines that were neither legally binding nor directly publicly accessible.

As there was no domestic law regulating the use of covert listening devices at the relevant time, the interference in this case was not in accordance with the law as required by article 8, paragraph 2, of the Convention. Therefore, there had been a violation of article 8 in this regard. In the light of this conclusion, the Court was not required to determine whether the interference was at the same time necessary in a democratic society for one of the aims enumerated in the same provision.

Regarding the telephone metering of the telephone in Mr. B.'s flat, the applicants submitted that it constituted an interference with their rights under article 8 of the Convention, referring to a previous case against the United Kingdom. They conceded that the information was disclosed in accordance with the applicable domestic law, namely the Telecommunications Act, 1984 and the Data Protection Act, 1984. However, neither of these legislative provisions, nor any common law rule, provided the safeguards envisaged in the Court's case law, in particular as regarded the use to which the material could be put, the conditions under which it would be stored and provision for its destruction. They argued that the Telecommunications Act merely exempted telephone operatives from prosecution if they disclosed information in

326

connection with a criminal offence. Equally, the Data Protection Act rendered personal data liable to disclosure for the purpose of preventing or detecting crime. Neither Act stipulated any of the restraints on abuse to be found, for instance, in the Police Act, 1997 in relation to covert recordings. Accordingly, the interference with the rights under article 8 was effected otherwise than in accordance with the law.

The Government acknowledged that those who used the telephone had an expectation of privacy in respect of the numbers dialled and that obtaining detailed billing information concerning that telephone constituted an interference with the rights of Mr. P. G. and Mr. J. H. under article 8. The obtaining of the information was, however, necessary in a democratic society in the interests of the public safety, for the prevention of crime and/or the protection of the rights of others. The investigation concerned a very serious crime, Mr. P. G. and Mr. J. H. had guns for use in the intended robbery and, as Mr. B. was surveillance conscious, conventional surveillance would not suffice. The only use of the information was to corroborate the times recorded by police officers in respect of the covert listening device in the flat.

In the Government's view, the interference was also in accordance with the law as there was a statutory prohibition in the Telecommunications Act, 1984 against disclosure of such information, save where a specific exception was satisfied. Similarly, under the Data Protection Act, 1984 governing the storage, processing and disclosure of personal data, there was a strict regime, however permitting disclosure for the purposes of the apprehension or prosecution of offenders. Accordingly, the disclosure to, and use by, the police of the itemized telephone bill was made in accordance with domestic law. Material not covered by the Data Protection Act would have been stored or destroyed according to the policy of the police force in question. In this case, under the police policy and procedure guideline system, the billing records concerning serious crime would have been retained in paper form for six years or longer at the discretion of a detective inspector.

The Court observed that it was not in dispute that the obtaining by the police of information relating to the numbers called on the telephone in Mr. B.'s flat interfered with the private lives or correspondence, in the sense of telephone communications, of Mr. P. G. and Mr. J. H. when making use of the telephone in the flat or being telephoned from the flat. The Court noted, however, that metering, not *per se* offending against article 8 if for example done by the telephone company for billing purposes, was by its very nature to be distinguished from the interception of communications that might be undesirable and illegitimate in a democratic society unless justified.

The Court further examined whether the interference in the present case was justified under article 8, paragraph 2, notably whether it was in accordance with the law

II:5

and necessary in a democratic society for one or more of the purposes enumerated in that paragraph.

The expression "in accordance with the law" required, firstly, that the impugned measure should have some basis in domestic law. Secondly, it referred to the quality of the law in question, requiring that it should be accessible to the person concerned, who moreover had to be able to foresee its consequences for him, and that it was compatible with the rule of law. The Court here made reference to its case law.

Both parties agreed that the obtaining of the billing information was based on statutory authority, in particular the Telecommunications Act, 1984 and the Data Protection Act, 1984. The first requirement therefore posed no difficulty. The applicants argued that the second requirement was not fulfilled in their case, as there were insufficient safeguards in place concerning the use, storage and destruction of the records.

The Court observed that the quality of law criterion in this context referred essentially to considerations of foreseeability and lack of arbitrariness. What was required by way of safeguards would depend, to some extent at least, on the nature and extent of the interference in question. In this case, the information obtained concerned the telephone numbers called from Mr. B.'s flat between two specific dates. It did not include any information about the contents of those calls or who made or received them. The data obtained, and the use that could be made of it, were therefore strictly limited.

While it did not appear that there were any specific statutory provisions, as opposed to internal policy guidelines, governing storage and destruction of such information, the Court was not persuaded that the lack of such detailed formal regulation raised any risk of arbitrariness or misuse. Nor was it apparent that there was any lack of foreseeability. Disclosure to the police was permitted under the relevant statutory framework where necessary for the purposes of the detection and prevention of crime. The material was used at the applicants' trial on criminal charges to corroborate other evidence relevant to the timing of telephone calls. It was not apparent that the applicants did not have an adequate indication as to the circumstances in, and conditions on, which the public authorities were empowered to resort to such a measure. The Court concluded that the measure in question was in accordance with the law.

As to whether the measure was necessary in a democratic society, the Court noted that the applicants had not sought to argue that the measure was not in fact justified as necessary for the protection of public safety, the prevention of crime and the protection of the rights of others. The information was obtained and used in the context of an investigation into, and trial of, a suspected conspiracy to commit armed robberies. No issues of proportionality had been identified. Accordingly, the measure was justified under article 8, paragraph 2, as necessary in a democratic society for the purposes identified above. The Court concluded that there had been no violation of article 8 of the Convention in respect of the applicants' complaints about the metering of the telephone in this case.

Regarding the use of listening devices in the police station, the applicants complained that their voices were recorded secretly when being charged in the police station and held in their cells. They submitted that what was said was irrelevant. This ranged from giving personal details to a conversation about football instigated by a police officer. They considered that it was the circumstances in which the words were spoken that was significant. There was a breach of privacy if the speaker believed that he was only speaking to the person addressed and had no reason to believe the conversation was being broadcast or recorded. The key issue in their view was whether the speaker knew or had any reason to suspect that the conversation was being recorded. In the present case, the police knew that the applicants had refused to provide voice samples voluntarily. They sought to trick to them into speaking in an underhand procedure being wholly unregulated, arbitrary and attended by bad faith. It was also irrelevant that the recording was used for forensic purposes rather than to obtain information about the speaker, as it was the covert recording itself, not the use made of it, that amounted to the breach of privacy.

The applicants further submitted that the use of the covert listening devices was not in accordance with the law, as there was no domestic law regulating the use of such devices and no safeguards provided within the law to protect against abuse of such surveillance methods. They rejected any assertion that the police could rely on any general power to obtain and store evidence.

The Government submitted that the use of the listening devices in the cells and when Mr. P. G. and Mr. J. H. were being charged did not disclose any interference, as these recordings were not made to obtain any private or substantive information. The aural quality of their voices was not part of private life. It was rather a public, external feature. In particular, the recordings when Mr. P. G. and Mr. J. H. were charged, a formal process of criminal justice in the presence of at least one police officer, did not concern private life. They could not have had any expectation of privacy in that context. In any event, to the extent that the Court might find that the recordings did engage article 8 of the Convention, any interference was so negligible as not to amount to a violation of their rights under that provision. By analogy from a previous case against the United Kingdom, if the obtaining of samples of breath, blood or urine would not raise problems under article 6, the obtaining of voice samples would equally not offend articles 6 or 8 of the Convention.

II:5

Assuming that there was an interference with any right under article 8, the Government contended that it was justified under paragraph 2 as necessary in a democratic society to protect public safety, prevent crime and/or protect the rights of others. It relied on, *inter alia*, the fact that the investigation concerned a very serious crime; that Mr. P. G. and Mr. J. H. were known to have guns; that the voice samples were needed to establish fairly whether the voices recorded in the flat belonged to Mr. P. G. and Mr. J. H.; and that the judge ruled at the trial that the voice samples represented relevant, reliable and probative evidence of identity of those planning the robbery. The measure was proportionate, as it did not involve any act of trespass, the use of the samples was limited to identification, and Mr. P. G. and Mr. J. H. had the opportunity at trial to challenge their admissibility. Any interference was also conducted in accordance with the law, as the making of the recordings after arrest was an exercise by the police of their normal common law powers to obtain and store evidence. It had not been found by the trial judge to contravene any requirements regarding cautioning or interview codes.

The Court observed that private life was a broad term not susceptible to exhaustive definition. Making references to its case law, it had already held that elements such as gender identification, name and sexual orientation and sexual life were important elements of the personal sphere protected by article 8. This article also protected a right to identity and personal development and the right to establish and develop relationships with other human beings and the outside world. It might include activities of a professional or business nature. There was therefore a zone of interaction of a person with others, even in a public context, which might fall within the scope of private life.

A number of elements were relevant to a consideration of whether a person's private life was concerned in measures effected outside the person's home or private premises. Since there were occasions when people knowingly or intentionally involved themselves in activities, which were or might be recorded or reported in a public manner, a person's reasonable expectations as to privacy might be a significant, though not necessarily conclusive factor. A person walking down the street would, inevitably, be visible to any member of the public also present. Monitoring by technological means of the same public scene, for example a security guard viewing through close circuit television, was of a similar character. Private life considerations might arise, however, once any systematic or permanent record came into existence of such material from the public domain. It was for this reason that files gathered by security services on a particular individual fell within the scope of article 8 of the Convention, even where the information had not been gathered by any intrusive or covert method, as found in a previous judgment. In this context, the Court had referred to the Convention for the Protection of Individuals with regard to Automatic Processing of Personal Data, in force since 1985. This Council of Europe treaty had the purpose to secure in the territory of each State party for every individual respect for his rights and fundamental freedoms and, in particular, his right to privacy with regard to the automatic processing of personal data relating to him, being defined as any information relating to an identified or identifiable individual. The Court also made reference to another judgment, where the storing of information about the applicant on a card in a file was found to be an interference with private life, even though it contained no sensitive information and had probably never been consulted.

In the case of photographs, the Commission previously had regard to, for the purpose of delimiting the scope of protection afforded by article 8 against arbitrary interference by public authorities, whether the taking of the photographs amounted to an intrusion into the individual's privacy; whether the photographs related to private matters or public incidents; and whether the material obtained was envisaged for a limited use or was likely to be made available to the general public. Where photographs were taken of an individual at a public demonstration in a public place and retained by the police in a file, the Commission found no interference with private life, giving weight to the fact that the photographs were taken and retained as a record of the demonstration and that no action had been taken to identify the persons photo-graphed on that occasion by means of data processing.

In its case law, the Court had on numerous occasions found that the covert taping of telephone conversations fell within the scope of article 8 of the Convention in both aspects of the right guaranteed, namely the respect for private life and correspondence. While it was generally the case that the recordings were made for the purpose of using the content of the conversations in some way, the Court was not persuaded that recordings taken for use as voice samples could be regarded as falling outside the scope of the protection afforded by article 8. A permanent record had nonetheless been made of the person's voice. It was subject to a process of analysis directly relevant to identifying that person in the context of other personal data. Though it was true that when being charged, Mr. P. G. and Mr. J. H. answered formal questions in a place where police officers were listening to them, the recording and analysis of their voices on this occasion had still to be regarded as concerning the processing of personal data about them.

The Court concluded therefore that the recording of the applicants' voices when being charged and when in their police cell disclosed an interference with their right to respect for private life within the meaning of article 8, paragraph 1, of the Convention.

As to compliance with the requirements of article 8, paragraph 2, the Court examined, firstly, whether the interference was in accordance with the law. This criterion

II:5

imported two main requirements. There had to be some basis in domestic law for the measure, and the quality of the law had to be such as to provide safeguards against arbitrariness.

The Court recalled that the Government relied as the legal basis for the measure on the general powers of the police to store and gather evidence. While it might be permissible to rely on the implied powers of police officers to note evidence and collect and store exhibits for steps taken in the course of an investigation, it was trite law that specific statutory or other express legal authority was required for more invasive measures, whether searching private property or taking personal body samples. The Court had found in previous cases that the lack of any express basis in law for the interception of telephone calls on public and private telephone systems and for using covert surveillance devices on private premises did not conform with the requirement of lawfulness. It considered that no material difference arose where the recording device was operated, without the knowledge or consent of the individual concerned, on police premises. The underlying principle that domestic law should provide protection against arbitrariness and abuse in the use of covert surveillance techniques applied equally in that situation.

The Court noted that legislation in the United Kingdom now contained provisions concerning covert surveillance on police premises. However, at the relevant time, there existed no statutory system to regulate the use of covert listening devices by the police on their own premises. Therefore, the interference was not in accordance with the law as required by article 8, paragraph 2, of the Convention. There had been a violation of this provision. In these circumstances, an examination of the necessity of the interference was no longer required.

The Court also responded to other allegations submitted by the applicants. Those parts of the judgment are not included in this summary of the case.

As to article 41 of the Convention, allowing the Court to afford just satisfaction to the injured party, under specified circumstances, when there had been a violation of the Convention, the Court recalled that the right of Mr. P. G. and Mr. J. H. to respect for private life was violated in several aspects and that they had no effective remedy under domestic law. It considered that they must thereby have suffered some feelings of frustration and invasion of privacy not sufficiently compensated by a finding of violation. It therefore awarded Mr. P. G. and Mr. J. H. 1,000 pounds sterling each in respect of non-pecuniary damage. The Court also made an award of 12,000 pounds in respect of costs and expenses.

PART III

Police Functions and Protection of Human Rights

1. Introduction to Police Functions and Protection of Human Rights

The protection of individuals and groups from abuse of power by the State is central to our idea of human rights, and to the purposes of the institutions featured in this book. When state officials exercise their powers, human rights must be respected. Some of the most significant jurisprudence arising out of acts or omissions by police, of which the cases featured in this book are only a selection, concerns the use of force, treatment of detainees, deprivation of liberty and invasions of privacy. That is why the largest part of the book is devoted to police powers and respect for human rights.[1]

However, as is argued in the general introduction to this publication, the relationship between human rights and policing is not adequately represented solely by notions of power and respect.[2] The purposes of policing also have to be taken into account, and it is generally recognized that these are, primarily, to prevent and detect crime; to maintain and, where necessary, restore order; and to provide aid and assistance in emergencies. It is, therefore, important to look at human rights and policing in the context of what police do and the circumstances or conditions in which they do it. What police do, or in other words, the functions of policing, is the subject matter of this part of the book. The circumstances and conditions in which police work include policing in times of conflict, disturbance and tension, separately dealt with in the subsequent and last part of the book.[3]

Whereas there are clear and direct links between the exercise of a specific police power and each of the rights dealt with in part II, that is not the case in respect of the rights considered in this part of the book. Nevertheless, they are all, in various ways, of great relevance to policing, and they can all be affected, for good or for ill, by policing. For example, the ways in which police investigate crime can reinforce or subvert the right to a fair trial; the readiness and the ability of police to investigate crimes committed against people because of their religion or belief can safeguard or impair the right to freedom of thought, conscience and religion; and the methods adopted by police in maintaining or restoring public order can reinforce or undermine

---

[1] See part II (*supra*, pp. 33-332).
[2] See part I, chap. 1, sect. E (*supra*, pp. 30-32).
[3] See part IV (*infra*, pp. 525-636).

the rights to freedom of opinion and expression as well as freedom of assembly and association. Furthermore, the right to a fair trial is an essential component of the rule of law, and all of the rights treated in this part of the book are fundamental to the functioning of democracies. These are obvious reasons why police should understand their importance, and should protect them.

Ways in which police protect human rights, contributing to conditions necessary for the enjoyment of all human rights, and protecting specific human rights, are discussed in the general introduction. This means that police protect everyone's rights, and it would be extremely helpful to the cause of human rights and to the purposes of policing if this were explicitly acknowledged, and routinely listed, as one of the functions of policing.

An important aspect of human rights protection, of which police should be acutely aware, is the protection against discrimination on grounds of race. As indicated in the general introduction to this book, examples of the jurisprudence of the Committee on the Elimination of Racial Discrimination are included in this introduction.[4] They are included here primarily because the International Convention on the Elimination of All Forms of Racial Discrimination, under which the Committee is established, places a variety of obligations on States parties which are not expressed as rights to be enjoyed by individuals or groups of people. It seems, therefore, appropriate to include the Committee's jurisprudence here rather than in the subsequent chapters of the part, each of which devoted to a specific human right.

The preamble to the Convention reaffirms that discrimination between human beings on grounds of race, colour or ethnic origin is capable of disturbing peace and security among peoples and the harmony of persons living side by side even within one and the same State. These are all compelling reasons for police to act against discrimination on such grounds, especially when they have at their disposal measures under their national laws that prohibit words or deeds intended to, or likely to, stir up racial hatred.

In its general recommendation XIII (42) on training of law enforcement officials in the protection of human rights,[5] the Committee pointed out that the fulfilment of State parties' obligations under the Convention was very much dependent upon national law enforcement officials exercising police powers, especially the powers of arrest and detention, and upon whether they were properly informed about the obligations of their State under the Convention. Law enforcement officials should re-

---

[4] See part I, chap. 1, sect. D (*b*) (*supra*, pp. 11-12).
[5] See United Nations, *Official Records of the General Assembly, Forty-eighth Session, Supplement No. 18* (A/48/18), chap. VIII, sect. B.

ceive intensive training to ensure that in the performance of their duties, they respect as well as protect human dignity and maintain and uphold the human rights of all persons without distinction as to race, colour or national or ethnic origin.[6]

Recently, the Committee has adopted general recommendation XXXI (67) on the prevention of racial discrimination in the administration and functioning of the criminal justice system.[7] In this general recommendation, the Committee has identified, *inter alia*, steps to be taken to prevent racial discrimination with regard to victims of racism and with regard to accused persons who are subject to judicial proceedings, including during questioning, interrogation, arrest, pre-trial detention and trial. Some of the statements and recommendations made here by the Committee are of particular relevance to police and express fundamental principles to be applied by law enforcement agencies respecting and protecting human rights. For example, States parties to the Convention should take the necessary steps to to prevent questioning, arrest and searches which in reality are based solely on the physical appearance of a person, that person's colour or features or membership of a racial or ethnic group, or any profiling which exposes him or her to greater suspicion. Other points include those designed to prevent and punish torture and ill-treatment of such persons; to ensure the principles of proportionality and necessity in the use of force against them; to secure their fundamental rights when they are arrested; and to ensure their enjoyment of all the guarantees of a fair trial and equality before the law.

A few of the cases considered by the Committee under article 14 of the Convention have raised issues relevant to policing. Two of these cases have been selected as examples in this context.

In the case *L. K.* v. *the Netherlands*,[8] the author, a Moroccan citizen residing in the Netherlands, was subjected to threats and intimidation in 1989 by a crowd of local residents when he visited a house with a view to leasing it. Several of them said that they wanted no more foreigners in the locality, and others intimated to him that if he were to accept the house, they would set fire to it and damage his car. The author alleged that when he attempted to file a complaint with the police, they initially refused to register it. Although provisions of the Dutch criminal code were applicable to the actions of some of the street residents, no one was successfully prosecuted, in spite of an appeal by counsel for Mr. L. K. to a court of appeal and correspondence with the Minister of Justice.

---

[6] *Ibidem*, para. 2.
[7] *Ibidem, Sixtieth Session, Supplement No. 18* (A/60/18), para. 460.
[8] *Ibidem, Forty-eighth Session, Supplement No. 18* (A/48/18), annex IV, communication No. 4/1991, opinion adopted on 16 March 1993.

III:1

The author submitted that the remarks and statements of the local residents constituted acts of racial discrimination within the meaning of article 1, paragraph 1, of the Convention. He contended, *inter alia*, that the judicial authorities and the public prosecutor had not been sufficiently determined and expeditious in their handling of the case. The police investigation was neither thorough nor complete. He alleged violations of article 2, paragraph 1 (*d*), *juncto* articles 4 and 6 of the Convention.

After having taken into account the observations of the State party, the Committee found that the remarks and threats made to Mr. L. K. constituted incitement to racial discrimination and to acts of violence against persons of another colour or ethnic origin, contrary to article 4 (*a*) of the Convention, and that the investigation into these incidents by the police and prosecution authorities had been incomplete.

The Committee pointed out that when threats of racial violence were made, and especially when they were made in public and by a group, it was incumbent upon the State to investigate with due diligence and expedition. In this case, the State party failed to do this. The Committee found that that in view of the inadequate response to the incidents, the police and judicial proceedings had not afforded Mr. L. K. effective protection and remedies within the meaning of article 6 of the Convention. The Committee recommended the State party to review its policy and procedures concerning the decision to prosecute in cases of alleged racial discrimination, in the light of its obligations under article 4 of the Convention. Furthermore, it recommended the State party to provide Mr. L. K. with relief commensurate with the moral damage he had suffered.

In the other case, *Kashid Ahmad* v. *Denmark*,[9] the author, a Danish citizen of Pakistani origin, claimed to be a victim of violations by Denmark of articles 2, paragraph 1 (*d*), and 6 of the Convention. In 1998, he and his brother were waiting outside an examination room at a school, where a friend of theirs was taking an exam, when a teacher asked them to leave. When they refused, the teacher informed the headmaster, who called the police. The headmaster publicly referred to Kashid Ahmad and his brother as "a bunch of monkeys". When the author told him that he was going to complain about the manner in which he had been treated, the teacher expressed doubts about the effectiveness of such a complaint and said that the author and his brother were "a bunch of monkeys" who could not express themselves correctly.

Counsel for Kashid Ahmad filed a complaint with the police, but they subsequently informed him that they had interviewed the headmaster and the teacher and con-

---

[9] *Ibidem, Fifty-fifth Session, Supplement No. 18* (A/55/18), annex III, sect. A, communication No. 16/1999, opinion adopted on 13 March 2000.

cluded that the expressions used were outside the scope of the penal code. The case would be discontinued. Counsel then requested the police to have the case brought before the State attorney, but the the the decision of the police was upheld. The author submitted that the case had not been examined properly by the national authorities and that he had not obtained an apology or sufficient satisfaction or reparation.

After having taken into account the observations of the State party, the Committee noted that the teacher had not denied calling Kashid Ahmad and his brother "monkeys" and that the headmaster had not denied saying something similar. It was also established that these utterances were made in a school corridor in the presence of several witnesses. Thus, the Committee was of the opinion that the author was insulted in public, at least by the headmaster. The Committee also noted that the district public prosecutor had not established whether Kashid Ahmad had been insulted on the grounds of his national or ethnic origin, in violation of the provisions of article 2, paragraph 1 (*d*), of the Convention. In the Committee's opinion, if the police had not discontinued their investigations, it might have been established whether Kashid Ahmad had indeed been insulted on racial grounds.

From information submitted by the State party in another context, the Committee gathered that people had been convicted by Danish courts for breaches of the criminal code for insulting or degrading statements similar to the ones uttered in this case. Therefore, the Committee did not share the opinion of the State party that the statements in question did not fall within the criminal code.

Owing to the failure of the police to continue their investigations, and the final decision of the public prosecutor against which there was no right of appeal, Kashid Ahmad had been denied any opportunity to establish whether his rights under the Convention were violated. From this it followed that the author had been denied effective protection against racial discrimination and remedies attendant thereupon by the State party. In the light of these findings, the facts as presented constituted a violation of article 6 of the Convention. The Committee recommended the State party to ensure that the police and the public prosecutors properly investigate accusations and complaints related to acts of racial discrimination, which should be punishable by law according to article 4 of the Convention.

The following chapters of this part of the book deal with, respectively, the right to a fair trial; the right to freedom of thought, conscience and religion; the right to freedom of opinion and expression; and the right to freedom of peaceful assembly and association.

2. Right to a Fair Trial

A. INTRODUCTION

The purpose of the right to a fair trial is to secure the proper administration of justice. It is expressed briefly and concisely in article 10 of the Universal Declaration of Human Rights. Everyone is entitled in full equality to a fair and public hearing by an independent and impartial tribunal, in the determination of his rights and obligations and of any criminal charges against him.

The more detailed provisions of the corresponding articles in the International Covenant on Civil and Political Rights and the regional human rights treaties protect a series of distinct rights that are minimum guarantees necessary for a fair trial. However, before those rights can be brought into play, an individual must have been provided with the opportunity to have his or her case heard in the first place. In other words, there is a right to a hearing, a right of access to a tribunal. The right to a fair trial is a complex right that has been comprehensively interpreted and developed by courts and bodies established under international human rights treaties.

Furthermore, a number of non-treaty instruments contain provisions that are necessary to secure the right to a fair trial. For example, the Basic Principles on the Independence of the Judiciary set out a number of principles formulated to assist States in their task of securing and promoting the independence of the judiciary; the Basic Principles on the Role of Lawyers were adopted to assist States in their task of promoting and ensuring the proper role of lawyers; and the Guidelines on the Role of Prosecutors were formulated to assist States in their task of securing and promoting the effectiveness, impartiality and fairness of prosecutors in criminal proceedings.

A further measure to protect the independence of the judiciary was taken by the United Nations Commission on Human Rights in 1994 when it decided to create a monitoring mechanism.[1] The Commission noted both the increasing frequency of attacks on the independence of judges, lawyers and court officials and the link existing between the weakening of safeguards for the judiciary and lawyers and the gravity

---

[1] See Commission on Human Rights resolution 1994/41 of 4 March 1994 (United Nations, *Official Records of the Economic and Social Council, 1994, Supplement No. 4* (E/1994/24 and Corr.1), chap. II, sect. A).

III:2

and frequency of violations of human rights. The Special Rapporteur on the independence of judges and lawyers, accordingly appointed, implements a thematic special procedure of the Commission.

Under the mandate, the Special Rapporteur shall inquire into any substantial allegations submitted to him or her and report on the conclusions drawn; he or she shall indentify and record not only attacks on the independence of the judiciary, lawyers and court officials, but also progress achieved in protecting and enhancing their independence, and make concrete recommendations; and he or she shall study, for the purpose of making proposals, important and topical questions of principle with a view to protecting and enhancing the independence of the judiciary and lawyers.

Specific provisions on juvenile justice reinforce the right to a fair trial for juveniles. For example, the United Nations Standard Minimum Rules for the Administration of Juvenile Justice (The Beijing Rules) set out measures to ensure that juveniles accused of crimes are dealt with according to the principles of a fair and just trial. Article 40 of the Convention on the Rights of the Child requires States parties to ensure that every child alleged as or accused of having infringed the criminal law shall be guaranteed, *inter alia*, that the matter shall be determined without delay by a competent, independent and impartial authority or judicial body in a fair hearing according to the law.

Police, whether acting autonomously or under the direction and control of a prosecutor or an investigator with judicial powers, investigate crime for the purpose of gathering evidence to be considered by a court of trial. A lawful and ethical police investigation can support the right to a fair trial, but an unlawful and unethical investigation can subvert that right even before a trial has commenced. Furthermore, an important element of the right to a fair trial is the right of access to a tribunal, the right to a hearing. It is important to ensure that police action or inaction does not prevent an individual from having a case heard before a tribunal.

Some of the minimum guarantees for a fair trial embodied in human rights treaties have significant implications for the investigative process. For example, the right to be tried without undue delay means that investigations must be concluded as quickly and efficiently as possible. A number of factors beyond the control of the police may delay a trial, but police have a duty to ensure that the way in which their investigation is conducted is not the cause of failure to meet the obligation.

The right of an accused person to examine, or have examined, witnesses against him and to obtain the attendance and examination of witnesses on his behalf is especially relevant when a police investigation discovers a witness who has evidence supporting the case of an accused person. For the guarantee to be met, the accused person should be given the opportunity to secure the attendance and examination of that witness.

The right of everyone not to be compelled to testify against himself or to confess guilt may either be protected or violated in the investigative process by the ways in which a suspect is treated as a detainee, and particularly how he or she is interviewed. An essential element of a fair trial is the presumption of innocence, and it is this presumption, together with the requirement to respect human rights and to obey the law, that should dictate the behaviour of police officials towards people suspected of crime with whom they are dealing.

The detection of crime through investigation and evidence gathering is the first necessary step in a judicial process leading to the conviction and punishment of those found to be guilty of crime. When the investigation is conducted effectively and lawfully, that result may be achieved. When it is not so conducted, the result may be that innocent people are convicted of crimes they did not commit, and the guilty remain undetected and unpunished.

The right to a fair trial is immensely important because it is one of the cornerstones of democratic societies governed by the rule of law. Police have a duty to protect that right as a desirable end in itself, and also to reinforce and protect the great civilized and civilizing values on which those societies are built.

B. REVIEW OF CASES

(*a*) Human Rights Committee

Article 14 of the International Covenant on Civil and Political Rights protects the right to a fair trial. Although primarily applicable to courts and tribunals, the provisions of this long and detailed article aimed at ensuring the proper administration of justice also have an obvious bearing on police.

In paragraph 1, it is stipulated that all persons shall be equal before the courts and tribunals. In the determination of any criminal charge against him, or of his rights and obligations in a suit at law, everyone has an entitlement to a fair and public hearing by a competent, independent and impartial tribunal established by law. The paragraph also sets out the conditions under which press and public may be excluded from all or part of a trial. These include reasons of morals, public order or national security in a democratic society. However, any judgment rendered in a criminal case or in a suit at law must be made public except where the interest of juveniles requires otherwise or the proceedings concern matrimonial disputes or the guardianship of children.

III:2

Paragraph 2 expresses the fundamental principle of presumption of innocence. Everyone charged with a criminal offence shall have the right to be presumed innocent until proved guilty according to law

In the remainder of the article, paragraphs 3 to 7, the following provisions are of particular relevance in this context. In the determination of any criminal charge against him, everyone shall be entitled to a number of minimum guarantees set out in paragraph 3. These include to be informed promptly and in detail in a language he understands of the nature and cause of the charge against him; to have adequate time and facilities for the preparation of his defence and to communicate with counsel of his own choosing; to be tried without undue delay; to examine or have examined the witnesses against him; and not be compelled to testify against himself or to confess guilt. Paragraph 7 contains the basic rule of *ne bis in idem*. No one shall be liable to be tried or punished again for an offence for which he has already been finally convicted or acquitted in accordance with the law and penal procedure of each country.

In time of public emergency threatening the life of the nation, States parties may take measures derogating from its obligations under article 14, but only on the conditions set forth in article 4 of the Covenant.

In its general comment No. 13 (21) concerning article 14 of the Covenant,[2] the Human Rights Committee made a number of important pronouncements on the right to a fair trial. Of particular significance to police were the following comments. By reason of the presumption of innocence, laid down in article 14, paragraph 2, the burden of proof of the charge was on the prosecution, and the accused had the benefit of doubt. No guilt could be presumed until the charge had been proved beyond reasonable doubt. Furthermore, the presumption of innocence implied a right to be treated in accordance with this principle. It was therefore a duty for all public authorities to refrain from prejudging the outcome of a trial.[3] In considering the safeguard provided in article 14, paragraph 3 (*g*), that the accused might not be compelled to testify against himself or to confess guilt, the provisions of articles 7 and 10, paragraph 1, should be borne in mind. In order to compel the accused to confess or to testify against himself, methods violating these provisions were frequently used. The law should require that evidence provided by means of such methods or any other form of compulsion was wholly unacceptable.[4]

---

[2] See United Nations, *Official Records of the General Assembly, Thirty-ninth Session, Supplement No. 40* (A/39/40 and Corr.1 and 2), annex VI.

[3] *Ibidem*, para. 7.

[4] *Ibidem*, para. 14.

In the case *Gridin* v. *Russian Federation*,[5] summarized in section C,[6] the Committee found that, *inter alia*, the presumption of innocence principle had been violated. The author, Dimitriy Leonodovich Gridin, a Russian student, was arrested in 1989 on charges of attemped rape and murder. When in detention, he was also charged with multiple assaults. A court found him guilty of the charges and sentenced him to death, later commuted to life imprisonment. His appeals were rejected.

The Committee found that he had been a victim of a violation of article 14, paragraph 2, of the Covenant because of public statements made before the trial by high-ranking law enforcement officials portraying him as guilty. With reference to its pronouncement in general comment No. 13 (21), that it was the duty for all public authorities to refrain from prejudging the outcome of a trial, the Committee considered that the authorities had failed to exercise the restraint that article 14, paragraph 2, required. It also found a violation of article 14, paragraph 3 (*b*), because the victim had been denied access to legal counsel and then interrogated. These were, of course, events that had occurred before the trial. Furthermore, the Committee considered that article 14, paragraph 1, had been violated because of the way in which the trial had been conducted.

Two cases involving allegations of violations of the provision that no one should be compelled to testify against himself or to confess guilt, laid down in article 14, paragraph 3 (*g*), are reviewed below.

In the case *John Campbell* v. *Jamaica*,[7] the author, a Jamaican citizen, had been sentenced to death in 1983 following conviction for murder of his wife. At the trial, Mr. Campbell's juvenile son refused to testify against his father and, as a consequence, was detained overnight in police headquarters. He continued to refuse to testify the next day, and the judge adjourned the trial. When it resumed, the son broke down and testified against his father but later retracted his evidence.

In its deliberations on this case, the Committee pointed out that under article 14 of the Covenant, everyone was given the right to a fair and public hearing in the determination of a criminal charge against him. An indispensable aspect of the fair trial principle was the equality of arms between the prosecution and the defence. The Committee observed that the detention of witnesses with a view to obtaining their testimony was an exceptional measure to be regulated by strict criteria in law and in

---

[5] *Ibidem, Fifty-fifth Session, Supplement No. 40* (A/55/40), vol. II, annex IX, sect. O, communication No. 770/1997, views adopted on 20 July 2000.

[6] See part III, chap. 2, sect. C (*a*) (*infra*, pp. 374-378).

[7] See United Nations document A/48/40 (Part II), annex XII, sect. G, communication No. 307/1988, views adopted on 24 March 1993.

practice. It was not apparent from the information before the Committee that special circumstances existed to justify the detention of Mr. Campbell's minor child. Moreover, in the light of his retraction, serious questions arose about possible intimidation and about the reliability of the testimony obtained under these circumstances. The Committee therefore concluded that the author's right to a fair trial had been violated and that the appropriate remedy entailed release.

In an individual opinion, one member concurred with the Committee's findings, but he offered other reasons for finding a violation of the author's right to a fair trial. He pointed out that article 14, paragraph 3, of the Covenant contained further guarantees for those charged with a criminal offence. In particular, paragraph 3 (*e*) guaranteed that an accused should have the right, in full equality, to examine or have examined the witnesses against him and to obtain the attendance and examination of witnesses on his behalf under the same conditions as witnesses against him. In his opinion, however, the issue in this case was not whether the principle of equality of arms was violated with respect to hearing Mr. Campbell's son as a witness, but whether his examination was compatible with the principles of due process of law and fair trial. He recalled first that when the author's son was heard as a witness by the court, he was merely 13 years of age, and he was expected to recount truthfully an event which had occurred nearly three years earlier, when he was 10, and which might seriously incriminate his father. Secondly, measures of coercion were employed against him to make him testify and otherwise comply with his obligations as a witness.

Particular care had to be exercised in relation to child witnesses, in view of their vulnerability, and every effort should be made to conduct the hearing in as considerate and sympathetic a way as possible. He recalled that article 24 of the Covenant entitled every child to such measures of protection as were required by his status as a minor, and he concluded that the violation was in fact the violation of the rights of a witness, but its negative impact on the conduct of the trial was such that it rendered it unfair within the meaning of article 14, paragraph 1, of the Covenant.

In the case *R. T. Muñoz Hermoza* v. *Peru*,[8] the author, Rubén Toribio Muñoz Hermoza, a Peruvian citizen, was a former sergeant of the Guardia Civil. He alleged that he had been temporarily suspended from the force on 25 September 1978 on false accusations of having insulted a superior. When he was brought before a judge on 28 September 1978 on that charge, he was immediately released for lack of evi-

---

[8] See United Nations, *Official Records of the General Assembly, Forty-fourth Session, Supplement No. 40* (A/44/40), annex X, sect. D, communication No. 203/1986, views adopted on 4 November 1988.

dence. Nevertheless, by an administrative decision of 30 January 1984 he was discharged from service.

The author claimed that he, after having served in the force for over 20 years, had been arbitrarily deprived of his livelihood and of his acquired rights, including accrued retirement rights, thus leaving him in a state of destitution, particularly considering that he had eight children to feed and clothe. He then spent 10 years going through numerous and diverse domestic administrative and judicial instances seeking reinstatement in the force, without success.

In considering the merits of this case, the Committee noted that the concept of a fair hearing, as set out in article 14, paragraph 1, of the Covenant, necessarily entailed that justice should be rendered without undue delay. It reviewed the multifarious domestic procedures followed by the author, observing in particular that an administrative review kept pending for seven years constituted an unreasonable delay. The Committee concluded that such a seemingly endless sequence of instances and the repeated failure to implement decisions were incompatible with the principle of a fair hearing.

The events of the case, in so far as they continued or occurred after 3 January 1981, when the Optional Protocol to Covenant entered into force in respect of Peru, disclosed a violation of article 14, paragraph 1, of the Covenant. The Committee was also of the view that the State party was under an obligation, in accordance with the provisions of article 2 of the Covenant, to take effective measures to remedy the violations suffered by Mr. Muñoz Hermoza, including the payment of adequate compensation. Four members of the Committee filed individual opinions in the case.

Under article 14, paragraph 3 (*b*), of the Covenant, everyone charged with a criminal offence is entitled to have adequate time and facilities for the preparation of his defence and to communicate with a counsel of his own choosing. In the case *Paul Anthony Kelly* v. *Jamaica*,[9] the author, a Jamaican citizen, was awaiting execution at the time of submission of his complaint. He claimed to be a victim of a violation by the State party of, *inter alia*, article 14, paragraph 3 (*b*), of the Covenant, as he was denied access to his lawyer until five days after having been taken into custody, and for other reasons connected with his appeal against conviction.

When this aspect of the communication was brought to the attention of the State party by the Committee, the State promised to investigate the allegation but failed to report to the Committee on its findings. It did however admit that under Jamaican law,

---

[9] *Ibidem, Fifty-first Session, Supplement No. 40* (A/51/40), vol. II, annex VIII, sect. O, communication No. 537/1993, views adopted on 17 July 1996.

III:2

Paul Anthony Kelly had the right to consult with an attorney following his arrest. According to the file, made available to the State party for comments, Mr. Kelly, when brought to the police station, told the police officers that he wanted to speak to his lawyer, but the police officers ignored the request for five days. In the circumstances, the Committee concluded that the author's right under article 14, paragraph 3 (*b*), to communicate with counsel of his choice had been violated.

Ultimately, the Committee found violations of various provisions of article 14 of the Covenant, including paragraph 3 (*b*), and concluded that Paul Anthony Kelly was entitled to an effective remedy that should entail his release.

The provision in article 14, paragraph 3 (*c*), of the Covenant, entitling everyone charged with a criminal offence to be tried without undue delay, overlaps with that in article 9, paragraph 3, guaranteeing pre-trial detainees a right to be tried within a reasonable time or to release. In this respect, article 9, paragraph 3, is concerned with the length of detention before trial, whereas article 14, paragraph 3 (*c*), regulates the actual time between arrest and trial, regardless of whether or not the person is detained.

Article 9, paragraph 3, of the Covenant also requires anyone arrested or detained on a criminal charge to be brought promptly before a judge or other officer authorized by law to exercise judicial power. It was this aspect of the article that was at issue in the case *Paul Kelly* v. *Jamaica*.[10] This case, summarized in connection with the right to liberty and security of person,[11] also raised issues under, *inter alia*, article 14, paragraph 3 (*c*), of the Covenant. The author, a Jamaican citizen awaiting execution, was arrested on 20 August 1981 and detained without formal charges being brought against him until 15 September 1981 when he was charged with murder. He was subsequently convicted and sentenced to death.

In respect of article 9, paragraph 3, the Committee found that detention for some five weeks before Paul Kelly was brought before a judge, or judicial officer entitled to decide on the lawfulness of his detention, violated the requirement in that paragraph. Regarding article 14, paragraph 3 (*c*), the Committee could not conclude that a lapse of a year and a half between the arrest and the start of the trial constituted undue delay, as there was no suggestion that pre-trial investigations could have been concluded earlier or that Paul Kelly complained in this respect to the authorities. Two members of the Committee filed individual opinions in the case.

---

[10] *Ibidem, Forty-sixth Session, Supplement No. 40* (A/46/40), annex XI, sect. D, communication No. 253/1987, views adopted on 8 April 1991.

[11] See part II, chap. 4, sect. C (*e*) (*supra*, pp. 252-255).

The case *Michael and Brian Hill* v. *Spain*,[12] another case summarized in connection with the right to liberty and security of person,[13] concerned article 14, paragraph 3 (*c*), of the Covenant as well as various paragraphs of article 9. The authors, British citizens residing in the United Kingdom, were arrested on 15 July 1985 and formally charged on 19 July 1985. Their trial did not start until November 1986, and their appeal was not disposed of until July 1988. The State party argued that the delay of three years between arrest and final appeal was due to the complexities of the case, but it provided no information showing the nature of the alleged complexities. Michael and Brian Hill were claimed to have firebombed a bar in Gandía, Spain. Having examined all the information available to it, the Committee failed to see in which respect the case could be regarded as complex. The sole witness was an eyewitness who gave evidence at the hearing in July 1985, and there was no indication that any further investigation was required after that hearing was completed. In these circumstances, the Committee found that the State party had violated the authors' right under article 14, paragraph 3 (*c*), to be tried without undue delay.

In contrast, the case *Dieter Wolf* v. *Panama*[14] was more complex in that it concerned the issue of 12 uncovered cheques for varying amounts between 25 and 3,000 US dollars. The author, a German citizen, was arrested in 1984, and he was detained at a Panamanian penitentiary when he submitted his communication. In this case, there was a delay of four and a half years between arrest and rendering of the judgment. The Committee stated that with respect to the author's right under article 14, paragraph 3 (*c*), to be tried without unreasonable delay, it could not conclude that the proceedings had suffered from undue delays. The Committee observed that investigations into allegations of fraud might be complex and that the author had not shown that the facts did not necessitate prolonged proceedings. However, the Committee found other violations of the Covenant in the case, including article 14, paragraphs 1 and 3 (*b*) and (*d*).

The case *Bernard Lubuto* v. *Zambia*,[15] summarized in section C,[16] concerned the conviction of Mr. Lubuto, a Zambian citizen and author of the communication, for aggravated robbery, committed in 1980, for which he was sentenced to death. In this

---

[12] See United Nations, *Official Records of the General Assembly, Fifty-second Session, Supplement No. 40* (A/52/40), vol. II, annex VI, sect. B, communication No. 526/1993, views adopted on 2 April 1997.

[13] See part II, chap. 4, sect. C (*f*) (*supra*, pp. 255-258).

[14] See United Nations, *Official Records of the General Assembly, Forty-seventh Session, Supplement No. 40* (A/47/40), annex IX, sect. K, communication No. 289/1988, views adopted on 26 March 1992.

[15] *Ibidem, Fifty-first Session, Supplement No. 40* (A/51/40), vol. II, annex VIII, sect. B, communication No. 390/1990, views adopted on 31 October 1995.

[16] See part III, chap. 2, sect. C (*b*) (*infra*, pp. 378-381).

case, there was an eight-year delay between arrest and dismissal of appeal. The State party requested the Committee to take into consideration the State's situation as a developing country and the problems it encountered in the administration of justice. The shortcomings were attributable to the difficult economic situation in the country. The Committee pointed out that the Covenant rights constituted minimum standards that all States parties had agreed to observe. It found a violation of article 14, paragraph 3 (*c*), of the Covenant. The Committee was also of the view that facts in the case disclosed a violation of article 6 on the right to life, invoked by the author. One member of the Committee filed an individual opinion in the case.

This case is interesting because of the Committee's view on the imposition of the death penalty, which may only be imposed for the most serious crimes, and the questions it raised about a State's resources and its ability to secure respect for civil and political rights. Under article 2 of the International Covenant on Economic, Social and Cultural Rights, each State party undertakes to take steps, to the maximum of its available resources, with a view to achieving progressively the full realization of the rights recognized in the Covenant. However, the International Covenant on Civil and Political Rights makes no such allowances for the incremental realization of the rights it protects, a fact made clear in the response of the Committee to the State's submission in the case. Whilst there are no, or few, resource implications in securing respect for some civil and political rights, the prohibition of torture, for example, simply requires that state officials desist from committing the crime, resources are required to run an effective police service and an efficient justice system.

The insistence of the Committee on compliance with the requirements to limit pre-trial detention and to expedite justice, in spite of difficulties encountered in the administration of justice, is also apparent in the case *Sextus* v. *Trinidad and Tobago*.[17] The author, Sandy Sextus, a national of Trinidad and Tobago, claimed that he on 21 September 1988 was arrested on suspicion of murdering his mother-in-law on the same day. The complaint centred on alleged excessive delays in the judicial process and the conditions of detention suffered by him at various stages in that process. As to the allegation of delay, the author contended that his rights under articles 9, paragraph 3, and 14, paragraph 3 (*c*), of the Covenant were violated in that there was a 22-month delay in bringing his case to trial.

In its observations to the Committee concerning the merits of the claims of delay, the State party submitted that the relevant periods were not unreasonable in the circumstances then prevailing in the State's territory in the years immediately follow-

---

[17] See United Nations, *Official Records of the General Assembly, Fifty-sixth Session, Supplement No. 40* (A/56/40), vol. II, annex X, sect. I, communication No. 818/1998, views adopted on 16 July 2001.

ing an attempted coup. The increase in crime had placed great pressures on the courts in that period, with backlogs resulting. Difficulties experienced in the timely preparation of complete and accurate court records caused delays in bringing cases to trial and in hearing appeals. The Committee considered, however, that in this case substantial reasons had to be shown to justify a 22-month delay until trial. Mr. Sextus was arrested on the day of the offence, charged with murder and held until trial, and the factual evidence was straightforward and apparently required little police investigation. The State party had pointed only to general problems and instabilities following a coup attempt, and it had acknowledged delays that ensued. In the circumstances, the Committee concluded that the author's rights under, *inter alia*, articles 9, paragraph 3, and 14, paragraph 3 (*c*), of the Covenant had been violated. One member of the Committee filed an individual opinion in the case.

In the case *Lloyd Grant* v. *Jamaica*,[18] the Committee considered the provision in article 14, paragraph 3 (*e*), entitling everyone charged with a criminal offence to examine, or have examined, the witnesses against him and to obtain the attendance and examination of witnesses on his behalf under the same conditions as witnesses against him. The author was a Jamaican citizen awaiting execution. He and his brother were tried and convicted of murder in 1986 and sentenced to death. A court of appeal later dismissed Lloyd Grant's appeal, but his brother was acquitted. The author contended that he was unable to secure the attendance of witnesses on his behalf, in particular the attendance of his girlfriend.

The Committee noted from the trial transcript that Lloyd Grant's attorney did contact the girlfriend and, on the second day of the trial, made a request to the judge to have her called to court. The judge then instructed the police to contact this witness, who had no means to attend. The Committee was of the opinion that in the circumstances, and bearing in mind that the case involved the death penalty, the judge should have adjourned the trial and issued a subpoena to secure the attendance of the witness in court. Furthermore, the Committee considered that the police should have made transportation available to her. To the extent that failure of the witness to appear in court was attributable to the State party's authorities, the Committee found that the criminal proceedings against Lloyd Grant were in violation of article 14, paragraphs 1 and 3 (*e*), of the Covenant.

Ultimately, the Committee found that the facts before it disclosed violations of articles 6 and 14, paragraphs 1, 3 (*b*), (*d*) and (*e*), of the Covenant, and it was of the view that Lloyd Grant was entitled to a remedy entailing his release.

---

[18] *Ibidem, Forty-ninth Session, Supplement No. 40* (A/49/40), vol. II, annex IX, sect. H, communication No. 353/1988, views adopted on 31 March 1994.

III:2

In the case *G. Peart and A. Peart* v. *Jamaica*,[19] summarized in section C,[20] the authors, Andrew Peart and Garfield Peart, Jamaican citizens convicted and sentenced in 1988 to death on a murder charge, claimed, *inter alia*, a failure to make the statement of a witness for the prosecution available to the defence. The Committee considered that this failure seriously obstructed the defence in its cross-examination of the witness, thereby precluding a fair trial of the defendants, and that there had been a violation of article 14, paragraph 3 (*e*), of the Covenant. Furthermore, as death sentences had been passed in this case without due respect for the requirement of fair trial, there had consequently also been a violation of article 6 of the Covenant. The Committee was of the view that the remedy should be the authors' release. This case is also interesting because of the authors' accounts of their treatment whilst imprisoned following conviction and the Committee's response to this.

Under article 14, paragraph 3 (*g*), of the Covenant, everyone charged with a criminal offence is entitled not to be compelled to testify against himself or to confess guilt. In the case *Sánchez López* v. *Spain*,[21] the author, Antonio Sánchez López, claimed that in 1990, his car, which he was driving, was photographed after being detected exceeding the speed limit by police radar. On being required under the provisions of a legislative decree to identify the driver, Mr. Sánchez López declined to do so and was fined. He then appealed the case, claiming that the imposition of the fine constituted a violation of the right to presumption of innocence, the right not to confess guilt and the right not to testify against oneself, all of which being recognized in the Spanish Constitution. When the appeal was rejected, the author submitted a communication to the Committee alleging that he had been the victim of a violation of article 14, paragraph 3 (*g*), in that he had been obliged to confess guilt to the extent that the request for identification was addressed to the owner of the vehicle, who was in fact the driver responsible for the offence. He further maintained that one of the fundamental elements of the presumption of innocence in article 14, paragraph 2, namely the placing of the burden of proof on the prosecution and not the defence, had been violated. It was in fact incumbent on the authorities themselves to identify the driver presumed to be responsible for the offence.

The Committee considered that the author had been punished for non-cooperation with the authorities and not for the traffic offence and that a penalty for failure to cooperate with the authorities in this way fell outside the scope of application of the

---

[19] *Ibidem, Fiftieth Session, Supplement No. 40* (A/50/40), vol. II, annex X, sect. E, communications No. 464/1991 and No. 482/1991, views adopted on 19 July 1995.
[20] See part III, chap. 2, sect. C (*c*) (*infra*, pp. 382-385).
[21] See United Nations, *Official Records of the General Assembly, Fifty-fifth Session, Supplement No. 40* (A/55/40), vol. II, annex X, sect. D, communication No. 777/1997, decision adopted on 18 October 1999.

provisions of the Covenant referred to in the communication. Accordingly, the Committee decided that the communication was inadmissible under article 1 of the Optional Protocol to the Covenant.

In the case *Albert Berry* v. *Jamaica*,[22] also cited in connection with the right to liberty and security of person,[23] the author, a Jamaican national awaiting execution, complained that the State party had violated, *inter alia*, articles 7 and 14, paragraph 3 (*g*), of the Covenant in that he had been threatened that he would be shot if he did not make and sign a confession statement. On 27 March 1984, he had been arrested on a charge of murder and subsequently convicted and sentenced to death. On 15 June 1984, the preliminary hearing was held.

As to this claim under article 14, paragraph 3 (*g*), *juncto* article 7, of the Covenant, the Committee recalled that the wording of article 14, paragraph 3 (*g*), that no one should be compelled to testify against himself or to confess guilt, had to be understood in terms of the absence of any direct or indirect physical or psychological pressure from the investigating authorities on the accused with a view to obtaining a confession of guilt. *A fortiori*, it was unacceptable to treat an accused person in a manner contrary to article 7 of the Covenant in order to extract a confession. The Committee noted that the author claimed that the investigating officer had threatened to shoot him and forced him to sign a prepared statement. This claim had not been contested by the State party. On the other hand, the Committee noted that the investigating officer testified during the trial that Mr. Berry had made his statement after police cautioning. The Committee observed that in order to reconcile these different versions, the written depositions made and used during the preliminary hearing were required.

The Committee further observed that counsel had requested the State party, on several occasions, to make available to him the transcript of Mr. Berry's preliminary hearing, including the depositions of witnesses, and that finally, after several reminders, he was informed by the judicial authorities that they were unable to locate them. These allegations had not been denied by the State party and, therefore, due weight had to be given to the author's claims. The Committee found that the facts in the case disclosed violations of article 14, paragraph 3 (*g*), *juncto* article 7, and a number of other provisions of the Covenant. Mr. Berry was entitled to an appropriate remedy entailing his release.

---

[22] *Ibidem, Forty-ninth Session, Supplement No. 40* (A/49/40), vol. II, annex IX, sect. D, communication No. 330/1988, views adopted on 7 April 1994.

[23] See part II, chap. 4, sect. B (*a*) (*supra*, pp. 215-216).

III:2

(*b*) Working Group on Arbitrary Detention

It is recalled that the Working Group on Arbitrary Detention regards deprivation of liberty as arbitrary in the following cases:

(*a*) When it manifestly cannot be justified on any legal basis, such as continued detention after the sentence has been served or despite an applicable amnesty act (category I);

(*b*) When the deprivation of liberty is the result of a judgment or sentence for the exercise of the rights or freedoms proclaimed by articles 7, 13, 14, 18, 19, 20 and 21 of the Universal Declaration of Human Rights and also, in respect of States parties, in articles 12, 18, 19, 21, 22, 25, 26 and 27 of the International Covenant on Civil and Political Rights (category II); and

(*c*) When the complete or partial non-observance of the international standards relating to a fair trial set forth in the Universal Declaration and in the relevant international instruments accepted by the States concerned is of such gravity as to confer the deprivation of liberty, of whatever kind, an arbitrary character (category III).

In order to evaluate the arbitrary character of cases of deprivation of freedom entering into category III, the Working Group considers, in addition to the general principles set out in the Universal Declaration, several criteria drawn from the Body of Principles for the Protection of All Persons under Any Form of Detention or Imprisonment and, for States parties, the criteria laid down particularly in articles 9 and 14 of the Covenant.

When the Working Group concludes that a person has been arbitrarily deprived of his or her liberty, the Government concerned is typically requested to take the necessary steps to remedy the situation and to bring it into conformity with the standards and principles set forth in the Universal Declaration and, where applicable, the Covenant. States non-parties to the Covenant are encouraged to become a party to it.

From the jurisprudence of the Working Group, five cases of arbitrary detention arising out of failures to respect the right to a fair trial are included in this review.

A case in which an officer allegedly had been arrested, held in pre-trial detention and convicted, exclusively because he had exercised his right to freedom of expression, opinion No. 27/2001 (*Morocco*),[24] is summarized in section C[25] and also cited

---

[24] See United Nations document E/CN.4/2003/8/Add.1, p. 27, opinion adopted on 3 December 2001.

in connection with the right to freedom of opinion and expression.[26] It concerned Mustapha Adib, a former captain of the Moroccan armed forces. He refused to become involved in corrupt dealings when he served in the armed forces. As a consequence, he suffered various forms of harassment. On 5 December 1999, he was arrested and eventually sentenced to a term of imprisonment and dismissal from the army for having expressed his views to a journalist who later published them.

The Working Group was concerned that Mustapha Adib had been judged by a military tribunal. The independence of such tribunals from the executive power was often in doubt. In this case, the tribunal had acted in a way that cast doubts on its impartiality by infringing the presumption of innocence of the accused and by hindering his defence. The deprivation of Mustapha Adib's liberty was declared arbitrary, as being in contravention of articles 9 and 10 of the Universal Declaration and articles 9 and 14 of the Covenant, to which Morocco was a party. It fell within category III of the categories applicable to the consideration of cases submitted to the Working Group

In a case that included allegations of a deposition obtained by force, opinion No. 14/1999 (*Palestine*),[27] it was claimed that Youssef Al-Rai and Ashaher Al-Rai, two Palestinian cousins, were arrested on 3 September 1995 on suspicion of having killed two villagers in July 1995. On 13 September 1995, they were sentenced to seven years' imprisonment for murder. Their trial allegedly lasted no more than half an hour. It was held in a state security court composed of three military judges. The court appointed a soldier as the legal representative of the accused. The two cousins could not speak with their lawyer, and he was unable to defend them during the trial.

According to the source, the only evidence justifying the two men's sentence was the deposition by another prisoner who had been questioned by the Israeli authorities on 2 September 1995. These authorities transmitted his deposition to the Palestinian security services. After his release in 1995, and again during a press conference on 17 September 1998, he said that he had lied. In fact, he had never met the two cousins. On 24 September 1998, he publicly admitted that he had been forced to give false evidence against the cousins, under torture.

The allegations had not been refuted by the Palestinian Authority, despite an opportunity to do so. In accordance with its methods of work, the Working Group pronounced, it was able to consider whether the right to a fair trial provided for in arti-

---

[25] See part III, chap. 2, sect. C (*d*) (*infra*, pp. 385-390).

[26] See part III, chap. 4, sect. B (*b*) (*infra*, pp. 445-446).

[27] See United Nations document E/CN.4/2000/4/Add.1, p. 65, opinion adopted on 15 September 1999.

III:2

cle 10 of the Universal Declaration and in the Body of Principles had been violated in the present case.

The Working Group considered that the sentence in this case was based on a deposition obtained by force. Under article 5 of the Universal Declaration, no one should be subjected to torture or to cruel, inhuman or degrading treatment or punishment. In admitting as evidence a deposition obtained by force, the Palestinian judicial authorities had violated that provision, as well as articles 9 and 10 of the Universal Declaration, guaranteeing the right to a fair trial, and principles 21 and 27 of the Body of Principles, setting out, *inter alia*, that no detained person should be subject to violence, threats or methods of interrogation which might impair his capacity of decision or his judgement and that non-compliance with these principles should be taken into account in determining the admissibility of evidence. The authorities had also violated principle 17 of the Body of Principles, providing that a detained person should be entitled to have the assistance of a legal counsel, as well as principle 36 on the presumption of innocence. The Working Group found that the violation was of such gravity as to confer an arbitrary character on the detention of Youssef and Ashaher Al-Rai, falling within category III. Palestine was not a party to the Covenant.

In another case, opinion No. 1/2001 (*Uzbekistan*),[28] there were allegations of torture and fabrication of evidence. It was claimed that Munavar Hasanov, 70 years old, was arrested on 18 November 1999 by members of the Uzbek police on charges of possessing leaflets printed by a banned Islamic organization. During interrogation he agreed to sign a confession statement, it was alleged, to put an end to the torture of his son, Ismail Hasanov, that he reportedly was forced to witness. Furthermore, the police later confronted the son with his father and threatened to continue to beat the father unless the son signed a confession statement, which he did.

On 16 February 2000, a regional court sentenced Munavar Hasanov to three years in prison for anti-constitutional activity, solely on the basis of leaflets found in his house. He denied possession of the leaflets and insisted that the police had conducted the search without a warrant and that they had fabricated and planted evidence in his house. He identified, in the courtroom, the officer who had allegedly put the leaflets in his home. It was said that the judge studiously ignored his intervention. The three-year sentence was later extended by six months on charges that he had violated internal prison rules by not shaving his beard and not removing his skullcap while passing a guard.

---

[28] See United Nations document E/CN.4/2002/77/Add.1, p. 36, opinion adopted on 16 May 2001.

In the light of the allegations presented by the source, which had not been denied by the Government, despite the opportunity to do so, the Working Group found that the rights of Munavar and Ismail Hasanov, under articles 9 and 10 of the Universal Declaration and articles 9, 10 and 14 of the Covenant, to which Uzbekistan was a party, had been violated during their detention. Their rights to a fair trial had not been respected. The Working Group concluded that the non-observance of their rights to a fair trial was of such gravity as to confer an arbitrary character upon the deprivation of their liberty, falling within category III.

A case about denial of the right to a fair hearing, opinion No. 29/2001 (*Ethiopia*),[29] concerned the arrest, on 13 November 1997, of Gebissa Lemessa Gelelcha, a 59-year-old former accountant at the Ethiopian office of the United Kingdom-based Save the Children Fund and founder of the Human Rights League, together with other founder members of the League. They were taken to a police investigation centre, although not initially charged with any offence. 11 days after their arrest, a judge ordered that they should be allowed access to their relatives, lawyers and medical care.

According to the source, the League was formed in 1996, among the Oromo community in Addis Ababa, with the stated objectives of enlightening citizens about human rights, reporting on human rights violations and providing legal aid to victims of human rights violations. It had applied for official registration and was about to hold a workshop on human rights standards when its board members were arrested.

Mr. Lemessa had been held in detention for four and a half years, reportedly charged with offences relating to armed conspiracy with the Oromo Liberation Front. His trial, held in camera, had continued for four years and no verdict had been issued. He was being held in detention, according to the source, simply for his work in favour of promoting human rights and denouncing violations of the Universal Declaration.

The Working Group took due note of the Government's comments to the effect that the detention of Mr. Lemessa was apparently justified by his involvement in terrorist activities. The Working Group noted, however, that he had been imprisoned since 1997, without having been charged or convicted, and that he had been arrested and detained on a number of occasions in the past for periods of up to eight years before being released, without being charged or convicted. These repeated periods of detention without charge or conviction gave credence to the version of events advanced by the source. Furthermore, regardless of the allegation that the detainee had personally committed serious crimes, his prolonged detention without trial could not be regarded as having any basis in law, given that he had been denied the right to a fair

---

[29] See United Nations document E/CN.4/2003/8/Add.1, p. 38, opinion adopted on 3 December 2001.

III:2

trial. The Working Group further noted that to date, the person concerned had not been given an opportunity to challenge the legality of his detention.

The Working Group believed that a violation of the individual's right to a fair hearing had occurred. This violation was of such gravity as to confer on the deprivation of liberty an arbitrary character, contravening articles 9 and 10 of the Universal Declaration and articles 9 and 14 of the Covenant, to which Ethiopia was a party, and falling within category III.

Finally, another case of denial of a fair hearing, opinion No. 2/2002 (*Myanmar*),[30] concerned Aung San Suu Kyi, the leader of a political party and known advocate of political change in Myanmar, exclusively by peaceful means. She was arrested on 22 September 2000 by military intelligence personnel. No arrest warrant was shown during her arrest, which took place as she was about to board a train. It was believed that she was arrested on charges of attempting to violate a travel ban preventing her from leaving Yangon, the capital of Myanmar, and on charges relating to the State Protection Act. This Act allowed for restrictions to be imposed on the fundamental rights of a citizen if he or she had performed, was performing or was believed to be performing an act endangering the State's sovereignty and security, as well as public law and order. However, there had to be a potential danger to the State from that person.

Aung San Suu Kyi was placed under house arrest without being formally charged with any offence and without standing trial. She was prevented from leaving her house and from receiving any visitors except with express authorization from the Government. Her telephone was cut off. For the most part, she was being held incommunicado. However, the United Nations Special Rapporteur on the situation of human rights in Myanmar and a European Union delegation were authorized to meet her in early 2001.

Previously, on 20 July 1989, Aung San Suu Kyi had also been placed under house arrest. Her case was then submitted to the Working Group. In its decision No. 8/1992 (*Myanmar*),[31] it ruled that the measure of house arrest then applied was a deprivation of liberty equivalent to detention, which, in addition, was of an arbitrary character and falling within categories II and III. She was not released until 1995.

Based on the comments of the Government, it appeared that it did not consider the current situation in the case as amounting to deprivation of liberty. Yet, the Working

---

[30] See United Nations document E/CN.4/2003/8/Add.1, p. 50, opinion adopted on 19 June 2002.
[31] See United Nations document E/CN.4/1993/24, annex I, p. 43.

Group had made its position clear in this regard in a number of cases, including in its earlier decision concerning the house arrest imposed on Aung San Suu Kyi. Furthermore, in its deliberation No. 1/1993 on house arrest, it had stated in unambiguous terms that house arrest might be compared to deprivation of liberty, provided that it was carried out in closed premises which the person was not allowed to leave.[32] On the basis of the information provided by the source, not contested by the Government, the Working Group concluded that the circumstances of house arrest imposed in this case amounted to deprivation of liberty.

In the view of the Working Group, this deprivation of liberty was arbitrary. The source believed that the arrest of Aung San Suu Kyi was based on charges relating to several provisions of the State Protection Act. The Government had neither confirmed nor refuted this assumption. The Working Group considered that there was no legal basis whatsoever for her arrest and detention. Furthermore, the Government had not contested that she was in custody without having been charged and without being given the opportunity to have her case heard by a competent authority in a fair proceeding.

The Government had not disputed that the house arrest of Aung San Suu Kyi was largely motivated by her political convictions and activities. Consequently, the Working Group rendered its opinion that the deprivation of liberty in this case was arbitrary, as being in contravention of articles 9, 10, 19 and 20 of the Universal Declaration and falling within categories II and III. Myanmar was not a party the Covenant.

(*c*) African Commission on Human and Peoples' Rights

Article 7 of the African Charter on Human and Peoples' Rights protects the right to a fair trial. Under paragraph 1, every individual shall have the right to have his cause heard. This comprises the right to an appeal to competent national organs against acts violating his fundamental rights; the presumption of innocence; the right to defence; and the right to be tried within a reasonable time by an impartial court or tribunal.

Paragraph 2 states that no one may be condemned for an act or omission not constituting a legally punishable offence at the time it was committed, and no penalty may be inflicted for an offence for which no provision was made at the time it was committed. Punishment can only be imposed on the offender.

---

[32] *Ibidem*, para. 20.

III:2

There is no provision in the Charter allowing States parties to derogate from their treaty obligations.

The case *Krischna Achutan and Amnesty International* v. *Malawi*,[33] also cited in connection with the right to life[34] and with the prohibition of torture,[35] raised issues under article 7 of the Charter. The first communication was filed with the African Commission on Human and Peoples' Rights by Krischna Achutan on behalf of Aleke Benda, his father-in-law, and the two others by Amnesty International on behalf of Orton and Vera Chirwa.

Mr. Banda, a prominent political figure, had at the time of the communication been imprisoned for over 12 years without legal charge or trial. According to the author, Mr. Banda was being held "at the pleasure of the Head of State". The Commission noted that Mr. Banda was not allowed recourse to the national courts to challenge the violation of his fundamental right to liberty as guaranteed by article 6 of the Charter. Furthermore, he was detained indefinitely without trial. The Commission found that Mr. Banda's imprisonment violated article 7, paragraph 1 (*a*) and (*d*), of the Charter.

Mr. and Mrs. Chirwa had been abducted from Zambia, where they lived in exile, and taken into custody by Malawi security officials. They were subsequently sentenced to death for treason, later commuted to life imprisonment. They were tried before a traditional court without being defended by counsel. The Commission found that this constituted a violation of article 7, paragraph 1 (*c*), of the Charter.

(*d*) Inter-American Court of Human Rights

Article 8 of the American Convention on Human Rights protects the right to a fair trial. Under paragraph 1, everyone has the right to a hearing with due guarantees and within a reasonable time by a competent, independent and impartial tribunal, previously established by law, in the substantiation of any accusation of a criminal nature made against him or for the determination of his rights and obligations of a civil, labour, fiscal or any other nature.

Paragraph 2 contains the fundamental principle of presumption of innocence until proved guilty according to law and a number of minimum rights set forth to protect those who are charged with a criminal offence. These rights of the accused include

---

[33] See *Review of the African Commission on Human and Peoples' Rights*, vol. 5 (1995), p. 186, communications No. 64/92, No. 68/92 and No. 78/92.
[34] See part II, chap. 2, sect. B (*c*) (*supra*, p. 53).
[35] See part II, chap. 3, sect. B (*d*) (*supra*, pp. 142-143).

to be notified in detail of the charges against him; to have adequate time and means for the preparation of his defence; to defend himself personally or to be assisted by legal counsel of his own choosing; to examine witnesses present in the court and to obtain the appearance, as witnesses, of experts or other persons who may throw light on the facts; and not to be compelled to witness against himself or to plead guilty.

Paragraphs 3 to 5 set out further principles for a fair trial: a confession of guilt made by the accused shall be valid only if made without coercion of any kind; an accused acquitted by a judgment that is not appealable shall not be retried for the same cause; and criminal proceedings shall be public unless to protect the interests of justice.

In time of war, public danger or other emergency threatening the independence or security, States parties may take measures derogating from its obligations under article 8, but only on the conditions set forth in article 27 of the Convention.

From the jurisprudence of the American Court of Human Rights, three cases are included in this review. No case arising out of article 8 of the Convention has been selected for a case summary.

The violations of the right to a fair trial in these cases arose principally because of the failures of States parties to carry out effective investigations into allegations of human rights violations. The cases involved serious infringements of other provisions in the Convention, such as the right to life, the prohibition of torture and the right to personal liberty. State authorities obstructed, impeded or delayed investigations by various means, including, in one of the cases, the kidnapping of an investigative judge.

The *Genie Lacayo* case *(Nicaragua)*[36] concerned the violation of, *inter alia*, article 8 of the Convention because of a denial of justice arising out of a failure of the authorities to carry out an impartial investigation into a killing. In the application of the Inter-American Commission on Human Rights, it was stated that on 28 October 1990, Jean-Paul Genie Lacayo, aged 16, was travelling by car to his home in Managua, the capital of Nicaragua, when he came upon a convoy of vehicles transporting military personnel who, in response to his attempts to pass them, shot and killed him. The young man's car had been machine-gunned by weapons from two or more vehicles, and 51 cartridge shells of AK-47 ammunition were found at the site. On the car, 19 bullet impacts were found, all made while the car was in motion, and three shots were fired at short range once it had stopped.

---

[36] See Inter-American Court of Human Rights, Series C: *Decisions and Judgments*, No. 30 (1998), petition No. 10792, judgment of 29 January 1997.

III:2

In considering the merits of the case, the Court observed that article 8 of the Convention established the main lines of what was known as due process of law or the right to legal defence. It included the right of every person to a hearing, with due guarantees and within a reasonable time, by a competent, independent and impartial tribunal, previously established by law.

In order to establish a violation of article 8 in this case, it was necessary, first of all, to establish whether the procedural rights of the accusing party, Raymond Genie Peñalba, the victim's father, had been respected in the trial to determine those responsible for the death of Jean-Paul Genie Lacayo.

The Court considered that there was abundant evidence to show that certain military authorities had either obstructed or refused to collaborate adequately in the investigations by the Attorney-General's office and with a judge of first instance. In fact, the situation reached the point where that court was constrained to contact the President of the Republic by letter to intercede with the military authorities for them to afford the facilities needed for the inspection of a military unit and that unit's weapons, vehicles and weapons log. The judge in charge of the case had encountered problems, generated by the authorities, in collecting the evidence he considered necessary for the proper trial of the case, and this constituted a violation of article 8, paragraph 1, of the Convention. The Court also found another violation of the same provision, because delays at various stages of the proceedings exceeded the limits of reasonableness prescribed in the article.

The Court concluded that Nicaragua had violated article 8, paragraph 1, in connection with article 1, paragraph 1, of the Convention, to the detriment of Mr. Genie Peñalba.

The *Blake* case (*Guatamala*)[37] concerned the forced disappearance and killing of a journalist, Nicholas Blake, and a photographer, both United States citizens residing in Guatemala, by agents of the State. They disappeared on 28 or 29 March 1985, and their remains were discovered seven years later. The case raised issues under a number of articles of the Convention, including article 4 on the right to life, article 7 on the right to personal liberty and article 8 on the right to a fair trial.

In respect of the latter provision, the Commission pointed out that the Guatemalan authorities had failed to fulfil the obligation to provide simple, prompt and effective judicial recourse to Mr. Blake's relatives. They had impeded the clarification of the cause of Mr. Blake's death and disappearance, and they had delayed the investigation of the facts and the institution of any judicial proceedings. In fact, the relatives

---

[37] *Ibidem*, No. 36 (2000), petition No. 11219, judgment of 24 January 1998.

were deprived of the right to an independent judicial process within a reasonable time, and they were consequently prevented from obtaining fair compensation. According to the Commission, no judgment had yet been issued 12 years after Mr. Blake's forced disappearance began. It further stated that the violation of article 8 of the Convention went beyond the problem of reasonable time, inasmuch as justice was also obstructed by the State authorities. They deliberately concealed the information they had received.

The Court considered that article 8, paragraph 1, of the Convention had to be given a broad interpretation based on both the letter and the spirit of the provision. It had also to be appreciated in accordance with article 29 (c) of the Convention, which stated that none of its provisions should be interpreted as precluding other rights or guarantees inherent in the human personality or derived from representative, democratic form of government.

Citing article 1, paragraph 2, of the Declaration on the Protection of All Persons from Enforced Disappearance, the Court pronounced that article 8, paragraph 1, of the Convention also included the rights of the victim's relatives to judicial guarantees. Any act of forced disappearance placed the victim outside the protection of the law and caused grave suffering to him and to his family. Consequently, this provision of the Convention recognized the right of Mr. Blake's relatives to have his disappearance and death effectively investigated by the Guatemalan authorities; to have those responsible prosecuted for committing such unlawful acts; to have the relevant punishment, where appropriate, meted out; and to be compensated for the damages and injuries they sustained.

The Court declared, by seven votes to one, that Guatemala violated, to the detriment of the relatives of Mr. Blake, article 8, paragraph 1, in relation to article 1, paragraph 1, of the Convention. Likewise, it also declared, unanimously, that Guatemala violated the right to humane treatment enshrined in article 5 of the Convention. Furthermore, the Court declared that the State was obliged to use all the means at its disposal to investigate the acts denounced and to punish those responsible for Mr. Blake's disappearance and death. The State was also obliged to pay a fair compensation to the relatives of Mr. Blake and reimburse them for the expenses incurred in their representations to the Guatemalan authorities in connection with this process.

In another case against the same State, the *Paniagua Morales* et al. case (*Guatemala*)[38], known as the *"white van"* case, beacuse that type of vehicle was part of the *modus operandi*, the Court had to rule on whether Guatemala had violated various provisions of the Convention by acts of abduction, arbitrary detention, inhuman

---

[38] *Ibidem*, No. 37 (2000), petition No. 10154, judgment of 8 March 1998.

III:2

treatment, torture and murder committed by treasury police agents against Ana Eliz-abeth Paniagua Morales and 10 other victims in the years 1987 and 1988. In respect of the right to a fair trial set forth in article 8 of the Convention, the Commission al-leged that Guatamala had failed to respect the right of all the victims in the case and their relatives to be heard by a competent, independent and impartial judge or tribu-nal in order to establish their rights.

On 19 and 20 July 1988, a judge investigating the crimes ordered the arrest of a number of people who were treasury police agents at the time of the events leading to the case. Thereafter, he was kidnapped and released two days later. On returning to his duties, he revoked the orders of provisional imprisonment against all of the suspects. The decisions ordering the release of those implicated were appealed, but they were deemed by the court of appeal to be consistent with the law. After this de-cision, no significant progress was made with the investigation.

According to the Commission, the kidnapping of the judge and the threats he re-ceived meant that he could not then fulfil the requirements established in article 8 of the Convention, as proven by the subsequent events in the case. It was the duty of the State to ensure the existence of effective judicial remedies and measures to re-store the independence and impartiality of the court following the judge's abduction. In failing to investigate this incident and to replace the judge in his functions, Guate-mala had failed to observe its obligation to provide an effective judicial remedy. Furthermore, the Commission claimed, the decision taken by domestic courts to re-lease the suspects of the crimes was unjustified, arbitrary and contrary to the evi-dence on record.

In its final arguments, the Commission concluded that there had been multiple viola-tions of article 8 of the Convention in this case. It went on to say that the domestic proceeding was not conducted within the reasonable time required by the Conven-tion, since no final decision had yet been reached, nor had those responsible been punished. The Commission pointed out that the judicial proceeding had not even been initiated in the cases concerning the kidnapping of the judge and the kidnap-ping and murder of two other people.

The Court found it proven that there was widespread fear among those involved in the *"white van"* case, corroborated by the eyewitnesses' reluctance to testify before the judge in the case and the failure to conduct a thorough investigation into his kid-napping. The Court considered that it was neither necessary nor pertinent to examine the possible connection of the judge's kidnapping with the case. It simply noted that the kidnapping was not duly investigated and that no decision was taken on the sug-gestion that the judge had been threatened and coerced during his captivity.

In accordance with criteria previously established by the Court with regard to the concept of reasonable time in judicial processes, the Court was of the view that the proceeding, still at the pre-trial stage, had far exceeded the principles of reasonable time set forth in the Convention. The Court considered that the *"white van"* case was not heard by an independent and impartial tribunal or within a reasonable time. The State had not provided the due guarantees to ensure the victims due process in determining their rights. Responsibility for this omission rested with the State, which had the duty to make those guarantees.

The Court concluded that Guatemala had violated article 8, paragraph 1, in relation to article 1, paragraph 1, of the Convention, to the detriment of Ana Elizabeth Paniagua Morales and five other victims. It also found violations of a number of other articles of the Convention. The Court further ruled that the State had to conduct a genuine and effective investigation to determine the persons responsible for the human rights violations established in the judgment and, where appropriate, punish them. The State was also obliged to make reparation for the consequences of the declared violations and pay fair compensation to the victims and, where appropriate, to their next of kin.

(*e*) European Court of Human Rights

Article 6 of the Convention for the Protection of Human Rights and Fundamental Freedoms protects the right to a fair trial. Under paragraph 1, in the determination of his civil rights and obligations or of any criminal charge against him, everyone is entitled to a fair and public hearing within a reasonable time by an independent and impartial tribunal established by law. Any judgment shall be pronounced publicly, but the press and public may be excluded from all or part of the trial for a variety of reasons, including public order and national security in a democratic society.

Paragraph 2 contains the fundamental principle of presumption of innocence until proved guilty according to law.

In paragraph 3, finally, a number of minimum rights are set forth to protect those who are charged with a criminal offence. These rights include to be informed promptly, in a language the person charged understands and in detail, of the nature and cause of the accusation against him; to have adequate time and facilities to prepare his defence; to defend himself in person or through legal assistance of his own choosing; to examine or have examined witnesses against him and to obtain the attendence and examination of witnesses on his behalf under the same conditions as witnesses against him; and, where needed, to have the free assistance of an interpreter.

III:2

In time of war or other public emergency threatening the life of the nation, States parties may take measures derogating from its obligations under article 6, but only on the conditions set forth in article 15 of the Convention.

In the *Engel and Others* case (*the Netherlands*),[39] also cited in connection with the right to freedom opinion and expression,[40] the distinction between criminal proceedings and disciplinary proceedings was considered, a point of some interest to police agencies, as most of them conduct hearings in respect of breaches of their own internal discipline codes. The applicants, Cornelis J. M. Engel and four other Netherlands nationals, were, in 1971, conscript soldiers serving in different non-commisioned ranks in the Netherlands armed forces. Penalties had been imposed on them by their commanding officers for offences against military discipline. The applicants complained, *inter alia*, that proceedings before the military authorities were not in conformity with the requirements of article 6 of the Convention.

In deciding on the applicability of article 6 to these circumstances, the European Court of Human Rights, in plenary session, considered whether this article ceased to be applicable just because the competent organs of a State party classified as disciplinary an act or omission, or whether it applied in certain cases notwithstanding this classification. The Court accepted that States' classification of offences was relevant, but observed that greater importance attached to the nature of the offence and the degree of severity of the penalty.

In applying these criteria to the various offences with which the applicants had been charged, the Court held, by eleven votes to two, that in the case of three of the applicants there had been a breach of article 6, paragraph 1, of the Convention in respect of hearings that took place *in camera*.

The Court has considered a number of important cases on the right of access to a tribunal. In the case *Osman* v. *the United Kingdom*,[41] also cited in connection with the right to life,[42] the applicants, Mulkiye Osman and her son, Ahmet Osman, both British nationals, alleged that the dismissal by a court of appeal of their negligence action against the police on grounds of public policy amounted to a restriction on their right of access to a court in breach of article 6, paragraph 1, of the Convention.

---

[39] See *Publications of the European Court of Human Rights*, Series A: *Judgments and Decisions*, vol. 22 (1977), applications No. 5100/71, No. 5101/71, No. 5102/71, No. 5354/72 and No. 5390/72, judgment of 8 June 1976.
[40] See part III, chap. 4, sect. B (*d*) (*infra*, pp. 457-458).
[41] See European Court of Human Rights, *Reports of Judgments and Decisions*, 1998-VIII, p. 3124, application No. 23452/94, judgment of 28 October 1998.
[42] See part II, chap. 2, sect. B (*e*) (*supra*, pp. 62-63).

The dismissal of their appeal was based on a rule excluding liability of police for alleged negligence in respect of the investigation and suppression of crime, as opposed to cases of assault or false imprisonment, in order to avoid defensive policing and the diversion of police manpower.

The Court, sitting as a grand chamber, recalled that the reasons which led the domestic courts to lay down an exclusionary rule to protect the police from negligence actions were based on the view that the interests of the community as a whole were best served by a police service whose efficiency and effectiveness in the battle against crime were not jeopardized by the constant risk of exposure to tortious liability for policy and operational decisions. The Court observed that although the aim of such a rule might be accepted as legitimate in terms of the Convention, as being directed to the maintenance of the effectiveness of the police service and hence to the prevention of disorder or crime, it had nevertheless to have particular regard to the scope and especially the application of the rule in the case at issue.

In fact, the Court observed, the way in which the rule had been applied in this case only served to confer a blanket immunity on the police during the investigation and suppression of crime. It amounted to an unjustifiable restriction of the right of an applicant to have a determination on the merits of a claim against the police in deserving cases. The court of appeal had regarded the exclusionary rule as an absolute defence to the applicants' civil action against police. It gave no consideration to competing public-interest considerations at stake. For example, the case involved allegations that police had been gravely negligent in failing to protect the life of a child. In the Court's view, such considerations required to be examined on their merits, and not dismissed in the application of a rule in a way tantamount to granting immunity to police. The rule's application in this case was considered to be a disproportionate interference with the applicants' right of access to a court. Accordingly, there had been a violation of article 6, paragraph 1, of the Convention.

The requirements for a fair procedure have been considered in a number of the Court's judgments, including in the *Schenk* case *(Switzerland)*[43] where the applicant, Pierre Schenk, a Swiss national, had been convicted of commissioning another man in 1981 to kill his wife. Telephone conversations between the two men were recorded without prior order by the competent judge, and the applicant alleged that his right to a fair trial had been infringed by reason of the use of the disputed recording in evidence.

---

[43] See *Publications of the European Court of Human Rights*, Series A: *Judgments and Decisions*, vol. 140 (1988), application No. 10862/84, judgment of 12 July 1988.

III:2

The Court, in plenary session, observed that whilst article 6 of the Convention guaranteed the right to a fair trial, it did not lay down any rules on the admissibility of evidence as such. That was, therefore, primarily a matter for regulation under national law. The Court could not exclude as a matter of principle, and in the abstract, that unlawfully obtained evidence of the kind referred to in this case might be admissible. It had only to ascertain whether Mr. Schenk's trial as a whole was fair.

The Court noted that the rights of the defence were not disregarded, citing examples, and it attached weight to the fact that the recording of the telephone conversation was not the only evidence on which the conviction was based. In fact, the criminal court had taken account of a combination of evidential elements before reaching its opinion. Accordingly, the Court concluded, by thirteen votes to four, that the use of the disputed recording in evidence had not deprived the applicant of a fair trial in contravention of article 6, paragraph 1, of the Convention. Nor did the use of the recording, the Court unanimously held, constitute a breach of the principle of the presumption of innocence set forth in article 6, paragraph 2.

An issue under article 8, protecting the right to privacy, also arose in this case in respect of the making and use of the disputed recording. The Commission had declared inadmissible the complaint regarding the making of the recording, but the Court pointed out that nothing would prevent it from considering the question of the use made of it. However, the Court held by fifteen votes to two, this was not necessary, as the issue had been subsumed, and already dealt with, under the question of the use made of the recording during the judicial investigation and the trial.

The question of fairness also arose in the *Barberà, Messegué and Jabardo* case *(Spain)*.[44] The applicants, Francesc-Xavier Barberá, Antonino Messegué and Ferrán Jabardo, all nationals of Spain, had been arrested in connection with the killing in 1977 of a 77-year-old Catalan businessman by a terrorist organization. Whilst in police custody, they signed statements admitting their part in the killing. During the proceedings before the examining judge, however, they retracted their confessions, two of them claiming to have been subjected to torture. Subsequently, after a trial lasting for only one day, all three applicants were convicted, two of murder and other charges and one of aiding and abetting a murder, and sentenced to long terms of imprisonment.

In considering the applicants' claim that their trial had been unfair, the Court, in plenary session, examined the way in which the evidence had been taken and the conduct of the trial proceedings. The Court had reservations about some crucial aspects

---

[44] *Ibidem*, vol. 146 (1989), applications No. 10588/83, No. 10589/83 and No. 10590/83, judgment of 6 December 1988.

of these matters, including the confessions of the accused. When they made their confessions to the police, the Court observed, they had already been charged but did not have the assistance of a lawyer, although they did not appear to have waived their right to one. Accordingly these confessions, which had been obtained during a long period of custody in which they were held incommunicado, gave rise to reservations on the part of the Court.

The Court concluded that the proceedings in question, taken as a whole, did not satisfy the requirements of a fair and public hearing. Consequently, it held, by ten votes to eight, that there had been a violation of article 6, paragraph 1, of the Convention. The Court also considered the alleged breach of article 6, paragraph 2, on the presumption of innocence, but it held, unanimously, that there had been no violation of the Convention in that respect.

In the case *Saunders* v. *the United Kingdom*,[45] the Court, sitting as a grand chamber, considered the question of self-incrimination and the right to silence. The applicant, Ernest Saunders, a British citizen, had been subjected to proceedings in which he was legally required to give statements during an investigation into corporate fraud. The statements were later used in his criminal trial.

On this point, the Court recalled that although not specifically mentioned in article 6 of the Convention, the right to silence and the right not to incriminate oneself were generally recognized international standards. They lay at the heart of the notion of a fair procedure under that article. Citing its case law, the Court observed that their rationale lay, *inter alia*, in the protection of the accused against improper compulsion by the authorities, thereby contributing to the avoidance of miscarriages of justice and to the fulfilment of the aims of article 6. The right not to incriminate oneself, in particular, presupposed that the prosecution in a criminal case sought to prove the case against the accused without resort to evidence obtained through methods of coercion or oppression in defiance of the will of the accused. In this sense, the right was closely linked to the presumption of innocence contained in article 6, paragraph 2, of the Convention.

The right not to incriminate oneself was, however, primarily concerned with respecting the will of an accused person to remain silent. As commonly understood in the legal systems of the States parties to the Convention and elsewhere, it did not extend to the use in criminal proceedings of material which might be obtained from the accused through the use of compulsory powers but which had an existence independent of the will of the suspect, such as, *inter alia*, documents acquired pursuant to a

---

[45] See European Court of Human Rights, *Reports of Judgments and Decisions*, 1996-VI, p. 2044, application No. 19187/91, judgment of 17 December 1996.

III:2

warrant, breath, blood and urine samples and bodily tissue for the purpose of DNA testing.

The Court concluded that the evidence available to it supported the claim that the transcripts of the answers of Mr. Saunders were used in the course of the proceedings in a manner sought to incriminate him. It found, by sixteen votes to four, that the applicant had been deprived of a fair hearing in violation of article 6, paragraph 1, of the Convention.

Access to a lawyer is another important element of the right to a fair trial. In the case *John Murray* v. *the United Kingdom*,[46] the applicant, a British citizen, had been arrested by police in 1990 under emergency legislation introduced to counter acts of terrorism. His access to a solicitor was delayed on the authority of a detective superintendent, also under emergency legislation. The delay was authorized for a period of 48 hours on the basis that the detective superintendent had reasonable grounds to believe that the exercise of the right of access would, *inter alia*, interfere with the gathering of information about the commission of acts of terrorism or make it more difficult to prevent an act of terrorism.

Following his trial and conviction, the applicant complained, *inter alia*, that he had been denied access to his solicitor in violation of article 6, paragraph 3 (*c*), of the Convention. The Court, sitting as a grand chamber, observed that it had not been disputed by the Government that article 6 applied even at the stage of the preliminary investigation into an offence by the police. In this respect, the Court recalled its finding in a previous case that article 6, especially paragraph 3, might be relevant before a case was sent for trial if, and so far as, the fairness of the trial was likely to be seriously prejudiced by an initial failure to comply with its provisions. As it had pointed out in that judgment, the manner in which article 6, paragraph 3 (*c*), was to be applied during the preliminary investigation depended on the special features of the proceedings involved and on the circumstances of the case.

The Court then observed that national laws might attach consequences to the attitude of an accused, at the initial stages of police interrogation, which were decisive for the prospects of the defence in any subsequent criminal proceedings. Article 6 would normally require, in such circumstances, that the accused should be allowed to benefit from the assistance of a lawyer at the initial stages of police interrogation. However, this right, not explicitly set out in the Convention, might be subject to restrictions for good cause. In each case, the question was whether the restriction, in the light of the entirety of the proceedings, had deprived the accused of a fair hearing.

---

[46] *Ibidem*, 1996-I, p. 30, application No. 18731/91, judgment of 8 February 1996.

Ultimately, the Court concluded, by twelve votes to seven, that there had been a breach of article 6, paragraph 1, in conjunction with article 6, paragraph 3 (*c*), of the Convention regarding the applicant's lack of access to a lawyer during the first 48 hours of his police detention.

In addition to the requirement that a hearing should be fair, article 6, paragraph 1, of the Convention stipulates that it must take place within a reasonable time. In the *Zimmermann and Steiner* case (*Switzerland*),[47] the applicants, Werner Zimmermann and Johann Steiner, two Swiss nationals, alleged that the length of the proceedings relative to the hearing of their administrative-law appeal to the Federal Court, from 18 April 1977 to 15 October 1980, had exceeded what was within reasonable time under that provision.

The Court stated that the reasonableness of the length of proceedings coming within the scope of article 6, paragraph 1, of the Convention had to be assessed in each case according to the particular circumstances. The Court had to have regard, *inter alia*, to the complexity of the factual or legal issues raised by the case, to the conduct of the applicants and the competent authorities and to what was at stake for the former. Furthermore, only delays attributable to the State might justify a finding of a failure to comply with this requirement.

Having regard to all circumstances of the case, the Court found that the lapse of time, nearly three and a half years, was excessive and in violation of article 6, paragraph 1, of the Convention.

The principle that everyone charged with a criminal offence shall be presumed innocent until proved guilty according to law has been considered in many judgments of the Court. In the case *Allenet de Ribemont* v. *France*,[48] summarized in section C,[49] the applicant, Patrick Allenet de Ribemont, a French national, claimed, *inter alia*, that statements made by the Minister of the Interior and two senior police officials at a press conference in 1976 had infringed his right to presumption of innocence secured in article 6, paragraph 2, of the Convention.

The Court observed that the presumption of innocence might be infringed not only by a judge or court but also by other public authorities. In the present case, the Court found, by eight votes to one, that there had been a violation of this principle in respect of the statements at the press conference. In this judgment, the Court also in-

---

[47] See *Publications of the European Court of Human Rights*, Series A: *Judgments and Decisions,*, vol. 66 (1983), application No. 8737/79, judgment of 13 July 1983.

[48] *Ibidem*, vol. 308 (1995), application No. 15175/89, judgment of 10 February 1995.

[49] See part III, chap. 2, sect. C (*e*) (*infra*, pp. 390-395).

III:2

voked the right to freedom of expression, guaranteed by article 10 of the Convention, noting that it included the freedom to receive and impart information. In this respect, the Court said that article 6, paragraph 2, could not prevent the authorities from informing the public about criminal investigations in progress, but it required that they did so with discretion and circumspection if the presumption of innocence was to be respected.

The principle contained in article 6, paragraph 3 (*c*), of the Convention that everyone charged with a criminal offence has the right to defend himself in person or through legal assistance of his own choosing was invoked in the case *S. v. Switzerland*,[50] summarized in section C.[51] The applicant, Mr. S., a Swiss national, complained, *inter alia*, that he had not been allowed to communicate with his lawyer freely and without supervision. The Court noted that unlike some national laws and unlike article 8, paragraph 2 (*d*), of the American Convention on Human Rights, the European Convention did not expressly guarantee the right of a person charged with a criminal offence to communicate with defence counsel without hindrance. However, citing two other international instruments, the Court observed that this right was nevertheless set forth within the Council of Europe. In the present case, restrictions had been imposed for over seven months on contacts between Mr. S. and his court-appointed defense counsel. The Court pronounced that the right of an accused to communicate with his advocate out of hearing of a third person was part of the basic requirements of a fair trial in a democratic society. It found a violation of article 6, paragraph 3 (*c*), of the Convention.

Under article 6, paragraph 3 (*d*), of the Convention, everyone charged with a criminal offence has the right to examine or have examined witnesses against him and to obtain the attendance and examination of witnesses on his behalf under the same conditions as witnesses against him. Some cases brought under this provision concern the use of anonymous witnesses. In the *Kostovski* case (*the Netherlands*),[52] the applicant, Slobodan Kostovski, a Yugoslav citizen, had a long criminal record. He was identified by two witnesses as having taken part in a bank robbery in 1982 during a period in which he had escaped from prison. Because they feared reprisals, the witnesses wished to remain anonymous. At the trials that followed, neither witness gave evidence, although the court based its finding of guilt on reports of the police and examining magistrate derived from their evidence. The applicant alleged a

---

[50] See *Publications of the European Court of Human Rights*, Series A: *Judgments and Decisions*, vol. 220 (1992), applications No. 12629/87 and No. 13965/88, judgment of 28 November 1991.

[51] See part III, chap. 2, sect. C (*f*) (*infra*, pp. 395-400).

[52] See *Publications of the European Court of Human Rights*, Series A: *Judgments and Decisions*, vol. 166 (1989), application No. 11454/85, judgment of 20 November 1989.

breach of article 6 of the Convention, notably in that he was not given the opportunity to have questions put to the anonymous witnesses and was unable to challenge their statements.

The Court, in plenary session, observed that in principle, all the evidence had to be produced in the presence of the accused at a public hearing with a view to adversarial argument. The Court further stated that as on previous occasions, it did not underestimate the importance of the struggle against organized crime. The growth of such crime undoubtedly demanded the introduction of appropriate measures. However, the right to a fair administration of justice held such a prominent place in a democratic society that it could not be sacrificed to expediency. The Convention did not preclude reliance, at the investigation stage of criminal proceedings, on sources such as anonymous informants. The subsequent use of anonymous statements as sufficient evidence to found a conviction, as in the present case, was, however, a different matter. It involved limitations on the rights of the defence which were irreconcilable with the guarantees contained in article 6. The Court concluded that there had been a violation of article 6, paragraph 3 (*d*), taken together with article 6, paragraph 1, of the Convention.

In the *Windisch* case (*Austria*),[53] the applicant, Harald Windisch, an Austrian citizen, had been arrested and charged with burglary in 1985. After the crime had been committed, two women went to the police and, on receiving assurances that their anonymity would be respected, stated that they had seen two men near the scene of the crime. One of the men had a handkerchief held in front of his face. Subsequently, the police arrested Mr. Windisch and held a covert confrontation in which the women, seated in a car, identified him from a distance of ten metres. During the confrontation, Mr. Windisch held a handkerchief over his face. The applicant complained that he had been convicted solely on the basis of evidence given by two anonymous witnesses who had not given evidence at his trial.

In considering the application, the Court said that the collaboration of the public was undoubtedly of great importance for the police in their struggle against crime. In this connection, it reiterated that the Convention did not preclude reliance, at the investigation stage, on sources such as anonymous informants, but that it was another matter subsequently to use their statements to found a conviction.

The Court stressed that in this case no one had observed the actual commission of the offence. The information given and the identification made by the two anonymous witnesses was the only evidence indicating the presence of Mr. Windisch at the scene of the crime. This was the central issue during the investigation and at the

---

[53] *Ibidem*, vol. 186 (1991), application No. 12489/86, judgment of 27 September 1990.

III:2

hearings. In convicting Mr. Windisch, the domestic court had relied to a large extent on this evidence. In these circumstances, the use of it involved such limitations on the rights of the defence that the applicant could not be said to have received a fair trial.

The same issues arose in the case *Doorson* v. *the Netherlands*,[54] summarized in section C,[55] where the applicant, Désiré Wilfried Doorson, a Netherlands national, claimed, *inter alia*, that he had been a victim of violations of article 6 of the Convention. In this case, the anonymous witnesses were questioned by an investigating judge in the presence of Mr. Doorson's counsel. At that stage, counsel was able to ask the witnesses questions he considered to be in the interests of the defence. The Court also noted that counterbalancing procedures were adopted during the trial to compensate the handicaps under which the defence had to work and that the national court did not base its finding of guilt solely or to a decisive extent on the evidence of the two anonymous witnesses. None of the alleged shortcomings led the Court to conclude that the applicant did not receive a fair trial, nor could it find that the proceedings as a whole were unfair. By seven votes to two, the Court found no violation of the right to a fair trial.

Another interesting aspect of this case is the observation the Court made on the interests of witnesses and victims, pointing out that they were, in principle, protected by the Convention in other provisions than article 6. This implied that the States parties should organize their criminal justice proceedings in such a way that those interests were not unjustifiably imperilled.

C. CASE SUMMARIES

(a) *Gridin* v. *Russian Federation* (Human Rights Committee)[56]

The author of the communication was Dimitriy Leonodovich Gridin, a Russian student. He submitted the communication to the Human Rights Committee on 27 June 1996, claiming to be a victim of a violation by Russia of article 14, paragraphs 1, 2 and 3 (*b*), (*e*) and (*g*), of the International Covenant on Civil and Political Rights. The case also appeared to raise issues under articles 9 and 10 of the Covenant.

---

[54] See European Court of Human Rights, *Reports of Judgments and Decisions*, 1996-II, p. 446, application No. 20524/92, judgment of 26 March 1996.

[55] See part III, chap. 2, sect. C (*g*) (*infra*, pp. 400-404).

[56] See United Nations, *Official Records of the General Assembly, Fifty-fifth Session, Supplement No. 40* (A/55/40), vol. II, annex IX, sect. O, communication No. 770/1997, views adopted on 20 July 2000.

The facts

The author submitted, *inter alia*, the following. He was arrested on 25 November 1989 on charges of attempted rape and murder. He was later charged with six other assaults. On 3 October 1990, a regional court found him guilty of the charges and sentenced him to death. He made a number of appeals, but they were all rejected. On 3 December 1993, his death sentence was commuted to life imprisonment.

He alleged that a warrant for his arrest was not issued until 29 November 1989, over three days after he was detained, and that he was denied access to a lawyer, despite his requests, until 6 December 1989. He claimed that he was interrogated for a period of 48 hours, without being given any food and without being allowed to sleep. His glasses had also been taken away from him, and he could not see much because of his shortsightedness. During the interrogation, he was beaten. He stated that he was told that his family was letting him down and that the only way to avoid the death penalty would be to confess. He then confessed to the six charges as well as to three other charges.

He claimed that the handling of the evidence violated the Russian criminal procedure code. His clothes were transported to the laboratory in the same bag as those of the victims, and therefore no value could be attached to the outcome of the examination that fibres of his clothes were found on the victims' clothes. He also claimed that there were irregularities in the identification process in that he was led through the hall where the victims were sitting on the day of the identification and that when one of the victims failed to point him out as the perpetrator, the investigator took her hand and pointed to the author. It was further submitted that the description by the victims of their attacker completely differed from the author's appearance.

He further claimed that his right to presumption of innocence was violated. Between 26 and 30 November 1989, radio stations and newspapers announced that he was the feared lift-boy murderer, who had raped several girls and murdered three of them. Also, on 9 December 1989, the head of the police announced that he was sure that the author was the murderer, and this was broadcasted on television. Moreover, the author alleged that the investigator pronounced him guilty in public meetings before the court hearing. According to the author, the court room was crowded with people who were screaming that he should be sentenced to death. He also stated that the social prosecutors and the victims were threatening the witnesses and the defence and that the judge did not do anything to stop this. Because of this, there was no proper opportunity to examine the main witnesses in court.

On the first day of the hearing, he pleaded not guilty. He was then placed in a lock-up. He complained that he was never allowed to discuss the case with his law-

III:2

yer in private. He also complained that the witnesses who could have confirmed his alibi were not examined in court. Moreover, some statements given during the preliminary examination disappeared from the record.

The State party submitted that in order to respond to the Committee's request, the office of the Russian Federation Procurator had reviewed Mr. Gridin's case. It verified the statements of the victims and witnesses, the examination of the place where the incidents occurred and the conditions under which Mr. Gridin was identified. The State party contended that the claims that the author was innocent and that the investigation methods used violated his rights to a defence, as well as the issue of public pressure, were all reviewed by the Supreme Court in its capacity as an appeal court and considered to be unfounded.

The State party further contended that neither Mr. Gridin nor his lawyer had ever raised the issue of police coercion before the courts and that Mr. Gridin was represented by a lawyer throughout the preliminary investigation, during which he provided detailed information in respect of the crimes. According to the State party, Mr. Gridin only retracted these statements in court due to pressure placed on him by members of his family.

With respect to the allegation that the author was unable to read the statements, because he was denied reading glasses, the State party noted from the court records that he had stated he could read at a distance of 10 to 15 centimetres without glasses. Furthermore, the investigators provided him with glasses. Consequently, the State party rejected any violation of the Covenant in this respect.

Finally, the State party stated that Mr. Gridin was questioned in the presence of the defence lawyer who was assigned to him in accordance with the law. The State party noted that Mr. Gridin was arrested on 25 November 1989 and, on 1 December 1989, his mother wrote requesting that the defence lawyer should be invited to participate in the investigations. On 5 December 1989, an agreement was concluded between Mr. Gridin's relatives and the lawyer who, from that time, was allowed to participate.

Issues and proceedings before the Committee

As to the allegations of ill-treatment and police coercion during the investigation period and certain court action deficiencies, the Committee found the claims unsubstantiated for the purposes of admissibilty. After declaring the remaining claims admissible, it proceeded with the examination of their merits.

With respect to the allegation that the author was arrested without a warrant and that it was only issued more than three days after the arrest, in contravention of national legislation stipulating that a warrant had to be issued within 72 hours of arrest, the Committee noted that this matter had not been addressed by the State party. In this regard, the Committee considered that in the circumstances of the case, the author had been deprived of his liberty in violation of a procedure established by law. Consequently, it found that the facts before it disclosed a violation of article 9, paragraph 1, of the Covenant.

Regarding the author's claim that he was denied a fair trial in violation of article 14, paragraph 1, of the Covenant, in particular because of the failure by the trial court to control the hostile atmosphere and pressure created by the public in the court room, making it impossible for defence counsel to properly cross-examine the witnesses and present his defence, the Committee noted that the Supreme Court referred to this issue, but it failed to specifically address it when it heard Mr. Gridin's appeal. The Committee considered that the conduct of the trial, as described, violated the author's right to a fair trial within the meaning of article 14, paragraph 1.

As to the allegation of a violation of the presumption of innocence, including public statements, given wide media coverage, made by high-ranking law enforcement officials portraying the author as guilty, the Committee noted that the Supreme Court referred to the issue, but it failed to deal with it specifically when it heard the appeal of Mr. Gridin. The Committee referred to the statement in its general comment on article 14 of the Covenant that it was a duty for all public authorities to refrain from prejudging the outcome of a trial. In the present case, the Committee considered that the authorities had failed to exercise the restraint that article 14, paragraph 2, required of them and that the author's rights were thus violated.

With respect to the allegation that the author did not have a lawyer available to him for the first five days after he was arrested, the Committee noted that the State party had responded that he was represented in accordance with the law. However, it had not refuted the author's claim that he requested a lawyer soon after his detention and that his request was ignored. Neither had it refuted his claim that he was interrogated without the benefit of consulting a lawyer, after he repeatedly requested such a consultation. The Committee found that denying the author access to legal counsel after he had requested such access and interrogating him during that time constituted a violation of his rights under article 14, paragraph 3 (*b*), of the Covenant. Furthermore, the Committee considered that the fact that the author was unable to consult with his lawyer in private, an allegation not refuted by the State party, also constituted a violation of the same provision.

III:2

Regarding the remaining allegations, the Committee noted that the Supreme Court had addressed the specific allegations by the author that the evidence was tampered with, that he was not properly identified by the witnesses and that there were discrepancies between the trial and its records. However, the rejection by the court of these specific allegations did not address the fairness of the trial as a whole, and therefore it did not affect the Committee's finding that article 14, paragraph 1, of the Covenant had been violated.

The Committee was of the view that the facts before it disclosed a violation of articles 9, paragraph 1, and 14, paragraphs 1, 2 and 3 (*b*), of the Covenant. Furthermore, in accordance with article 2, paragraph 3 (*a*), the State party was under an obligation to provide Mr. Gridin with an effective remedy, entailing compensation and his immediate release. The State party was also under an obligation to ensure that similar violations did not occur in the future. The Committee wished to receive from the State party, within 90 days, information about the measures taken to give effect to these views.

(*b*) *Bernard Lubuto* v. *Zambia*
(Human Rights Committee)[57]

The author of the communication was Bernard Lubuto, a Zambian citizen, who was awaiting execution in a maximum security prison in Zambia. He submitted the communication to the Human Rights Committee on 1 January 1990. Although the author did not invoke specific provisions of the Covenant, it appeared from the allegations and the facts he submitted that he claimed to be a victim of a violation by Zambia of articles 6, 7 and 14 of the International Covenant on Civil and Political Rights.

The facts

The author submitted, *inter alia*, the following. He was sentenced to death on 4 August 1983 for aggravated robbery, committed on 5 February 1980. On 10 February 1988, the Supreme Court of Zambia dismissed his appeal.

The evidence presented during the trial was that on 5 February 1980, he and two co-accused robbed a man of a motor vehicle. One of the co-accused held the victim at gunpoint. He and the other co-accused were standing nearby in the bushes. Although gunshots were fired, no one was injured. He was later identified at an identification parade. The prosecution produced a statement, signed by the author, in which he admitted his involvement in the robbery.

---

[57] *Ibidem, Fifty-first Session, Supplement No. 40* (A/51/40), vol. II, annex VIII, sect. B, communication No. 390/1990, views adopted on 31 October 1995.

He testified during the trial that he had been arrested by the police on 4 February 1980, after a fight in a tavern. He was kept in the police station overnight. On the morning of 5 February, when he was about to be released, he was told that a robbery had taken place. He was taken to an office, where a witness said that he answered the description of the robber. He was then returned to the cells, but he continued to deny any involvement in the robbery. On 7 February 1980, he participated in an i-dentification parade and was identified as one of the robbers by the witness with whom he had been confronted earlier at the police station.

His testimony was rejected by the trial court, as the entries in the police register showed, *inter alia*, that he had been arrested late in the evening of 5 February 1980.

He claimed that his trial was unfair, as there were discrepancies in the witnesses' statements; that his legal aid lawyer advised him to plead guilty and that when he refused, the lawyer failed to cross-examine the witnesses; and that the death sentence imposed on him was disproportionate, since no one was killed or injured during the robbery.

He further claimed that he was tortured by the police to force him to give a statement. He alleged that he was beaten with a hose pipe and cable wires; that sticks were put between his fingers and that his fingers were then hit on the table; and that a gun was tied with a string to his penis and that he was then forced to stand up and walk. These allegations were made at the trial, but the judge considered, on the basis of the evidence, that the statement to the police had been given freely and voluntarily.

On 30 June 1994, the Committee declared the communication admissible insofar as it appeared to raise issues under articles 6, 7 and 14, paragraphs 3 (*c*) and 5, of the Covenant. The State party was requested not to carry out the death sentence against Mr. Lubuto while his communication was under consideration by the Committee.

In a submission on the merits, the State party acknowledged that the proceedings in Mr. Lubuto's case had taken rather a long time. However, it requested the Committee to take into consideration the State party's situation as a developing country and the problems it encountered in the administration of justice. This was not an isolated case. It took considerable time for both civil and criminal cases to be disposed of by the courts because of the lack of administrative support available to the judiciary. Judges had to write out every word verbatim during hearings because of the absence of transcribers. There were further delays when these records were typed and then proffered by the judges. The State party also referred to the costs involved in preparing court documents.

III:2

The State party further pointed out that the work load of courts had increased and that due to the bad economic situation in the country, it had not been possible to provide the equipment and services necessary to expedite the disposal of cases. However, computers had recently been acquired in order to improve the situation.

The State party concluded that the delays suffered by the author in the determination of his case were inevitable owing to the situation it had described. It submitted that there had been no violation of article 14, paragraph 5, of the Covenant, since the author's appeal had, ultimately, been heard by the Supreme Court.

Regarding the author's claim that the imposition of the death sentence was disproportionate since no one had been killed or wounded during the robbery, the State party submitted that his conviction was in accordance with Zambian law. Because armed robberies were prevalent in the country and victims suffered a traumatic experience, the State party viewed aggravated robbery involving the use of a firearm as a serious offence whether or not a person was injured. Furthermore, the State party submitted that Mr. Lubuto's sentence was pronounced by the competent courts and that under the Constitution, the President of the Republic of Zambia could exercise the prerogative of mercy. A decision on this prerogative was awaited in Mr. Lubutu's case.

With regard to the author's claim that he had been tortured by the police, the State party submitted that torture was prohibited under Zambian law and that a victim of torture could seek redress under both criminal and civil law. Mr. Lubuto had not made use of these possibilities, and the State party suggested that had his allegations been true, his counsel at the trial would have certainly advised him to do so.

The State party further explained that if an accused person alleged during trial that he had been tortured in order to extract a confession, the court was obliged to conduct a trial within the trial to determine whether the confession was voluntary or not. This procedure was followed in Mr. Lubuto's case, and it appeared from the trial transcript that the judge had concluded that the accused had not been assaulted. There was no record of Mr. Lubuto having been medically treated for injuries which might have been caused by maltreatment.

Finally, the State party confirmed that pursuant to the Committee's request, the appropriate authorities had been instructed not to carry out the death sentence against the author while his case was before the Committee.

III:2

Issues and proceedings before the Committee

The Committee noted that the author had been convicted and sentenced to death under a law that provided for the imposition of the death penalty for aggravated robbery in which firearms were used. Accordingly, the issue to be decided was whether the sentence was compatible with article 6, paragraph 2, of the Covenant, allowing for the imposition of the death penalty only for the most serious crimes. Considering that in this case the use of firearms had not led to the death or wounding of any person and that the court could not under the law take this into account in imposing sentence, the Committee was of the view that the mandatory imposition of the death sentence under these circumstances violated article 6, paragraph 2.

The Committee further noted the State party's explanations concerning the delay in the trial proceedings against the author. The Committee acknowledged the difficult economic situation of the State party, but it wished to emphasize that the rights set forth in the Covenant constituted minimum standards that all States parties had agreed to observe. Under article 14, paragraph 3 (*c*), of the Covenant, all accused should be entitled to be tried without delay, and this requirement applied equally to the right of review of conviction and sentence guaranteed by article 14, paragraph 5. The Committee considered that the period of eight years between the author's arrest and the final decision of the Supreme Court, dismissing his appeal, was incompatible with the requirements of article 14, paragraph 3 (*c*).

Regarding the author's claim that he was heavily beaten and tortured upon arrest, the Committee noted that this allegation was before the judge who rejected it on the basis of the evidence. The Committee considered that the information before it was not sufficient to establish a violation of article 7 of the Covenant in this case.

In conclusion, the Committee was of the view that the facts before it disclosed a violation of articles 6, paragraph 2, and 14, paragraph 3 (*c*), of the Covenant. One member of the Committee expressed an individual opinion.

Furthermore, under article 2, paragraph 3 (*a*), of the Covenant, Mr. Lubuto was entitled to an appropriate and effective remedy, entailing a commutation of sentence. The State party was also under an obligation to take appropriate measures to ensure that similar violations did not occur in the future. The Committee wished to receive from the State party, within 90 days, information about the measures taken to give effect to these views.

III:2

(c) *G. Peart and A. Peart* v. *Jamaica*
(Human Rights Committee)[58]

The authors of the communications were Garfield Peart and Andrew Peart, Jamaican citizens, who, at the time of submission, were awaiting execution in Jamaica. They submitted their communications, referring to closely related events affecting them, to the Human Rights Committee on 17 July 1991 and 12 November 1991, respectively. They claimed to be victims of a violation by Jamaica of, *inter alia*, articles 6, 7, 10 and 14 of the International Covenant on Civil and Political Rights. The Committee decided to deal jointly with the communications.

The facts

The authors submitted, *inter alia*, the following. Andrew Peart was arrested on 14 July 1986 and charged with murder. Garfield Peart was arrested on 5 March 1987 in connection with the same murder. On 26 January 1988, after a trial lasting six days, the two brothers were convicted and sentenced to death. Subsequent appeal and petition to appeal were dismissed.

The principal witness for the prosecution was 15 years old at the time of the trial. He testified that he, on 24 June 1986, together with Andrew Peart, the murder victim and a fourth person, had gone to Andrew Peart's house, where Garfield Peart was also present, sitting outside in the yard. It was night, and there was no lighting. The witness saw an attack on the victim in which Andrew Peart and Garfield Peart were involved. Garfield Peart had threatened the victim with a gun. The witness and the fourth person left the scene to hide. He then heard gunshots and a voice saying, "make sure he is dead". The witness was discovered by Andrew Peart, who tied him up and threatened him, but he managed to escape.

The authors' defence was based on alibi. Upon his arrest, Garfield Peart had immediately denied involvement and said that he had been at a cinema with friends when the incident took place. At the trial, he made an unsworn statement from the dock, repeating what he had told the arresting officer. He added that while at the cinema, he had received a message from his child's mother that a shooting had taken place at his house. His alibi was supported by the sworn evidence of two women. In an unsworn statement from the dock, Andrew Peart contended that on the night of the murder, he had been in the company of his girlfriend until 11 p.m. and that he had been framed.

---

[58] *Ibidem, Fiftieth Session, Supplement No. 40* (A/50/40), vol. II, annex X, sect. E, communications No. 464/1991 and No. 482/1991, views adopted on 19 July 1995.

The authors claimed that the trial against them was unfair. They pointed out that they were convicted upon the uncorroborated evidence of the principal witness. They submitted that the trial transcript contained a suggestion that another eyewitness was not called, because his evidence would not have supported that of the principal witness. It was submitted that the principal witness had made a written statement to the police on the night of the incident containing material discrepancies from the evidence that he had given at the trial. This statement was not released to the defence, even though the prosecutor was obliged under Jamaican law to provide the defence with a copy of any such statement. During the trial, the authors' lawyer had applied to see the original statement, but the judge refused the application. A copy of the statement first came into the possession of their counsel in February 1991. In the statement, the principal witness did not identify Garfield Peart as one of the attackers, and he mentioned another person as the one who shot the victim. It was submitted that without hearing evidence as to the contents of the statement, the jury was not in a position to give a fair and proper verdict.

The authors further claimed that they were not put on an identification parade, although they had asked for one, and that the judge should therefore have disallowed the dock identification made by the principal witness. It was stated that the witness might have been mistaken in his identification of Garfield Peart as being present, because he knew that he lived at the premises.

The authors also claimed that they were victims of a violation of article 6 on the right to life, since they had been sentenced to death following a trial not being in accordance with the provisions of the Covenant.

Garfield Peart further claimed that his prolonged detention on death row, under degrading conditions, was in violation of articles 7 and 10 of the Covenant. Both authors submitted that the prison conditions were hard and inhuman and that they were not being offered treatment aimed at reformation and rehabilitation. It appeared from a report prepared by a non-governmental organization that Andrew Peart was injured by prison warders during the riots of May 1990. Garfield Peart referred to an incident on 4 May 1993 when he was badly beaten during the course of an extensive search of the prison, allegedly because his brother Andrew was a witness in a murder case involving some senior warders. All his personal belongings were destroyed. Upon indication of a prison warder, a soldier beat him with a metal detector on his testicle. Later he was taken to the sick bay and given painkillers, but no doctor came to see him. He reported the incident to the acting superintendent, who, however, disclaimed responsibility. His counsel wrote to the Jamaican Commissioner of Police, also to no avail. Garfield Peart stated that he had exhausted all domestic remedies in this respect and claimed that the remedies of filing complaints were not effective.

III:2

The Committee decided that the communications were admissible inasmuch as they appeared to raise issues under articles 7, 10 and 14, paragraphs 1 and 3 (*e*), of the Covenant, in relation to Garfield Peart and Andrew Peart, as well as under article 9, paragraph 3, in relation to Andrew Peart.

Issues and proceedings before the Committee

With regard to the evidence given by the principal witness for the prosecution, the Committee noted that it appeared from the trial transcript that during cross-examination by the defence, the witness admitted that he had made a written statement to the police on the night of the incident. Counsel then requested a copy of this statement, which the prosecution refused to give. The trial judge subsequently held that defence counsel had failed to put forward any reason why a copy of the statement should be provided. The trial proceeded without a copy of the statement being made available to the defence.

From the copy of the statement, which came into counsel's possession only after the appeal had been rejected and the initial petition for special leave to appeal submitted, it appeared that the witness named another man as the one who shot the deceased; that he implicated Andrew Peart as having had a gun in his hand; and that he did not mention Garfield Peart's participation or presence during the killing. The Committee noted that the evidence of the only eyewitness produced at the trial was of primary importance in the absence of any corroborating evidence. It considered that the failure to make the police statement of the witness available to the defence seriously obstructed the defence in its cross-examination of the witness, thereby precluding a fair trial of the defendants. The Committee found, therefore, that the facts before it disclosed a violation of article 14, paragraph 3 (*e*), of the Covenant.

With regard to the authors' allegations about maltreatment on death row, the Committee noted that the State party had indicated that it would investigate the allegations, but the results of the investigations had not been transmitted to the Committee. Due weight had therefore to be given to the authors' allegations, to the extent that they were substantiated. The Committee noted that the authors mentioned specific incidents, in May 1990 and May 1993, during which they were assaulted by prison warders or soldiers and, moreover, that Andrew Peart had been receiving death threats. In the Committee's view, this amounted to cruel treatment within the meaning of article 7 of the Covenant, also entailing a violation of article 10, paragraph 1.

Furthermore, the Committee was of the opinion that the imposition of a sentence of death upon conclusion of a trial in which the provisions of the Covenant had not been respected constituted, if no further appeal against the sentence was possible, a violation of article 6 of the Covenant. The provision that a sentence of death might be imposed only in accordance with the law and not contrary to the provisions of the Covenant implied that the procedural guarantees prescribed in the Covenant had to be observed, including the right to a fair hearing by an independent tribunal, the presumption of innocence, the minimum guarantees for the defence and the right to review of conviction and sentence by a higher tribunal. In the present case, since the final sentence of death was passed without due respect for the requirement of fair trial, there had consequently also been a violation of article 6 of the Covenant.

In conclusion, the Committee was of the view that the facts before it disclosed a violation of articles 7, 10, paragraph 1, and 14, paragraph 3 (*e*), and consequently article 6, of the Covenant. No other violations were found in this case.

Furthermore, in capital punishment cases, the obligation of States parties to observe rigorously all the guarantees for a fair trial set out in article 14 of the Covenant admitted of no exception. The failure to make the police statement of the prosecution witness available to the defence obstructed the defence in its cross-examination of this witness, in violation of article 14, paragraph 3 (*e*). Thus, Garfield Peart and Andrew Peart had not received a fair trial within the meaning of the Covenant. Consequently, they were entitled, under article 2, paragraph 3 (*a*), of the Covenant, to an effective remedy. The Committee took note of the commutation of the authors' death sentences on 18 April 1995, but it was of the view that in the circumstances of the case, the remedy should be the authors' release. The State party was also under an obligation to ensure that similar violations did not occur in the future. The Committee wished to receive from the State party, within 90 days, information about the measures taken to give effect to these views.

(*d*) Opinion No. 27/2001 (*Morocco*)
(Working Group on Arbitrary Detention)[59]

The communication, addressed to the Government of Morocco on 13 June 2001, concerned Mustapha Adib, a former captain of the Moroccan armed forces. Allegedly, he had been arrested, held in pre-trial detention and convicted exclusively because of the fact that he, when serving in the armed forces, had made use of his right to freedom of expression. Morocco was a party to the International Covenant on Civil and Political Rights.

The Working Group on Arbitrary Detention welcomed the cooperation of the Government. Having transmitted the Government's reply to the source and received its

---

[59] See United Nations document E/CN.4/2003/8/Add.1, p. 27, opinion adopted on 3 December 2001.

III:2

comments, the Working Group believed that it was in a position to render an opinon on the facts and circumstances of the case.

The facts

According to the source, Mustapha Adib, born in 1968 and of Moroccan nationality, was arrested by military personnel on 5 December 1999 at a military airbase where he, a captain of the armed forces, was posted at the time. When responsible for e-quipment at another airbase, he had occasion to witness illegal trafficking in fuel, or-ganized by the most senior officer of the base. The unit received a fuel consignment for the operation of a large radar system. The traffic consisted in diverting and sell-ing the fuel oil received free to a neighbouring gas station. Some 120 tonnes of fuel oil were believed to have been involved over a period of 10 months.

As the person responsible for supplies, the captain was required by his superiors to sign fuel vouchers. When he refused to become involved in corrupt dealings, he suf-fered various forms of pressure and then penalties for refusing to obey.

In October 1998, he reported the illegal trafficking to the Crown Prince, as coordina-tor of the armed forces. After an inquiry, the Permanent Tribunal of the Royal Armed Forces found the senior officers mentioned in the report guilty of diverting fuel supplies, complicity and failure to report offences. Mustapha Adib, on the other hand, was exonerated of any involvement in the trafficking he had reported. Looked upon thenceforth, however, as a "black sheep" in the army, he was subjected to har-assment, bullying, close confinement and various other forms of punishment. He re-ceived four disciplinary sanctions and was subsequently transferred to two other air-bases in quick succession.

Finally, Mustapha Adib decided to appeal against the disciplinary sanctions. Ac-cording to the source, those appeals merely made matters worse. A request for dis-charge from the army was refused. Feeling that he had exhausted all possible reme-dies, he contacted a journalist with the French daily *Le Monde* specializing in Magh-reb affairs. An interview took place on 30 November 1999. On 5 December, before anything was published, Mustapha Adib was arrested. He was sentenced to 60 days' confinement in a military prison, starting from 10 December 1999.

On 16 December 1999, *Le Monde* published an article under the title "Moroccan officers denounce corruption in the army", signed by the journalist. Mustapha Adib was cited as one of the sources of the information. The gendarmerie opened an in-vestigation, and he was placed in pre-trial detention on 17 January 2000.

The source added that the Permanent Tribunal of the Royal Armed Forces, in a judgment on 17 February 2000, found Mustapha Adib guilty of a violation of military rules and contempt of the army under the military justice code. He received the maximum sentence applicable, five years' imprisonment, and was discharged from the army. On 21 February 2000, he initiated the only appeal action possible, for judicial review of his case by the Supreme Court. On 24 June 2000, the Supreme Court annulled the judgment for lack of reasons regarding the absence of attenuating circumstances and referred the case back to the Permanent Tribunal, with a different composition. On 6 October 2000, Mustapha Adib was sentenced by the Tribunal to two and a half years' imprisonment and to dismissal from the army. By a decision of 22 February 2001, the Supreme Court rejected his appeal against that judgment, thus making it irrevocable.

Still according to the source, Mustapha Adib was not given a fair trial before the Permanent Tribunal. His presumed innocence was violated, and the Tribunal displayed a lack of impartiality with regard to the hearing of witnesses. By ordering him to appear in civilian dress, it had ignored the ruling of the Supreme Court, which had annulled his dismissal. The source also alleged that the Permanent Tribunal acceded to all the prosecution's requests and systematically rejected all those put forward by the defence. No preliminary hearing was held for the accused to explain his case. At the time of the second hearing before the Supreme Court, the captain's counsel had not been informed of the case brought by the prosecution.

The source considered that the arrest, pre-trial detention and conviction of Mustapha Adib were due exclusively to the fact that he had made use of his right to freedom of expression. The restriction imposed on him was not referred to expressly in Moroccan law, which made no provision for restricting the right to denounce corrupt behaviour. On the contrary, it was his duty to report corrupt deeds that were prejudicial to the army's reputation. The effect of such restrictions was to stifle any attempts to report facts punishable under Moroccan law and to cover up corruption, rather than to punish contempt of the army or the violation of military rules.

In its reply, the Government merely recalled the facts that had led to Mustapha Adib's conviction for violating military rules and contempt of the army by the Permanent Tribunal and the various trials that had led to his last sentence of two and a half years' imprisonment.

The source maintained in his rejoinder that Mustapha Adib had not enjoyed a fair trial before the Permanent Tribunal and that his pre-trial detention and conviction were due solely to the fact that he had used his right to freedom of expression.

III:2

Issues and proceedings before the Working Group

With regard to the violation of the right to a fair trial, the Working Group noted that the Government in its reply had not rejected or even discussed the facts and allegations contained in the communication, particularly those concerning the reasons for the arrest, detention and conviction of Mustapha Adib and those concerning the details of the trial proceedings.

Thus there was no denial of the fact that the Permanent Tribunal, on the basis of an administrative decision to dismiss the captain and giving in to the demands of the prosecutor, had obliged the accused to appear in civilian dress, whereas, in its final judgment, it had again ordered his dismissal. That appeared to suggest that dismissal could be decided only by the Tribunal. Therefore, prior to that ruling, the accused could still claim to belong to the army and was entitled to appear in uniform.

It was not denied, either, that the accused had been removed from the court room and judged *in absentia* and without his lawyers being present, since they withdrew once he had been removed, only because he had protested against the systematic rejection of his counsel's requests, particularly the request to call witnesses, and had called for a fair trial.

It appeared that Mustapha Adib had been judged by a military tribunal, a type of court whose independence from the executive power was often in doubt owing to its composition and the form of appointment of its members. In addition, it acted in this particular case in a way that cast doubts on its impartiality by infringing the presumption of innocence of the accused and by hindering his defence.

In this respect and in conformity with its methods of work, the Working Group considered that under article 14, paragraph 1, of the Covenant, if a trial was not conducted by a competent, independent and impartial tribunal, the gravity of the violation of the right to a fair trial was such as to confer on the deprivation of liberty an arbitrary character.

The Working Group added, however, that in commenting on the arbitrary character of the captain's deprivation of liberty, it took account of the special circumstances of the case. Therefore, its conclusions should not be interpreted as a position of principle regarding the incompatibility of justice rendered by military courts and the standards of fair trial.

With regard to the enjoyment of the right to freedom of expression, the Working Group said that a doubt arose as to how far the freedom of expression of the person concerned extended in view of the fact that he was on active military service and expressed himself through the media.

Under article 19 of the Covenant, the enjoyment of the right to freedom of expression might, generally speaking, be subject to certain restrictions if necessary for respect of the rights or reputations of others, for the protection of national security, of public order or of public health or morals. According to the Covenant, however, these restrictions had to be expressly provided by law. The Human Rights Committee had in the past taken the view that when a State imposed certain restrictions on the exercise of freedom of expression, these might not put in jeopardy the right itself.

With regard to the specific case of military personnel, it was generally recognized that the right to freedom of expression of officials, police officers and those of the armed forces should be subject to certain restrictions owing to the special nature of the obligations and responsibilities by which they were bound. In the case in hand, Mustapha Adib, in a letter addressed to the Moroccan authorities and to the international community to protest against his conviction and detention, had recognized that Moroccan military personnel, under the regulations of the armed forces, were generally forbidden to publish.

Yet, even if there had been a breach of regulations, the question of the disproportionality of the sanction, 60 days of military confinement and five years' imprisonment, including two and a half non-suspensive, in relation to the fault committed, which might have merited no more than a disciplinary sanction, still remained and deserved to be examined.

However, considering that neither the information supplied by the source, nor that supplied by the Government, shed sufficient light on the matter, the Working Group was not, in the circumstances, in a position to express an opinion regarding the compatibility of the restriction with the provisions of article 19 of the Covenant or the proportionality of the sanction inflicted on the captain for his violation.

In conclusion, the Working Group rendered the opinion that the deprivation of liberty of Mustapha Adib was arbitrary, as being in contravention of articles 9 and 10 of the Universal Declaration of Human Rights and articles 9 and 14 of the Covenant. It fell within category III of the categories applicable to the consideration of cases submitted to the Working Group.

In view of the circumstances, and since the deprivation of liberty had been declared arbitrary within category III, the Working Group did not consider it necessary to decide whether the deprivation of liberty also fell within category II.

III:2

Consequent upon the opinion rendered, the Working Group requested the Government of Morocco to take the necessary steps to remedy the situation and to bring it into conformity with the standards and principles set forth in the Universal Declaration and in the Covenant.

(e) *Allenet de Ribemont* v. *France* (European Court of Human Rights)[60]

The case was referred to the European Court of Human Rights on 21 January 1994 by the European Commission of Human Rights. It originated in an application against the French Republic lodged with the Commission on 24 May 1989 by Patrick Allenet de Ribemont, a French national. The object of the request was to obtain a decision as to whether the facts of the case disclosed a breach by the respondent State of its obligations under article 6, paragraphs 1 and 2, of the Convention for the Protection of Human Rights and Fundamental Freedoms.

The facts

On 24 December 1976, Jean de Broglie, a member of parliament and former minister, was murdered in front of the home of Mr. Allenet de Ribemont. Mr. de Broglie had just been visiting his financial adviser, Pierre De Varga, who lived in the same building and with whom Mr. Allenet de Ribemont was planning to become the joint owner of a restaurant. The scheme was financed by means of a loan taken out by the victim. He had passed on the borrowed sum to Mr. Allenet de Ribemont, who was responsible for repaying the loan.

A judicial investigation was commenced. On 27 and 28 December 1976, the crime squad at Paris police headquarters arrested a number of people, including Mr. De Varga. On the 29 December, it arrested Mr. Allenet de Ribemont.

On 29 December 1976, at a press conference on the subject of the French police budget for the coming years, Michel Poniatowski, the Minister of the Interior, Jean Ducret, the director of the Paris criminal investigation department and Pierre Ottavioli, the head of the crime squad, referred to the inquiry that was under way. Two French television channels reported this press conference in their news programmes. The transcript of the relevant extract of one of those programmes, *TF1 News*, read as follows:

---

[60] See *Publications of the European Court of Human Rights*, Series A: *Judgments and Decisions*, vol. 308 (1995), application No. 15175/89, judgment of 10 February 1995.

Mr. Roger Giquel, newsreader: ... Be that as it may, here is how all the aspects of the de Broglie case were explained to the public at a press conference given by Mr. Michel Poniatowski yesterday evening.

Mr. Poniatowski: The haul is complete. All the people involved are now under arrest after the arrest of Mr. De Varga-Hirsch. It is a very simple story. A bank loan guaranteed by Mr. de Broglie was to be repaid by Mr. Varga-Hirsch and Mr. de Ribemont.

A journalist: Superintendent, who was the key figure in this case? De Varga?

Mr. Ottavioli: I think it must have been Mr. De Varga.

Mr. Ducret: The instigator, Mr. De Varga, and his acolyte, Mr. de Ribemont, were the instigators of the murder. The organizer was Detective Sergeant Simoné and the murderer was Mr. Frèche.

Mr. Giquel: As you can see, those statements include a number of assertions. That is why the police are now being criticized by Ministry of Justice officials. Although Superintendent Ottavioli and Mr. Ducret were careful to (end of recording).

In the *Antenne 2 News*, the remarks of Mr. Poniatowski, Mr. Ducret and Mr. Ottavioli at the press conference were also broadcast, and a journalist gave an account of the background to the case and of the circumstances of the crime. He explained that the loan had been guaranteed by a life insurance policy taken out by Mr. de Broglie; that in the event of his death, the sum insured was to be paid to Mr. De Varga-Hirsch and Mr. Allenet de Ribemont; that a police officer had admitted organizing the murder, lending a gun for the killing and hiring the contract killer. The journalist then described how the investigation had led to the arrest of the suspects.

On 14 January 1977, Mr. Allenet de Ribemont was charged with aiding and abetting intentional homicide and taken into custody. He was released on 1 March 1977, and a discharge order was issued on 21 March 1980.

On 23 March 1977, Mr. Allenet de Ribemont submitted a claim to the Prime Minister based on article 6, paragraph 2, of the Convention. He sought compensation of 10 million French francs for the non-pecuniary and pecuniary damage he maintained to have sustained on account of the statements by the Minister of the Interior and senior police officials at the press conference. On 20 September 1977, he applied to an administrative court for review of the Prime Minister's implicit refusal of his

III:2

claim and renewed his claim for compensation, but the court ruled that the application was inadmissible.

The author then sought remedy before various other national judicial authorities, but without success.

In his application lodged with the Commission, Mr. Allenet de Ribemont alleged the infringement of his right to benefit from the presumption of innocence secured in article 6, paragraph 2, of the Convention. He also complained, under article 13, that he had not had an effective remedy enabling him to obtain redress for the damage he had allegedly sustained on account of those statements. Furthermore, he complained, under article 6, paragraph 1, that the domestic courts had not been independent and that the court proceedings had taken too long. The final appeal was dismissed more than 11 years and a half since the first claim lodged with the Prime Minister.

The Commission declared the application admissible as to the complaints based on disregard of the presumption of innocence and the length of the proceedings. In its report, it expressed the opinion that there had been a violation of article 6, paragraphs 1 and 2, of the Convention.

The law

As to the alleged violation of article 6, paragraph 2, of the Convention, providing that everyone charged with a criminal offence should be presumed innocent until proved guilty according to law, the applicant complained of the remarks made by the Minister of the Interior and the senior police officers accompanying him at the press conference of 29 December 1976.

Regarding the applicability of that provision, the Government contested, in substance, that it was applicable, relying on a previous judgment of the Court. The Government maintained that the presumption of innocence could be infringed only by a judicial authority. This presumption could be shown to have been infringed only where, at the conclusion of proceedings ending in a conviction, the court's reasoning suggested that it regarded the defendant as guilty in advance.

The Commission had acknowledged that the principle of presumption of innocence was above all a procedural safeguard in criminal proceedings. However, it took the view that the scope of this principle was more extensive, in that it imposed obligations not only on criminal courts determining criminal charges but also on other authorities.

The Court stated that its task was to determine whether the situation found in this case affected the applicant's right under article 6, paragraph 2, of the Convention. Citing some of its previous judgments, it pointed out that the presumption of innocence enshrined in that provision was one of the elements of the fair criminal trial that was required by article 6, paragraph 1. It would be violated if a judicial decision concerning a person charged with a criminal offence reflected an opinion that he was guilty before he had been proved guilty according to law. It sufficed, even in the absence of any formal finding, that there was some reasoning suggesting that the court regarded the accused as guilty.

However, the Court observed, the scope of article 6, paragraph 2, of the Convention was not limited to the eventuality mentioned by the Government. There had been violations of this provision found in two previous cases before the Court, although the national courts concerned had closed the proceedings in the first of those cases, because the limitation period had expired, and had acquitted the applicant in the second. The Court then cited other cases in which it had similarly held article 6, paragraph 2, to be applicable where the domestic courts did not have to determine the question of guilt. Moreover, further citing its case law, the Court reiterated that the Convention had to be interpreted in such a way as to guarantee rights which were practical and effective as opposed to theoretical and illusory. This also applied to the right enshrined in article 6, paragraph 2.

The Court considered that the presumption of innocence might be infringed not only by a judge or court but also by other public authorities.

At the time of the press conference, on 29 December 1976, Mr. Allenet de Ribemont had just been arrested by the police. Although he had not yet been charged with aiding and abetting intentional homicide, his arrest and detention in police custody formed part of the judicial investigation begun a few days earlier by an investigating judge. This made him a person charged with a criminal offence within the meaning of article 6, paragraph 2, of the Convention. The two senior police officers present were conducting the inquiries in the case. Their remarks, made in parallel with the judicial investigation and supported by the Minister of the Interior, were explained by the existence of that investigation and had a direct link with it. Article 6, paragraph 2, therefore applied in this case.

Regarding the compliance in this case with article 6, paragraph 2, the Court first mentioned that freedom of expression, guaranteed by article 10 of the Convention, included the freedom to receive and impart information. Article 6, paragraph 2, could not therefore prevent the authorities from informing the public about criminal investigations in progress, but it required that they did so with all the discretion and circumspection necessary for the presumption of innocence to be respected.

III:2

Like the applicant, the Commission considered that the remarks made by the Minister of the Interior and, in his presence and under his authority, by the police superintendent in charge of the inquiry and the director of the criminal investigation department were incompatible with the presumption of innocence. In those remarks, Mr. Allenet de Ribemont was held up as one of the instigators of Mr. de Broglie's murder.

The Government maintained that such remarks came under the head of information about criminal proceedings in progress and were not such as to infringe the presumption of innocence, since they did not bind the courts and could be proved false by subsequent investigations. The facts of the case bore this out, as the applicant had not been formally charged until two weeks after the press conference and the investigating judge had eventually decided that there was no case to answer.

The Court noted that some of the highest-ranking officers in the French police had referred to Mr. Allenet de Ribemont, without any qualification or reservation, as one of the instigators of a murder and thus an accomplice in that murder. This was clearly a declaration of his guilt which, firstly, encouraged the public to believe him guilty and, secondly, prejudged the assessment of the facts by the competent judicial authority. The Court therefore held, by eight votes to one, that there had been a breach of article 6, paragraph 2, of the Convention.

As to the alleged violation of article 6, paragraph 1, of the Convention, the applicant complained of the length of the compensation proceedings he brought in the administrative and then in the ordinary courts. The applicability of this provision was not contested.

The Court recalled that the reasonableness of the length of the proceedings was to be determined in the light of the circumstances of the case and with reference to the criteria laid down in its case law, in particular the complexity of the case, the conduct of the applicant and that of the competent authorities. On the latter point, the importance of what was at stake for the applicant in the litigation had to be taken into account.

Having considered these factors, the Court concluded that the complexity of the case and the applicant's conduct were not in themselves sufficient to explain the length of the proceedings. The overall delay was essentially due to the way in which the national authorities handled the case, particularly their refusal to grant the requests by Mr. Allenet de Ribemont for production of a vital piece of evidence. Regard being had to the importance of what was at stake for the applicant, and even though the proceedings in the court of appeal and the Court of Cassation, taken separately, did not appear excessively long, a total lapse of time of approximately 11 years and 8 months could not be regarded as reasonable. Accordingly, the Court unanimously held that there had been a breach of article 6, paragraph 1, of the Convention.

Under the then article 50 of the Convention, allowing the Court to afford just satisfaction to an injured party, under specified circumstances, when there had been a violation of the Convention, the Court took the following decision. Taking into account the various relevant factors and making its assessment on an equitable basis, as required by article 50, the Court, by eight votes to one, awarded Mr. Allenet de Ribemont a total sum of 2,000,000 French francs. The applicant was also awarded, unanimously, 100,000 francs, plus value-added tax, for costs and expenses.

(f) S. v. Switzerland
(European Court of Human Rights)[61]

The case was referred to the European Court of Human Rights on 8 October 1990 by the European Commission of Human Rights and on 12 December 1990 by the Government of the Swiss Confederation. It originated in two applications against Switzerland lodged with the Commission on 18 November 1986 and 28 May 1988 by Mr. S., a Swiss national. The applicant requested the Court not to disclose his identity.

The object of the Commission's request and of the Government's application was to obtain a decision as to whether the facts of the case disclosed a breach by the respondent State of the requirements of articles 6, paragraph 3 (*b*) and (*c*), and 5, paragraph 4, of the Convention for the Protection of Human Rights and Fundamental Freedoms.

The facts

In the autumn of 1980, a protest movement broke out in the town of Winterthur directed against the sale of nuclear power stations to a Latin American country, then under a military regime. It continued in 1981 in the form of demonstrations against the holding of an international arms fair, writing graffiti and occupying buildings as a protest against the housing shortage. In the years 1983 and 1984, there was a series of cases of arson and attacks using explosives, causing damage to several public and private buildings, including the house of a cabinet minister, then the head of the Department of Justice and Police.

A special police unit was set up to coordinate the investigation into these crimes. It shadowed individuals, tapped telephones and regularly emptied the dustbins of a

---

[61] *Ibidem*, vol. 220 (1992), applications No. 12629/87 and No. 13965/88, judgment of 28 November 1991.

III:2

commune which was thought to be sheltering those responsible. A number of people were subsequently arrested, including, on 21 November 1984, Mr. S, but he succeded in escaping. He was re-arrested on 30 March 1985 and charged with the use of explosives in connection with the attack on the house of the cabinet minister. On 10 April 1985, Mr. S. was questioned by federal public prosecutor officials, but he exercised his right to silence.

After questioning Mr. S. on 28 May 1985, the district attorney accused him of causing an explosion at the cabinet minister's house and starting a fire at a civil defence centre. He was remanded in custody on the grounds of the risk of flight and collusion with his co-accused. On 7 June 1985, Mr. S. was further accused of arson at two rifle ranges, flooding business premises and criminal damage to property by means of graffiti.

On 10 June 1985, Mr. Garbade was designated as court-appointed defence counsel for Mr. S. with retrospective effect from 4 May. On 8 May 1985, the applicant had been able to confer freely with Mr. Garbade for about half an hour. However, as from 15 May, visits took place under the supervision of a police official. Three of the letters of Mr. S. to his lawyer were intercepted and used for the purpose of graphological reports. On 31 May 1985, Mr. S. spoke with Mr. Garbade in the presence of a policeman who took notes and stopped the interview after an hour, on the grounds that they were no longer speaking about the case and that he had other business to see to.

In a letter of 12 June 1985, the district attorney informed the principal public prosecutor of the canton that he considered these measures necessary in view of the risk that the lawyer of Mr. S. might collude with other lawyers or other co-accused. He relied on an article of the canton's criminal procedure code, according to which an accused who was held in custody was permitted written and oral contact with defence counsel, insofar as the purpose of the investigation was not jeopardized. Once his detention had exceeded 14 days, an accused must not be refused permission to consult defence counsel freely and without supervision, unless there were special reasons, in particular a danger of collusion. After the close of the investigation, an accused had this right without restriction.

On 27 June 1985, the indictments division of a court of appeal gave the defence counsel permission to examine three police reports and several transcripts of statements by the co-accused at the court's registry, but not to take copies of them. From that date until January 1986, Mr. Garbade did not have access to any other documents in the case file. There continued to be numerous disputes between the lawyer and those carrying out the surveillance measures.

Subsequently, detention on remand of Mr. S. was extended until 12 September 1986 in order to prevent him from colluding with his co-accused, who had meanwhile been released, and tampering with evidence. In October 1985, Mr. Garbade saw some extracts from the final police report of 8 August 1985, but he did not have access to the case file until January 1986.

As from 3 June 1985, Mr. S. launched a series of appeals to domestic courts, up to and including the Federal Court, against the surveillance measures and against his continued detention. These were all dismissed at various levels on the grounds that he might collude with other accused people, that he might flee and that Mr. Garbade might unintentionally collude with lawyers representing the other accused.

In two appeals to the Federal Court, Mr. S. relied on article 6, paragraph 3 (*b*), in conjunction with article 5, paragraph 4, of the Convention, alleging that the surveillance of the interviews made his right to take proceedings, within the meaning of the latter provision, illusory and that his right to a fair hearing was deprived of substance regarding the review of the lawfulness of his detention on remand. In particular, the surveillance prevented any confidential conversation with his lawyer aimed at refuting the evidence collected during the investigation. Furthermore, he did not have access to the case file, and his lawyer was unable to take a copy of it.

The Federal Court dismissed the first appeal on the grounds, *inter alia*, that Mr. Garbade, whose task it was to draw up the application for release from detention, had had access to the case file, so that the rights of Mr. S. in the proceedings on the extension of his pre-trial detention had not been infringed. The Federal Court added that counsel would, at the preparation for trial at the latest, have the right to a copy of the case file for his client if he asked for this. Dismissing the second appeal, the Federal Court held that only article 4 of the Federal Constitution and article 6, paragraph 3 (*c*), of the Convention were relevant, but not article 6, paragraph 3 (*b*), as the surveillance had not prejudiced preparation for the trial. The Federal Court concluded that surveillance of Mr. Garbade's contacts with his client was in accordance with the Constitution and the Convention.

The surveillance of visits and correspondence was ended during the course of a second series of appeals against these measures. Ultimately, the Federal Court dismissed a public-law appeal brought by Mr. S, finding that there had been a danger of collusion.

On 11 December 1989, a court of appeal found Mr. S. guilty of a number of crimes, including manufacturing explosives, arson, theft and criminal damage. He was sentenced to seven years' imprisonment, the 1,291 days spent in custody on remand being deducted, and to payment of costs and expenses. Mr. S. then appealed, but the

III:2

appeal court upheld its judgment of 11 December 1989. By an appeal to a court of cassation, the enforcement of the judgment was suspended.

In his applications lodged with the Commission, Mr. S. complained, *inter alia*, that he had not been allowed to communicate with his lawyer freely and without supervision. In this respect, he relied on article 6, paragraph 3 (*b*) and (*c*), of the Convention. He also claimed that the surveillance measures had made his right to bring proceedings before a court, within the meaning of article 5, paragraph 4, illusory.

The Commission found these complaints admissible. It concluded that there had been a violation of article 6, paragraph 3 (*c*), of the Convention in that the applicant from 31 May 1985 to 10 January 1986 had been unable to converse freely with his lawyer. No separate issue was raised with reference to articles 6, paragraph 3 (*b*), and 5, paragraph 4.

The law

As to the alleged violation of article 6, paragraph 3 (*c*), of the Convention, providing everyone charged with a criminal offence the right to defend himself in person or through legal assistance of his own choosing, the applicant criticized the Swiss authorities for having exercised surveillance of his meetings with Mr. Garbade. He also criticized them for having authorized Mr. Garbade to consult only a minute fraction of the case file, with the alleged effect that it had been difficult for him to challenge the decisions by which his detention on remand was extended. Free communication between a lawyer and his detained client was a fundamental right essential in a democratic society, above all in the most serious cases. There was a contradiction between naming a court-appointed defence counsel at the start of an investigation, because of the seriousness of the alleged offences, and preventing him from carrying out his task freely.

The Government, citing the Commission's report, pointed out that an accused's right to communicate with his counsel without hindrance, insofar as it was implicitly guaranteed by article 6, paragraph 3 (*c*), of the Convention, might call for such regulation as to restrict the exercise of the right in certain cases. The particularly drastic restriction imposed in this case was justified, according to the Government, by the exceptional circumstances of the case. The grounds for the decisions of the Swiss courts, which were best in a position to assess the situation, provided two decisive arguments in support of the very unusual length of the surveillance: firstly, the extraordinarily dangerous character of the accused, whose methods had features in common with those of terrorists, and the existence of systematic offences against public and social order; and, secondly, the risk of collusion between Mr. Garbade and the co-accused. The court of appeal had stated that such a risk was increased when a defendant exercised his right to silence. Finally, the applicant had not in any way shown that the surveillance complained of by him had adversely affected his defence.

The Court noted that unlike some national laws and unlike article 8, paragraph 2 (*d*), of the American Convention on Human Rights, the European Convention did not expressly guarantee the right of a person charged with a criminal offence to communicate with defence counsel without hindrance. That right was set forth, however, within the Council of Europe. The Court cited the Standard Minimum Rules for the Treatment of Prisoners, approved by the United Nations Economic and Social Council and annexed to a Committee of Ministers resolution, and the European Agreement Relating to Persons Participating in Proceedings of the European Commission and Court of Human Rights, binding on no less than 20 member States, including Switzerland from 1974.

The Court considered that an accused's right to communicate with his advocate out of hearing of a third person was part of the basic requirements of a fair trial in a democratic society and followed from article 6, paragraph 3 (*c*), of the Convention. If a lawyer would be unable to confer with his client and receive confidential instructions from him without such surveillance, his assistance would lose much of its usefulness, whereas the Convention was intended to guarantee rights that were practical and effective.

The risk of collusion relied on by the Government did, however, merit consideration by the Court. According to the Swiss courts, there were indications pointing to such a risk in the person of defence counsel. There was reason to fear that Mr. Garbade would collaborate with another defendant's counsel, who had informed the office of the district attorney that all the lawyers proposed to coordinate their defence strategy.

Such a possibility, however, notwithstanding the seriousness of the charges against the applicant, could not in the Court's opinion justify the restriction in issue, and no other reason had been adduced cogent enough to do so. There was nothing extraordinary in a number of defence counsels collaborating with a view to coordinating their defence strategy. Moreover, neither the professional ethics of Mr. Garbade, who had been designated as court-appointed defence counsel, nor the lawfulness of his conduct were at any time called into question in this case. Furthermore, the restriction in issue had lasted for over seven months.

The Court dismissed the argument that Mr. S. was not prejudiced by the measures in question, as he was, in fact, able to make several applications for provisional release. Making reference to its case law, the Court observed that a violation of the Conven-

III:2

tion did not necessarily imply the existence of damage. It concluded that there had been a violation of article 6, paragraph 3 (*c*).

As to the alleged violation of article 6, paragraph 3 (*b*), of the Convention, the applicant had originally invoked this provision claiming that the surveillance of his conferences with his lawyer had deprived him of his right to have adequate time and facilities for the preparation of his defence. However, he no longer relied on this provision before the Court, and there was no need for the Court to consider the question of its own motion.

Finally, as to the alleged violation of article 5, paragraph 4, of the Convention, the applicant, as an alternative complaint, stated that the impossibility of conferring freely with his defence counsel had rendered illusory his right to challenge the extension of his detention, thereby entailing a breach of the requirements of that article.

Having regard to the conclusion that there had been a violation of article 6, paragraph 3 (*c*), of the Convention, the Court saw no need to consider the matter from the point of view of article 5, paragraph 4.

Under the then article 50 of the Convention, allowing the Court to afford just satisfaction to an injured party, under specified circumstances, when there had been a violation of the Convention, the Court considered that Mr. S. must have suffered some non-pecuniary damage and awarded him 2,500 Swiss francs. It also awarded the applicant 12,500 francs for costs and expenses.

(g) *Doorson* v. *the Netherlands*
(European Court of Human Rights)[62]

The case was referred to the European Court of Human Rights on 8 December 1994 by the European Commission of Human Rights. It originated in an application against the Kingdom of the Netherlands lodged with the Commission on 27 June 1992 by Désiré Wilfried Doorson, a Netherlands national. The object of the request was to obtain a decision as to whether the facts of the case disclosed a breach by the respondent State of its obligations under article 6, paragraphs 1 and 3, of the Convention for the Protection of Human Rights and Fundamental Freedoms.

---

[62] See European Court of Human Rights, *Reports of Judgments and Decisions*, 1996-II, p. 446, application No. 20524/92, judgment of 26 March 1996.

The facts

In August 1987, the prosecuting authorities decided to take action against drug traffickers in Amsterdam. The police had compiled sets of photographs of people suspected of being drug dealers, and these were shown to about 150 drug addicts in order to obtain statements from them. However, because of fear of retaliation by drugs dealers, most of the addicts to whom photographs were shown were only prepared to make statements on condition that their identity was not disclosed to drugs dealers.

In each set of photographs shown, there was one of a person known to be innocent. Statements made by people who identified this photograph as that of a drug dealer were regarded as unreliable and discounted.

In September 1987, the police received information from a person referred to by the police under a code number that Mr. Doorson was engaged in drug trafficking. Mr. Doorson's identification photograph, which had been taken in 1985, was thereupon included by the police in the collection of photographs shown to drug addicts. A number of drug addicts subsequently stated to police that they recognized Mr. Doorson from his photograph and that he had sold drugs. Six of these drug addicts remained anonymous, referred to by the police under code names. The identity of two others was disclosed.

On 12 April 1988, Mr. Doorson was arrested on suspicion of having committed drug offences and subsequently kept in detention on remand. On 13 April, he was shown the photograph taken of him by the police, and he recognized it as a photograph of himself. A preliminary investigation was opened. After a number of hearings, a regional court, on 13 December 1988, convicted Mr. Doorson of drug trafficking and sentenced him to 15 months' imprisonment. He then appealed this judgment. Again after a number of hearings, a court of appeal, on 6 December 1990, quashed the regional court's judgment, as it was adopting a different approach with regard to the evidence. However, it found Mr. Doorson guilty of the deliberate sale of quantities of heroin and cocaine and sentenced him to 15 months' imprisonment. Two issues considered at length during the various hearings was the evidence of anonymous informants and the reliability of the evidence of drug abusers.

Mr. Doorson then filed an appeal to the Supreme Court, but it was rejected on 24 March 1992.

In the application lodged with the Commission, Mr. Doorson claimed that he had been a victim of violations of article 6, paragraphs 1 and 3 (*d*), of the Convention in that he had been convicted on the evidence of witnesses who had not been heard in his presence and whom he had not had the opportunity to question; in that the court

III:2

of appeal had accepted the evidence of the anonymous witnesses on the basis of the statement of an investigating judge who, at a previous stage of the proceedings, had participated in a decision to prolong his detention on remand; and in that the court of appeal had refused to hear an expert witness called by the defence, but had agreed to hear an expert witness called by the prosecution. He also alleged a lack of respect for his private life, in violation of article 8, paragraph 1, of the Convention, in that his photograph had been shown to third parties without any basis in law.

The Commission declared the application admissible insofar as it concerned article 6, paragraphs 1 and 3 (*d*), of the Convention. In its report, it expressed the opinion that there had been no violation of those provisions.

The law

As to the alleged violation of article 6, paragraph 1, taken together with article 6, paragraph 3 (*d*), of the Convention, the applicant claimed that the taking and hearing of, and reliance on, evidence from certain witnesses during the criminal proceedings against him infringed the rights of the defence. These provisions provided, *inter alia*, that in the determination of any criminal charge, everyone was entitled to a fair hearing by an impartial tribunal and that everyone charged with a criminal offence had the right to examine or have examined witnesses against him and to obtain the attendance and examination of witnesses on his behalf under the same conditions as witnesses against him. Neither the Commission nor the Government endorsed the applicant's view.

The Court decided to examine the complaints under article 6, paragraphs 1 and 3 (*d*), taken together, as the requirements of article 6, paragraph 3, were to be seen as particular aspects of the right to a fair trial guaranteed by article 6, paragraph 1.

The Court reiterated that the admissibility of evidence was primarily a matter for regulation by national law, and as a general rule, it was for the national courts to assess the evidence before them. Making reference to its case law, the Court stated that its task under the Convention was not to give a ruling as to whether statements of witnesses were properly admitted as evidence, but rather to ascertain whether the proceedings as a whole, including the way in which evidence was taken, were fair.

The Court agreed with the Commission that no issue arose in relation to the fact that an investigating judge heard two anonymous witnesses in the absence of the applicant's counsel in the course of the preliminary judicial investigation, since these two witnesses were heard in counsel's presence during the subsequent appeal proceedings.

As the Court had held on previous occasions, the Convention did not preclude reliance, at the investigation stage, on sources such as anonymous informants. The subsequent use of their statements by the trial court to found a conviction was, however, capable of raising issues under the Convention. As was already implicit in a previous judgment, such use was not under all circumstances incompatible with the Convention.

The Court declared that article 6 of the Convention did not explicitly require the interests of witnesses in general, and those of victims called upon to testify in particular, to be taken into consideration. However, their life, liberty or security of person might be at stake, as might their interests coming generally within the ambit of article 8. Such interests of witnesses and victims were in principle protected by other, substantive, provisions of the Convention, which implied that the States parties should organize their criminal justice proceedings in such a way as to not unjustifiably imperil those interests. Against this background, principles of fair trial also required that in appropriate cases the interests of the defence were balanced against those of witnesses or victims called upon to testify.

In the case under consideration, the Court felt that there was relevant and sufficient reason to preserve the anonymity of two specific witnesses because of the need to obtain evidence from them and because of the requirement to protect them against the possibility of reprisals. The maintenance of the anonymity of these witnesses presented the defence with difficulties which criminal proceedings should not normally involve. Nevertheless, the Court stated, no violation of article 6, paragraph 1, taken together with article 6, paragraph 3 (*d*), of the Convention could be found if it was established that the handicaps, under which the defence laboured, were sufficiently counterbalanced by the procedures followed by the judicial authorities.

In this case, the anonymous witnesses were questioned at the appeals stage in the presence of counsel by an investigating judge who was aware of their identity, even if the defence was not. The judge noted circumstances on the basis of which the court of appeal was able to draw conclusions as to the reliability of their evidence. In this respect, the present case was to be distinguished from a previous one before the Court. Counsel was not only present, but he was able to ask the witnesses questions he considered to be in the interests of the defence except insofar as they might lead to the disclosure of their identity, and these questions were all answered. In this respect also, the present case differed from that of the previous case.

The Court stated that although it was normally desirable that witnesses should identify a person suspected of serious crimes in person if there was any doubt about his identity, it should be noted in the present case that the two anonymous witnesses concerned in this aspect of the case identified Mr. Doorson from a photograph which

III:2

he himself had acknowledged to be of himself. Moreover, both gave descriptions of his appearance and dress.

It followed from these considerations that in the circumstances, the counterbalancing procedure followed by the judicial authorities in obtaining the evidence of the two witnesses had to be considered sufficient to have enabled the defence to challenge the evidence of the anonymous witnesses and attempt to cast doubt on the reliability of their statements. It did so in open court by, amongst other things, drawing attention to the fact that both were drug addicts.

Finally, the Court stated that it should be recalled that even when counterbalancing procedures were found to compensate sufficiently the handicaps under which the defence laboured, a conviction should not be based either solely or to a decisive extent on anonymous statements. That, however, was not the case here. It was sufficiently clear that the national court did not base its finding of guilt solely or to a decisive extent on the evidence of the two anonymous witnesses.

Furthermore, evidence obtained from witnesses under conditions in which the rights of the defence could not be secured to the extent normally required by the Convention should be treated with extreme care. The Court was satisfied that this was done in the criminal proceedings leading to Mr. Doorson's conviction, as was reflected in the express declaration by the court of appeal that it had treated the statements of the two witnesses with the necessary caution and circumspection.

The Court then considered other aspects of the trial, including the admission as evidence of the statement of a witness whose presence it had been impossible to secure at the trial, but whose statement could be corroborated by other evidence. The Court found no unfairness in this respect. Neither did it find that the fairness of the criminal proceedings was adversely affected by the decision of the court of appeal not to hear an expert witness called by the defence, but to hear one such witness called by the prosecution. The court had refused to hear the expert witness called by the defence, because he would have been unable to contribute to the elucidation of the facts of the case. He would have been able to testify generally to the effect that statements made to the police by drug addicts were often unreliable. The evidence of the expert witness called by the prosecution, a police official, concerned the way in which the police went about obtaining statements from drug addicts and ensuring that these were as reliable as possible.

In conclusion, the Court said that none of the alleged shortcomings considered on their own led it to conclude that the applicant had not received a fair trial. Moreover, it could not find, even if the alleged shortcomings were considered together, that the proceedings as a whole were unfair. Accordingly, the Court held, by seven votes to two, that there had been no violation of article 6, paragraph 1, taken together with article 6, paragraph 3 (*d*), of the Convention.

3. Right to Freedom of Thought, Conscience and Religion

A. INTRODUCTION

Under article 18 of the Universal Declaration of Human Rights, everyone has the right to freedom of thought, conscience and religion. This right includes freedom to change religion or belief and freedom, either alone or in community with others and in public or private, to manifest religion or belief in teaching, practice, worship and observance.

The core element of this right concerns the inner state of mind of an individual. It is when individuals seek to manifest their religion or belief that the right is sometimes subverted, and this is problematic, because freedom of thought and conscience are fundamental to the functioning of democracies and, with freedom of religion, essential to securing respect for human dignity and for the individual.

The right to freedom of thought, conscience and religion is protected by article 18 of the International Covenant on Civil and Political Rights and by provisions included in regional treaties of general application, for example, article 9 of the Convention for the Protection of Human Rights and Fundamental Freedoms. Similarly, the right is given legal force in article 14 of the Convention on the Rights of the Child. Under this provision, the States parties shall respect the right of the child to freedom of thought, conscience and religion as well as the rights and duties of the parents and, when applicable, legal guardians to provide direction to the child in the exercise of his or her right in a manner consistent with the evolving capacities of the child. Such treaty provisions allow, however, for lawful limitations on the freedom to manifest one's religion or beliefs in order to secure other benefits, such as public safety, order and the rights and freedoms of others.

In addition to these instruments, a number of other human rights treaties embody legally binding provisions on religion and belief. For example, article 5 of the International Convention on the Elimination of All Forms of Racial Discrimination requires States parties to guarantee the right of everyone, without distinction as to race, colour, or national or ethnic origin, to equality before the law, including the enjoyment of the right to freedom of thought, conscience and religion. In a regional context, Protocol No. 12 to the Convention for the Protection of Human Rights and Funda-

III:3

mental Freedoms reinforces the general principle of non-discrimination. Under article 1 of the Protocol, the enjoyment of any right set forth by law shall be secured without discrimination on a number of specified grounds, including those of religion and political or other opinion. Furthermore, it requires that no one shall be discriminated against by any public authority on any of these grounds. This treaty is open to States parties to the Convention and entered into force in 2005.

The right to freedom of thought, conscience and religion is further elaborated in a universal non-treaty instrument, the Declaration on the Elimination of All Forms of Intolerance and of Discrimination Based on Religion or Belief, in which the protection of this right, as expressed in article 18, paragraphs 1 to 3, of the Covenant, is reiterated in its article 1. Under article 2 of the Declaration, no one shall be subject to discrimination by any State, institution, group of persons or person on the grounds of religion or other belief. The expression "intolerance and discrimination based on religion or belief" means in this Declaration any distinction, exclusion, restriction or preference based on religion or belief and having as its purpose or as its effect nullification or impairment of the recognition, enjoyment or exercise of human rights and fundamental freedoms on an equal basis. The Declaration then sets out a number of detailed provisions designed to protect the right and to eliminate intolerance and discrimination on grounds of religion or belief.

The United Nations Commission on Human Rights, being seriously concerned by frequent, reliable reports from all parts of the world which revealed that, because of governmental actions, universal implementation of the Declaration had not yet been achieved, established in 1986 a thematic special procedure for the examination of incidents and governmental actions in all parts of the world inconsistent with the provisions of the Declaration and for the recommendation of remedial measures.[1] In carrying out the mandate, the Special Rapporteur on religious intolerance was to seek credible and reliable information from Governments, as well as from specialized agencies, intergovernmental organizations and non-governmental organizations, including communities of religion or belief. The Special Rapporteur was invited to respond effectively to credible and reliable information and to carry out the work with discretion and independence. In 2000, the Commission decided to change the title to Special Rapporteur on freedom of religion or belief.

Under the methods of work, the Special Rapporteur carries out, *inter alia*, the following activities.[2] She adresses the question of the relationship between the State

---

[1] See Commission on Human Rights resolution 1986/20 of 10 March 1986 (United Nations, *Official Records of the Economic and Social Council, 1986, Supplement No. 2* (E/1986/22), chap. II, sect. A).

[2] See United Nations documents E/CN.4/2005/61 and Corr.1, paras. 13 and 14.

and religious communities and the question of non-discrimination between religious communities, as well as intrerreligious and intrareligious tolerance. She undertakes activities that may be articulated around the principles of protection and prevention. She communicates with a wide range of interlocutors to ensure receipt of accurate information; draws the attention of States to possible violations through communications in individual cases, including urgent appeals; undertakes country visits to get in-depth understanding of specific contexts and practices and to provide constructive feedback to the country; collects information on contentious issues and gives indications on how to consider them under international human rights law; and collects information, comments on legislative frameworks in member States and identifies best practices. In carrying out her mandate, she pays special attention to vulnerable groups, such as women, and monitors the impact that State policies have on their situation.

The Special Rapporteur reports annually on her activities to the Commission. She also submits interim reports to the General Assembly of the United Nations.

Issues of religion and discrimination on grounds of religion or belief are sometimes linked to the protection of minority groups or people who in some way are distinctive. The International Labour Organization Convention concerning Indigenous and Tribal Peoples in Independent Countries (No. 169) was adopted in recognition of the aspirations of such peoples to exercise control over their own institutions, ways of life and economic development and to maintain and develop identities, languages and religions within the framework of the States in which they live.

Article 5 of the Convention states, *inter alia*, that in applying its provisions, the social, cultural, religious and spiritual values and practices of indigenous and tribal peoples shall be recognized and protected, and due account shall be taken of the nature of the problems which face them both as groups and as individuals.

In the Framework Convention for the Protection of National Minorities, a treaty signed under the auspices of the Council of Europe, it is stated in the preambular text that a pluralist and genuinely democratic society should not only respect the ethnic, cultural, linguistic and religious identity of each person belonging to a national minority, but also create appropriate conditions enabling them to express, preserve and develop this identity. Under article 7 of the Convention, the States parties shall ensure respect for the right of every person belonging to a national minority to, *inter alia*, freedom of thought, conscience and religion. Article 8 further stipulates that the States parties undertake to recognize that every person belonging to a national minority has the right to manifest his or her religion or belief and to establish religious institutions, organizations and associations.

III:3

The Declaration on the Rights of Persons Belonging to National or Ethnic, Religious and Linguistic Minorities is a non-treaty instrument of universal application, proclaimed by the General Assembly of the United Nations in recognition of the need to ensure even more effective implementation of international human rights instruments with regard to the rights of persons belonging to minorities.

Protection of the right to freedom of thought, conscience and religion is also reinforced by provisions of non-treaty instruments addressed to police officials. Article 2 of the Code of Conduct for Law Enforcement Officials requires law enforcement officials to respect and protect human dignity and maintain and uphold the human rights of all persons. In the explanatory commentary to this article, reference is made to a number of relevant international instruments, first of all the Universal Declaration of Human Rights and the International Covenant on Civil and Political Rights, both of which containing articles protecting the right to freedom thought, conscience and religion. Article 43 of the European Code of Police Ethics is more specific. It requires that police, in carrying out their activities, shall always bear in mind everyone's fundamental rights, such as freedom of thought, conscience, religion, expression, peaceful assembly, movement and the peaceful enjoyment of possessions

Clearly, a State can violate the right to freedom of thought, conscience and religion through its laws or practices or fail to protect the right when, for example, adherents of a religion are prevented from lawfully manifesting their belief by those hostile to it. It is essential that police should recognize the intrinsic importance of this right and its wider significance, for they are one of the means by which a State may protect the right or prevent or reduce social tension or disorder arising out of any failure to do so.

B. REVIEW OF CASES

(a) Human Rights Committee

Article 18 of the International Covenant on Civil and Political Rights protects the right to freedom of thought, conscience and religion. Under paragraph 1, everyone shall have the right to freedom of thought, conscience and religion. This right includes the freedom to have or to adopt a religion or belief of one's choice and the freedom, either individually or in community with others and in public or private, to manifest one's religion or belief in worship, observance, practice and teaching.

Paragraph 2 prohibits subjecting anyone to coercion which would impair his freedom to have or to adopt a religion or belief of his choice. In paragraph 3 it is stated that the freedom to manifest one's religion or beliefs may be subject only to such limitations as are prescribed by law and are necessary to protect public safety, order, health or morals, or the fundamental rights and freedoms of others. Paragraph 4, finally, requires States parties to the Covenant to have respect for the liberty of parents and, where applicable, legal guardians to ensure the religious and moral education of their children in conformity with their own convictions.

The provisions of article 18 are protected from derogation under article 4 of the Covenant. Not even in time of public emergency threatening the life of the nation may a State party take measures derogating from its obligations under article 18.

In its general comment No. 22 (48) on article 18 of the Covenant,[3] the Human Rights Committee observed that the right to freedom of thought, conscience and religion, including the freedom to hold beliefs, in article 18, paragraph 1, was far-reaching and profound. It encompassed the freedom of thought on all matters, personal conviction and the commitment to religion or belief, whether manifested individually or in community with others.

Three cases considered by the Committee in respect of the right to freedom of thought, conscience and religion have been found relevant to the purposes of this publication. In none of these cases was a violation found.

In the case *L. T. K.* v. *Finland*,[4] the author, a Finnish citizen, claimed to be a victim of a breach by Finland of articles 18 and 19 of the Covenant, stating that his status as conscientious objector to military service had not been recognized. In 1983, he had been criminally prosecuted because of his refusal to perform military service and sentenced to a term of imprisonment. He had claimed serious moral considerations based on his ethical convictions for being unable to perform such service, armed or unarmed.

The Committee noted that the author was not prosecuted and sentenced because of his beliefs or opinions as such, but because he had refused to perform military service. It observed that the Covenant did not provide for the right to conscientious objection. Neither article 18 nor article 19 of the Covenant could be construed as implying such a right, especially taking into account the provision in article 8, paragraph 3 (*c*) (ii), that the term "forced or compulsory labour" should not include any service of a military character and, in countries where conscientious objection was recognized, any national service required by law of conscientious objectors. The Committee concluded that the facts submitted by the author in substantiation of his

---

[3] See United Nations document A/48/40 (Part I), annex VI.
[4] See United Nations, *Official Records of the General Assembly, Fortieth Session, Supplement No. 40* (A/40/40), annex XXI, communication No. 185/1984, decision adopted on 9 July 1985.

claim did not raise an issue under any of the provisions of the Covenant. Accordingly, the claim was incompatible with the provisions of the Covenant. The Committee decided that the communication was inadmissible.

Eight years later, the Committee, in its general comment No. 22 (48), stated that the Covenant did not explicitly refer to a right of conscientious objection. The Committee believed, however, that such a right could be derived from article 18, inasmuch as the obligation to use lethal force might seriously conflict with the freedom of conscience and the right to manifest one's religion or belief. When this right was recognized by law or practice, there should be no differentiation among conscientious objectors on the basis of the nature of their particular beliefs. Likewise, there should be no discrimination against conscientious objectors because they had failed to perform military service. The Committee invited the States parties to report on the conditions under which persons could be exempted from military service on the basis of their rights under article 18 of the Covenant and on the nature and length of alternative national service.[5]

These observations suggest that the Committee may now come to a different decision than they did in the *L. T. K.* case.

In the case *K. Singh Bhinder* v. *Canada*,[6] the author, Karnel Singh Bhinder, a naturalized Canadian citizen born in India, claimed to be a victim of a violation by Canada of article 18 of the Covenant. A Sikh by religion, he wore a turban in his daily life and refused to wear safety headgear during his work. This resulted, in 1978, in the termination of his labour contract with the Canadian National Railway Company, where he worked as a maintenance electrician. The author claimed that his right to manifest his religious beliefs under article 18, paragraph 1, had been restricted by virtue of the enforcement of the hard hat regulations. This limitation did not meet the requirements of article 18, paragraph 3. In particular, he argued, the limitation was not necessary to protect public safety, since any safety risk ensuing from his refusal to wear safety headgear was confined to himself.

The Committee noted that in this case, legislation, although on the face of it neutral in that it applied to all persons without distinction, was said to operate in fact in a way discriminating against persons of the Sikh religion. Whilst the author had claimed a violation of article 18 of the Covenant, the Committee also examined the issue in relation to article 26. Under this provision, all persons are equal before the

---

[5] See United Nations document A/48/40 (Part I), annex VI, para. 11.
[6] See United Nations, *Official Records of the General Assembly, Forty-fifth Session, Supplement No. 40* (A/45/40), vol. II, annex IX, sect. E, communication No. 208/1986, views adopted on 9 November 1989.

law and entitled without any discrimination to equal protection of the law. In this respect, the law shall prohibit any discrimination and guarantee to all persons equal and effective protection against discrimination on any ground such as race, colour, sex, language, religion, political or other opinion, national or social origin, property, birth or other status.

In the view of the Committee, whether one approached the issue from the perspective of article 18 or article 26 of the Covenant, the same conclusion had to be reached. If the requirement that a hard hat should be worn was regarded as raising issues under article 18, then it was a limitation that was justified by reference to the grounds laid down in article 18, paragraph 3. If the same requirement was seen as a discrimination de facto against persons of the Sikh religion under article 26, then, applying criteria well established in the jurisprudence of the Committee, the legislation requiring workers in federal employment to be protected from injury and electric shock by the wearing of hard hats was to be regarded as reasonable and directed towards objective purposes that were compatible with the Covenant.

The Committee was, therefore, of the view that the facts placed before it did not disclose a violation of any provision of the Covenant. However, it may be noted that the Committee did not spell out exactly how the hard hat requirement conformed to article 18, paragraph 3. In particular, it is arguable how Mr. Bhinder's non-compliance with that requirement could threaten public safety, order, health or morals, or the fundamental rights and freedoms of others.

In the case *M. A. B., W. A. T. and J.-A. Y. T.* v. *Canada*,[7] the Committee ruled inadmissible a communication submitted by three Canadian citizens claiming to be victims of violations by Canada of a number of articles of the Covenant, including article 18, on account of their prosecution under Canadian narcotic control law. They were members of an organization named "Assembly of the Church of the Universe" whose beliefs and practices involved the care, cultivation, possession, distribution, maintenance, integrity and worship of the "Sacrament" of the Church, which was, in fact, marijuana. Since the foundation of the Church, several of its members, including the alleged victims in the case, had come into conflict with the law because of their relationship with, and worship of, marijuana.

In this case, summarized in section C,[8] the Committee rejected the argument that a belief consisting in the worship and distribution of a narcotic drug could be brought within the scope of article 18 of the Covenant.

---

[7] *Ibidem, Forty-ninth Session, Supplement No. 40* (A/49/40), vol. II, annex X, sect. DD, communication No. 570/1993, decision adopted on 8 April 1994.
[8] See part III, chap. 3, sect. C (*a*) (*infra*, pp. 417-419).

III:3

(*b*) European Court of Human Rights

Article 9 of the Convention for the Protection of Human Rights and Fundamental Freedoms protects the right to freedom of thought, conscience and religion. Under paragraph 1, this right includes freedom to change one's religion or belief and freedom, either alone or in community with others and in public or private, to manifest one's religion or belief, in worship, teaching, practice and observance.

Paragraph 2 states that freedom to manifest one's religion or beliefs shall be subject only to such limitations as are prescribed by law and are necessary in a democratic society in the interests of public safety, for the protection of public order, health or morals or for the protection of the rights and freedoms of others.

Unlike the equivalent provisions in the International Covenant on Civil and Political Rights, the provisions of article 9 of the Convention are not non-derogable. In time of war or other public emergency threatening the life of the nation, States parties may take measures derogating from its obligations under article 9, but only on the conditions set forth in article 15 of the Convention.

In the case *Kokkinakis* v. *Greece*,[9] the European Court of Human rights made some significant prouncements on the importance of the freedom of thought, conscience and religion.

The applicant in this case, Minos Kokkinakos, a Greek national, had for a long time been a Jehovah's Witness. In 1986, he and his wife called at the home of the wife of the cantor at a local Orthodox church, and they engaged in a discussion with her. The cantor informed the police who arrested them. They were convicted under a Greek law prohibiting proselytism. They appealed, but the conviction of Mr. Kokkinakos was upheld.

The Court considered that the impugned measure was in pursuit of a legitimate aim under article 9, paragraph 2, of the Convention, namely the protection of the rights and freedoms of others, relied on by the Government. In determining whether the measur taken at the national level was justified in principle and proportionate, the Court distinguished between bearing Christian witness and improper proselytism. The former corresponded to true evangelism, but the latter represented a corruption and deformation of it. It might take the form of offering material or social advantages with a view to gaining new members for a Church or exerting improper pressure on people in distress or need, and it might even entail the use of violence or

---

[9] See *Publications of the European Court of Human Rights*, Series A: *Judgments and Decisions*, vol. 260-A (1993), application No. 14307/88, judgment of 25 May 1993.

brainwashing. More generally, it was not compatible with the respect for the freedom of thought, conscience and religion of others.

In deciding, by six votes to three, that there had been a violation of article 9 of the Convention, the Court held that the the conviction of Mr. Kokkinakos was not proportionate to the legitimate aim pursued. The Greek courts had not sufficiently specified how the applicant had used improper means during the proselytism, and thus they had failed to establish a pressing social need for the conviction.

Generally on the right to freedom of thought, conscience and religion, as enshrined in article 9 of the Convention, the Court pronounced that this freedom was one of the foundations of a democratic society within the meaning of the Convention. It was, in its religious dimension, one of the most vital elements that go to make up the identity of believers and their conception of life, but it was also a precious asset for atheists, agnostics, sceptics and the unconcerned. The pluralism indissociable from a democratic society, which had been dearly won over the centuries, depended on it.

While religious freedom was primarily a matter of individual conscience, it also implied, *inter alia*, the freedom to manifest one's religion. Bearing witness in words and deeds was bound up with the existence of religious convictions. According to article 9, the Court said, the freedom to manifest one's religion was not only exercisable in community with others, in public and within the circle of those whose faith one shared, but could also be asserted alone and in private. Furthermore, it included in principle the right to try to convince, for example, one's neighbour through teaching, failing which, moreover, the freedom to change one's religion or belief, also enshrined in article 9, would be likely to remain a dead letter.

In the case *Kalaç* v. *Turkey*,[10] summarized in section C,[11] the applicant, Faruk Kalaç, a Turkish national and practising Muslim, born in 1939, had pursued a career as judge advocate in the air force. He submitted that his compulsory retirement in 1990 from this post infringed his freedom of religion on the ground that it was based on his religious beliefs and practices.

In coming to its decision that there had been no violation in this case of article 9 of the Convention, the Court observed that in choosing to pursue a military career, Mr. Kalaç was accepting, of his own accord, a system of military discipline that by its very nature implied the possibility of placing on certain of the rights and freedoms of members of the armed forces limitations incapable of being imposed on civilians.

---

[10] See European Court of Human Rights, *Reports of Judgments and Decisions*, 1997-IV, p. 1199, application No. 20704/92, judgment of 1 July 1997.

[11] See part III, chap. 3, sect. C (*b*) (*infra*, pp. 419-421).

III:3

In any event, the Court accepted the Government's argument that the order for his dismissal was not based on his religious opinions and beliefs or the way he had performed his religious duties, but on his conduct and attitude. According to the Turkish authorities, this conduct breached military discipline and infringed the principle of secularism, the foundation of the Turkish nation, which it was the task of the armed forces to guarantee.

The case *Metropolitan Church of Bessarabia and Others* v. *Moldova*,[12] summarized in section C,[13] concerned the allegations by the Metropolitan Church of Bessarabia and 12 Moldovan nationals, in particular, that the refusal by the Moldovan authorities to recognize the applicant Church, formed in 1992, infringed their freedom of religion and association and that the Church was the victim of discrimination on the ground of religion.

Particularly noteworthy in this judgment is what the Court pronounced on the preservation of pluralism, the proper functioning of democracy and resolving a country's problems through dialogue, without recourse to violence. The Court pointed out that it was the role of the authorities in circumstances of tension not to remove the cause of tension by eliminating pluralism, but to ensure that the competing groups tolerated each other.

In conclusion, the Court considered that the refusal to recognize the applicant Church had such consequences for the applicants' freedom of religion that it could not be regarded as proportionate to the legitimate aim pursued or, accordingly, as necessary in a democratic society. There had been a violation of article 9 of the Convention.

This case hinged upon national law, and the way in which it was applied, and upon government policy. It could only have been resolved, ultimately, by the courts and the Government. However, given the tension and conflict, police inevitably became involved. The applicants reported a number of incidents during which members of the clergy or adherents of the Church were allegedly intimidated or prevented from manifesting their beliefs. Six of these incidents, all referring to police, are described in the summary.

This case is a good illustration of the principle that in such circumstances, the role of the police is to maintain the rule of law and public order so that the matter can be resolved, and the underlying causes of tension and disorder removed or reduced,

---

[12] See European Court of Human Rights, *Reports of Judgments and Decisions*, 2001-XII, p. 81, application No. 45701/99, judgment of 13 December 2001.

[13] See part III, chap. 3, sect. C (*c*) (*infra*, pp. 422-432).

through political action. In carrying out this role, police need to retain absolute impartiality and independence of action.

C. CASE SUMMARIES

(a) *M. A. B., W. A. T. and J.-A. Y. T.* v. *Canada* (**Human Rights Committee**)[14]

The authors of the communication were M. A. B., W. A. T. and J.-A. Y. T., three Canadian citizens and members of an organization named "Assembly of the Church of the Universe", based in Canada. They submitted the communication to the Human Rights Committee on 14 October 1993, claiming to be victims of violations by Canada of articles 9 and 18 and a number of other provisions of the International Covenant on Civil and Political Rights.

The facts

The authors submitted, *inter alia*, the following. They were leading members and plenipotentiaries of the Assembly of the Church of the Universe, whose beliefs and practices, according to the authors, necessarily involved the care, cultivation, possession, distribution, maintenance, integrity and worship of the "Sacrament" of the Church. Whereas they also referred to this "Sacrament" as "God's tree of life", it was generally known under the designation *cannabis sativa* or marijuana.

Since the foundation of the Church, several of its members had come into conflict with the law, as their relationship with, and worship of, marijuana fell within the scope of application of the provisions of the Canadian Narcotic Control Act.

On 17 October 1990, a constable of the Royal Canadian Mounted Police entered the Church's premises in Hamilton, Ontario under the pretext of wishing to join the Church and to purchase the "Church Sacrament". She was offered a few grams of marijuana, which led to the arrest of W. A. T. and J.-A. Y. T. All of the marijuana and money found in their possession were confiscated, and they were ordered to stand trial before a jury, under the terms of section 4 of the Narcotic Control Act. Further investigations into the activities and properties of the Church also led to the arrest and detention of M. A. B.

---

[14] See United Nations, *Official Records of the General Assembly, Forty-ninth Session, Supplement No. 40* (A/49/40), vol. II, annex X, sect. DD, communication No. 570/1993, decision adopted on 8 April 1994.

III:3

The trial of W. A. T. and J.-A. Y. T. was scheduled to commence on 1 November 1993 and the trial of M. A. B. on 14 November 1993. Another action, based on unspecified charges against M. A. B. filed in the course of 1987, was scheduled to be heard during the week beginning 13 December 1993. It was thus obvious that the authors had not yet exhausted available domestic remedies in Canada.

It should be noted that the judicial authorities, before deciding to hear the authors' cases, sought to dismiss their arguments on the basis of frivolousness. From the authors' submission, it appeared that all of their claims based upon alleged violations of their freedom of religion and conscience were indeed dismissed by the Canadian courts.

The authors complained that they were denied a fair and public hearing before an impartial and independent tribunal. They contended that their previous court actions and constitutional challenges in the Federal Court of Canada, directed against the action or inaction of the Ontario courts and the Attorney-General, both at the provincial and federal levels, had not been heard. It was apparent from the authors' submission that they contended that there was no independent or impartial forum in Canada to hear their complaint.

The authors further contended that a number of rights had been violated, including their right not to be subjected to arbitrary arrest and detention; their right to freedom of thought, conscience and religion and to manifest these beliefs in worship, practice and religion; and their right to be free from any coercion which would impair their freedom to have or to adopt a religion or belief of their choice.

The authors requested the Committee to intercede to stop the proceedings instituted against them. They also requested, *inter alia*, the Committee to issue a writ of prohibition preventing the Canadian Government and its agencies from persecuting and prosecuting the authors regarding the manifestation of their religious beliefs in worship, observance, practice and teaching pertaining to the cultivation, distribution and use of the "Church Sacrament".

Issues and proceedings before the Committee

In deciding whether or not this communication was admissible under the Optional Protocol to the International Covenant on Civil and Political Rights, the Committee examined whether the facts as submitted would raise *prima facie* issues under any provision of the Covenant. It concluded that they did not. In particular, a belief consisting primarily or exclusively in the worship and distribution of a narcotic drug could not conceivably be brought within the scope of article 18 of the Covenant, nor could arrest for the possession and distribution of a narcotic drug conceivably come within the scope of article 9, paragraph 1, concerning freedom from arbitrary arrest and detention.

The Committee further observed that the conditions for declaring a communication admissible included, *inter alia*, that the claims submitted had to be sufficiently substantiated and that they did not constitute an abuse of the right of submission. The authors' communication revealed that these conditions had not been met. In particular, the allegations against the judicial authorities of Canada were of a sweeping nature and had not been substantiated in such a way as to show how the authors would qualify as victims within the meaning of article 1 of the Optional Protocol to the Covenant. This situation justified doubts about the seriousness of the authors' claims under article 14 of the Covenant and led the Committee to conclude that they constituted an abuse of the right of submission under article 3 of the Optional Protocol.

The Committee therefore decided that the communication was inadmissible under articles 2 and 3 of the Optional Protocol.

(b) Kalaç v. Turkey
(European Court of Human Rights)[15]

The case was referred to the European Court of Human Rights on 19 April 1996 by the European Commission of Human Rights and on 3 July 1996 by the Government of the Republic of Turkey. It originated in an application against Turkey lodged with the Commission on 13 July 1992 by Faruk Kalaç, a Turkish national. The object of the Commission's request and of the Government's application was to obtain a decision as to whether the facts disclosed a breach by the respondent State of its obligations under article 9 of the Convention for the Protection of Human Rights and Fundamental Freedoms.

The facts

Mr. Kalaç, born in 1939, was a judge advocate in the air force. In 1990, he was serving, with the rank of group captain, as the high command's director of legal affairs.

By an order of 1 August 1990, the Supreme Military Council ordered the retirement of three officers, including Mr. Kalaç, and 28 non-commissioned officers for breaches of discipline and scandalous conduct. The decision, which was based on various types of legislation governing the armed forces, made the specific criticism in Mr. Kalaç's case that his conduct and attitude revealed that he had adopted unlawful fun-

---

[15] See European Court of Human Rights, *Reports of Judgments and Decisions*, 1997-IV, p. 1199, application No. 20704/92, judgment of 1 July 1997.

III:3

damentalist opinions. In a judgement of 30 May 1991, the Supreme Administrative Court of the Armed Forces ruled, by four votes to three, that it did not have jurisdiction to entertain the application by Mr. Kalaç to set aside the order of 1 August 1990 on the ground that under article 125 of the Constitution, decisions of the Supreme Military Council were final and not subject to judicial review.

The law

The applicant submitted that his compulsory retirement from his post as judge advocate infringed his freedom of religion on the ground that it was based on his religious beliefs and practices. He relied on article 9 of the Convention, protecting the right to freedom of thought, conscience and religion.

The applicant argued that domestic law gave no indication of what the expression "unlawful fundamentalist opinions", given as grounds for his compulsory retirement, should be understood to mean. As a practising Muslim, he prayed five times a day and kept the fast of Ramadan. The documents produced by the Government, for the first time when the proceedings were already before the Court, did not constitute evidence of his alleged membership of the Muslim fundamentalist Süleyman sect. He had been unaware of its existence. Moreover, the Supreme Military Council's decision infringed the principle of judges' security of tenure, set forth in article 139 of the Constitution.

The Government argued that the question whether Mr. Kalaç should be allowed to remain a member of the armed forces lay at the heart of the problem submitted to the Court. His compulsory retirement was not an interference with his freedom of conscience, religion or belief. It was intended to remove from the military legal service a person who had manifested his lack of loyalty to the foundation of the Turkish nation, namely secularism, which it was the task of the armed forces to guarantee. Mr. Kalaç belonged to the Süleyman sect as a matter of fact, if not formally. He participated in the activities of the Süleyman community, which was known to have unlawful fundamentalist tendencies. Various documents showed that Mr. Kalaç had given it legal assistance, had taken part in training sessions and had intervened on a number of occasions in the appointment of servicemen who were members of the sect.

The Government further pointed out that facilities to practise one's religion within the armed forces in Turkey were provided for both Muslims and the adherents of other faiths. However, the protection of article 9 of the Convention could not extend, in the case of a serviceman, to membership of a fundamentalist movement, insofar as the activities of its members were likely to upset the army's hierarchical equilibrium.

The Commission took the view that the compulsory retirement of Mr. Kalaç constituted interference with the right guaranteed by article 9, paragraph 1, of the Convention. It concluded that there had been a breach of that provision on the ground that the interference was not prescribed by law within the meaning of article 9, paragraph 2, finding that the relevant provisions did not afford adequate protection against arbitrary decisions.

The Court reiterated that while religious freedom was primarily a matter of individual conscience, it also implied, *inter alia*, freedom to manifest one's religion not only in community with others, in public and within the circle of those whose faith one shared, but also alone and in private. Article 9 of the Convention listed a number of forms which the manifestation of one's religion or belief might take, namely worship, teaching, practice and observance. Nevertheless, article 9 did not protect every act motivated or inspired by a religion or belief. Moreover, in exercising his freedom to manifest his religion, an individual might need to take his specific situation into account.

In choosing to pursue a military career, Mr. Kalaç was accepting, of his own accord, a system of military discipline that by its very nature implied the possibility of placing on certain of the rights and freedoms of members of the armed forces limitations incapable of being imposed on civilians, as the Court had pronounced in a previous judgment. States might adopt for their armies disciplinary regulations forbidding this or that type of conduct, in particular an attitude inimical to an established order reflecting the requirements of military service.

It was not contested that the applicant, within the limits imposed by the requirements of military life, was able to fulfil the obligations which constituted the normal forms through which a Muslim practised his religion. For example, he was in particular permitted to pray five times a day and to perform his other religious duties, such as keeping the fast of Ramadan and attending Friday prayers at the mosque.

The Supreme Military Council's order was, moreover, not based on the religious opinions and beliefs of Mr. Kalaç or the way in which he had performed his religious duties, but on his conduct and attitude. According to the Turkish authorities, this conduct breached military discipline and infringed the principle of secularism.

The Court accordingly concluded that the applicant's compulsory retirement did not amount to an interference with the right guaranteed by article 9 of the Convention, since it was not prompted by the way he manifested his religion. Therefore, there was no breach of that article.

III:3

(c) *Metropolitan Church of Bessarabia and Others* v. *Moldova*
(European Court of Human Rights)[16]

The case was transmitted to the European Court of Human Rights on 1 November 1998. It originated in an application against the Republic of Moldova lodged with the European Commission of Human Rights on 3 June 1998 by the Metropolitan Church of Bessarabia and 12 Moldovan nationals, named in the judgment. The applicants alleged in particular that the refusal by the Moldovan authorities to recognize the Metropolitan Church of Bessarabia infringed their freedom of religion and association and that this Church was the victim of discrimination on the ground of religion. They invoked, *inter alia*, articles 9 and 14 of the Convention for the Protection of Human Rights and Fundamental Freedoms.

The facts

The Metropolitan Church of Bessarabia was an autonomous Orthodox Church having canonical jurisdiction in the territory of the Republic of Moldova. The other applicants were members of the eparchic council of the Church.

On 14 September 1992, the individual applicants formed the applicant Church. According to its articles of association, it took the place, from the canon-law point of view, of the Metropolitan Church of Bessarabia that had existed until 1944. In December 1992, it was attached to the patriarchate of Bucharest.

The applicant Church adopted articles of association which determined, among other matters, the composition and administration of its organs, the training, recruitment and disciplinary supervision of its clergy, the ecclesiastical hierarchy and rules concerning its assets. The principles governing the organization and operation of the Church were defined in the preamble to the articles of association.

At the time of the application, the Church had established 117 communities in Moldovan territory, three communities in Ukraine, one in Lithuania, one in Latvia, two in the Russian Federation and one in Estonia. The communities in Latvia and Lithuania had been recognized by the State authorities and had legal personality. Nearly one million Moldovan nationals were affiliated to the Church, which had more than 160 clergy. The Church was recognized by all the Orthodox patriarchates with the exception of that of Moscow.

Pursuant to Moldova's legislation on religious denominations, requiring denominations active in the territory to be recognized by means of a government decision, the

---

[16] *Ibidem*, 2001-XII, p. 81, application No. 45701/99, judgment of 13 December 2001.

Church applied for recognition in 1992. It received no reply. It made two further applications in 1995, but these were refused by the Religious Affairs Department.

The applicants launched a series of legal challenges to this refusal up to, and including, the Supreme Court of Justice, which considered that the case was simply an administrative dispute within a single Church. It could be settled only by the Metropolitan Church of Moldova, since any interference by the State in the matter might aggravate the situation. The Supreme Court held that the State's refusal to intervene in this conflict was compatible with article 9, paragraph 2, of the Convention.

On 15 March 1999, the applicants again applied to the Government for recognition. The Prime Minister refused on the ground that the Metropolitan Church of Bessarabia was not a religious denomination in the legal sense, but a schismatic group within the Metropolitan Church of Moldova. He informed the applicants that the Government would not allow their application until a religious solution to the conflict had been found, following the negotiations in progress between the patriarchates of Russia and Romania.

In addition to legal proceedings on this matter, there were discussions and consultations at the political level. For example, the Government asked several of its ministries for their opinion about whether or not to recognize the applicant Church. They all responded that they were in favour of, or had no objection to, its recognition. However, the Religious Affairs Department expressed concern on a number of grounds, including that the activity of the group was causing religious and socio-political tension in Moldova. If nothing were done to put a stop to its activities, the result would be destabilization not just of the Orthodox Church, but the whole of Moldovan society

In an opinion on the application by the Republic of Moldova for membership of the Council of Europe, the Parliamentary Assembly of that organization noted Moldova's willingness to fulfil the commitments it had entered into when it lodged its application. These commitments, reaffirmed before the adoption of the opinion, included an undertaking to confirm complete freedom of worship for all citizens without discrimination and to ensure a peaceful solution to the dispute between the Moldovan Orthodox Church and the Bessarabian Orthodox Church.

The applicants reported a number of incidents, not disputed by the Government, during which members of the clergy or adherents of the applicant Church were allegedly intimidated or prevented from manifesting their beliefs. This was illustrated, *inter alia*, by the following incidents.

III:3

- The chairman of a parish council was urged by the mayor to persuade the villagers to accept the removal of a priest of the Church from office, but he refused. The chairman was then arrested, pinned down by five policemen, thrown into a police van and taken to the town hall where he was savagely beaten. He was then taken into police custody where he was upbraided for showing favour to the Church. He was not informed of the reasons for his arrest and was released after being detained for three days. Thereafter, the priest left the parish.

- Following a number of actions directed against a parish priest, several people, led by a priest of the Metropolitan Church of Moldova, violently assaulted the priest drawing blood and asked him to join their Church. They also attacked the priest's wife, tearing her clothes. The priest managed to escape into the church where a service was taking place, but he was pursued by his assailants who began to fight with the congregation. A police official sent to the scene managed to persuade the aggressors to leave the church.

- Following the death of a parish priest, an individual applicant in the present case was appointed as his replacement. A church was then occupied by representatives of the Metropolitan Church of Moldova who locked it and prevented the adherents of the applicant Church from entering. The police issued a summons against this applicant for organizing a public meeting in front of the church without first obtaining the authorization required for public meetings. A judge later discontinued the proceedings on the ground that the applicant had not organized a meeting, but had merely celebrated a mass in his capacity as priest at the request of about a hundred believers who were present. The judge also noted that the mass had been celebrated on the square, as the church door had been locked.

- A grenade was thrown into the house of a member of the clergy of the Church. He was later threatened by six people unknown to him, and he lodged a criminal complaint. In a letter to the President of Moldova, the Minister of the Interior expressed his regret about the slow progress of the investigations into that person's complaints, and he informed him that disciplinary penalties had been imposed on the police officers responsible for the inquiry.

- Late one night, a parish priest was woken by the sound of people trying to force open the presbytery door. He was threatened with death if he did not give up the idea of creating a new parish. When later threatened with death by a priest of the Metropolitan Church of Moldova, he complained to the police.

- A parish priest and his family received threats on a number of occasions from various priests of the Metropolitan Church of Moldova. The windows of his house were broken, and he was attacked in the street and beaten by strangers who told him not to meddle with "those things" any more. The priest consulted a forensic physician who issued a certificate detailing the injuries that had been inflicted on him. He subsequently lodged a criminal complaint with the police.

The law

As to the alleged violations of article 9 of the Convention, the applicants claimed that the refusal by the Moldovan authorities to recognize the Metropolitan Church of Bessarabia infringed their freedom of religion, since only religions recognized by the Government could be practised in Moldova. They asserted in particular that their freedom to manifest their religion in community with others was frustrated by the fact that they were prohibited from gathering together for religious purposes and by the complete absence of judicial protection of the assets of the Church. They relied on article 9 of the Convention, protecting the right to freedom of thought, conscience and religion.

The Court noted that, according to the Moldovan legislation on religious denominations, only religions recognized by government decision might be practised. It observed that not being recognized, the applicant Church could not operate. In particular, its priests could not conduct divine service, its members could not meet to practise their religion and not having legal personality, it was not entitled to judicial protection of its assets.

The Court therefore considered that the refusal by the Moldovan Government to recognize the Church, upheld by the decision of the Supreme Court of Justice, constituted interference with the right of the Church and the other applicants to freedom of religion, as guaranteed by article 9, paragraph 1, of the Convention.

In order to determine whether or not that interference entailed a breach of the Convention, the Court had then to decide whether it satisfied the requirements of article 9, paragraph 2. It had to be prescribed by law, to pursue a legitimate aim for the purposes of that provision and to be necessary in a democratic society.

The Court made reference to its established case law to the effect that the terms "prescribed by law" and "in accordance with the law", in articles 8 to 11 of the Convention, not only required that the impugned measures had some basis in domestic law, but also referred to the quality of the law in question. It had to be sufficiently accessible and foreseeable as to its effects to enable the individual to regulate his conduct. Furthermore, the law had to indicate with sufficient clarity the scope of any legal discretion granted to the executive in order to afford a measure of legal protection against arbitrary interferences by public authorities with the rights guaranteed by the Convention.

III:3

In the present case, the Court noted that the law required religious denominations to be recognized by a government decision. Only denominations whose practices and rites were compatible with the Moldovan Constitution and legislation might be recognized. Without giving a categorical answer to the question whether these provisions satisfied the requirements of foreseeability and precision, the Court was prepared to accept that the interference in question was prescribed by law before deciding whether it pursued a legitimate aim and was necessary in a democratic society.

The Government submitted that the refusal to allow the application for recognition lodged by the applicants was intended to protect public order and public safety. The Moldovan State had an ethnically and linguistically varied population, and religion was a factor conducive to stability. Consequently, recognition of the Moldovan Orthodox Church, which was subordinate to the patriarchate of Moscow, had enabled the entire population to come together within that Church. If the applicant Church should be recognized, that tie was likely to be loosened and the Orthodox Christian population dispersed among a number of Churches. Moreover, under cover of the applicant Church, which was subordinate to the patriarchate of Bucharest, political forces acting hand-in-glove with Romanian interests favourable to reunification between Bessarabia and Romania were working. Recognition of the Church would therefore revive old Russo-Romanian rivalries within the population, thus endangering social stability and even Moldova's territorial integrity.

The applicants denied that the measure complained of had been intended to protect public order and public safety. They alleged that the Government had not shown that the Church had constituted a threat to public order and public safety.

Making reference to its case law, the Court considered that States were entitled to verify whether a movement or association carried on, ostensibly in pursuit of religious aims, activities that were harmful to the population or to public safety. The Court concluded that the interference complained of in this case pursued a legitimate aim under article 9, paragraph 2, of the Convention, namely the protection of public order and public safety.

Regarding the requirement "necessary in a democratic society", the Court referred to its settled case law to the effect that, as enshrined in article 9 of the Convention, freedom of thought, conscience and religion was one of the foundations of a democratic society within the meaning of the Convention. It was, in its religious dimension, one of the most vital elements that go to make up the identity of believers and their conception of life, but it was also a precious asset for atheists, agnostics, sceptics and the unconcerned. The pluralism indissociable from a democratic society, which had been dearly won over the centuries, depended on it.

While religious freedom was primarily a matter of individual conscience, it also implied, *inter alia*, the freedom to manifest one's religion alone and in private or in community with others, in public and within the circle of those whose faith one shared. Bearing witness in words and deeds was bound up with the existence of religious convictions. That freedom entailed, the Court reiterated, the freedom to hold or not to hold religious beliefs and to practise or not to practise a religion. Article 9 of the Convention listed a number of forms which the manifestation of one's religion or belief might take, namely worship, teaching, practice and observance. Nevertheless, as the Court had found in a previous judgment, article 9 did not protect every act motivated or inspired by a religion or belief.

The Court had also said that in a democratic society in which several religions coexisted within one and the same population, it might be necessary to place restrictions on this freedom in order to reconcile the interests of the various groups and ensure that everyone's beliefs were respected. However, in exercising its regulatory power in this sphere and in its relations with the various religions, denominations and beliefs, the State had a duty to remain neutral and impartial. At stake here, the Court reiterated, was the preservation of pluralism and the proper functioning of democracy. One of the principle characteristics of the latter was the possibility it offered of resolving a country's problems through dialogue without recourse to violence, even when they were irksome. Accordingly, the role of the authorities in such circumstances was not to remove the cause of tension by eliminating pluralism, but to ensure that the competing groups tolerated each other.

The Court further observed that in principle the right to freedom of religion for the purposes of the Convention excluded assessment by the State of the legitimacy of religious beliefs or the ways in which those beliefs were expressed. State measures favouring a particular leader or specific organs of a divided religious community or seeking to compel the community or part of it to place itself, against its will, under a single leadership, would also constitute an infringement of the freedom of religion. In democratic societies, the State did not need to take measures to ensure that religious communities remained or were brought under a unified leadership. Similarly, where the exercise of the right to freedom of religion or of one of its aspects was subject under domestic law to a system of prior authorization, involvement in the procedure for granting authorization of a recognized ecclesiastical authority could not be reconciled with the requirements of article 9, paragraph 2, of the Convention.

Moreover, since religious communities traditionally existed in the form of organized structures, article 9 had to be interpreted in the light of article 11 of the Convention, safeguarding associative life against unjustified State interference. Seen in that perspective, the right of believers to freedom of religion, including the right to manifest one's religion in community with others, encompassed the expectation that believers

III:3

would be allowed to associate freely, without arbitrary State intervention. Indeed, the autonomous existence of religious communities was indispensable for pluralism in a democratic society and was thus an issue at the very heart of the protection afforded by article 9.

In addition, making reference to its case law, the Court said that one of the means of exercising the right to manifest one's religion, especially for a religious community in its collective dimension, was the possibility of ensuring judicial protection of the community, its members and its assets. Consequently, article 9 had to be seen not only in the light of article 11, but also of article 6 of the Convention.

According to its settled case law, the Court left to States parties to the Convention a certain margin of appreciation in deciding whether, and to what extent, an interference was necessary, but that went hand in hand with European supervision of both the relevant legislation and the decisions applying it. The Court's task was to ascertain whether the measures taken at national level were justified in principle and proportionate.

In order to determine the scope of the margin of appreciation in the present case, the Court reiterated that it had to take into account what was at stake, namely the need to maintain true religious pluralism, which was inherent in the concept of a democratic society. Similarly, a good deal of weight had to be given to that need when determining, as article 9, paragraph 2, of the Convention required, whether the interference corresponded to a pressing social need and was proportionate to the legitimate aim pursued. In exercising its supervision, the Court had to consider the interference complained of on the basis of the file as a whole.

The Government submitted that the interference complained of was necessary in a democratic society, because in recognizing the applicant Church, the State would have to give up its position of neutrality in religious matters. Furthermore, the refusal to recognize it was necessary for national security and Moldovan territorial integrity, regard being had to the fact that the Church engaged in political activities, working towards the reunification of Moldova with Romania, with the latter country's support. The Government substantiated its assertions by mentioning articles in the Romanian press favourable to recognition of the Church by the Moldovan authorities and reunification of Moldova with Romania. The Church was supported by openly pro-Romanian Moldovan parties denying the specificity of Moldova, thus destabilizing the Moldovan State. The refusal to recognize the Church had also been necessary to preserve social peace and understanding among believers. The aggressive attitude of the Church, which sought to draw other Orthodox Christians to it and to swallow up the other Churches, had led to a number of incidents which, without police intervention, could have caused injury or loss of life.

The applicants submitted that the refusal to recognize the Metropolitan Church of Bessarabia was not necessary in a democratic society. There was nothing in the file to show that the applicants had carried on, intended or sought to carry on activities capable of undermining Moldovan territorial integrity, national security or public order.

Non-recognition had made it impossible for the members of the Church to practise their religion. The State provided its protection only to recognized denominations, and only those denominations could defend their rights in the courts. Consequently, the clergy and members of the Church had not been able to defend themselves against the physical attacks and persecution they had suffered, and the Church had not been able to protect its assets. The applicants denied that the State had tolerated the Church and its members. They alleged, on the contrary, not only that State agents had permitted acts of intimidation which members of the Church had suffered at the hands of other believers, but also that, in a number of cases, State agents had participated in such acts.

The Court then examined in turn the arguments put forward by the respondent Government in justification of the interference and the proportionality of that interference in relation to the aims pursued. It noted that the Moldovan Constitution guaranteed the freedom of religion and enunciated the principle of autonomy of religious denominations *vis-à-vis* the State. The legislation on religious denominations laid down a procedure for the recognition of such denominations. The Government submitted that it was in order to comply with these principles, including the duty of neutrality as between denominations, that the applicant Church had been refused recognition and instead told first to settle its differences with the already recognized Church from which it wished to split, namely the Metropolitan Church of Moldova.

The Court noted first of all that the applicant Church lodged a first application for recognition in 1992 to which no reply was forthcoming and that it was only later, in 1993, that the State recognized the Metropolitan Church of Moldova. That being so, the Court found it difficult, at least for the period preceding recognition of the latter Church, to understand the Government's argument that the applicant Church was only a schismatic group within the Metropolitan Church of Moldova, which had been recognized.

In any event, the Court observed that the State's duty of neutrality and impartiality, as defined in its case law, was incompatible with any power on the State's part to assess the legitimacy of religious beliefs. It required the State to ensure that conflicting groups tolerated each other, even where they originated in the same group. In the present case, the Court considered that by taking the view that the applicant Church was not a new denomination and by making its recognition depend on the will of an

III:3

ecclesiastical authority that had been recognized, the Government had failed to discharge its duty of neutrality and impartiality. Consequently, the argument that refusing recognition was necessary in order to uphold Moldovan law and the Moldovan Constitution had to be rejected.

Regarding the argument of threat to territorial integrity, the Court noted in the first place that in the Church's articles of association, in particular in the preamble thereto, it defined itself as an autonomous local Church, operating within Moldovan territory in accordance with the laws of that State. Its name was a historical one having no link with current or previous political situations. Although its activity was mainly religious, the Church stated that it was also prepared to cooperate with the State in the fields of culture, education and social assistance. It further declared that it had no political activity. The Court considered those principles to be clear and perfectly legitimate.

At the hearing before the Court, the Government nevertheless submitted that in reality the Church was engaged in political activities contrary to Moldovan public policy and that, if it should be recognized, such activities would endanger Moldovan territorial integrity.

The Court reiterated that it could not be ruled out that an organization's programme might conceal objectives and intentions different from those it proclaimed. In verifying that it did not, the Court had to compare the content of the programme with the organization's actions and the positions it defended. In the present case, the Court noted that there was nothing in the file warranting the conclusion that the Church carried on activities other than those stated in its articles of association. As to the invoked press articles, although their content, as described by the Government, revealed ideas favourable to reunification of Moldova with Romania, they could not be imputed to the Church. Moreover, the Government had not argued that the Church had prompted such articles.

Similarly, in the absence of any evidence, the Court could not conclude that the Church was linked to the political activities of Moldovan organizations allegedly working towards unification of Moldova with Romania. Furthermore, it noted that the Government had not contended that the activity of these associations and political parties was illegal.

As for the possibility that the Church, once recognized, might constitute a danger to national security and territorial integrity, the Court considered that this was a mere hypothesis which, in the absence of corroboration, could not justify a refusal to recognize it.

The Court noted that the Government did not dispute that incidents had taken place at meetings of the adherents and members of the clergy of the Church. In particular, conflicts had occurred when priests belonging to the Church tried to celebrate mass in places of worship to which the adherents and clergy of the Metropolitan Church of Moldova laid claim for their exclusive use or in places where certain persons were opposed to the presence of the Church on the ground that it was illegal.

On the other hand, the Court noted that there were certain points of disagreement between the applicants and the Government about what took place during these incidents. Without expressing an opinion on exactly what took place during the events concerned, the Court noted that the refusal to recognize the Church played a role in the incidents.

The Government submitted that although the authorities had not recognized the Church, they acted in a spirit of tolerance and permitted it to continue its activities without hindrance. In particular, its members could meet, pray together and manage assets. As evidence, they cited the numerous activities of the Church.

The Court noted that under the law, only religions recognized by a government decision might be practised in Moldova. In particular, only a recognized denomination had legal personality, might produce and sell specific liturgical objects and engage clergy and employees. In addition, associations whose aims were wholly or partly religious were subject to the obligations arising from the legislation on religious denominations.

That being so, the Court noted that in the absence of recognition, the Church might neither organize itself nor operate. Lacking legal personality, it could not bring legal proceedings to protect its assets, which were indispensable for worship, while its members could not meet to carry on religious activities without contravening the legislation on religious denominations. Regarding the tolerance allegedly shown by the Government towards the Church and its members, the Court could not regard such tolerance as a substitute for recognition, since recognition alone was capable of conferring rights on those concerned.

The Court further noted that on occasion, the applicants had not been able to defend themselves against acts of intimidation, since the authorities had fallen back on the excuse that only legal activities were entitled to legal protection.

Lastly, it noted that when the authorities had recognized other liturgical associations, they had not applied the criteria used in order to refuse to recognize the applicant Church and that no justification had been put forward by the Government for this difference in treatment.

III:3

In conclusion, the Court considered that the refusal to recognize the Church had such consequences for the applicants' freedom of religion that it could not be regarded as proportionate to the legitimate aim pursued or, accordingly, as necessary in a democratic society. There had been a violation of article 9 of the Convention.

As to the alleged violations of other articles of the Convention, the Court found that there had been a violation of article 13 on the right to an effective remedy, as the applicants had been unable to obtain redress from a national authority in respect of their complaint relating to their right to freedom of religion. Concerning the remaining allegations, the Court found no cause to examine them separately.

In respect of article 41 of the Convention, allowing the Court to afford just satisfaction to an injured party, under specified circumstances, when there had been a violation of the Convention, the Court considered that the violations it had found in this case must undoubtedly have caused the applicants non-pecuniary damage which it assessed, on an equitable basis, at 20,000 euros. The Court also awarded the applicants the sum of 7,025 euros for costs and expenses, plus any sum which might be chargeable in value-added tax.

4. Right to Freedom of Opinion and Expression

A. INTRODUCTION

The right to freedom of opinion and expression is of great significance to the individual and to society as a whole. It is essential for an individual's development and human dignity, and for genuine political democracy in a society. It is expressed in article 19 of the Universal Declaration of Human Rights. Under this provision, everyone has the right to freedom of opinion and expression. This right includes freedom to hold opinions without interference and to seek, receive and impart information and ideas through any media and regardless of frontiers.

The right to freedom of opinion and expression is protected by article 19 of the International Covenant on Civil and Political Rights and by provisions in regional treaties of general application, such as article 13 of the American Convention on Human Rights and article 10 of the Convention for the Protection of Human Rights and Fundamental Freedoms. In respect of children, there is similar protection afforded in article 13 of the Convention on the Rights of the Child. The right of children to freedom of expression is further reinforced by article 12 of the Convention. States parties shall assure to the child who is capable of forming his or her own views the right to express those views freely in all matters affecting the child, the views of the child being given due weight in accordance with the age and maturity of the child.

Treaty provisions giving legal force to the right to freedom of opinion and expression embody limitation clauses that allow for restrictions on the right. In article 19 of the Covenant, for example, it is stated that the exercise of the right to freedom of expression carries with it special duties and responsibilities. It may therefore be subject to certain restrictions, provided by law and necessary for various reasons that include national security or public order. Under article 20, any propaganda for war shall be prohibited by law, as shall any advocacy of national, racial or religious hatred that constitutes incitement to discrimination, hostility or violence.

Apart from these instruments, there are provisions in other treaties protecting the right to freedom of opinion and expression. Under article 5 of the International Convention on the Elimination of All Forms of Racial Discrimination, for example, the States parties undertake to guarantee the right of everyone, without distinction as to

III:4

race, colour, or national or ethnic origin, to equality before the law, including the enjoyment of the right to freedom of opinion and expression. However, there are provisions embodying significant restrictions on this right in article 4 of the Convention. States parties condemn all propaganda and all organizations which are based on ideas or theories of superiority of one race or group of persons of one colour or ethnic origin, or which attempt to justify or promote racial hatred and discrimination in any form. They undertake to adopt immediate and positive measures designed to eradicate all incitement to, or acts of, such discrimination. To this end, and with due regard to the principles in the Universal Declaration and article 5 of the Convention, they shall declare an offence punishable by law, *inter alia*, all dissemination of ideas based on racial superiority or hatred. Furthermore, they shall declare illegal and prohibit propaganda activities that promote and incite racial discrimination, and they shall recognize participation in such activities as an offence punishable by law.

As in the case of the right to freedom of thought, conscience and religion, special protection is afforded national minorities in respect of the right to freedom of opinion and expression, for example, in the Framework Convention for the Protection of National Minorities. Under article 7 of this regional treaty, the States parties shall ensure respect for the right of every person belonging to a national minority to, *inter alia*, freedom of expression. In article 9 of the Convention, they undertake to recognize that this right includes freedom to hold opinions and to receive and impart information and ideas in the minority language without interference by public authorities and regardless of frontiers. Furthermore, they shall ensure, within the framework of their legal systems, that persons belongning to a national minority are not discriminated against in their access to media.

The Special Rapporteur on the promotion and protection of the right to freedom of opinion and expression implements a thematic special procedure of the United Nations Commission on Human Rights. Under the mandate, originally established in 1993,[1] the Special Rapporteur is requested to gather all relevant information, wherever it might occur, of discrimination against, threats or use of violence and harassment, including persecution and intimidation, directed at professionals in the field of information, as a matter of high priority, and at other persons seeking to exercise or to promote the exercise of the right to freedom of opinion and expression. The Special Rapporteur is further requested to seek and receive credible and reliable information from Governments, non-governmental organizations and from any other parties who have knowledge of these cases.

---

[1] See Commission on Human Rights resolution 1993/45 of 5 March 1993 (United Nations, *Official Records of the Economic and Social Council, 1993, Supplement No. 3* (E/1993/23 and Corr. 2, 4 and 5), chap. II, sect. A).

The methods of work of the Special Rapporteur describe the activities carried out under the mandate.[2] He seeks information using a wide range of sources and considers communications in dialogue with the Governments concerned. He adopts an urgent action procedure for cases that are of life-threatening nature. He seeks to hold consultations with all persons and organizations of interest to him in the fulfilment of the mandate, and he undertakes on-site visits. Finally, he carries out his mandate in cooperation with others implementing human rights procedures, such as the Special Rapporteur on freedom of religion or belief and the Working Group on Arbitrary Detention.

The Special Rapporteur reports annually to the Commission on the activities relating to the mandate. The reports contain recommendations and provide suggestions on ways and means to promote and protect better the right to freedom of opinion and expression in all its manifestations.

Under article 1 of the Declaration on the Right and Responsibility of Individuals, Groups and Organs of Society to Promote and Protect Universally Recognized Human Rights and Fundamental Freedoms, a non-treaty instrument, everyone has the right, individually and in association with others, to promote and to strive for the protection and realization of human rights and fundamental freedoms at the national and international levels. This right includes, as set forth in article 6 of the Declaration, *inter alia*, to know, seek, obtain, receive and hold information about all human rights and fundamental freedoms; to publish, impart or disseminate freely to others views, information and knowledge in respect of such rights and freedoms; and to study, discuss, form and hold opinions on the observance, both in law and in practice, of all human rights and fundamental freedoms and to draw public attention to those matters.

In 2000, the United Nations Commission on Human Rights, in considering the question of human rights defenders,[3] noted with deep concern that in many countries, persons and organizations engaged in promoting and defending human rights and fundamental freedoms were often subjected to threats, harassment, insecurity, arbitrary detention and extrajudicial executions. The Commission requested the Secretary-General of the United Nations to appoint a special representative to report on the situation of human rights defenders in all parts of the world and on possible means to enhance their protection in full compliance with the Declaration. The Spe-

---

[2] See United Nations document E/CN.4/1995/32, paras. 56-70.

[3] See Commission on Human Rights resolution 2000/61 of 26 April 2000 (United Nations, *Official Records of the Economic and Social Council, 2000, Supplement No. 3* (E/2000/23 and Corr.1), chap. II, sect. A).

cial Representative submits annual reports on the activities to the Commission and to the General Assembly of the United Nations.

Protection of the right to freedom of opinion and expression is also reinforced by provisions, addressed to police officials, of the same non-treaty instruments as referred to in the introduction to the chapter on the right to freedom of thought, conscience and religion.[4] Article 2 of the Code of Conduct for Law Enforcement Officials sets out a general requirement for law enforcement officials to respect and protect human dignity and maintain and uphold human rights, including, pursuant to the explanatory commentary to this article, the right to freedom of opinion and expression as protected by the Universal Declaration of Human Rights and the International Covenant on Civil and Political Rights. Article 43 of the European Code of Police Ethics requires police, in carrying out their activities, always to bear in mind everyone's fundamental rights, among them the freedom of expression.

These provisions are important, because the majority of cases summarized and/or reviewed in this chapter of the book concern suppression, or attempts at suppression, by Governments of the right to freedom of expression of political opponents or of people criticizing forms of government, government policies or state institutions. Furthermore, in some instances, police are the means by which Governments violate or attempt to violate this right. It is vitally important that police officials recognize the importance of the right to freedom of opinion and expression to individuals, and its significance to the wider society. No good purpose, including national security and pubic order, is served by unjustified suppression of this right. In fact, to undermine this right is to undermine democracy and the rule of law.

B. REVIEW OF CASES

(*a*) Human Rights Committee

Article 19 of the International Covenant on Civil and Political Rights protects the right to freedom of opinion and expression. Under paragraph 1, everyone shall have the right to hold opinions without interference. Paragraph 2 stipulates that everyone shall have the right to freedom of expression. This right includes freedom to seek, receive and impart information and ideas of all kinds, regardless of frontiers, either orally, in writing or in print, in the form of art, or through any other media of one's choice.

Paragraph 3 states that the exercise of the rights provided for in paragraph 2 carries with it special duties and responsibilities. It may, therefore, be subject to certain re-

---

[4] See part III, chap. 3, sect. A (*supra*, p. 410).

strictions, but these shall only be such as are provided by law and are necessary for the respect of the rights or reputations or others or for the protection of national security, public order or of public health or morals. Particular restrictions are prescribed in article 20 of the Covenant.

In time of public emergency threatening the life of the nation, States parties may take measures derogating from their obligations under article 19, but only on the conditions set forth in article 4 of the Covenant.

In its general comment No. 10 (19) on article 19,[5] the Human Rights Committee pointed out that the Covenant did not permit any exception or restriction to the right to freedom of opinion set forth in paragraph 1.[6] Concerning the right to freedom of expression in paragraph 2, the Committee pronounced that the inter-play between the principle of freedom of expression and any limitations and restrictions determined the actual scope of the individual's right.[7]

A number of cases brought under this article involve attempts by Governments to deny the freedom of expression to political opponents. For example, in the case *Monja Jaona* v. *Madagascar*,[8] the author was a 77-year-old Malagasy national and leader of a political opposition party. In the presidential elections held on 7 November 1982 in Madagascar, he was the candidate of his party. Following the re-election of the incumbent President, Mr. Jaona challenged the results and called for new elections at a press conference. Shortly afterwards, he was placed under house arrest and subsequently detained at a military camp. He was not informed of the grounds for his arrest, and there was no indication that charges were ever brought against him or investigated. He was later on released and then elected deputy to the National People's Assembly in elections held on 28 August 1983. Counsel for Mr. Jaona alleged violations of, *inter alia*, articles 9 and 19 of the Covenant.

The State party submitted that Mr. Jaona had been placed under house arrest on the basis of a law relating to the dissolution of certain associations and to the placing under house arrest of persons convicted of subversive activities. It adduced no evidence, however, that this law was applicable in the case of Mr. Jaona. The Committee could not conclude that the author was engaged in any activities prohibited by the law in question. It concluded that the facts before it disclosed a violation of arti-

---

[5] See United Nations, *Official Records of the General Assembly, Thirty-eighth Session, Supplement No. 40* (A/38/40), annex VI.
[6] *Ibidem*, para. 1.
[7] *Ibidem*, para. 3.
[8] *Ibidem, Fortieth Session, Supplement No. 40* (A/40/40), annex IX, communication No. 132/1982, views adopted on 1 April 1985.

III:4

cle 19, paragraph 2, of the Covenant, because Mr. Jaona had suffered persecution on account of his political opinions. In respect of his arrest and detention, the Committee also found violations of article 9, paragraphs 1 and 2, of the Covenant.

In the case *Aduayom* et al. v. *Togo*,[9] the Committee dealt jointly with communications submitted by three Togolese citizens. Adimayo M. Aduayom and Sofianou T. Diasso were teachers and Yawo S. Dobou inspector in the Ministry of Post and Telecommunications. They were separately arrested by police or agents of the Gendarmerie Nationale on 18 September, 17 December and 30 September 1985, respectively. They were each charged with the offence of leze majesty, for insult of the Head of State in his exercise of powers. The charges against them were later dropped, and they were released. Subsequently, they all unsuccessfully requested reinstatement in their former posts.

The authors claimed that they had been arrested and detained contrary to article 9, paragraph 1, of the Covenant. This was implicitly conceded by the State party when it dropped all the charges against them. They further contended that the State party had violated article 19, because they were persecuted for having carried, read or disseminated documents that contained no more than an assessment of Togolese politics, either at the domestic or foreign policy level.

In respect of the claim under article 19 of the Covenant, the Committee observed that it had remained uncontested that the authors were first prosecuted and later not reinstated in their posts, between 1986 and 1991, *inter alia*, for having read and, respectively, disseminated information and material critical of the Togolese Government in power and of the system of governance prevailing in Togo. The Committee observed that the freedom of information and freedom expression were cornerstones in any free and democratic society. It was in the essence of such societies that its citizens had to be allowed to inform themselves about alternatives to the political system/parties in power and that they might criticize or openly and publicly evaluate their governments without fear of interference or punishment, within the limits set by article 19, paragraph 3. On the basis of the information before the Committee, it appeared that the authors were not reinstated in the posts they had occupied prior to their arrest because of such activities. There was no indication that the authors' activities represented a threat to the rights or reputations of others or to national security or public order. In the circumstances, the Committee concluded that there had been violations by Togo of articles 19 and 25 (*c*) of the Covenant in respect of each author. One member of the Committee filed an individual opinion in the case.

---

[9] *Ibidem, Fifty-first Session, Supplement No. 40* (A/51/40), vol. II, annex VIII, sect. C, communications No. 422/1990, No. 423/1990 and No. 424/1990, views adopted on 12 July 1996.

In the case *Henry Kalenga* v. *Zambia,*[10] the author, a Zambian citizen who had promoted protest campaigns against government policies, was arrested on 11 February 1986 by the police. A police detention order was then issued against him pursuant to a regulation of the Preservation of Public Security Act. This order was later on replaced by a presidential detention order issued under the same legislation, allowing the President of Zambia to authorize the administrative detention of persons accused of political offences for an indefinite period of time for purposes of preserving public security. Mr. Kalenga was subsequently kept in police detention on charges of being one of the founding members and having sought to disseminate the views of a political organization considered to be illegal under Zambia's one-party Constitution then in force. He was also charged with preparing subversive activities aimed at overthrowing the regime of Kenneth Kaunda, the then President of Zambia. Mr. Kalenga was eventually released on 3 November 1989, following a presidential order.

The author contended that at the time of his arrest he was not engaged in any political activities aimed at undermining the Government. He had merely been promoting campaigns protesting against the Government's national education, military and economic policies. The subversive activities he was accused of amounted to no more than burning the card affiliating him with the President's political party. The author alleged violations of, *inter alia*, articles 9 and 19 of the Covenant.

In respect of issues under article 19 of the Covenant, the Committee was of the opinion that the uncontested response of the Zambian authorities to Mr. Kalenga's attempts to express his opinions freely and to disseminate the tenets of his political organization constituted a violation of his rights under that article. The Committee also found violations of the provisions concerning the prohibition of arbitrary arrest and rights of persons arrested, the right to humane treatment as a detainee and the right to freedom of movement in articles 9, 10 and 12, respectively.

Whilst the author in this case had been detained under a public security act, the State party did not invoke article 19, paragraph 3, of the Covenant allowing for restrictions on the right to freedom of expression necessary to protect, *inter alia*, national security or public order.

This provision, however, was invoked in the case *Albert Womah Mukong* v. *Cameroon,*[11] summarized in connection with the prohibition of torture[12] and also cited in

---

[10] See United Nations document A/48/40 (Part II), annex XII, sect. L, communication No. 326/1988, views adopted on 27 July 1993.
[11] See United Nations, *Official Records of the General Assembly, Forty-ninth Session, Supplement No. 40* (A/49/40), vol. II, annex IX, sect. AA, communication No. 458/1991, views adopted on 21 July 1994.

III:4

connection with the right to liberty and security of person.[13] The author, a journalist, writer and long-time opponent of the one-party system in Cameroon, alleged violations of, *inter alia*, articles 7, 9 and 19 of the Covenant. In respect of the latter provision, he claimed to have been persecuted for his advocacy of multi-party democracy and the expression of opinions inimical to the Government of Cameroon. His arrests in 1988 and 1990 were allegedly linked to these activities. The State party replied that restrictions on the author's freedom of expression were justified under the terms of article 19, paragraph 3, of the Covenant.

The Committee observed that any restriction on the right to freedom of expression pursuant to article 19, paragraph 3, had cumulatively to meet the following conditions: it had to be provided for by law; it had to address one of the aims enumerated in paragraphs 3 (*a*) and (*b*); and it had to be necessary to achieve the legitimate purpose. While the State party had indicated that the restrictions on Mr. Mukong's freedom of expression were provided for by law, it still had to be determined whether the measures taken against him were necessary for the safeguard of national security and/or public order.

The Committee considered that it was not necessary to safeguard an alleged vulnerable state of national unity by subjecting Mr. Mukong to arrest, continued detention and treatment in violation of the prohibition of torture in article 7 of the Covenant. It further considered that the legitimate objective of safeguarding, and indeed strengthening, national unity under difficult political circumstances could not be achieved by attempting to muzzle advocacy of multi-party democracy, democratic tenets and human rights. In this regard, the question of deciding which measures might meet the necessity test in such situations did not arise. The Committee concluded that there had been a violation of article 19 of the Covenant. It also found violations by Cameroon of articles 7 and 9, paragraph 1.

Article 19, paragraph 3, of the Covenant was also invoked by the State party in the case *Jong-Kyu Sohn* v. *the Republic of Korea*,[14] summarized in section C.[15] The author, a Korean trade union leader, was convicted of contravening labour legislation for, at a meeting on 9 February 1991, having joined in issuing a statement supporting a strike and condemning the Government's threat to send in troops to break the strike. The author alleged a violation of article 19, paragraph 2.

---

[12] See part II, chap. 3, sect. C (*b*) (*supra*, pp. 158-161).

[13] See part II, chap. 4, sect. B (*a*) (*supra*, p. 207).

[14] See United Nations, *Official Records of the General Assembly, Fiftieth Session, Supplement No. 40* (A/50/40), vol. II, annex X, sect. L, communication No. 518/1992, views adopted on 19 July 1995.

[15] See part III, chap. 4, sect. C (*a*) (*infra*, pp. 459-463).

In this case, the Committee noted that both national security and public order had been invoked. However, it considered that the State party had failed to specify the precise nature of the threat it contended that Mr. Sohn's exercise of his freedom of expression posed. The Committee found that none of the arguments advanced by the State party sufficed to render the restriction of the author's right to freedom of expression compatible with article 19, paragraph 3, of the Covenant. The facts of the case disclosed a violation by the Republic of Korea of article 19, paragraph 2.

In addition to the Committee's considerations and conclusions, this case is also interesting because of the submissions made by the the author and the State party. For example, the author made reference to the jurisprudence of the Committee on Freedom of Association of the Governing Body of the International Labour Office in respect of workers' freedom of expression as an essential component of the freedom of association.

In the case *Robert Faurisson* v. *France*,[16] the Committee found no violation of article 19, paragraph 3, of the Covenant. The author, with dual French/British citizenship, was a professor of literature who doubted the existence of gas chambers for extermination purposes at Auschwitz and in other Nazi concentration camps, although he did not contest the use of gas chambers for purposes of disinfection. In 1991, he was removed from his chair at a French university.

On 13 July 1990, the French legislature passed the so-called "Gayssot Act", amending a law on the freedom of the press by adding an article that made it an offence to contest the existence of the category of crimes against humanity as defined in the London Charter of 8 August 1945. On the basis of that Charter, Nazi leaders were tried and convicted by the International Military Tribunal at Nuremberg from 1945 to 1946. The author contended that the Gayssot Act curtailed his right to freedom of expression and academic freedom in general. He considered that the law targeted him personally and complained that the provision in question constituted unacceptable censorship, obstructing and penalizing historical research. Subsequent to an interview published in September 1990, in which he reiterated his personal conviction that there were no homicidal gas chambers for the extermination of Jews in Nazi concentration camps, Mr. Faurisson was convicted of an offence under the Act and fined.

In its observations on the mertits, the State party submitted, *inter alia*, that a former Minister of Justice had aptly summarized the position of the Government that had

---

[16] See United Nations, *Official Records of the General Assembly, Fifty-second Session, Supplement No. 40* (A/52/40), vol. II, annex VI, sect. I, communication No. 550/1993, views adopted on 8 November 1996.

introduced the Gayssot Act by stating that it was impossible not to devote oneself fully to the fight against racism. He added that racism did not constitute an opinion but an aggression and that every time racism was allowed to express itself publicly, public order was immediately and severely threatened. The Act did not punish the expression of an opinion, but the denial of a historical reality universally recognized. In the State party's opinion, the adoption of the provision was necessary not only to protect the rights and the reputations of others, but also to protect public order and morals.

As in the other cases in which article 19, paragraph 3, of the Convention had been invoked, the Committee observed that any restriction on the right to freedom of expression had cumulatively to meet the conditions for restrictions set out in that provision.

The Committee pointed out that the restriction on Mr. Faurisson's freedom of expression was indeed provided by law. The Gayssot Act was, as read, interpreted and applied to his case by the French courts, in compliance with the provisions of the Covenant. In assessing whether the restrictions placed on his freedom of expression by his criminal conviction were applied for the purposes provided for by the Covenant, the Committee noted the following. The rights for the protection of which restrictions on the right to freedom of expression were permitted by article 19, paragraph 3, might relate to the interests of other persons or to those of the community as a whole. Since the statements made by Mr. Faurisson were of a nature as to raise or strengthen anti-Semitic feelings, the restriction served the respect of the Jewish community to live free from fear of an atmosphere of anti-Semitism. The Committee concluded, therefore, that the restriction of the author's freedom of expression was permissible under article 19, paragraph 3 (*a*), of the Covenant. Finally, noting the State party's argument that the introduction of the Act was intended to serve the struggle against racism and anti-Semitism, the Committee was satisfied that the restriction of Mr. Faurisson's freedom of expression was necessary within the meaning of article 19, paragraph 3, of the Covenant. Seven members of the Committee filed individual opinions in the case, all concurring opinions.

The case *Auli Kivenmaa* v. *Finland,*[17] is summarized in connection with the right to freedom of peaceful assembly and association.[18] However, it also raised issues in relation to article 19 of the Covenant. Ms. Kivenmaa, secretary general of a Finnish political youth organization, and members of her organization had on 3 September 1987, on the occasion of a visit of a foreign head of State, distributed leaflets and

---

[17] *Ibidem, Forty-ninth Session, Supplement No. 40* (A/49/40), vol. II, annex IX, sect. N, communication No. 412/1990, views adopted on 31 March 1994.
[18] See part III, chap. 5, sect. C (*a*) (*infra*, pp. 500-508).

raised a banner critical of the human rights record of the visiting head of State. She was subsequently charged with, and convicted of, violating the Act on Public Meetings by holding such a meeting without prior notification. The author alleged a violation of articles 15 and 19, alternatively, article 21 of the Covenant.

Ms. Kivenmaa denied that what took place was a public meeting within the meaning of the Act on Public Meetings. She characterized the incident as an exercise of her right to freedom of expression, which was regulated by other legislation not requiring prior notification. She contended that her conviction was, therefore, in violation of article 19 of the Covenant. She alleged that the way in which the courts found her actions to come within the scope of the Act on Public Meetings constituted *ex analogia* reasoning and was, therefore, insufficient to justify the restriction of her right to freedom of expression as being provided by law within the meaning of article 19, paragraph 3.

In this respect, the Committee observed that the right for an individual to express his political opinions, including obviously his opinions on the question of human rights, formed part of the freedom of expression guaranteed by article 19 of the Covenant. In this particular case, the Committee noted, the author of the communication exercised this right by raising a banner. It was true that article 19 authorized the restriction by law of the right to freedom of expression in certain circumstances. However, in this specific case, the State party had neither referred to a law allowing this freedom to be restricted, nor established how the restriction applied to Ms. Kivenmaa was necessary to safeguard the rights and national imperatives set forth in article 19, paragraphs 2 (*a*) and (*b*), of the Covenant. Therefore, there had been a violation of that article. The Committee also found that the facts before it disclosed a violation by Finland of article 21.

It should be noted, however, that one member of the Committee filed an individual opinion in which he disagreed with the conclusions of the Committee in the case. His observations on the nature of the relationship between the right to freedom of expression and the right to freedom of peaceful assembly are particularly interesting. This dissenting opinion is included in the case summary.

Finally, concerning the jurisprudence of the Committee on article 19 of the Covenant, the authors in the cases *S. G. v. France*[19] and *G. B. v. France*,[20] both French citizens residing in Brittany, were arrested in 1987 on charges of having defaced

---

[19] See United Nations, *Official Records of the General Assembly, Forty-seventh Session, Supplement No. 40* (A/47/40), annex X, sect. F, communication No. 347/1988, decision adopted on 1 November 1991.

[20] *Ibidem*, sect. G, communication No. 348/1989, decision adopted on 1 November 1991.

III:4

several road signs. Their actions were part of a campaign led by the movement "Stourm ar Brezhoneg" (Fight for the Breton Language) whose aim was the posting of bilingual road signs, in Breton and French, throughout Brittany. They were each convicted of crimes connected with the incidents, fined and sentenced to terms of imprisonment, suspended.

Both authors submitted that they were victims of a violation by France of, *inter alia*, article 19, paragraphs 1 and 2, of the Covenant. However, in each case, the Committee observed that the defacing of road signs did not raise issues under article 19. It decided to declare the communications inadmissible under article 2 of the Optional Protocol to the Covenant. One member of the Committee filed identical individual opinions in the two cases.

(*b*) Working Group on Arbitrary Detention

It is recalled that the Working Group on Arbitrary Detention regards deprivation of liberty as arbitrary in the following cases:

(*a*) When it manifestly cannot be justified on any legal basis, such as continued detention after the sentence has been served or despite an applicable amnesty act (category I);

(*b*) When the deprivation of liberty is the result of a judgment or sentence for the exercise of the rights or freedoms proclaimed by articles 7, 13, 14, 18, 19, 20 and 21 of the Universal Declaration of Human Rights and also, in respect of States parties, in articles 12, 18, 19, 21, 22, 25, 26 and 27 of the International Covenant on Civil and Political Rights (category II); and

(*c*) When the complete or partial non-observance of the international standards relating to a fair trial set forth in the Universal Declaration and in the relevant international instruments accepted by the States concerned is of such gravity as to confer the deprivation of liberty, of whatever kind, an arbitrary character (category III).

In order to evaluate the arbitrary character of cases of deprivation of freedom entering into category III, the Working Group considers, in addition to the general principles set out in the Universal Declaration, several criteria drawn from the Body of Principles for the Protection of All Persons under Any Form of Detention or Imprisonment and, for States parties, the criteria laid down particularly in articles 9 and 14 of the Covenant.

When the Working Group concludes that a person has been arbitrarily deprived of his or her liberty, the Government concerned is typically requested to take the necessary steps to remedy the situation and to bring it into conformity with the standards and principles set forth in the Universal Declaration and, where applicable, the Covenant. States non-parties to the Covenant are encouraged to become a party to it.

No cases from the jurisprudence of the Working Group have been selected for a summary in this chapter, but opinion No. 27/2001 (*Morocco*),[21] a case summarized in connection with the right to a fair trial,[22] is also of interest on the matter of the right to freedom of expression. It concerned an officer who allegedly had been arrested, held in pre-trial detention and convicted, exclusively because he had exercised his freedom of expression. Mustapha Adib, a former captain of the Moroccan armed forces, refused to become involved in corrupt dealings when he served in the armed forces. Consequently, he suffered various forms of harassment. He was eventually sentenced to a term of imprisonment and dismissal from the army for having expressed his views to a journalist who in 1999 published an article in the French daily *Le Monde* based on, *inter alia*, that interview.

In view of the fact that Mustapha Adib had been on active military service and expressed himself through the media, the Working Group said that a doubt arose as to how far his freedom of expression extended. It made reference to the restrictions allowed under article 19 of the Covenant, to which Morocco was a party. With regard to the specific case of military personnel, the Working Group stated, it was generally recognized that the right to freedom of expression of officials, police officers and those of the armed forces should be subject to certain restrictions owing to the special nature of the obligations and responsibilities by which they were bound. In this case, the officer had recognized that under the regulations of the armed forces, he was generally forbidden to publish.

The Working Group observed that even if there had been a breach of regulations, the question of the disproportionality of the sanction, 60 days of military confinement and five years' imprisonment, including two and a half non-suspensive, in relation to the fault committed, which might have merited no more than a disciplinary sanction, still remained and deserved to be examined. However, considering that neither the information supplied by the source, nor that supplied by the Government, shed sufficient light on the matter, the Working Group was not, in the circumstances, in a position to express an opinion regarding the compatibility of the restriction with the provisions of article 19 of the Covenant or the proportionality of the sanction inflicted on Mustapha Adib for his violation. However, it found his deprivation of liberty arbitrary as violating the right to a fair trial, in contravention of articles 9 and 10 of

---

[21] See United Nations document E/CN.4/2003/8/Add.1, p. 27, opinion adopted on 3 December 2001.

[22] See part III, chap. 2, sect. C (*d*) (*supra*, pp. 385-390).

III:4

the Universal Declaration and articles 9 and 14 of the Covenant and falling within category III of the categories applicable to the consideration of cases submitted to the Working Group.

Two further cases of arbitrary detention are included in this review. They concern suppression of the activities of human rights defenders.

In the first case, opinion No. 32/2000 (*Uzbekistan*),[23] it was alleged that on 12 May 1999 in Tashkent, a group of police officers in plain clothes entered the flat of Makhbuba Kasymova, a human rights defender, and searched it although she was not there at the time. Ms. Kasymova was one of a small group of human rights defenders who had monitored the wave of arrests and trials that followed a series of bomb explosions in February 1999 in Tashkent and the murders of officials in late 1997 in the Fergana valley. The police officers questioned her husband, two of her daughters and another person staying in the flat. The latter was detained after a hand grenade and a small quantity of drugs were allegedly found. No warrant was shown, nor did the officers reveal their identity, as required under the law.

According to the source, in the following days, Ms. Kasymova was repeatedly questioned in the city internal affairs department. On several occasions, the interrogations lasted for many hours, without a break, and ended late at night. On 19 May 1999, she was taken under guard directly from that office to the assembly hall of her local neighbourhood council, where some 200 people had gathered to denounce her publicly. It was reported that she was pointed out to them as "one of the sort of people who killed your sons". Excerpts of this meeting were allegedly shown on national television, and she and her independent human rights organization, unregistered, were presented as being supporters of terrorism.

Shortly after this "show trial", Ms. Kasymova was formally charged with concealing a crime. She remained at liberty, on bail. In early June 1999, while the criminal investigation was still under way, an additional charge of misappropriation of money was brought against her.

On 13 July 1999, Ms. Kasymova attended the district court. She had not been informed that her trial was imminent and thus had not yet engaged a lawyer. However, she brought with her to the court building the Human Rights Watch representative in Uzbekistan. The trial against her began forthwith, without prior notice, in the absence of any defence witness and with a lawyer assigned by the court. Three hours later, the proceedings concluded with the handing down of a five-year sentence for

---

[23] See United Nations document E/CN.4/2002/77/Add.1, p. 10, opinion adopted on 27 November 2001.

concealment of a crime and for misappropriation of funds. She was immediately transferred to a prison.

On the basis of the allegations made, not denied by the Government although given the opportunity to do so, the Working Group noted that the conviction and detention of Ms. Kasymova were motivated exclusively by her human rights activities. In acting as she did, she was only peacefully exercising her right to freedom of expression, as guaranteed by article 19 of the Universal Declaration and article 19 of the Covenant, to which Uzbekistan was a party.

In view of this, the Working Group was of the opinion that an analysis of the irregularities of the legal proceedings preceding the final conviction was unnecessary, although the source saw those proceedings as violations of international norms, notably articles 9 and 14 of the Covenant. The Working Group found that the deprivation of Ms. Kasymova's liberty was arbitrary in that it contravened the provisions of article 19 of the Universal Declaration and article 19 of the Covenant, falling within category II.

The other case, opinion No. 19/1999 (*China*),[24] concerned Li Hai, a human rights defender, who had collected the names and particulars of victims of human rights violations since the late 1980s and conveyed such information to independent human rights organizations based abroad. He was apprehended on 31 May 1995 but not formally arrested until 5 April 1996, when he was charged with leaking State secrets. His trial took place on 21 May 1996, and he was sentenced to nine years' imprisonment and two years' deprivation of all his political rights. His appeal was rejected in January 1997.

It appeared to the Working Group that, without prejudice to the question whether Li Hai had enjoyed guarantees of the right to a fair trial as stated in the Government's reply, he was accused of having sought out and amassed a large volume of State secrets for foreign organizations, in breach of Chinese law. However, no details were given on the nature of such secrets, and the claim that he was collecting names and particulars of individual cases of human rights violation was not contested.

Before expressing an opinion on this case, the Working Group considered that it should answer the question whether or not information on allegations or, *a fortiori*, evidence of human rights violations could legally be characterized as State secrets.

---

[24] See United Nations document E/CN.4/2000/4/Add.1, p. 78, opinion adopted on 16 September 1999.

III:4

The Working Group found that under article 5 (*c*) of the Declaration on the Right and Responsibility of Individuals, Groups and Organs of Society to Promote and Protect Universally Recognized Human Rights and Fundamental Freedoms, everyone had the right to communicate with non-governmental or intergovernmental organizations for the purpose of promoting and protecting human rights and fundamental freedoms. According to article 6 (*a*) of the Declaration, everyone had the right, individually and in association with others, to know, seek, obtain, receive and hold information about all human rights and fundamental freedoms, including having access to information as to how those rights and freedoms were given effect in domestic legislative, judicial or administrative systems.

Many procedures established by the United Nations and, in particular, by the Economic and Social Council and the Commission on Human Rights with a view to guaranteeing the promotion and protection of human rights, encouraged and legitimized the collection of such information. Characterizing it as State secrets would suggest that the Office of the United Nations High Commissioner for Human Rights was a body keeping a large volume of such secrets. The Covenant and, in particular, its article 41 on the remedy of inter-State communications, invited States themselves, not only individuals, to bring situations of human rights violations to the attention of the Human Rights Committee.

The Working Group was of the opinion that such a characterization of the information would be contrary to the international procedural standards prescribed in the field of human rights and that it could therefore not be regarded as constituting an offence. Not being State secrets, it was information within the meaning of article 19 of the Universal Declaration, which provided that freedom of expression included freedom to hold opinions without interference and to seek, receive and impart information and ideas through any media and regardless of frontiers. Since its dissemination, even outside the territory, was guaranteed by that provision, such an initiative could not, of itself, constitute an offence, much less an aggravating circumstance.

In other words, the Working Group considered that collecting and disseminating information relating to allegations and, *a fortiori*, to evidence of human rights violations were ways of exercising the right to freedom of expression protected by article 19 of the Universal Declaration. In the light of international standards, this legal analysis demonstrated that Li Hai was sentenced to a term of imprisonment for having exercised the right to freedom of expression, including the right to impart information regardless of frontiers, guaranteed to every person by that provision.

In view of this, the Working Group rendered the opinion that the deprivation of liberty of Li Hai was arbitrary, since it was contrary to article 19 of the Universal Declaration and fell within category II. China was not a party to the Covenant.

448

(*c*) Inter-American Court of Human Rights

Article 13 of the American Convention on Human Rights protects the right to free-dom of thought and expression. Under paragraph 1, everyone has the right to free-dom of thought and expression, including the freedom to seek, receive and impart information and ideas of all kinds, regardless of frontiers, either orally, in writing, in print, in the form of art or through any other medium of one's choice.

Paragraph 2 states that the exercise of the right to freedom of thought and expression shall not be subject to prior censorship. However, it shall be subject to subsequent imposition of liability, as expressly established by law, to the extent necessary to en-sure the respect for he rights or reputations of others or the protection of national se-curity, public order or public health or morals. However, under paragraph 4, public entertainments may be subject by law to prior censorship for the sole purpose of reg-ulating access to them for the moral protection of childhood and adolescence.

Paragraph 3 prohibits restricting the right of expression by indirect methods or means, such as the abuse of government or private controls over newsprint, radio broadcasting frequencies or equipment used in the dissemination of information or by any other means tending to impede the communication and circulation of ideas and opinions.

Paragraph 5, finally, requires that any propaganda for war and any advocacy of na-tional, racial or religious hatred constituting incitement to lawless violence or to any other similar illegal action against any person or group of persons on any grounds, including those of race, colour, religion, language or national origin, shall be consid-ered as offences punishable by law.

In time of war, public danger or other emergency threatening the independence or security of the State party, it may take measures derogating from its obligations un-der article 13, but only on the conditions set forth in article 27 of the Convention.

One case from the jurisprudence of the Inter-American Court of Human Rights con-cerning article 13 of the Convention, the *Ivcher Bronstein* case (*Peru*),[25] is relevant to the purposes of this book and is summarized in section C.[26] It is an important and interesting case in which the victim, Baruch Ivcher Bronstein, a naturalized Peruvian citizen, was majority shareholder, director and president of Channel 2 of the Peruvi-an television network. In 1997, the Inter-American Commission on Human Rights

---

[25] See Inter-American Court of Human Rights, Series C: *Decisions and Judgments,* No. 74 (2002), petition No. 11762, judgment of 6 February 2001.
[26] See part III, chap. 4, sect. C (*b*) (*infra*, pp. 463-469).

III:4

alleged, he was arbitrarily deprived of his nationality title in order to remove him from the editorial control of the Channel and restrict his freedom of expression. He had manifested this freedom by denouncing grave violations of human rights and acts of corruption in reports in *Contrapunto*, a programme on Channel 2. As a result of these reports, he was subjected to threats and harassment by various State authorities recommending him to change the editorial line. The Commission claimed violations by Peru of article 13 and a number of other articles of the Convention.

In its judgment, the Court insisted that it was essential that journalists who worked in the media should enjoy protection and independence to exercise their functions comprehensively. They kept society informed, and it was an indispensable requirement to enable society to enjoy full freedom. Citing an earlier advisory opinion, the Court linked public order in a democratic society with the guarantee of the widest possible circulation of news, ideas and opinions, as well as the widest access to information by society as a whole. It pointed out that freedom of expression constituted the primary and basic element of the public order of a democratic society. This was not conceivable without free debate and the possibility of dissenting voices to be fully heard.

Bearing in mind that a primary function of policing is the maintenance of public order, this is an extremely significant observation. It identifies one of the essential characteristics of, and prerequisites for, public order in a democratic society, and it indicates that one of the ways in which police and other state authorities in such a society should maintain public order is through the active protection of human rights.

The Court concluded that the State had violated article 13, paragraphs 1 and 3, of the Convention with regard to Mr. Ivcher Bronstein. It also found other violations of the Convention in this case.

(*d*) European Court of Human Rights

Article 10 of the Convention for the Protection of Human Rights and Fundamental Freedoms protects the right to freedom of expression. Under paragraph 1, this right shall include freedom to hold opinions and to receive and impart information and ideas without interference by public authority and regardless of frontiers. It is also stated in this paragraph that the article does not prevent States from requiring the licensing of broadcasting, television or cinema enterprises.

Paragraph 2 states that since the exercise of these freedoms carries with it duties and responsibilities, it may be subject to such formalities, conditions, restrictions or penalties as are prescribed by law and are necessary in a democratic society, in the interests of national security, territorial integrity or public safety, for the prevention of disorder or crime, for the protection of health or morals, for the protection of the reputation or rights of others, for preventing the disclosure of information received in confidence or for maintaining the authority and impartiality of the judiciary.

In time of war or other public emergency threatening the life of the nation, States parties may take measures derogating from their obligations under article 10 on the conditions set forth in article 15 of the Convention.

In the case *Zana* v. *Turkey*,[27] the applicant, Mehdi Zana, was a Turkish national and former mayor of Diyarbakir in southeast Turkey. In an interview with journalists in August 1987, he had made some remarks in support of the Workers' Party of Kurdistan (PKK), published in a national daily. He claimed, *inter alia*, that his conviction by a national security court on account of this statement had infringed his right to freedom of expression. The European Court of Human Rights, sitting as a grand chamber, noted that indisputably there was in the case an interference with Mr. Zana's excercise of his freedom of expression. This interference contravened article 10 of the Convention unless it was prescribed by law, had an aim or aims legitimate under paragraph 2 of that article and was necessary in a democratic society for achieving such an aim or aims.

Having considered that the impugned interference was prescribed by law and pursued legitimate aims, the Court made some significant pronouncements regarding the necessity of the interference. It reiterated the fundamental principles that emerged from its judgments relating to article 10 of the Convention. Freedom of expression constituted one of the essential foundations of a democratic society and one of the basic conditions for its progress and for each individual's self-fulfilment. Subject to paragraph 2 of that article, it was applicable not only to information or ideas that were favourably received or regarded as inoffensive or as a matter of indifference, but also to those that offended, shocked or disturbed. Such were the demands of that pluralism, tolerance and broadmindedness without which there was no democratic society. As set forth in article 10, this freedom was subject to exceptions, which had, however, to be construed strictly, and the need for any restrictions had to be established convincingly.

The adjective "necessary", within the meaning of article 10, paragraph 2, implied the existence of a pressing social need. The States parties had a certain margin of appreciation in assessing whether such a need existed, but it went hand in hand with European supervision, embracing both the legislation and the decisions applying it, even

---

[27] See European Court of Human Rights, *Reports of Judgments and Decisions*, 1997-VII, p. 2533, application No. 18954/91, judgment of 25 November 1997.

those given by an independent court. The Court was therefore empowered to give the final ruling on whether a restriction was reconcilable with the freedom of expression as protected by article 10 of the Convention.

In exercising its supervisory jurisdiction, the Court had to look at the impugned interference in the light of the case as a whole, including the content of the remarks held against the applicant and the context in which he made them. In particular, it had to determine whether the interference in issue was proportionate to the legitimate aims pursued and whether the reasons adduced by the national authorities to justify it were relevant and sufficient. In doing so, the Court had to satisfy itself that the national authorities applied standards which were in conformity with the principles embodied in article 10 and, moreover, that they based themselves on an acceptable assessment of the relevant facts.

In applying these principles to the present case, the Court held, by twelve votes to eight, that there had not been a breach of article 10 of the Convention. It considered that the interference was proportionate to the legitimate aims pursued. In doing so, the Court had regard to, *inter alia*, that the interview coincided with murderous attacks carried out by the PKK on civilians in southeast Turkey, a region with extreme tension at the time. In those circumstances, Mr. Zana's support of the PKK, in an interview published in a major national daily, had to be regarded as likely to exacerbate an already explosive situation in that region. In respect of the right to a fair trial, however, the Court found violations of article 6 of the Convention.

In the case *Thorgeir Thorgeirson* v. *Iceland*,[28] summarized in section C,[29] the applicant, an Icelandic citizen, was a writer. It concerned the publication in 1983 of two articles by Thorgeir Thorgeirson on police brutality in an Icelandic daily. At the request of the Reykjavik Police Association, the public prosecutor investigated statements made in these articles, and Mr. Thorgeirson was eventually convicted of a criminal offence of defamation.

Noting that the articles were phrased in particularly strong terms, the Court observed, however, that they referred to a matter of serious public concern. Having regard to their purpose and the impact they were designed to have, the Court was of the opinion that the language used could not be regarded as excessive. Finding, by eight votes to one, a violation of article 10 of the Convention, the Court considered that the conviction and sentence were capable of discouraging open discussion of

---

[28] See *Publications of the European Court of Human Rights*, Series A: *Judgments and Decisions*, vol. 239 (1992), application No. 13778/88, judgment of 25 June 1992.
[29] See part III, chap. 4, sect. C (*c*) (*infra*, pp. 470-476).

matters of public concern. The interference complained of was not proportionate to the legitimate aim pursued and, therefore, not necessary in a democratic society.

In the case Özgür Gündem v. *Turkey*,[30] also summarized in section C,[31] the four applicants, respectively, editors and owners of the Turkish daily *Özgür Gündem*, alleged that there had been a concerted and deliberate assault on their freedom of expression through a campaign of targeting journalists, distributors and others associated with the newspaper with its main office located in Istanbul. For the serious attacks and harassment, eventually forcing the closure of the newspaper in 1994, they held the Turkish authorities directly or indirectly responsible.

The Court concluded that the State had failed to take adequate protective and investigative measures to protect the exercise by *Özgür Gündem* of its freedom of expression. Furthermore, the State had imposed measures on the newspaper, through a search-and-arrest operation and through numerous prosecutions and convictions in respect of issues of the newspaper, which were disproportionate and unjustified in the pursuit of any legitimate aim. As a result of these cumulative factors, the newspaper ceased publication. Accordingly, the Court held, there had been a breach of article 10 of the Convention.

Particularly interesting in this case are the Court's observations on the scope of the positive obligation on States to protect the right to freedom of expression. There it acknowledged the difficulties involved in policing modern societies and the choices that must be made in terms of priorities and resources.

Some of the prosecutions related to identifying officials participating in the fight against terrorism. The Court observed that it was true that some articles alleged serious misconduct by the officials named and were capable of exposing them to public contempt. However, it had not been taken into account that the names of the officials and their role in fighting terrorism were already in the public domain. This meant that the interest in protecting their identity was substantially diminished, and the potential damage that the restriction aimed at preventing was minimal. To the extent that the authorities had relevant reasons to impose criminal sanctions, these could not be regarded as sufficient to justify the restrictions placed on the newspaper's freedom of expression.

---

[30] See European Court of Human Rights, *Reports of Judgments and Decisions*, 2000-III, p. 1, application No. 23144/93, judgment of 16 March 2000.
[31] See part III, chap. 4, sect. C (*d*) (*infra*, pp. 476-486).

III:4

This issue also arose in another case against the same State party, *Sürek* v. *Turkey* (No. 2).[32] In this case, the applicant, Kamil Tekin Sürek, a Turkish national, was the major shareholder in a company which owned a weekly review published in Istanbul. The review's issue of 26 April 1992 contained a news report of a press conference by a delegation, including two former Turkish parliamentarians and two foreign delegates, on its visit to a village in the wake of tensions in the area. The news report included an article reporting the local governor as having told the delegation that a chief of police had given an order to open fire on the people. It further reported a dialogue between the two former Turkish parliamentarians and a gendarme commander. Being the owner of the review, Mr. Sürek was subsequently convicted and fined for an offence, under an act on the prevention of terrorism, of revealing the identity of officials mandated to fight terrorism and thus rendering them terrorist targets. He claimed to be a victim of a violation of article 10 of the Convention, as well as of article 6, paragraph 1, in respect of the right to a fair hearing.

The Court, sitting as a grand chamber, heard this case together with 12 other cases against Turkey related to the right to freedom of expression. Although not reported, the Court's judgment in the present case has been selected for a review because of its particular relevance for police.

The Court noted that Mr. Sürek's conviction and sentence related, in the first place, to the fact that his publication had reported that the governor had affirmed that a chief of police had given an order to open fire against the people. Secondly, it had quoted one of the former parliamentarians as having stated that a named gendarme commander had told the other former parliamentarian: "Your death would give us pleasure. Your blood would not quench my thirst". Thus, the report in the publication clearly implied serious misconduct on the part of the police and gendarme officers in question. Although the statements were not presented in a manner which could be regarded as incitement to violence against the officers concerned or the authorities, they were capable of exposing the officers to strong public contempt. Moreover, the news report was published in the context of the security situation in southeast Turkey where, since approximately 1985, serious disturbances had raged between the security forces and the members of the PKK involving a very heavy loss of life and the imposition of emergency rule in much of the region.

Consequently, the Court saw no reason to doubt that the applicant's conviction was supported by reasons relevant for the purposes of the necessity test under article 10, paragraph 2, of the Convention. As to whether the reasons relied on could also be considered sufficient, the Court observed that the impugned news report simply reiterated what a police officer and a gendarme officer were said to have ordered or af-

---

[32] See European Court of Human Rights, application No. 24122/94, judgment of 8 July 1999.

firmed on specific occasions. Assuming that the assertions were true, the Court considered that in view of the seriousness of the misconduct in question, the public had a legitimate interest in knowing not only the nature of the conduct, but also the identity of the officers. However, the defences of truth and public interest could not have been pleaded under relevant Turkish law. Furthermore, it was undisputed that the press declaration on which the news report was based had already been reported in other newspapers and that the information was already in the public domain. Thus, the interest in protecting the identity of the officers concerned had been substantially diminished, and the potential damage that the restriction was aimed at preventing had already been done. Finally, the Court considered that the conviction and sentence were capable of discouraging the contribution of the press to open discussion on matters of public concern.

The Court concluded that it did not find the objective of the Government in protecting the officers against terrorist attack sufficient to justify the restrictions placed on Mr. Sürek's right to freedom of expression under article 10 of the Convention. In the absence of a fair balance between the interests in protecting the freedom of the press and those in protecting the identity of the public officials in question, the interference complained of was disproportionate to the legitimate aims pursued. The Court therefore held, by sixteen votes to one, that there had been a violation of article 10 of the Convention, as well as of article 6, paragraph 1.

The publication of a matter already in the public domain was also considered by the Court in an earlier case, *Vereniging Weekblad* Bluf! v. *the Netherlands*.[33] The applicant in this case was an association based in Amsterdam which, at the material time, published *Bluf!*, a weekly for a left-wing readership. In the spring of 1987, the editorial staff came into possession of a report by the internal security service (BVD). Dated 1981 and marked "Confidential", it was designed mainly to inform BVD staff and other officials carrying out work for the service about the organisation's activities. It showed that the BVD at that time was interested in, among other groups, the Communist Party of the Netherlands and the anti-nuclear movement.

The editor of *Bluf!* proposed to publish the report with a commentary as a supplement to issue No. 267 of the weekly on 29 April 1987. However, on that day, before the journal was published or sent out to subscribers, the applicant association's premises were searched, and the entire print run of issue No. 267, including the supplement, was seized. The police apparently did not take away the offset plates remaining on the printing presses. During that night, unknown to the authorities, the staff of the association reprinted the issue that had been seized, and some 2,500 cop-

---

[33] See *Publications of the European Court of Human Rights*, Series A: *Judgments and Decisions*, vol. 306-A (1995), application No. 16616/90, judgment of 9 February 1995.

ies were sold in the streets of Amsterdam the next day, a national holiday. In order to avoid public disorder, the authorities decided not to stop it. Subsequently, a domestic court allowed an application by the public prosecutor for an order to withdraw issue No. 267 of *Bluf!* from circulation.

The applicant association maintained that the seizure and subsequent withdrawal from circulation of the issue had infringed its right to freedom of expression under article 10 of the Convention. The Court noted that the impugned measures amounted to interferences by a public authority in the applicant's exercise of its freedom to impart information and ideas. Having concluded that the interferences were prescribed by law and were designed to protect national security, a legitimate aim under article 10, paragraph 2, it went on to consider whether they were necessary in a democratic society.

The Court accepted that because of the nature of the duties performed by the internal security service, whose value was not disputed, such an institution had to enjoy a high degree of protection where the disclosure of information about its activities was concerned. Nevertheless, it was open to question whether the information in the report was sufficiently sensitive to justify preventing its distribution. The document in question was six years old at the time of the seizure. Furthermore, it was of a fairly general nature, the head of the security service having himself admitted that in 1987 the various items of information, taken separately, were no longer State secrets. Lastly, the report was marked simply "Confidential", representing a low degree of secrecy. It was in fact a document intended for BVD staff and other officials carrying out work for the service.

The Court did not consider that it had to determine whether the seizure carried out on 29 April 1987, taken alone, could be regarded as necessary. The withdrawal from circulation, on the other hand, had to be considered in the light of the events as a whole. After the newspaper had been seized, the publishers reprinted a large number of copies and sold them in the streets of Amsterdam, which were very crowded. Consequently, the information in question had already been widely distributed when the journal was withdrawn from circulation.

In respect of the latter, the Court, citing previous judgments, pointed out that it had already held that it was unnecessary to prevent the disclosure of certain information seeing that it had already been made public or had ceased to be confidential. Whilst the extent of publicity was different in this case, the information in question was made accessible to a large number of people able in their turn to communicate it to others. Furthermore, the events were commented on by the media. That being so, the protection of the information as a State secret was no longer justified, and the withdrawal of issue No. 267 of *Bluf!* no longer appeared necessary to achieve the legitimate aim pursued. In short, as the measure was not necessary in a democratic society, there had been a breach of article 10 of the Convention. The Court did note, however, that it would have been quite possible to prosecute the offenders.

The rights of public officials under article 10 of the Convention have been considered by the Court in a number of cases. In the *Engel and Others* case (*the Netherlands*),[34] also cited in connection with the right to a fair trial, the applicants, Cornelis J. M. Engel and four other Netherlands nationals, were conscript soldiers in 1971 serving in different non-commisioned ranks in the Netherlands armed forces. Penalties had been imposed on them by their commanding officers for various offences. Two of the applicants complained that the punishment imposed on them for having published and distributed articles deemed to undermine military discipline had contravened, *inter alia*, article 10 of the Convention.

As to the two applicants' collaboration in the publication and distribution of a journal published by an association of conscript servicemen, the Court, in plenary session, found that the disputed penalty represented an interference with the exercise of their freedom of expression and that it was prescribed by law. It further emphasized that the concept of order, as envisaged by article 10, paragraph 2, not only referred to public order, but also covered the order that had to prevail within the confines of a specific social group. This was so, for example, when, as in the case of the armed forces, disorder in that group could have repercussions on the order in society as a whole. It followed that the penalties imposed on the soldiers met this condition if, and to the extent that, their purpose was the prevention of disorder within the Netherlands armed forces.

Acknowledging that the freedom of expression guaranteed by article 10 of the Convention applied to servicemen just as it did to other persons within the jurisdiction of the States parties, the Court, however, pointed out that the proper functioning of an army was hardly imaginable without legal rules designed to prevent servicemen from undermining military discipline, for example by writings.

The Court observed that it must not disregard either the particular characteristics of military life, the specific duties and responsibilities incumbent on members of the armed forces or the margin of appreciation that article 10, paragraph 2, of the Convention left to the States parties. With regard to the penalties inflicted on the two applicants by the military authorities, the Court found that there was no question of depriving them of their freedom of expression, but only of punishing the abusive exer-

---

[34] *Ibidem*, vol. 22 (1977), applications No. 5100/71, No. 5101/71, No. 5102/71, No. 5354/72 and No. 5370/72, judgment of 8 June 1976.
[35] See part III, chap. 2, sect. B (*d*) (*supra*, p. 366).

cise of that freedom on their part. Consequently, there had been no violation of article 10.

Similar issues arose in the case *Vereinigung demokratischer Soldaten Österreichs and Gubi* v. *Austria*.[36] The Austrian authorities had prohibited the distribution of a monthly magazine, aimed at the soldiers serving in the Austrian army, that contained information and articles, often of a critical nature, on military life. The applicants were an Austrian association that published the magazine and a member of the same association, Berthold Gubi, an Austrian national and soldier. They complained, *inter alia*, of the prohibition imposed in respect of the magazine, and Mr. Gubi complained specifically of an order requiring him to cease distributing a certain issue of the magazine in the barracks.

In respect of the applicant association, the Court found, by six votes to three, a violation of article 10 of the Convention. It reiterated that freedom of expression was also applicable to information or ideas that offended, shocked or disturbed the State or any section of the population. Such were the demands of that pluralism, tolerance and broadmindedness without which there was no democratic society. The same was true, the Court observed, when the persons concerned were servicemen, because article 10 applied to them just as it did to other persons within the jurisdiction of the States parties. The Court further added, as it had stated in other judgments, that the proper functioning of an army was hardly imaginable without legal rules designed to prevent servicemen from undermining military discipline, for example by writings.

The Government sought support for its case from the content of the magazine. It was critical and satirical, and it had represented a threat to discipline and to the effectiveness of the army. However, in the Court's opinion, such an assertion had to be illustrated and substantiated by specific examples. None of the issues of the magazine submitted in evidence recommended disobedience or violence, or even questioned the usefulness of the army. Admittedly, most of the issues set out complaints, put forward proposals for reforms or encouraged the readers to institute legal complaints or appeals proceedings. However, despite their often polemical tenor, it did not appear that they overstepped the bounds of what was permissible in the context of a mere discussion of ideas, which had to be tolerated in the army of a democratic State just as it had to be in the society that such an army served.

Also in respect of Mr. Gubi, the Court found, by eight votes to one, a violation of article 10 of the Convention. Having noted the content of the issue in question, the Court concluded that the magazine could scarcely be seen as a serious threat to mili-

---

[36] See *Publications of the European Court of Human Rights*, Series A: *Judgments and Decisions*, vol. 302 (1995), application No. 15153/89, judgment of 19 December 1994.

tary discipline. Consequently, the order prohibiting this applicant to distribute the issue was disproportionate to the aim pursued.

C. CASE SUMMARIES

(a) *Jong-Kyu Sohn* v. *the Republic of Korea*
(Human Rights Committee)[37]

The author of the communication was Jong-Kyu Sohn, a citizen of the Republic of Korea. He submitted the communication to the Human Rights Committee on 7 July 1992, claiming to be a victim of a violation by the Republic of Korea of article 19, paragraph 2, of the International Covenant on Civil and Political Rights.

The facts

The author submitted, *inter alia*, the following. He had been president of a trade union since 1990 and was a founding member of the Solidarity Forum of Large Company Trade Unions. On 8 February 1991, a strike was called at the Daewoo Shipyard Company, and the Government announced that it would send in police troops to break the strike. Following that announcement, he had a meeting, on 9 February 1991, with other members of the Solidarity Forum, in Seoul, 400 kilometres from the place where the strike took place. At the end of the meeting, they issued a statement in which they supported the strike and condemned the Government's threat to send in troops. That statement was transmitted to the workers at the Daewoo Shipyard by facsimile. The Daewoo Shipyard strike ended peacefully on 13 February 1991.

On 10 February 1991, the author, together with some 60 other members of the Solidarity Forum, was arrested by the police when leaving the premises where the meeting had been held. On 12 February 1991, he and six others were charged with contravening an article of the Labour Dispute Adjustment Act. This provision prohibited others than the concerned employer, employees or trade union, or persons having legitimate authority attributed to them by law, to intervene in a labour dispute for the purpose of manipulating or influencing the parties concerned. He was also charged with contravening legislation on assembly and demonstration, but his communication did not relate to that.

---

[37] See United Nations, *Official Records of the General Assembly, Fiftieth Session, Supplement No. 40* (A/50/40), vol. II, annex X, sect. L, communication No. 518/1992, views adopted on 19 July 1995.

III:4

On 9 August 1991, a judge of a criminal court found him guilty as charged and sentenced him to one and a half years' imprisonment and three years' probation. His appeals against the conviction were later dismissed by the appeal section of the same court and, finally, by the Supreme Court.

In his complaint, the author argued that the provision he was convicted of having contravened was used to punish support for the labour movement and to isolate the workers. He also argued that the provision had never been used to charge those who took the side of management in a labour dispute. He claimed that the vagueness of the provision, which prohibited any act to influence the parties, violated the principle of legality (*nullum crimen, nulla poena sine lege*).

The author further argued that the provision was incorporated into the law to deny the right to freedom of expression to supporters of labourers or trade unions. In this respect, he made reference to the Labour Union Act, which prohibited third party support for the organization of a trade union. He concluded that any support to labourers or trade unions might thus be punished, by the Labour Dispute Adjustment Act at the time of strikes and by the Labour Union Act at other times.

The author claimed that his conviction violated article 19, paragraph 2, of the Covenant. He emphasized that the way in which he exercised his right to freedom of expression did not infringe the rights or reputations of others, nor did it threaten national security, public order or public health or morals.

In deciding on the admissiblity of the communication, the Committee noted that the author was arrested, charged and convicted not for any physical support for the strike in progress, but for participating in a meeting where verbal expressions of support were given. It considered that the facts submitted by the author might raise issues under article 19 of the Covenant and declared the communication admissible.

In its observations on the merits of the complaint, the State party emphasized that the author had not only attended the meeting of the Solidarity Forum on 9 February 1991, but had also actively participated in distributing propaganda on 10 or 11 February 1991, and, on 11 November 1990, he was involved in a violent demonstration during which Molotov cocktails were thrown.

The State party invoked article 19, paragraph 3, of the Covenant, providing that the right to freedom of expression might be subject to certain restrictions, *inter alia*, for the protection of national security or public order.

The author noted that the State party had not specified what part of the statements of the Solidarity Forum threatened public security and public order and for what reasons. He contended that a general reference to public security and public order did not justify the restriction of his freedom of expression. In this connection, he recalled that the statements of the Solidarity Forum contained arguments for the legitimacy of the strike concerned, strong support for the strike and criticism of the employer and of the Government for threatening to break the strike by force.

The author denied that the statements by the Solidarity Forum had posed a threat to the national security and public order of South Korea. He could not see how the expression of support for the strike and criticism of the employer and the Government in handling the matter could threaten national security. Moreover, the author argued that public order was not threatened by the statements given by the Solidarity Forum, but, on the contrary, the right to express one's opinion freely and peacefully enhanced public order in a democratic society.

The author noted that the Committee on Freedom of Association of the Governing Body of the International Labour Office had recommended that the Government should repeal the provision prohibiting the intervention by a third party in labour disputes. That provision was incompatible with the Constitution of the International Labour Organization, which guaranteed workers' freedom of expression as an essential component of the freedom of association.

The State party explained that the labour movement in the Republic of Korea could be generally described as being politically oriented and ideologically influenced. In this connection, it was stated that labour activists in Korea did not hesitate in leading workers to extreme actions by using force and violence and engaging in illegal strikes in order to fulfil their political aims or carry out their ideological principles. Furthermore, the State party argued, there had been frequent instances where the idea of a proletarian revolution had been implanted in the minds of workers.

The State party stated that if a third party interfered in a labour dispute to the extent that the party actually manipulated, instigated or obstructed the decisions of workers, such a dispute was being distorted towards other objectives and goals. The State party explained that in view of the general nature of the labour movement, it had felt obliged to maintain the law concerning the prohibition of third party intervention.

Moreover, the State party submitted, the written statement distributed in February 1991 to support the Daewoo Shipyard Trade Union was used as a disguise to incite a nation-wide strike of all workers. The State party argued that in the case where a national strike would take place, in any country, regardless of its security situation, there was considerable reason to believe that the national security and public order of the nation would be threatened.

III:4

Issues and proceedings before the Committee

The Committee took note of the State party's argument that Mr. Sohn had participated in a violent demonstration in November 1990 for which he was convicted under the applicable legislation. The Committee also noted that the author's complaint did not concern this particular conviction, but only his conviction for having issued the statement of the Solidarity Forum in February 1991. The Committee considered that the two convictions concerned two different events, which were not related. The issue before the Committee was, therefore, only whether Mr. Sohn's conviction under the Labour Dispute Adjustment Act for having joined in issuing a statement supporting the strike at the Daewoo Shipyard Company and condemning the Government's threat to send in troops to break the strike violated article 19, paragraph 2, of the Covenant.

This provision of the Covenant, guaranteeing the right to freedom of expression, included the freedom to seek, receive and impart information and ideas of all kinds, regardless of frontiers, either orally, in writing or in print, in the form of art, or through any other media. The Committee considered that the author, by joining others in issuing a statement supporting the strike and criticizing the Government, was exercising his right to impart information and ideas within the meaning of article 19, paragraph 2, of the Covenant.

The Committee observed that any restriction of the right to freedom of expression pursuant to article 19, paragraph 3, had cumulatively to meet the following conditions: it had to be provided for by law; it had to address one of the aims enumerated in article 19, paragraph 3 (*a*) and (*b*); and it had to be necessary to achieve the legitimate purpose. While the State party had stated that the restrictions were justified in order to protect national security and public order and that they were provided for by law, under the Labour Dispute Adjustment Act, the Committee had still to determine whether the measures taken against Mr. Sohn were necessary for the purpose stated.

The Committee noted that the State party had invoked national security and public order by reference to the general nature of the labour movement and by alleging that the statement issued by Mr. Sohn in collaboration with others was a disguise for the incitement to a national strike. The Committee considered that the State party had failed to specify the precise nature of the threat that it contended was posed by Mr. Sohn's exercise of his freedom of expression. It found that none of the arguments advanced by the State party sufficed to render the restriction of Mr. Sohn's right to freedom of expression compatible with article 19, paragraph 3, of the Covenant.

In conclusion, the Committee found that the facts before it disclosed a violation of article 19, paragraph 2, of the Covenant. The Committee was also of the view that

Mr. Sohn was entitled, under article 2, paragraph 3 (*a*), of the Covenant, to an effective remedy, including appropriate compensation, for having been convicted for exercising his right to freedom of expression. The Committee further invited the State party to review the Labour Dispute Adjustment Act. The State party was under an obligation to ensure that similar violations did not occur in the future. The Committee wished to receive from it, within 90 days, information about the measures taken to give effect to these views.

(*b*) *Ivcher Bronstein* case (*Peru*)
(Inter-American Court of Human Rights)[38]

On 31 March 1999, the Inter-American Commission on Human Rights submitted an application to the Inter-American Court of Human Rights against the Republic of Peru. It originated in a petition received on 9 June 1997 by the Commission. The purpose of the application was for the Court to decide whether the State had violated the rights of Baruch Ivcher Bronstein in respect of the right to a fair trial in article 8, the freedom of thought and expression in article 13, the right to nationality in article 20, the right to property in article 21 and the right to judicial protection in article 25, all of them in relation to the obligation to respect rights in article 1, paragraph 1, of the American Convention on Human Rights.

According to the facts described by the Commission, the State, in 1997, arbitrarily deprived Mr. Ivcher Bronstein, a naturalized Peruvian citizen, majority shareholder, director and president of Channel 2 of the Peruvian television network, of his nationality title in order to remove him from the editorial control of the Channel and restrict his freedom of expression, which he manifested by denouncing grave violations of human rights and acts of corruption.

The Commission therefore requested the Court to call on Peru to restore and guarantee to Mr. Ivcher Bronstein the enjoyment of all his rights, in particular to order that his Peruvian nationality title should be reinstated; that his enjoyment and exercise of his right to own shares in the company operating Channel 2 should be restored; that his enjoyment and exercise of the right to freedom of expression should be guaranteed and, in particular, that the acts of harassment and persecution against him, his family and his company should cease; and that the necessary legislative and administrative measures should be adopted to make full reparation and compensate him for all the material and moral damages the acts of the Peruvian administrative and judicial organs had caused him.

---

[38] See Inter-American Court of Human Rights, Series C: *Decisions and Judgments,* No. 74 (2002), petition No. 11762, judgment of 6 February 2001.

III:4

The Commission also petitioned the Court to order the State to adopt the necessary legislative and administrative measures to avoid a recurrence of events of this nature and to investigate and punish those responsible for the violations of the fundamental rights of Mr. Ivcher Bronstein.

Proceedings and conclusions of the Court

With the application brief, the Commission submitted 43 attachments, comprising 433 documents, eight videos and numerous newspaper articles. During the public hearing, the Commission submitted one video, two books and 34 documents.

During the public hearing, the Court received the statements of witnesses and the report of an expert, specialized in constitutional affairs, offered by the Commission. Some of these statements, summarized in the judgment, contained allegations that police and other security agencies had been involved in acts of harassment.

For example, Mr. Ivcher Bronstein testified that an agent of the army intelligence service had told him that the authorities were investigating his connection with the Ecuadorian army, had mentioned that he was a naturalized Israeli and warned him that he should take care, because there were those who wanted to kill him. The head of imports at a factory owned by Mr. Ivcher Bronstein stated that in connection with alleged customs and tax offences, police and army helicopters had flown very low over the factory for about three months and that when she was in prison, police had arrived with balaclava helmets and flashlights at about 2 a.m. or 3 a.m., shone the flashlights on her face and not let her sleep. They had also done this when she was in a clinic. Furthermore, a sociologist and journalist whose publications regularly referred to military issues, the intelligence services, cases of corruption and human rights violations testified that he had received death threats from the intelligence services of the armed forces.

As to the alleged violation of article 13 of the Convention, protecting the freedom of thought and expression, the Comission claimed, *inter alia*, the following. The primary objective of the deprivation of Mr. Ivcher Bronstein's nationality title was to violate his right to freedom of expression. The fact that Channel 2 under his direction transmitted news reports critical of the Government and that when he was separated from it, the journalists who produced those programmes were dismissed, thus terminating the transmission of such news reports, showed that the deprivation of his nationality was a means of reprisal and served to silence investigative journalism.

Furthermore, systematic repressive practices were carried out in Peru, designed to silence investigative journalists who had denounced irregularities in the conduct of the Peruvian Government, the armed forces and the national intelligence service.

The exercise of freedom of expression was not protected, in practice, by effective judicial guarantees that allowed the investigation, punishment and reparation of abuses and crimes against journalists. The overall evaluation of the attacks on investigative journalism revealed the existence of a plan designed to persecute and harass investigative journalists by the intelligence services, the security forces and other State institutions. This was shown by the persistence over time and the similarity of the campaigns of harassment and persecution, as well as the similarity of the investigation and denunciation activities of the victims.

The State did not submit any arguments on this issue, since it did not submit any defense, nor did it attend the hearings to which it was summoned.

Regarding the content of the right to freedom of thought and expression set forth in article 13 of the Convention, the Court, making reference to its jurisprudence, observed that those protected by this provision had not only the right and freedom to express their own thoughts. They had also the right and freedom to seek, receive and disseminate information and ideas of all types. Consequently, the freedom of expression had both an individual and a social dimension. It required, on the one hand, that no one might be arbitrarily harmed or impeded from expressing his own thought, and therefore it represented a right of each individual. However, it also implied, on the other hand, a collective right to receive any information and to know the expression of the thought of others. These two dimensions had to be guaranteed simultaneously.

With regard to the first dimension of the right embodied in article 13, the individual right, the Court stated that freedom of expression was not exhausted in the theoretical recognition of the right to speak or write. It also included, inseparably, the right to use any appropriate method to disseminate thought and allow it to reach the greatest number of persons. In this respect, the expression and dissemination of thought and information were indivisible. Consequently, a restriction of the possibilities of dissemination represented directly, and to the same extent, a limit to the right to free expression.

Regarding the second dimension of the right, the social element, the Court indicated that freedom of expression was a medium for the exchange of ideas and information between persons. It included the right to try and communicate one's points of view to others, but it also implied everyone's right to know opinions, reports and news. For the ordinary citizen, the right to know about other opinions and the information that others had was as important as the right to impart their own.

The Court considered both dimensions to be of equal importance. They should be guaranteed simultaneously in order to give total effect to the right to freedom of ex-

III:4

pression in the terms of article 13 of the Convention. The Court observed that the importance of this right was further underlined when examining the role that the media played in a democratic society, when a true instrument of freedom of expression and not a way of restricting it. Consequently, it was vital that the media could gather the most diverse information and opinions.

Furthermore, the Court stated, it was essential that the journalists who worked in the media should enjoy the necessary protection and independence to exercise their functions comprehensively, because they kept society informed, and this was an indispensable requirement to enable society to enjoy full freedom.

The Court had understood this in a previous advisory opinion by indicating that the same concept of public order in a democratic society required the guarantee of the widest possible circulation of news, ideas and opinions, as well as the widest access to information by society as a whole. Freedom of expression constituted the primary and basic element of the public order of a democratic society, and this was not conceivable without free debate and the possibility of dissenting voices to be fully heard.

The European Court of Human Rights had also recognized this criterion in stating that freedom of expression constituted one of the essential pillars of democratic society and a fundamental condition for its progress and the personal development of each individual. This freedom should not only be guaranteed with regard to the dissemination of information and ideas that were received favourably or considered inoffensive or indifferent, but also with regard to those that offended, were unwelcome or shocked the State or any sector of the population. According to the European Court, this was of particular importance when applied to the press. It not only implied that it was the task of the media to transmit information and ideas on matters of public interest, but also that the public had the right to receive them.

When evaluating an alleged restriction or limitation to freedom of expression, the American Court stated that it should not restrict itself to examining the act in question. It should also examine this act in the light of the facts of the case as a whole, including the circumstances and context in which they occurred. Taking this into consideration, the Court examined whether, in the context of the instant case, there was a violation of the right to freedom of expression in respect of Mr. Ivcher Bronstein.

It noted that the European Court had emphasized that article 10, paragraph 2, of the Convention for the Protection of Human Rights and Fundamental Freedoms, protecting the right to freedom of expression, left a very reduced margin to any restriction of political discussion or discussion of matters of public interest. According to this Court, the acceptable limits to criticism were broader with regard to the Government than in relation to the private citizen or even a politician. In a democratic system, the acts or omissions of the Government should be subject to rigorous examination, not only by the legislative and judicial authorities, but also by public opinion.

In the instant case, it had been established that in 1997, Mr. Ivcher Bronstein was the majority shareholder of the company operating Peruvian television's Channel 2. Moreover, he was director and chairman of the board and authorized to take editorial decisions on programming. In April 1997, in its programme *Contrapunto*, Channel 2 aired investigative reports of national interest, such as reports on possible torture committed by members of the army intelligence service against an agent, the alleged assassination of another agent and the extremely high revenues an adviser to the Peruvian intelligence service allegedly had obtained.

The testimonies of witnesses, including Mr. Ivcher Bronstein, demonstrated the extensive audience that Channel 2 had in 1997 throughout the country. Both Mr. Ivcher Bronstein and the journalists who worked for *Contrapunto* were fully entitled to investigate and disseminate events of public interest, such as those denounced, in the exercise of the right to freedom of expression protected by article 13 of the Convention.

In the same way, it had been shown that as a consequence of the editorial line assumed by Channel 2, Mr. Ivcher Bronstein was the object of threatening actions of various types. For example, after the emission of one of the reports mentioned, the joint command of the armed forces issued an official communiqué in which it denounced Mr. Ivcher Bronstein for conducting a defamatory campaign intended to slander the armed forces. On the same day, Peru's executive branch issued a supreme decree regulating the law on nationality and establishing the possibility of cancelling the nationality of naturalized Peruvians.

It had also been proved that only days after Channel 2 had announced the presentation of an investigative report on the unlawful recording of the telephone conversations of opposition candidates, the Director General of the National Police Force advised that the file in which the nationality title of Mr. Ivcher Bronstein was processed could not be found. Furthermore, it had not been certified that he had renounced his Israeli nationality. As a result, it was arranged to annul his Peruvian nationality title by a directorial resolution.

In view of the foregoing, the Court noted, a judge ordered the suspension of the exercise of Mr. Ivcher Bronstein's rights as majority shareholder and president of the company operating Channel 2, and his appointment as a director of the company was revoked. An extraordinary shareholders meeting was judicially convened to e-

III:4

lect a new board, and Mr. Ivcher Bronstein was prohibited from transferring his shares. Moreover, the judge granted the provisional administration of the company to the minority shareholders until a new board was appointed, thus taking the control of Channel 2 away from Mr. Ivcher Bronstein.

It had been verified that after the minority shareholders of the company assumed its administration, the journalists who had been working for *Contrapunto* were prohibited from entering the Channel and the programmes's editorial line was modified.

In the context of these facts, the Court observed that the resolution annulling the nationality title of Mr. Ivcher Bronstein constituted an indirect means of restricting his freedom of expression, as well as that of the journalists who worked and conducted investigations for *Contrapunto* of Peruvian television's Channel 2.

By separating Mr. Ivcher Bronstein from the control of Channel 2 and excluding the *Contrapunto* journalists, the State had not only restricted their right to circulate news, ideas and opinions. It had also affected the right of all Peruvians to receive information, thus limiting their freedom to exercise political options and develop fully in a democratic society. The Court concluded that the State had violated the right to freedom of expression embodied in article 13, paragraphs 1 and 3, of the Convention with regard to Mr. Ivcher Bronstein.

As to the alleged non-compliance by the State with the obligation to respect rights under article 1, paragraph 1, of the Convention, the Commission claimed that the arbitrary deprivation of the nationality title of Mr. Ivcher Bronstein and the other acts violating his rights constituted an additional violation by the State of that provision.

Based on this article, the Court had already in a previous case established that the State was obliged to respect the rights and freedoms recognized in the Convention and to organize the public authorities in order to ensure to all persons subject to its jurisdiction the free and full exercise of human rights. According to the legal norms on state responsibility applicable under international human rights law, the act or omission of any public authority, whatsoever its rank, constituted an act which might be attributed to the State and engaged its responsibility in the terms of the of the Convention.

The Court observed that pursuant to what had been established in the judgment, the State had violated, *inter alia*, article 13 of the Convention with regard to Mr. Ivcher Bronstein. Consequently, it had failed to comply with its general obligation to respect the rights and freedoms recognized in the Convention and to ensure their free and full exercise as stipulated in article 1, paragraph 1.

Under article 63, paragraph 1, of the Convention, the Court, when there had been a violation of a right or freedom protected by the Convention, was to rule that the injured party should be ensured the enjoyment of his right or freedom violated. It was also to rule, if appropriate, that the consequences of the measure or situation that constituted the breach of such a right or freedom should be remedied and fair compensation paid to the injured party.

In this case, the Court had already established that Peru violated article 13 of the Convention, as well as a number of other articles not included in this summary. As a consequence of these violations, the Court ruled, the victim should be guaranteed the enjoyment of his violated rights and freedoms. The Court noted that a ministerial resolution had declared null and void the previous resolution annulling Mr. Ivcher Bronstein's nationality. Consequently, the Court considered that the State had already responded to the Commission's request concerning the reinstatement of the nationality title of Mr. Ivcher Bronstein.

In respect of the right to property, the Court believed that the State should facilitate the conditions whereby Mr. Ivcher Bronstein, whose Peruvian nationality had been restored, could take the necessary steps to recover the use and enjoyment of his rights as majority shareholder of the company operating Channel 2, in the terms of domestic legislation.

With regard to article 13 of the Convention, the Court considered that the State should guarantee Mr. Ivcher Bronstein the right to seek, investigate and disseminate information and ideas through Peruvian television's Channel 2.

The Court also made a statement on the obligation of States parties to prevent, investigate, identify and punish the masterminds and accessories to human rights violations. Based on that, the Court reiterated, the State had the obligation to avoid and combat impunity, defined as the overall lack of investigation, tracking down, capture, prosecution and conviction of those responsible for violating the rights protected by the Convention. Consequently, Peru should investigate the facts that resulted in the violations established in the judgment in order to identify and punish those responsible.

Finally, as to damages in this case, the Court found, particularly taking into account the acts of persecution suffered by Mr. Ivcher Bronstein, that it would be fair to grant him 20,000 United States dollars in compensation for moral damages. The Court also found it fair to grant him the amount of 50,000 dollars in reimbursement of the costs and expenses incurred in the domestic and the international jurisdictions.

III:4

(c) *Thorgeir Thorgeirson* v. *Iceland*
(European Court of Human Rights)[39]

The case was referred to the European Court of Human Rights on 8 March 1991 by the European Commission of Human Rights. It originated in an application against the Republic of Iceland lodged with the Commission on 19 November 1987 by Thorgeir Thorgeirson, an Icelandic citizen. The object of the Commission's request was to obtain a decision as to whether the facts of the case disclosed a breach by the respondent State of its obligations under articles 6, paragraph 1, and 10 of the Convention for the Protection of Human Rights and Fundamental Freedoms.

The facts

The applicant was a writer residing in Reykjavik. From 1979 to 1983, a number of incidents occurred in Iceland involving allegations of police brutality, and about 10 of them were reported to the police. The last of these complaints, made in the autumn of 1983 by a journalist, led to the prosecution of three members of the Reykjavik police of whom two were acquitted and one convicted. His case received extensive coverage by the press and gave rise to considerable discussion on the relations between the public and the police. This caused Thorgeir Thorgeirson to publish two articles on police brutality in an Icelandic daily on 7 and 20 December 1983, respectively.

The first article, which took the form of an open letter to the Minister of Justice, included the following statements:

> (1) Recently a problem which has been bothering - if not obsessing - me for several years has suddenly been highlighted by the press. One of the journalists of your very own progressive party-newspaper [...] had a painful experience and returned with some injuries from the Reykjavik night-life jungle. [...]

> (2) [...] The photographs of his facial injuries, spread across four newspaper columns, have, of course, shocked us.

> (3) We do not want to accept that our policemen have damaged this journalist's handsome face in this way. All he was doing, he tells us, was innocently looking for his overcoat when the beasts in uniform in the aforementioned jungle attacked him.

---

[39] See *Publications of the European Court of Human Rights*, Series A: *Judgments and Decisions*, vol. 239 (1992), application No. 13778/88, judgment of 25 June 1992.

(5) [This] case, brought to our attention by the press, is but the tip of the iceberg. Beneath it, in the dark sea of silence, lurks a problem nine times bigger.

(6) That is the part I would like to bring to your attention, because you are the Minister of Justice and thus in command of those wild beasts in uniform that creep around, silently or not, in the jungle of our town's night-life.

(8) Several years ago I had to spend several weeks on a ward in our local hospital. In a room leading off the same corridor was a man in his twenties lying in his bed. He was a promising and charming young person, but he was paralysed to the extent that he could not move any part of his body, other than his eyes. He was able to read with the aid of special machinery and a helping hand to turn the pages for him.

I was told that his chance of recovery was minimal.

(9) The young man's room-mates told me that his injuries had been inflicted by bouncers of a restaurant and some policemen. At first I could not believe this, so I enquired among the hospital staff and - Yes, they were right; we had there a victim of the Reykjavik night-squad.

(10) The image of this paralysed youngster somehow followed me out of the hospital and I couldn't help talking about his case. I then found out that most people had various stories of persons who had had a similar or even worse experiences with the beasts in uniform. Individuals reduced to a mental age of a new-born child as a result of strangleholds that policemen and bouncers learn and use with brutal spontaneity instead of handling people with prudence and care. There are so many such stories, identical in substance, that you can hardly dismiss them merely as lies any more. Another thing that goes with those stories as inevitably as brutality follows stupidity is the statement that suing a policeman in such a case would be hopeless. The investigation would be undertaken by another department of the police and there be carried out by an élite group who see it as their duty to wash all policemen clean of any accusations made against them.

(11) The victims of the police brutes remain forgotten, without hope, as the years pass without their causes ever being seriously discussed.

(12) Now this might be one of those rare occasions. It is the reason for this letter of mine.

III:4

(13) I have little doubt that there is something essentially wrong in a system where the people in charge seem to disregard all sense of justice and misinterpret their duties by allowing brutes and sadists to act out their perversions - no matter who is the victim. [...]

(15) My opinion is that the real problem lies with a system where policemen investigate other policemen's violations of correct professional conduct. [...]

(20) I have the gut feeling that our Police Problem could be compared with the so-called Youth Problem in the sense that comparatively few individuals are responsible for this negative public opinion of them. Furthermore, those individuals could not be said to be typical of either group - nor the most intelligent.

(21) I have seen the policemen in this town perform many a good deed and therein I have met many an exemplary fellow. We cannot do without them. But I feel I owe it to the young man I met at the local hospital to muster my courage and put forward this proposal: let us try cleaning up this mess so that those who, ready to risk their lives, embark on the adventure of the jungle of the Reykjavik night-life in the future can at least be assured that a policeman in uniform is not among the perils therein.

There are enough other wild beasts.

The second article was a response to comments made by a police official, chairman of the Reykjavik Police Association, during a television programme in which he read a statement referring to the first article. Extracts from this article read as follows:

(14) Since Tuesday many people have telephoned me and expressed the opinion that the policemen's show on television was a disastrous exhibition of national characteristics for our children to see.

(15) They should have been in uniform, someone said. Their behaviour was so typical of what is gradually becoming the public image of our police force defending itself: bullying, forgery, unlawful actions, superstitions, rashness and ineptitude.

In just those words.

In response to these articles, the Ministry of Justice sent Mr. Thorgeirson a letter dated 9 January 1984. He was informed that the problems raised in the articles were being reviewed at various levels and that the matter was on the agenda of the Parliament so that the Minister of Justice could report to it in the near future on the studies and proposals which had been made in this field.

By letter of 27 December 1983, the Reykjavik Police Association asked the public prosecutor to investigate the allegations. Accordingly, on 21 May 1984, he sent the case to criminal investigation police to examine whether the publications constituted defamation within the meaning of the general penal code. On 18 June 1984, the police interrogated Mr. Thorgeirson who was assisted by his lawyer. On 13 August 1985, the public prosecutor issued a bill of indictment charging Mr. Thorgeirson with defamation of unspecified members of the Reykjavik police, contrary to the penal code. Some passages of the two articles were considered to be defamatory.

On 9 September 1985, an indictment was served on Mr. Thorgeirson, summoning him to appear at a criminal court. After a number of hearings, he was convicted and sentenced to pay a fine. He was also ordered to pay all the costs of the case, including his counsel's fees. Both Mr. Thorgeirson and the prosecutor appealed to the Supreme Court of Iceland. It heard the case on 22 September 1987, but the conviction and the punishment were upheld.

The law

As to the alleged violation of article 6, paragraph 1, of the Convention, on the right to a fair trial, the applicant claimed that he had not received a hearing by an impartial tribunal within the meaning of that provision. The public prosecutor had, in accordance with Icelandic law, been absent from a number of sittings of the criminal court, allegedly resulting in the judge also taking on a role as representative of the prosecution. This claim was contested by the Government and not accepted by the Commission.

The Court did not consider, in the circumstances, that such fears as the the applicant might have had, on account of the prosecutor's absence, regarding the court's lack of impartiality could be held justified. It found unanimously that there had been no violation of article 6, paragraph 1, of the Convention.

As to the alleged violation of article 10 of the Convention, protecting the right to freedom of expression, the applicant claimed to be a victim of a violation as a result of the defamation proceedings instituted against him and his subsequent conviction. The allegation was accepted by the Commission but contested by the Government.

The Court considered that Mr. Thorgeirson's conviction and sentence for defamation by the criminal court, as upheld by the Supreme Court, constituted an interfer-

III:4

ence with his right to freedom of expression, and this was not disputed. Such an interference entailed a violation of article 10 of the Convention unless it was prescribed by law, had an aim or aims legitimate under paragraph 2 of that article and was necessary in a democratic society for this aim or these aims.

After noting the relevant domestic law and the way in which it had been applied by the domestic courts, the Court concluded that the interference was prescribed by law. It also noted that it was not disputed that the applicant's conviction and sentence were aimed at protecting the reputation of others and thus had an aim that was legitimate under article 10, paragraph 2, of the Convention.

In considering whether or not the interference was necessary in a democratic society, the Court recalled that freedom of expression constituted one of the essential foundations of a democratic society. Subject to article 10, paragraph 2, of the Convention, it was applicable not only to information or ideas that were favourably received or regarded as inoffensive or as a matter of indifference, but also to those that offended, shocked or disturbed. As the Court had stated in a previous judgment, the freedom of expression, as enshrined in article 10, was subject to a number of exceptions which, however, had to be narrowly interpreted, and the necessity for any restrictions had to be convincingly established.

In the present case, the Court noted that Mr. Thorgeirson had expressed his views by having them published in a newspaper. Making reference to its case law, the Court said that regard had therefore to be had to the pre-eminent role of the press in a State governed by the rule of law. Whilst the press must not overstep the bounds set, *inter alia*, for the protection of the reputation of others, it was nevertheless incumbent on it to impart information and ideas on matters of public interest. Not only did it have the task of imparting such information and ideas. The public also had a right to receive them. Were it otherwise, the press would be unable to play its vital role of "public watchdog".

On the questions of general principle raised by the Government, the Court observed that there was no warrant in its case law for distinguishing, in the manner suggested by the Government, between political discussion and discussion of other matters of public concern. Its submission which sought to restrict the right to freedom of expression on the basis of the recognition in article 10 that its exercise carried with it duties and responsibilities failed to appreciate that such exercise could be restricted only on the conditions provided for in paragraph 2 of that article.

Regarding the specific circumstances of the case, the Court was unable to accept the Government's argument that the statements in Mr. Thorgeirson's articles lacked an objective and factual basis. The first article took as its starting-point one specific case of ill-treatment which had given rise to extensive public debate and led to the conviction of the policeman responsible. It was undisputed that this incident did actually occur.

With regard to the other factual elements contained in the articles, the Court noted that these consisted essentially of references to stories or rumours, emanating from persons other than the applicant, or public opinion, involving allegations of police brutality. For instance, it was the room-mates of the young man at the hospital who had recounted, and the hospital personnel who had confirmed, that he had been injured by the police. It had not been established that this story was altogether untrue and merely invented. Again, according to the first article, Mr. Thorgeirson had found out that most people knew of various stories of that kind which were so similar and numerous that they could hardly be treated as mere lies.

In short, Mr. Thorgeirson was essentially reporting what was being said by others about police brutality. He was convicted by the criminal court of an offence under the penal code, partly because of failure to justify what it considered to be his own allegations, namely that unspecified members of the Reykjavik police had committed a number of acts of serious assault resulting in disablement of their victims, as well as forgery and other criminal offences. Insofar as Mr. Thorgeirson was required to establish the truth of his statements, he was, in the Court's opinion, faced with an unreasonable, if not impossible, task.

The Court was also not convinced by the Government's contention that the principal aim of Mr. Thorgeirson's articles was to damage the reputation of the Reykjavik police as a whole. In the first place, his criticisms could not be taken as an attack against all the members, or any specific member, of the Reykjavik police force. As stated in the first article, Mr. Thorgeirson assumed that comparatively few individuals were responsible and that an independent investigation would hopefully show that a small minority of policemen were responsible. Secondly, as the Court had observed, Mr. Thorgeirson was essentially reporting what was being said by others.

These circumstances, combined with a perusal of the first article, confirmed his contention that his principal purpose was to urge the Minister of Justice to set up an independent and impartial body to investigate complaints of police brutality. The second article, written in response to certain statements made by a police officer during a television programme, had to be seen as a continuation of the first article.

The articles bore on a matter of serious public concern, and they were framed in particularly strong terms. However, having regard to their purpose and the impact that they were designed to have, the Court was of the opinion that the language used could not be regarded as excessive. Finally, the Court considered that the conviction and sentence were capable of discouraging open discussion of matters of public concern.

The Court concluded that the reasons advanced by the Government did not suffice to show that the interference complained of was proportionate to the legitimate aim pursued. It was therefore not necessary in a democratic society. Accordingly, the Court held, by eight votes to one, that there had been a violation of article 10 of the Convention.

Under the then article 50 of the Convention, allowing the Court to afford just satisfaction to an injured party, under specified circumstances, when there had been a violation of the Convention, the Court considered that the applicant was entitled to be reimbursed, for costs and expenses, the sum of 530,000 Icelandic crowns.

(*d*) Özgür Gündem v. *Turkey* (European Court of Human Rights)[40]

The case was referred to the European Court of Human Rights on 8 March 1999 by the European Commission of Human Rights. It originated in an application against the Republic of Turkey lodged with the Commission on 9 December 1993 by three Turkish nationals, named in the judgment, and a Turkish limited company. The first two applicants were, respectively, the editor-in-chief and the assistant editor-in-chief of the Turkish newspaper *Özgür Gündem* of which the third and fourth applicants were the owners. The Commission later decided not to pursue the examination of the application insofar as it concerned the first applicant, since she had died in 1997.

The application concerned the applicants' allegations that there had been a concerted and deliberate assault on their freedom of expression through a campaign of targeting journalists and others involved in *Özgür Gündem*. The applicants relied on articles 10 and 14 of the Convention for the Protection of Human Rights and Fundamental Freedoms and on article 1 of the first Protocol to the Convention.

The facts

The daily *Özgür Gündem* had its main office located in Istanbul. It was a Turkish-language publication with an estimated national circulation of up to 45,000 copies and a further unspecified international circulation. It incorporated its predecessor, the weekly *Yeni Ülke*, which was published between 1990 and 1992. *Özgür Gündem*

---

[40] See European Court of Human Rights, *Reports of Judgments and Decisions*, 2000-III, p. 1, application No. 23144/93, judgment of 16 March 2000.

was published from 30 May 1992 until April 1994. It was succeeded by another newspaper, *Özgür Ülke*.

The case concerned the applicants' allegations that *Özgür Gündem* was the subject of serious attacks and harassment which forced its eventual closure and for which the Turkish authorities were directly or indirectly responsible.

The applicants made detailed submissions to the Commission, listing the attacks made on journalists, distributors and others associated with the newspaper. The Government, in its submissions to the Commission, denied that some of these attacks had occurred.

The following incidents were not contested: Seven people connected with *Özgür Gündem* were killed in circumstances originally regarded as killings by unknown perpetrators. These people, journalists, staff members and others, were listed in the judgment with the dates and manner of their deaths. Details of eight attacks between November 1992 and October 1993 on newsagents' premises and individuals selling *Özgür Gündem* were also set out in the judgment. These included arson attacks on premises and knife attacks on newspaper boys. A ninth attack, consisting of a bomb explosion on 2 December 1994 at the Istanbul office of the newspaper's successor, *Özgür Ülke*, killing one employee and injuring 18 others, was also included.

The applicants listed a large number of other incidents, arson attacks, attacks and threats on newsagents, distributors and newspaper boys, which the Government stated either had not occured or concerning which it had received no information or complaint. They also referred to the disappearance of a journalist on 7 August 1993 and to the detention and ill-treatment of many journalists. In one these cases, the Court had found that the journalist had been subjected to inhuman and degrading treatment while in custody.

The applicants, and others acting on behalf of the newspaper and its employees, addressed numerous petitions to the authorities concerning the threats and attacks that they claimed had occurred. These included letters from one of the applicants to the Prime Minister, the Deputy Prime Minister and the Minister of the Interior, informing them of the attacks and requesting investigations to be opened and measures of protection to be taken. There was no reply to the vast majority of these letters.

Written complaints were made by persons from the newspaper about specific attacks, incidents and threats concerning which the Government stated that it had received no information or complaint, including the attacks on children distributing the newspaper in Diyarbakir during 1993, the death of a newsagent in Diyarbakir on

III:4

27 September 1993 and attacks on distributors by people with meat axes, also in Diyarbakir, in September 1993.

Following a request for security measures received by the Diyarbakir police on 2 December 1993, police escorted employees of the two companies dealing with the distribution of newspapers to the distribution stores. Measures were also taken with respect to deliveries of the newspaper from the stores to newsagents. The Government submitted to the Commission that no other requests for protection were received. Following the explosion on 2 December 1994 at the office of *Özgür Ülke* and a request from the owner, security measures, including patrolling, were taken by the authorities.

On 10 December 1993, the police conducted a search of the office of *Özgür Gündem* in Istanbul. During the operation, they took into custody those present in the building, 107 persons, including two of the applicants, and seized all the documents and archives.

Two search-and-seizure documents, dated 10 December 1993, record that the police found two guns, ammunition, two sleeping bags and 25 gas masks. In a further search-and-seizure document dated 10 December 1993, it was stated that the following items had been found: photographs, described as kept in envelopes with a label "PKK Terrorist Organization"; a tax receipt stamped with the name ERNK, a wing of the Workers' Party of Kurdistan (PKK), for 400,000,000 Turkish liras, found in the desk of one of the applicants; and numerous printed and hand-written documents, including an article on Abdullah Öcalan. A document dated 24 December 1993, signed by a public prosecutor at the Istanbul national security court, listed the following material as having been seized: in a sealed envelope, the military identification card of a dead soldier; in a sealed box, 1,350 injection kits, one typewriter, one video-cassette and one audio-cassette; and 40 books found at the house of one of the applicants. As a result of these measures, the publication of the newspaper was disrupted for two days.

In an indictment dated 5 April 1994, charges were brought against three of the applicants and seven others, alleging that they were members of the PKK, had assisted the PKK and made propaganda in its favour. According to the Government, the editor and the manager were convicted, on 12 December 1996 by a national security court, of aiding and abetting the PKK. The editor had previously been convicted of involvement with the PKK, in or about the end of December 1990, and had been released from prison in 1992.

Numerous prosecutions were brought against the newspaper, including the relevant editor, the owner and publisher and the authors of the impugned articles, alleging that offences had been committed through the publication of various articles. The prosecutions resulted in many convictions, carrying sentences imposing fines and prison terms, orders of confiscation of issues of the newspaper and orders of closure of the newspaper for periods of three days to a month.

The prosecutions were brought under provisions rendering it an offence, *inter alia*, to publish material insulting or vilifying the Turkish nation, the Republic or specific State officers or authorities; material provoking feelings of hatred and enmity on grounds of race, region of origin or class; and materials constituting separatist propaganda, disclosing the names of officials involved in fighting terrorism or reporting the declarations of terrorist organizations.

On 3 July 1993, *Özgür Gündem* published a press release announcing that the newspaper was charged with offences which, cumulatively, were punishable by fines totalling 8,617,441,000 Turkish liras and prison terms ranging from 155 years and 9 months to 493 years and 4 months.

During a period of 68 days in 1993, 41 issues of the newspaper were ordered to be seized. In 20 cases, closure orders were issued, three for a period of one month, 15 for a period of 15 days and two for 10 days.

The applicants further stated, and this was not contested by the Government, that there had been prosecutions in respect of 486 out of 580 issues of the newspaper and that pursuant to convictions by the domestic courts, the owner had been fined up to 35 billion liras, while journalists and editors together had had imposed sentences totalling 147 years' imprisonment and fines reaching 21 billion liras.

Both parties provided the Commission with copies of judgments and decisions by the courts relating to the proceedings brought in respect of the newspaper. These involved 112 prosecutions brought between 1992 and 1994. Details of the articles in issue and the judgments given in 21 cases were summarized in the Commission's report.

The applicants provided the Commission with a copy of the so-called "Susurluk report", produced at the request of the Prime Minister within his office. After receiving the report in January 1998, he made it available to the public, although 11 pages and certain annexes were withheld.

Susurluk was the scene of a road accident in November 1996 involving a car in which a member of parliament, a former deputy director of the Istanbul security services, a notorious far-right extremist, a drug trafficker wanted by Interpol and his girlfriend had been travelling. The latter three were killed. The fact that they had all

III:4

been travelling in the same car had so shocked public opinion that it had been neces-sary to start more than 16 judicial investigations at different levels and a parliamen-tary inquiry.

In the introduction, it was stated that the report was not based on a judicial investiga-tion and did not constitute a formal investigative report. It was intended for informa-tion purposes and purported to do no more than describe certain events that had oc-curred mainly in southeast Turkey, tending to confirm the existence of unlawful dealings between political figures, government institutions and clandestine groups.

The report analyzed a series of events, such as murders carried out under orders, the killings of well-known figures or supporters of the Kurds and deliberate acts by a group of informants supposedly serving the State. It concluded that there was a con-nection between the fight to eradicate terrorism in the region and the underground relations that had been formed as a result, particularly in the drug-trafficking sphere. The report included passages that concerned matters affecting radical periodicals distributed in the region.

The report ended with numerous recommendations, such as improving coordination and communication between the different branches of the security, police and intelli-gence departments; identifying and dismissing security force personnel implicated in illegal activities; limiting the use of confessors; reducing the number of village guards; terminating the use of a special operations bureau outside the southeast re-gion and incorporating it into the police outside that area; opening investigations in-to various incidents; and taking steps to suppress gang and drug-smuggling activi-ties.

The law

As to the alleged violation of article 10 of the Convention, protecting the right to freedom of expression, the applicants complained that the newspaper *Özgür Gün-dem* was forced to cease publication due to the campaign of attacks on journalists and others associated with the newspaper and due to the legal steps taken against the newspaper and its staff.

The applicants claimed that the Turkish authorities had, directly or indirectly, sought to hinder, prevent and render impossible the production of *Özgür Gündem* by the en-couragement of, or acquiescence in, unlawful killings and forced disappearances, by harassment and intimidation of journalists and distributors and by failure to provide any, or any adequate, protection for journalists and distributors when their lives were clearly in danger and despite requests for such protection.

They relied on the findings in the Commission's report that there was a disturbing pattern of attacks on persons concerned with *Özgür Gündem*. Through the failure by authorities to take measures of protection and to conduct adequate investigations in relation to the apparent pattern of attacks on the newspaper and persons connected with it, they did not comply with their positive obligation to secure to the applicants their right to freedom of expression guaranteed under article 10 of the Convention.

The Government emphasized that *Özgür Gündem* was the instrument of the terrorist organization PKK and espoused the aim of that organization to destroy the territorial integrity of Turkey by violent means. It disputed that any reliance could be placed on previous judgments of the Court or on the Susurluk report in deducing that there was any official complicity in any alleged attacks. In particular, that report was not a judicial document and had no probative value.

The Government submitted that the Commission based its findings on general presumptions unsupported by any evidence and that the applicants had not substantiated their claims of a failure to protect the lives and physical integrity of persons attached to *Özgür Gündem*. Nor had they substantiated that the persons attacked were related to the newspaper. The Government disputed that any positive obligation extended to the protection and promotion of the propaganda instrument of a terrorist organization. It asserted that in any event, necessary measures were taken in response to individual complaints, investigations being carried out by public prosecutors as required.

The Court observed that the Government had disputed the Commission's findings concerning the pattern of attacks in general terms without specifying which were, or in what way they were, inaccurate. It noted that the Government denied specifically that any weight could be given to the Susurluk report and its description of acquiescence and connivance by State authorities in unlawful activities, some of which targeted *Özgür Gündem* and journalists.

In a previous case against Turkey, in which it was alleged that the security forces had connived in an attack on two people who were involved in the sale and distribution of *Özgür Gündem* in Diyarbakir, the Court had found that the Susurluk report did not provide a basis for enabling the perpetrators of the attack on the victims in the case to be identified. It did find that the report gave rise to serious concerns and that it was not disputed in the case that there had been a number of serious attacks on journalists, newspaper kiosks and distributors of *Özgür Gündem*. The Susurluk report might indeed not be relied on for establishing to the required standard of proof that State officials were implicated in any particular incident. However, the Court considered that the report, which was drawn up at the request of the Prime Minister and which he decided should be made public, had to be regarded as a serious attempt to provide information on, and analyze problems associated with, the

III:4

fight against terrorism from a general perspective and to recommend preventive and investigative measures. On that basis, the report could be relied on as providing factual substantiation of the fears expressed by the applicants from 1992 onwards that the newspaper and persons associated with it were at risk from unlawful violence.

Having regard to the parties' submissions and the findings of the Commission in its report, the Court was satisfied that from 1992 to 1994 there were numerous incidents of violence, including killings, assaults and arson attacks, involving *Özgür Gündem* and journalists, distributors and other persons associated with it. The concerns of the newspaper and its fears that it was the victim of a concerted campaign tolerated, if not approved, by State officials were brought to the attention of the authorities. It did not appear, however, that any measures were taken to investigate this allegation. Nor did the authorities respond by any protective measures, save in two instances.

The Court had long held that, although the essential object of many provisions of the Convention was to protect the individual against arbitrary interference by public authorities, there might in addition be positive obligations inherent in an effective respect of the rights concerned. Making reference to its case law, the Court said that it had found that such obligations might arise under articles 8 and 11 of the Convention. Obligations to take steps to undertake effective investigations had also been found to accrue in the context of articles 2 and 3, while a positive obligation to take steps to protect life might also exist under article 2.

The Court recalled the key importance of freedom of expression as one of the preconditions for a functioning democracy. Genuine, effective exercise of this freedom did not depend merely on the State's duty not to interfere, but might require positive measures of protection, even in the sphere of relations between individuals. In determining whether or not a positive obligation existed, regard had to be had to the fair balance to be struck between the general interest of the community and the interests of the individual, the search for which was inherent throughout the Convention. The scope of this obligation would inevitably vary, having regard to the diversity of situations obtaining in the States parties, the difficulties involved in policing modern societies and the choices that had to be made in terms of priorities and resources. Nor must such an obligation be interpreted in such a way as to impose an impossible or disproportionate burden on the authorities, as the Court had stated in previous judgments.

In the present case, the authorities were aware that *Özgür Gündem*, and persons associated with it, had been subject to a series of violent acts and that the applicants feared that they were being targeted deliberately in efforts to prevent the publication and distribution of the newspaper. However, the vast majority of the petitions and requests for protection submitted by the newspaper or its staff remained unanswered.

The Government had only been able to identify one protective measure concerning the distribution of the newspaper which was taken while the newspaper was still in existence. The steps taken after the bomb attack on 2 December 1994 at the Istanbul office concerned the newspaper's successor. The Court found, having regard to the seriousness of the attacks and their widespread nature, that the Government could not rely on the investigations ordered by individual public prosecutors into specific incidents. It was not convinced by the Government's contention that these investigations provided adequate or effective responses to the applicants' allegations that the attacks were part of a concerted campaign which was supported, or tolerated, by the authorities.

The Court noted the Government's submissions concerning its strongly held conviction that *Özgür Gündem* and its staff supported the PKK and acted as its propaganda tool. This did not, even if true, provide a justification for failing to take steps effectively to investigate and, where necessary, provide protection against unlawful acts involving violence.

The Court concluded that the Government had failed, in the circumstances, to comply with their positive obligation to protect *Özgür Gündem* in the exercise of its freedom of expression.

Concerning the police operation on 10 December 1993 at the premises of *Özgür Gündem* in Istanbul, the applicants relied on the findings in the Commission's report that the search-and-arrest operation, during which all the employees were detained and the archives, library and administrative documents seized, disclosed an interference with the newspaper's freedom of expression for which there was no convincing justification. In their submissions to the Commission, they stated that there were innocent explanations for the allegedly incriminating material found on the premises.

The Government pointed to the materials seized during the search, including injection kits, gas masks, an ERNK receipt and the identity card of a dead soldier, which, they submitted, were indisputable proof of the links between the newspaper and the PKK. It referred to the conviction on 12 December 1996 of the editor and the manager for aiding the PKK. They also asserted that of the 107 people apprehended at the Istanbul office, 40 could claim no connection with the newspaper, which gave additional grounds for suspicions of complicity with the terrorist organization.

The Court found that the operation, which resulted in newspaper production being disrupted for two days, constituted a serious interference with the applicants' freedom of expression. It accepted that the operation was conducted according to a procedure prescribed by law for the purpose of preventing crime and disorder within the meaning of article 10, paragraph 2, of the Convention. It did not, however, find that

III:4

a measure of such dimension was proportionate to this aim. No justification had been provided for the seizure of the newspaper's archives, documentation and library. Nor had the Court received an explanation for the fact that every person found on the newspaper's premises had been taken into custody, including the cook, cleaner and heating engineer. The presence of 40 persons who were not employed by the newspaper was not, in itself, evidence of any sinister purpose or of the commission of any offence.

As stated in the Commission's report, the necessity for any restriction in the exercise of freedom of expression had to be convincingly established. The Court concluded that the search operation, as conducted by the authorities, had not been shown to be necessary in a democratic society for the implementation of any legitimate aim.

Concerning the legal measures taken in respect of issues of *Özgür Gündem*, the applicants claimed that the Government had also sought to hinder, prevent and render impossible the production and distribution of the newspaper by means of unjustified legal proceedings. The Court examined in detail five of these proceedings.

In respect of prosecutions concerning the offence of insulting the State and the military authorities, the Court found that the measures taken were not necessary in a democratic society for the pursuit of any legitimate aim. In respect of prosecutions concerning the offence of provoking racial and regional hostility, the Court found no relevant and sufficient reasons for imposing criminal convictions and penalties in respect of this offence and that the interference was not justified under article 10, paragraph 2, of the Convention. In respect of prosecutions for reporting statements of the PKK, the Court found that the measures complained of were reasonably proportionate to the legitimate aims of preventing crime and disorder and could be justified as necessary in a democratic society within the meaning of article 10, paragraph 2. In respect of prosecutions for statements constituting separatist propaganda, the Court concluded that the restrictions imposed on the newspaper's freedom of expression disclosed in these cases were disproportionate to the aim pursued and could not be justified as necessary in a democratic society.

Finally, in respect of prosecutions for identifying officials participating in the fight against terrorism, the Court observed that the convictions and sentences had been imposed, because the articles had identified by name certain officials in connection with alleged misconduct, namely, the death of a politician's son during detention, the allegation of official acquiescence in the killing of a journalist, the forcible evacuation of villages, the intimidation of villagers, the bombing of Sirnak and the revenge killing of two persons after a PKK raid on a gendarmerie headquarters. However, it was significant that in two of the articles, the officials named were not in fact alleged to be responsible for the misconduct, but merely implicated in the surrounding events. In particular, concerning the death during detention, the Sirnak security director was cited as having previously reassured the family that the man would be released safely and the Sirnak chief public prosecutor was reported as being unavailable for comment. While three village guards were named in the article concerning the revenge killing, it was alleged that the gendarmes had killed the two people.

It was true, the Court observed, that the other three articles alleged serious misconduct by the officials named and were capable of exposing them to public contempt. However, as for the other articles, the truth of their content was apparently not a factor taken into account, and, if true, the matters described were of public interest. Nor was it taken into account that the names of the officials and their role in fighting terrorism were already in the public domain. Thus, the governor of the state of emergency region who was named in one article was a public figure in the region, while the gendarmerie commanders and village guards named in the other articles would have been well known in their districts. Consequently, the interest in protecting their identity was substantially diminished, and the potential damage that the restriction aimed at preventing was minimal. Citing a previous judgment against Turkey, the Court said that to the extent, therefore, that the authorities had relevant reasons to impose criminal sanctions, these could not be regarded as sufficient to justify the restrictions placed on the newspaper's freedom of expression. Accordingly, these measures could not be justified in terms of article 10, paragraph 2, of the Convention.

The Court concluded that the respondent State had failed to take adequate protective and investigative measures to protect *Özgür Gündem* in the exercise of its freedom of expression and that it had imposed measures on the newspaper, through the search-and-arrest operation of 10 December 1993 and through numerous prosecutions and convictions in respect of issues of the newspaper, which were disproportionate and unjustified in the pursuit of any legitimate aim. As a result of these cumulative factors, the newspaper ceased publication. Accordingly, there had been a breach of article 10 of the Convention.

As to the alleged violation of article 14 of the Convention, prohibiting discrimination, the applicants claimed that the measures imposed on *Özgür Gündem* disclosed discrimination.

The Court recalled that it had found a violation of article 10 of the Convention. However, in reaching the conclusion that the measures imposed in respect of 29 articles and news reports were not necessary in a democratic society, it was satisfied that they pursued the legitimate aims of protecting national security and territorial integrity or that of the prevention of crime or disorder. There was no reason to believe that the restrictions on freedom of expression which resulted could be attribut-

III:4

ed to a difference of treatment based on the applicants' national origin or to association with a national minority. Accordingly, the Court concluded that there had been no breach of article 14 of the Convention.

Article 41 allowed the Court to afford just satisfaction to an injured party, under specified circumstances, when there had been a violation of the Convention. The Court held, by six votes to one, that the respondent State was to pay to the applicant company 9,000,000,000 Turkish liras for pecuniary damage; to the two remaining applicant individuals 5,000 pounds sterling each for non-pecuniary damage; and to the applicants 16,000 pounds sterling for costs and expenses, less the amount received by way of legal aid from the Council of Europe.

5. Right to Freedom of Peaceful Assembly and Association

A. INTRODUCTION

Freedom of peaceful assembly and association and freedom of opinion and expression are essential political rights, enabling participation in democratic political processes. However, their importance extends beyond the purely political sphere, because the exercise of these rights can be necessary to secure other rights of all categories. In fact, they are among the first rights to be suppressed by Governments seeking to introduce more repressive forms of governance.

Article 20 of the Universal Declaration of Human Rights states that everyone has the right to freedom of peaceful assembly and association and that no one may be compelled to belong to an association. On workers' rights, it is stated in article 23, paragraph 4, that everyone has the right to form and join trade unions for the protection of his interests.

The right to freedom of peaceful assembly is protected by article 21 and the right to freedom of association by article 22 of the International Covenant on Civil and Political Rights. Similar protection is afforded under regional treaty provisions, such as article 11 of the Convention for the Protection of Human Rights and Fundamental Freedoms. In respect of children, as stated in article 15 of the Convention on the Rights of the Child, States parties recognize the rights of the child to freedom of association and to freedom of peaceful assembly. Restrictions may be placed on the exercise of these rights. Under article 21 of the Covenant, for example, restrictions are allowed when they are imposed in conformity with the the law and are necessary in a democratic society in the interests of, *inter alia*, national security, public safety or public order.

Other treaties deal with particular aspects of the right to freedom of peaceful assembly and association. Under article 5 of the International Convention on the Elimination of All Forms of Racial Discrimination, for example, the States parties undertake to guarantee the right of everyone, without distinction as to race, colour, or national or ethnic origin, to equality before the law, including the enjoyment of the right to freedom of peaceful assembly and association, as well as the right to form and join trade unions. The enjoyment of these rights is, however, subject to the restrictions

III:5

set forth in article 4 of the Convention, mentioned in connection with the right to freedom of opinion and expression.[1]

In respect of international labour standards, the right to freedom of association is a core principle. Under the auspices of the International Labour Organization, a number of conventions reinforcing this right have been adopted, including the Convention concerning Freedom of Association and Protection of the Right to Organise (No. 87) and the Convention concerning the Application of the Principles of the Right to Organise and to Bargain Collectively (No. 98), both regarded as fundamental human rights conventions.

In a regional context, article 7 of the Framework Convention for the Protection of National Minorities stipulates that States parties shall ensure respect for the right of every person belonging to a national minority to, *inter alia*, freedom of peaceful assembly and to freedom of association. Under article 17 of the Convention, the States parties undertake not to interfere with the right of every person belonging to a national minority to estblish and maintain free and peaceful contacts across frontiers with persons lawfully staying in other States, as well as not to interfere with the right of such persons to participate in the activities of non-governmental organizations, both at the national and international levels.

Human rights defenders are afforded special protection by the Declaration on the Right and Responsibility of Individuals, Groups and Organs of Society to Promote and Protect Universally Recognized Human Rights and Fundamental Freedoms. Under article 1 of this non-treaty instrument, everyone has the right, individually and in association with others, to promote and to strive for the protection and realization of human rights and fundamental freedoms at the national and international levels.

Protection of the right to freedom of peaceful assembly and association is also reinforced by provisions, addressed to police officials, of the same non-treaty instruments as referred to in the introduction to the chapter on the right to freedom of thought, conscience and religion.[2] Article 2 of the Code of Conduct for Law Enforcement Officials requires law enforcement officials to respect and protect human dignity and maintain and uphold the human rights of all persons, including, under the explanatory commentary to the article, the right to freedom of peaceful assembly and association set forth in the Universal Declaration of Human Rights and the International Covenant on Civil and Political Rights. Article 43 of the the European Code of Police Ethics requires police, in carrying out their activities, always to bear in mind everyone's fundamental rights, such as the freedom of peaceful assembly.

---

[1] See part III, chap. 4, sect. A (*supra*, p. 434).
[2] See part III, chap. 3, sect. A (*supra*, p. 410).

The Basic Principles on the Use of Force and Firearms contain some important provisions concerning the right to peaceful assembly. Principle 12 states that as everyone is allowed to participate in lawful and peaceful assemblies, in accordance with the Universal Declaration and the Covenant, Governments and law enforcement agencies and officials shall recognize that force and firearms may be used only in accordance with principles 13 and 14. Under principle 13, in the dispersal of assemblies that are unlawful but non-violent, law enforcement officials shall avoid the use of force or, where that is not practicable, shall restrict such force to the minimum extent necessary. Principle 14 stipulates that in the dispersal of violent assemblies, law enforcement officials may use firearms only when less dangerous means are not practicable and only to the minimum extent necessary. Law enforcement officials shall not use firearms in such cases, except under the conditions stipulated in principle 9. In essence, law enforcement officials shall not use firearms against persons except in self-defence or defence of others against the imminent threat of death or serious injury.

Principally, because of their function to maintain order, police are uniquely placed to avoid and to prevent violations of the right to peaceful assembly and association, and to protect this right. Indeed, in the explanatory memorandum published together with the European Code of Police Ethics, on article 43 referring to the right to freedom of peaceful assembly and other rights, it is pointed out that the police play a major part in safeguarding these rights, either directly through safeguarding democratic arrangements or indirectly through their general responsibility for upholding the rule of law. Without these rights, democracy becomes an empty notion without any basis in reality.

B. REVIEW OF CASES

(*a*) Human Rights Committee

Article 21 of the International Covenant on Civil and Political Rights protects the right to peaceful assembly. This right shall be recognized, and no restrictions may be placed on the exercise of the right other than those imposed in conformity with the law and which are necessary in a democratic society in the interests of national security or public safety, public order, the protection of public health or morals or the protection of the rights and freedoms of others.

Article 22 of the Covenant protects the right to freedom of association. Under paragraph 1, everyone shall have the right to freedom of association with others, including the right to form and join trade unions for the protection of his interests. Paragraph 2 prohibits placing restrictions on the exercise of this right other than those prescribed by law and necessary in a democratic society for the same purposes as

III:5

those listed in article 21. It should be noted, however, that this paragraph includes the provision that article 22 shall not prevent the imposition of lawful restrictions on members of the armed forces and of the police in their exercise of this right. Paragraph 3, finally, states that the guarantees provided for in the International Labour Organization Convention concerning Freedom of Association and Protection of the Right to Organise (No. 87) may not be prejudiced because of this article of the Covenant.

In time of public emergency threatening the life of the nation, States parties may take measures derogating from their obligations under articles 21 and 22, but only on the conditions set forth in article 4 of the Covenant.

In the jurisprudence of the Human Rights Committee, there is one case under article 21 and no case under article 22 found to be relevant to the purposes of this publication.

The case *Auli Kivenmaa* v. *Finland*,[3] summarized in section C,[4] raised issues under articles 19 and 21 of the Covenant. The case has also been cited in connection with the right to freedom of opinion and expression.[5] Ms. Kivenmaa, secretary general of a Finnish political youth organization, and another 25 members of her organization had on 3 September 1987, on the occasion of a visit of a foreign head of State, amid a larger crowd, gathered outside the palace where the leaders were meeting, distributed leaflets and raised a banner critical of the human rights record of the visiting head of State. She was charged with and convicted of holding a public meeting without prior notification. She contended that she had not organized a public meeting, but only demonstrated her criticism of the alleged human rights violations. The author alleged a violation by Finland of articles 15 and 19, alternatively, article 21 of the Covenant.

Regarding the invocation of article 21, the Committee concluded that the gathering of several individuals at the site of the welcoming ceremonies, publicly announced in advance, could not be regarded as a demonstration. Concerning the State party's contention that displaying a banner turned their presence into a demonstration, the Committee noted that any restriction upon the right to assemble had to fall within the limitation provisions of article 21. The application of Finnish legislation on demonstrations to such a gathering could not be considered as an application of a restric-

---

[3] See United Nations, *Official Records of the General Assembly, Forty-ninth Session, Supplement No. 40* (A/49/40), vol. II, annex IX, sect. N, communication No. 412/1990, views adopted on 31 March 1994.

[4] See part III, chap. 5, sect. C (*a*) (*infra*, pp. 500-508).

[5] See part III, chap. 4, sect. B (*a*) (*supra*, pp. 442-443).

tion permitted by article 21, and there had been a violation of that article, as well as of article 19 of the Covenant.

In an individual opinion, one member of the Committee strongly argued against the reasoning behind these conclusions, as he did not share the Committee's legal assessment of the facts. As to article 21 of the Covenant, he believed that the conclusion was based on an erroneous appreciation of the facts and, even more so, on an erroneous view of what constituted a peaceful assembly in the sense of that article. He set out his views on what constituted such an assembly. In his remarks on article 19, he considered the relationship between articles 19 and 21 of the Covenant. Citing an analysis of political and related rights, he agreed with an observation made by the State party on this point, namely that the right of peaceful assembly seemed to be one specific aspect of the more general right to freedom of expression.

This individual opinion is included in the case summary because of the insights into the concept of peaceful assembly and the way in which the provisions of articles 21 and 19 of the Covenant are applied to the circumstances of the case.

(*b*) Committee on Freedom of Association

The right to freedom of peaceful assembly and association is clearly an indispensable right for trade unionists and trade unions, as well as for employers and their organizations. As concerns the freedom of association, two International Labour Organization (ILO) conventions are of particular interest as expressing fundamental human rights principles. Article 2 of the Convention concerning Freedom of Association and Protection of the Right to Organise (No. 87) stipulates that workers and employers shall, without any discrimination, have the right to establish and, subject to the organizations' rules, join organizations of their own choosing and without previous authorization. Under article 3, the organizations shall enjoy autonomy in their internal affairs, and the public authorities shall refrain from any interference restricting this right or impeding its lawful exercise. The Convention concerning the Application of the Principles of the Right to Organise and to Bargain Collectively (No. 98) further protects the right to freedom of association. Both include a provision that it shall be determined by national laws or regulations to which extent the guarantees provided for in the respective Convention shall apply to the armed forces and the police.

The principles of freedom of association are, however, applicable to any State member of the ILO irrespective of whether or not it has ratified these Conventions. In the ILO Declaration on Fundamental Principles and Rights at Work, the International Labour Conference recalled, in 1998, that all members had an obligation arising from the very fact of membership of the ILO to respect, to promote and to realize, in

III:5

good faith and in accordance with the Constitution, the principles concerning the fundamental rights set forth in ILO conventions recognized as fundamental. To this category belong Conventions No. 87 and No. 98 on freedom of association and the effective recognition of the right to collective bargaining.

The great importance attached to the right to freedom of peaceful assembly and association in the fields of industrial relations and labour law is reflected in the jurisprudence of the Committee on Freedom of Association of the Governing Body of the International Labour Office. This right protects a wide range of activities essential to trade unionists and employers. The Committee's reports on cases before it show many examples of how state authorities have endeavoured to interfere with such activities in various ways, including suppressing or intervening in demonstrations, marches and meetings, as well as unauthorized entry into premises. Whilst recognizing the need to maintain public order, the Committee has insisted that the response of an authority has to be proportionate to the situation faced.

In a report on case No. 1014 (*Dominican Republic*),[6] the Committee examined complaints by a trade union, including an allegation that when members of the union had gathered to hear leaders' reports, the police appeared and assaulted the workers, beating 17 and arresting 14. In response to this allegation, the Committee recalled that freedom from government interference in the holding and proceedings of trade union meetings constituted an essential element of trade union rights. The public authorities should refrain from any interference which would restrict this right or impede its exercise, unless public order was disturbed thereby or its maintenance seriously and imminently endangered.

A report on case No. 1510 (*Paraguay*)[7] concerned allegations of anti-union discrimination affecting trade union members and large groups of workers endeavouring to organize or join a trade union. The alleged actions included massive dismissals, illegal arrests and detentions of trade union leaders and violent repression by the army of workers at strike, resulting in two deaths and dozens of injuries. The Government did not reply to the allegations.

The Committee, noting specific allegations that trade union leaders were illegally arrested while legitimately exercising their right to strike or demonstrate, observed that it had always considered that workers should enjoy the right to strike and the right to peaceful demonstration to defend their occupational interests. It also emphasized that the preventive detention of trade unionists implied serious interference in

---

[6] See International Labour Office, *Official Bulletin*, vol. LXIV, Series B, No. 3 (1981), p. 130, interim report.

[7] *Ibidem*, vol. LXXIII, Series B, No. 2 (1990), p. 160, interim report.

trade union activities and should be accompanied by appropriate judicial safeguards to be implemented within a reasonable period. As to the allegegation of the violent repression of a strike, the Committee recalled that a climate of violence, such as that reflected by the violent death or injury of trade unionists, constituted a serious obstacle to the exercise of freedom of association.

In the report on case No.1285 (*Chile*),[8] also cited in connection with the right to liberty and security of person,[9] the Committee considered a number of allegations, including physical attack on a trade union leader, arbitrary detention, responses of the authorities to demonstrations and raids on trade union premises. In response to the latter allegation, the Committee reiterated the principle that the right of inviolability of union premises also necessarily implied that the public authorities could not enter such premises without prior authorization or without having obtained a legal warrant to do so. An objection was also raised in relation to a law punishing any person who, without permission, promoted or called for collective public acts in streets, squares and other places in public use and who promoted or incited demonstrations of any other kind that allowed or facilitated a breach of the public peace. In this connection, the Committee pointed out that the requirement of administrative permission to hold public meetings and demonstrations was not objectionable *per se* from the standpoint of the principles of freedom of association. The maintenance of public order was not incompatible with the right to hold demonstrations so long as the authorities responsible for public order reached agreement with the organizers of a demonstration concerning the place where it would be held and the manner in which it would take place.

A report on case No. 1598 (*Peru*),[10] and two other cases against the same State, also cited in connection with the right to life,[11] concerned killings, arrests and detentions, disappearances, physical ill-treatment and torture of trade union leaders and members. With regard to the violent intervention of the police at a trade union meeting, resulting in the death of one worker and in four others receiving bullet wounds, and the police repression of a march by medical doctors on strike, resulting in three persons receiving gunshot wounds, the Committee brought to the attention of the Government the fact that the authorities should resort to the use of force only in situations where law and order was seriously threatened. The Committee expressed the opinion that the intervention of the forces of law and order should be in due proportion to the danger to law and order it was attempting to control. Governments should

---

[8] *Ibidem*, vol. LXVIII, Series B, No. 3 (1985), p. 115, definitive report.
[9] See part II, chap. 4, sect. B (*c*) (*supra*, p. 223).
[10] See International Labour Office, *Official Bulletin*, vol. LXXVIII, Series B, No. 1 (1995), p. 38, request report.
[11] See part II, chap. 2, sect. B (*b*) (*supra*, pp. 50-51).

III:5

take measures to ensure that the competent authorities received adequate instructions so as to eliminate the danger entailed by the use of excessive violence when controlling demonstrations which might result in a disturbance of the peace.

With regard to allegations concerning the suspension of the right of assembly in certain areas affected by labour disputes, the Committee called the attention of the Government to the principles under which the right to organize trade union meetings was an essential aspect of trade union rights. Measures taken by the authorities to ensure observance of the law should not, therefore, prevent trade unions from organizing meetings during labour disputes.

In a report on case No. 1888 (*Ethiopia*),[12] also cited in connection with the right to life[13] and with the right to liberty and security of person,[14] the Committee considered a number of serious allegations, including interference in the internal administration of a trade union. The Committee recalled that workers, without distinction whatsoever, should have the right to establish and join organizations of their own choosing; that they should have the right to elect their representatives in full freedom, to organize their activities and to formulate their programmes; that the public authorities should refrain from any interference restricting these rights or impeding their lawful exercise; and that workers should enjoy adequate protection against acts of anti-union discrimination. Noting with serious concern that these conditions did not exist at the time in Ethiopia, the Committee recalled that it was incumbent upon the Government to ensure that these fundamental rights and principles regarding freedom of association were respected, in law and in practice.

In a report on case No. 2090 (*Belarus*),[15] the Committee examined various complaints alleging interference by government authorities with trade union activities and elections. In one complaint, it was alleged that the state authorities issued a ban on trade union members entering the union premises and refused to grant them passes or recognition in order to deprive the union of its right to engage freely in its activities. It was further alleged that district officials, without a court order and in the absence of any trade union representative, entered union premises and broke open cupboards in which union papers and property were kept. The premises were then sealed and the entrances blocked off, locks were fitted on all doors and property was removed.

---

[12] See International Labour Office, *Official Bulletin*, vol. LXXXIII, Series B, No. 2 (2000), p. 60, interim report.

[13] See part II, chap. 2, sect. B (*b*) (*supra*, pp. 51-52).

[14] See part II, chap. 4, sect. B (*c*) (*supra*, p. 224).

[15] See International Labour Office, *Official Bulletin*, vol. LXXXIV, Series B, No. 3 (2001), p. 68, interim report.

In response to this complaint, the Committee recalled the importance it attached to the principles that any search of trade union premises without a court order constituted an extremely serious infringement of freedom of association and that the occupation or sealing of trade union premises should be subject to independent judicial review before being undertaken by the authorities in view of the significant risk that such measures might paralyze trade union activities. Furthermore, the access of trade union members to their union premises should not be restricted by the state authorities. The Committee therefore requested the Government to take the necessary measures to initiate an independent investigation into the allegations raised by the trade union in this regard and to ensure that any remaining confiscated property and papers were promptly returned to the union.

In the report on case No. 2184 (*Zimbabwe*),[16] summarized in section C,[17] the Committee examined a complaint alleging unauthorized police entry into trade union premises in order to prevent a meeting of the union's executive council from taking place, unjustifiable interference in trade union activities and lack of respect for the principles of freedom of association. Recalling some of its decisions and principles, the Committee requested the Government to ensure that the principles of non-interference by the authorities in the meetings and internal affairs of trade unions were respected and to implement a court order to the effect that police intervention in the meetings of trade unions might be avoided in the future.

A report on case No. 2189 (*China*),[18] also summarized in section C,[19] concerned complaints about a series of responses by the authorities, including the police, to demonstrations and other events in the context of labour disputes. It can be seen from the summary that the Committee attached great importance to the principle that such responses should be in due proportion to the danger to law and order that the authorities were attempting to control. In light of the numerous allegations concerning the excessive use of force by the police in various disputes taking place in different parts of the country, the Committee requested the Government to consider preparing relevant instructions for the forces of law and order aimed at eliminating the danger of resorting to the use of excessive violence when controlling demonstrations. On a more general note, giving full consideration to the context of an economy in transition and the Government's determination to achieve simultaneous development in economic and social fields, the Committee considered that it was precisely within that context that the only durable solution to the apparently increasing so-

---

[16] *Ibidem*, vol. LXXXV, Series B, No. 3 (2002), p. 250, definitive report.
[17] See part III, chap. 5, sect. C (*b*) (*infra*, pp. 508-511).
[18] See International Labour Office, *Official Bulletin*, vol. LXXXVI, Series B, No. 1 (2003), p. 101, interim report.
[19] See part III, chap. 5, sect. C (*c*) (*infra*, pp. 511-518).

III:5

cial conflict experienced in the country was through full respect for the right of workers to establish independent organizations of their own choosing.

These cases considered by the Committee, and indeed those cited in preceding chapters of this publication, should prompt police leaders to ensure that any proposed interventions in the affairs of workers' or employers' organizations and in labour and industrial relations disputes are appropriate and justifiable in policing terms. Furthermore, when an intervention is justified to prevent or investigate crime or to maintain or restore order, it should be lawful and proportionate to the danger to law and order. Respect for and protection of the rights of all individuals and groups within society is a prerequisite for a social order based on, and derived from, the rule of law.

(c) European Court of Human Rights

Article 11 of the Convention for the Protection of Human Rights and Fundamental Freedoms protects the right to freedom of peaceful assembly and to freedom of association with others, including, as stipulated in paragraph 1, the right to form and to join trade unions for the protection of one's interests.

Paragraph 2 states that no restrictions shall be placed on the exercise of these rights other than such as are prescribed by law and are necessary in a democratic society in the interests of national security or public safety, for the prevention of disorder or crime, for the protection of health or morals or for the protection of the rights and freedoms of others. The same paragraph also states that the article shall not prevent the imposition of lawful restrictions on the exercise of these rights by members of the armed forces, of the police or of the administration of the State.

In time of war or other public emergency threatening the life of the nation, States parties may take measures derogating from their obligations under article 11 on the conditions set forth in article 15 of the Convention.

Although originating in applications declared inadmissible by the European Commission of Human Rights, two cases have been included in this review because of the significant statements relevant to police made by the Commission in these decisions.

In the case *Rassemblement jurassien and Unité jurassienne* v. *Switzerland*,[20] the applicants, two Swiss non-profit organizations, alleged violations of, *inter alia*, article

---

[20] See European Commission of Human Rights, *Decisions and Reports*, No. 17 (1980), p. 93, application No. 8191/78, decision of 10 October 1979.

11 of the Convention. It concerned the ban on two occasions in 1977 on all political meetings within the boundaries of a municipality. The Commission pronounced that the right to peaceful assembly was a fundamental right in a democratic society and like the right to freedom of expression, one of the foundations of such a society, as stated by the European Court of Human Right in a previous judgment. It covered both private meetings and meetings in public thoroughfares. Concerning the latter, the Commission said that their subjection to a prior authorization procedure did not normally encroach on the essence of the right. Such a procedure was in keeping with the requirements of article 11, paragraph 1, of the Convention if only in order that the authorities might be in a position to ensure the peaceful nature of a meeting and, accordingly, did not as such constitute interference with the exercise of the right.

The Commission then found that a temporary ban imposed on all public demonstrations in a specified municipality, based on the situation obtaining at the time, was in accordance with article 11, paragraph 2, of the Convention. It considered that the principle of proportionality was not infringed in this case, and it was not convinced that less stringent measures than those taken would have been suited to the situation.

In the case *Christians against Racism and Fascism* v. *the United Kingdom*,[21] the applicant, an association constituted at the initiative of several church organizations, had been affected by a general ban on public processions for two months in 1978 imposed by the police, following public order disturbances involving an extremist political party. The ban had been imposed to prevent further outbreaks of violence. The Commission found it to be justified, but it observed that under article 11, paragraph 1, of the Convention, the right to freedom of peaceful assembly was secured to everyone who had the intention of organizing a peaceful demonstration. In the Commission's opinion, the possibility of violent counter-demonstrations or the possibility of extremists with violent intentions, not members of the organizing association, joining the demonstration could not as such take the right to peaceful assembly away. Even if there was a real risk of a public procession resulting in disorder by developments outside the scope of those organizing it, such a procession would not, for this reason alone, fall outside the scope of article 11, paragraph 1. Furthermore, the Commission pointed out, any restriction placed on such an assembly had to be in conformity with the terms of paragraph 2 of that article.

The Commission then set out the circumstances under which a general ban for a specific period was permissible under article 11 of the Convention. A general ban on demonstrations could only be justified if there was a real danger of their resulting in disorder which could not be prevented by other less stringent measures. In this connection, the authority had also to take into account the effect of a ban on processions

---

[21] *Ibidem*, No. 21 (1981), application No. 8440/78, decision of 16 July 1980.

III:5

which did not by themselves constitute a danger for the public order. Only if the disadvantage of the ban was clearly outweighed by the security considerations justifying it, and if there was no possibility of avoiding such undesirable side effects by a narrow circumscription of the ban's scope in terms of territorial application and duration, could the ban be regarded as being necessary within the meaning of article 11, paragraph 2.

In the case *Plattform "Ärzte für das Leben" v. Austria*,[22] summarized in section C,[23] the Court considered the positive obligation on States to protect the right to peaceful assembly. The applicant, an Austrian association of doctors campaigning against abortion, alleged violations of, *inter alia*, article 11 of the Convention, as the association had not been sufficiently protected by police during two demonstrations held in 1980 and 1982, respectively. It also relied, under article 13, on the right to an effective remedy for violations of rights and freedoms set forth in the Convention. The Commission declared the application admissible in respect of article 13, but the other complaints were declared inadmissible as being manifestly ill-founded.

In order to establish whether article 13 of the Convention applied, the Court had to decide whether there was an arguable claim that article 11 had been violated, notwithstanding that the Commission had dismissed it as manifestly ill-founded. In order to do this, it had to give an interpretation of article 11. The Court thus held that this provision sometimes did require positive measures to be taken to protect the right to peaceful assembly and that in the instant case, the Austrian authorities had not failed to take reasonable and appropriate measures to do so. Accordingly, no arguable claim that article 11 was violated had been made out, and article 13 did not apply.

In determining this matter, the Court found that it did not have to assess the expediency or effectiveness of the tactics adopted by the police on these occasions. Police tactics were, however, considered by the Commission in its decision on the admissibility of the application,[24] and it is interesting to note its observations in this respect.

The fact that the police authorities did not actively intervene against the disturbances of the association's demonstration had been explained by the Government as being based on considerations of proportionality. An immediate police intervention would almost inevitably have led to physical violence. In choosing between different meth-

---

[22] See *Publications of the European Court of Human Rights*, Series A: *Judgments and Decisions*, vol. 139 (1988), application No. 10126/82, judgment of 21 June 1988.

[23] See part III, chap. 5, sect. C (*d*) (*infra*, pp. 519-524).

[24] See European Commission of Human Rights, *Decisions and Reports*, No. 44 (1985), p. 65, application No. 10126/82, decision of 17 October 1985.

ods of protecting a demonstration, limitation of preventive policing measures to the control of physical violence and the taking of repressive measures against any other kind of disturbance might in fact be indicated. This was particularly so if, as it was claimed in the present case, there was a likelihood of preventive policing measures themselves provoking an outburst of violence. The Austrian authorities thus could not be blamed for the fact that in view of this risk, they applied considerations of proportionality and dispersed the counter-demonstrators only when this could be done without violent confrontation. By acting in this way, the authorities in fact aimed at preventing disorder on a larger scale than actually occurred, an aim which was clearly covered by the prevention of disorder clause in article 11, paragraph 2, of the Convention.

Finally, in the case *Ezelin* v. *France*,[25] the Court considered the question of restrictions in article 11, paragraph 2, of the Convention and stated that these could not be interpreted as not including measures taken after a meeting. The applicant, Roland Ezelin, a French national and practising lawyer in Guadeloupe, took part in a public demonstration on 12 February 1983 which had been authorized. During the demonstration, insulting remarks were made to the police, and offensive graffiti were painted on public buildings. Although there was no evidence that Mr. Ezelin had engaged in this type of behaviour, disciplinary proceedings were subsequently taken against him and he was reprimanded. Relying on articles 10 and 11 of the Convention, the applicant claimed that the disciplinary sanction imposed on him seriously interfered with his rights to freedom of expression and to freedom of peaceful assembly.

The Court concluded that there had been an interference with Mr. Ezelin's right to peaceful assembly and that the interference was prescribed by law and had a legitimate aim, the prevention of disorder. The Court then had to decide whether the interference was necessary in a democratic society. It observed that the proportionality principle demanded a balance to be struck between the requirements of the purposes listed in article 11, paragraph 2, of the Convention and those of the free expression of opinions by word, gesture or even silence by persons assembled on the streets or in other public places. The pursuit of a just balance must not result in practising lawyers being discouraged, for fear of disciplinary sanctions, from making clear their beliefs on such occasions.

Admittedly, the Court further observed, the penalty imposed on Mr. Ezelin was at the lower end of the scale of disciplinary penalties. It had mainly moral force, since it did not entail any ban, even a temporary one, on practising the profession or on sitting as a member of the Bar Council. The Court considered, however, that the

---

[25] See *Publications of the European Court of Human Rights*, Series A: *Judgments and Decisions*, vol. 202 (1991), application No. 11800/85, judgment of 26 April 1991.

III:5

freedom to take part in a peaceful assembly, in this instance a demonstration that had not been prohibited, was of such importance that it could not be restricted in any way, even for a practising lawyer, so long as the person concerned did not himself commit any reprehensible act on such an occasion.

In short, the sanction complained of, however minimal, did not appear to have been necessary in a democratic society. The Court held, by six votes to three, that there had been a violation of article 11.

C. CASE SUMMARIES

(a) Auli Kivenmaa v. Finland
(Human Rights Committee)[26]

The author of the communication was Auli Kivenmaa, a Finnish citizen and secretary general of a political youth organization. She submitted the communication to the Human Rights Committee on 7 March 1990, claiming to be a victim of a violation by Finland of articles 15 and 19, alternatively, article 21 of the International Covenant on Civil and Political Rights.

The facts

The author submitted, *inter alia*, the following. On 3 September 1987, on the occasion of a visit of a foreign head of State and his meeting with the President of Finland, she and about 25 members of her organization, amid a larger crowd, gathered across the Presidential Palace where the leaders were meeting, distributed leaflets and raised a banner critical of the human rights record of the visiting head of State. The police immediately took the banner down and asked who was responsible. She identified herself and was subsequently charged with violating the Act on Public Meetings by holding a public meeting without prior notification. This Act made it a punishable offence to call a public meeting without notification to the police at least six hours before the meeting.

Although she argued that she had not organized a public meeting, but only demonstrated her criticism of the alleged human rights violations by the visiting head of State, a court, on 27 January 1988, found her guilty of the charge and fined her. The court did not address her defence that the conviction would be in violation of the Covenant. On 19 September 1989, a court of appeal upheld this judgement, arguing,

---

[26] See United Nations, *Official Records of the General Assembly, Forty-ninth Session, Supplement No. 40* (A/49/40), vol. II, annex IX, sect. N, communication No. 412/1990, views adopted on 31 March 1994.

inter alia, that the Act on Public Meetings, in the absence of other legal provisions, was applicable also in the case of demonstrations; that the entry into force of the Covenant had not repealed or amended the Act; that the Covenant allowed restrictions, provided by law, of the rights to freedom of expression and freedom of assembly; and that the requirement of prior notification was justified in the case, because the demonstration was organized against a visiting head of State. On 21 February 1990, the Supreme Court denied leave to appeal, without further motivation.

The author denied that what took place was a public meeting within the meaning of the Act on Public Meetings. Rather, she characterized the incident as an exercise of her right to freedom of expression, regulated in Finland by the Freedom of the Press Act and not requiring prior notification. Therefore, she contended, her conviction was in violation of article 19 of the Covenant. She alleged that the way in which the courts had found her actions to come within the scope of the Act on Public Meetings constituted *ex analogia* reasoning and was, therefore, insufficient to justify the restriction of her right to freedom of expression as being provided by law within the meaning of article 19, paragraph 3. Moreover, she contended, such an application of the Act to the circumstances of the case amounted to a violation of article 15 of the Covenant, since there was no law making it a crime to hold a political demonstration. The author further argued that even if the event could be interpreted as an exercise of the freedom of assembly, she was still not under an obligation to notify the police, as the demonstration did not take the form of a public meeting, nor a public march, as defined by the Act.

On 20 March 1992, the Committee declared the communication admissible insofar as it might raise issues under articles 15, 19 and 21 of the Covenant. In its decision, the Committee requested the State party to clarify whether there was any discrimination between those who cheered and those who protested against the visiting head of State. In particular, the Committee requested clarification as to whether any other groups or subgroups in the larger crowd welcoming the visiting head of State also distributed leaflets or displayed banners, whether they gave prior notification to the police pursuant to the Act on Public Meetings and, if not, whether they were similarly prosecuted.

In its submission on the merits of the communication, the State party referred to the questions put to it by the Committee and stated that there was only a small crowd of people assembled in front of the Presidential Palace. Besides Ms. Kivenmaa's group, there were journalists and some curious passers-by. Except for Ms. Kivenmaa and her friends, there was no other group or subgroup present that could be characterized as demonstrators, distributing leaflets or displaying banners. No other groups had given prior notification to the police of their intent to hold a public meeting.

III:5

The State party submitted that the right to freedom of expression might be restricted by the authorities, as long as these restrictions did not affect the heart of the right. With regard to the present case, the State party argued that Ms. Kivenmaa's freedom of expression had not been restricted. She was allowed freely to express her opinions, for instance by circulating leaflets, and the police did not, after having received information about the organizer of the public meeting, hinder her and her group from continuing their activities. The State party therefore denied that the Act on Public Meetings was applied *ex analogia* to restrict the right to freedom of expression.

In this context, the State party argued that a demonstration necessarily entailed the expression of an opinion, but by its specific character, it was to be regarded as an exercise of the right of peaceful assembly. In this connection, the State party argued that article 21 of the Covenant had to be seen as *lex specialis* in relation to article 19. Therefore, the expression of an opinion in the context of a demonstration had to be considered under article 21, and not under article 19 of the Covenant.

The State party agreed with the author that article 15 of the Covenant in principle also prohibited *ex analogia* application of a law to the disadvantage of a person charged with an offence. It argued, however, that in the present case, Ms. Kivenmaa was not convicted of expressing her opinion, but merely of her failure to give prior notification of a demonstration, as was required by the Act on Public Meetings.

With regard to the author's allegation that she was a victim of a violation of article 21 of the Covenant, the State party recalled that this article allowed restrictions on the exercise of the right to peaceful assembly. In Finland, the Act on Public Meetings guaranteed the right to assemble peacefully in public, while ensuring public order and safety and preventing abuse of the right of assembly. Under the Act, public assembly was understood to be the coming together of more than one person for a lawful purpose in a public place to which others than those invited also had access. The State party submitted that the Act, in the established interpretation, also applied to demonstrations arranged as public meetings or street processions. The Act required prior notification to the police, at least six hours before the beginning of any public meeting at a public place in the open air. The State party emphasized that the Act did not apply to a peaceful demonstration by only one person.

The State party further submitted that the prior notification requirement enabled the police to take the necessary measures to make it possible for the meeting to take place, for instance by regulating the flow of traffic, and to protect the group in their exercise of the right to freedom of assembly. In this context, the State party contended, when a foreign head of State was involved, it was of utmost practical importance that the police should be notified prior to the event. The State party argued that the right of public assembly was not restricted by the requirement of a prior notification to the police. In this connection, it referred to jurisprudence of the European Court of Human Rights. The State party emphasized that the prior notification was necessary to guarantee the peacefulness of the public meeting.

Regarding the specific circumstances of the present case, the State party was of the opinion that the actual behaviour of the author and her friends amounted to a public meeting within the meaning of the Act on Public Meetings. In this context, the State party submitted that although the word "demonstration" was not expressly named in the Act, this did not signify that demonstrations were outside the scope of its application. Furthermore, the State party noted that article 21 of the Covenant did not specifically refer to demonstrations as a mode of assembly either. Finally, it was argued, the requirement of prior notification was in conformity with the second sentence of article 21. In this context, the State party submitted that the requirement was prescribed by law and was necessary in a democratic society in the interests of legitimate purposes, especially in the interest of public order.

The author's submission challenged the State party's description of the facts and referred to the court records in her case. According to these records, witnesses testified that approximately one hundred persons were present on the square, among whom were persons welcoming the foreign head of State and waving miniature flags. No action was taken by the police against them, but the police removed the banner displayed by her and her friends. According to her, this indicated that the police interfered with her and her friends' demonstration because of the contents of the opinion expressed, in violation of article 19 of the Covenant.

The author further challenged the State party's contention that the police did not hinder her and her group in the expression of their opinion. She emphasized that the entrance of the foreign head of State into the Presidential Palace was a momentary event. The measures by the police, taking away the banner immediately after it was erected and questioning her, dramatically decreased her possibilities to express her opinion effectively.

Regarding the alleged violation of article 15 of the Covenant, the author referred to her earlier submissions and maintained that applying *ex analogia* the Act on Public Meetings to a demonstration such as the one organized by her was in violation of article 15 of the Covenant. In this context, the author submitted that the State party's argument that article 21 of the Covenant did not include a reference to demonstrations either was irrelevant, since article 15 only prohibited analogous interpretation to the disadvantage of an accused in criminal procedures.

III:5

The author challenged the State party's contention that it should have been evident to her that she was under an obligation to notify the police of the demonstration. She argued that this was only firmly established by the court's decision in her own case. The general interpretation to which the State party referred was insufficient as basis for her conviction. The author finally submitted that the description of a public meeting, within the meaning of the Act, used by the State party was unacceptably broad and would cover almost any outdoor discussion between at least three persons.

In conclusion, the author stated that she did not contest that restrictions on the exercise of the right of peaceful assembly might be justified and that prior notification of public meetings was a legitimate form of such restrictions. However, she did challenge the concrete application of the Act on Public Meetings in her case. She contended that this outdated, vague and ambiguous statute, not amended since 1921, was used as the legal basis for police interference with her expressing concern about the human rights situation in the country of the visiting head of State. She claimed that this interference was not in conformity with the law, nor necessary in a democratic society within the meaning of article 21 of the Covenant. In this connection, it was again stressed that by taking away the banner, the police interfered with the most effective method for her to express her opinion.

Issues and proceedings before the Committee

The Committee found that a requirement to notify the police of an intended demonstration in a public place six hours before its commencement might be compatible with the permitted limitations laid down in article 21 of the Covenant. In the circumstances of this specific case, it was evident from the information provided by the parties that the gathering of several individuals at the site of the welcoming ceremonies for a foreign head of State on an official visit, publicly announced in advance by the State party authorities, could not be regarded as a demonstration. Insofar as the State party contended that displaying a banner turned their presence into a demonstration, the Committee noted that any restrictions upon the right to assemble had to fall within the limitation provisions of article 21. A requirement to pre-notify a demonstration would normally be for reasons of national security or public safety, public order, the protection of public health or morals or the protection of the rights and freedoms of others. Consequently, the application of Finnish legislation on demonstrations to such a gathering could not be considered as an application of a restriction permitted by article 21 of the Covenant.

The right for an individual to express his political opinions, including obviously his opinions on the question of human rights, formed part of the freedom of expression guaranteed by article 19 of the Covenant. In this particular case, the author of the communication exercised this right by raising a banner. It was true that article 19 authorized the restriction by law of freedom of expression in certain circumstances. However, in this specific case, the State party had neither referred to a law allowing this freedom to be restricted, nor had it established how the restriction applied to Ms. Kivenmaa was necessary to safeguard the rights and national imperatives set forth in article 19, paragraph 2 (*a*) and (*b*), of the Covenant.

The Committee noted that while claims under article 15 had been made, no issues under this provision arose in the present case.

In conclusion, the Committee was of the view that the facts before it disclosed a violation of articles 19 and 21 of the Covenant. Pursuant to article 2 of the Covenant, the State party was under an obligation to provide Ms. Kivenmaa with an appropriate remedy and to adopt such measures as might be necessary to ensure that similar violations did not occur in the future. The Committee wished to receive information, within 90 days, on any relevant measures taken by the State party in respect of these views.

In an individual opinion, one member of the Committee formed strongly dissenting views. He said that he was regrettably unable to agree with the substantive decision that Finland had violated articles 19 and 21 of the Covenant, because he did not share at all the Committee's legal assessment of the facts.

As to the question of a possible violation of article 21, he believed that the Committee's finding that by applying the Act on Public Meetings to Ms. Kivenmaa and ultimately imposing a fine on her, the State party had breached article 21 of the Covenant was based on an erroneous appreciation of the facts and, even more so, on an erroneous view of what constituted a peaceful assembly in the sense of article 21.

He agreed that a requirement to notify the police of an intended demonstration in a public place six hours before its commencement might be compatible with the permitted limitations laid down in article 21 of the Covenant. The legal issue, he said, therefore centred on the question of whether or not Ms. Kivenmaa's actions, the fact that she and about 25 members of her organization, amid a larger crowd, gathered, distributed leaflets and raised a banner, ought to be qualified as a public meeting in the sense of the Act or, for that matter, as a peaceful assembly in the sense of article 21 of the Covenant.

In that respect, he said that he was not able to follow the Committee's reasoning that it was evident from the information provided by the parties that the gathering of several individuals at the site of the welcoming ceremonies for a foreign head of State on an official visit, publicly announced in advance by the State party authorities,

III:5

could not be regarded as a demonstration. It was not contested by the author that she and a group of people of her organization summoned by her went to the Presidential Palace explicitly for the purpose of distributing leaflets and raising a banner and thus publicly to denounce the presence, in Finland, of a foreign head of State whose human rights record they criticized. If this did not constitute a demonstration, indeed a public gathering within the scope of article 21 of the Covenant, what else would constitute a peaceful assembly in that sense and, accordingly, a public meeting in the sense of the Act?

Furthermore, he cited a commentary in which it was stated on article 21, *inter alia*, that the term "assembly" was not defined but rather presumed in the Covenant. Therefore, it had to be interpreted in conformity with the customary, generally accepted meaning in national legal systems, taking into account the object and purpose of this traditional human right. Only intentional, temporary gatherings of several persons for a specific purpose were afforded the protection of freedom of assembly. This was exactly the case, he argued, with Ms. Kivenmaa's manifestation in front of the Presidential Palace. The decisive element for the determination of an assembly, as opposed to a more or less accidental gathering, obviously was the intention and the purpose of the individuals coming together. The author was estopped from arguing that she and her group were bystanders like the other crowd, apparently attracted by the appearance of a foreign head of State visiting the President of Finland. She and her group admittedly joined the event to make a political demonstration. This was the sole purpose of their appearing before the Presidential Palace. The State party, therefore, rightly stated that this was, conceptually, a demonstration.

He was also unable to follow the Committee's argument where an attempt was made to create a link between the purpose, and thus the legality, of the restrictive legislation as such and its application in a concrete case. To say that a requirement to pre-notify a demonstration would normally be for reasons of national security, etc., and then to conclude that consequently, the application of the Finnish legislation on demonstrations to such a gathering could not be considered as an application of a restriction permitted by article 21 of the Covenant was, to say at least, contradictory.

If the restricting legislation, the Act, as such was considered as being within the limits of article 21, a fact not contested by the author and recognized by the Committee, the relevant law had obviously to be applied in a uniform manner to all cases falling under its scope. In other words, if the Act and the obligation therein contained to notify any public meeting prior to its commencement was a valid restriction on the exercise of the right to assembly, permitted under article 21 of the Covenant, then its formal application could not be considered as a violation of the Covenant, whatever the actual reasons, in the mind of the authorities, for demanding the notification.

He concluded that the Finnish authorities, therefore, did not violate article 21 of the Covenant by insisting that Ms. Kivenmaa should address an appropriate notification to the authorities prior to her demonstrating in front of the Presidential Palace and by fining her subsequently for not having made such a notification.

As to the question of a possible violation of article 19, he recalled the Committee's conclusion that as Ms. Kivenmaa had exercised her right to freedom of expression by waiving a banner and this had been removed by the police, there had been a violation of this article. In this respect, he argued that the removal of the banner should be placed in the context of the whole event. Ms. Kivenmaa and her group demonstrated, distributed leaflets and waived a banner; the police intervened in order to establish the identity of the person leading the demonstration; the banner was taken down by the police; the demonstration was allowed to continue; Ms. Kivenmaa herself and her group went on to distribute their leaflets and presumably gave vent in public to their opinion concerning the visiting head of State; and there was no further intervention by the police. Hence, he concluded, the taking down of the banner was the only fact to be retained in view of a possible violation of article 19. The Committee had opted for a very simple *façon de voir*. Take away the banner and you necessarily violate the right to freedom of expression. This view did not take into account the intimate and somewhat complex relationship between articles 19 and 21 and, for that matter, also article 18 of the Covenant.

He observed that the right of peaceful assembly would seem to be just one facet of the more general right to freedom of expression. In that regard, he cited an analysis of political and related rights, in which it was stated that there would hardly be freedom of assembly in any real sense without freedom of expression. Assembly was indeed a form of expression. If, therefore, there were in force in any given State party legal norms on the right to assembly, in conformity with article 21 of the Covenant, including restrictions of that right permitted under the article, such legislation would apply to a public meeting or peaceful assembly rather than legislation on the exercise of freedom of expression. In that sense, the observation by the State party that article 21 had to be seen as *lex specialis* in relation to article 19 was correct.

He regretted that the Committee had not addressed this legal problem. It had contented itself with the somewhat oversimplified statement that just by removing the displayed banner, the State party violated Ms. Kivenmaa's right to freedom of expression. He doubted that the Committee would still have found a violation of article 19 of the Covenant if it had found no violation of article 21.

Finally, as to he question of a possible violation of article 15, he noted that although the Committee, in its admissibility decision, clearly retained article 15 among the articles that might have been violated by the State party, it had completely failed to address the issue of that article in its final views. He concluded that the Committee should have included, in those views, a statement to the effect that Finland had not violated this article.

(b) Case No. 2184 (Zimbabwe)
(Committee on Freedom of Association)[27]

The complaint against the Government of Zimbabwe was submitted on 15 March 2002 by the International Confederation of Free Trade Unions (ICFTU). The Government sent its observations in a communication dated 26 June 2002.

Zimbabwe had ratified the Convention concerning the Application of the Principles of the Right to Organise and to Bargain Collectively (No. 98) and the Convention concerning Protection and Facilities to be Afforded to Workers' Representatives in the Undertaking (No. 135), but not the Convention concerning Freedom of Association and Protection of the Right to Organise (No. 87).

The facts

The complainant alleged acts of unauthorized police entry into trade union premises in order to prevent a meeting of the union's executive council from taking place.

The ICFTU stated that on 14 March 2002, at approximately 2 p.m., policemen in plain clothes entered by force into the headquarters of the Zimbabwe Congress of Trade Unions (ZCTU) in Harare in order to monitor a meeting of its executive council. When reminded that they were not invited and should therefore leave the ZCTU premises, they threatened that unless they were allowed in, they would use force to disband the meeting. The complainant alleged that as the union leadership stuck to its position, the police prevented the ZCTU from proceeding with the meeting.

The complainant alleged moreover that the situation of trade unionists in Zimbabwe was extremely precarious. According to the complainant, several trade unionists had been victimized both during the electoral campaign and the period leading to it, while the President during the electoral campaign allegedly expressed the intention to deregister the ZCTU. The complainant further noted that unionized workers had been massively involved in civic and political activities calling for a change in the political leadership in Zimbabwe, as workers were bearing the brunt of the mismanagement of the national economy and were prompted to agitate for change because

---

[27] See International Labour Office, *Official Bulletin*, vol. LXXXV, Series B, No. 3 (2002), p. 250, definitive report.

of the erosion of their purchasing power, high unemployment, the breakdown in social and medical facilities and the looming problem of famine.

The Government replied that far from forcing its way in the ZCTU meeting, the police simply approached the ZCTU leadership in order to ascertain the nature of the gathering and that at that point, the ZCTU executive council abandoned the meeting citing police interference. The Government informed the Committee that it acted in accordance with the Public Order and Security Act that required prior notification of public meetings and authorized their monitoring by the police. With regard to the legal basis of its action, the Government informed the Committee that after the aborted meeting, the ZCTU filed a petition to the High Court of Zimbabwe, which ruled that ZCTU meetings were not covered by the Act.

The Government was of the view that the aborted ZCTU meeting was not a genuine trade union meeting, but rather a meeting aimed at planning mass action against the Government, as shown by the fact that the organization called for a stay away two days later. The Government emphasized that the stay away did not concern issues of employment but political goals. According to the Government, the ZCTU was an appendage to an opposition political party which had lost the latest presidential elections and connived with the ZCTU to embark on mass actions to topple the elected Government. As it had communicated to the ZCTU leadership, the Government did not interfere in genuine trade union meetings, but if it had good cause to believe that the meetings were of a political nature and in contravention of the Public Order and Security Act, it would not hesitate to deal with the situation, particularly when the action was aimed at removing the Government by violence.

The Committee's conclusions and recommendations

The Committee on Freedom of Association noted that the complainant alleged that on 14 March 2002, at approximately 2 p.m., representatives of the Zimbabwean Republic Police in plain clothes entered the ZCTU headquarters in Harare, threatened that they would use force to disband the meeting unless they were allowed in the premises and finally prevented the ZCTU from proceeding with a scheduled meeting.

The Committee noted that the Government had stated that the police simply approached the ZCTU leadership in order to ascertain the nature of the gathering, in accordance with the Public Order and Security Act that prohibited public meetings without prior notice to the police, and that the decision to abandon the meeting was taken by the ZCTU itself. The Committee also noted that according to the Government, the aborted ZCTU meeting was not a genuine trade union meeting but rather a meeting of a political nature. The Committee further noted that according to the

III:5

Government, the ZCTU called the aborted meeting in order to plan a stay away, which took place two days later, in an effort to embark on mass action to topple the Government. The Committee observed that the Government had not sent information supporting its views on this.

The Committee further observed that the High Court of Zimbabwe had ruled that the meeting of the ZCTU was exempted from the Public Order and Security Act. Moreover, the High Court found that the ZCTU meeting did not qualify as a public gathering as defined by this Act. Therefore, it found that the police did not have a right to monitor the meeting and issued an order prohibiting the police from sitting at or attending the meeting of the ZCTU general council, to be held on the next day, and any similar meeting in the future.

The Committee recalled that the entry by police or military forces into trade union premises, without a judicial warrant, constituted a serious and unjustifiable interference in trade union activities. The right of the inviolability of trade union premises also necessarily implied that the public authorities might not insist on entering such premises without prior authorization or without having obtained a legal warrant to do so. The Committee further recalled that respect for the principles of freedom of association required that the public authorities exercised great restraint in relation to intervention in the internal affairs of trade unions.

The Committee noted with grave concern the allegations of the complainant concerning the intention of the authorities to deregister the ZCTU and the attitude against trade unionists before and during the electoral campaign. It observed that the Government had not made observations in this respect.

In the light of these conclusions, the Committee invited the Governing Body of the International Labour Office to approve a number recommendations.

The Government was reminded that the entry by police into trade union premises without a judicial warrant constituted a serious and unjustifiable interference in trade union activities and that respect for the principles of freedom of association required that the public authorities exercised great restraint in relation to intervention in the internal affairs of trade unions.

The Government was requested to ensure that the principles of non-interference by the authorities in the meetings and internal affairs of trade unions were respected and to implement the order of the High Court of Zimbabwe to the effect that police intervention in the meetings of trade unions might be avoided in the future.

Noting with grave concern the allegations of the complainant concerning the attitude against trade unionists before and during the electoral campaign and the intention of the authorities to deregister the ZCTU, the Government was strongly urged to refrain from any action in this respect.

(c) Case No. 2189 (China)
(Committee on Freedom of Association)[28]

The complaint against the Government of China was submitted on 27 March, 2 June, 19 August 2002 and 10 January 2003 by the International Confederation of Free Trade Unions (ICFTU). The International Metalworkers' Federation (IMF) associated itself with the complaint and, on 3 April 2002, made additional allegations. The Government sent a reply to some of the allegations in a communication dated 26 September 2002.

China had not ratified the Convention concerning Freedom of Association and Protection of the Right to Organise (No. 87), nor the Convention concerning the Application of the Principles of the Right to Organise and to Bargain Collectively (No. 98).

The facts

In its communication dated 27 March 2002, the ICFTU lodged a formal complaint against the People's Republic of China for violations of the principles of freedom of association, on the basis of the facts detailed in the report of the case and in attached documents, including two letters sent on 15 and 27 March 2002 to the President of China. These letters concerned repressive measures, including threats, intimidation, intervention by security forces, beatings, detentions, arrests and other mistreatment meted out to leaders, elected representatives and members of independent workers' organizations in three provinces. All the described events occurred in the course of March 2002.

In its reply, the Government provided information in response to the complainants' allegations, set out in detail in the report of the case. The Government stated that in the months preceding the submission of its response, it had made an extensive investigation of the relevant individuals and incidents, including visits to such relevant departments as the Ministries of Public Security, State Security and Judiciary Affairs, the All-China Federation of Trade Unions and local governments.

---

[28] *Ibidem*, vol. LXXXVI, Series B, No. 1 (2003), p. 101, interim report.

III:5

The Government concluded that the facts concerned in this case were already fairly clear. There should be no need for discussion by the Committee on Freedom of Association. Nevertheless, in the spirit of promoting cooperation and enhancing understanding, the Government expressed its willingness to maintain dialogue with the Committee.

The Committee's conclusions and recommendations

The Committee noted that the allegations in this case referred to the use of repressive measures, including threats, intimidation, intervention by security forces, beatings, detentions, arrests and other mistreatment meted out to leaders, elected representatives and members of independent workers' organisations at the Ferrous Alloy Factory in Liaoning Province and the Daqing Petroleum Company in Heilongjiang Province, as well as violent police intervention in a workers' demonstration at Guangyuan Textile Factory and the sentencing of advocates of workers' rights in Sichuan Province. Finally, the complainants alleged the detention, arrest and mistreatment in Shanxi Province of an independent labour activist for trying to set up a federation for retired workers.

In respect of events related to the Ferrous Alloy Factory, the Committee noted with concern the specific allegations regarding the arrest and detention of four leaders and representatives of the independent workers' organization at the factory, on charges of illegal demonstration, following a mass demonstration in support of over 10,000 retrenched workers. The arrests on 20 March 2002 of three of the representatives were reportedly accompanied by violent and forceful police intervention, resulting in numerous injuries to many of the demonstrators. The complainant made further allegations of arrests and detentions, as well as of police violence and beatings in respect of subsequent demonstrations.

The Committee also noted with deep concern the allegations that the health of one of the detainees was in a very serious condition and the suspicions of torture or other mistreatment surrounding his detention. In particular, allegedly, he was suffering from a stroke caused by the onset of heart disease, itself following his brutal treatment at the hands of the police. After a brief hospitalization, he was returned to the detention centre where, despite the continuing deterioration of his health, he had been denied access to medical treatment, including a return to hospital or release on medical parole. Allegations of mistreatment and beatings were also made by the complainant in respect of other detainees. Finally, the Committee noted a case of alleged disappearance.

Concerning the demonstrations, brought about by the consequences of the factory's bankruptcy, the Government indicated that an investigation group was immediately organized to look into the claims put forward by the workers concerning corruption at the enterprise and financial compensation for wages and social security. The Committee further noted the Government's report of measures taken to punish corrupt individuals, mobilize funds to ensure workers' basic living needs and to assist in the re-employment of the laid-off workers.

More generally, the Committee noted the various explanations given by the Government concerning the consequences of the process of transition from a planned economy to a socialist market economy and the multiple steps taken to solve the resulting problems and to protect workers' basic rights. While stating that it had always protected and paid attention to the democratic rights of all citizens, including the right to freedom of association, the Government added that the incidents that were the subject of this complaint were simply labour disputes resulting from the adjustment of interests during the reduction of the enterprise workforce and were in no way related to freedom of association.

The Government linked this general context to the particular case of the the factory workers, stating that the four detained representatives took advantage of certain workers who were making an appeal to the authorities and repeatedly planned activities of terrorism and sabotage, severely threatening public security, disrupting public order and damaging public property. The Government stated that they were summoned for trial in accordance with the law on charges of holding illegal meetings, parades and demonstrations. Forcible measures were applied by the public security authorities. The Government concluded that the ICFTU allegations were at variance with the facts and constituted a misinterpretation of them.

While taking due note of the explanations given by the Government concerning the measures taken to respond to workers' demands and to ensure basic living needs, the Committee noted with regret that very little information had been provided in respect of the only issue before it for which it had any competence, the question of ensuring respect for the basic principles of freedom of association. This sparseness of information was all the more regretted in light of the detailed information provided by the complainants concerning the role and activities of the four factory workers' representatives. While noting the Government's general indication that these representatives allegedly planned illegal activities to disturb public order and endanger public security, the Committee observed that the Government provided no detail as to the specific illicit nature of their activities, yet admitted that the entire context was one of a labour dispute.

In these circumstances, the Committee had to recall that the detention of trade union leaders or members for reasons connected with their activities in defence of the interests of workers constituted a serious interference with civil liberties in general and

III:5

with trade union rights in particular. Further, noting that the Government had not supplied any information in reply to the specific allegations of violent police intervention in the workers' demonstrations, other than to state that the public security officials had applied forcible measures against the alleged lawbreakers, the Committee recalled that workers should enjoy the right to peaceful demonstration to defend their occupational interests. The authorities should resort to the use of force only in situations where law and order was seriously threatened. The intervention of the forces of law and order should be in due proportion to the danger to law and order the authorities were attempting to control. Governments should take measures to ensure that the competent authorities received adequate instructions so as to eliminate the danger entailed by the use of excessive violence when controlling demonstrations which might result in a disturbance of the peace.

As for the brief detentions of a worker representative and an arrested leader's wife, the Committee recalled that the arrest, even if only briefly, of trade union leaders and trade unionists for exercising legitimate trade union activities constituted a violation of the principles of freedom of association.

As for the arrest and detention of the four worker representatives, in light of the insufficiency of the Government's reply as to the precise nature of the activities resulting in the disturbance of public order and endangered public security and the fact that the initial charge of illegal demonstration was converted to subversion, a crime reportedly carrying a penalty of up to life imprisonment or even the death penalty, nine months after the incident and two weeks before trial, the Committee requested the Government to provide specific and detailed information on the charges brought against these four representatives. In the meantime, the Committee recalled that the sentencing of trade unionists to long periods of imprisonment, very often on the grounds of disturbance of public order, in view of the general nature of the charges, might make it possible to repress activities of a trade union nature.

Concerning allegations regarding a lawyer's lack of access to his client, one of the detainees, the Committee recalled that detained trade unionists, like anyone else, should benefit from normal judicial proceedings and have the right to due process. In particular, they should have the the the right to be informed of the charges brought against them, the right to have adequate time and facilities for the preparation of their defence and to communicate freely with counsel of their own choosing, as well as the right to a prompt trial by an impartial and independent judicial authority.

In respect of events related to the Daqing Petroleum Company, the Committee noted the allegations concerning the intimidation and threats by some 1,000 police and paramilitary forces against workers during a sit-in demonstration at the company's headquarters. According to the complainant, workers at this demonstration were detained for up to two weeks and released on the condition that they would no longer participate in the demonstrations. The Committee noted with particular concern the allegations that several representatives of an independently formed provisional union committee for retrenched workers of the company and another 60 workers involved in protest actions in the city were reportedly detained on 11 March 2002 and were still unaccounted for. The complainant also alleged the arrest and detention of an unidentified 50-year-old woman and a retired worker whose whereabouts were unknown.

The Committee noted the background information provided by the Government on the dispute in the Daqing oilfields and the explanation that workers had changed their mind in respect of a compensation payment offered during a restructuring process of the company and had demanded to be re-employed. According to the Government, these workers stopped trains, started an assault on the office building of the company and smashed cars. While indicating that in order to maintain proper order and prevent deterioration of the situation, the police were sent in to carry out their duty, the Government added that no clashes occurred between the police and demonstrators. Subsequently, a tripartite investigation group, according to the Government, comprising representatives of relevant ministries and commissions, the trade union and the enterprise, was established, and various measures were proposed in respect of social security insurance and conditions for re-employment. The Government added that there was information indicating that those who had terminated their labour contracts had accepted these measures.

While noting the efforts made by the Government to resolve this dispute through a tripartite investigation group, the Committee noted with regret that other than a general statement to the effect that there were no clashes between the police and demonstrators, the Government had not replied to the allegations concerning the detention of several representatives of the independently formed provisional union committee and some 60 other workers involved in the protest actions in the city, as well as an unidentified 50-year-old woman and a retired worker, all of whom, according to the complainant, were still unaccounted for. The Committee recalled that the detention of trade union leaders or members for reasons connected with their activities in defence of the interests of workers constituted a serious interference with civil liberties in general and with trade union rights in particular.

As to the police intervention at a strike at the Guangyuan Textile Factory, the sentencing of workers' advocates in Sichuan Province and the detention of an independent labour activist in Shanxi Province, the Committee made the following observations.

III:5

In Sichuan Province, the allegations referred to police intervention in a strike action at the Guangyuan Textile Factory, where several strikers were beaten up by the police at the picket line outside the factory and about a dozen detained. The complainants also alleged that two democratic opposition activists, and possibly a third activist, had been sentenced to heavy prison terms for acting on behalf of the organizing workers.

The Committee noted that according to the Government, the factory workers, unsatisfied with the compensation they had received when the textile mill went bankrupt, had repeatedly gathered inside and around the grounds of the factory, blocking the major routes of traffic in the city and disturbing the normal social order. According to the Government, the issues of compensation were solved through mediation by a tripartite investigation group.

While noting the Government's general indication that the workers had disturbed the normal social order in the city, the Committee had to recall the importance it attached to the principle that the intervention of the forces of law and order should be in due proportion to the danger to law and order that the authorities were attempting to control. Governments should take measures to ensure that the competent authorities received adequate instructions so as to eliminate the danger entailed by the use of excessive violence when controlling demonstrations which might result in a disturbance of the peace.

Finally, the Committee noted that the Government had not replied to the allegations concerning the two democratic opposition activists, and possibly a third one, who had reportedly been sentenced to heavy prison terms for acting on behalf of the organizing workers, nor to the allegations that an independent labour activist, formerly a state employee at a machinery factory, was detained on 1 June 2002 in Shanxi Province for trying to set up a federation for retired workers and charged with incitement to subvert state power.

On a more general note, and giving full consideration to the context of transition described by the Government and its determination to achieve simultaneous development in economic and social fields, the Committee considered that it was precisely within this context that the only durable solution to the apparently increasing social conflict experienced in the country was through full respect for the right of workers to establish organizations of their own choosing by ensuring, in particular, the effective possibility of forming, in a climate of full security, organizations independent both of those already existing and of any political party. While noting the Government's statement that freedom of association was guaranteed through explicit provisions in the Constitution, under labour law and trade union law, the Committee referred to its conclusions in previous reports on cases against the same State. It had concluded that many provisions of the Trade Union Act were contrary to the fundamental principles of freedom of association and had requested the Government to take the necessary steps to ensure that those provisions were modified.

In conclusion, the Committee strongly believed that the development of free and independent organizations and negotiation with all those involved in social dialogue was indispensable to enable a government to confront its social and economic problems and resolve them in the best interests of the workers and the nation. Indeed, a balanced economic and social development required the existence of strong and independent organizations which could participate in the process of development.

In the light of these conclusions, the Committee invited the Governing Body of the International Labour Office to approve a number of recommendations.

The Government was requested to institute an impartial and independent investigation into the allegations of violent police intervention in respect of the demonstrations in relation to the workers' struggle at the Ferrous Alloy Factory. The Government was asked to provide detailed information to the Committee on the outcome of this investigation and to indicate the measures taken to compensate any injured workers.

The Government was further requested to institute an independent investigation into the allegations concerning the serious condition of the health of a detained worker representative and the torture or mistreatment surrounding his detention. The Government was asked to inform the Committee of the outcome of this investigation and of any measures taken in the event that it was found that this person had been mistreated while in detention, including the measures taken to ensure that he received any necessary medical treatment.

The Government was requested to institute an independent investigation into the allegations that another worker representative was beaten during his brief detention and to inform the Committee of the outcome of this investigation and of any measures taken in the event that it was found that he had been mistreated. The Government was also requested to provide any information it might have in respect of the whereabouts of a person allegedly disappeared.

Given the Government's indication that the events occurring at the Ferrous Alloy Factory fell within the context of a labour dispute, the Government was requested to drop all charges relating to terrorism, sabotage and subversion.

The Government was further requested to provide specific and detailed information on the charges brought against the four worker representatives. In the meantime, it was requested to take the necessary steps for the immediate release of any of the factory workers' representatives still detained and to ensure that the charges brought against them were dropped. The Government was also requested to keep the Committee informed in this regard.

The Government was requested to ensure that due process of the law was guaranteed in respect of all the workers' representatives named in the complaint. It was also requested to reply specifically to the allegations that representatives of the provisional union committee for retrenched workers of the Daqing Petroleum Company and some 60 other workers involved in protest actions in the city, as well as an unidentified 50-year-old woman and a retired worker, were detained. The Government was further requested to provide any information at its disposal concerning arrests which might have been made in connection with the protests in Daqing, whether any individuals were still being detained and any charges which might have been brought against them.

In light of the numerous allegations in this complaint concerning the excessive use of force by the police in various disputes taking place in different parts of the country, the Government was requested to consider preparing relevant instructions for the forces of law and order aimed at eliminating the danger of resorting to the use of excessive violence when controlling demonstrations.

The Government was further requested to provide detailed information concerning the two democratic opposition activists who had reportedly been sentenced to heavy prison terms for acting on behalf of the organizing workers and on the allegations that an independent labour activist was detained in Shanxi Province for trying to set up a federation for retired workers. The Government was asked, in particular, to provide information concerning the health of the latter detainee and the allegations of his mistreatment in detention.

Finally, the Government was requested once again to examine the possibility of a direct contacts mission being undertaken to the country in order to promote the full implementation of freedom of association. The Committee expressed the hope that the Government would respond positively to this suggestion, which had been made in a constructive spirit with a view to assisting the Government to find appropriate solutions to the existing problems.

(d) Plattform "Ärzte für das Leben" v. Austria
(European Court of Human Rights)[29]

The case was referred to the European Court of Human Rights on 14 May 1987 by the European Commission of Human Rights. It originated in an application against Austria lodged with the Commission on 13 September 1982 by an Austrian association, Plattform "Ärzte für das Leben". The purpose of the Commission's request was to obtain a decision from the Court as to whether the facts of the case disclosed a breach by the respondent State of its obligations under article 13 of the Convention for the Protection of Human Rights and Fundamental Freedoms.

The facts

The applicant was an association of doctors who were campaigning against abortion and seeking to bring about reform of the Austrian legislation on the matter. In 1980 and 1982, it held two demonstrations which were disrupted by counter-demonstrators despite the presence of a large contingent of police.

The association decided to hold a religious service on 28 December 1980 at a church in Upper Austria, after which there would be a march to the surgery of a doctor who carried out abortions. As required under the Assembly Act, it gave notice, on 30 November 1980, to the district's police authority. The police made no objection and gave the participants permission to use the public highway. The police did, however, have to ban two other planned demonstrations announced subsequently by supporters of abortion, as these demonstrations were to be held at the same time and in the same place as the association's demonstration.

As the organizers feared that incidents might occur nonetheless, they sought, shortly before the beginning of the march, to change their plans, in consultation with the local authorities. They gave up the idea of demonstrating outside the doctor's surgery. Instead, they decided to march to an altar erected on a hillside quite a distance away from the church and hold a religious ceremony there.

The police representatives pointed out to the organizers that the main body of the police officers had already been deployed along the route originally planned and that, because of the lie of the land, the new route was not suited to crowd control. They did not refuse to provide protection. However, they stated, irrespective of the route chosen or to be chosen, it would be impossible to prevent counter-demonstrators from throwing eggs and disrupting both the march and the religious service.

---

[29] See *Publications of the European Court of Human Rights*, Series A: *Judgments and Decisions*, vol. 139 (1988), application No. 10126/82, judgment of 21 June 1988.

III:5

During the mass, a large number of counter-demonstrators, who, it seemed, had not given the notice required under the Assembly Act, assembled outside the church and were not dispersed by the police. They disrupted the march to the hillside by mingling with the marchers and shouting down their recitation of the rosary. The same thing happened at the service celebrated in the open air. Some 500 people attempted to interrupt it using loudspeakers and threw eggs and clumps of grass at the congregation.

At the end of the ceremony, when tempers had risen to the point where physical violence nearly broke out, special riot-control units, having until then been standing by without intervening, formed a cordon between the opposing groups, and this enabled the procession to return to the church.

In a letter to the safety authority in Upper Austria, the chairman of the association described the counter-demonstrators' behaviour as relatively peaceful. On other occasions, the association's opponents had attacked its members and assaulted policemen.

On 21 January 1981, the association lodged a disciplinary complaint alleging that the local police had failed to provide sufficient protection for the demonstration. The safety authority in Upper Austria considered that the behaviour of the police had been irreproachable, and it decided not to take any disciplinary measures against them. It referred to the difficulty of completely protecting an open-air demonstration from verbal abuse and from missiles not likely to cause the participants any physical harm. The authority added that, in not intervening, the police had been prompted by the concern to avoid more serious trouble.

The association subsequently lodged an appeal with the Constitutional Court. In its submission, the local authorities' failure to act had in the instant case allowed an infringement of the freedoms of assembly and religious observance guaranteed by the Austrian Constitution. In a judgment on 1 March 1982, the Constitutional Court held that it had no jurisdiction. Consequently, it declared the appeal inadmissible. It noted that the association's complaint was clearly not directed against a decision or acts of direct administrative coercion within the meaning of the Constitution.

The association did not take any ordinary criminal proceedings by lodging a complaint or by bringing a subsidiary private prosecution. The safety authority in Upper Austria and the local police, however, opened investigation proceedings against a person or persons unknown for disruption of a meeting. For its part, a private organization for the protection of human dignity lodged a complaint against one of the counter-demonstrators, a member of parliament, alleging obstruction of a religious ceremony and incitement to hatred under the criminal code as well as an offence against the Assembly Act. Complaints were also lodged against two other people. The public prosecutor, however, discontinued the proceedings under the criminal procedure code. One person caught in the act of throwing eggs was fined under another law.

The competent police authority gave permission for a second demonstration against abortion to be held on 1 May 1982 in the cathedral square in Salzburg. An anniversary meeting was due to be held in the square by the Socialist Party on the same day, but it had to be cancelled, because notice of it had been given after the applicant association had given notice of its own meeting. The demonstration began at 2.15 p.m. and ended with an hour of prayers inside the cathedral.

At about 1.30 p.m., some 350 people angrily shouting their opposition had passed through the three archways that provided access to the square and gathered outside the cathedral. 100 policemen formed a cordon around the association demonstrators to protect them from direct attack. Other trouble was caused by sympathizers of an extreme right-wing party who voiced their support for the association. The police asked the association's chairman to order these people to disperse, but without success. In order to prevent the religious ceremony being disrupted, the police cleared the square.

No proceedings were taken after these incidents, and in view of the Constitutional Court's decision on 1 March 1982, the association considered that a second appeal would have served no purpose.

In its application to the Commission, the association claimed that it had not had sufficient police protection during its demonstrations on 28 December 1980 and on 1 May 1982, respectively. It submitted that there had been violations of articles 9, 10 and 11 of the Convention. It also relied on article 13, claiming that the Austrian legal system did not provide an effective remedy before a national authority to ensure the effective exercise of those rights.

The complaints under articles 9, 10, and 11 of the Convention was declared inadmissible by the Commission as being manifestly ill-founded. On the other hand, the complaint under article 13 was declared admissible, but the Commission held in its report that there had been no violation of this article.

The law

The applicant stated that no effective remedy was available to it in Austria for its complaint under article 11 of the Convention. It relied on article 13 providing that everyone whose rights and freedoms as set forth in the Convention were violated

III:5

should have an effective remedy before a national authority notwithstanding that the violation had been committed by persons acting in an official capacity.

The Government's main submission was that article 13 of the Convention applied only where a substantive provision of the Convention had been infringed. As evidence of this, the Government cited the French text, containing the words "ont été violés", which in their view were clearer than the corresponding English terms "are violated".

The Court did not accept this submission. Under its case law, article 13 secured an effective remedy before a national authority to anyone claiming on arguable grounds to be the victim of a violation of his rights and freedoms as protected in the Convention. Any other interpretation would render it meaningless.

Although the Commission declared the complaint inadmissible as being manifestly ill-founded in respect of article 11 of the Convention, it considered the complaint arguable for the purposes of article 13. The Government thought it contradictory to declare one and the same complaint to be manifestly ill-founded under a substantive provision and yet arguable under article 13.

The Court did not propose to give an abstract definition of the notion of arguability. In order to ascertain whether article 13 of the Convention was applicable in the instant case, it was sufficient that the Court should determine, in the light of the facts of the case and the nature of the legal issue or issues raised, whether the claim that the requirements of article 11 had not been complied with was arguable notwithstanding that the Commission had dismissed it as manifestly ill-founded. Citing a previous judgment, the Court said that the Commission's decision on admissibility might provide the Court with useful pointers as to the arguability of the relevant claim.

Before the Commission, the applicant complained that the Austrian authorities had disregarded the true meaning of freedom of assembly by having failed to take practical steps to ensure that its demonstrations passed off without any trouble. In the Government's submission, article 11 did not create any positive obligation to protect demonstrations. Freedom of peaceful assembly, enshrined in Austrian law, was mainly designed to protect the individual from direct interference by the State. Unlike some other provisions in the Convention, and the Austrian Constitution, article 11 did not apply to relations between individuals. At all events, the choice of the means to be used in a given situation was a matter for the State's discretion.

In its decision on admissibility, the Commission dealt at length with the question whether article 11 of the Convention impliedly required the State to protect demonstrations from those wishing to interfere with or disrupt them. It answered this question in the affirmative.

The Court considered that it did not have to develop a general theory of the positive obligations that might flow from the Convention, but before ruling on the arguability of the applicant's claim, it had to give an interpretation of article 11.

A demonstration might annoy or give offence to persons opposed to the ideas or claims that it was seeking to promote. The participants had, however, to be able to hold the demonstration without having to fear that they would be subjected to physical violence by their opponents. Such a fear would be liable to deter associations or other groups supporting common ideas or interests from openly expressing their opinions on highly controversial issues affecting the community. In a democracy, the right to counter-demonstrate could not extend to inhibiting the exercise of the right to demonstrate.

Genuine and effective freedom of peaceful assembly could not, therefore, be reduced to a mere duty on the part of the State not to interfere. A purely negative conception would not be compatible with the object and purpose of article 11 of the Convention. This article, like article 8, sometimes required positive measures to be taken, even in the sphere of relations between individuals, if needed.

Concurring with the Government and the Commission, the Court found that Austrian law was concerned to protect demonstrations by such positive action. For example, under the criminal code, there was an offence for any person to disperse, prevent or disrupt a meeting that had not been prohibited. The Assembly Act, which empowered the authorities in certain cases to prohibit, bring to an end or disperse by force an assembly, also applied to counter-demonstrations.

While it was the duty of States parties to take reasonable and appropriate measures to enable lawful demonstrations to proceed peacefully, they could not guarantee this absolutely, and they had a wide discretion in the choice of the means to be used, as the Court had pronounced in other judgments. In this area, the obligation they entered into under article 11 of the Convention was an obligation as to measures to be taken and not as to results to be achieved.

In the applicant's submission, the police remained entirely passive at each of the two demonstrations in issue. The Government and the Commission disagreed. In their view, immediate intervention was not justified in the absence of any serious assaults and would inevitably have provoked physical violence. The Court did not have to assess the expediency or effectiveness of the tactics adopted by the police on these

III:5

occasions, but only to determine whether there was an arguable claim that the appropriate authorities failed to take the necessary measures.

Regarding the incidents on 28 December 1980, the Court noted that the two demonstrations planned by supporters of abortion, due to be held at the same time and place as the association's demonstration of which notice had been given on 30 November 1980, had been prohibited. Furthermore, a large number of uniformed and plain-clothes policemen had been deployed along the route originally planned, and the police representatives did not refuse the association their protection even after it decided to change the route despite their objections. Lastly, no damage was done, nor were there any serious clashes. The counter-demonstrators chanted slogans, waved banners and threw eggs or clumps of grass, which did not prevent the procession and the open-air religious service from proceeding to their conclusion. Special riot-control units placed themselves between the opposing groups when tempers had risen to the point where violence threatened to break out.

For the 1982 demonstration in Salzburg, the organizers had chosen the date of 1 May, the day of the traditional Socialist march which had to be cancelled regarding the cathedral square, because the association had given notice of its demonstration earlier. Furthermore, 100 policemen were sent to the scene to separate the participants from their opponents and avert the danger of direct attacks. They cleared the square so as to prevent any disturbance of the religious service.

It thus clearly appeared that the Austrian authorities did not fail to take reasonable and appropriate measures.

No arguable claim that article 11 of the Convention was violated had thus been made out. Therefore, article 13 did not apply in the instant case. For these reasons, the Court held that there had been no violation of article 13.

PART IV

Police Behaviour in Times of Armed Conflict, Disturbance and Tension

1. Introduction to Police Behaviour in Times of Armed Conflict, Disturbance and Tension

Situations of armed conflict and internal disturbance and tension present acute challenges, difficulties and dangers to police and other security forces. The ways in which they respond to such situations can either lower or heighten tensions in societies, quell or exacerbate disturbances, or make armed conflicts more or less bloody. Overreaction can make the difficult and dangerous task of policing in such situations even more difficult and dangerous by, for example, alienating individuals or sections of a community to such an extent that they are prepared to support or even become members of disaffected groups who may be involved in terrorism or other acts of violence. It can undermine the values of a democratic society governed by the rule of law which police are supposed to be protecting against subversion or violent attack.

Lawful, humane and intelligent policing, on the other hand, can be a significant factor in preventing social tensions from escalating into violence and in reducing intercommunal bitterness and hostility in post-conflict situations. When peace is being restored, the extent to which, and the time within which, police are able to secure, maintain or rebuild that trust, consent and cooperation of the people which is necessary for effective policing depends crucially on the conduct of police during any period of conflict or disturbance.

The purpose of this part of the book is to consider cases from international human rights institutions arising out of police actions in times of armed conflict, disturbance and tension as well as cases in which individuals have been held to account for international crimes in such situations. The cases considered in previous parts of the book have arisen out of police responses to ordinary criminality and to the types of situation to which this part is devoted. Hence, the views of human rights institutions on what is considered to be permissible or impermissible in times of armed conflict, disturbance and tension have already been elucidated to some extent in this book. It has been made clear that some of the most important and significant cases on, for example, the right to life and the prohibition of torture have arisen in situations where peace and order have broken down.

Whilst, therefore, aspects of police behaviour in such situations have been considered in cases cited within the frameworks of the exercise of police powers and the performance of police functions, it is crucially important to give especial emphasis

527

to policing in times of armed conflict, disturbance and social tension by devoting this final part of the book to it. Police will be more effective in their efforts to maintain or restore peace and social order, so that the underlying causes of the unrest or discontent can be resolved through political processes, if their responses are lawful, humane and intelligent. Their role is to manage a difficult and dangerous situation, not to become a part of the problem.

When an armed conflict is not internal, but between States, policing also needs to be given especial consideration. Clearly, the extent to which, and the ways in which, a State is involved in an international armed conflict affects the nature of any police involvement, and the various possibilities are numerous. For example, a State may be fighting a war far away from its borders, with few implications for its police. On the other hand, an international armed conflict may be taking place within the territory of a State; a State may have been invaded and occupied by another State's military forces; or a State may be involved in an armed conflict in a neighbouring State. All of these, and other, possibilities have many and different implications for policing and the behaviour of police. Furthermore, that behaviour would be regulated not only by international human rights law, but also by international humanitarian law applicable in armed conflicts, also known as the laws of war.

Recent conflicts involving grave and systematic violations of human rights and humanitarian law have called for particular enforcement mechanisms under international law to be considered. In 1993, acting under Chapter VII of the Charter of the United Nations, the Security Council established the International Tribunal for the former Yugoslavia for the sole purpose of prosecuting persons responisble for serious violations of international humanitiarian law committed in the territory of the former Yugoslavia since 1991.[1] Correspondingly, in 1994, the Security Council established the International Criminal Tribunal for Rwanda for prosecuting persons responsible for genocide and other serious violations of international humanitarian law in the territory of Rwanda and Rwandan citizens responsible for genocide and other such violations committed in the territory of neighbouring States in 1994.[2]

These measures taken under international law have been followed and further developed by the establishment of the International Criminal Court, seated in The Hague, the Netherlands. The Rome Statute of the International Criminal Court, a treaty in force since 2002, states in article 1 that the Court shall be a permanent institution with the power to exercise its jurisdiction over persons for the most serious crimes of international concern, complementary to national criminal jurisdictions. Under article 5, paragraph 1, the Court has jurisdiction in accordance with the Statute with

---

[1] See part I, chap. 1, sect. D (*f*) (*supra*, pp. 17-19).
[2] See part I, chap. 1, sect. D (*g*) (*supra*, pp. 19-22).

respect to the crime of genocide, crimes against humanity, war crimes and the crime of aggression.

A brief account of some elements of international humanitarian law is set out below, because, for a more complete understanding of this part of the book, it is important that police should be aware of the fundamental principles on which its provisions are based. They should also know how some terms and concepts are defined, especially those of combatant and civilian, and how police fit within these categories, and be able to compare and contrast humanitarian law with human rights law. Examples of rules of conduct prescribed by international humanitarian law are not included here for reasons of space. However, such provisions are cited in the jurisprudence of international courts and bodies, and these have been retained in the reviews and summaries of cases in the ensuing chapters.

The present introduction, and the accounts of the cases, may encourage those responsible for developing and conducting educational and training programmes for police to include elements of international humanitarian law relevant to police in their programmes. It is important to do so, because it is legally applicable in both international and non-international armed conflicts, and because some of its principles and provisions are relevant to policing conflict just below the threshold of armed conflict and to policing other less serious or less durable forms of social disorder, even though they are not legally applicable in such circumstances. Furthermore, a variety of forms of conflict and social disorder may arise within the context of a society experiencing actual armed conflict.

Police officials need to understand and apply principles and provisions of humanitarian law, and human rights law, in times of armed conflict and internal disturbance and tension as a matter of good professional practice, in order that they may behave correctly, benefit from the forms of protection to which they are entitled, promote the protection of others and enforce or encourage correct behaviour on the part of others where this is possible and appropriate. It is also the case that some police officials will be given the task of investigating alleged breaches of international humanitarian law either during a conflict or when it has ceased. Furthermore, some police officials may be in a position to gather evidence of such breaches, perhaps during the course of a conflict and before any investigation has been launched. Evidence of this nature could be used to support prosecutions before domestic courts and international tribunals. In this respect, articles 86 to 102 of the Rome Statute contain a series of provisions on international cooperation and judicial assistance. Evidence gathered during or soon after a conflict would assist compliance with these provisions and enhance the investigation and prosecution of genocide, crimes against humanity and war crimes.

IV:1

International humanitarian law applicable in armed conflicts has developed relatively recently in its present form, but it has its origins in antiquity when, for example, military leaders would sometimes order captured enemy fighters to be spared and the enemy civilian population to be treated humanely. Practices of this kind gradually developed into a body of customary law which parties to a conflict are legally bound to respect. One principle of customary law is that the right of belligerents to adopt means of injuring the enemy is not unlimited. This principle affects, for example, the use of weapons. It prohibits belligerents from using weapons that give rise to unnecessary suffering or superfluous injury. Another such principle is that of proportionality. When taking action against a legitimate military objective, belligerents are required to have regard to the impact on civilians not being targeted. A third example is the principle of discrimination, which is about care in the selection of methods, weaponry and targets.

International humanitarian law now consists of two sets of treaty law, the so-called "Hague Law" and "Geneva Law", respectively, as well as a number of customary rules based on the above principles. The two strands of treaty law are distinguished in that Hague Law governs the conduct of hostilities, the permissible means and methods of warfare, whereas Geneva Law is concerned with the protection of victims of war. Since they first entered into force, many of the Hague regulations have been developed or superseded by Geneva Law. In fact, the distinction between the two sets of treaty law is nowadays not quite so marked, as they are merging to some extent through provisions evolved in Geneva Law.

The four Geneva Conventions of 12 August 1949 make provision for combatants who become victims of war as sick, wounded or shipwrecked casualties, in the first and second Conventions; for prisoners of war in the third Convention; and for the protection of civilians in time of war in the very long and detailed fourth Convention. All provisions of the Geneva Conventions concern the protection of victims of international armed conflicts except article 3 common to the Conventions, which is applicable in armed conflicts not of an international character. In 1977, two Protocols to the Geneva Conventions were adopted. The Protocol Additional to the Geneva Conventions of 12 August 1949, and relating to the Protection of Victims of International Armed Conflicts (Protocol I), updates and elaborates existing rules of combat as well as rules for the protection of war victims, bringing about a partial fusion of Hague Law and Geneva Law. The Protocol Additional to the Geneva Conventions of 12 August 1949, and relating to the Protection of Victims of Non-International Armed Conflicts (Protocol II), supplements the provisions of common article 3. Like the Geneva Conventions, the additional Protocols are treaties which are legally binding on States having ratified or acceded to them.

The purposes of international humanitarian law are, in short, to regulate the conduct of hostilities and to protect victims of armed conflicts. It imposes obligations on parties to armed conflicts and comes into force only when armed conflict occurs. For example, the four Geneva Conventions and Protocol I apply in cases of declared war or of any other armed conflict arising between two or more States parties from the beginning of such a situation, even if a state of war is not recognized by one of them. The treaties also cover armed conflicts in which people are fighting against colonial domination and alien occupation and against racial regimes in the exercise of their right of self-determination.

It is clear from the preceding parts of this book that the overriding purpose of international human rights law is to secure the lawful rights and freedoms of individuals. To that end, obligations are imposed on governments in relation to individuals and groups within the functional jurisdiction of the States they govern. It limits and controls the exercise of power by States in relation to individuals and groups. Human rights law applies in all places and at all times, in times of peace as well as in times of conflict. Its scope and effectiveness may be diminished through measures taken by States, which derogate from their obligations, during periods of national emergency threatening the life of the nation, but it remains applicable. Some provisions protecting the most fundamental human rights may even be non-derogable, such as provisions on the right to life and the prohibition of torture.

The differences in fields of application mean that international human rights law and international humanitarian law are essentially complementary. For example, human rights law can be seen as operating in the normal state of society and then merging, through measures of derogation, with humanitarian law as social order becomes disrupted or breaks down. Even when war breaks out, the human rights regime, albeit diminished, does not become inoperative. It remains ready to return to full effect as the normal state of society is restored.

It is important that police officials should understand the distinction between combatants and civilians and their own status in these terms. Broadly, under article 4 of the Geneva Convention relative to the Treatment of Prisoners of War (Geneva Convention III) and articles 43 and 44 of Protocol I, members of the armed forces of a party to an international armed conflict, other than medical and religious personnel, are combatants, and any combatant captured by the adverse party is a prisoner of war. Such armed forces must be organized, placed under a command responsible to that party for the conduct of its subordinates and subject to an internal disciplinary system which enforces compliance with the rules of international law applicable in armed conflict.

IV:1

Compliance with these rules implies, in particular, that combatants are obliged to distinguish themselves from the civilian population by a uniform or by some other distinctive sign, at least while they are engaged in an attack or in a military operation preparatory to an attack. In exceptional circumstances, owing to the nature of hostilities, they may distinguish themselves as combatants by carrying arms openly.

Under article 50 of Protocol I, a civilian is any person who is not a member of armed forces, and where there is doubt as to whether or not a person is a civilian, that person is to be considered a civilian.

Civil police forces are not armed forces in the sense in which that term is used in these definitions. It is clear that civil police forces have civilian status and that members of those forces have civilian and not combatant status. This point is reinforced by article 43, paragraph 3, of Protocol I under which a party to a conflict shall notify other parties whenever it incorporates a paramilitary or armed law enforcement agency into its armed forces. In order for a police official to be accorded combatant status, he or she must be a member of an armed law enforcement agency formally assimilated into the armed forces of a party to a conflict. Such an act of incorporation, coupled with notification to other parties, radically alters the status of members of the law enforcement agency. It also confirms the civilian status of members of agencies to which this provision has not been applied. The non-combatant status of police is also underscored by other provisions.

Article 3 common to the Geneva Conventions extends basic humanitarian protection to certain categories of people by applying principles on which the four Geneva Conventions are based to armed conflicts not of an international character occurring in the territory of a State party. In such cases, each party to the conflict is bound to apply its provisions as a minimum.

The fundamental principle of humane treatment is embodied in subparagraph (1). This provision also defines those protected under the article as persons taking no active part in hostilities, including members of armed forces who have laid down their arms and those placed *hors de combat* by sickness, wounds, detention, or any other cause.

Protocol II develops and supplements common article 3 without modifying its existing conditions of application. The material field of application of the Protocol is set out in its article 1, paragraph 1. The Protocol applies to all armed conflicts which are not covered by Protocol I, relating to international armed conflicts, and which take place in the territory of a State party between its armed forces and dissident armed forces or other organized armed groups which, under responsible command, exercise such control over a part of its territory as to enable them to carry out sustained and concerted military operations and to implement the Protocol.

Under article 1, paragraph 2, the Protocol does not apply to situations of internal disturbances and tensions, such as riots, isolated and sporadic acts of violence and other acts of a similar nature, as not being armed conflicts. Thus the upper and lower limits of the field of application of the Protocol are established.

The personal field of application of the Protocol is defined in article 2, paragraph 2, as all persons affected by an armed conflict as defined in article 1. A person who takes a direct part in hostilities is not regarded as affected by an armed conflict. The only protection for those who take part in hostilities is set out in article 4, paragraph 1, which prohibits orders that there shall be no survivors. In the same provision, it is made clear that all of the other provisions of the Protocol are designed to protect those who do not take a direct part or who have ceased to take part in hostilities. This point is reinforced by article 13, paragraph 3, which concerns the protection of civilians. They shall enjoy the protection afforded by the Protocol unless and for such time as they take a direct part in hostilities.

On the question of status, it should be noted that the notion of combatant, and therefore of combatant status, does not exist in non-international armed conflict. Those engaged in such an armed conflict are either members of armed forces, police forces or other security forces of a State, who have legitimate power to use lawful force, or members of insurrectionary forces whose use of force for insurgent purposes is unlawful. Members of insurrectionary forces are punishable under criminal law for such unlawful use of force, their act of insurrection and other criminal acts they may commit.

Under the terms and conditions of common article 3 and Protocol II, three categories of internal conflict can be distinguished. The first category, identified in article 1 of the Protocol, embraces those high-intensity internal armed conflicts in which rebel forces have control of territory. The Protocol regulates this type of conflict in some detail, supplementing considerably the provisions of common article 3 which, nevertheless, also apply. At a lower intensity are those conflicts which fall below the threshold of Protocol II and to which only the provisions of common article 3 apply. Finally, below that level, is the category specifically excluded by article 1, paragraph 2, of the Protocol, situations of internal disturbances and tensions.

Internal disturbances and tensions are exemplified in this article as riots, isolated and sporadic acts of violence and other acts of a similar nature, as not being armed conflicts. However, there remains some difficulty in distinguishing between armed conflicts and internal disturbances, particularly where the scale of violence fluctuates around that manifested in those internal disturbances and tensions specifically excluded by the article. Furthermore, whilst this threshold is not included in the provisions of common article 3, the article clearly deals with armed conflicts involving hostilities between armed forces. In any event, when civil conflict does occur, the demarcation between civil war and disturbances and tensions is not always clear, and the need to alleviate the suffering of victims remains, however the conflict may be categorized, as does the legal and moral obligation to comply with human rights and humanitarian standards.

One of the strengths of international humanitarian law in protecting people in times of armed conflict is that its fundamental principles and its specific provisions are directly relevant to the situation of victims of armed conflict. Furthermore, the scope of human rights law can be limited through measures of derogation taken by States in times of public emergency. Given that some forms of internal disturbance, in terms of their intensity and the numbers of victims created, can be almost indistinguishable from a non-international armed conflict, it can be argued that it is a matter of good professional policing to comply with relevant principles and provisions of humanitarian law, as well as those of human rights law, when dealing with situations of internal disturbance. The protection of victims and the process of post-conflict reconciliation would both be enhanced if this were to be the case.

Children are afforded special protection under international humanitarian law. For example, parties to a conflict are required, *inter alia*, to take the necessary measures to ensure that children under the age of 15 years, who are orphaned or separated from their families as a result of war, are not left to their own resources and that their maintenance, the exercise of their religion and their education are facilitated in all circumstances.

Concerning children, international humanitarian law is reinforced by article 38 of the Convention on the Rights of the Child. Under paragraph 1, States parties undertake to respect and to ensure respect for those rules of international humanitarian law applicable to them in armed conflicts which are relevant to the child. Paragraph 2 stipulates that States parties shall take all feasible measures to ensure that persons under 15 years do not take a direct part in hostilities. Under paragraph 3, States parties shall refrain from recruiting any person who has not attained the age of 15 years into their armed forces, and in recruiting among those persons who have attained the age of 15 years but not 18 years, States parties shall endeavour to give priority to those who are oldest. Finally, in paragraph 4, it is pronounced that in accordance with their obligations under international humanitarian law to protect the civilian population in armed conflicts, States parties shall take all feasible measures to ensure protection and care of children who are affected by an armed conflict.

The Optional Protocol to the Convention on the Rights of Child on the involvement of children in armed conflict, in force since 2002, raises the age of possible recruitment of persons into armed forces and their participation in hostilities in relation to what is stipulated in article 38 of the Convention. The protection of children afforded by this article is reinforced by provisions of the Optional Protocol prescribing, *inter alia*, that members of armed forces under the age of 18 years shall not take a direct part in hostilities, nor be compulsorily recruited into the armed forces of a State party, and that armed groups distinct from the armed forces of a State shall not under any circumstances recruit or use in hotilities persons under that age. This treaty is subject to ratification and is open to accession by any State. In a regional context, children, especially girls under the age of 18 years, are afforded similar protection under article 11 of the Protocol to the African Charter on Human and Peoples' Rights on the Rights of Women in Africa.

The following chapters of this part of the book deal with respect for and protection of human rights and international crimes, respectively, in times of armed conflict, disturbance and tension.

2. Respect for and Protection of Human Rights

A. INTRODUCTION

In the three opening paragraphs of the preamble to the Universal Declaration of Human Rights, it is pronounced that recognition of the inherent dignity and of the equal and inalienable rights of all members of the human family is the foundation of freedom, justice and peace in the world; that disregard and contempt for human rights have resulted in barbarous acts which have outraged the conscience of mankind, and the advent of a world in which human beings shall enjoy freedom of speech and belief and freedom from fear and want has been proclaimed as the highest aspiration of the common people; and that it is essential, if man is not to be compelled to have recourse, as a last resort, to rebellion against tyranny and oppression, that human rights should be protected by the rule of law.

These preambular paragraphs are cited here, because, unlike the preceding chapters of this book, this chapter does not focus on a specific human right. All human rights, including those considered hitherto, are vulnerable in times of armed conflict, disturbance and tension. Therefore, it is appropriate to recall that recognition of human dignity and human rights is the foundation of freedom, justice and peace; that mankind has committed, and continues to commit, barbarous acts; and that tyranny and oppression, and rebellion against those twin evils, remain constant features of our world. The actions of state and non-state actors have been as criminally bloody and brutal in the opening years of this century as they were throughout the last. In particular, human rights and humanitarian standards, in fact all civilized values, remain threatened through acts of terrorism and through clumsy, opportunistic, unlawful and brutal responses to them.

In the introduction to this part of the book,[1] the challenges, dangers and difficulties of policing in times of armed conflict, disturbance and tension are acknowledged, and reasons why police should behave lawfully and humanely in those times are emphasized. Some of the many tasks that may fall to police when armed conflict breaks out are alluded to, as are the primary roles of police when there are disturbances and tensions. When social order breaks down, it is the task of police to restore order. When there is social tension police can be one of the necessary means by which it is

---

[1] See part IV, chap. 1 (*supra*, pp. 527-535).

IV:2

prevented from escalating into violence. In both situations they can protect people, and they can contribute to the conditions necessary for the protection of all human rights.

The Geneva Conventions of 12 August 1949 have been cited in the case law of international human rights institutions, for example, in three of the cases summarized and/or reviewed in this chapter of the book. Two of these were considered by the Working Group on Arbitrary Detention and one by the Inter-American Court of Human Rights. The other cases cited occurred in the context of disturbances or tensions. Some of the disturbances were of sufficient intensity to be on the threshold of internal armed conflicts, although it is unlikely that any of the States involved would have agreed that the situation had deteriorated to that extent.

Derogation from human rights obligations in times of emergency to secure the survival of the nation is acknowledged and allowed for under some human rights treaties.

Article 4 of the International Covenant on Civil and Political Rights contains provisions on derogation during a state of emergency. Under paragraph 1, States parties may take measures derogating from their obligations under the Covenant in time of public emergency which threatens the life of the nation. However, the state of emergency has to be officially proclaimed by the State, and the measures taken must be strictly required by the exigencies of the situation. Furthermore, the measures must not be inconsistent with the State's other obligations under international law and not involve discrimination solely on the ground of race, colour, sex, language, religion or social origin.

Paragraph 2 states that no derogation may be made under article 4 from articles 6, 7, 8, paragraphs 1 and 2, 11, 15, 16 and 18 of the Covenant. The list of non-derogable provisions in this paragraph is extended, by article 6, paragraph 2, of the Second Optional Protocol to the Covenant, to include the abolition of the death penalty under article 1, paragraph 1, of the Protocol, without prejudice, however, to the possibility of making a reservation for the application of the death penalty in time of war.

Paragraph 3, finally, establishes the procedure to be applied by a State party when it avails itself of the right of derogation.

In its general comment No. 29 (72) on derogations from provisions of the Covenant during a state of emergency,[2] the Human Rights Committee made a number of sig-

---

[2] See United Nations, *Official Records of the General Assembly, Fifty-sixth Session, Supplement No. 40* (A/56/40), vol. I, annex VI.

nificant pronouncements intended to assist States parties to meet the requirements of article 4. The Committee pointed out that the article was of paramount importance for the system of protection for human rights under the Covenant. It allowed for a State party unilaterally and temporarily to derogate from part of its obligations, but the measure taken and its material consequences were subject to a specific regime of safeguards.

Among the observations made by the Committee in analyzing article 4, some should be mentioned in this context. The Committee pointed out that no derogation might be inconsistent with the State's other obligations under international law, particularly the rules of international humanitarian law. Article 4 might not be invoked as a justification for acting in violation of humanitarian law or peremptory norms of international law, for instance, by taking hostages, by imposing collective punishment, through arbitrary deprivations of liberty or by deviating from fundamental principles of fair trial, including the presumption of innocence. In assessing the scope of legitimate derogation from the Covenant, one criterion could be found in the definition of certain human rights violations as crimes against humanity, recently codified in the Rome Statute of the International Criminal Court. Furthermore, in some provisions not listed as non-derogable, there were elements that could not be made subject to lawful derogation under article 4. One example mentioned was the provision that all persons deprived of their liberty should be treated with humanity and with respect for the inherent dignity of the human person, prescribed in article 10 of the Covenant, which expressed, the Committee believed, a norm of general international law not subject to derogation.

Article 27 of the American Convention on Human Rights also provides for derogation in time of emergency. Under paragraph 1, a State party may take measures derogating from its obligations under the Convention in time of war, public danger or other emergency that threatens its independence or security. However, such derogations are only allowed to the extent and for the period of time strictly required by the exigencies of the situation. Such measures must not be inconsistent with the State's other obligations under international law and must not involve discrimination on the ground of race, colour, sex, language, religion or social origin.

Paragraph 2 lists a number of non-derogable provisions. No derogation shall be made under articles 3, 4, 5, 6, 9, 12, 17, 18, 19, 20, and 23, or of the judicial guarantees essential for the protection of such rights. Paragraph 3 sets out the procedure to be applied by a State party when it avails itself of the right of derogation.

Similar provisions are set out in Article 15 of the Convention for the Protection of Human Rights and Fundamental Freedoms. Under paragraph 1, a State party may take measures derogating from its obligations under the Convention in time of war

IV:2

or other public emergency threatening the life of the nation. However, such derogations are only allowed to the extent strictly required by the exigencies of the situation, provided that such measures are not inconsistent with the State's other obligations under international law.

The non-derogable provisions are listed in paragraph 2. No derogation shall be made under article 15 from article 2, except in respect of deaths resulting from lawful acts of war, or from articles 3, 4, paragraph 1, and 7 of the Convention. Furthermore, the application of this provision has been extended by article 3 of Protocol No. 6 to the Convention and article 2 of Protocol No. 13 to the Convention, both in respect of the abolition of the death penalty, and by article 4 of Protocol No. 7 to the Convention in respect of the right not to be tried or punished twice. Paragraph 3, finally, includes the provisions establishing the procedure to be applied by States parties making use of the right of derogation.

The African Charter on Human and Peoples' Rights contains no specific provision entitling a State party to derogate from any of its obligations. However, many of the articles contain so-called "claw back" clauses under which a State is entitled to restrict the rights embodied by the provisions to the extent permitted by domestic law.

Not every situation of conflict, disorder or tension is of sufficient gravity to justify derogation from the provisions of human rights treaties. When conditions for derogation are not met, the entire range of human rights applies and States remain bound by their treaty obligations to respect those rights. However, restrictions, as opposed to derogations, may be imposed on some rights through a wider application of the limitation clauses attached to some articles of human rights treaties. For example, it may be felt that the right to peaceful assembly should be lawfully restricted in the interests of national security or public order, as provided for in article 21 of the Covenant. Even when conditions for derogation do exist, derogation to the fullest possible extent is not necessarily justifiable, and governments have to exercise judgement as to which rights people within their jurisdiction will be denied during a public emergency

It should also be recognized that measures of derogation can be a seriously limiting factor on human rights protection, their effect extending beyond those rights subject to derogation and affecting non-derogable rights. For example, those safeguards designed to secure judicial supervision of detainees following arrest or detention on criminal charges may be diminished following derogation from articles protecting the right to liberty of person and prohibiting arbitrary arrest under the Covenant and the regional treaties. Torture or ill treatment of detainees, and even unlawful killings, can occur as a consequence of the limitation of this form of supervision. However, these dangers can be reduced by proper scrutiny of the effects of emergency

540

legislation by treaty bodies when they have cause to consider measures of derogation in particular cases, thereby ensuring that such safeguards are retained to some extent.

In respect of the prohibition of torture, a non-derogable provision, it should be recalled that article 2 of the Convention against Torture and Other Cruel, Inhuman or Degrading Treatment or Punishment states that no exceptional circumstances whatsoever, whether a state of war or a threat of war, internal political instability or any other public emergency, may be invoked as a justification of torture. Principle 1 of the Principles on the Effective Prevention and Investigation of Extra-Legal, Arbitrary and Summary Executions and article 7 of the Declaration on the Protection of All Persons from Enforced Disappearance contain similar provisions in respect of extrajudicial killings and enforced disappearances, respectively.

B. REVIEW OF CASES

(*a*) Human Rights Committee

Given the frequency and intensity of various forms of conflict, disturbance and tension that occur in countries throughout the world, and the fact that human rights are particularly vulnerable when they do, it is not surprising that many of the cases considered by the Human Rights Committee arise out of such situations. Indeed, a number of the cases from its jurisprudence that are summarized and/or reviewed in preceding chapters of this book derive from situations of internal conflict, disturbance or tension, especially cases on the right to life, the prohibition of torture and the right to liberty and security of person.

For example, the case *María Fanny Suárez de Guerrero* v. *Colombia*,[3] summarized in connection with the right to life,[4] concerned the premeditated and calculated slaughter by police of seven unarmed people, among them Mrs. Suárez de Guerrero. The police operation was carried out on 13 April 1978 at a house where a kidnapped person was believed to be held prisoner. In formulating its views, the Committee noted that a legislative decree, invoked by the State party, referred to a situation of disturbed public order in Colombia. It also noted that on 18 July 1980, in order to comply with the requirements of article 4, paragraph 3, of the International Covenant on Civil and Political Rights, the Government of Colombia had notified the Secretary-General of the United Nations that in view of the state of siege in all the national territory since 1976, temporary measures had been adopted, which had the

---

[3] *Ibidem, Thirty-seventh Session, Supplement No. 40* (A/37/40), annex XI, communication No. 45/1979, views adopted on 31 March 1982.
[4] See part II, chap. 2, sect. C (*a*) (*supra*, pp. 67-72).

IV:2

effect of limiting the application of articles 19, paragraph 2, and 21 of the Covenant. The Committee observed that the present case was not concerned with these provisions. Furthermore, there were several rights recognized by the Covenant which could not be derogated from by a State party. The non-derogable rights included articles 6 and 7 of the Covenant, invoked in this case.

Three other cases from the Committee's jurisprudence, cited in connection with the right to life, may also be mentioned in this context. In the case *Herrera Rubio* v. *Colombia,*[5] the author, Joaquín Herrero Rubio, claimed, *inter alia*, that he had been arrested on 17 March 1981 by members of the Colombian armed forces on suspicion of being a "guerrillero"; in the case *Guillermo Ignacio Dermit Barbato and Hugo Haroldo Dermit Barbato* v. *Uruguay,*[6] it was alleged that one of the victims, who despite having completed a sentence of imprisonment in July 1980, was kept in detention pursuant to so-called "prompt security measures" and later found dead; and in the case *Rickly Burrell* v. *Jamaica,*[7] it was claimed that the victim, a prisoner on death row, was shot and killed on 31 October 1993 by a warder during a prison riot.[8]

Two more of the Committee's cases, not summarized nor reviewed in previous chapters of the book, are included in this review. None have been selected for summary.

In the case *Jayawardena* v. *Sri Lanka,*[9] the author, Jayalath Jayawardena, a Sri Lankan citizen, was a member of the United National Party in Sri Lanka. At the time of his initial communication, in February 2000, he was an opposition member of Parliament. In December 2001, his party obtained a majority in Parliament, and he was appointed Minister of Rehabilitation, Resettlement and Refugees. Since 1998, the President of Sri Lanka had made a series of public accusations, during interviews with the media, to the effect that Jayalath Jayawardena was involved with the Liberation Tigers of Tamil Eelam (LTTE). These allegations were given wide publicity by radio and television corporations, and they appeared in a national newspaper.

---

[5] See United Nations, *Official Records of the General Assembly, Forty-third Session, Supplement No. 40* (A/43/40), annex VII, sect. B, communication No. 161/1983, views adopted on 2 November 1987.

[6] *Ibidem, Thirty-eighth Session, Supplement No. 40* (A/38/40), annex IX, communication No. 84/1981, views adopted on 21 October 1982.

[7] *Ibidem, Fifty-first Session, Supplement No. 40* (A/51/40), vol. II, annex VIII, sect. R, communication No. 546/1993, views adopted on 18 July 1996.

[8] See part II, chap. 2, sect. B (*a*) (*supra*, pp. 44-45, 46 and 47, respectively).

[9] See United Nations, *Official Records of the General Assembly, Fifty-seventh Session, Supplement No. 40* (A/57/40), vol. II, annex IX, sect. BB, communication No. 916/2000, views adopted on 22 July 2002.

The author complained that allegations made by the President about his alleged involvement with the LTTE put his life at risk, and he had no opportunity to sue the President because of rules of immunity. The author further claimed that in refusing to grant him sufficient security despite the fact that he was receiving death threats, the State party did not protect his life, and it failed to investigate any of the complaints he had made to the police on the issue of the death threats received against him.

In response to Jayalath Jayawardena's concerns about his security, the Secretary-General of Parliament on 2 March 2000 requested the Ministry of Defence to provide Jayalath Jayawardena with additional personal security because of threats to his life. He subsequently received two extra security guards, a lesser number than was usually provided to government members of Parliament whose security was threatened, and certain security devices, also usually made available, were not provided.

On 8 June 2001, a State-owned newspaper published an article in which it was stated that Jayalath Jayawardena's name had appeared in a magazine as a spy for the LTTE. After this incident, the author alleged, he had received around 100 death threats over the telephone and was followed by several unidentified persons in unmarked vehicles. As a result of these calls, his family was in a state of severe psychological shock. He made a complaint to the police requesting extra security, but this was not granted. On 18 July 2001, the author alleged, he was followed by an unidentified gunman close to his constituency office, and he lodged a complaint with the police on the same day, but no action was taken. On 31 August 2001, a live hand grenade was found at a junction near his residence.

In respect of the author's claim that the allegations made publicly by the President of Sri Lanka put his life at risk, the Committee noted that the State party had not contested the fact that these statements were in fact made. It did contest that Jayalath Jayawardena was the recipient of death threats subsequent to the President's allegations. However, on the basis of the detailed information provided by the author, the Committee was of the view that due weight had to be given to the author's allegations that such threats were received after the statements and that he feared for his life. For these reasons, and because the statements were made by the Head of State acting under immunity enacted by the State party, the Committee took the view that Sri Lanka was responsible for a violation of Jayalath Jayawardena's right to security of person under article 9, paragraph 1, of the Covenant. Six members of the Committee disagreed as to the admissibility of this claim by the author.

With regard to the author's claim that the State party violated his rights under the Covenant by failing to investigate his complaints to the police in respect of death threats he had received, the Committee noted the State party's contention that Jaya-

IV:2

lath Jayawardena did not receive any death threats and that no complaints or reports of such threats were received. However, the State party did not provide any specific arguments or materials to refute the author's detailed account of at least two complaints made by him to the police. In the circumstances, the Committee concluded that the failure of the State party to investigate these threats to life violated Jayalath Jayawardena's right to security of person under article 9, paragraph 1, of the Covenant.

Pursuant to article 2, paragraph 3 (*a*), of the Covenant, the author was entitled to an appropriate remedy.

Finally, in another recent case against the same State party, the case *Nallaratnam v. Sri Lanka,*[10] there were allegations of, *inter alia,* torture and forced confessions resulting in violations of article 14 of the Covenant. The author, Nallaratnam Singarasa, a Sri Lankan national and member of the Tamil community, had been arrested on suspicion of supporting the Liberation Tigers of Tamil Eelam (LTTE). He was detained pursuant to an order by the Minister of Defence under prevention of terrorism legislation.

Three police officials, assisted by a former Tamil militant, interrogated Nallaratnam Singarasa. He alleged that he was subjected to torture and ill-treatment and that he was questioned in broken Tamil by the police officers. He was held in incommunicado detention, and subsequently he made a statement to the police. The author further alleged that, later, he was produced before an assistant superintendent of police and one of the officials who had previously interrogated him. He was asked numerous questions, but as he could not speak Sinhalese, the police official interpreted between Tamil and Sinhalese. Nallaratnam Singarasa was then requested to sign a statement which had been translated and typed in Sinhalese by the official. He refused to sign, as he could not understand it, and he alleged that the assistant superintendent then forcibly put his thumbprint on the typed statement. The prosecution later produced this statement as evidence of Nallaratnam Singarasa's alleged confession. He had neither external interpretation nor legal representation at this time. Based solely on the alleged confession, he was finally convicted and sentenced to 35 years' imprisonment

Concerning the author's claim of a violation of article 14, paragraph 3 (*f*), of the Covenant, due to the absence of an external interpreter during the alleged confession, the Committee noted that this provision provided for the right to an interpreter during the court hearing only, a right which was granted to the author. However, as

---

[10] *Ibidem, Fifty-ninth Session, Supplement No. 40* (A/59/40), vol. II, annex IX, sect. AA, communication No. 1033/2001, views adopted on 21 July 2004.

clearly appeared from the court proceedings, the confession took place in the sole presence of two investigating officers. One of them typed the statement and provided interpretation between Tamil and Sinhalese. The Committee concluded that Nallaratnam Singarasa was denied a fair trial in accordance with article 14, paragraph 1, of the Covenant by solely relying on a confession obtained in such circumstances.

As to the claim of a violation of the author's rights under article 14, paragraph 3 (*g*), of the Covenant, in that he was forced to sign a confession and subsequently had to assume the burden of proof that it was extracted under duress and was not voluntary, the Committee considered the principles underlying the right protected in this provision. It referred to its previous jurisprudence that the wording in the article, that no one should be compelled to testify against himself or to confess guilt, had to be understood in terms of the absence of any direct or indirect physical or psychological coercion from the investigating authorities on the accused with a view to obtaining a confession of guilt. The Committee considered that it was implicit in this principle that the prosecution proved that the confession was made without duress. It also noted relevant aspects of Sri Lankan law, including a provision in prevention of terrorism legislation that placed on the accused the burden of proving whether the confession was voluntary. The Committee concluded that Sri Lanka had violated article 14, paragraphs 2 and 3 (*g*), read together with articles 2, paragraph 3, and 7 of the Covenant.

The Committee also found a violation by the State party of other provisions of article 14 of the Covenant in this case.

In accordance with article 2, paragraph 3 (*a*), of the Covenant, the State party was under an obligation to provide the author with an effective and appropriate remedy, including release or retrial and compensation. The State party was also under an obligation to avoid similar violations in the future. It was required to ensure that the prevention of terrorism legislation was made compatible with the provisions of the Covenant.

(*b*) Committee against Torture

One case from the jurisprudence of the Committee against Torture, the case *Hajrizi Dzemajl* et al. v. *Serbia and Montenegro*,[11] is included in this chapter of the book. It is summarized at some length in section C,[12] and it is also cited in connection with

---

[11] *Ibidem, Fifty-eighth Session, Supplement No. 44* (A/58/44), annex VI, sect. A, complaint No. 161/2000, decision adopted on 21 November 2002.

[12] See part IV, chap. 2, sect. C (*a*) (*infra*, pp. 562-572).

IV:2

the prohibition of torture.[13] The presentation of the facts by the complainants in this case, 65 nationals of Serbia and Montenegro, all of Roma origin, is worthy of attention, especially on account of its reference to the jurisprudence of various human rights institutions, as is the application by the Committee of the standards of the Convention against Torture and Other Cruel, Inhuman or Degrading Treatment or Punishment to the circumstances of the case.

On 15 April 1995, several hundred non-Roma people attacked a Roma settlement. This resulted in the levelling of the entire settlement and the burning or complete destruction of all proporties belonging to its Roma residents. A number of police officers were present at the scene of these events when they occured, but they did not intervene. Investigations into the incident were discontinued, and no perpetrators were tried by any court. The State failed to enable the victims to obtain redress and to provide them with compensation. The complainants alleged violations by Serbia and Montenegro of a number of articles of the Convention.

The Committee considered that the burning and destruction of houses, in the circumstances, constituted acts of cruel, inhuman or degrading treatment or punishment, committed with the acquiescence of police officers, in violation of article 16, paragraph 1, of the Convention. In an individual opinion, two members of the Committee expressed the view that the acts amounted to torture within the meaning of article 1, paragraph 1. The Committee also found violations of articles 12 and 13.

The circumstances described by the complainants, and relied on by the Committee in its deliberations, indicate a spectacular failure of the police and other authorities to prevent public disorder in a situation of extreme tension, to protect a community from harassment and physical attack and to bring to justice people guilty of very serious crimes. The rule of law was undermined, as was one of the primary purposes of a state, to provide security for those living within its jurisdiction. The circumstances set out in this case indicate a complete negation of the idea of policing.

The fact that the victims belonged to the Roma minority in Serbia and Montenegro was emphasized in the complaint and in the individual opinion. The two dissenting members of the Committee pointed out that because of the vulnerability of this ethnic group in many parts of Europe, States had to afford them greater protection. This is a particularly important point to make about members of minority groups everywhere. Discrimination against, and mistreatment of, minority groups is a major cause of tension in many societies, and police and other social agencies must work to reduce that tension and act promptly and decisively to protect minority groups from harassment and violence.

---

[13] See part II, chap. 3, sect. B (*b*) (*supra*, p. 139).

(*c*) **Working Group on Arbitrary Detention**

It is recalled that the Working Group on Arbitrary Detention regards deprivation of liberty as arbitrary in the following cases:

(*a*) When it manifestly cannot be justified on any legal basis, such as continued detention after the sentence has been served or despite an applicable amnesty act (category I);

(*b*) When the deprivation of liberty is the result of a judgment or sentence for the exercise of the rights or freedoms proclaimed by articles 7, 13, 14, 18, 19, 20 and 21 of the Universal Declaration of Human Rights and also, in respect of States parties, in articles 12, 18, 19, 21, 22, 25, 26 and 27 of the International Covenant on Civil and Political Rights (category II); and

(*c*) When the complete or partial non-observance of the international standards relating to a fair trial set forth in the Universal Declaration and in the relevant international instruments accepted by the States concerned is of such gravity as to confer the deprivation of liberty, of whatever kind, an arbitrary character (category III).

In order to evaluate the arbitrary character of cases of deprivation of freedom entering into category III, the Working Group considers, in addition to the general principles set out in the Universal Declaration, several criteria drawn from the Body of Principles for the Protection of All Persons under Any Form of Detention or Imprisonment and, for States parties, the criteria laid down particularly in articles 9 and 14 of the Covenant.

When the Working Group concludes that a person has been arbitrarily deprived of his or her liberty, the Government concerned is typically requested to take the necessary steps to remedy the situation and to bring it into conformity with the standards and principles set forth in the Universal Declaration and, where applicable, the Covenant. States non-parties to the Covenant are encouraged to become a party to it.

From the jurisprudence of the Working Group, three cases of arbitrary detention in times of armed conflict, disturbance and tension are cited in this chapter of the book.

In a case concerning the repeated use of administrative detention against an individual, decision No. 16/1994 (*Israel*),[14] summarized in section C,[15] the Government ar-

---

[14] See United Nations document E/CN.4/1995/31/Add.2, p. 16, decision adopted on 28 September 1994.

[15] See part IV, chap. 2, sect. C (*b*) (*infra*, pp. 573-575).

gued that it would jeopardize the safety of witnesses to bring the detainee to trial. The source claimed that Sha'ban Rateb Jabarin, a Palestinian para-legal and human rights activist, had been detained seven times since 1979 for alleged terrorist activities, on six of these occasions without being brought to trial. Since 21 June 1994, he had been held in administrative detention for six months.

In deciding that there had been arbitrary detentions in this case, the Working Group insisted that individual liberty could not be sacrificed because of the Government's inability either to collect evidence or to present it in an appropriate form. Arguing that the detainee should be charged and brought to trial, the Working Group said that the Government should not use the power of administrative detention to achieve its purposes without a formal trial. The use of administrative detention was otherwise punitive and not preventive.

In its reply to the Working Group, the Government invoked article 78 of the Geneva Convention relative to the Protection of Civilian Persons in Time of War (Geneva Convention IV), as well as a domestic security provisions order. Article 78 of Geneva Convention IV states, *inter alia*, that if the occupying power considers it necessary, for imperative reasons of security, to take safety measures concerning protected persons, it may, at the most, subject them to assigned residence or to internment. However, the Working Group pointed out, this provision could not be used to justify the administrative detention of Mr. Jabarin, as in the case of occupied territory, the applicability of many provisions of the Convention, including article 78, ceased one year after the general close of military operations.

The Working Group concluded that the detention of Mr. Jabarin, on all the occasions he was not brought to trial and since 21 June 1994, was arbitrary, as being in contravention of articles 9 and 10 of the Universal Declaration and articles 9 and 14 of the Covenant, to which Israel was a party. It fell within category III of the principles applicable to the consideration of cases submitted to the Working Group.

In another case that occurred in the context of what had been an international armed conflict, decision No. 59/1993 (*Kuwait*),[16] it was alleged that Omar Shehada Abu-Shanab, a Palestinian citizen using a Jordanian passport and, during the Gulf war, a nurse at a hospital in Kuwait, was arrested on 10 March 1991. He was then held incommunicado until his trial on 9 June 1991. He was sentenced to 15 years' imprisonment for having collaborated with the enemy during the Gulf war. In the communication, it was claimed that the charge against him was unjust, since in the course of his duties as a nurse, he simply acted in a humanitarian spirit, without making dis-

---

[16] See United Nations document E/CN.4/1995/31/Add.1, p. 22, decision adopted on 9 December 1993.

tinctions between the sick and wounded for whom he was caring in that war situation on the ground that they belonged to one side or the other. It was added that he was tortured and forced to make false statements when being held incommunicado.

The Government responded that no person with the name given was in detention or had been tried. However, ultimately, the Working Group concluded that Omar Shehada Abu-Shanab was in detention in Kuwait and that the detention was arbitrary. He had been accused and sentenced for the lawful exercise of the medical occupation in which he was engaged in the hospital, a right embodied in article 23, paragraph 1, of the Universal Declaration. It was quite clear, the Working Group stated, that free choice of employment presupposed the free performance of work in conditions in conformity with the specific rules for the activity in question. It was recognized that in a war situation it was not lawful for medical personnel to extend the required humanitarian care only to the wounded of one side. Such action was contrary to the Geneva Conventions relating to the treatment of wounded prisoners and to civilians affected by the conflict.

Consequently, the Working Group decided that the detention of Omar Shehade Abu-Shanab was arbitrary, as being in contravention of articles 9 and 23 of the Universal Declaration and articles 9, 10 and 14 of the Covenant and falling within category III. Kuwait was not a party to the Covenant.

If the Government did not report that it had taken the necessary measures to remedy the situation, or if it continued to insist that the person referred to in the decision was not in detention, within a period of 30 days, the information would be transmitted to the United Nations Working Group on Enforced or Involuntary Disappearances.

Finally, in a case arising in the context of severe social tension and disturbances, opinion No. 25/2001 (*Pakistan*),[17] summarized in section C,[18] the authorities appeared unwilling or unable to protect the victim, members of his community, his lawyer and trial judges from threats, intimidation and actual violence. The source claimed that Ayub Masih, a Christian Pakistani citizen, on 14 October 1996 had been arrested by the police and subsequently accused and convicted of blasphemy, largely because he belonged to a religious minority, on the basis of a provision of a law which itself was clearly discriminatory.

The Working Group found that the procedure conducted against Mr. Masih did not respect the fundamental rights of a person charged with a crime. For example, he

---

[17] See United Nations document E/CN.4/2003/8/Add.1, p. 22, opinion adopted on 30 November 2001.
[18] See part IV, chap. 2, sect. C (*c*) (*infra*, pp. 576-579).

IV:2

was not provided with documentary or other evidence against him, nor was he informed of his rights as an accused; the verdict against him was based on the testimony of a single, biased witness; the threats by extremists against him and his defence lawyer during trial and appeal and the hostile atmosphere intimidated the accused and counsel alike; and blasphemy cases insulting the Muslim religion could, under Pakistani law, only be heard by Muslim judges. Such serious deficiencies basically stripped the procedure of its requisite fair character.

The Working Group concluded that the deprivation of liberty of Mr. Masih was arbitrary, as being in contravention of articles 9 and 10 of the Universal Declaration and falling within category III. Pakistan was not a party to the Covenant.

As can be seen in this case, the failure of the authorities to ensure internal security and to respond effectively to social tension and disorder had implications that extended far wider than the circumstances of the particular case.

(*d*) African Commission on Human and Peoples' Rights

In the jurisprudence of the African Commission on Human and Peoples' Rights, there are some decisions concerning communications arising out of situations of armed conflict, disturbance and tension in States parties to the African Charter on Human and Peoples' Rights. In this chapter of the book, four cases of the Commission are cited. They relate to alleged grave and massive human rights violations in Zaire, Chad, Togo and Mauritania, respectively.

In the case *Free Legal Assistance Group* et al. v. *Zaire*,[19] summarized in section C,[20] the Commission considered four communications in which the complainants, six altogether, made allegations involving multiple violations of human rights in Zaire. There was no substantive response from the Government of Zaire. Invoking article 58 of the Charter, the Commission held in this case that the communications revealed the existence of serious and massive violations of human rights.

The Commission found violations of a number of human rights provisions in the Charter that are typically infringed in situations of armed conflict, disturbance and tension, such as the right to life, article 4; the prohibition of torture and other ill-treatment, article 5; and the right to liberty and security of person, article 6. However, it also found violations of articles 16 and 17 of the Charter.

---

[19] See *Review of the African Commission on Human and Peoples' Rights*, vol. 6 (1996-1997), p. 183, communications No. 25/89, No. 47/90, No. 56/91 and No. 100/93.
[20] See part IV, chap. 2, sect. C (*d*) (*infra*, pp. 579-582).

Article 16 affirms that every individual shall have the right to enjoy the best attainable state of physical and mental health, and States parties are required to take the necessary measures to protect the health of their people. In this respect, the Commission found that the failure of the Government to provide basic services such as safe drinking water and electricity and the shortage of medicine, as alleged, constituted a violation of this article.

Article 17 requires that every individual shall have the right to education. The Commission held that the closures of universities and secondary schools as described constituted a violation of this provision.

Unlike the International Covenant on Civil and Political Rights, the American Convention on Human Rights and the Convention for the Protection of Human Rights and Fundamental Freedoms, the Charter embodies economic, social and cultural rights, such as those protected under articles 16 and 17, as well as civil and political rights.

In the case *Commission Nationale des Droits de l'Homme et des Libertés* v. *Chad*,[21] the African Commission found that there had been serious and massive violations of human rights in Chad. In the complaint, it was alleged, *inter alia*, that journalists were harassed, attacked by unidentified individuals claimed to be security service agents; that several people had been arbitrarily arrested and illegally detained; and that there were several accounts of killings, disappearances and torture as a result of the civil war involving the security services and other groups.

The complainant claimed that not only had agents of the Government committed violations of the Charter, but that the State had failed to protect the rights in the Charter from violation by other parties. The Government claimed that no violations were committed by its agents and that it had no control over violations committed by other parties, as Chad was in a state of civil war.

The Commission recalled that under article 1 of the Charter, the States parties had not only to recognize the rights, duties and freedoms enshrined in the Charter, but they had also to undertake measures to give effect to them. In other words, if a State party neglected to ensure the rights in the Charter, this could constitute a violation, even if the State or its agents were not the immediate cause of the violation.

The Commission pointed out that the Charter, unlike other human rights instruments, did not allow for States parties to derogate from their treaty obligations dur-

---

[21] See *Review of the African Commission on Human and Peoples' Rights*, vol. 6 (1996-1997), p. 190, communication No. 74/92.

IV:2

ing emergency situations. Thus, not even a civil war in Chad could be used as an excuse by the State for violating or permitting violations of human rights protected by the Charter.

In this case, Chad had failed to provide security and stability in the country, thereby allowing serious and massive violations of human rights. The national armed forces were participants in the civil war, and there had been several instances in which the Government had failed to intervene to prevent the assassination and killing of specific individuals. The Commission held that even where it could not be proved that agents of the Government had committed violations, the Government had a responsibility to secure the safety and the liberty of its citizens and to conduct investigations into murders. Chad was, therefore, responsible for the violations of the Charter.

The complainant alleged violations of the right to life, article 4; the prohibition of torture and other ill-treatment, article 5; the right to liberty and security of person, article 6; the right to a fair trial, article 7; and the right to freedom of expression, article 10. There was no substantive response from the Government of Chad, just a blanket denial of responsibility.

Based on the events alleged by the complainant, the Commission found that there had been violations of articles 4, 5, 6 and 7 of the Charter.

Unlike the Governments in the two previous cases, the Government of Togo did enter into a dialogue with the Commission in respect of the case *Jean Yaovi Degli* et al. v. *Togo*,[22] three communications considered jointly by the Commmission. The complainants alleged grave and massive violations of various rights protected by the Charter.

In the first communication, Jean Yaovi Degli alleged that Nikabour Bikagni, an army corporal, was arrested on 7 October 1992 and subjected to torture and maltreatment. Under duress he made a confession that he was planning a coup against the Government of Togo.

The second communication consisted of a report of a mission sent to Togo in 1992 by the Union Interafricaine des Droits de l'Homme. This report included information on the attempt on the life of an opposition leader; the assassination of the driver of the Prime Minister; extortion and killings in villages in the north of Togo; a shooting incident which resulted in at least 14 deaths; and another shooting which caused at least four deaths. The communication also mentioned the discovery of

---

[22] *Ibidem*, vol. 5 (1995), p. 188, communications No. 83/92, No. 88/93 and No. 91/93.

more than 15 bodies which were found mutilated and bound in the waters around Lomé, the capital of Togo.

In the third communication, the Commission Internationale de Juristes alleged that on 30 January 1993, the Togolese military shot and killed 20 peaceful demonstrators in Lomé. This was related to a general breakdown of law and order resulting in numerous violations of human rights by the security forces. Abuses by the security forces caused 40,000 Togolese to flee the country.

The African Commission sent a delegation to Togo, and it was adduced that the alleged acts were committed under a previous administration. It was satisfied that the present administration had dealt with the issues satisfactorily.

In the case *Malawi African Association* et al. v. *Mauritania*,[23] also cited in connection with the prohibition of torture,[24] the Commission considered 38 communications filed against Mauritania. The complainants alleged numerous cases of grave and massive violations of human rights attributed to the Mauritanian State.

The communications related to the situation prevailing in Mauritania between 1986 and 1992. The population of Mauritania was described as being composed essentially of Moors, living in the northern part of the country, and various black ethnic groups, as well as Haratines, freed slaves, who physically resembled the black population but were closely associated with the Moors. Following a coup d'etat in 1984, which brought an army colonel to power, the Government was criticized by members of black ethnic groups for marginalizing black Mauritanians and by groups of Moors who favoured closer ties with the Arab world.

These communications set out details of horrifying violations of human rights protected by the Charter, notably the right to life in article 4 and and the prohibition of torture and other ill-treatment in article 5. In respect of article 4 of the Charter, the Commission stated, *inter alia*, that denying people food and medical attention, burning them in sand and subjecting them to torture to the point of death revealed a shocking lack of respect for life. Evidence of various arbitrary executions also satisfied the Commission of repeated violations of article 4. All communications detailed instances of torture and cruel, inhuman and degrading treatment, and the Government did not produce any argument to counter these allegations. The Commission concluded that there was proof of widespread utilization of torture and other ill-

---

[23] See Organization of African Unity document AHG/222 (XXXVI), annex V, p. 138, communications No. 54/91, No. 61/91, No. 96/93, No. 98/93, Nos. 164/97-196/97 and No. 210/98.
[24] See part II, chap. 3, sect. B (*d*) (*supra*, pp. 143-144).

IV:2

treatment in violation of article 5 of the Charter. The Commission also found a violation of this provision due to practices analogous to slavery. It emphasized that unremunerated work was tantamount to a violation of the right to respect for dignity inherent in the human being, and it considered that the conditions to which descendants of slaves were subjected clearly constituted exploitation and degradation of man.

The Commission also found massive violations of article 6 of the Charter protecting the right to liberty and security of person. The complainants alleged, *inter alia*, that hundreds of people were detained in connection with events that took place in 1989 and that a wave of arrests at the end of 1990 resulted in the detention of hundreds of people without charge or trial. Allegedly, the fate of many people remained unknown.

Violations of some or all of these rights are characteristic of situations of armed conflict, disturbance or tension. However, in this case, as well as in the above *Free Legal Assistance Group* et al. case, it is interesting to note that the Commission has insisted on the responsibility of States parties to the Charter to secure also other rights in these situations.

In the present case, for example, the Commission applied the provisions of article 16 of the Charter, protecting the right to health, to the situation of detainees. It observed that the State's responsibility to ensure this right in the event of detention was even more evident to the extent that detention centres were its exclusive preserve. Hence, the physical integrity and welfare of detainees was the responsibility of the competent public authorities. The Commission noted that some prisoners had died as a result of the lack of medical attention; that the general state of health of the prisoners had deteriorated due to the lack of sufficient food; and that they had neither blankets nor adequate hygiene. The Commission considered that the State was directly responsible for this state of affairs and that there had been violations of article 16.

The Commission also found violations of article 18, paragraph 1, of the Charter, requiring the State to protect the family, on the grounds that holding people in solitary confinement during detention, which was in any event arbitrary, deprived detainees of their right to a family life; of article 12, paragraph 1, giving every individual the right to freedom of movement and residence within the borders of the State, because black Mauritanians were evicted from their houses and deprived of their citizenship; and of article 14, guaranteeing the right to property, because of the confiscation and looting of the property of black Mauritanians and the expropriation or destruction of their land and houses.

Treatment of black Mauritanians also led the Commission to find violations of article 2 of the Charter, entitling every individual to the enjoyment of the rights and freedoms recognized and guaranteed in the Charter without distinction on a number of grounds, including race, ethnic group and colour. Furthermore, it found a violations of article 19, providing that all peoples shall be equal and shall enjoy the same respect and have the same rights and that nothing shall justify the domination of a people by another. In this respect, the Commission observed that the question of the domination of one section of the population by another was at the heart of the abuses alleged in the different communications.

The responsibility of the State to secure the safety of all its citizens was recalled by the Commission when it found a violation of article 23 of the Charter, setting out the right of all peoples to national and international peace and security. The Mauritanian Government had argued that the conflict through which the country passed was the result of the actions of certain groups for which it was not responsible. However, the Commission observed, it was indeed the Mauritanian public forces that had attacked Mauritanian villages, and even if they were rebel forces, the responsibility for protection was incumbent on the State. In making this point, the Commission referred to its decision in the above *Commission Nationale des Droits de l'Homme et des Libertés* case and concluded that unprovoked attacks on villages constituted a denial of the right to live in peace and security.

Finally, the Commission declared that during the years 1989 to 1992, there were grave or massive violations of human rights as proclaimed in the Charter, in particular of, *inter alia*, articles 2, 4, 5, 6, 12, 14, 16 and 18. It also made a number of recommendations to the Government.

(e) Inter-American Court of Human Rights

From the jurisprudence of the Inter-American Court of Human Rights, two cases are cited in this review.

The *Bámaca Velásquez* case (*Guatemala*),[25] summarized in section C[26] and also cited in connection with the right to life[27] and the prohibition of torture,[28] concerned the human rights of Efraín Bámaca Velásquez, a guerrilla force commander captured in 1992 by agents of the State's armed forces during an internal armed conflict. In its

---

[25] See Inter-American Court of Human Rights, Series C: *Decisions and Judgments*, No. 70 (2001), petition No. 11129, judgment of 25 November 2000.
[26] See part IV, chap. 2, sect. C (*e*) (*infra*, pp. 582-593).
[27] See part II, chap. 2, sect. B (*d*) (*supra*, pp. 55-56).
[28] See part II, chap. 3, sect. B (*e*) (*supra*, pp. 148 and 149).

IV:2

application, the Inter-American Commission on Human Rights asked the Court to decide whether the State had violated a number of rights of Mr. Bámaca Velásquez, including those embodied in article 3 common to the Geneva Conventions of 12 August 1949. The Commission also requested the Court to call on the State to adopt the necessary reforms to the training programmes and regulations of the Guatemalan armed forces so that military operations were conducted in conformity with the laws and customs applicable to internal conflicts.

In responding to the Commission's request concerning the rights in common article 3, the Court noted that it had been proved that there was an internal armed conflict in Guatemala at the time of the facts of the case. Instead of releasing the State from its obligations to respect and guarantee human rights, the Court observed, this required the State to act in accordance with such obligations. The Court further stated that although it lacked the competence to declare that a State was internationally accountable for the violation of international treaties that did not grant it such competence, it could observe that certain acts or omissions violating human rights, protected by treaties it was competent to apply and interpret, also violated other international instruments for the protection of the individual, such as the Geneva Conventions and, in particular, their common article 3.

The Court pointed out the similarity between the content of common article 3 and the provisions of the American Convention on Human Rights and other international instruments regarding non-derogable human rights, such as the right to life and the right not to be subjected to torture or cruel, inhuman or degrading treatment. It also cited a previous case in which it had indicated that relevant provisions of the Geneva Conventions might be taken into account when interpreting the American Convention.

All of these observations are extremely important and relevant to police behaviour in times of armed conflict and, indeed, in times of internal disturbance. They reinforce the requirement to respect human rights and humanitarian law standards in such difficult and dangerous times. They also reinforce the need for police to be aware of those elements of international humanitarian law, relevant to the type of conflict in which they may be engaged, and their status in such a conflict.

In its consideration of this case, the Court also recalled what it had indicated on previous occasions, that although the State had the right and obligation to guarantee its security and maintain public order, its powers were not unlimited. It had the obligation, at all times, to apply procedures that were in accordance with the law and to respect the fundamental rights of each individual in its jurisdiction.

The Court unanimously found that the State had violated a number of articles of the Convention and that it had not complied with its obligation under the Inter-American Convention to Prevent and Punish Torture. Four judges filed individual opinions in the case.

The distressing circumstances described in the *Del Caracazo* case (*Venezuela*)[29] are interesting and relevant to this review, because they show how the deployment of inexperienced military forces, not trained or equipped for dealing with public disorder, and failures of command and control over these and police officials resulted in atrocities being inflicted on the population.

The facts of the case, as set out by the Commission, were that the President of Venezuela announced, on 16 February 1989, a series of measures to refinance the external debt through the International Monetary Fund. In response to the effects of some of these measures, an undetermined number of people from the poorer sectors of the population began, on 27 February 1989, a series of disturbances, mainly burning urban transportation vehicles, looting and destroying commercial properties, at various locations. At that time, however, a sector of the metropolitan police was on strike and, consequently, did not intervene promptly to control the disturbances.

The armed forces were then entrusted with controlling the situation, and to this end, about 9,000 soldiers were brought in from the interior of the country. These were young men, 17 and 18 years of age, recruited in February 1989, and it was clear that the armed forces were not prepared to assume control of public order. The young men who were sent were a danger to the life and physical integrity of the population, owing to their youth and inexperience. Similarly, it was evident that these young soldiers were equipped with assault weapons, 7.62 mm light automatic rifles, to control the civilian population, and AMX-13 armored vehicles. The officers used 9 mm heavy-duty guns.

A state of emergency was declared, and the State security bodies, together with the metropolitan police, the national guard and the army, carried out a series of operations to repress acts of violence. According to official figures, the events of February and March 1989 left 276 dead, numerous injured, several disappeared and heavy material losses. However, this list was invalidated by the subsequent appearance of mass graves. Two non-governmental organizations that carried out investigations *in situ*, as well as international experts, agreed that most of the deaths were due to indiscriminate firing by agents of the Venezuelan State, while others resulted from extrajudicial executions.

---

[29] See Inter-American Court of Human Rights, Series C: *Decisions and Judgments*, No. 58 (2000), petition No.11455, judgment of 11 November 1999.

IV:2

The Commission requested the Court to declare that Venezuela had violated the right to life of 36 people, the right to personal liberty of five people and the right to humane treatment of three people, all of whom were named in the judgment. It also requested the Court to declare that Venezuala had violated the right to a fair trial and judicial protection of the 44 victims in this case, because their next of kin and lawyers were not heard with due guarantees and within a reasonable time by a competent tribunal, since access to the case files was restricted for over 10 years. The victims and their next of kin did not have access to a simple, prompt and effective recourse against the actions that violated their fundamental rights.

Furthermore, the Commission requested the Court to order Venezuela, *inter alia*, to conduct investigations in order to identify, prosecute and criminally punish those responsible for extrajudicial killings and unlawful burial of corpses, to hand over the remains of victims to the next of kin as well as to pay the costs and to reimburse the expenses incurred by the representatives of the victims in litigating the case at the national and the international level.

Ultimately, during a public hearing before the Court, the State acknowledged the facts described by the Commission in its application, accepted the legal consequences that derived from them and fully acknowledged its international responsibility in the case.

Consequently, the Court considered that the facts set out by the Commission had been proved. It concluded that the State had incurred responsibility for violations of the right to life in article 4, the right to humane treatment in article 5, the right to personal liberty in article 7, the right to a fair trial in article 8, the right to judicial protection in article 25 and the provision on suspension of guarantees in article 27, in accordance with article 1, paragraph 1, on the obligation to respect rights, and article 2, on domestic legal effects, of the Convention, to the detriment of the people cited in the judgment.

Noting the State's declaration with regard to the investigations initiated in order to identify, prosecute and punish those responsible for the facts mentioned in the application, the Court urged the State to continue them.

(*f*) European Court of Human Rights

Two cases from the jurisprudence of the European Court of Human Rights have been selected for inclusion in this review. They both relate, in particular, to article 2 of the Convention for the Protection of Human Rights and Fundamental Freedoms, protecting the right to life.

The case *Ergi* v. *Turkey*,[30] summarized in section C,[31] concerned the killing on 29 September 1993 of a young woman, Havva Ergi, the applicant's sister, who was struck in the head by a bullet whilst she was on the balcony of her home in a village in southeast Turkey. The applicant, Muharrem Ergi, a Turkish citizen of Kuridish origin, brought the application on his own behalf and that of his sister and her daughter. There were differing versions as to the circumstances that led to the death of Havva Ergi. The applicant claimed that it was the result of a retaliatory operation by the security forces against the village, whilst the Government asserted that there had been a clash between its forces and members of the Workers Party of Kurdistan (PKK) around the village and that the bullet killing her had not originated from the military side.

The European Court of Human Rights held that it had not been established that the applicant's sister was killed by the security forces. However, it nevertheless found a violation article 2 of the Convention on account of the planning and conduct of the security forces' operation and in the failure of the State authorities to conduct an adequate and effective investigation into the circumstances surrounding the death of Havva Ergi. The Court observed that the responsibility of the State was not confined to circumstances where there was significant evidence that misdirected fire from agents of the State had killed a civilian. It might also be engaged where they failed to take all feasible precautions in the choice of means and methods of a security operation mounted against an opposing group with a view to avoiding and, in any event, to minimizing incidental loss of civilian life. The Court had to consider whether the security forces' operation had been planned and controlled in such a way as to avoid or minimize, to the greatest extent possible, any risk to the lives of the villagers, including from the fire-power of the PKK members. In stating that it had to take into account the planning and control of the operation, the Court cited its judgment in one of its leading cases on article 2, *McCann and Others* v. *the United Kingdom*,[32] summarized in connection with the right to life.[33]

The Court did not refer to international humanitarian law in its judgment in the present case, and no argument was being made here as to its applicability in southeast Turkey at the time of the incident leading to this case. Nevertheless, it is interesting to note the provisions of the Protocol Additional to the Geneva Conventions of 12 August 1949, relating to the Protection of Victims of Non-International Armed Con-

---

[30] See European Court of Human Rights, *Reports of Judgments and Decisions*, 1998-IV, p. 1751, application No. 23818/94, judgment of 28 July 1998.

[31] See part IV, chap. 2, sect. C (*f*) (*infra*, pp. 594-596).

[32] See *Publications of the European Court of Human Rights*, Series A: *Judgments and Decisions*, vol. 324 (1996), application No. 18984/91, judgment of 27 September 1995.

[33] See part II, chap. 2, sect. C (*d*) (*supra*, pp. 86-104).

flicts (Protocol II) which are alluded to in the introduction to this part of the book.[34] For example, article 13, paragraph 1, of the Protocol requires that the civilian population and individual civilians shall enjoy general protection against the dangers arising from military operations, and under paragraph 2 of the same article, the civilian population as such, as well as individual civilians, shall not be the object of attack.

Regardless of its applicability, it is clearly good practice for police to take into account relevant provisions of international humanitarian law in the planning and conduct of operations involving armed engagements, especially where well-armed terrorists or other types of armed opposition groups are concerned. Rules of international humanitarian law have immediate relevance to these types of operations. In any event, the distinction is not always clear between armed conflicts to which Protocol II applies and internal disturbances and tensions, such as riots, isolated and sporadic acts of violence and other acts of a similar nature, which are excluded by article 1, paragraph 2, of the Protocol.

Concerning the planning of, and briefing for, operations involving armed engagements, it should always be possible to show what positive steps had been taken to protect the right to life and, where appropriate, what provisions of international humanitarian law had been taken into account. In the *Ergi* case, the Court found that it could reasonably be inferred that insufficient precautions had been taken to protect the lives of the civilian population in the light of the failure of the authorities to adduce direct evidence on the planning and conduct of the operation.

Apart from finding, unanimously, a violation of article 2 of the Convention, the Court also found, by eight votes to one, violations of articles 13 and 25, paragraph 1, in this case. Furthermore, the Court held that the respondent State was to compensate, by eight votes to one, Mr. Ergi and, unanimously, his niece for non-pecuniary damage and, also unanimously, for costs and expenses.

The other case, *Güleç* v. *Turkey*,[35] concerned the killing on 4 March 1991 of Ahmet Güleç, aged 15, the applicant's son, by security forces during an operation to quell a violent demonstration in a town in an eastern Turkey province. The applicant, Hüseyin Güleç, a Turkish national, alleged that the death of his son had been caused by bullets fired by the security forces and that he had not been able to lodge a complaint with the criminal courts against their members because of the administrative authorities' decision to discontinue proceedings.

---

[34] See part IV, chap. 1 (*supra*, pp. 530-534).
[35] See European Court of Human Rights, *Reports of Judgments and Decisions*, 1998-IV, p. 1698, application No. 21593/93, judgment of 27 July 1998.

In its judgment, the Court commented on the security forces' tactics and on the lack of equipment that would have enabled them to adopt a graduated and proportionate response to the situation.

The European Commission of Human Rights conducted an investigation on the spot and heard oral evidence in Strasbourg. It concluded that the security forces had deployed an armoured vehicle equipped with a machine gun which had opened fire in the street where the demonstration was taking place, either in the air or at the ground, in order to disperse the demonstrators. Ahmet Güleç had been hit by a fragment of a bullet, fired from the armoured vehicle, which had ricocheted off the ground or a wall. However, the Commission did not believe that the machine gun, a combat weapon with a very rapid rate of fire, had been used to kill demonstrators intentionally. It accepted that the form the demonstration had taken was such that it could be described as a riot within the meaning of article 2, paragraph 2 (*c*), of the Convention, but it expressed the view that the use of a combat weapon during a demonstration for the purpose of restoring order could not be regarded as proportionate.

The Court accepted the facts as set out by the Commission, and it accepted that the demonstration was far from peaceful, as was evidenced by the damage to property in the town and the injuries sustained by some members of the security forces. The Court observed that, confronted with serious acts of violence, the security forces, who were not present in sufficient strength, called for reinforcements, and at least two armoured vehicles were deployed. Whereas the driver of one such vehicle asserted that he had fired into the air, several witnesses said that shots had been fired at the crowd. Although this allegation was denied by the Government, the Court noted that it was corroborated by the fact that nearly all the wounded demonstrators were hit in the legs. This would have been perfectly consistent with ricochet wounds from bullets with a downward trajectory which could have been fired from the turret of an armoured vehicle.

The Court, like the Commission, accepted that the use of force might have been justified under article 2, paragraph 2 (*c*), of the Convention. However, it insisted, a balance had to be struck between the aim pursued and the means employed to achieve it. The security forces had used a very powerful weapon, because they apparently did not have truncheons, riot shields, water cannon, rubber bullets or tear gas. The Court stated that the lack of such equipment was all the more incomprehensible and unacceptable, because this province of Turkey, as the Government had pointed out, was in a region where a state of emergency had been declared and where, at the material time, disorder could have been expected.

IV:2

The Court unanimously concluded that in the circumstances of the case, the force used to disperse the demonstrators, which caused the death of Ahmet Güleç, was not absolutely necessary within the meaning of article 2 of the Convention. It also concluded that there had been a breach of that article on account of the lack of a thorough investigation into the circumstances of his death. Furthermore, the Court held, by seven votes to two, that the respondent State was to compensate for non-pecuniary damage and, unanimously, for costs and expenses.

C. CASE SUMMARIES

(a) *Hajrizi Dzemajl* et al. v. *Serbia and Montenegro*
(Committee against Torture)[36]

The complainants in this case were 65 people, all nationals of Serbia and Montenegro and of Roma origin. They submitted the complaint to the Committee against Torture on 11 November 1999, claiming that Serbia and Montenegro had violated articles 1, paragraph 1, 2, paragraph 1, 12, 13, 14 and 16, paragraph 1, of the Convention against Torture and Other Cruel, Inhuman or Degrading Treatment or Punishment.

The facts

The complainants submitted, *inter alia*, the following. On 14 April 1995 at about 10 p.m., the police department in Danilovgrad received a report indicating that two Roma minors had raped a girl, an ethnic Montenegrin. In response to this report, at about midnight, the police entered and searched a number of houses in the Bozova Glavica Roma settlement. They took into custody all of the young male Roma men present in the settlement, all of them among the complainants to the Committee.

At the same time, 200 ethnic Montenegrins, led by relatives and neighbours of the raped girl, assembled in front of the police station and publicly demanded that the municipal assembly should adopt a decision expelling all Roma from Danilovgrad. The crowd shouted slogans addressed to the Roma, threatening to exterminate them and burn down their houses.

Later, two Roma minors confessed under duress. On 15 April 1995, between 4 and 5 a.m., all of the detainees except those who confessed were released from police custody. Before their release, they were warned by the police to leave Danilovgrad im-

---

[36] See United Nations, *Official Records of the General Assembly, Fifty-eighth Session, Supplement No. 44* (A/58/44), annex VI, sect. A, complaint No. 161/2000, decision adopted on 21 November 2002.

mediately with their families, because they would be at risk of being lynched by their non-Roma neighbours.

At the same time, a police officer, named in the decision, went to the Bozova Glavica Roma settlement and told the residents that they had to evacuate the settlement immediately. The officer's announcement caused panic. Most residents of the settlement fled towards a nearby highway, where they could take buses for Podgorica, the Montenegrin capital. Only a few men and women remained in the settlement to safeguard their homes and livestock. At about 5 a.m., the police officer returned to the settlement, accompanied by a police inspector. The officers told the remaining Roma still in their homes, including some of the complainants, to leave Danilovgrad immediately, as no one could guarantee their safety or provide them with protection.

Later on that day, at about 8 a.m., a group of non-Roma residents of Danilovgrad entered the Bozova Glavica Roma settlement, hurling stones and breaking windows of houses owned by the complainants. Those Roma who had still not left the settlement, all of them among the complainants, hid in the cellar of one of the houses from which they eventually managed to flee through the fields and woods towards Podgorica.

In the course of the same morning, a police car repeatedly patrolled the deserted Bozova Glavica settlement. Groups of non-Roma residents of Danilovgrad gathered in different locations in the town and in the surrounding villages. At about 2 p.m., the non-Roma crowd arrived in the Bozova Glavica settlement, in cars and on foot. Soon a crowd of at least several hundred non-Roma assembled in the then deserted Roma settlement. According to different sources, between 400 and 3,000 persons were present

Between 2 and 3 p.m., the crowd continued to grow and some began to shout: "We shall evict them!"; "We shall burn down the settlement!"; and "We shall raze the settlement!". Shortly after 3 p.m., the demolition of the settlement began. The mob, with stones and other objects, first broke windows of cars and houses belonging to Roma and then set them on fire. The crowd also destroyed and set fire to the haystacks, farming and other machines, animal feed sheds and stables, as well as all other objects belonging to the Roma. They hurled explosive devices and Molotov cocktails that they had prepared beforehand, and they threw burning cloths and foam rubber into houses through the broken windows. Shots and explosions could be heard amid the sounds of destruction. At the same time, valuables were looted and cattle slaughtered. The devastation endured unhindered for hours.

Throughout the course of these events, police officers present failed to act in accordance with their legal obligations. Shortly after the attack began, rather than interven-

IV:2

ing to halt the violence, the police officers simply moved their car to a safe distance and reported to their superior officer. As the violence unfolded, police officers did no more than feebly seek to persuade some of the attackers to calm down pending a final decision of the municipal assembly with respect to the popular request to evict Roma from the Bozova Glavica settlement.

The outcome of the anti-Roma rage was that the whole settlement was levelled and all properties belonging to its Roma residents were burnt or completely destroyed. Although the police did nothing to halt the destruction of the Roma settlement, they did ensure that the fire did not spread to any of the surrounding buildings, which belonged to the non-Roma.

The police and the investigating magistrate of the local court in Danilovgrad subsequently drew up an on-site investigation report regarding the damage caused by those who took part in the destruction of the Bozova Glavica Roma settlement. Official police documents, as well as statements given by a number of police officers and other witnesses, both before the court and in the initial stage of the investigation, indicated that eight non-Roma residents of Danilovgrad, named in the decision, were among those who took part in the destruction of the settlement. Moreover, there was evidence that five police officers, also named in the decision, were all present as the violence unfolded and did nothing or not enough to protect the Roma residents of Bozova Glavica or their property.

Several days following the incident, the debris of the Roma settlement was completely cleared away by heavy construction machines of a public utility company. All traces of the existence of the Roma in Danilovgrad were obliterated.

Following the attack and pursuant to the relevant domestic legislation, the police department in Podgorica, on 17 April 1995, filed a criminal complaint with the public prosecutor's office in Podgorica. The complaint alleged that a number of unknown perpetrators had committed the criminal offence of causing public danger contrary to the Montenegrin criminal code and, *inter alia*, explicitly stated that there were reasonable grounds to believe that in an organized manner and by using naked flames, they had caused a fire to break out on 15 April 1995 which completely consumed dwellings and other properties belonging to persons who used to reside in the Bozova Glavica settlement.

On 17 April 1995, the police brought in 20 individuals for questioning. On 18 April 1995, a memorandum was drawn up by the police department which quoted the statement of one of the detainees, named in the decision. He noticed flames in a hut, and that led him to conclude that the crowd had started setting fire to huts. He found several pieces of foam rubber which he lit with his lighter and threw them, alight, into two huts. One of them caught fire. On the basis of this testimony and the official police memorandum, the police department on 18 April 1995 ordered that person to be remanded in custody on the grounds that there were reasons to believe that he had committed the criminal offence of causing public danger contrary to the criminal code.

On 25 April 1995, the public prosecutor instituted proceedings against him only with respect to the incident at the origin of the complaint. He was charged with causing public danger under the criminal code. The same indictment charged another named man with illegally obtaining firearms in 1993. This offence was unrelated to the incident at issue notwithstanding the evidence implicating him in the destruction of the Bozova Glavica Roma settlement.

Throughout the investigation, the investigating magistrate of the court in Danilovgrad heard a number of witnesses. All of them stated that they had been present as the violence unfolded, but they were not able to identify a single perpetrator. On 22 June 1995, the investigating magistrate heard a police officer, named in the decision. Contrary to the official memorandum that he personally had drawn up on 16 April 1995, the officer then stated that he had not seen anyone throwing an inflammable device, nor could he identify any of the individuals involved.

On 25 October 1995, the public prosecutor in Podgorica requested the investigating magistrate of the court in Danilovgrad to undertake additional investigation into the facts of the case. Specifically, the prosecutor proposed that new witnesses should be heard, including those officers from the police department in Danilovgrad who had been entrusted with protecting the Bozova Glavica Roma settlement. The investigating magistrate then heard additional witnesses. They all stated that they had seen none of the individuals who had caused the fire. The investigating magistrate took no further action.

On 23 January 1996, the public prosecutor in Podgorica dropped all charges against the man who had been remanded in custody, due to the lack of evidence. On 8 February 1996, the investigating magistrate of the court in Danilovgrad issued a decision to discontinue the investigation. Up to the submission of the complaint, the authorities took no further steps to identify and/or punish those responsible for the incident at issue, civilians and police officers alike.

In violation of domestic legislation, the complainants were not served with the court decision to discontinue the investigation. They were thus prevented from assuming the capacity of a private prosecutor and to continue with the prosecution of the case. On 6 September 1996, all complainants filed a civil claim for damages, pecuniary and non-pecuniary, but more than five years after the submission of this claim, these proceedings were still pending.

The complainants, having been driven out of their homes and their property having been completely destroyed, fled to the outskirts of Podgorica. During the first few weeks following the incident, they hid in parks and abandoned houses. Local Roma from Podgorica supplied them with basic food and told them that groups of angry non-Roma men had been looking for them in the Roma suburbs in Podgorica. From this time on, the banished Danilovgrad Roma had continued to live in Podgorica in abject poverty, in makeshift shelters or abandoned houses, and had been forced to work at the city dump or to beg for a living.

The complainants submitted that the State party had violated article 2, paragraph 1, read in conjunction with articles 1 and 16, paragraph 1, and articles 12, 13 and 14, taken alone or together with article 16, paragraph 1, of the Convention.

With regard to the admissibility of the complaint under article 22 of the Convention, and more particularly the exhaustion of local remedies, the complainants submitted that given the level of wrongs suffered and alongside the jurisprudence of the European Court of Human Rights, only a criminal remedy would be effective. Civil and/or administrative remedies would not provide sufficient redress.

The complainants further noted that the authorities had the obligation to investigate, or at least to continue their investigation, if they considered the available evidence insufficient. Moreover, even though the complainants acknowledged that they had never filed a criminal complaint against those responsible for the attack, they contended that both the police and the prosecuting authorities were sufficiently aware of the facts to initiate and conduct the investigation ex officio. The complainants therefore concluded that there was no effective remedy.

Referring to a number of excerpts from non-governmental organizations and governmental sources, the complainants first requested that they, taking into account the situation of the Roma in Serbia and Montenegro, should be considered as victims of systematic police brutality and the dire human rights situation in general. The complainants alleged that the authorities had violated the Convention under either article 2, paragraph 1, read in conjunction with article 1 embodying the definition of torture, or article 16, paragraph 1, in respect of other acts of cruel, inhuman or degrading treatment or punishment, because the police during the events stood by and watched as the situation unfolded. In this regard, the complainants considered that the particularly vulnerable character of the Roma minority had to be taken into account in assessing the level of ill-treatment that had been committed. They suggested that a given level of physical abuse was more likely to constitute degrading or inhuman treatment or punishment when motivated by racial animus.

With regard to the fact that the acts had mostly been committed by non-State actors, the complainants relied on a review of international jurisprudence on the principle of due diligence and recalled the current state of international law with regard to positive obligations that were incumbent on States. They submitted that the purpose of the provisions of the Convention was not limited to negative obligations for States parties, but included positive steps that had to be taken in order to avoid that torture and other related acts being committed by private persons.

The complainants further contended that the acts of violence occurred with the consent or acquiescence of the police whose duty under the law was to secure their safety and afford them protection.

Moreover, the complainants alleged a violation of article 12 of the Convention, read alone or taken together with article 16, paragraph 1, if the acts committed did not amount to torture, because the authorities failed to conduct a prompt, impartial, and comprehensive investigation capable of leading to the identification and punishment of those responsible. Citing the jurisprudence of the Committee, it was submitted that the State party had the obligation to conduct not just any investigation, but a proper investigation, even in the absence of the formal submission of a complaint, since they were in possession of abundant evidence. The complainants further suggested that the impartiality of the investigation depended on the level of independence of the body conducting it. In this case, it was alleged that the level of independence of the investigative magistrate of the court was not sufficient.

Finally, the complainants alleged violations of articles 13 and 14 of the Convention, read alone and/or taken together with article 16, paragraph 1, because their right to complain and to have their case promptly and impartially examined by the competent authorities was violated and because of the absence of redress and of fair and adequate compensation, respectively.

The State party contended that the complaint was inadmissible, because the case had been conducted according to the national legislation in force and because all available legal remedies had not been exhausted.

The Committee declared the complaint admissible. Notwithstanding the Committee's call for observations on the merits, the State party made no further submission.

The complainants submitted additional comments on the merits. They transmitted detailed information on different questions asked by the Committee, namely, on the presence and behaviour of the police during the events, the actions that had been taken towards the local population, the relations between the different ethnic groups, as well as their respective titles of property.

With regard to the general situation of the Roma minority in Serbia and Montenegro, the complainants contended that it had remained largely unchanged after the departure of President Milosevic. Referring to two reports by non-governmental organizations, the complainants submitted that the situation of Roma in the State party was very preoccupying and emphasised that there had been a number of serious incidents against Roma over the last few years. No significant measures to find or prosecute the perpetrators or to compensate the victims had been taken by the authorities.

With regard to the property titles, the complainants explained that most were lost or destroyed during the events of 14 and 15 April 1995, and this was not challenged by the State party's authorities during the civil proceedings.

The complainants then made a thorough analysis of the scope of application of articles 1, paragraph 1, and 16, paragraph 1, of the Convention. They first submitted that the European Court of Human Rights had ascertained in its case law that article 3 of the Convention for the Protection of Human Rights and Fundamental Freedoms, embodying the prohibition of torture, also covered the infliction of mental suffering by creating a state of anguish and stress by means other than bodily assault.

Moreover, the complainants reiterated that the assessment of the level of ill-treatment also depended on the vulnerability of the victim and should thus also take into account the sex, age, state of health or ethnicity of the victim. As a result, the Committee should consider the Roma ethnicity of the victims in their appreciation of the violations committed, particularly in Serbia and Montenegro. They also reiterated that a given level of physical abuse was more likely to constitute a treatment prohibited by article 16 of the Convention if it was motivated by racial considerations.

Concerning the devastation of human settlements, the complainants referred to two cases before the European Court with factual circumstances similar to the one at issue. The Court had considered that the burning and destruction of homes as well as the eviction of their inhabitants from the village constituted acts that were contrary to article 3 of the European Convention.

Concerning the perpetrators of the alleged violations of articles 1 and 16 of the Convention, the complainants submitted that although only a public official or a person acting in an official capacity could be the perpetrator of an act in the sense of either of these provisions, both stated that the act of torture or of other ill-treatment might also be inflicted with the consent or acquiescence of a public official. While not disputing that the acts had not been committed by the police officers or that the latter had not instigated them, the complainants considered that the acts had been committed with their consent and acquiescence. The police were informed of what was going to happen on 15 April 1995 and were present on the scene at the time of the attack, but they did not prevent the perpetrators from committing their wrongdoing.

With regard to the positive obligations of States to prevent and suppress acts of violence committed by private individuals, the complainants referred to a general comment by the Human Rights Committee on article 7 of the International Covenant on Civil and Political Rights, prohibiting the use of torture or cruel, inhuman or degrading treatment or punishment. This provision covered acts committed by private individuals, which implied a duty for States to take appropriate measures to protect everyone against such acts. The complainants also referred to three other instruments with provisions having a similar purpose, namely the Code of Conduct for Law Enforcement Officials, the Basic Principles on the Use of Force and Firearms by Law Enforcement Officials and the Framework Convention for the Protection of National Minorities.

On the same issue, the complainants cited a judgment of the Inter-American Court of Human Rights. An illegal act violating human rights but initially not directly imputable to a State could lead to international responsibility for the State, not because of the act itself but because of the lack of due diligence to prevent the violation or to respond to it as required.

Similarly, the European Court of Human Rights had addressed this issue in a judgment. It had stated that article 2 of the European Convention, protecting the right to life, might also imply in certain well-defined circumstances a positive obligation on the authorities to take preventive operational measures to protect an individual whose life was at risk from the criminal acts of another individual. Where there was an allegation that the authorities had violated their positive obligation to protect the right to life in the context of their duty to prevent and suppress offences against the person, it had to be established to its satisfaction that the authorities knew or ought to have known at the time of the existence of a real and immediate risk to the life of an identified individual or individuals from the criminal acts of a third party and that they failed to take measures within the scope of their powers which, judged reasonably, might have been expected to avoid that risk. Having regard to the nature of the right protected by article 2, a right fundamental in the scheme of the Convention, it was sufficient for an applicant to show that the authorities did not do all that could be reasonably expected of them to avoid a real and immediate risk to life of which they had or ought to have had knowledge.

The complainants further contended that the extent of the obligation to take preventive measures might increase with the immediacy of the risk to life. In support of this argument, they relied extensively on another judgment of the European Court. States had an obligation to take every reasonable step in order to prevent a real and immediate threat to the life and integrity of a person when the actions could be perpetrated by a person or group of persons with the consent or acquiescence of public authorities. Furthermore, States had an obligation to provide an effective remedy, including a proper and effective investigation, with regard to actions committed by non-State actors undertaken with the consent or acquiescence of public authorities.

The complainants also underlined that the obligation of States parties to the European Convention went well beyond mere criminal sanctions for private individuals who had committed acts contrary to article 3 of that Convention. In one case, the authorities had been aware of the serious ill-treatment and neglect suffered by the applicants over a period of years at the hands of their parents and failed, despite the means reasonably available to them, to take any effective steps to bring it to an end. The European Commission of Human Rights held in this case that the State had therefore failed in its positive obligation under article 3 to provide the applicants with adequate protection against inhuman and degrading treatment.

In conclusion, the complainants submitted that they had indeed been subjected to acts of community violence inflicting on them great physical and mental suffering amounting to torture and/or cruel, inhuman and degrading treatment or punishment. They further stated that this happened for the purpose of punishing them for an act committed by a third person, the rape of the young girl, and that the community violence, or rather the racist attack, at issue took place in the presence of, and thus with the consent or acquiescence of, the police whose duty under law was precisely the opposite, to secure their safety and afford them protection.

Finally, relying on the jurisprudence of the European Court and that of the Human Rights Committee, the complainants argued that by not contesting the facts or the legal arguments developed in the complaint and further submissions, the State party had tacitly accepted the claims at issue.

Issues and proceedings before the Committee

The Committee considered the complaint under article 22 of the Convention in the light of all information made available to it by the parties concerned. In the absence of any submission from the State party following the decision on admissibility, the Committee relied on the detailed submissions made by the complainants. It recalled in this respect that a State party had an obligation under the Convention to cooperate with the Committee and to submit written explanations or statements clarifying the matter and the remedy, if any, that might have been granted.

As to the legal qualification of the facts that had occurred on 15 April 1995, as they were described by the complainants, the Committee first considered that the burning and destruction of houses constituted, in the circumstances, acts of cruel, inhuman or degrading treatment or punishment. The nature of these acts was further aggravated by the fact that some of the complainants were still hidden in the settlement when the houses were burnt and destroyed, by the particular vulnerability of the alleged victims and by the fact that the acts were committed with a significant level of racial motivation.

The Committee further considered that the complainants had sufficiently demonstrated that the police did not take any appropriate steps in order to protect the complainants, although they had been informed of the immediate risk that the complainants were facing and had been present at the scene of the events. This implied acquiescence in the sense of article 16 of the Convention. In this respect, the Committee had reiterated on many instances its concerns about inaction by police and law enforcement officials who failed to provide adequate protection against racially motivated attacks when such groups had been threatened. Although the acts referred to by the complainants were not committed by public officials themselves, the Committee considered that those acts were committed with their acquiescence. Therefore, they constituted a violation of article 16, paragraph 1, of the Convention by the State party.

The Committee went on to analyze other alleged violations in the light of the finding that the facts described by the complainants constituted acts within the meaning of article 16, paragraph 1, of the Convention.

As to the alleged violation of article 12 of the Convention, the Committee was of the opinion, as it had underlined in previous cases, that a criminal investigation had to seek both to determine the nature and circumstances of the alleged acts and to establish the identity of any person who might have been involved therein. In the present case, the Committee noted that no perpetrator, nor any member of the police forces, had been tried by the courts of the State party, despite the participation of at least several hundred non-Roma in the events of 15 April 1995 and the presence at the time of a number of police officers at the scene of those events. In these circumstances, the Committee was of the view that the investigation conducted by the State authorities did not satisfy the requirements of article 12 of the Convention.

As to the alleged violation of article 13 of the Convention, the Committee considered that the absence of an investigation also constituted a violation of that article.

IV:2

Moreover, the Committee was of the view that the State party's failure to inform the complainants of the results of the investigation, *inter alia*, by not serving on them the decision to discontinue the investigation, effectively prevented them from assuming private prosecution of their case. In the circumstances, the Committee found that this constituted a further violation of article 13.

As to the alleged violation of article 14 of the Convention, protecting the rights of victims to redress and compensation, the Committee noted that the scope of application of this provision only referred to torture in the sense of article 1. It did not cover other forms of ill-treatment. Moreover, article 16, paragraph 1, of the Convention, while specifically referring to articles 10, 11, 12, and 13, did not mention article 14. Nevertheless, this did not mean that the State party was not obliged to grant redress and fair and adequate compensation to the victim of an act in breach of article 16. The positive obligations that flowed from this provision included such an obligation. The Committee was therefore of the view that the State party had failed to observe its obligations under article 16 of the Convention by failing to enable the complainants to obtain redress and to provide them with fair and adequate compensation.

The Committee concluded that the facts before it disclosed a violation of articles 16, paragraph 1, 12 and 13 of the Convention.

The Committee urged the State party to conduct a proper investigation into the facts that occurred on 15 April 1995, prosecute and punish the persons responsible for those acts and provide the complainants with redress, including fair and adequate compensation. It also urged the State to inform it, within 90 days, of the steps taken in response to the Committee's views.

In an individual opinion, two members of the Committee expressed the view that the illegal incidents for which the State party was responsible constituted torture within the meaning of article 1, paragraph 1, of the Convention, not merely cruel, inhuman or degrading treatment as covered by article 16. The failure of the State authorities to react to violent evictions, forced displacement and the destruction of homes and property by individuals amounted to unlawful acquiescence which, in their judgement, violated article 1, paragraph 1, particularly read in conjunction with article 2, paragraph 1, of the Convention. What the victims suffered amounted to a presumption of severe suffering, certainly mental but also inescapably physical in nature, even if the victims were not subjected to direct physical aggression. Thus, they considered that the incidents at issue should have been categorized as torture. In coming to this conclusion, they pointed out, *inter alia*, that all the inhabitants of the settlement who were violently displaced belonged to the Roma ethnic group, known to be especially vulnerable in many parts of Europe, and States had therefore to afford them greater protection.

(*b*) Decision No. 16/1994 (*Israel*)
(Working Group on Arbitrary Detention)[37]

The communication, addressed to the Government of Israel on 18 July 1994, concerned Sha'ban Rateb Jabarin, described by the source as a Palestinian para-legal and human rights activist. It was claimed that since 1979, he had been detained seven times for alleged terrorist activities, on six of these occasions without being brought to trial. Since 21 June 1994, he had been held in administrative detention for six months. Israel was a party to the International Covenant on Civil and Political Rights, with effect from 3 January 1992.

The Working Group on Arbitary Detention welcomed the cooperation of the Government. Having transmitted the Government's reply to the source and received its comments, the Working Group believed that it was in a position to take a decision on the facts and circumstances of the case.

The facts

On 7 July 1992, following the detention of Sha'ban Rateb Jabarin, the Chairman of the Working Group sent an urgent appeal to the Minister for Foreign Affairs of Israel. On 10 July 1992, Mr. Jabarin was released. Later, he was again arrested and detained without charge. On 4 May 1994, a letter was addressed by the Chairman of the Working Group to the Permanent Representative of Israel to the United Nations office at Geneva. The office of the Permanent Representative later informed the Working Group that Mr. Jabarin on 5 May 1994 had been released from administrative detention. On 21 June 1994, he was again detained, and yet another communication was addressed by the Chairman of the Working Group to the Minister for Foreign Affairs asking for information concerning Mr. Jabarin's situation and the legal basis of his detention. An appeal was also made in that communication to the Government of Israel to consider his release from prison and to do its utmost to guarantee his right to liberty and security.

On 10 March 1994, Mr. Jabarin was allegedly arrested without a warrant, and six months' administrative detention was imposed on him, apparently pursuant to a military order. He was subsequently detained in prison without having been charged with any offence. The source claimed that the reason for his detention was his involvement in the writing of a publication on violence by Jewish settlers in the Hebron area. The source also claimed that no judicial or other procedures existed to challenge the legality of the arrest or detention, as military courts refused to hear ju-

---

[37] See United Nations document E/CN.4/1995/31/Add.2, p. 16, decision adopted on 28 September 1994.

IV:2

dicial proceedings in the nature of *habeas corpus* or *amparo*. It was also claimed that rules of evidence and procedure, as well as restrictions on the powers of an appeal's committee, made it difficult for a detainee to challenge the order effectively. Such orders were rarely set aside on appeal. The source maintained that Mr. Jabarin was detained for his non-violent activities in the exercise of his right to freedom of expression and opinion.

In its response, the Government informed the Working Group that Mr. Jabarin was held in administrative detention from 10 March 1994 until 8 May 1994. The Government strongly denied that Mr. Jabarin was an innocent man devoting his efforts to an organization engaged in the field of human rights. It insisted that he had never been detained for his work with that organization. According to the Government, Mr. Jabarin had been, for many years, a senior member of the Popular Front for the Liberation of Palestine (PFLP), a terrorist organization committed to using violence in order to bring about the destruction of the State of Israel. The Government also maintained that since the Israeli-Palestinian Declaration of Principles was signed in September 1993, the PFLP's declared objective had been to derail the peace process by acts of terror. The Government claimed to be in possession of substantial evidence to the effect that in his capacity as a senior operative of the PFLP, Mr. Jabarin had been, and continued to be, connected with its violent activities.

The Government explained that failure to bring Mr. Jabarin to trial was due to its concern for the lives and welfare of several witnesses to the case. Consequently, he had, periodically and for a limited period of time, been placed under administrative detention in accordance with article 78 of the Geneva Convention relative to the Protection of Civilian Persons in Time of War (Geneva Convention IV), as well as a domestic security provisions order. On one occasion, in 1985, Mr. Jabarin had been tried without endangering witnesses. He was then convicted of recruiting new members for the PFLP and for arranging guerrilla training outside of Israel. He was sentenced to 24 months' imprisonment, 9 months of which were served and 15 months suspended.

The Government contended that Mr. Jabarin had not discontinued his terrorist involvement. He had maintained his position in the leadership of the PFLP. The Government admitted that he had been arrested on 21 June 1994 and placed in administrative detention for six months. He could not be brought to trial, as that would endanger the safety of witnesses were they to give evidence.

The source responded that Israel had chosen to criminalize membership of the PFLP, a Palestinian political party, and that if Mr. Jabarin was accused of criminal activities, the Government should bring him to trial. The source also questioned the use of article 78 of Geneva Convention IV and the security provisions order to justify administrative detention.

Issues and proceedings before the Working Group

The Working Group observed that the Israeli Government had chosen to detain Mr. Jabarin and not to put him on trial, because it feared that the lives of witnesses would be endangered if they would give evidence against him. However, individual liberty could not be sacrificed because of the Government's inability either to collect evidence or to present it in an appropriate form.

If the PFLP was a terrorist organization committed to using violence in order to bring about the destruction of the State of Israel and if the Government had sufficient evidence to indicate that Mr. Jabarin was involved in terrorist activities, the Government should charge Mr. Jabarin and bring him to trial. The Government should not use the power of administrative detention to achieve its purposes without a formal trial. The use of administrative detention was otherwise punitive and not preventive.

Reliance by the Government on article 78 of Geneva Convention IV and the security provisions order was also unjustified. The latter could only be used as a preventive measure, but not in relation to an offence for which a person could be charged and tried. As far as the provisions of Geneva Convention IV were concerned, article 6 provided that in the case of occupied territory, the applicability of many provisions of the Convention, including article 78, ceased one year after the general close of military operations. Article 78 could therefore not be used to justify Mr. Jabarin's administrative detention.

The Working Group decided that the detention of Mr. Jabarin, on all the occasions on which he was not brought to trial and since 21 June 1994, was arbitrary, as being in contravention of articles 9 and 10 of the Universal Declaration of Human Rights and articles 9 and 14 of the Covenant. It fell within category III of the principles applicable to the consideration of cases submitted to the Working Group.

The Working Group requested the Government of Israel to take the necessary steps to remedy the situation in order to bring it into conformity with the provisions and principles of the Universal Declaration and the Covenant.

IV:2

(c) Opinion No. 25/2001 (*Pakistan*)
(Working Group on Arbitrary Detention)[38]

The communication, addressed to the Government of Pakistan on 18 October 2001, concerned Ayub Masih, a Christian Pakistani citizen. Allegedly, he had been arrested and subsequently accused and convicted of blasphemy, largely because he belonged to a religious minority, on the basis of a provision of a law which itself was clearly discriminatory. Pakistan was not a party to the International Covenant on Civil and Political Rights.

The Working Group on Arbitrary Detention welcomed the cooperation of the Government. Having transmitted the Government's reply to the source and received its comments, the Working Group believed that it was in a position to take a decision on the facts and circumstances of the case.

The facts

According to the information submitted to the Working Group, Ayub Masih was arrested on 14 October 1996 by the police. No judicial decision or arrest warrant was presented at the time of his arrest.

The source claimed that Mr. Masih's family had applied for land under a government programme for distributing parcels of land to provide housing for homeless people. The local landlord and other residents of the village apparently resented this prospect, as previously Christian families had lived on land provided by Muslim landowners in exchange for labour. Implementation of this land allocation programme would deprive the village landowners of the benefits of Christian labour.

It was submitted that Mr. Masih was arrested when a Muslim neighbour told police that Mr. Masih had offended him by stating Christianity was "right" and suggesting he should read British author Salman Rushdie's *Satanic Verses*. Mr. Masih denied all these accusations. On the day of his arrest, the other villagers forced the entire Christian population of the village, 14 families in all, to leave their homes and abandon their belongings. The authorities allocated Mr. Masih's house to the complainant, who had apparently been living there ever since. Bishop John Joseph of Faisalbad observed that the allegations against Mr. Masih were motivated by a dispute between Muslim and Christian villagers. He pointed out that neither Mr. Masih nor the complainant could read English and would know little about the Rushdie book.

---

[38] See United Nations document E/CN.4/2003/8/Add.1, p. 22, opinion adopted on 30 November 2001.

On 6 November 1997, the complainant shot and injured Mr. Masih in the halls of the court, after which the trial was held in camera. The police reportedly refused to register a complaint against the perpetrator, despite eyewitness testimonies by family members. On 8 January 1998, the trial began. On 20 April 1998, Mr. Masih was sentenced to death and to a fine of 100,000 rupees. He immediately filed an appeal before a high court. On the day of the verdict, extremists gathered near the court threatened Mr. Masih's lawyer with dire consequences for pursuing the case. It was reported that Bishop John Joseph of Faisalbad on 6 May 1998 shot and killed himself in front of the court to protest against Mr. Masih's conviction.

In January 1999, Mr. Masih was allegedly attacked and injured in the prison by four other inmates. No action appeared to have been taken against the attackers. The source reported that on 24 July 2001, the high court finally heard Mr. Masih's appeal, over three years and three months after being convicted. On the day of the hearing, the courtroom was filled with extremists who made death threats against the court and Mr. Masih's lawyer. Shortly thereafter, two judges affirmed the judgment, and an appeal was made to the Supreme Court of Pakistan.

The source cited the particular provision of the penal code giving rise to the sentence. Whoever by words, either spoken or written, by visible representation or by any imputation, innuendo or insinuation directly or indirectly defiled the sacred name of the Holy Prophet (PBUH) should be punished with death, or imprisonment for life, and should also be liable to fine.

It was submitted that in October 1990, the Federal Shariah Court ruled that the penalty for contempt of the Holy Prophet (PBUH) was death. Under Pakistani law, the Federal Shariah Court was a religious body whose rulings were binding on the Government of Pakistan. Thus, life imprisonment was no longer an available sentence for persons convicted of blasphemy under the penal code. The only possible punishment available in such cases was death. Moreover, according to the criminal procedure code, judges presiding at blasphemy trials had to be Muslims. This was the only section in the Pakistani criminal system for which a religious qualification of the judge was prescribed.

Summarizing its position, the source pointed out that the detention of Mr. Masih was arbitrary. He was accused and convicted, largely because he belonged to a religious minority, on the basis of a provision of a law which itself was clearly discriminatory. Therefore, his conviction implied a violation of Mr. Masih's rights to equal protection and non-discrimination.

It was submitted that Mr. Masih requested written documentation regarding the charges and evidence against him. He was not provided with any such documenta-

IV:2

tion or evidence. He was never informed of his rights during the proceedings. It was also submitted that by refusing to conduct an independent investigation and by allowing the testimony of a single, biased witness, the court shifted the burden of proof onto the defendant who was expected to prove he did not commit the alleged offence. This shifting of the burden of proof was reinforced by the requirement that judges hearing blasphemy cases had to be Muslims.

Moreover, the threats and atmosphere surrounding Mr. Masih's trial and appeal denied him any chance of having a fair trial. The source considered that the courts hearing the case and appeal were unable to make their decisions in an independent and impartial manner, because the judges themselves felt that their personal integrity and safety were at risk. The source recalled that a judge was assassinated on 19 October 1997 in his office after acquitting two persons accused of blasphemy.

The description by the Government of the facts of the case giving rise to Mr. Masih's conviction were quite close to but more detailed than that given by the source. According to the Government, the complainant, overcome with emotion upon hearing the derogatory remarks of Mr. Masih, seized him and took him to the police. The Government did not comment on or refute the allegations of the source on how the proceedings against the accused were conducted.

Issues and proceedings before the Working Group

The Working Group found that the procedure conducted against Mr. Masih did not respect the fundamental rights of a person charged with a crime. He was not provided with documentary or other evidence against him, nor was he informed of his rights as an accused. This prevented him from properly preparing his defence. The verdict against him was based on the testimony of a single, biased witness. The threats by extremists against him and his defence lawyer during trial and appeal, and the hostile atmosphere, characterized, *inter alia*, by the fact that the complainant shot at him in the courtroom without apparently being sanctioned by the court, intimidated the accused and counsel alike, thereby restricting the effectiveness of the defence. To all this was added the fact that under Pakistani law, blasphemy cases insulting the Muslim religion could only be heard by Muslim judges. This undermined credibility in a fair and impartial trial being conducted. These serious deficiencies in proceedings, where capital punishment was provided by law as a mandatory penalty if the accused was found guilty, basically stripped the procedure of its requisite fair character.

In conclusion, the Working Group rendered the opinion that the deprivation of liberty of Mr. Masih was arbitrary, as being in contravention of articles 9 and 10 of the

Universal Declaration of Human Rights. It fell within category III of the categories applicable to the consideration of cases submitted to the Working Group.

Consequent upon the opinion rendered, the Working Group requested the Government to take the necessary steps to remedy the situation of Mr. Masih. The Working Group believed that under the circumstances, a retrial, the granting of a pardon or a commutation of sentence would be an appropriate remedy. It recommended the Government to consider ratifying the International Covenant on Civil and Political Rights.

(*d*) *Free Legal Assistance Group* **et al. v.** *Zaire* (African Commission on Human and Peoples' Rights)[39]

The communications were filed with the African Commission on Human and Peoples' Rights by the Free Legal Assistance Group, dated 17 March 1989, the Austrian Committee Against Torture, dated 29 March 1989, and the Centre Haitien des Droits et Libertés, dated 20 April 1989, all members of the World Organization Against Torture; by the Lawyers' Committee for Human Rights in New York, dated 16 October 1990; by the Jehovah's Witnesses of Zaire, dated 27 March 1991; and by the Union Interafricaine des Droits de l'Homme, dated 20 March 1993, respectively, against Zaire under the African Charter of Human and Peoples' Rights. The complainants alleged a number violations of human rights in Zaire.

The facts

In the communication filed by the Free Legal Assistance Group *et al.*, it was alleged that on or about 19 January 1989, 15 people were tortured by a military unit. On 19 April 1989, when several people protested against their treatment, they were detained and held indefinitely.

The communication filed by the Lawyers' Committee for Human Rights alleged arbitrary arrests, arbitrary detentions, torture, extrajudicial executions, unfair trials, severe restrictions placed on the right to association and peaceful assembly as well as suppression of the freedom of the press.

The communication submitted by the Jehovah's Witnesses of Zaire alleged the persecution of Jehovahs' Witnesses, including arbitrary arrests, appropriation of church property and exclusion from access to education.

---

[39] See *Review of the African Commission on Human and Peoples' Rights*, vol. 6 (1996-1997), p. 183, communications No. 25/89, No. 47/90, No. 56/91 and No. 100/93.

IV:2

In the communication submitted by the Union Interafricaine des Droits de l'Homme, finally, there were allegations of torture, executions, arrests, detention, unfair trials, restrictions on freedom of association and freedom of the press. It was also alleged that public finances were mismanaged; that the failure of the Government to provide basic services was degrading; that there was a shortage of medicines in the country; that the universities and secondary schools had been closed for two years; that freedom of movement was violated; and that ethnic hatred was incited by the official media.

The Commission requested that a mission consisting of two of its members should be received in Zaire, with the objective of discovering the extent and cause of human rights violations and endeavouring to help the Government to ensure full respect for the Charter. The Government of Zaire did not respond to the request.

The communications were brought, separately and in various ways, to the attention of the State. In spite of reminders and other notifications sent by the Commission, no responses were forthcoming.

The law

After deliberations, as envisioned by article 58 of the Charter, the Commission considered that the communications in the case revealed the existence of serious and massive violations of human rights.

The Commission then observed that article 56 of the Charter required that the complainants had exhausted local remedies before the Commission could take up a case, unless such remedies were practically unavailable or unduly prolonged. This requirement was founded on the principle that a government should have notice of a human rights violation in order to have the opportunity to remedy the situation before being called before an international body. In this case, the Government had had ample notice of the violation. The Commission had never held this requirement to apply literally in cases where it was impractical or undesirable for the complainant to seize the domestic courts in the case of each violation. This was the situation here, given the vast and varied scope of the violations alleged and the general situation prevailing in Zaire.

The Commission declared the communications admissible.

On the merits, the Commission first pronounced that the main goal of the communications procedure was to initiate a positive dialogue, resulting in an amicable resolution between the complainant and the State party concerned. A prerequisite for amicably remedying violations of the Charter was the good faith of the parties concerned, including their willingness to participate in a dialogue.

In the present case, there had been no substantive response from the Government of Zaire, despite numerous notifications of the communications sent by the Commission. Recalling its previous decisions setting out the principle that where allegations of human rights abuse went uncontested by the government concerned, even after repeated notifications, the Commission had to decide on the facts provided by the complainant and to treat those facts as given. As the Government of Zaire did not wish to participate in a dialogue, the Commission had to continue its consideration of the case, although, regrettably, on the basis of facts and opinions submitted by the complainants alone.

In respect of article 5 of the Charter, protecting the right of every individual not be subjected to, *inter alia*, torture, cruel, inhuman or degrading punishment and treatment, the Commission held that the alleged torture of 15 people by a military unit constituted a violation of this provision. The indefinite detention of those who protested against torture of these people violated article 6 on the right to liberty and securiy of person.

Article 4 of the Charter, protecting the right to life, was violated in respect of alleged extrajudicial executions.

Provisions of the right to a fair trial contained in article 7 of the Charter were found to have been violated in the unfair trials described in one of the communications.

The alleged harassment of the Jehovah's Witnesses constituted a violation of article 8 of the Charter on the right to freedom of religion, as the Government had presented no evidence that the practice of their religion in any way threatened law and order. The arbitrary arrests of believers of this religion likewise constituted a contravention of article 6.

The torture, executions, arrests, detention, unfair trials, restrictions on freedom of association and freedom of the press, as described in one of the communications, violated the relevant articles of the Charter.

Article 16 of the Charter, protecting the right to health, was also taken into consideration by the Commission. The failure of the Government to provide basic services such as safe drinking water and electricity and the shortage of medicine, as alleged in one communication, was held to constitute a violation of this article. The Commission also held that closures of universities and secondary schools, as described in the same communication, constituted a violation of article 17.

IV:2

In conclusion, the Commission held that the facts constituted serious and massive violations of the Charter, namely of articles 4, 5, 6, 7, 8, 16 and 17. The Commission brought the matter to the attention of the Assembly of Heads of State and Government of the Organization of African Unity under article 58 of the Charter.

(e) *Bámaca Velásquez* case (*Guatemala*)
(Inter-American Court of Human Rights)[40]

On 30 August 1996, the Inter-American Commission on Human Rights submitted an application to the Inter-American Court of Human Rights against the Republic of Guatemala. It originated in a petition received on 5 March 1993 by the Commission. The purpose of the application was for the Court to decide whether the State had violated the rights of Efraín Bámaca Velásquez in respect of the right to juridical personality in article 3, the right to life in article 4, the right to humane treatment in article 5, the right to personal liberty in article 7, the right to a fair trial in article 8, the right to judicial protection in article 25 and the obligation to respect rights in article 1 of the American Convention on Human Rights, as well as in respect of articles 1, 2 and 6 of the Inter-American Convention to Prevent and Punish Torture and article 3 common to the Geneva Conventions of 12 August 1949.

The Commission also requested the Court to call on the State to identify and punish those responsible for the violations, to adopt the necessary reforms to the training programmes and regulations of the Guatemalan armed forces so that military operations were conducted in conformity with the laws and customs applicable to internal conflicts and to compensate the victim's next of kin. In its final arguments, the Commission additionally requested the Court to declare that article 8 of the Inter-American Convention to Prevent and Punish Torture had been violated.

Proceedings and conclusions of the Court

In summarizing the facts set out in the Commission's application, the Court said that Efraín Bámaca Velásquez, known as "Comandante Everardo", formed part of the Revolutionary Organization of the People in Arms (ORPA), one of the guerrilla groups that made up the Guatemalan National Revolutionary Unit (URNG). He led this group's Luis Ixmatá Front. On 12 March 1992, he disappeared after an encounter between the army and the guerrilla in the western part of Guatemala. He was alive when the Guatemalan armed forces took him prisoner. They imprisoned him secretly in several military installations, tortured and eventually executed him. Moreover, the State concurred in denial of justice and concealment, by failing to provide

---

[40] See Inter-American Court of Human Rights, Series C: *Decisions and Judgments*, No. 70 (2001), petition No. 11129, judgment of 25 November 2000.

any legal protection or compensation for the crimes perpetrated against Mr. Bámaca Velásquez, to investigate adequately his disappearance and death and to punish those responsible.

The Commission and the State presented documentary evidence, and the Court heard the oral testimony of witnesses, an expert in the administration of justice in Guatemala, a forensic anthropologist, lawyers, members of guerrilla movements, and members and former members of the Guatemalan armed forces.

Having evaluated the evidence, the Court proceeded to consider the relevant facts. It found, *inter alia*, the following to have been proved. At the time when the events took place, Guatemala was convulsed by an internal conflict. In 1992, the ORPA guerrilla group operated on four fronts in Guatemala, one of which was the Luis Ix-matá Front commanded by Efraín Bámaca Velásquez. On 15 February 1992, the Quetzal Task Force, established by the army to combat the guerrillas in the south-western zone of the country, began its activities. It was the practice of the army to capture guerrillas and keep them in clandestine confinement in order to obtain information that was useful for the army, through physical and mental torture. These guerrillas were frequently transferred from one military detachment to another. After several months, they were used as guides to determine where the guerrilla were active and to identify individuals who were fighting with the guerrillas. Many of those detained were then executed, which completed the figure of forced disappearance.

At the time of the events, various former guerrillas were collaborating with the army and providing it with useful information. On 12 March 1992, there was an armed encounter between guerrilla fighters belonging to the Luis Ixmatá Front and members of the army during which Efraín Bámaca Velásquez was captured alive. He was wounded and taken by his captors to a military detachment. During his confinement there, he remained tied up with his eyes covered, and he was submitted to unlawful coercion and threats while being interrogated. He was eventually transferred to another military base where he, during July 1992, was interrogated and tortured. He was the last time seen in the infirmary of that military base, tied to a metal bed.

As a result of these events, several judicial proceedings were initiated in Guatemala, including petitions for *habeas corpus*, a special pre-trial investigation procedure and various criminal lawsuits. None of these was effective, and the whereabouts of Mr. Bámaca Velásquez remained unknown. On various occasions, as a result of the judicial proceedings, exhumation procedures were carried out in order to find his body. However, there were no positive results because of obstruction by State agents.

The phenomenon of forced disappearance of persons was referred to by the Commission in its final written arguments. It stated that the arbitrary detention, solitary

IV:2

confinement, isolation and torture of the victim in this type of situation were followed, in most cases, by the execution of the victim and the concealment of his corpse, accompanied by an official silence, denials and obstruction. The family, friends and companions remained anxious and uncertain about the fate of the victim. Forced disappearance attempted to erase any trace of the crime in order to ensure the total impunity of those who committed it.

The Commission then argued that although Guatemala had signed, but not ratified, the Inter-American Convention on Forced Disappearance of Persons, this treaty had entered into effect in 1996 and that this Convention constituted an important instrument to classify and understand forced disappearances and to interpret the American Convention on Human Rights, pursuant to its article 29. Furthermore, the Commission stated, in Latin America most victims of dirty wars did not die in combat or accidentally in crossfire between the armed rebel groups and the army. Many of them were confined in clandestine detention centres, tortured and buried without dignity or respect in unnamed graves or thrown from aeroplanes into the sea.

According to the Commission, there was in Guatemala, at the time of the facts of this case, a State practice that amounted to the phenomenon of forced disappearance. Mr. Bámaca Velásquez was a victim of this practice.

In article II of the Inter-American Convention on Forced Disappearance of Persons, forced disappearance was defined as

> the act of depriving a person or persons of his or their freedom, in whatever way, perpetrated by agents of the State or by persons or groups of persons acting with the authorization, support or acquiescence of the State, followed by an absence of information or a refusal to acknowledge that deprivation of freedom or to give information on the whereabouts of that person, thereby impeding his or her recourse to the applicable legal remedies and procedural guarantees.

The Commission also made reference to a provision in the Guatemalan criminal code establishing the crime of forced disappearance.

Citing its case law, the Court observed that involuntary or forced disappearance constituted a multiple and continuing violation of a number of rights protected by the American Convention on Human Rights. Not only did it produce an arbitrary deprivation of liberty, but it also endangered personal integrity, safety and the very life of the detainee. Moreover, it placed the victim in a state of complete defencelessness, resulting in other related crimes.

This phenomenon also showed a disregard by the State of its duty to organize its apparatus so as to guarantee the rights recognized in the Convention. Therefore, when it implemented or tolerated activities that resulted in forced or involuntary disappearances, when it did not investigate them adequately and did not punish those responsible, the State violated the obligation to respect the rights protected by the Convention. Furthermore, the secret execution of those detained, and concealment of the corpse, had as one of their purposes the elimination of material evidence of the crime to ensure the impunity of those responsible.

Due to the nature of the phenomenon and its probative difficulties, the Court in previous cases had established that if it had been proved that the State had promoted or tolerated the practice of forced disappearance of persons and the case of a specific person could be linked to this practice, either by circumstantial or indirect evidence, or both, or by logical inference, then this specific disappearance might be considered to have been proven.

In the present case, the Court considered it proven that the army had a practice of capturing guerrillas, detaining them clandestinely without advising the competent, independent and impartial judicial authorities, physically and mentally torturing them in order to obtain information and, eventually, killing them. The Court also deemed it to have been proved that the disappearance of Mr. Bámaca Velásquez was related to this practice.

In view of the fact that these actions were attributable to agents of the State, the international legal obligations of Guatemala as a State party to the Convention were at issue. Furthermore, it had been shown that the various domestic remedies invoked had not resulted in the prosecution and punishment of those responsible. Guatemala had even accepted its international responsibility in this respect, stating that it had still not been possible for the competent bodies to identify the persons or person criminally responsible for the unlawful acts that were the subject of this application.

As it had been proved that the detention and disappearance of Mr. Bámaca Velásquez occured and that they might be attributed to the State, the Court would examine these facts in the light of the Convention.

As to the alleged violation of article 7 of the Convention, protecting the right to personal liberty, the Commission claimed that the detention of Mr. Bámaca Velásquez by agents of the Guatemalan armed forces and his captivity in a clandestine centre, without presenting him before the judicial authorities, violated that right.

Citing its case law, the Court reiterated that article 7 regulated the necessary guarantees to safeguard personal liberty. With regard to arbitrary arrest or imprisonment, the Court had found that, although some forms might be legal, they might still be considered to be incompatible with respect for the fundamental rights of the individual, because they were, for example, unreasonable, unforeseeable or out of proportion.

The Court observed that like the European Court of Human Rights, it had stated that the prompt judicial supervision of detentions was of particular importance in order to prevent arbitrariness. An individual who had been deprived of his freedom without any type of judicial supervision should be liberated or immediately brought before a judge, because the essential purpose of article 7 of the Convention was to protect the liberty of the individual against interference by the State. The European Court had stated that although the word "immediately" should be interpreted according to the special characteristics of each case, no situation, however grave, granted the authorities the power to unduly prolong the period of detention without affecting article 5, paragraph 3, of the Convention for the Protection of Human Rights and Fundamental Freedoms. It had emphasized that failure to acknowledge the detention of an individual was a complete denial of the guarantees that had to be granted and an even greater violation of the same article. The Inter-American Court had indicated that by protecting personal liberty, a safeguard was also provided for both the physical liberty of the individual and his personal safety, in a context where the absence of guarantees might result in the subversion of the rule of law and deprive those arrested of the minimum legal protection.

In cases of forced disappearance of persons, the Court had stated, *inter alia*, that this represented a phenomenon of arbitrary deprivation of liberty, an infringement of a detainee's right to be taken without delay before a judge and to invoke the appropriate procedures to review the legality of the arrest, all in violation of article 7 of the Convention.

The Court established as proven that Mr. Bámaca Velásquez had been detained by the Guatemalan army in clandestine detention centres for at least four months, thus violating article 7. Although this was a case of the detention of a guerrilla during an internal conflict, the detainee should have been ensured the guarantees that existed under the rule of law, and he should have been submitted to a legal proceeding. In previous cases, the Court had already stated that although the State had the right and obligation to guarantee its security and maintain public order, it had to execute its actions within limits and according to procedures that preserved both public safety and the fundamental rights of the human person.

The Court concluded that the State had violated article 7 of the Convention to the detriment of Mr. Bámaca Velásquez.

As to the alleged violation of article 5 of the Convention, protecting the right to humane treatment, the Commission claimed that the forced disappearance of Mr. Bámaca Velásquez and his confinement in a clandestine detention centre constituted a violation of that right, because they represented cruel and inhuman treatment that according to the Court's jurisprudence, injured the physical and moral integrity of the person and his dignity.

The Court considered that it should proceed to examine the possible violation of article 5 of the Convention from two different perspectives. First, it should examine whether or not there was a violation of paragraphs 1 and 2 of the article to the detriment of Mr. Bámaca Velásquez. Then it should evaluate whether the next of kin of the victim were also subjected to the violation of their right to humane treatment.

It had been proved that Mr. Bámaca Velásquez was detained by members of the army and that his detention had not been communicated to a competent judge or to his next of kin. The Court recalled that it had already established that a person who was unlawfully detained was in an exacerbated situation of vulnerability creating a real risk that his other rights, such as the right to humane treatment and to be treated with dignity, would be violated. It then referred to a number of cases in which it had pronounced on prolonged isolation and solitary confinement. The Court had stated that in international human rights law, incommunicado detention was considered to be an exceptional instrument and that its use during detention might constitute an act against human dignity.

With regard to the treatment of Mr. Bámaca Velásquez by the State authorities during his detention, the Court had taken into account evidence given by former guerrillas which indicated that he had been tortured by State agents at the various military bases where he was kept captive.

The Court referred to earlier cases in which it had ruled that in situations of forced disappearance, the State's defense could not rely on the failure of the plaintiff to present evidence in the proceedings. In such cases, the State controlled the means to clarify the facts that have occurred in its jurisdiction. Therefore, it was in practice necessary to rely on the cooperation of the State itself in order to obtain the required evidence.

The evidence gathered in the present case led the Court to consider proved the abuses committed against Mr. Bámaca Velásquez during his detention in various military installations. The Court then had to determine whether such abuses constituted torture or cruel, inhuman or degrading treatment. Clearly, it was important to state that both types of acts were strictly prohibited under any circumstance.

IV:2

The Court had previously observed that when a State faced a situation of internal upheaval, this should not result in restrictions in the protection of the physical integrity of the person. Specifically, the Court had indicated that any use of force that was not strictly necessary to ensure proper behaviour on the part of the detainee constituted an assault on the dignity of the person in violation of article 5 of the Convention.

According to article 1 of the Convention against Torture and Other Cruel, Inhuman or Degrading Treatment or Punishment, the Court noted, torture implied deliberately inflicting punishment or physical or mental suffering in order to intimidate, punish, investigate or prevent crimes, punish their commitment or any other end.

Article 2 of the Inter-American Convention to Prevent and Punish Torture defined torture as any act intentionally performed whereby physical or mental pain or suffering was inflicted on a person for purposes of criminal investigation, as a means of intimidation, as personal punishment, as a preventive measure, as a penalty or to any other purpose. Torture should also be understood to be the use of methods upon a person intended to obliterate the personality of the victim or to diminish his physical or mental capacities, even if they did not cause him physical pain or mental anguish. Furthermore, it was added, the concept of torture should not include physical or mental pain or suffering that was inherent in or solely the consequence of lawful measures, provided that they did not include the performance of the acts or use of the methods referred to in the provision.

The Court considered that the acts denounced in this case were deliberately prepared and inflicted in order to obtain information from Mr. Bámaca Velásquez which was relevant for the army. According to the evidence, the victim had been submitted to grave acts of physical and mental violence during a prolonged period of time for the said purpose and thus intentionally placed in a situation of anguish and intense physical suffering which could only be qualified as both physical and mental torture.

Concerning the right to humane treatment of the victim's next of kin, the Court recalled previous occasions on which it had concluded that the next of kin of victims of human rights violations had themselves become victims. In one case, for example, the Court ruled that the victims' mothers had suffered owing to the negligence of the authorities in establishing the victims' identities. The authorities had neglected to locate the relatives of the victims immediately and notify them of the deaths, thus delaying the opportunity to bury them according to their traditions, and they had failed to investigate the crimes and punish those responsible. In that case, the victims' next of kin also suffered because of the treatment of the corpses. These were discovered in an uninhabited place, showing signs of extreme violence and exposed to the weather and the attention of animals. Such treatment of the victims' remains constituted cruel and inhuman treatment for the families.

The Court also referred to the jurisprudence of the European Court of Human Rights. That Court had accepted that when fundamental human rights were violated, the persons closest to the victim might also be considered victims. Recently, it had developed the concept further, emphasizing that the following were some of the issues to be considered: the closeness of the family relationship; the degree to which the family member was a witness to the events related to the disappearance; the way in which the family member was involved in attempts to obtain information about the disappearance of the victim; and the State's response to the steps undertaken.

Similarly, the United Nations Human Rights Committee, interpreting the International Covenant on Civil and Political Rights, had stated that the next of kin of disappeared people should be considered victims of ill-treatment, among other violations. In one case, the Committee stated that it understood the profound grief and anguish that the author of the communication had suffered, owing to the disappearance of her daughter and the continued uncertainty about her fate and her whereabouts.

Taking into account the circumstances of the case under consideration, and in particular the continued obstruction of efforts to learn the truth, the concealment of the corpse, the obstruction of the attempted exhumation procedures by various public authorities, the official refusal to provide relevant information and the ignorance of the whereabouts of Mr. Bámaca Velásquez, the Court considered that the suffering to which the next of kin had been subjected clearly constituted cruel, inhuman or degrading treatment, violating article 5, paragraphs 1 and 2, of the Convention.

The Court concluded that the State had violated these provisions to the detriment of Mr. Bámaca Velásquez and also that of his next of kin.

As to the alleged violation of article 4 of the Convention, protecting the right to life, the Commission claimed that in presuming that Mr. Bámaca Velásquez was dead, the agents of the Guatemalan armed forces had violated that right when they executed him while he was secretly detained by the army.

The Court noted that it had already been proved that Mr. Bámaca Velásquez had been captured and retained in the hands of the army and that this was a case of forced disappearance. Citing a previous judgment, the Court had already made it clear that any person deprived of liberty had the right to live in conditions of detention that were compatible with his personal dignity and that the State had to guarantee his right to life and to humane treatment. Consequently, the State, as responsible for detention establishments, was the guarantor of such rights of those detained.

The Court then referred to a statement by the Human Rights Committee in a general comment on article 6 of the Covenant. The protection against arbitrary deprivation

IV:2

of life, explicitly required by article 6, paragraph 1, was of paramount importance. The Committee considered that States parties should take measures not only to prevent and punish deprivation of life by criminal acts, but also to prevent arbitrary killing by their own security forces. The deprivation of life by the authorities of the State was a matter of utmost gravity. Therefore, the State had strictly to control and limit the circumstances in which a person might be deprived of his life by such authorities.

In this case, the circumstances of the detention of Mr. Bámaca Velásquez, the fact that he was a was a guerrilla commander, the State practice of forced disappearances and extrajudicial executions and the passage of eight years and eight months since he was captured caused the Court to presume that he had been executed.

As the Court had indicated, although the State had the right and obligation to guarantee its security and maintain public order, its powers were not unlimited, because it had the obligation, at all times, to apply procedures that were in accordance with the law and to respect the fundamental rights of each individual in its jurisdiction.

The Court concluded that the State had violated article 4 of the Convention to the detriment of Mr. Bámaca Velásquez.

As to the alleged violations of articles 8 and 25 of the Convention, protecting the right to a fair trial and the right to judicial protection, respectively, in relation to article 1 on the obligation to respect rights, the Commission claimed that the State, in a number of ways, had violated those rights to to the detriment of Mr. Bámaca Velásquez and his next of kin.

The Court pointed out that although numerous domestic recourses had been attempted in order to determine the whereabouts of Mr. Bámaca Velásquez, such as the petitions for *habeas corpus*, the special pre-trial investigation procedure and the criminal actions, none of them had been effective, and his whereabouts remained unknown.

It further observed that it was not sufficient to embody such recourses in law, they had also to be effective. They had to give results or responses to violations of the rights established in the Convention. Citing its case law, the Court stated that among the essential judicial guarantees, *habeas corpus* represented the ideal means of guaranteeing liberty, controlling respect for the life and integrity of a person and preventing his disappearance. It was also a means of protecting the individual from torture or other cruel, inhuman or degrading punishment or treatment. However, three petitions for *habeas corpus* were filed in this case, but they did not protect the victim from the acts committed against him by State agents.

The Court had previously indicated that as part of their general obligations under the Convention, States had a positive obligation of guarantee, according to article 1, paragraph 1, with regard to persons within their jurisdiction. This required States parties to remove any impediments that might prevent individuals from enjoying their rights under the Convention. Any State tolerating circumstances or conditions that prevented individuals from having recourse to legal remedies designed to protect their rights was consequently in violation of that provision. The Court concluded that the State in this case had violated articles 8 and 25, in relation to article 1, paragraph 1, of the Convention.

As to the alleged failure to comply with article 1, paragraph 1, of the Convention in relation to article 3 common to the Geneva Conventions, providing protection in conflicts not of an international character, the Commission claimed, *inter alia*, the following. The State had violated its obligation to respect and guarantee the rights established in the Convention. Even when a State faced a rebel movement or terrorism that truly threatened its independence or security, forced disappearances, summary executions and torture were strictly forbidden under article 27, paragraph 2, of the Convention. In accordance with common article 3, providing for prohibitions against violations of the right to life and ensuring protection against torture and summary executions, and the provisions of the Convention, Mr. Bámaca Velásquez should have received humane treatment.

The Court considered it to be proven that when the events of this case took place, there was an internal armed conflict in Guatemala. The Court observed that this fact, instead of releasing the State from its obligations to respect and guarantee human rights, required it to act in accordance with such obligations. Therefore, as required by article 3 common to the Geneva Conventions, the State should grant those persons who were not participating directly in the hostilities, or who had been placed *hors de combat* for whatever reason, humane treatment, without any unfavourable distinctions. In particular, attempts against the life and personal integrity of those protected by common article 3 were prohibited at any place and time.

The Court could not declare that a State was internationally accountable for the violation of international treaties that it was not competent to apply and interpret. However, it could observe that certain acts or omissions that violated human rights, protected by treaties it was competent to apply and interpret, also violated other international instruments for the protection of the individual, such as the Geneva Conventions and, in particular, their common article 3.

Indeed, the Court observed, there was a similarity between the content of common article 3 and the provisions of the Convention and other international instruments regarding non-derogable human rights, such as the right to life and the right not to be

IV:2

subjected to torture or cruel, inhuman or degrading treatment. It had already indicated in a previous judgment that relevant provisions of the Geneva Conventions might be taken into account when interpreting the American Convention.

According to article 1, paragraph 1, of the Convention, Guatemala was obliged to respect the rights and freedoms recognized in the Convention and to make the necessary legislative, executive and administrative arrangements so as to guarantee persons within its jurisdiction the free and full exercise of human rights. This was essential, because an act or omission of a public authority might involve the responsibility of the State in the terms set out in the Convention.

The Court had confirmed that there existed in Guatemala a situation of impunity with regard to the facts of this case, because despite the State's obligation to prevent and investigate, it did not do so. Citing a previous judgment, the Court understood impunity to be the total lack of investigation, prosecution, capture, trial and conviction of those responsible for violations of the rights protected by the Convention, in view of the fact that the State had the obligation to use all the legal means at its disposal to combat that situation, since impunity fostered chronic recidivism of human right violations and total defencelessness of victims and their relatives.

In its case law, the Court had clearly indicated that the obligation to investigate had to be fulfilled in a serious manner and not as a mere formality preordained to be ineffective. An investigation had to have an objective and be assumed by the State as its own legal duty, not as a step taken by private interests depending upon the initiative of the victim or his family or upon their offer of proof, without an effective search for the truth by the Government.

The Court noted that the violations of the right to personal liberty and security, to life, to physical, mental and moral integrity and to judicial guarantees and protection, established in the judgment, were attributable to Guatemala, which had the obligation to respect these rights and to guarantee them. Consequently, Guatemala was responsible for the non-observance of article 1, paragraph 1, in relation to violations of articles 4, 5, 7, 8 and 25 of the Convention.

As to the alleged violation of article 3 of the Convention, protecting the right to recognition of juridical personality, the Court did not find that the State had violated that right.

Finally, as to the alleged violation of articles 1, 2, 6 and 8 of the Inter-American Convention to Prevent and Punish Torture, developing the principles contained in article 5 of the American Convention, the Commission claimed that the treatment which Mr. Bámaca Velásquez had suffered constituted torture in the terms of the former instrument.

The Court declared that it had the responsibility to exercise its competence to apply the Inter-American Convention to Prevent and Punish Torture, ratified by Guatemala in 1987. Indeed, it had previously had the occasion to apply this Convention and to conclude that a State was responsible for violations of its provisions.

In this case, it had been shown that Mr. Bámaca Velásquez was tortured whilst secretly imprisoned in military installations. It was clear that the State had not effectively prevented such acts, and by not investigating them, it had failed to punish those responsible. Article 8 of the Convention expressly embodied the State's obligation to proceed immediately *de oficio* in cases such as this one. However, the State had not acted in accordance with these provisions.

It had also been confirmed that despite the numerous proceedings initiated in order to discover the whereabouts of Mr. Bámaca Velásquez, these were ineffective. The denial of judicial protection proven also signified that the State had not prevented or effectively investigated the torture to which the victim was being submitted. Consequently, the State had failed to fulfill its commitments made under the Convention.

Therefore, the Court concluded, the State had failed to comply with its obligations to prevent and punish torture in the terms of articles 1, 2, 6 and 8 of the Convention to the detriment of Mr. Bámaca Velásquez.

In sum, the Court unanimously found that the State had violated articles 4, 5, 7, 8 and 25 of the Convention and that it had not complied with its obligations under article 1, paragraph 1, of the American Convention on Human Rights as well as under articles 1, 2, 6 and 8 of the Inter-American Convention to Prevent and Punish Torture. Four judges filed individual opinions.

The Court decided that the State should order an investigation to determine the persons responsible for the human rights violations referred to in the judgment. The State should also publicly disseminate the results of such investigation and punish those responsible. The Court further decided that the State should remedy the damages caused by the violations under article 63, paragraph 1, of the Convention.

(f) *Ergi* v. *Turkey*
(European Court of Human Rights)[41]

The case was referred to the European Court of Human Rights on 9 July 1997 by the European Commission of Human Rights. It originated in an application against the Republic of Turkey lodged with the Commission on 25 March 1994 by Muharrem Ergi, a Turkish national, who brought the application on his own behalf and that of his deceased sister, Havva Ergi, and her young daughter. The object of the request was to obtain a decision as to whether the facts of the case disclosed a breach by the respondent State of its obligations under, *inter alia*, article 2 of the Convention for the Protection of Human Rights and Fundamental Freedoms.

The facts

The applicant, a Turkish citizen of Kurdish origin, lived in a village in southeast Turkey. He stated that his house was in the middle of the village. On 29 September 1993, his father and sister, Havva Ergi, were sleeping on the balcony on the upper part of the house. When gunfire broke out, they took shelter inside the house, but Havva Ergi went out onto the veranda to collect something. She was hit in the head by a bullet when she was on the threshold and died immediately.

There were divergent versions as to the circumstances which led to the killing. The applicant claimed that it was the result of a retaliatory operation by the security forces against the village. The Government asserted that there had been a clash between those forces and members of the Workers Party of Kurdistan (PKK) around the village and that the bullet killing her had not originated from the military side.

The applicant complained of the unlawful killing of his sister by soldiers. He relied, *inter alia*, on article 2 of the Convention, protecting the right to life.

After having declared the application admissible, the Commission in its report found that in relation to article 2, there had been a violation on account of the planning and conduct of the security forces' operation and the failure to carry out an effective investigation into the death of the applicant's sister.

The law

As to the alleged violation of article 2 of the Convention, the Court noted that on the Government's own account, the security forces had carried out an ambush operation

---

[41] See European Court of Human Rights, *Reports of Judgments and Decisions*, 1998-IV, p. 1751, application No. 23818/94, judgment of 28 July 1998.

and engaged in an armed clash with the PKK in the vicinity of the village. The Government disputed that the bullet killing Havva Ergi was fired by the security forces. The Court, like the Commission, considered that there was an insufficient factual and evidentiary basis on which to conclude that the applicant's sister was, beyond reasonable doubt, intentially killed by the security forces in the circumstances alleged by the applicant.

The Court then, however, moved on to consider alleged failure to comply with other requirements of article 2 of the Convention. It was not convinced by the Government's submission that it was inappropriate for the Court to review whether the planning and conduct of the operation was consistent with that article.

In this regard, the Court recalled that the text of article 2, read as a whole, demonstrated that paragraph 2 did not primarily define instances where it was permitted intentionally to kill an individual, but described situations where it was permitted to use force that might result, as an unintended outcome, in the deprivation of life. The force used had to be strictly proportionate to the achievement of the aims set out in that paragraph. In keeping with the importance of this provision in a democratic society, the Court had, in making its assessment, to subject deprivations of life to the most careful scrutiny, particularly where deliberate lethal force was used. It had to take into consideration not only the actions of the agents of the State actually administering the force, but also all the surrounding circumstances, including such matters as the planning and control of the actions under examination, as the Court had found in a previous judgment. Furthermore, under article 2 read in conjunction with article 1 of the Convention, stipulating the obligation of States parties to respect human rights, the State might be required to take certain measures in order to secure an effective enjoyment of the right to life.

In the light of such considerations, the Court observed, the responsibility of the State was not confined to circumstances where there was significant evidence that misdirected fire from agents of the State had killed a civilian. It might also be engaged where they failed to take all feasible precautions in the choice of means and methods of a security operation mounted against an opposing group with a view to avoiding and, in any event, to minimizing incidental loss of civilian life.

Thus, even though it had not been established beyond reasonable doubt that the bullet killing Havva Ergi had been fired by the security forces, the Court had to consider whether their operation had been planned and conducted in such a way as to avoid or minimize, to the greatest extent possible, any risk to the lives of the villagers, including from the fire power of the PKK members.

IV:2

The Court considered that it was probable that the bullet killing Havva Ergi had been fired from the south or southwest, that the security forces had been present in the south and that there had been a real risk to the lives of the civilian population through being exposed to cross fire between the security forces and the PKK. In the light of the failure of the State authorities to adduce direct evidence on the planning and conduct of the operation, the Court found that it could reasonably be inferred that insufficient precautions had been taken to protect the lives of the civilian population

Furthermore, concerning the alleged inadequacy of the investigation, the Court stated that it had attached particular weight to the procedural requirement implicit in article 2 of the Convention. The obligation to protect the right to life under that article, again read in conjunction with article 1, required that there should be some form of effective official investigation when individuals had been killed as a result of the use of force by agents of the State. This obligation was not confined to cases where it had been established that the killing was caused by such an agent. The mere knowledge of the killing on the part of the authorities gave rise to an obligation to carry out an effective investigation into the circumstances surrounding the death.

The authorities had failed to comply with this requirement. Neither the prevalence of violent armed clashes nor the high incidence of fatalities could displace the obligation to ensure that an effective, independent investigation was conducted into the deaths arising out of clashes involving the security forces, in particular in cases such as the present where the circumstances in many respects were unclear.

The Court unanimously found that the Turkish authorities had failed to protect Havva Ergi's right to life on account of the defects in the planning and conduct of the security forces' operation and the lack of an adequate and effective investigation. Accordingly, there had been a violation of article 2 of the Convention. The Court also found, by eight votes to one, violations of articles 13 and 25, paragraph 1.

Under the then article 50 of the Convention, allowing the Court to afford just satisfaction to an injured party, under specified circumstances, when there had been a violation of the Convention, the Court held, by eight votes to one, that the respondent State was to pay, in respect of non-pecuniary damage, 1,000 pounds sterling to the applicant and, unanimously, 5,000 pounds to Havva Ergi's daughter, or to the guardian on her behalf. In respect of costs and expenses, the Court unanimously held that the State should pay the applicant 12,000 pounds together with any value-added tax that might be chargeable, less the amount received by way of legal aid from the Council of Europe.

3. International Crimes

A. INTRODUCTION

Whereas the preceding chapters of this book focus on human rights, this chapter focuses on crimes. However, some human rights violations, for example in respect of the right to life and the prohibition of torture, are also very serious crimes. They are crimes everywhere and at all times, in times of peace as well as in times of war, and when there is tension and disorder within societies. This chapter deals with crimes committed in times of war and, in particular, serious breaches of international humanitarian law committed in the territory of the former Yugoslavia since 1991 and genocide and crimes against humanity committed in Rwanda in 1994.

The principle reason for focusing on crimes committed in such circumstances is that there is a number of cases relevant to police in which people have been convicted and sentenced by the International Tribunal for the former Yugoslavia[1] and the International Criminal Tribunal for Rwanda,[2] respectively.

Under article 1 of the Statute of the International Tribunal for the former Yugoslavia, this Tribunal is empowered to prosecute persons responsible for serious violations of international humanitarian law committed in the territory of the former Yugoslavia since 1991, in accordance with the provisions of the Statute. The specific crimes for which the International Tribunal may prosecute persons are set out in articles 2 to 5 of the Statute.

Article 2 refers to grave breaches of the Geneva Conventions of 12 August 1949 and lists acts against persons or property protected under the provisions of the relevant Geneva Convention. These include wilful killing, torture or inhuman treatment, wilfully causing great suffering or serious injury to body or health and taking civilians as hostages.

Article 3 refers to violations of the laws and customs of war. Such violations include, but are not limited to, five listed categories, such as employment of poisonous weapons or other weapons calculated to cause unnecessary suffering, wanton de-

---

[1] See part I, chap. 1, sect. D (*f*) (*supra*, pp. 17-19).
[2] See part I, chap. 1, sect. D (*g*) (*supra*, pp. 19-22).

struction of cities, towns or villages, or devastation not justified by military necessity, and plunder of public or private property.

Article 4 deals with genocide. In paragraph 2 of the article, genocide is defined as any of a number of acts, listed in the paragraph, committed with the intent to destroy, in whole or in part, a national, ethnical, racial or religious group as such. The acts listed include killing members of the group, causing serious bodily or mental harm to members of the group and deliberately inflicting on the group conditions of life calculated to bring about its physical destruction in whole or in part. Under paragraph 3, the following acts are punishable: genocide; conspiracy to commit genocide; direct and public incitement to commit genocide; attempt to commit genocide; and complicity in genocide.

Article 5, finally, refers to crimes against humanity, namely crimes, listed in the article, committed in armed conflict, whether international or internal in character, and directed against any civilian population. The crimes are murder, extermination, enslavement, deportation, imprisonment, torture, rape, persecutions on political, racial and religious grounds as well as other inhumane acts.

Under article 7, paragraph 1, of the Statute, any person who planned, instigated, ordered, committed or otherwise aided or abetted in the planning, preparation or execution of a crime, referred to in articles 2 to 5, shall be individually responsible for the crime. Such responsibility is reinforced by provisions in article 7, paragraphs 2 to 4, stipulating, respectively, that the official position of any accused person shall not relieve the person of criminal responsibility, nor shall the fact that the act was committed by a subordinate, if certain requirements are met, or the fact that the accused acted pursuant to an order of a Government or of a superior. However, the fact that the act was ordered may be considered in mitigation of punishment.

Under article 1 of the Statute of the International Criminal Tribunal for Rwanda, this Tribunal has the power to prosecute persons responsible for serious violations of international humanitarian law committed in the territory of Rwanda, and Rwandan citizens responsible for such violations committed in the territory of neighbouring States between 1 January and 31 December 1994, in accordance with the provisions of the Statute. The specific crimes for which the International Tribunal may prosecute persons are set out in articles 2 to 4 of the Statute.

Article 2 gives the International Tribunal the power to prosecute persons committing genocide or other acts as defined in the article. Genocide and the other prohibited acts are identical to those described in article 4, paragraphs 2 and 3, of the Statute of the International Tribunal for the former Yugoslavia.

Article 3, dealing with crimes against humanity, empowers the International Tribunal to prosecute persons responsible for specified crimes when committed as part of a widespread or systematic attack against any civilian population on national, political, ethnic, racial or religious grounds. In contrast to the Statute of the International Tribunal for the former Yugoslavia, no reference is made to armed conflict, but the specified crimes are the same.

Article 4 refers to violations of article 3 common to the Geneva Conventions of 12 August 1949 and the Protocol Additional to the Geneva Conventions of 12 August 1949, and relating to the Protection of Victims of Non-International Armed Conflicts (Protocol II). The International Tribunal has the power to prosecute persons committing or ordering to be committed serious violations of common article 3, applicable in conflicts not of an international character, and the provisions of Protocol II. Such violations include, but are not limited to: violence to life, health and physical or mental well-being of persons, in particular murder as well as cruel treatment such as torture, mutilation or any form of corporal punishment; collective punishments; taking of hostages; acts of terrorism; outrages upon personal dignity, in particular humiliating and degrading treatment, rape, enforced prostitution and any form of indecent assault; pillage; the passing of sentences and the carrying out of executions without previous judgment pronounced by a regularly constituted court, affording all the judicial guarantees recognized as indispensable by civilized peoples; and threats to commit any such acts.

Under article 6, paragraph 1, of the Statute, any person who planned, instigated, ordered, committed or otherwise aided or abetted in the planning, preparation or execution of a crime, referred to in articles 2 to 4, shall be individually responsible for the crime. Such responsibility is reinforced by provisions in article 6, paragraphs 2 to 4, stipulating, respectively, that the official position of any accused person shall not relieve the person of criminal responsibility, nor shall the fact that the act was committed by a subordinate, if certain requirements are met, or the fact that the accused acted pursuant to an order of a Government or of a superior. However, the fact that the act was ordered may be considered in mitigation of punishment.

As indicated in the introduction to this part of the book,[3] one of the reasons why police officials need to understand principles and provisions of humanitarian law, and human rights law, in times of armed conflict and internal disturbance and tension, is that they may be required to investigate crimes arising out of such situations. Investigations of this kind may occur in an international context where, for example, police officials are included in teams of forensic and legal experts, or in a domestic context.

---

[3] See part IV, chap. 1 (*supra*, p. 529).

IV:3

In respect of domestic investigations, it is important to note that each one of the four Geneva Conventions obliges States parties to provide effective penal sanctions for persons committing or ordering to be committed grave breaches of the Conventions. They are also required to search for such persons and bring them, regardless of nationality, before their own courts or hand them over for trial to another State party concerned under articles 49, 50, 129 and 146 of the respective Convention. Article 85 of the Protocol Additional to the Geneva Conventions of 12 August 1949, and relating to the Protection of Victims of International Armed Conflicts (Protocol I), states that the provisions relating to the repression of breaches and grave breaches of the Conventions shall apply to the repression of breaches and grave breaches of the Protocol. This article, and article 11 of the Protocol, extend the list of acts defined as grave breaches.

These provisions are clearly relevant to police, because law enforcement and investigation of crimes are police matters. Enforcement of domestic law embodying the provisions required by the Conventions, either during or in the aftermath of an international armed conflict, requires the application of police skills within a singular legal, social and political context.

There are no comparable provisions in Protocol II, protecting victims of non-international armed conflicts. However, many of the acts prohibited by this Protocol amount to crimes under the domestic laws of the States parties and as such would be investigated by police.

B. REVIEW OF CASES

(*a*) International Tribunal for the former Yugoslavia

From the jurisprudence of the International Tribunal for the Prosecution of Persons Responsible for Serious Violations of International Humanitarian Law Committed in the Territory of the Former Yugoslavia since 1991, three cases are included in this chapter of the book.

The case *Prosecutor* v. *Anto Furundzija*,[4] summarized in section C[5] and also cited in connection with the prohibition of torture,[6] concerned the trial of the local commander of a special unit of the military police within the armed forces of the Croatian Community of Herzeg-Bosna, known as the Croatian Defence Council. Under

---

[4] See case No. IT-95-17/1-T, judgment of 10 December 1998 (trial chamber); see also case No. IT-95-17/1-A, judgment of 21 July 2000 (appeals chamber).
[5] See part IV, chap. 3, sect. C (*infra*, pp. 616-636).
[6] See part II, chap. 3, sect. A (*supra*, pp. 126-127).

the amended indictment, the accused, in his capacity as a commander, and another soldier interrogated a Bosnian Moslem civilian. During the questioning, she had a knife rubbed against her inner thigh and lower stomach, and the perpetrator, the other soldier, threatened to put his knife inside her vagina if she did not tell the truth. Allegedly, the accused continued to interrogate her and another victim, a Bosnian Croat who had previously assisted her family. They were beaten on the feet with a baton. Furthermore, she was forced to have oral and vaginal sexual intercourse with the other soldier while the accused stood by, failing to intervene in any way. In relation to these alleged acts, the accused was charged with two counts of violations of the laws or customs of war, as recognized by article 3 of the Statute of the International Tribunal: torture and outrages upon personal dignity, including rape.

The incidents took place on or around 15 May 1993 in the context of a non-international armed conflict involving the armed forces of the Republic of Bosnia and Herzegovina, a State declared independent on 6 March 1992, and the armed forces of the Croatian Community of Herzeg-Bosna, which considered itself an independent political entity inside the Republic of Bosnia and Herzegovina.

A trial chamber of the International Tribunal found Anto Furundzija, as co-perpetrator, guilty of a violation of the laws or customs of war in respect of torture and, for aiding and abetting, a violation of the laws or customs of war in respect of outrages upon personal dignity, including rape. He was sentenced to ten and eight years of imprisonment, respectively, to be served concurrently, *inter se*. His appeal was dismissed by the appeals chamber of the International Tribunal.

This case is important and interesting for the purposes of this book for a number of reasons. For example, during the course of its lengthy judgment, the trial chamber recalled the test to be applied in determining the existence of an armed conflict, and it examined the scope of article 3 of the Statute. This provision refers to violations of the laws and customs of war. In applying the law to the circumstances of this case, the trial chamber delivered a comprehensive account of torture under international law. In particular, it considered torture under international humanitarian law and human rights law and identified some specific elements that pertain to torture as considered from the viewpoint of international criminal law relating to armed conflicts. The trial chamber also discussed rape as torture and as a distinct crime under international criminal law. In its judgment, the trial chamber described torture, variously, as this odious practice, this heinous phenomenon, vicious and ignominious, and this despicable practice.

In considering how to distinguish perpetration of torture from aiding an abetting torture, the trial chamber took into account modern trends in State practices of torture. It pointed out that in modern times, the infliction of torture typically involved a large

IV:3

number of people, each performing his or her individual function, and it elaborated very clear principles for identifying the individual criminal responsibility of those involved.

The two other cases included here do not involve police operations directly, but they concern matters of great importance to, in particular, the questions of command responsibility and duress as a defence to a criminal charge, respectively. Whereas the principles on command responsibility are clear, and there is agreement on these, the same is not the case with the concept of duress. Nevertheless, the observations and findings in respect of the latter could be referred to by police officials investigating crimes committed in the context of armed conflict for erudite and authoritative guidance. In any event, it is certainly clear that police leaders should not issue unlawful orders, and certainly not unlawful orders accompanied by duress.

Command responsibility is fundamental to the subject matter of this part of the book, and in the case *Prosecutor v. Zejnil Delalic, Zdravko Mucic, Hazim Delic and Esad Landzo*, also known as the *"Celebici"* case,[7] it was pronounced upon by a trial chamber of the International Tribunal. The findings on command responsibility in this case were later endorsed by the appeals chamber of the International Tribunal and have subsequently been cited in other judgments

The trial related to events which took place in 1992 in a prison camp in the village of Celebici in central Bosnia and Herzegovina. The four accused in the case were charged with numerous counts of grave breaches of the Geneva Conventions of 12 August 1949 under article 2 of the Statute and with violations of the laws or customs of war under article 3. The victims were Bosnian Serb detainees in the Celebici camp. The trial of the four accused commenced on 10 March 1997 and covered a period of some 19 months.

The crimes alleged in the indictment were serious violations of international humanitarian law, and they involved many complex issues of fact and law previously unaddressed by any international judicial body. Zejnil Delalic and Zdravko Mucic were primarily charged as superiors with responsibility, pursuant to article 7, paragraph 3, of the Statute, for crimes committed by their subordinates. Hazim Delic and Esad Landzo were primarily charged with individual criminal responsibility pursuant to article 7, paragraph 1, as direct participants in certain crimes alleged, including acts of murder, torture and rape.

---

[7] See case No. IT-96-21-T, judgment of 16 November 1998 (trial chamber); see also case No. IT-96-21-A, judgment of 20 February 2001 (appeals chamber), case No. IT-96-21-T*bis*-R117, judgment of 9 October 2001 (trial chamber) and case No. IT-96-21-A*bis*, judgment of 8 April 2003 (appeals chamber).

The trial chamber found that the armed conflict in Bosnia and Herzegovina at the relevant time was international, as the Bosnian Serb forces fighting in Bosnia and Herzegovina were under the control of the Federal Republic of Yugoslavia.

The pronouncement of the trial chamber on the concept of command responsibility was the first decision by an international judicial body on that doctrine since the cases decided in the wake of the Second World War. It concluded that the doctrine of command responsibility encompassed both military and civilian superiors on the basis of *de jure* as well as de facto positions of authority.

The trial chamber observed that although no explicit reference was made to the concept of command responsibility in the Statute, its governing principles had been incorporated into article 7, paragraph 3. In this provision, it was stated that the fact that any of the acts referred to in articles 2 to 5 of the Statute was committed by a subordinate did not relieve his superior of criminal responsibility if he knew or had reason to know that the subordinate was about to commit such acts, or had done so, and the superior failed to take the necessary and reasonable measures to prevent such acts or to punish the perpetrators of them.

Before turning its attention to the construction of this provision, the trial chamber considered briefly the legal character of this species of criminal responsibility and its status under customary international law more generally. It observed that it was a well-established norm of customary and conventional international law that military commanders and other persons occupying positions of superior authority might be held criminally responsible for the unlawful conduct of their subordinates. Such criminal liability might arise out of the positive acts of the superior, sometimes referred to as direct command responsibility, or from his culpable omissions, indirect command responsibility or command responsibility *strictu sensu*. Thus, a superior might be held criminally responsible not only for ordering, instigating or planning criminal acts carried out by his subordinates, but also for failing to take measures to prevent or repress the unlawful conduct of his subordinates. The trial chamber noted the distinct legal character of the two types of superior responsibility.

While the criminal liability of a superior for positive acts followed from general principles of accomplice liability, the criminal responsibility of superiors for failing to take measures to prevent or repress the unlawful conduct of their subordinates was best understood when seen against the principle that criminal responsibility for omissions was incurred only where there existed a legal obligation to act.

The trial chamber pointed out that in the case of military commanders, under article 87 of the Protocol Additional to the Geneva Conventions of 12 August 1949, and relating to the Protection of Victims of International Armed Conflicts (Protocol I), in-

IV:3

ternational law imposed an affirmative duty on superiors to prevent persons under their control from committing violations of international humanitarian law. Ultimately, it was this duty that provided the basis for, and defined the contours of, the imputed criminal responsibility under article 7, paragraph 3, of the Statute.

In the period following the Second World War until the present time, the trial chamber observed, the doctrine of command responsibility had not been applied by any international judicial body. Nonetheless, there could be no doubt that the concept of the individual criminal responsibility of superiors for failure to act was today firmly placed within the corpus of international humanitarian law. Through the adoption of Protocol I, the principle had now been codified and given a clear expression in international conventional law. Thus, article 87 of the Protocol gave expression to the duty of commanders to control the acts of their subordinates and to prevent or, where necessary, to repress violations of the Geneva Conventions or the Protocol. The concomitant principle under which a superior might be held criminally responsible for the crimes committed by his subordinates where the superior had failed to properly exercise this duty was formulated in article 86 of the Protocol. The trial chamber concluded that the principle of individual criminal responsibility of superiors for failure to prevent or repress the crimes committed by subordinates formed part of customary international law.

The trial chamber then considered the elements of individual criminal responsibility under article 7, paragraph 3, of the Statute. It concluded that it was possible to identify the essential elements of command responsibility for failure to act: there existed a superior-subordinate relationship; the superior knew or had reason to know that the criminal act was about to be or had been committed; and the superior failed to take the necessary and reasonable measures to prevent the criminal act or punish the perpetrator of it. These elements were then considered in turn.

The trial chamber observed that the requirement of the existence of a superior-subordinate relationship was particularly problematic in a situation, such as that of the former Yugoslavia during the period relevant to this case, where previously existing formal structures had broken down and where, during an interim period, the new, possibly improvised, control and command structures might be ambiguous and ill-defined. It concluded that persons effectively in command of such informal structures, with power to prevent and punish the crimes of persons who were in fact under their control, might under certain circumstances be held responsible for their failure to do so. Individuals in positions of authority, whether civilian or within military structures, might incur criminal responsibility under the doctrine of command responsibility on the basis of their de facto as well as *de jure* positions as superiors. The mere absence of formal legal authority to control the actions of subordinates should therefore not be understood to preclude the imposition of such responsibility.

Concerning the responsibility of non-military superiors, it was apparent to the trial chamber from the text of article 7, paragraph 3, of the Statute that no express limitation was made restricting the scope of this type of responsibility to military commanders or situations arising under a military command. In contrast, the use of the generic term "superior" in this provision, together with its juxtaposition to the affirmation of the individual criminal responsibility of heads of State or government or responsible government officials in article 7, paragraph 2, clearly indicated that its applicability extended beyond the responsibility of military commanders to encompass also political leaders and other civilian superiors in positions of authority. Thus, the trial chamber concluded, the applicability of the principle of superior responsibility in article 7, paragraph 3, extended not only to military commanders, but also to individuals in non-military positions of superior authority.

The trial chamber then turned to the requisite character of the superior-subordinate relationship. In its opinion, a situation of command was a necessary precondition for the imposition of command responsibility. However, it had to be recognized that the existence of such a position could not be determined by reference to formal status alone. Instead, the factor determining liability for this type of criminal responsibility was the actual possession, or non-possession, of powers of control over the actions of subordinates. Accordingly, formal designation as a commander should not be considered to be a necessary prerequisite for command responsibility to attach, as such responsibility might be imposed by virtue of a person's de facto, as well as *de jure*, position as a commander.

While, therefore, the trial chamber concluded that a superior, whether military or civilian, might be held liable under the principle of superior responsibility on the basis of his de facto position of authority, the fundamental considerations underlying the imposition of such responsibility had to be borne in mind. The doctrine of command responsibility was ultimately predicated upon the power of the superior to control the acts of his subordinates. A duty was placed upon the superior to exercise this power so as to prevent and repress the crimes committed by his subordinates, and a failure by him to do so in a diligent manner was sanctioned by the imposition of individual criminal responsibility in accordance with the doctrine. It followed that there was a threshold at which persons ceased to possess the necessary powers of control over the actual perpetrators of offences and, accordingly, could not properly be considered their superiors within the meaning of article 7, paragraph 3, of the Statute. The trial chamber observed that while it had at all times to be alive to the realities of any given situation and be prepared to pierce such veils of formalism that might shield those individuals carrying the greatest responsibility for heinous acts, great care had to be taken lest an injustice be committed in holding individuals responsible for the acts of others in situations where the link of control was absent or too remote.

IV:3

Accordingly, the trial chamber took the view that in order for the principle of superior responsibility to be applicable, it was necessary that the superior had effective control over the persons committing the underlying violations of international humanitarian law, in the sense of having the material ability to prevent and punish the commission of these offences. With the caveat that such authority could have a de facto as well as a *de jure* character. The doctrine of superior responsibility extended to civilian superiors only to the extent that they exercised a degree of control over their subordinates which was similar to that of military commanders.

Concerning the mental element of command responsibility, knew or had reason to know, the trial chamber observed that the doctrine of superior responsibility did not establish a standard of strict liability for superiors for failing to prevent or punish the crimes committed by their subordinates. Instead, article 7, paragraph 3, of the Statute provided that a superior might be held responsible only where he knew or had reason to know that his subordinates were about to or had committed the acts referred to under articles 2 to 5. A construction of this provision in light of the content of the doctrine under customary law led the trial chamber to conclude that a superior might possess the *mens rea* required to incur criminal liability where he had actual knowledge, established through direct or circumstantial evidence, that his subordinates were committing or about to commit crimes referred to under articles 2 to 5 of the Statute; or where he had in his possession information of a nature, which at the least would put him on notice of the risk of such offences by indicating the need for additional investigation in order to ascertain whether such crimes were committed or were about to be committed by his subordinates.

Concerning the third element, necessary and reasonable measure, the trial chamber observed that the legal duty resting upon all individuals in positions of superior authority required them to take all necessary and reasonable measures to prevent the commission of offences by their subordinates or, if such crimes had been committed, to punish the perpetrators of them. It was the view of the trial chamber that any evaluation of the action taken by a superior to determine whether this duty had been met was so inextricably linked to the facts of each particular situation that any attempt to formulate a general standard *in abstracto* would not be meaningful.

The trial chamber insisted that it had to be recognized that international law could not oblige a superior to perform the impossible. Hence, a superior might only be held criminally responsible for failing to take such measures that were within his powers. The question then arose of what actions were to be considered to be within the superior's powers in this sense. As the corollary to the standard adopted by the trial chamber with respect to the concept of superior, it concluded that a superior should be held responsible for failing to take such measures that were within his material possibility.

In its verdict, the trial chamber found Zejnil Delalic not guilty of the charges against him. The prosecution had failed to prove that he had command authority and, therefore, superior responsibility over the Celebici prison camp, its commander, deputy commander or guards. He could not be held responsible for the crimes alleged to have been committed in that camp. The three other accused were found guilty of various charges of grave breaches of the Geneva Conventions and violations of the laws or customs of war. They were sentenced to various terms of imprisonment. In respect of superior responsibility of Zdravko Mucic, the trial chamber concluded that he was the de facto commander of the camp exercising de facto authority. Accordingly, he was criminally responsible for the acts of personnel in the Celebici camp on the basis of the principle of superior responsibility. In the case of Hazim Delic, however, the trial chamber did not find that he lay within the chain of command to issue orders to subordinates or to prevent or punish criminal acts of subordinates.

The prosecution as well as the parties found guilty by the trial chamber appealed against the judgment. As to superior responsibility, the appeals chamber of the International Tribunal dismissed the grounds of appeal submitted by the parties. In respect of sentencing, the appeals chamber remitted the case to a newly constituted trial chamber. In the new sentencing judgment, Zdravko Mucic was sentenced to nine years of imprisonment, Hazim Delic to 18 years and Esad Landzo to 15 years. This judgment was subsequently confirmed by the appeals chamber.

In the case *Prosecutor* v. *Drazen Erdemovic*,[8] the accused allegedly had committed a crime against humanity under article 5 of Statute or a violation of the laws and customs of war under article 3. Drazen Erdemovic, born in 1971, was a member of a sabotage detachment of the Bosnian Serb army. On 16 July 1995, he was sent with other members of his unit to a collective farm. Once there, they were informed that later that day Muslim men from 17 to 60 years of age would be brought to the farm in buses. The men were unarmed civilians who had surrendered to members of the Bosnian Serb army or police after the fall of the so-called "safe area" at Srebrenica. Members of the military police took the civilians off the buses in groups of ten and escorted them to a field next to the farm buildings. There they were lined up with their backs to a firing squad. The men were then killed by Drazen Erdemovic and other members of his unit with the help of soldiers from another brigade.

At his initial appearance before a trial chamber of the International Tribunal on 31 May 1996, the accused pleaded guilty to the count of a crime against humanity. He

---

[8] See case No. IT-96-22-T, judgment of 29 November 1996 (trial chamber); see also case No. IT-96-22-A, judgment of 7 October 1997 (appeals chamber) and case No. IT-96-22-T*bis*, judgment of 5 March 1998 (trial chamber).

IV:3

added, as an explanation to his guilty plea, that he had to to commit the crime, as if he had refused, he would have been killed together with the victims. When he initially refused, he was told that if he was sorry for the victims, he had to line up with them, and he would be killed too. He said that he was not sorry for himself, but for his family, his wife and son who was then nine months of age. He emphasized that he could not have refused, because he would have been killed.

The trial chamber accepted the guilty plea and dismissed the count of a violation of the laws or customs of war. However, in response to his explanation, it observed that the very contents of a declaration which was ambiguous or equivocal might affect the plea's validity. It considered, therefore, that it had to examine the possible defence for the elements invoked.

The trial chamber referred to article 7, paragraph 4, of the Statute. Under this provision, the fact that a defendant acted pursuant to a superior order should not relieve him of criminal responsibility, but it might be considered in mitigation of punishment. However, in respect of the physical and moral duress accompanied by the order from a military superior, the Statute provided no guidance. Accordingly, the trial chamber examined how the International Military Tribunal at Nuremberg and other international military courts delivering judgments after the Second World War had distinguished between exculpatory duress justifying the crime and duress as a grounds for a mitigation of sentence.

As part of this examination, the trial chamber cited a review of international military case law by a United Nations commission. It showed that the military tribunals of nine nations after the Second World War considered the issue of duress as constituting a complete defence. After an analysis of some 2,000 decisions by these military tribunals, the commission identified three features which were always present and which it laid down as essential conditions for duress to be accepted as a defence for a violation of international humanitarian law: the act charged was done to avoid an immediate danger both serious and irreparable; there was no adequate means of escape; and the remedy was not disproportionate to the evil.

The trial chamber concluded that while justification on account of moral duress and the state of necessity pursuant to an order from a superior might not be excluded absolutely, its conditions of application were especially strict. The acts invoked, if proven, had to be assessed according to very rigorous criteria and appreciated *in concreto* and involve, in particular, the lack of moral choice by the accused when placed in a situation where he could not resist.

The elements drawn from the facts of this case and the hearing did not enable the trial chamber to consider that evidence existed warranting a full exculpation of the accused's responsibility. The elements invoked by the defence could, nevertheless, be taken into account as grounds for a mitigation of sentence. On this basis, it confirmed the validity of the guilty plea. Ultimately, however, the trial chamber noted that in respect of the acts involving the accused, which might be a basis for allowing urgent necessity stemming from duress and a superior order to be considered as mitigating circumstances, the defence had provided no testimony to corroborate what Drazen Erdemovic had said. Accordingly, it was unable to accept the plea of urgent necessity as a mitigating factor.

In fact, in sentencing the accused to 10 years of imprisonment, the trial chamber took into account the following mitigating circumstances: his age at the time when the crimes were committed and his low military rank; the remorse he expressed, his willingness to surrender and the cooperation he had provided to the prosecution; and the fact that he did not pose a threat and had a corrigible personality.

Drazen Erdemovic appealed against this sentencing judgment, seeking either acquittal or revision of the sentence. In the appeals chamber of the International Tribunal, the judges differed on a number of the issues raised, both as to reasoning and as to result. It unanimously rejected the application for acquittal and, with four votes to one, the application for revision of the sentence. However, it ordered, with four votes to one, the case to be remitted to another trial chamber of the International Tribunal to give the appellant an opportunity to replead.

On the question of duress, the appeals chamber, by three votes to two, found that duress did not afford a complete defence to a soldier charged with a crime against humanity and/or a war crime involving the killing of innocent human beings.

In a separate and dissenting opinion, one judge contended, on the basis of a survey of copious international case law, that no special rule excluding duress in case of murder had evolved in international criminal law. He maintained that the only logical conclusion to be drawn from the absence of such a rule was that the general rule on duress must apply. Consequently, duress might also be admitted, subject to various stringent requirements, for crimes involving the killing of innocent persons.

On the notion and requirements of duress, he noted, *inter alia*, that it was also important to mention that in the case law, duress was commonly raised in conjunction with superior orders. However, there was no necessary connection between the two. Superior orders might be issued without being accompanied by any threats to life or limb. In these circumstances, if the superior order was manifestly illegal under international law, the subordinate was under a duty to refuse to obey the order. If, following such a refusal, the order was reiterated under a threat to life or limb, then the defence of duress might be raised and superior orders lose any legal relevance. Equal-

IV:3

ly, duress might be raised entirely independently of superior orders, for example, where the threat issued from a fellow serviceman. Thus, where duress was raised in conjunction with manifestly unlawful superior orders, the accused might only have a defence if he first refused to obey the unlawful order and then only carried it out after a threat to life or limb.

Furthermore, he argued, the relevant case law was almost unanimous in requiring four strict conditions to be met for duress to be upheld as a defence, namely: the act charged was done under an immediate threat of severe and irreparable harm to life or limb; there was no adequate means of averting such evil; the crime committed was not disproportionate to the evil threatened, in other words, the crime committed under duress had to be, on balance, the lesser of two evils, for example, in the case of killing in order to avert an assault; and the situation leading to duress must not have been voluntarily brought about by the person coerced.

On 14 January 1998, Drazen Erdemovic appeared before a new trial chamber and pleaded guilty to violations of the laws or customs of war. In determining the sentence, this trial chamber found that the magnitude of the crime and the accused's role in it were aggravating circumstances. It also concluded that various mitigating factors were present, including Drazen Erdemovic's personal circumstances, his admission of guilt, remorse, cooperation with the prosecution and the existence of duress. The trial chamber sentenced him to five years' imprisonment.

(*b*) International Criminal Tribunal for Rwanda

From the jurisprudence of the International Criminal Tribunal for the Prosecution of Persons Responsible for Genocide and Other Serious Violations of International Humanitarian Law Committed in the Territory of Rwanda and Rwandan Citizens Responsible for Genocide and Other Such Violations Committed in the Territory of Neighbouring States between 1 January and 31 December 1994, two cases are reviewed in this chapter of the book. They concern, primarily, genocide and crimes against humanity. Two of those convicted were in positions of authority, namely burgomaster (*bourgmestre*) and prefect (*préfet*), respectively, and therefore questions of command responsibility arose. In each of the cases, police and gendarmes were used by the perpetrators as means to commit some of their crimes. The judgments show how police officials committed murder and other inhumane acts and failed to prevent others. Law and order had completely collapsed, and the police were part of the problem.

In the case *Prosecutor* v. *Jean Paul Akayesu*,[9] the accused was the former burgomaster of a commune in Rwanda. Prior to his appointment as burgomaster, he was a teacher and school inspector in the same commune.

The Republic of Rwanda was divided into 11 prefectures, and these were further divided into communes. The prefect was the highest local representative of the Government and had control over the Government and its agencies throughout the prefecture. In each commune, there existed a council of the commune led by the burgomaster of that commune. The burgomaster was subject to the hierarchical authority of the prefect, but, and subject to this authority, he was in charge of governmental functions within his commune. The prefect was responsible for maintaining the peace, public order and security within the prefecture. In fulfilling his duty to maintain peace, the prefect could demand assistance from the army and the national gendarmerie. The burgomaster had authority over those members of the national gendarmerie who were stationed in his commune. Each commune also had communal police engaged by the burgomaster. Normally, the burgomaster had exclusive authority over the members of the communal police. In case of public calamities, however, the prefect could claim the police officials of the communal police and place them under his direct control.

Jean-Paul Akayesu was indicted on 15 counts of genocide, crimes against humanity and violations of article 3 common to the Geneva Conventions of 12 August 1949 and the Protocol Additional to the Geneva Conventions of 12 August 1949, and relating to the Protection of Victims of Non-International Armed Conflicts (Protocol II). The alleged crimes included murder, extermination, torture and other inhumane acts as well as outrages upon personal dignity, in particular rape.

The crimes were committed in the context of a non-international armed conflict involving the Rwandan Armed Forces and the Rwandan Patriotic Front. The trial chamber of the International Tribunal found that Jean Paul Akayesu, in his capacity as burgomaster, was responsible for maintaining law and public order in the commune. He had effective authority over the communal police. In addition to the criminal responsibility that attached from committing or participating in the commission of any of the crimes under the jurisdiction of the International Tribunal, article 6, paragraph 3, of its Statute provided that a superior was criminally responsible for the acts of subordinates if the superior knew or had reason to know that the subordinate was about to commit such acts or had actually done so and yet failed to prevent or punish such acts.

---

[9] See case No. ICTR-96-4-T, judgment of 2 September 1998 and decision of 2 October 1998 (trial chamber); see also case No. ICTR-96-4-A, judgment of 1 June 2001 (appeals chamber).

IV:3

In interpreting this provision, the trial chamber reviewed the findings of other tribunals. It found that in the case of civilians, the application of the principle of individual criminal responsibility remained contentious. Against this background, the trial chamber held that it was appropriate to assess on a case-by-case basis the power of authority actually devolved upon the accused in order to determine whether or not he had the power to take all necessary and reasonable measures to prevent the commission of the alleged crimes or to punish the perpetrators of them.

The accused was charged cumulatively with more than one crime in relation to the same sets of facts in all but one count. For example, the events described in one part of the indictment were the subject of three counts, of genocide, complicity in genocide and crimes against humanity, respectively. The trial chamber's factual findings on the counts in this part of the indictment are reviewed here to exemplify the case as a whole.

In the indictment it was stated, *inter alia*, that on or about 19 April 1994, the men who, on Jean Paul Akayesu's instructions, were searching for a named person destroyed his house and burned down his mother's house. They then went to search the house of his brother-in-law in another commune and there found the named person's three brothers. They tried to escape, but Jean Paul Akayesu blew his whistle to alert local residents to the attempted escape and ordered the people to capture the brothers. After they were captured, the accused ordered and participated in the killing of the three men.

One witness testified that a mob of people had detained the three brothers and had beaten them. Although he did not see the beatings, he saw the injuries that had been inflicted. The brothers had open, bleeding wounds, and their clothes were torn. They were made to sit on a lawn. Following a conversation, the accused said: "We need to finish these people off." He confirmed this response by saying that they needed to be shot. Police officials then made the three brothers lie on their stomachs. The crowd of people that had gathered were asked to step back, and all three brothers were shot at close range behind their heads by the officials.

The trial chamber found no evidence that Jean Paul Akayesu blew the whistle to alert local residents to the attempted escape of the brothers, but it found all of the other facts alleged in this part of the indictment proved beyond reasonable doubt. It held that these acts rendered the accused criminally responsible for having ordered, committed, aided and abetted in the preparation or execution of the killings of members of the Tutsi group and the infliction of serious bodily and mental harm on members of that group. The trial chamber found that the acts were committed by the accused with the specific intent to destroy the Tutsi group as such and constituted the crime of genocide, but not that of complicity. Furthermore, the killings constituted extermination committed as part of a widespread or systematic attack on civilians on ethnic grounds and as such constituted a crime against humanity.

As to the verdict, the trial chamber found Jean Paul Akayesu guilty of nine of the counts on which he was charged and not guilty of six counts in his indictment.

In a separate decision, the trial chamber sentenced Jean Paul Akayesu to life imprisonment for each of the crimes of genocide, incitement to commit genocide and crimes against humanity (extermination). He was sentenced to 15 years' imprisonment for each of three crimes against humanity (murder); 10 years' imprisonment for crimes against humanity (torture); 15 years' imprisonment for crimes against humanity (rape); and 10 years' imprisonment for crimes against humanity (other inhumane acts). The Trial Chamber decided that the sentences should be served concurrently. Therefore, it sentenced Jean Paul Akayesu to a single sentence of life imprisonment.

The appeals chamber of the International Tribunal dismissed each of the grounds of appeal raised by Jean-Paul Akayesu and affirmed the verdict and sentence by the trial chamber.

In the case *Prosecutor* v. *Clément Kayishema and Obed Ruzindana*,[10] Clément Kayishema was charged criminally responsible for genocide, crimes against humanity and violations of common article 3 and Protocol II, 24 counts altogether. He was also, or alternatively, held individually responsible as a superior for the criminal acts of his subordinates with respect to each of the crimes charged. Additionally, Obed Ruzindana was indicted on six of the counts. The alleged crimes included murder, extermination and other inhumane acts. Clément Kayishema was the prefect of Kibuye and Obed Ruzindana a commercial trader during the time when the crimes occurred.

The case arose out of four massacres which occurred at two churches, a sports stadium and in the area of Bisesero, respectively. Thousands of men, women and children were killed and numerous people injured. Police and gendarmerie were involved in atrocities at all of the sites and were the agents by which the accused committed some of their crimes. The trial chamber's findings on the massacres that occurred in the area of Bisesero, and the circumstances that led to it, are reviewed here to exemplify the case as a whole.

---

[10] See case No. ICTR-95-1-T, judgment of 21 May 1999 and decision of 21 May 1999 (trial chamber); see also case No. ICTR-95-1-A, judgment of 1 June 2001 (appeals chamber).

IV:3

The area of Bisesero spanned over two communes of the Kibuye prefecture. From a-bout 9 April to 30 June 1994, people in thousands sought refuge in that area. They were predominantly Tutsis trying to escape from attacks on the Tutsi group that had occurred throughout the prefecture. The attackers used guns, grenades, machetes, spears, pangas, cudgels and other weapons to kill the Tutsis in Bisesero. At various times, the men, women and children seeking refuge there attempted to defend them-selves from these attacks with stones, sticks and other crude weapons.

These atrocities formed the bases of six of the counts of the indictment. At various locations and times throughout April, May and June 1994, and often in concert, Clé-ment Kayishema and Obed Ruzindana brought to the area of Bisesero members of the national gendarmerie, communal police and an unofficial paramilitary group, composed almost exclusively of extremist Hutus, as well as armed civilians and di-rected them to attack the people seeking refuge there. In addition, at various loca-tions and times, also often in concert, Clément Kayishema and Obed Ruzindana per-sonally attacked and killed such persons.

In respect of this massacre, the indictment alleged one count of genocide and three counts of crimes against humanity. Two counts alleged, respectively, a violation of common article 3 and of Protocol II.

On hearing testimony from witnesses about situations in which the accused acted in concert, the trial chamber found that at one location, for example, they were present at the massacres and helped transport other assailants to the location; instigated the attack on the Tutsis gathered there; orchestrated the method of attack; led the at-tacks; and personally participated in them. Additionally, with regard to Clément Ka-yishema, the trial chamber found that the prosecution had proved that his subordi-nates, including members of the national gendarmerie, the communal police and the paramilitary group and local officials, had participated in the massacres.

After hearing evidence of an attack at another location in the same area, in which scores of Tutsis were killed, the trial chamber found that both Clément Kayishema and Obed Ruzindana were present and played a leading role in directing the perpe-trators of the massacre. It also found that gendarmes, paramilitaries and various local officials were present and participated.

Giving an account of a large-scale attack in which Clément Kayishema acted sepa-rately from Obed Ruzindana, one witness testified that the accused arrived in a car with other civic authorities, soldiers, gendarmes, communal police officials, para-militaries and civilians. He was carrying a long gun and gave instructions to the at-tackers. He then proceeded with others to the top of a hill from where he shot at a fleeing Tutsi, killing him instantaneously. The attack continued until the evening.

The witness described how the slaughtered bodies on the hill were like small insects which had been killed off by insecticide. On that day, he lost many members of his family, including his mother, wife, nine children, four sisters and their children, five of his brother's children, two brothers and their wives.

Burgomasters and other members of the administration, gendarmes, soldiers, communal police officials, prison wardens, paramilitaries and armed civilians were identified at the massacre sites. The trial chamber found that they participated in the atrocities at these sites. The question for it to address, therefore, was whether Clément Kayishema exercised *de jure* or de facto control over these assailants. The trial chamber was mindful of the need to view his *de jure* powers with an appreciation of the chaotic situation that prevailed at the time. Accordingly, any consideration as to the *de jure* powers exercised by Clément Kayishema had to be subject to an elucidation of the de facto power, or lack thereof, that he held over the assailants. The trial chamber found that it was beyond question that the prefect exercised *de jure* authority over burgomasters, communal police and members of the national gendarmerie. The Rwandan law was very clear in that respect.

Concerning de facto control, the trial chamber, referring to the jurisprudence of the International Tribunal for the former Yugoslavia, observed that even where a clear hierarchy based upon *de jure* authority was not present, this did not prevent the finding of command responsibility. Equally, the mere existence of *de jure* power did not always necessitate the imposition of command responsibility. The culpability that the doctrine of command responsibility gave rise to had ultimately to be predicated upon the power that the superior exercised over his subordinates in a given situation.

The trial chamber noted that defence witnesses did not actually contest the control that the prefect exercised over the law-enforcing and administrative bodies. The facts of the case also reflected that Clément Kayishema exercised de facto control over all of the assailants participating in the massacres. In the Bisesero area, for example, it was testified that he was directing the massacre of Tutsis and that he arrived at a location leading a number of soldiers, gendarmes and armed civilians, addressed them by megaphone and then instructed them to attack. Upon his orders, the massacres began. These facts had been proven beyond a reasonable doubt.

This was indicative of the pivotal role Clément Kayishema played in leading the execution of the massacres. It was clear that for all crime sites denoted in the indictment, he had *de jure* authority over most of the assailants and de facto control of them all. It had also been proved beyond reasonable doubt that the attacks, with one exception, were commenced upon his orders. They were attacks clearly orchestrated by him and only executed upon his direction. The trial chamber found, therefore, that Clément Kayishema was criminally responsible, pursuant to article 6, paragraph

IV:3

3, of the Statute, for the crimes committed by his *de jure* and de facto subordinates at the various locations.

As to the verdict, the trial chamber found, unanimously, Clément Kayishema guilty of four counts of genocide and Obed Ruzindana guilty of one. However, by two votes to one, it did not find the accused guilty of the counts of crimes against humanity in respect of murder and extermination, as these crimes were considered to be fully subsumed in the crime of genocide. Unanimously, it found the accused not guilty of the remaining counts.

In a separate decision, the trial chamber sentenced Clément Kayishema to life imprisonment and Obed Ruzindana to 25 years of imprisonment.

The appeals chamber of the International Tribunal dismissed the grounds of appeal raised by Clément Kayishema and Obed Ruzindana and affirmed the verdict and sentences by the trial chamber.

C. CASE SUMMARIES

(a) *Prosecutor v. Anto Furundzija*
(International Tribunal for the former Yugoslavia)[11]

The accused in this case was Anto Furundzija, a citizen of Bosnia and Herzegovina, born in 1969. His trial commenced on 8 June 1998 before a trial chamber of the International Tribunal for the Prosecution of Persons Responsible for Serious Violations of International Humanitarian Law Committed in the Territory of the Former Yugoslavia since 1991. The trial was concluded on 12 November 1998.

Facts and proceedings

On 10 November 1995, a judge of the International Tribunal confirmed the indictment against the accused, charging him with a grave breach of the Geneva Conventions of 12 August 1949 and violations of the laws or customs of war. The accused was charged with three individual counts of, respectively, torture and inhumane treatment; torture; and outrages upon personal dignity, including rape. These charges were in respect of acts alleged to have been committed at the headquarters of the Jokers, a special unit within the armed forces of the Croatian Community of Herzeg-Bosna, known as the Croatian Defence Council. The judge ordered that there should be no disclosure of the indictment.

---

[11] See case No. IT-95-17/1-T, judgment of 10 December 1998 (trial chamber); see also case No. IT-95-17/1-A, judgment of 21 July 2000 (appeals chamber).

The accused was arrested on 18 December 1997 by members of SFOR, the multinational stabilization force, acting pursuant to a warrant for arrest issued by the International Tribunal. The accused was immediately transferred to the International Tribunal and detained in its detention unit in The Hague.

On 2 June 1998, an amended indictment was filed. One of the grave breach counts and associated allegations was withdrawn.

Under the amended indictment, the accused was shown as the local commander of a special unit of the military police, the Jokers. In this capacity, he and another soldier, accused B., interrogated witness A., a Bosnian Moslem civilian. During the questioning, she had a knife rubbed against her inner thigh and lower stomach, and the perpetrator threatened to put his knife inside her vagina if she did not tell the truth. Allegedly, the accused continued to interrogate witness A. and victim B., a Bosnian Croat who had previously assisted witness A.'s family. They were beaten on the feet with a baton. Furthermore, witness A. was forced to have oral and vaginal sexual intercourse with accused B. while the accused stood by, failing to intervene in any way.

In relation to these alleged acts, the amended indictment charged the accused with two counts of violations of the laws or customs of war, as recognized by article 3 of the Statute of the International Tribunal: torture and outrages upon personal dignity, including rape.

Having opened on 8 June 1998, the hearings closed on 29 June 1998. Thereafter, the prosecution disclosed two documents to the defence. One was a redacted certificate dated 11 July 1995 and the other a witness statement dated 16 September 1995 from a psychologist from the Medica Women's Therapy Centre in Zenica, Bosnia and Herzegovina, concerning witness A. and the treatment she had received at the Medica Centre.

On 10 July 1998, the defence filed a motion to strike the testimony of witness A. due to what it considered to be misconduct on the part of the prosecution or, in the event of a conviction, for a new trial. The prosecution filed its response to the motion on 13 July 1998. In a decision of 16 July 1998, the trial chamber found that there had been serious misconduct on the part of the prosecution in breach of the Rules of Procedure and Evidence of the International Tribunal. Consequently, the defence was prejudiced. It ordered that the proceedings were to be re-opened in connection with the medical, psychological or psychiatric treatment or counselling received by witness A. after May 1993, and the prosecution was ordered to disclose any other connected documents.

IV:3

On 9 November 1998, the proceedings re-opened. The defence called four witnesses, including two expert witnesses, while the prosecution called two expert witnesses.

As to the factual allegations submitted by the prosecution, substantiating those set out in the amended indictment, it was claimed that witness A. was arrested on or around 15 May 1993 by members of the Jokers whose headquarters was in a well-known local village hostelry, known as the bungalow. They took witness A. to a house adjacent to the bungalow, the holiday cottage, where their living quarters were, and she was detained in a large room in the company of a group of soldiers.

The accused, a local commander of the Jokers, arrived at the holiday cottage and immediately began to interrogate witness A. about a list of Croatian names and the activities of her sons. During the questioning by the accused, one of the soldiers forced witness A. to undress and then rubbed his knife along her inner thigh and lower stomach and threatened to put his knife inside her vagina should she not tell the truth. The accused continued to interrogate witness A. throughout this threatening conduct.

Thereafter, witness A. was moved to another room in the holiday cottage. A Croatian soldier, known to the witness and identified in the amended indictment as victim B., but referred to hereafter as witness D., because he so appeared in these proceedings, was also brought into the room. He appeared to have been badly beaten. While the accused continued to interrogate witnesses A. and D., the same soldier who had earlier assaulted witness A. beat both of them with a baton on their feet and then forced witness A. to have oral and vaginal intercourse with him. The accused did nothing to prevent these acts.

In respect of legal arguments, the prosecution submitted that the accused might be held individually responsible for his participation in the alleged crimes pursuant to article 7, paragraph 1, of the Statute. Under this provision, a person who planned, instigated, ordered, committed or otherwise aided and abetted in the planning, preparation or execution of a crime referred to in articles 2 to 5 of the Statute should be individually responsible for the crime. The prosecution contended that such liability could be established by showing that the accused had intent to participate in the crime and that his act contributed to its commission. It was further submitted that such a contribution did not necessarily require participation in the physical commission of the crime, but that liability accrued where the accused was shown to have been intentionally present at a location where unlawful acts were being committed. Accordingly, the prosecution argued, the accused's alleged acts of encouragement, and his omissions, were sufficient to trigger his individual criminal responsibility under article 7, paragraph 1, for the crimes alleged.

The prosecution further submitted that the alleged acts by the accused constituted the crime of torture, as recognized in article 3 common to the Geneva Conventions. It was contended that by his conduct under the factual circumstances alleged, the accused, acting in an official capacity as a uniformed soldier on duty, intentionally inflicted severe physical or mental pain or suffering on witness A., a non-combatant, during an interrogation for the purpose of obtaining information and for the purpose of intimidation, thereby committing torture. The prosecution submitted that the elements of the crime of torture under common article 3 were met, as it was asserted that these events took place in the context of, and were directly linked to, an armed conflict between the armed forces of the Government of the Republic of Bosnia and Herzegovina, which declared itself independent on 6 March 1992, and the armed forces of the Croatian Community of Herzeg-Bosna, which considered itself an independent political entity inside the Republic.

The prosecution also submitted that the accused was individually criminally responsible for the alleged acts under article 4, paragraph 2 (*e*), of the Protocol Additional to the Geneva Conventions of 12 August 1949, and relating to the Protection of Victims of Non-International Armed Conflicts (Protocol II). Under this provision, outrages upon personal dignity, in particular humiliating and degrading treatment, rape, enforced prostitution and any form of indecent assault, were prohibited. The prosection made reference to a previous jurisdiction decision by the International Tribunal that customary international law imposed criminal liability for serious violations of common article 3 as supplemented by other general principles and rules on the protection of victims of internal armed conflict. It was submitted that the substantive offences prohibited by article 4 of Protocol II were part of customary law and that they enhanced the protection afforded by common article 3.

It was argued that by his interrogation of witness A., a non-combatant in the hands of an adverse party during a conflict, throughout which she was maintained in a state of forced nudity, obligated to submit to several sexual assaults, and was humiliated by attacks on her personal, including sexual, integrity, the accused committed outrages upon personal dignity within the meaning of article 4, paragraph 2 (*e*), of Protocol II.

Similarly, the prosecution argued that by the accused's conduct during the time that witness A., a non-combatant in the hands of an adverse party during an armed conflict, was subjected to vaginal, anal and oral forcible sexual penetration, the accused was criminally responsible for rape, as recognized under article 4, paragraph 2 (*e*), of Protocol II.

The defence did not concede the existence of an armed conflict for the purposes of bringing the alleged crimes within the jurisdictional scope of article 3 of the Statute.

IV:3

As to the specific allegations in the amended indictment, the defence contended that the accused was not guilty of the crimes alleged. It was asserted that the accused was not present for any sexual assault on witness A., and it submitted that her recollection of the events, which formed the basis for the charge against the accused, was unreliable. In support of these submissions, the defence relied upon alleged inconsistencies in the testimony of the witness.

In respect of the existence of an armed conflict, the prosecution stated, *inter alia*, that from about January 1993 until mid-July 1993, the armed forces of the Croatian Community of Herzeg-Bosna was engaged in an armed conflict with the Army of Bosnia and Herzegovina. The Croatian Community had declared itself an independent political entity inside the Republic of Bosnia and Herzegovina on 3 July 1992. During this time, the Croatian armed forces attacked villages inhabited mainly by Bosnian Moslems in the Lasva River Valley region in central Bosnia and Herzegovina. The accused was a member of the Jokers, the special unit of Croatian military police, which participated in the armed conflict in that region. These attacks led to the expulsion, detention, wounding and deaths of numerous civilians. The prosecution alleged that this was the context in which the crimes by the accused took place.

Evidence of the existence of an armed conflict was given by prosecution witnesses. They testified as to the increasing tension between the Croatian and Muslim communities, incidents of violence, the outbreak of fighting and the plight of the Moslem population who were subjected to harassment, expulsion from their homes and attacks.

The defence did not concede that a state of armed conflict existed at the relevant time, but called no evidence to counter the submissions of the prosecution. In his closing remarks, defence counsel submitted that the prosecution evidence had not demonstrated that there was an armed conflict in terms of front-lines and military objectives, but only that there was an attack by the Croatian armed forces on civilians.

As to factual findings, the trial chamber pronounced that it was not disputed that the test to be applied in determining the existence of an armed conflict was that set out by the International Tribunal in a previous appeal case. In the juridiction decision in that case, it was stated that an armed conflict existed whenever there was a resort to armed force between States or protracted armed violence between governmental authorities and organized armed groups or between such groups within a State. Applying that test, the trial chamber found that at the material time, being mid-May 1993, a state of armed conflict existed between the Croatian armed forces and the Army of Bosnia and Herzegovina. The trial chamber then had to determine whether a nexus existed between the alleged criminal conduct of the accused and the armed conflict.

The prosecution submitted that the accused participated in the armed conflict as a local commander of the Jokers. It was in this capacity that he was alleged to have interrogated witness A., a civilian, about her fighting-age sons and relations between Moslems and personnel of the Croatian armed forces. Several prosecution witnesses identified the accused as a commander of the Jokers.

Witness A. testified that during her interrogation, she was accused of cooperating with soldiers of the Croatian armed forces, in particular witness D. with whom she was confronted by the accused. He asked her if she knew two named men, and he accused her of having a certain code-name. The accused also demanded to know whether her children were in the Army of Bosnia and Herzegovina, and he threatened personally to kill them. Witness D. testified that he was beaten and interrogated by members of the Jokers, including the accused, about his arrest by the Army of Bosnia and Herzegovina and whether he had told them anything about the Jokers.

Although the defence did not contest that the accused was a member of the Jokers, its case was that he was not present during the sexual assaults on witness A., and he did not interrogate her. Moreover, the defence argued, there was no armed conflict to which the accused could be linked.

The trial chamber accepted the evidence of witness A. about the nature of her interrogation by the accused. She was a civilian in the hands of the Jokers being questioned by the accused, a commander of that unit. He was an active combatant and participated in expelling Moslems from their homes. He also participated in arrests such as those of witness D. and another witness. The trial chamber held that these circumstances were sufficient to link the alleged offences committed by the accused to the armed conflict.

As to the events at the bungalow and the holiday cottage, the prosecution case against the accused turned on the evidence of witness A. and, to a lesser extent, witness D. Both witnesses testified as to what happened to them in mid-May 1993 at the bungalow and the holiday cottage. The precise dates involved were a matter of dispute between the parties. The trial chamber was assured that these two vital witnesses had no contact with each other or knowledge of the whereabouts of the other since then.

In response, the case of the defence was that witness A. was mistaken. Due to the traumatic events that she endured and lapse of time, her memory regarding the events at issue was flawed. Suggestions were alleged to have been made to her during vulnerable stages of her physical and psychological recovery, therefore rendering her memory unreliable. This, it was argued, was demonstrated by inconsistencies in the statements she gave in 1993, 1995, 1997 and before the trial chamber in oral tes-

IV:3

timony. The defence further contended that witness A's testimony was directly contradicted by that of witness D., thereby making it unreliable, and another witness was called to challenge certain assertions made by that witness. The evidence of a medical expert witness, who did not examine any of the witnesses, but testified in these proceedings, was submitted to demonstrate the weakness of memory, in particular where shock was involved.

The defence did not deny that the accused was in the holiday cottage. There had been no denial that witness A. did in fact suffer the atrocities she claimed were committed against her. The defence was simply that her recollection of the events was inaccurate and that the accused was not present when she was being assaulted.

Before examining the evidence pertaining to these events, the trial chamber felt it necessary to establish the factual background and circumstances that led to witnesses A. and D. being together at the holiday cottage in May 1993.

Witness A. was a married woman of Bosnian Moslem origin. Fighting between the Croatian armed forces and the Army of Bosnia and Herzegovina broke out on 16 April 1993 where she lived. Through a series of events, witness A. came to be separated from her husband. She spoke of how, in spite of public warnings not to help Moslems, the man she later came to know as witness D. transferred her two sons to a safer building when she and others were taken to the headquarters of the Croatian armed forces. At a later stage, she and some friends of the family arranged to have her sons sent to another place. Witness A., upon cross-examination, denied that her children were in the Army of Bosnia and Herzegovina and that her husband had any involvement in the military.

Witness A. testified how she came to live in the family apartment with another person, a childhood friend of her children. He was of Croatian origin and had a military affiliation to the Croatian armed forces. Having promised to protect the mother of his friends in their absence, he moved into her apartment. On a day in May, which she said was 15 May 1993, several soldiers from an elite unit of the Croatian armed forces came to her apartment. They were dressed in black uniforms with the characteristic insignia of the Jokers, known to be a special task unit of the Croatian armed forces with a "terrifying" reputation. Witness A. was not molested at this time, but she was ordered to go with them. In her testimony, she recalled that it was at about 10.30 in the morning. She recounted being taken in a sports car to the bungalow, which had been turned into the headquarters of the Jokers in 1991.

Witness D. was a member of the Croatian armed forces, and much of his testimony was undisputed. Following the outbreak of hostilities, he was assigned guard duties around the area of the headquarters of the Croatian armed forces, which included several residential buildings. One of these buildings housed witness A.'s apartment. As one of the guards of that apartment block, witness D., on several occasions during the four to five days that he was stationed there, transferred the children of witness A. to a safer building and back again. On or around 8 May 1993, he was captured by the Army of Bosnia and Herzegovina and detained for several days, along with two others. During this time, he was interrogated about the Croatian armed forces in the region.

A document issued by the Joint Committee for the Release of Detainees demonstrated that witness D. was released on 16 May 1993 in a prisoner-of-war exchange. He was then interrogated by the Croatian armed forces and eventually released. Witness D. claimed that the accused, a soldier, identified as accused B, and another person picked him up by car as he was walking back home. He was told that they had been looking for him, and he was then driven to the bungalow.

At the bungalow, he told the trial chamber, he was held in detention and interrogated. The defence did not challenge the assertion by this witness that the accused questioned him about the circumstances of his arrest by the Army of Bosnia and Herzegovina and what he had revealed to them, nor that the accused also hit the witness. In the course of his detention at the bungalow, witness D. was subjected to serious physical assaults by accused B., for what he estimated to be three days, before his encounter with witness A., and the defence did not challenge his allegation that the accused was present for parts of the serious assaults on him. Another witness saw him on what appeared to have been his first day at the bungalow, before he showed visible signs of physical assault. Although witness D. did not mention seeing that witness at the bungalow at any time, the latter confirmed that he later witnessed some of the severe physical attacks which accused B. inflicted upon the witness. Both witnesses spoke of a style of beating, which involved hitting the toes and the top of the foot close to the ankle-bone with a baton. He also testified that he saw accused B. hit witness D. on the head and elsewhere on his body. He also corroborated witness D.'s testimony that the accused was present for some of the beatings that witness suffered.

After the hearing in the case was closed on 22 June 1998, the trial chamber ordered that the proceedings were to be re-opened in respect of the medical, psychological and psychiatric treatment or counselling received by witness A. after May 1993. The principal reason for this was serious misconduct on the part of the prosecution resulting in the defence being prejudiced.

In its judgment, the trial chamber placed the re-opened proceedings in procedural context and examined the evidence relating to the central issue of those proceedings, namely the extent to which the reliability of witness A.'s evidence might have been

IV:3

affected by any psychological disorder arising out of her traumatic ordeal. In this respect, it examined the evidence presented through expert witnesses for both the prosecution and the defence on the issue of post-traumatic stress disorder (PTSD) and its potential effect on memory.

The trial chamber found that witness A.'s memory regarding material aspects of the events was not affected by any disorder which she might have had. It accepted her evidence that she had sufficiently recollected these material aspects of the events. There was no evidence of any form of brain damage or that her memory was in any way contaminated by any treatment which she might have had. Indeed, it accepted the medical evidence that such treatment she might have had was of a purely preliminary nature. It also considered that the aim in therapy was not fact-finding. The trial chamber further bore in mind that even when a person was suffering from PTSD, this did not mean that he or she was necessarily inaccurate in the evidence given. There was no reason why a person with PTSD could not be a perfectly reliable witness.

Having considered the evidence, the trial chamber was satisfied beyond reasonable doubt that the following findings might be made.

On or about 16 May 1993, witness D. was arrested and taken to the bungalow by the accused and accused B., and he was interrogated and assaulted by both of them. Accused B. in particular beat him with his fists and on the feet and toes with a baton, in the presence of another witness, most of the time in the presence of the accused who was coming and going.

On or about 18 or 19 May 1993, witness A. was arrested and taken from her apartment by several members of an elite unit of soldiers attached to the Croatian armed forces and known as the Jokers. She was driven by car to the bungalow, the headquarters of the Jokers. Soldiers and several commanders of different units, among them the accused and accused B., were based there.

On arrival at the bungalow, witness A. was taken to a nearby house, the holiday cottage, which formed part of the bungalow complex. She entered a room described as the large room, which was where the Jokers lodged. She was told to sit down and was offered food. Around her, the soldiers, dressed in Jokers uniforms, awaited the arrival of the man referred to as the boss, who was going to deal with her. Witness A. then heard someone announce the arrival of Furundzija. The man she identified to the satisfaction of the trial chamber as being Anto Furundzija, the accused, entered the room holding some papers in his hands.

Witness A. was interrogated by the accused. She was forced by accused B. to undress and remain naked before a substantial number of soldiers. She was subjected to cruel, inhuman and degrading treatment and to threats of serious physical assault by accused B. in the course of her interrogation by the accused. The purpose of this abuse was to extract information from witness A. about her family, her connection with the Army of Bosnia and Herzegovina and her relationship with certain Croatian soldiers, and also to degrade and humiliate her. The interrogation by the accused and the abuse by accused B. were parallel to each other.

Witness A. was left by the accused in the custody of accused B, who proceeded to rape her, sexually assault her and to physically abuse and degrade her. Witness A. was subjected to severe physical and mental suffering and public humiliation.

The interrogation of witness A. continued in the pantry, once more before an audience of soldiers. Whilst naked but covered by a small blanket, she was interrogated by the accused. Accused B. subjected her to rape, sexual assaults and cruel, inhuman and degrading treatment. Witness D. was also interrogated by the accused, and accused B subjected him to serious physical assaults. He was made to watch rape and sexual assault perpetrated upon a woman whom he knew in order to force him to admit allegations made against her. In this regard, both witnesses were humiliated.

Accused B. beat witness D. and repeatedly raped witness A. while the accused was present in the room as he carried on his interrogations. When not in the room, he was present in the near vicinity, just outside an open door, and he knew that crimes including rape were being committed. In fact, the acts by accused B. were performed in pursuance of the accused's interrogation. It was clear that in the pantry both witness A. and witness D. were subjected to severe physical and mental suffering, and they were also publicly humiliated.

There was no doubt that the accused and accused B., as commanders, divided the process of interrogation by performing different functions. The role of the accused was to question, while accused B.'s role was to assault and threaten in order to elicit the required information from the witnesses.

Law and legal findings

As to the law, the trial chamber first made reference to article 3 of the Statute, which empowered the International Tribunal to prosecute persons violating the laws or customs of war. It noted that this provision had a very broad scope, as interpreted by the International Tribunal in a previous appeal case. It covered any serious violation of a rule of customary international humanitarian law entailing, under international customary or conventional law, the individual criminal responsibility of the person

IV:3

breaching the rule. It was immaterial whether the breach occured within the context of an international or internal armed conflict.

It followed that the list of offences contained in article 3 of the Statute was merely illustrative. This provision also covered serious violations of international rules of humanitarian law not included in that list. More than the other substantive provisions of the Statute, article 3 constituted an "umbrella rule". While the other provisions envisaged classes of offences they indicated in terms, article 3 made an open-ended reference to all international rules of humanitarian law. Pursuant to article 3, violations of any international rule of humanitarian law might be regarded as crimes falling under this provision of the Statute if the requisite conditions were met.

The trial chamber continued with detailed accounts of torture in international law. In respect of international humanitarian law, it observed that torture in times of armed conflict was specifically prohibited by international treaty law, in particular by the Geneva Conventions and their Additional Protocols.

Under the Statute, as interpreted in the previous appeal case, these treaty provisions might be applied as such by the International Tribunal if it was proved that at the relevant time, all the parties to the conflict were bound by them. Bosnia and Herzegovina had ratified all these instruments. Accordingly, at least common article 3 and article 4 of Protocol II, both explicitly prohibiting torture, were applicable as minimum fundamental guarantees of treaty law in the territory of Bosnia and Herzegovina at the time relevant to the indictment. In addition, in 1992, the parties to the conflict in Bosnia and Herzegovina undertook to observe the most important provisions of the Geneva Conventions, including those prohibiting torture. Thus, the provisions concerning torture applied as being treaty law in the territory of Bosnia and Herzegovina as between the parties to the conflict.

The trial chamber also noted that torture was prohibited as a war crime under the penal code of the Socialist Federal Republic of Yugoslavia, and the same violation had been made punishable in the Republic of Bosnia and Herzegovina by virtue of decree-law.

It further made reference to how a general prohibition against torture had evolved in customary international law. That the treaty provisions mentioned in the judgment had ripened into customary rules was evinced by various factors. Firstly, these treaties, in particular the Geneva Conventions, had been ratified by practically all States of the world. Admittedly those treaty provisions remained as such, and any contracting party was formally entitled to relieve itself of its obligations by denouncing the treaty, an occurrence extremely unlikely in reality. Nevertheless, the practically universal participation in these treaties showed that all States accepted among other things the prohibition of torture. In other words, this participation was highly indicative of the attitude of States to the prohibition of torture. Secondly, no State had ever claimed that it was authorized to practice torture in time of armed conflict, nor had any State shown or manifested opposition to the implementation of treaty provisions against torture. When a State had been taken to task, because its officials allegedly resorted to torture, it had normally responded that the allegation was unfounded, thus expressly or implicitly upholding the prohibition of this odious practice. Thirdly, the International Court of Justice had authoritatively, albeit not with express reference to torture, confirmed this custom-creating process. In a judgment, it had held that common article 3, *inter alia* prohibiting torture against persons taking no active part in hostilities, was now well-established as belonging to the corpus of customary international law and was applicable both to international and internal armed conflicts.

It therefore seemed incontrovertible to the trial chamber that torture in time of armed conflict was prohibited by a general rule of international law. In armed conflicts, this rule might be applied both as part of international customary law and, if the requisite conditions were met, as being treaty law, the content of the prohibition being the same.

The treaty and customary rules thus referred to imposed obligations upon States and other entities in an armed conflict. First and foremost, however, they addressed themselves to the acts of individuals, in particular to State officials, or more generally, to officials of a party to the conflict or else to individuals acting at the instigation or with the consent or acquiescence of a party to the conflict. Both customary rules and treaty provisions applicable in times of armed conflict prohibited any act of torture. Those who engaged in torture were personally accountable at the criminal level for such acts. As the International Military Tribunal at Nuremberg had put it in general terms, crimes against international law were committed by men, not by abstract entities, and only by punishing individuals who committed such crimes could the provisions of international law be enforced. The trial chamber pronounced that individuals were personally responsible, whatever their official position, even if they were heads of State or government ministers.

The trial chamber stressed that in international humanitarian law, depending on the specific circumstances of each case, torture might be prosecuted as a category of such broad international crimes as serious violations of humanitarian law, grave breaches of the Geneva Conventions, crimes against humanity or genocide. Under current international humanitarian law, in addition to individual criminal liability, State responsibility might ensue as a result of State officials engaging in torture or failing to prevent torture or to punish torturers. If carried out as an extensive practice of State officials, torture amounted to a serious breach on a widespread scale of an

IV:3

international obligation of essential importance for safeguarding the human being, thus constituting a particularly grave wrongful act generating State responsibility.

In respect of international human rights law, the trial chamber pointed out that the prohibition of torture laid down in international humanitarian law with regard to situations of armed conflict was reinforced by the body of international treaty rules on human rights. These rules banned torture both in armed conflict and in time of peace. In addition, treaties as well as resolutions of international organizations set up mechanisms designed to ensure that the prohibition was implemented and to prevent resort to torture as much as possible.

The trial chamber said it should be noted that the prohibition of torture laid down in human rights treaties enshrined an absolute right, which could never be derogated from, not even in time of emergency. On this ground, the prohibition also applied to situations of armed conflicts. This was linked to the fact that the prohibition of torture was a peremptory norm or *jus cogens*. The prohibition was so extensive that States were even barred by international law from expelling, returning or extraditing a person to another State where there were substantial grounds for believing that the person would be in danger of being subjected to torture.

These treaty provisions imposed upon States the obligation to prohibit and punish torture, as well as to refrain from engaging in torture through their officials. In international human rights law, which dealt with State responsibility rather than individual criminal responsibility, torture was prohibited as a criminal offence to be punished under national law. In addition, the trial chamber observed, all States parties to the relevant treaties had been granted, and were obliged to exercise, jurisdiction to investigate, prosecute and punish offenders. Thus, in human rights law too, the prohibition of torture extended to and had a direct bearing on the criminal liability of individuals.

The existence of this corpus of general and treaty rules proscribing torture showed that the international community, aware of the importance of outlawing this heinous phenomenon, had decided to suppress any manifestation of torture by operating both at the inter-State level and at the level of individuals. The trial chamber noted that no legal loopholes had been left.

The trial chamber then continued outlining main features of the prohibition against torture in international law. There existed today universal revulsion against torture. This revulsion, as well as the importance States attached to the eradication of torture, had led to the cluster of treaty and customary rules on torture acquiring a particularly high status in the international normative system, a status similar to that of principles such as those prohibiting genocide, slavery, racial discrimination, aggression, the acquisition of territory by force and the forcible suppression of the right of peoples to self-determination. The trial chamber observed that the prohibition of torture exhibited three important features, which were probably held in common with the other general principles protecting fundamental human rights.

Firstly, the prohibition even covered potential breaches. Given the importance that the international community attached to the protection of individuals from torture, the prohibition against torture was particularly stringent and sweeping. States were obliged not only to prohibit and punish torture, but also to forestall its occurrence. It was insufficient merely to intervene, the trial chamber observed, after the infliction of torture when the physical or moral integrity of human beings had already been irremediably harmed. Consequently, States were bound to put in place all those measures that might pre-empt the perpetration of torture. As had been authoritatively held by the European Court of Human Rights, international law intended to bar not only actual breaches, but also potential breaches of the prohibition against torture, as well as any inhuman and degrading treatment. It followed that international rules prohibited not only torture, but also the failure to adopt the national measures necessary for implementing the prohibition and the maintenance in force or passage of laws contrary to the prohibition.

Secondly, the prohibition imposed on States obligations *erga omnes*, obligations owed towards all the other members of the international community, each of which then having a correlative right. In addition, the trial chamber noted, the violation of such an obligation simultaneously constituted a breach of the correlative right of all members of the international community and gave rise to a claim for compliance accruing to each and every member, then having the right to insist on fulfilment of the obligation or in any case to call for the breach to be discontinued.

Where there existed international bodies charged with impartially monitoring compliance with treaty provisions on torture, these bodies enjoyed priority over individual States in establishing whether a certain State had taken all the necessary measures to prevent and punish torture and, if they had not, in calling upon that State to fulfil its international obligations. The existence of such international mechanisms made it possible for compliance with international law to be ensured in a neutral and impartial manner.

Finally, the prohibition had acquired the status of *jus cogens*. The trial chamber noted that while the *erga omnes* nature it had just mentioned appertained to the area of international enforcement, the other major feature of the principle proscribing torture related to the hierarchy of rules in the international normative order. Because of the importance of the values it protected, this principle had evolved into a peremptory norm or *jus cogens*, a norm that enjoyed a higher rank in the international hierar-

IV:3

chy than treaty law and even other customary rules. The most conspicuous consequence of this higher rank was that the principle at issue could not be derogated from by States through international treaties or local or special customs or even general customary rules not endowed with the same normative force.

Clearly, the *jus cogens* nature of the prohibition against torture articulated the notion that the prohibition had now became one of the most fundamental standards of the international community. Furthermore, this prohibition was designed to produce a deterrent effect, in that it signaled to all members of the international community and the individuals over whom they wielded authority that the prohibition of torture was an absolute value from which nobody must deviate.

The fact that torture was prohibited by a peremptory norm of international law had other effects at the inter-State and individual levels. It served to internationally delegitimize any legislative, administrative or judicial act authorizing torture. At the individual level, that of criminal liability, it seemed to the trial chamber that one of the consequences of the *jus cogens* character bestowed by the international community upon the prohibition of torture was that every State was entitled to investigate, prosecute and punish or extradite individuals accused of torture present in a territory under its jurisdiction.

In respect of the definition of torture, finally, the trial chamber noted that international humanitarian law did not provide a definition of the prohibition, albeit outlawing torture in armed conflict. Such a definition could instead be found in article 1, paragraph 1, of the Convention against Torture and Other Cruel, Inhuman or Degrading Treatment or Punishment, cited in the judgment.

The trial chamber reviewed international instruments and international jurisprudence bearing on the definition of torture. It noted that their broad convergence demonstrated that there was now general acceptance of the main elements contained in the definition set out in that Convention. It considered, however, that while the definition applied to any instance of torture, whether in time of peace or of armed conflict, it was appropriate to identify or spell out some specific elements that pertained to torture as considered from the specific viewpoint of international criminal law relating to armed conflicts. The trial chamber considered that the elements of torture in an armed conflict required that torture:

- consisted of the infliction, by act or omission, of severe pain or suffering, whether physical or mental; in addition

- this act or omission must be intentional;

- it must aim at obtaining information or a confession, or at punishing, intimidating, humiliating or coercing the victim or a third person, or at discriminating, on any ground, against the victim or a third person;

- it must be linked to an armed conflict; and

- at least one of the persons involved in the torture process must be a public official or must at any rate act in a non-private capacity, for example as a de facto organ of a State or any other authority-wielding entity.

As was apparent from this enumeration of criteria, the trial chamber considered that among the possible purposes of torture, one must also include that of humiliating the victim. This proposition was warranted by the general spirit of international humanitarian law: the primary purpose of this body of law was to safeguard human dignity. It was also supported by some general provisions of such important international treaties as the Geneva Conventions and their Additional Protocols, consistently aiming at protecting persons not taking part, or no longer taking part, in the hostilities from outrages upon personal dignity. In any event, the notion of humiliation was close to the notion of intimidation, explicitly referred to in the definition of torture.

The trial chamber, citing authorities, observed that the vicious and ignominious practice of torture could take on various forms. There was a momentum towards addressing, through legal process, the use of rape in the course of detention and interrogation as a means of torture and, therefore, as a violation of international law. Rape was resorted to either by the interrogator himself or by other persons associated with the interrogation of a detainee, as a means of punishing, intimidating, coercing or humiliating the victim, or obtaining information or a confession from the victim or a third person. Under human rights law, rape in such situations might amount to torture, as demonstrated, for example, by the the jurisprudence of the European Court of Human Rights.

As to the law, the trial chamber continued with similar accounts of rape and other sexual assaults in international law. In respect of international humanitarian law, it made reference to provisions of the Geneva Conventions and their Additional Protocols and observed that rape in time of war was specifically prohibited by treaty law. Other serious sexual assaults were expressly or implicitly prohibited in various provisions of the same treaties.

In the present case, at least common article 3, implicitly referring to rape, and article 4 of Protocol II, explicitly mentioning rape, applied as being treaty law, because Bosnia and Herzegovina had ratified these instruments. Furthermore, the parties to the conflict had undertaken to observe the most important provisions of the Geneva

IV:3

Conventions and to grant the protections afforded therein. In addition, the trial chamber noted that rape and inhuman treatment were prohibited as war crimes by penal code provisions applicable in Bosnia and Herzegovina.

The trial chamber traced the ways in which the prohibition of rape and serious sexual assault in armed conflict had also evolved in customary international law. It concluded that universally accepted norms of international law prohibiting rape and serious sexual assault, applicable in any armed conflict, had evolved. It was indisputable that rape and other serious sexual assaults in armed conflict entailed the criminal liability of the perpetrators.

In respect of international human rights law, the trial chamber observed that no international human rights instrument specifically prohibited rape or other serious sexual assaults. Nevertheless, these offences were implicitly prohibited by the provisions safeguarding physical integrity, which were contained in all relevant international treaties. The right to physical integrity was a fundamental right, undeniably part of customary international law. Furthermore, the trial chamber recalled, in certain circumstances, rape could amount to torture and had been found by international judicial bodies to constitute a violation of the norm prohibiting torture.

The trial chamber further recalled that the prosecution of rape was explicitly provided for in article 5 of the Statute as a crime against humanity. Rape might also amount to a grave breach of the Geneva Conventions, a violation of the laws or customs of war or an act of genocide, if the requisite elements were met, and might be prosecuted accordingly. Moreover, the Statute covered outrages upon personal dignity including rape.

In respect of the definition of rape, the trial chamber noted the unchallenged submission of the prosecution that rape was a forcible act and that no definition of rape could be found in international law. In order to arrive at an accurate definition of rape based on the criminal law principle of specificity, it looked for principles of criminal law common to the major legal systems of the world. It was apparent from this survey of national legislation that in spite of inevitable discrepancies, most legal systems in the common and civil law worlds consider rape to be the forcible sexual penetration of the human body by the penis or the forcible insertion of any other object into either the vagina or the anus.

The trial chamber did, however, discern a major discrepancy in the criminalization of forced oral penetration. Some States treated it as sexual assault, while it was categorized as rape in other States. In seeking an appropriate solution to this lack of uniformity, the trial chamber held that the forced penetration of the mouth by the male sexual organ constituted a most humiliating and degrading attack upon human dignity. It observed that the essence of the whole corpus of international humanitarian law as well as human rights law lay in the protection of the human dignity of every person irrespective of gender. The general principle of respect for human dignity was the basic underpinning and indeed the very *raison d'être* of international humanitarian law and human rights law. It was consonant with this principle that such an extremely serious sexual outrage as forced oral penetration should be classified as rape.

Thus, the trial chamber found that the following might be accepted as the objective elements of rape:

- the sexual penetration, however slight of the vagina or anus of the victim by the penis of the perpetrator or any other object used by the perpetrator, or of the mouth of the victim by the penis of the perpetrator;

- by coercion or force or threat of force against the victim or a third person.

In respect of individual criminal responsibility, the trial chamber noted that under article 7, paragraph 1, of the Statute not only the commission of rape or serious sexual assault, but also the planning, ordering or instigating of such acts, as well as aiding and abetting in the perpetration, were prohibited. The accused was charged with torture and outrages upon personal dignity, including rape. For the purposes of the present case, it was necessary to define aiding and abetting as used in the Statute.

The trial chamber observed that since no treaty law on the subject existed, it had to examine customary international law in order to establish the content of this head of criminal responsibility. In particular, it had to establish whether the alleged presence of the accused in the locations where witness A. was assaulted would be sufficient to constitute the *actus reus* of aiding and abetting, and the relevant *mens rea* required to accompany this action for responsibility to ensue had to be substantiated.

After reviewing at length international case law and international instruments on these questions, the trial chamber held the legal ingredients of aiding and abetting in international criminal law to be the following. The *actus reus* consisted of practical assistance, encouragement or moral support which had a substantial effect on the perpetration of the crime. The *mens rea* required the knowledge that these acts assisted the commission of the offence. This notion of aiding and abetting was to be distinguished from the notion of common design, where the *actus reus* consisted of participation in a joint criminal enterprise and the *mens rea* required intent to participate.

IV:3

The trial chamber concluded its legal analysis by outlining how to distinguish perpetration of torture from aiding and abetting torture. The definitions and propositions concerning aiding and abetting it had enunciated applied equally to rape and to torture, and indeed to all crimes. Nevertheless, the trial chamber deemed it useful to address the issue of who might be held responsible for torture as a perpetrator and who as an aider and abettor, since in modern times the infliction of torture typically involved a large number of people, each performing his or her individual function. It was appropriate to elaborate the principles of individual criminal responsibility applicable thereto. The trial chamber recalled that under current international law, individuals had to refrain from perpetrating torture or in any way participating in torture.

To determine whether an individual was a perpetrator or co-perpetrator of torture or had instead to be regarded as an aider and abettor, or even not to be regarded as criminally liable, the trial chamber observed that it was crucial to ascertain whether the individual who took part in the torture process also was partaking of the purpose behind torture. If he did not but gave some sort of assistance and support with the knowledge, however, that torture was being practised, then the individual might be found guilty of aiding and abetting in the perpetration of torture. Arguably, if the person attending the torture process neither shared in the purpose behind torture, nor in any way assisted in its perpetration, then he should not be regarded as criminally liable. Here, the trial chamber gave the example of the soldier whom a superior had ordered to attend a torture session in order to determine whether that soldier could stomach the sight of torture and thus be trained as a torturer.

These legal propositions, based on a logical interpretation of the customary rules on torture, were supported by a teleological construction of these rules. To demonstrate this point, the trial chamber observed that account had to be taken of some modern trends in many States practising torture. They tended to "compartmentalize" and "dilute" the moral and psychological burden of perpetrating torture by assigning to different individuals a partial, and sometimes relatively minor, role in the torture process. Thus, one person could order torture to be carried out; another could organize the whole process at the administrative level; yet another could ask questions while the detainee was being tortured; a fourth one could provide or prepare the tools for executing torture although another physically inflicted torture or caused mental suffering; someone else could furnish medical assistance so as to prevent the detainee from dying as a consequence of torture or from subsequently showing physical traces of the sufferings he had undergone; another person could process the results of interrogation known to be obtained under torture; and finally, yet another could procure the information gained as a result of the torture in exchange for granting the torturer immunity from prosecution.

Failing to take account of these modern trends, international law would prove unable to cope with this despicable practice. The rules of construction emphasizing the importance of the object and purpose of international norms led the trial chamber to conclude that international law rendered all the aforementioned persons equally accountable, although some might be sentenced more severely than others, depending on the circumstances. In other words, the nature of the crime and the forms that it took, as well as the intensity of international condemnation of torture, suggested that in the case of torture, all those who in some degree participated in the crime and in particular took part in the pursuance of one of its underlying purposes were equally liable.

The trial chamber stressed that this was to a large extent consistent with the provisions contained in particular in the Convention against Torture, from which it could be inferred that they prohibited not only the physical infliction of torture, but also any deliberate participation in this practice. It followed, *inter alia*, that if an official interrogated a detainee while another person was inflicting severe pain or suffering, the interrogator was as guilty of torture as the person causing the severe pain or suffering, even if he did not in any way physically participate in such infliction. Here the criminal law maxim of *quis per alium facit per se ipsum facere videtur*, or he who acts through others is regarded as acting himself, fully applied.

Furthermore, the trial chamber observed, it followed from the above that at least in those instances where torture was practised under the pattern described, that is with more than one person acting as co-perpetrators of the crime, accomplice liability might only occur within very narrow confines. Thus, it would seem that aiding and abetting in the commission of torture might only exist in such very limited instances as for example driving the torturers to the place of torture in full knowledge of the acts they were going to perform there; or bringing food and drink to the perpetrators at the place of torture, again in full knowledge of the activity they were carrying out there. In these instances, those aiding and abetting in the commission of torture could be regarded as accessories to the crime. By contrast, at least in the case under discussion, all other varying forms of direct participation in torture should be regarded as instances of co-perpetration of the crime and those co-perpetrators should all be held to be principals. Nevertheless, the varying degree of direct participation as principals might still be a matter to consider for sentencing purposes.

The trial chamber summarized its reasoning in the following way:

- to be guilty of torture as a perpetrator or co-perpetrator, the accused must participate in an integral part of the torture and partake of the purpose behind the torture, that is the intent to obtain information or a confession, to punish or intimidate, humiliate, coerce or discriminate against the victim or a third person; and

IV:3

- to be guilty of torture as an aider or abettor, the accused must assist in some way which has a substantial effect on the perpetration of the crime and with knowledge that torture was taking place.

As to the legal findings in the case, the trial chamber found Anto Furundzija, as co-perpetrator, guilty of a violation of the laws or customs of war in respect of torture and, for aiding and abetting, a violation of the laws or customs of war in respect of outrages upon personal dignity, including rape.

Sentencing

The trial chamber considered that the imposition of sentence had to take account of various mitigating and aggravating factors as well as the sentencing practices of the courts of the former Yugoslavia. For torture as a violation of the laws or customs of war, it sentenced Anto Furundzija to 10 years' imprisonment and for outrages upon personal dignity, including rape, as a violation of the laws or customs of war to eight years' imprisonment. The sentences were to be served concurrently, *inter se.*

Anto Furundzija appealed against these convictions and sentences. The appeals chamber unanimously rejected each ground of appeal, dismissed the appeal and confirmed the convictions and sentences.

TABLE OF CASES*

(*a*) Human Rights Committee

Adolfo Drescher Caldas v. *Uruguay*	209
Aduayom et al. v. *Togo*	438
Albert Berry v. *Jamaica*	215-216, 353
Albert Womah Mukong v. *Cameroon*	128-129, *158-161*, 207
	439-440
Auli Kivenmaa v. *Finland*	442-443, 490-491, *500-508*
Barbarin Mojica v. *the Dominican Republic*	202-203
Bernard Lubuto v. *Zambia*	349-350, *378-381*
Borisenko v. *Hungary*	213
Celis Laureano v. *Peru*	129-130, *161-163*
Chongwe v. *Zambia*	205, *247-248*
Dieter Wolf v. *Panama*	349
Elena Quinteros and	
M. C. Almeida de Quinteros v. *Uruguay*	130, 147
Eric Hammel v. *Madagascar*	214-215
Famara Koné v. *Senegal*	214
G. B. v. *France*	443-444
Gerald J. Griffin v. *Spain*	209-210
G. Peart and A. Peart v. *Jamaica*	352, *382-385*
Gridin v. *Russian Federation*	345, *374-378*
Guillermo Ignacio Dermit Barbato and	
Hugo Haroldo Dermit Barbato v. *Uruguay*	46, 542
Henry Kalenga v. *Zambia*	439
Herrera Rubio v. *Colombia*	44-45, 542
Hugo Rodríguez v. *Uruguay*	127-128, *155-158*
Hugo van Alphen v. *the Netherlands*	206
Ismet Celepli v. *Turkey*	201-202
Jayawardena v. *Sri Lanka*	542-544
John Campbell v. *Jamaica*	345-346
John Khemraadi Baboeram et al. v. *Suriname*	48
Jong-Kyu Sohn v. *the Republic of Korea*	440-441, *459-463*
K. Singh Bhinder v. *Canada*	412-413
Larry James Pinkney v. *Canada*	290-291
Leehong v. *Jamaica*	205-206
Lloyd Grant v. *Jamaica*	351
L. T. K. v. *Finland*	411-412
M. A. B., W. A. T. and J.-A. Y. T. v. *Canada*	413, *417-419*
Maria Fanny Suárez de Guerrero v. *Colombia*	43-44, *67-72*, 541-542

---

* Numbers after a case indicate page or pages where the case is cited. Numbers in italics refer to case summaries.

Michael and Brian Hill v. *Spain*	210, 213-214, *255-258*, 349
Miguel Angel Estrella v. *Uruguay*	290, *308-310*
Monja Joana v. *Madagascar*	437-438
Nallaratnam v. *Sri Lanka*	544-545
Neville Lewis v. *Jamaica*	213
Nicholas Toonen v. *Australia*	291-292, 303
Nicole Fillastre v. *Bolivia*	212
Nydia Bautista de Arellana v. *Colombia*	45-46
Paul Anthony Kelly v. *Jamaica*	347-348
Paul Kelly v. *Jamaica*	210-211, *252-255*, 348
Peter Grant v. *Jamaica*	209
Rickly Burrell v. *Jamaica*	47, 542
Robert Faurisson v. *France*	441-442
Rojas García v. *Colombia*	130-131, 289-290, *305-307*
Ronald H. van der Houwen v. *the Netherlands*	212
R. T. Muñoz Hermoza v. *Peru*	346-347
Sánchez López v. *Spain*	352-353
Sarma v. *Sri Lanka*	203-205
Sergio Rubén López Burgos v. *Uruguay*	131-132, 207
Sextus v. *Trinidad and Tobago*	350-351
S. G. v. *France*	443-444
Spakmo v. *Norway*	208, *250-252*
V. P. Domukovsky et al. v. *Georgia*	208, *248-250*
W. Delgado Páez v. *Colombia*	202, *244-246*

(*b*) Committee on the Elimination of Racial Discrimination

L. K. v. *the Netherlands*	337-338
Kashid Ahmad v. *Denmark*	338-339

(*c*) Committee against Torture

Encarnación Blanco Abad v. *Spain*	133-135
Gorki Ernesto Tapia Paez v. *Sweden*	137
Hajrizi Dzemajl et al. v. *Serbia and Montenegro*	139, 545-546, *562-572*
Ismail Alan v. *Switzerland*	136-137
Josu Arkauz Arana v. *France*	138
Qani Halimi-Nedzibi v. *Austria*	133
Radivoje Ristic v. *Yugoslavia*	135-136, *163-168*

(*d*) Working Group on Arbitrary Detention

Decision No. 8/1992 (*Myanmar*)	358
Decision No. 59/1993 (*Kuwait*)	548-549
Decision No. 16/1994 (*Israel*)	547-548, *573-575*
Decision No. 38/1994 (*Turkey*)	217-218, *258-262*

Decision No. 45/1995 (*Egypt*) 219
Decision No. 46/1995 (*China*) 220
Opinion No. 16/1997 (*Bolivia*) 219-220
Opinion No. 14/1999 (*Palestine*) 355-356
Opinion No. 19/1999 (*China*) 447-448
Opinion No. 32/2000 (*Uzbekistan*) 446-447
Opinion No. 37/2000 (*Mexico*) 218-219
Opinion No. 1/2001 (*Uzbekistan*) 356-357
Opinion No. 11/2001 (*Viet Nam*) 221-222
Opinion No. 18/2001 (*Mexico*) 218
Opinion No. 25/2001 (*Pakistan*) 549-550, *576-579*
Opinion No. 27/2001 (*Morocco*) 354-355, *385-390*, 445-446
Opinion No. 29/2001 (*Ethiopia*) 357-358
Opinion No. 2/2002 (*Myanmar*) 358-359

(*e*) International Tribunal for the former Yugoslavia

Prosecutor v. *Anto Furundzija* 126-127, 600-602, *616-636*
Prosecutor v. *Drazen Erdemovic* 607-610
Prosecutor v. *Zejnil Delalic, Zdravko Mucic,*
   Hazim Delic and Esad Landzo,
   the *"Celebici"* case 602-607

(*f*) International Criminal Tribunal for Rwanda

Prosecutor v. *Clément Kayishema and*
   Obed Ruzindana 613-616
Prosecutor v. *Jean-Paul Akayesu* 611-613

(*g*) Committee on Freedom of Association

Case No. 1007 (*Nicaragua*) 222-223
Case No. 1014 (*Dominican Republic*) 492
Case No. 1192 (*Philippines*) 50
Case No. 1208 (*Nicaragua*) 222-223
Case No. 1233 (*El Salvador*) 49-50
Case No. 1258 (*El Salvador*) 223
Case No. 1285 (*Chile*) 223, 493
Case No. 1308 (*Grenada*) 224
Case No. 1341 (*Paraguay*) 140
Case No. 1414 (*Israel*) 223-224
Case No. 1434 (*Colombia*) 51
Case No. 1508 (*Sudan*) 140-141
Case No. 1510 (*Paraguay*) 492-493
Case No. 1527 (*Peru*) 141
Case No. 1598 (*Peru*) 50-51, 493-494

Case No. 1700 (*Nicaragua*)	50
Case No. 1761 (*Colombia*)	52, *72-74*
Case No. 1888 (*Ethiopia*)	51-52, 224, 494
Case No. 2005 (*Central African Republic*)	141-142, *168-172*
Case No. 2074 (*Cameroon*)	224
Case No. 2090 (*Belarus*)	494-495
Case No. 2116 (*Indonesia*)	225, *262-266*
Case No. 2184 (*Zimbabwe*)	495, *508-511*
Case No. 2189 (*China*)	495-496, *511-518*

(*h*) African Commission on Human and Peoples' Rights

Commission Nationale des Droits de l'Homme et des Libertés v. *Chad*	551-552
Constitutional Rights Project and Civil Liberties Organisation v. *Nigeria*	225-227
Free Legal Assistance Group et al. v. *Zaire*	550-551, *579-582*
Jean Yaovi Degli et al. v. *Togo*	552-553
John D. Ouko v. *Kenya*	143
Krischna Achutan and Amnesty International v. *Malawi*	53, 142-143, 360
Malawi African Association et al. v. *Mauritania*	143-144, 553-555

(*i*) Inter-American Court of Human Rights

Bámaca Velásquez case (*Guatemala*)	55-56, 148, 149, 555-557
	582-593
Blake case (*Guatemala*)	362-363
Cantoral Benavides case (*Peru*)	146-147, 147-148, 149
	178-183
Castillo Páez case (*Peru*)	228, 230, *266-269*
Del Caracazo case (*Venezuela*)	557-558
Genie Lacayo case (*Nicaragua*)	361-362
Ivcher Bronstein case (*Peru*)	449-450, *463-469*
Neira Allegría et al. case (*Peru*)	56
Paniagua Morales et al. case (*Guatemala*), the *"white van"* case	363-365
Suárez Rosero case (*Ecuador*)	146, 229-231
Velásquez Rodrígues case (*Honduras*)	36-37, 54-55, 56, *74-85*
	146, 228
Villagrán Morales et al. case (*Guatemala*), the *"street children"* case	56-57, 145-146, 147, 148-149
	172-178, 231-232

(j) European Court of Human Rights

A. v. *France*	295-296, *310-313*
Aksoy v. *Turkey*	152-153, *184-186*, 240-241
Allenet de Ribemont v. *France*	371-372, *390-395*
Andronicou and Constantinou v. *Cyprus*	60-61
Barberà, Messagré and Jabordo case (*Spain*)	368-369
Brogan and Others case (*the United Kingdom*)	239-240, 244, *270-281*
Chappell case (*the United Kingdom*)	300-301
Ciulla case (*Italy*)	233-234, 236
Doorson v. *the Netherlands*	374, *400-405*
Dudgeon case (*the United Kingdom*)	304, 305
Engel and Others case (*the Netherlands*)	366, 457-458
Ergi v. *Turkey*	559-560, *594-596*
Ezelin v. *France*	499-500
Fox, Campbell and Hartley case (*the United Kingdom*)	236-237, 238-239
Güleç v. *Turkey*	560-562
Guzzardi case (*Italy*)	233, 235-236
Halford v. *the United Kingdom*	296-297, *313-322*
Ireland v. *the United Kingdom*	150-151, 152
John Murray v. *the United Kingdom*	370-371
K.-F. v. *Germany*	237, *282-286*
Kalaç v. *Turkey*	415-416, *419-421*
Klass and Others case (*Germany*)	293-294, 299
Kokkinakis v. *Greece*	414-415
Kostovski case (*the Netherlands*)	372-373
Lawless case (*Ireland*)	234-235, 235
Leander case (*Sweden*)	298-299
Lukanov v. *Bulgaria*	234
Mahmut Kaya v. *Turkey*	65, *104-112*
Malone case (*the United Kingdom*)	294-295
McCann and Others v. *the United Kingdom*	59-60, *86-104*, 559
McKerr v. *the United Kingdom*	61-62
Metropolitan Church of Bessarabia and Others v. *Moldova*	416, *422-432*
Murray v. *the United Kingdom*	301-302
Nachova and Others v. *Bulgaria*	65-66, *112-122*
Neumeister case (*Austria*)	242
Niemietz v. *Germany*	292-293
Norris case (*Ireland*)	304-305
Osman v. *the United Kingdom*	62-63, 65, 366-367
Özgür Gündem v. *Turkey*	453, *476-486*
Paul and Audrey Edwards v. *the United Kingdom*	63-65
P. G. and J. H. v. *the United Kingdom*	297, *322-332*
Plattform "Ärzte für das Leben" case (*Austria*)	498-499, *519-524*
Ribitsch v. *Austria*	154-155

641

Rotaru v. *Romania*   299-300
S. v. *Switzerland*   372, *395-400*
Saunders v. *the United Kingdom*   369-370
Schenk case (*Switzerland*)   367-368
Schiesser case (*Switzerland*)   241-242
Schönenberger and Durmaz case (*Switzerland*)   302-303
Selmouni v. *France*   147, 153-154, *186-197*
Sürek v. *Turkey* (No. 2)   454-455
Thorgeir Thorgeirson v. *Iceland*   452-453, *470-476*
Tomasi v. *France*   151-152
Vereinigung demokratischer Soldaten Österreichs
        and Gubi v. *Austria*   458-459
Vereniging Weekblad Bluf! v. *the Netherlands*   455-457
W. v. *Switzerland*   242-243
Windisch case (*Austria*)   373-374
Winterwerp case (*the Netherlands*)   238, 243
Zana v. *Turkey*   451-452
Zimmermann and Steiner case (*Switzerland*)   371

Christians against Rascism and Fascism
        v. *the United Kingdom*   497-498
        (declared inadmissible)
Greek case (*Greece*)   149-150, 150, 152
        (decided upon under article 32)
McVeigh, O'Neill and Evans v. *the United Kingdom*   235
        (decided upon under article 32)
Rassemblement jurassien and Unité jurassienne
        v. *Switzerland*   496-497
        (declared inadmissible)
Stewart v. *the United Kingdom*   58-59, 96
        (declared inadmissible)

TABLE OF INSTRUMENTS*

(a) Universal Declaration of Human Rights and universal human rights treaties

Universal Declaration of Human Rights

Adopted by the General Assembly of the United Nations
on 10 December 1948[1]

General	5, 10, 16-17, 127, 216-217, 262, 354, 357, 390, 410, 434, 436, 444-445, 488-489, 547, 575
Preamble	537
Article 2	6
Article 3	39, 199, 245
Article 5	14, 123, 217-218, 261, 356
Article 7	6, 17, 216, 354, 444, 547
Article 8	8
Article 9	199, 219-220, 355-359, 389 445-446, 548, 549-550, 575 578-579
Article 10	199, 219-220, 341, 355-359 389, 445-446, 548, 550, 575 578-579
Article 11	199, 219-220
Article 12	287
Article 13	17, 199, 216, 354, 444, 547
Article 14	17, 216, 354, 444, 547
Article 18	17, 216, 220, 222, 354, 407

---

* Numbers after general reference or specific provisions indicate page or pages where the instrument is accordingly cited. Numbers in italics refer to section of the book primarily focusing on the specific provision. In the notes, *Essential Texts* refers to *Essential Texts on Human Rights for the Police: A Compilation of International Instruments*, edited by Ralph Crawshaw and Leif Holmström (The Hague/London/Boston, Kluwer Law International, 2001), *RWI Compilation I* refers to *The Raoul Wallenberg Institute Compilation of Human Rights Instruments*, edited by Göran Melander and Gudmundur Alfredsson (The Hague/London/Boston, Martinus Nijhoff Publishers, 1997) and *RWI Compilation II* refers to *The Raoul Wallenberg Institute Compilation of Human Rights Instruments*, edited by Göran Melander, Gudmundur Alfredsson and Leif Holmström, second, revised edition (Leiden/Boston, Martinus Nijhoff Publishers, 2004).

[1] See General Assembly resolution 217 A (III) of 10 December 1948; *Essential Texts*, p. 17; and *RWI Compilation I*, p. 27 and *II*, p. 1.

	444, 547
Article 19	17, 216, 220, 222, 354, 359
	433, 444, 447-448, 547
Article 20	17, 216, 220, 354, 359, 444
	487, 547
Article 21	17, 216, 354, 444, 547
Article 23	487, 549

International Covenant on Economic, Social and Cultural Rights

Adopted by the General Assembly of the United Nations on 16 December 1966[2]

| General | 7 |
| Article 2 | 350 |

International Covenant on Civil and Political Rights

Adopted by the General Assembly of the United Nations on 16 December 1966[3]

General	10, 16, 46-48, 58, 67, 72, 123
	128-130, 141, 155, 157-159
	161, 163, 171, 202-204
	206-211, 213, 215-218, 220
	244-246, 249-250, 252, 255
	258, 262, 289-291, 307-309
	341, 349-350, 353-354, 356
	359, 376, 378, 381, 383-385
	389-390, 410-414, 417-418
	436, 442, 445, 448, 488-489
	538-539, 543, 545, 549-551
	573, 575-576, 579, 589
Preamble	10
Article 2	6, 8, 10, 45, 47, 128-129
	131-132, 157-158, 161-162
	163, 203, 205, 248, 250, 258

---

[2] See General Assembly resolution 2200 A (XXI) of 16 December 1966; United Nations, *Treaty Series*, vol. 993, No. I-14531; *Essential Texts*, p. 25; and *RWI Compilation I*, p. 33 and *II*, p. 9. The Covenant entered into force on 3 January 1976.

[3] See General Assembly resolution 2200 A (XXI) of 16 December 1966; United Nations, *Treaty Series*, vols. 999, No. I-14668, and 1059, No. A-14668 (corrigendum); *Essential Texts*, p. 37; and *RWI Compilation I*, p. 43 and *II*, p. 21. The Covenant entered into force on 23 March 1976.

	292, 307, 347, 378, 381, 385
	463, 505, 544-545
Article 3	7
Article 4	7, 39, 42, 71, 123, 127
	200-201, 288, 344, 411, 437
	490, 538, 539, 541
Article 6	39, *41-48*, 53, 57, *67-72*
	129, 203-206, 247-248, 255
	350-352, 378-379, 381-385
	538, 542, 589-590
Article 7	14, 44-45, 71, 123, *127-132*
	155-158, 158-161, 161-163
	180, 203-205, 207, 217-218
	261, 289-290, 305-307
	309-310, 344, 353, 378-379
	381-385, 440, 538, 542, 545
	569
Article 8	411, 538
Article 9	129, 131-132, 199-200
	200-216, 216, 219-220
	244-247, 247-248, 248-250
	250-252, 252-255, 255-258
	309, 348-351, 354-355
	357-358, 374, 377-378, 384
	389, 417, 419, 437-440, 444
	446-447, 543-544, 547-549
	575
Article 10	44-45, 204, 210, 220
	252-255, 258, 290, 309-310
	344, 357, 374, 382-385, 439
	539, 549
Article 11	538
Article 12	17, 201-202, 216, 354, 439
	444, 547
Article 13	215
Article 14	43, 211, 216, 218-220
	252-255, 261, 309, *343-353*
	354-355, 357-358, *374-378*
	378-381, 382-385, 388-389
	419, 444, 446-447, 544-545
	547-549, 575
Article 15	443, 490, 500, 501-503, 505
	507, 538
Article 16	538
Article 17	131, 287, *288-292, 305-307*
	308-310
Article 18	17, 216, 220, 222, 354

	407-408, *410-413, 417-419*
	444, 507, 538, 547
Article 19	17, 71, 129, 158, 161, 207
	216, 220, 222, 354, 389, 411
	433, *436-444*, 444-445, 447
	459-463, 490-491, 500-505
	507, 542, 547
Article 20	7, 433, 437
Article 21	17, 71, 216, 220, 354
	443-444, 487, *489-491*
	500-508, 540, 542, 547
Article 22	17, 216, 220, 354, 444, 487
	489-490, 547
Article 24	161-163, 346
Article 25	17, 216, 246, 250, 354, 438
	444, 547
Article 26	6, 17, 216, 354, 412-413
	444, 547
Article 27	17, 216, 354, 444, 547
Article 28	7, 10
Articles 41-43	10
Article 41	11, 448

*Optional Protocol to the International Covenant
on Civil and Political Rights*

Adopted by the General Assembly of the United Nations
on 16 December 1966[4]

General	10-11, 156, 163, 215, 250
	307, 309, 347, 418
Article 1	11, 131, 353, 419
Article 2	8, 419, 444
Article 3	419
Article 4	162

---

[4] See General Assembly resolution 2200 A (XXI) of 16 December 1966; United Nations, *Treaty Series*, vols. 999, No. I-14668, and 1059, No. A-14668 (corrigendum); *Essential Texts*, p. 59; and *RWI Compilation I*, p. 61 and *II*, p. 43. This Optional Protocol entered into force on 23 March 1976.

Second Optional Protocol to the International
Covenant on Civil and Political Rights,
aiming at the abolition of the death penalty

Adopted by the General Assembly of the United Nations
on 15 December 1989[5]

General	11, 42
Article 1	538
Article 4	11
Article 5	11
Article 6	538

International Convention on the Elimination
of All Forms of Racial Discrimination

Adopted by the General Assembly of the United Nations
on 21 December 1965[6]

General	7, 12, 336, 339
Preamble	336
Article 1	12, 338
Article 2	12, 338-339
Article 4	338-339, 434, 487
Article 5	407, 433-434, 487
Article 6	12, 338-339
Article 8	11
Articles 11-13	12
Article 14	12, 337

Convention on the Elimination of All Forms
of Discrimination against Women

Adopted by the General Assembly of the United Nations
on 18 December 1979[7]

General	7, 12

---

[5] See General Assembly resolution 44/128 of 15 December 1989; United Nations, *Treaty Series*, vol. 1642, No. A-14668; and *RWI Compilation I*, p. 65 and *II*, p. 49. This Optional Protocol entered into force on 11 July 1991.

[6] See General Assembly resolution 2106 A (XX) of 21 December 1965; United Nations, *Treaty Series*, vol. 660, No. I-9464; *Essential Texts*, p. 65; and *RWI Compilation I*, p. 255 and *II*, p. 207. The Convention entered into force on 4 January 1969.

[7] See General Assembly resolution 34/180 of 18 December 1979; United Nations, *Treaty Series*, vol. 1249, No. I-20378; and *RWI Compilation I*, p. 237 and *II*, p. 223. The Convention entered into force on 3 September 1981.

Article 1   13
Article 2   13
Article 17   13

Optional Protocol to the Convention
on the Elimination of All Forms of Discrimination
against Women

Adopted by the General Assembly of the United Nations
on 6 October 1999[8]

General   13-14
Article 1   13
Article 2   13

Convention against Torture and Other Cruel,
Inhuman or Degrading Treatment or Punishment

Adopted by the General Assembly of the United Nations
on 10 December 1984[9]

General   15, 123-124, 135, 139, 163
                                              165, 181, 258, 261, 546, 567
                                                                  630, 635
Preamble   14
Article 1   14, 123, 132, 139, 159, 181
                                               194-195, 546, 562, 566, 568
                                                            572, 588, 630
Article 2   14, 124, 132, 541, 562, 566
                                                                       572
Article 3   136-138
Article 4   9
Articles 5-9   132
Article 7   177
Articles 10-13   132, 572
Article 12   9, 14, 132-135, 139, 163
                                                    165-168, 177, 546, 562
                                                         566-567, 571-572
Article 13   14, 132-135, 139, 163, 165

[8] See General Assembly resolution 54/4 of 6 October 1999; United Nations, *Treaty Series*, vol. 2131, No. A-20378; and *RWI Compilation II*, p. 239. The Optional Protocol entered into force on 22 December 2000.

[9] See General Assembly resolution 39/46 of 10 December 1984; United Nations, *Treaty Series*, vol. 1465, No. I-24841; *Essential Texts*, p. 81; and *RWI Compilation I*, p. 549 and *II*, p. 445. The Convention entered into force on 26 June 1987.

	167-168, 546, 562, 566-567
	571-572
Article 14	14, 135, 163, 165, 168, 562
	566-567, 572
Article 15	14-15, 133, 217-218
	261-262
Article 16	14, 124, 132, 139, 167, 194
	546, 562, 566-568, 571-572
Article 17	14
Article 20	137
Article 21	15
Article 22	15, 566, 570

Optional Protocol to the Convention against Torture and Other Cruel, Inhuman or Degrading Treatment or Punishment

Adopted by the General Assembly of the United Nations on 18 December 2002[10]

| General | 124 |

Convention on the Rights of the Child

Adopted by the General Assembly of the United Nations on 20 November 1989[11]

General	7, 39
Article 1	39
Article 2	8
Article 6	39
Article 12	433
Article 13	433
Article 14	407
Article 15	487
Article 24	39
Article 37	200

---

[10] See General Assembly resolution 57/199 of 18 December 2002; and *RWI Compilation II*, p. 461. At present, the Optional Protocol has not entered into force.

[11] See General Assembly resolution 44/25 of 20 November 1989; United Nations, *Treaty Series*, vol. 1557, No. I-27531, and, as amended by General Assembly resolution 50/155 of 21 December 1995, vol. 2199, No. A-27531; *Essential Texts*, p. 97 (previous text); and *RWI Compilation I*, p. 279 (previous text) and *II*, p. 261. The Convention entered into force on 2 September 1990 and, as amended by General Assembly resolution 50/155, on 18 November 2002.

Article 38   39, 534-535

Article 40   342

Optional Protocol to the Convention
on the Rights of the Child
on the involvement of children in armed conflict

Adopted by the General Assembly of the United Nations
on 25 May 2000[12]

General   535

Article 1   39

Convention concerning Freedom of Association
and Protection of the Right to Organise

Adopted by the General Conference
of the International Labour Organisation,
at San Francisco, on 9 July 1948[13]

General   22-23, 49, 72, 169, 225, 262
                                                                488, 490-492, 508, 511

Article 2   491

Article 3   491

Convention concerning the Application
of the Principles of the Right to Organise
and to Bargain Collectively

Adopted by the General Conference
of the International Labour Organisation,
at Geneva, on 1 July 1949[14]

---

[12] See General Assembly resolution 54/263 of 25 May 2000; United Nations, *Treaty Series*, vol. 2173, No. A-27531; and *RWI Compilation II*, p. 285. This Optional Protocol entered into force on 12 February 2002.

[13] ILO Convention No. 87; see United Nations, *Treaty Series*, vol. 68, No. I-881, and, as amended by Final Articles Revision Convention, 1961 (No. 116), vol. 423, No. I-6083; and *RWI Compilation I*, p. 415 and *II*, p. 379. The Convention entered into force on 4 July 1950 and, as amended by Convention No. 116, on 5 February 1962.

[14] ILO Convention No. 98; see United Nations, *Treaty Series*, vol. 96, No. I-1341, and, as amended by Final Articles Revision Convention, 1961 (No. 116), vol. 423, No. I-6083; and *RWI Compilation II*, p. 387. The Convention entered into force on 18 July 1951 and, as amended by Convention No. 116, on 5 February 1962.

General   22-23, 49, 72, 169, 225, 262
                     265, 488, 491-492, 508, 511

Convention concerning Equal Remuneration
for Men and Women Workers
for Work of Equal Value

Adopted by the General Conference
of the International Labour Organisation,
at Geneva, on 29 June 1951[15]

General   7

Convention concerning Discrimination in Respect
of Employment and Occupation

Adopted by the General Conference
of the International Labour Organisation,
at Geneva, on 25 June 1958[16]

General   7

Convention concerning Protection and Facilities
to be Afforded to Workers' Representatives
in the Undertaking

Adopted by the General Conference
of the International Labour Organisation,
at Geneva, on 2 June 1971[17]

General   508

Convention concerning Indigenous
and Tribal Peoples in Independent Countries

Adopted by the General Conference
of the International Labour Organisation,
at Geneva, on 27 June 1989[18]

---

[15] ILO Convention No. 100; see United Nations, *Treaty Series*, vol. 165, No. I-2181; and *RWI Compilation II*, p. 427. The Convention entered into force on 23 May 1953.
[16] ILO Convention No. 111; see United Nations, *Treaty Series*, vol. 362, No. I-5181; and *RWI Compilation I*, p. 421 and *II*, p. 433. The Convention entered into force on 15 June 1960.
[17] ILO Convention No. 135; see United Nations, *Treaty Series*, vol. 883, No. I-12659. The Convention entered into force on 30 June 1973.

General	7, 409
Article 5	409

Convention against Discrimination
in Education

Adopted by the General Conference of the United Nations
Educational, Scientific and Cultural Organization,
at Paris, on 14 December 1960[19]

General	7

Rome Statute of the International Criminal Court

Adopted by the United Nations Diplomatic Conference
of Plenipotentiaries on the Establishment
of an International Criminal Court,
at Rome, on 17 July 1998[20]

General	39, 123, 539
Article 1	528
Article 5	528
Article 7	37, 204
Articles 86-102	529

Geneva Conventions of 12 August 1949

Adopted by the Diplomatic Conference
for the Establishment of International Conventions
for the Protection of Victims of War, at Geneva,
on 12 August 1949[21]

---

[18] ILO Convention No. 169; see United Nations, *Treaty Series*, vol. 1650, No. I-28383; and *RWI Compilation I*, p. 299 and *II*, p. 303. The Convention entered into force on 5 September 1991.
[19] See United Nations, *Treaty Series*, vol. 429, No. I-6193; and *RWI Compilation I*, p. 409 and *II*, p. 371. The Convention entered into force on 22 May 1962.
[20] *Ibidem*, vol. 2187, No. I-38544; and *RWI Compilation II*, p. 551. The Statute entered into force on 1 July 2002.
[21] *Ibidem*, vol. 75, No. I-970 (Geneva Convention for the Amelioration of the Condition of the Wounded and Sick in Armed Forces in the Field), No. I-971 (Geneva Convention for the Amelioration of the Condition of the Wounded, Sick and Shipwrecked Members of Armed Forces at Sea), No. I-972 (Geneva Convention relative to the Treatment of Prisoners of War) and No. I-973 (Geneva Convention relative to the Protection of Civilian Persons in Time of War); and for article 3 common to the Geneva Conventions of 12 August 1949, *Essential Texts*, p. 121. The four Geneva Conventions entered into force on 21 October 1950.

General   16-18, 39, 123, 530-532
                                                                 538, 549, 556, 591-592, 597
                                                                 600, 602, 604, 607, 616
                                                                 626-627, 631-632

Article 3 common to the Geneva Conventions
of 12 August 1949

General   20, 530, 532-534, 556, 582
                                                                 591, 599, 611, 613-614, 619
                                                                 626-627, 631

Geneva Convention for the Amelioration
of the Condition of the Wounded and Sick
in Armed Forces in the Field
(Geneva Convention I)

Article 49   600

Geneva Convention for the Amelioration
of the Condition of Wounded, Sick and
Shipwrecked Members of Armed Forces at Sea
(Geneva Convention II)

Article 50   600

Geneva Convention relative to the Treatment
of Prisoners of War
(Geneva Convention III)

Article 4   531
Article 129   600

Geneva Convention relative to the Protection
of Civilian Persons in Time of War
(Geneva Convention IV)

General   548, 575
Article 6   575
Article 78   548, 574-575
Article 146   600

*Protocols Additional to the Geneva Conventions
of 12 August 1949*

Adopted by the Diplomatic Conference on the Reaffirmation
and Development of International Humanitarian Law
Applicable in Armed Conflicts, at Geneva,
on 8 June 1977[22]

General   16, 39, 123, 626, 631

*Protocol Additional to the Geneva Conventions
of 12 August 1949, and relating to the Protection
of Victims of International Armed Conflicts
(Protocol I)*

General	530-531, 604
Article 11	600
Article 43	531-532
Article 44	531
Article 50	532
Article 85	600
Article 86	604
Article 87	603-604

*Protocol Additional to the Geneva Conventions
of 12 August 1949, and relating to the Protection
of Victims of Non-International Armed Conflicts
(Protocol II)*

General	20, 530, 532-533, 559-560
	599-600, 611, 613-614
Article 1	532-533, 560
Article 2	533
Article 4	533, 619, 626, 631
Article 13	533, 560

---

[22] *Ibidem*, vol. 1125, No. I-17512 (Protocol Additional to the Geneva Conventions of 12 August 1949, and relating to the Protection of Victims of International Armed Conflicts) and No. I-17513 (Protocol Additional to the Geneva Conventions of 12 August 1949, and relating to the Protection of Victims of Non-International Armed Conflicts); and for the latter Protocol, *Essential Texts*, p. 123. The two Protocols entered into force on 7 December 1978.

(*b*) **Regional human rights treaties**

African Charter on Human and Peoples' Rights

Adopted by the Assembly of Heads of State and Government
of the Organization of African Unity, at Nairobi,
on 27 June 1981[23]

General	24-25, 52-53, 58, 142-143
	225-227, 360, 540, 550-555
	579-581
Article 1	24, 551
Article 2	6, 555
Article 3	6
Article 4	*52-53*, 550, 552-553, 555
	581-582
Article 5	*142-144*, 550, 552-555
	581-582
Article 6	200, *225-227*, 360, 550, 552
	554-555, 581-582
Article 7	226-227, *359-360*, 552
	581-582
Article 8	581-582
Article 10	552
Article 12	554-555
Article 14	554-555
Article 16	550-551, 554-555, 581-582
Article 17	550-551, 581-582
Article 18	554-555
Article 19	555
Article 23	555
Article 30	24
Articles 31-44	24
Article 45	24
Articles 47-54	25
Articles 55-59	25
Article 56	580
Article 58	550, 580, 582
Article 60	25
Article 61	25

---

[23] *Ibidem*, vol. 1520, No. I-26363; *Essential Texts*, p. 147; and *RWI Compilation I*, p. 191 and *II*, p. 189. The Charter entered into force on 21 October 1986.

Protocol to the African Charter on Human and Peoples' Rights on the Establishment of an African Court on Human and Peoples' Rights

Adopted by the Assembly of Heads of State and Government of the Organization of African Unity, at Ouagadougou, on 9 June 1998[24]

General   24

Protocol to the African Charter on Human and Peoples' Rights on the Rights of Women in Africa

Adopted by the Assembly of Heads of State and Government of the African Union, at Maputu, on 11 July 2003[25]

General   24
Article 11   535

American Convention on Human Rights "Pact of San José, Costa Rica"

Signed by States Members of the Organization of American States, at San José, Costa Rica, on 22 November 1969[26]

General   26, 28, 37, 55, 58, 74, 77-78
                                   80-84, 146, 172, 177-178
                                 180-182, 230, 232, 267
                              361-365, 450, 468-469, 551
                              556-557, 584-585, 590-592
Article 1   6, 26, 54-55, 81-85, 146
                              172, 177-178, 228, 230, 232
                              267, 269, 362-363, 365, 463
                              468, 558, 582, 590-593
Article 2   26, 82, 558
Articles 3-25   26
Article 3   539, 582, 592
Article 4   *53-57, 74-85*, 146, 172, 177

---

[24] Visit http://www.africa-union.org; see *African Journal of International and Comparative Law*, vol. 12 (2000), p. 187. This Protocol entered into force on 25 January 2004.
[25] Visit http://www.africa-union.org. This Protocol entered into force on 25 November 2005.
[26] See OAS, *Treaty Series*, No. 36; United Nations, *Treaty Series*, vol. 1144, No. I-17955; *Essential Texts*, p. 165; and *RWI Compilation I*, p. 155 and *II*, p. 145. The Convention entered into force on 18 July 1978.

	228, 362, 539, 558, 582
	589-590, 592-593
Article 5	54, 74, 80-81, 85, *144-149*
	172-178, 178-183, 228, 363
	539, 558, 582, 587-589
	592-593
Article 6	539
Article 7	54, 56, 75, 80-81, 85, 200
	227-232, 266-269, 362, 558
	582, 585-586, 592-593
Article 8	228, *360-365,* 372, 399, 463
	558, 582, 590-593
Article 9	539
Article 12	539
Article 13	433, *449-450, 463-469*
Article 17	539
Article 18	539
Article 19	172, 539
Article 20	463, 539
Article 21	463
Article 23	539
Article 24	6
Article 25	8, 26, 228-231, 267-269
	463, 558, 582, 590-593
Article 26	27
Article 27	54, 56, 144, 227, 361, 449
	539, 558, 591
Article 29	363, 584
Article 33	26
Articles 34-37	26
Article 44	27
Article 45	27
Article 46	8
Articles 48-51	27
Articles 52-60	26
Article 61	27
Article 62	27
Article 63	27, 469, 593
Articles 66-69	27

Additional Protocol to the American Convention
on Human Rights in the Area of Economic,
Social and Cultural Rights
"Protocol of San Salvador"

Signed by States Members of the Organization
of American States, at San Salvador, El Salvador,
on 17 November 1988[27]

General	27
Article 19	27

Protocol to the American Convention
on Human Rights to Abolish the Death Penalty

Approved by the General Assembly of the Organization
of American States, at Asunción, Paraguay,
on 8 June 1990[28]

General	54

Inter-American Convention to Prevent
and Punish Torture

Signed by States Members of the Organization
of American States, at Cartagena de Indias, Colombia,
on 9 December 1985[29]

General	124, 144-145, 148-149, 178
	183, 232, 557, 593
Article 1	145, 148, 172, 177-178, 182
	582, 592-593
Article 2	144, 179, 181-183, 582, 588
	592-593
Article 3	145
Article 4	145
Article 5	145
Article 6	145, 148, 172, 177-179

---

[27] *Ibidem*, No. 69; and *RWI Compilation I*, p. 179 and *II*, p. 175. The Additional Protocol entered into force on 16 November 1999.

[28] *Ibidem*, No. 73; and *RWI Compilation I*, p. 189 and *II*, p. 187. This Protocol entered into force on 28 August 1991.

[29] *Ibidem*, No. 67; and *Essential Texts*, p. 195. The Convention entered into force on 28 February 1987.

658

	182-183, 582, 592-593
Article 7	145
Article 8	145, 148, 172, 177-179
	182-183, 582, 592-593

Inter-American Convention on Forced
Disappearance of Persons

Adopted by the General Assembly of the Organization
of American States, at Belém do Pará, Brazil,
on 9 June 1994[30]

General	37, 56, 584
Preamble	37
Article II	37, 584

Convention for the Protection of Human Rights
and Fundamental Freedoms
(European Convention on Human Rights)

Signed by States Members of the Council of Europe,
at Rome, on 4 November 1950[31]

General	6, 28-30, 107, 110, 149-154
	181, 185-186, 193-194, 232
	239, 244, 273-274, 277, 280
	284-285, 299-301, 313
	319-322, 367, 369-370
	372-374, 393, 399-400
	402-404, 408, 415, 425-428
	432, 482, 522, 551, 569
Preamble	277, 299
Article 1	29, 97, 110, 595-596
Articles 2-18	29
Article 2	*57-66, 86-104, 104-112*
	112-122, 482, 540, 558-562
	569, 594-596
Article 3	65, 104, 112, *149-155*, 175

---

[30] Visit http://www.oas.org. The Convention entered into force on 28 March 1996.

[31] See Council of Europe, *European Treaty Series*, No. 5 and, as amended by Protocol No. 11 to the Convention for the Protection of Human Rights and Fundamental Freedoms, restructuring the control machinery established thereby, No. 155; United Nations, *Treaty Series*, vols. 213, No. I-2889, and 2061, No. A-2889, respectively; *Essential Texts*, p. 203; and *RWI Compilation I*, p. 81 (previous text) and *II*, p. 61. The Convention entered into force on 3 September 1953 and, as amended by Protocol No. 11, on 1 November 1998.

177, 181-182, *184-186*
186-197, 241, 482, 540, 568
570
Article 4   540
Article 5   63, 200, *232-244, 270-281*
282-286, 302, 395, 398, 400
586
Article 6   63, 153, 166, 187, 191-192
196, 329, *365-374, 390-395*
395-400, 400-405, 428, 452
454-455, 470, 473
Article 7   540
Articles 8-11   59, 96, 425
Article 8   63, 287, *292-305, 310-313*
313-322, 322-332, 368
402-403, 482, 523
Article 9   407, *414-417, 419-421*
422-432, 521
Article 10   372, 393, 433, *450-459*, 466
470-476, 476-486, 499, 521
Article 11   427-428, 482, 487, *496-500*
519-524
Article 13   8, 65-66, 104, 109, 112-114
118, 166, 270, 281, 297, 314
320-321, 392, 432, 498, 519
521-522, 524, 560, 596
Article 14   6, 66, 104, 112-114,118-122
422, 476, 485-486
Article 15   58, 149, 185, 194, 233, 235
240, 273-274, 292, 366, 414
451, 496, 539-540
Article 19   28
Articles 20-23   28
Article 25   560, 596
Article 27   28
Article 28 (former)   97
Article 30   29
Article 31 (former)   97
Article 32   28
Article 32 (former)   30, 150, 235
Article 33   28
Article 34   28
Article 35   8, 28
Article 38   28
Article 40   28
Article 41   30, 112, 122, 196, 332, 432
486

Articles 42-46   29
Article 46   30
Article 50 (former)   104, 186, 281, 285, 313, 322
     395, 400, 476, 596

Protocol to the Convention for the Protection
of Human Rights and Fundamental Freedoms

Signed by States Members of the Council of Europe,
at Paris, on 20 March 1952[32]

General   185
Article 1   476

Protocol No. 4 to the Convention for the Protection
of Human Rights and Fundamental Freedoms,
securing certain rights and freedoms other than those
already included in the Convention and in the first
Protocol thereto

Signed by States Members of the Council of Europe,
at Strasbourg, on 16 September 1963[33]

General   185

Protocol No. 6 to the Convention for the Protection
of Human Rights and Fundamental Freedoms,
concerning the abolition of the death penalty

Signed by States Members of the Council of Europe,
at Strasbourg, on 28 April 1983[34]

---

[32] *Ibidem*, No. 9 and, as amended by Protocol No. 11 to the Convention for the Protection of Human Rights and Fundamental Freedoms, restructuring the control machinery established thereby, No. 155; United Nations, *Treaty Series*, vols. 213, No. I-2889, and 2061, No. A-2889, respectively; and *RWI Compilation I*, p. 97 (previous text) and *II*, p. 79. The present Protocol entered into force on 18 May 1954 and, as amended by Protocol No. 11, on 1 November 1998.

[33] *Ibidem*, No. 46 and, as amended by Protocol No. 11 to the Convention for the Protection of Human Rights and Fundamental Freedoms, restructuring the control machinery established thereby, No. 155; United Nations, *Treaty Series*, vols. 1496, No. A-2889, and 2061, No. A-2889, respectively; and *RWI Compilation I*, p. 101 (previous text) and *II*, p. 83. Protocol No. 4 entered into force on 2 May 1968 and, as amended by Protocol No. 11, on 1 November 1998.

[34] *Ibidem*, No. 114 and, as amended by Protocol No. 11 to the Convention for the Protection
(*continued*)

General	58
Article 3	540

Protocol No. 7 to the Convention for the Protection
of Human Rights and Fundamental Freedoms

Signed by States Members of the Council of Europe,
at Strasbourg, on 22 November 1984[35]

Article 4	540

Protocol No. 11 to the Convention for the Protection
of Human Rights and Fundamental Freedoms,
restructuring the control machinery established thereby

Signed by States Members of the Council of Europe,
at Strasbourg, on 11 May 1994[36]

General	28

Protocol No. 12 to the Convention for the Protection
of Human Rights and Fundamental Freedoms

Signed by States Members of the Council of Europe,
at Rome, on 4 November 2000[37]

General	407-408
Preamble	6
Article 1	6, 408

---

of Human Rights and Fundamental Freedoms, restructuring the control machinery established thereby, No. 155; United Nations, *Treaty Series*, vols. 1496, No. A-2889, and 2061, No. A-2889, respectively; and *RWI Compilation I*, p. 105 (previous text) and *II*, p. 87. Protocol No. 6 entered into force on 1 March 1985 and, as amended by Protocol No. 11, on 1 November 1998.

[35] *Ibidem*, No. 117 and, as amended by Protocol No. 11 to the Convention for the Protection of Human Rights and Fundamental Freedoms, restructuring the control machinery established thereby, No. 155; United Nations, *Treaty Series*, vols. 1525, No. A-2889, and 2061, No. A-2889, respectively; and *RWI Compilation I*, p. 109 (previous text) and *II*, p. 91. Protocol No. 7 entered into force on 1 November 1988 and, as amended by Protocol No. 11, on 1 November 1998.

[36] *Ibidem*, No. 155; United Nations, *Treaty Series*, vol. 2061, No. A-2889; and *RWI Compilation I*, p. 119. Protocol No. 11 entered into force on 1 November 1998.

[37] *Ibidem*, No. 177; and *RWI Compilation II*, p. 97. Protocol No. 12 entered into force on 1 April 2005.

*Protocol No. 13 to the Convention for the Protection
of Human Rights and Fundamental Freedoms,
concerning the abolition of the death penalty
in all circumstances*

Signed by States Members of the Council of Europe,
at Vilnius, on 3 May 2002[38]

General   58
Article 2   540

*European Agreement relating to Persons participating
in Proceedings of the European Commission
and Court of Human Rights*

Signed by States Members of the Council of Europe,
at London, on 6 May 1969[39]

General   399

*Convention for the Protection of Individuals
with regard to Automatic Processing of Personal Data*

Signed by States Members of the Council of Europe,
at Strasbourg, on 28 January 1981[40]

General   330

*European Convention for the Prevention of Torture and
Inhuman or Degrading Treatment or Punishment*

Signed by States Members of the Council of Europe,
at Strasbourg, on 26 November 1987[41]

---

[38] *Ibidem*, No. 187; United Nations, *Treaty Series*, vol. 2246, No. A-2889; and *RWI Compilation II*, p. 101. Protocol No. 13 entered into force on 1 July 2003.

[39] *Ibidem*, No. 67; United Nations, *Treaty Series*, vol. 788, No. I-11213. The Agreement entered into force on 17 April 1971.

[40] *Ibidem*, No. 108; United Nations, *Treaty Series*, vol. 1496, No. I-25702. The Convention entered into force on 1 October 1985.

[41] *Ibidem*, No. 126 and, as amended by Protocols No. 1 and No. 2 to the European Convention for the Prevention of Torture and Inhuman or Degrading Treatment or Punishment, Nos. 151 and 152; United Nations, *Treaty Series*, vols. 1561, No. I-27161, and 2206, No. A-27161; *Es-*
(*continued*)

General   124

*Framework Convention for the Protection
of National Minorities*

Signed by States Members of the Council of Europe,
at Strasbourg, on 1 February 1995[42]

General	7, 409, 434, 569
Preamble	409
Article 7	409, 434, 488
Article 8	409
Article 9	434
Article 17	488

(*c*) Non-treaty human rights instruments

Standard Minimum Rules for the Treatment of Prisoners

Approved by the Economic and Social Council
of the United Nations on 31 July 1957[43]

General	16, 129, 399
Rule 10	160
Rule 12	160
Rule 17	160
Rule 19	160
Rule 20	160

*Declaration on the Protection of All Persons from
Being Subjected to Torture and Other Cruel, Inhuman
or Degrading Treatment or Punishment*

Adopted by the General Assembly of the United Nations
on 9 December 1975[44]

---

sential Texts, p. 221 (previous text); and *RWI Compilation I*, p. 563 (previous text) and *II*, p. 477. The Convention entered into force on 1 February 1989 and, as amended by Protocols No. 1 and No. 2, on 1 March 2002.

[42] *Ibidem*, No. 157; United Nations, *Treaty Series*, vol. 2151, No. I-37548; and *RWI Compilation II*, p. 319. The Convention entered into force on 1 February 1998.

[43] See Economic and Social Council resolution 663 C (XXIV) of 31 July 1957; and *RWI Compilation I*, p. 457.

[44] See General Assembly resolution 3452 (XXX) of 9 December 1975; and *RWI Compilation I*, p. 545.

General   124

Code of Conduct for Law Enforcement Officials

Adopted by the General Assembly of the United Nations
on 17 December 1979[45]

General	47, 569
Article 2	410, 436, 488
Article 3	40
Article 4	287
Article 5	124

Declaration on the Elimination of All Forms
of Intolerance and of Discrimination
Based on Religion or Belief

Proclaimed by the General Assembly of the United Nations
on 25 November 1981[46]

General	7, 408
Article 1	408
Article 2	408

Basic Principles on the Independence of the Judiciary

Adopted by the Seventh United Nations Congress
on the Prevention of Crime and the Treatment of Offenders,
Milan, 26 August - 6 September 1985[47]

General	341

---

[45] See General Assembly resolution 34/169 of 17 December 1979; *Essential Texts*, p. 247; and *RWI Compilation I*, p. 429 and *II*, p. 487.

[46] See General Assembly resolution 36/55 of 25 November 1981; and *RWI Compilation I*, p. 275 and *II*, p. 255.

[47] See *Seventh United Nations Congress on the Prevention of Crime and the Treatment of Offenders, Milan, 26 August - 6 September 1985: report prepared by the Secretariat* (United Nations publication, Sales No. E.86.IV.1), chap. I, sect. D.2; and *RWI Compilation I*, p. 435 and *II*, p. 515.

United Nations Standard Minimum Rules
for the Administration of Juvenile Justice
(The Beijing Rules)

Adopted by the General Assembly of the United Nations
on 29 November 1985[48]
General 16, 342

Body of Principles for the Protection of All Persons
under Any Form of Detention or Imprisonment

Approved by the General Assembly of the United Nations
on 9 December 1988[49]

General 16, 143, 199, 216, 354, 356
444, 547
Principle 1 143
Principle 6 .... 125, 143
Principle 17 356
Principle 21 .... 125, 261, 356
Principle 27 356
Principle 36 356

Principles on the Effective Prevention and Investigation
of Extra-legal, Arbitrary and Summary Executions

Recommended by the Economic and Social Council
of the United Nations on 24 May 1989[50]

General 40, 47
Principle 1 541
Principle 9 95

---

[48] See General Assembly resolution 40/33 of 29 November 1985; and *RWI Compilation I*, p. 495.
[49] See General Assembly resolution 43/173 of 9 December 1988; *Essential Texts*, p. 265; and *RWI Compilation II*, p. 503.
[50] See Economic and Social Council resolution 1989/65 of 24 May 1989; *Essential Texts*, p. 293; and *RWI Compilation I*, p. 569.

Basic Principles on the Use of Force and Firearms
by Law Enforcement Officials

Adopted by the Eighth United Nations Congress
on the Prevention of Crime and the Treatment of Offenders,
Havana, 27 August - 7 September 1990[51]

General	40, 47, 489, 569
Principle 9	40, 95, 489
Principle 12	489
Principle 13	489
Principle 14	489
Principle 15	125

Basic Principles on the Role of Lawyers

Adopted by the Eighth United Nations Congress
on the Prevention of Crime and the Treatment of Offenders,
Havana, 27 August - 7 September 1990[52]

General	341

Guidelines on the Role of Prosecutors

Adopted by the Eighth United Nations Congress
on the Prevention of Crime and the Treatment of Offenders,
Havana, 27 August - 7 September 1990[53]

General	341
Guideline 16	218

United Nations Rules for the Protection of Juveniles
Deprived of their Liberty

Adopted by the General Assembly of the United Nations
on 14 December 1990[54]

---

[51] See *Eighth United Nations Congress on the Prevention of Crime and the Treatment of Offenders, Havana, 27 August - 7 September 1990: report prepared by the Secretariat* (United Nations publication, Sales No. E.91.IV.2), chap. I, sect. B.2; *Essential Texts*, p. 257; and *RWI Compilation I*, p. 439.

[52] *Ibidem*, sect. B.3; and *RWI Compilation I*, p. 445 and *II*, p. 525.

[53] *Ibidem*, sect. C.26; *Essentital Texts*, p. 325; and *RWI Compilation I*, p. 451 and *II*, p. 519.

[54] See General Assembly resolution 45/113 of 14 December 1990; *Essential Texts*, p. 277; and *RWI Compilation I*, p. 527.

General   16, 200

Declaration on the Protection of All Persons
from Enforced Disappearance

Proclaimed by the General Assembly of the United Nations
on 18 December 1992[55]

General	200
Preamble	37
Article 1	37, 363
Article 7	541
Article 13	9

Declaration on the Rights of Persons Belonging to
National or Ethnic, Religious and Linguistic Minorities

Proclaimed by the General Assembly of the United Nations
on 18 December 1992[56]

General   410

Declaration on the Right and Responsibility of
Individuals, Groups and Organs of Society to Promote
and Protect Universally Recognized Human Rights
and Fundamental Freedoms

Adopted by the General Assembly of the United Nations
on 9 December 1998[57]

General	435, 488
Article 1	435, 488
Article 5	448
Article 6	435, 448

---

[55] See General Assembly resolution 47/133 of 18 December 1992; and *Essential Texts*, p. 299.
[56] See General Assembly resolution 47/135 of 18 December 1992; and *RWI Compilation I*, p. 313.
[57] See General Assembly resolution 53/144 of 9 December 1998.

Principles on the Effective Investigation and
Documentation of Torture and Other Cruel, Inhuman
or Degrading Treatment or Punishment
(the Istanbul Principles)

Submitted to the United Nations High Commissioner
for Human Rights on 9 August 1999[58]

General   125

ILO Declaration on Fundamental Principles
and Rights at Work

Adopted by the International Labour Conference,
at Geneva, on 18 June 1998[59]
General   22, 491

European Code of Police Ethics

Adopted by the Committee of Ministers of the Council
of Europe on 19 September 2001[60]

General   40, 125
Article 36   125
Article 37   40
Article 41   288
Article 42   288
Article 43   410, 436, 488-489

(*d*) Other international instruments

Charter of the United Nations

Signed by States original Members of the United Nations
on 26 June 1945[61]

---

[58] See General Assembly resolution 55/89 of 4 December 2000, annex; and *Istanbul Protocol: Manual on the Effective Investigation and Documentation of Torture and Other Cruel, Inhuman or Degrading Treatment or Punishment* (Professional Training Series No. 8/Rev.1) (United Nations publication, Sales No. E.04.XIV.3), annex I.
[59] See International Labour Office, *Official Bulletin*, vol. LXXXI, Series A, No. 2 (1998), p. 73; and *RWI Compilation II*, p. 439.
[60] See *The European Code of Police Ethics: Recommendation Rec(2001)10 adopted by the Committee of Ministers of the Council of Europe on 19 September 2001 and explanatory memorandum* (Strasbourg, Council of Europe Publishing, 2002).

General	5, 15
Chapter VII	17, 20, 528

Statute of the International Tribunal for the former Yugoslavia

Adopted by the Security Council of the United Nations on 25 May 1993[62]

General	599, 633
Articles 1-7	17
Article 1	597
Articles 2-5	597-598, 603, 606, 618
Article 2	597, 602
Article 3	597, 601-602, 607, 617, 619
	625-626
Article 4	598
Article 5	598, 607, 632
Article 7	598, 602-606, 608, 618, 633
Article 9	18
Articles 11-17	18
Articles 18-24	19
Article 25	19
Article 26	19

Statute of the International Criminal Tribunal for Rwanda

Adopted by the Security Council of the United Nations on 8 November 1994[63]

---

[61] See *Yearbook of the United Nations, 1947-48* (United Nations publication, Sales No. 49.I. 13) and, as amended by General Assembly resolutions 1991 A and B (XVIII) of 17 December 1963, 2101 (XX) of 20 December 1965 and 2847 (XXVI) of 20 December 1971, United Nations, *Treaty Series*, vols. 557, No. I-8132, 638, No. A-8132 and 892, No. A-8132, respectively; and *RWI Compilation I*, p. 1 (excerpts) and *II*, p. 653. The Charter entered into force on 24 October 1945 and, as amended by General Assembly resolutions 1991 A and B (XVIII), 2101 (XX) and 2847 (XXVI), on 31 August 1965, 12 June 1968 and 24 September 1973, respectively.

[62] See Security Council resolution 827 (1993) of 25 May 1993 and, as amended, resolutions 1166 (1998) of 13 May 1998, 1329 (2000) of 30 November 2000, 1411 (2002) of 17 May 2002, 1431 (2002) of 14 August 2002, 1481 (2003) of 19 May 2003 and 1597 (2005) of 20 April 2005; and *RWI Compilation I*, p. 583 (previous text).

[63] See Security Council resolution 955 (1994) of 8 November 1994 and, as amended, resolu-
(*continued*)

Articles 1-6	20
Article 1	598
Articles 2-4	598, 599
Article 2	598
Article 3	599
Article 4	599
Article 6	599, 611, 615-616
Article 8	20
Article 10	20
Articles 11-16	20
Articles 17-23	21
Article 24	22
Article 25	22

tions 1165 (1998) of 30 April 1998, 1329 (2000) of 30 November 2000, 1411 (2002) of 17 May 2002, 1431 (2002) of 14 August 2002, 1503 (2003) of 28 August 2003 and 1512 (2003) of 27 October 2003; and *RWI Compilation I*, p. 593 (previous text).